Renewing Theology

Renewing Theology

Ignatian Spirituality and Karl Rahner,
Ignacio Ellacuría, and Pope Francis

J. Matthew Ashley

University of Notre Dame Press
Notre Dame, Indiana

Copyright © 2022 by the University of Notre Dame
Notre Dame, Indiana 46556
undpress.nd.edu
All Rights Reserved

Published in the United States of America

Paperback edition published in 2025

This book is made possible in part by support from
the Institute for Scholarship in the Liberal Arts, College of Arts and Letters,
University of Notre Dame.

Library of Congress Control Number: 2022935755

ISBN: 978-0-268-20317-7 (Hardback)
ISBN: 9780268203184 (Paperback)
ISBN: 978-0-268-20319-1 (WebPDF)
ISBN: 978-0-268-20316-0 (Epub)

GPSR Compliance Inquiries:
Lightning Source France,
1 Av. Johannes Gutenberg,
78310 Maurepas, France
compliance@lightningsource.fr
Phone: +33 1 30 49 23 42

To Kevin Burke, SJ:
friend, collaborator, Ignatian theologian

CONTENTS

Introduction:	The Poverty of Academic Theology	ix
CHAPTER 1.	Haven in a Heartless World or Well of Vision? Modernity and the Origins of Spirituality	1
CHAPTER 2.	Ignatian Spirituality: A Historical Overview	39
CHAPTER 3.	Ignatian Spirituality and the Limits of Modernity	79
CHAPTER 4.	Karl Rahner: Theology in a Secularized World	109
CHAPTER 5.	Ignacio Ellacuría: Theology under the Standard of Christ	173
CHAPTER 6.	Pope Francis: Theology as an Instrument of Consolation	233
CHAPTER 7.	Ignatius and the Theologians	289
	Notes	309
	Bibliography	369
	Index	387

Introduction
The Poverty of Academic Theology

Theology has always been a precarious discipline. This is in part because of its breathtaking audacity—to speak about God, no less! It is also because of its unavoidable dependence on cultural milieus, social institutions, and intellectual tools that it does not completely control. It arose out of the crucible of Christianity's first centuries, as that relatively obscure movement within Judaism became the dominant religion of late antiquity. Located first in the monastery and cathedral, theology entered a new phase with the birth and ascendancy of the medieval university. From the outset, many critics found theology in this iteration to be abstract and too far removed from the joys and fears of everyday believers. Some reformers, such as Jean Gerson, sought to make the university more conducive to a set of concerns that we now often group under the rubric of "spirituality."[1]

A century or so later, the critique was continued by the Modern Devotion, most well known for *The Imitation of Christ*. That book has a low opinion indeed of university theology, placing these words in the mouth of Christ: "I am God, who enable the humble-minded to understand more of the ways of the everlasting Truth in a single moment than ten years of study in the Schools. I teach in silence, without the clamour of controversy, without ambition for honours, without confusion of argument."[2]

Reformers, Protestant and Catholic alike, were aware of this problem. They strove in different ways to counter it, be it by repristinating monastic genres or by reinvigorating university theology with an infusion of the rhetorical arts, retrieved and refashioned by Renaissance humanism. These attempts notwithstanding, the following century was the century of orthodoxies and polemical theology, the century of scholasticisms, Catholic and Protestant. The problem of relating university theology (or seminary theology, for that matter) to the lives and needs of the majority of believers loomed over the theological landscape like a slumbering volcano, erupting periodically through the seventeenth and eighteenth centuries: thus, Pietism in Germany, Pascal and the Jansenists in France, or the Wesleyan reform in England.

Subsequent centuries brought new challenges. Theological subdisciplines developed, and once helpful distinctions became divisions and even oppositions. Moreover, from the Enlightenment on it was not only theology's ecclesial utility and contributions to individual holiness that was contested, but its very legitimacy as an academic discipline. Its defense on both scores headed the agenda of nineteenth-century Protestant "liberal theology." This worthy albeit often maligned movement endeavored to show both that the integrity and relevance of Christian faith could be speculatively defended and elaborated on modern grounds and that such a defense was vital not only as an apologetic strategy against its cultured despisers but also *ad intra* for the well-being of the faith itself. There were important developments along the same lines in Roman Catholic theology, but Pius IX and Leo XIII rejected that approach, embracing instead the neoscholastic revival of Libertore and Kleutgen as the proper response to the challenges the Church faced, both *ad intra* and *ad extra*.

In Catholicism, a way of understanding theology's role solidified during this time that has been described by Johann Baptist Metz: "The bishops teach; the priests care for; the (professional) theologians explain and defend doctrine and train the caretakers. And the rest? The people? They are chiefly the objects of this instructing and caretaking church."[3] Yet this solution, if solution it be, left unsolved the two problems that I have highlighted in this admittedly too brief history. First, a very real question subsists on whether and how theology has a future in increasingly secularized universities (even those still nominally affiliated with one or another Christian tradition). These universities are increasingly orienting themselves toward training the experts needed to keep late modernity's political, economic, and technological structures running smoothly. Thus, it is not just theology's avowed service to a particular cultural and historical tradition that makes it appear insufficiently "objective" for universities so conceived, but its insistence that its subject matter cannot be instrumentalized to the benefit of the smooth functioning of any set of human institutions and concepts, modern ones included. Will theology be dispersed into various component disciplines, which are "objective" enough to gain admission into these secular academies? Or will it withdraw from the university, restricting itself to the seminary? Or find new institutional settings, such as retreat houses or study centers, or root itself once again in the cloister and cathedral? Or in the ethereal landscape of websites and blogs?

Second, and more germane to the concerns of this book, will academic theology become more and more isolated from the joys, sorrows, needs, and gifts of believers outside the university gates? Here theology shares the dilemma of its sister discipline, philosophy. Pierre Hadot identified this dilemma in *Philosophy as a Way of Life*. He draws our attention to the difference between philosophy as it existed in the ancient schools and philosophy as it is often taught in the modern university: "Ancient philosophy proposed to mankind an art of living. By contrast, modern philosophy appears above all as the construction of a technical jargon reserved for specialists."[4] Has theology too become "the construction of a technical jargon reserved for specialists"? It certainly has become divided into subfields, each of which—rightly enough—holds itself accountable to the most exacting technical standards of its cognate discipline: scripture study to the various disciplines of textual analysis, literary critique, cultural anthropology, and so on; historical theology to a similar array of historical methodologies; moral and systematic theology to a spectrum of disciplines, including philosophy, psychology, anthropology, sociology, and even the natural sciences. This rigor is important, and theology is the better for the precision that comes with it. Yet, as a perhaps unintended result, is it any surprise that many Christians experience theology as an increasingly arcane and esoteric conversation carried on above their heads? Need we wonder that they find it difficult to experience theology anymore as a guide into an "art of living," an invitation to explore and deepen the response they have made, however tentatively, to the call to follow Christ?

To be sure, there are exceptions to this general story, and there are always theologians who rise to the challenge, combining both academic rigor and an empathic reach to include those outside the academy.

Nonetheless, it seems fair to say that there is a growing sense, even among its supporters, that academic theology needs renewal and reformulation if it is to respond to the needs of the Church and society today. This must encompass its specific institutional structures and pedagogical techniques, including the division of labor between different theological subdisciplines. However, it also includes the ways academic theology (both speculative and practical) identifies problems, marshals evidence, constructs arguments, defends and emends them in conversation with others, and communicates results and recommends action. But how to proceed? If it is to remain in the university, it is certainly important that theology continue to be scholarship of the highest caliber. If it cannot deal with its proximate subject matter—the material of scripture and tradition, the social and political configurations of religious faith today, the world in and for which faith necessarily lives—with the same rigor that the other disciplines deal with their *Sache*, then it deserves the reproaches often leveled at it (or, as is more often the case, the benign neglect). Moreover, theology can and should attend to the work of other disciplines in the university as they strive to improve the quality of teaching and to discussions within the university as a whole concerning its role in society. After all, theology is not the only discipline that feels vulnerable in the university today; the *kairos* that faces academic theology confronts the university as a whole as it grapples with the question of whether or not a tradition that is now at least nine centuries old has a future.

It is, however, equally important to respond to the second issue: How do we reestablish a living relationship between academic theology and the lives of Christians in the world outside the university gates? How do we reopen that vital circulation between the three elements that Friedrich von Hügel listed as integral to any living religion: the intellectual element, the historical-institutional element, and the "mystical-volitional" element, in which "religion is rather felt than seen or reasoned about, is loved and lived rather than analyzed, is action and power, rather than external fact or external verification."[5] Since the Enlightenment, theologians have tended to focus their energy on bringing the first two elements (intellectual and historical-institutional) into contact. Their worthy aim was to counter the growing suspicion that religion, particularly as communicated through historical traditions and lived out in concrete social institutions, simply cannot have an "intellectual element," that at the end of the day irrationality or mere opinion rules the minds of believers.

Without denying the importance of that challenge, the conviction that guides this book is that it must be met along with the second, and that means by tapping the "mystical-volitional" element of religion. The two tasks are not opposed, or even unconnected. Far from threatening to render faith even more "subjective" and "irrational," an appeal to the *experience* of the divine, as articulated in spiritual and/or mystical traditions, delineates an important locus from which to defend the cognitive integrity and relevance of religious faith.[6]

Thus, this is a book on spirituality and theology. In modernity, it is the genre of spirituality that has largely taken over the task of proposing "an art of living." Its separation from theology has been bemoaned for at least seventy years, and many contemporary theologians have continued to insist on the need to reintegrate spirituality into the practice and results of theology. Yet, it is not easy to see how this reintegration will happen, since the division is not just a terminological one that can be overcome at the whim of the academic wordsmith. Rather, as I argue in the first three chapters, the division between spirituality and theology flows from, reflects, and reinforces the social and cultural conditions of modernity. It cannot be overcome by theory alone but by a new praxis, both of doing theology and of practicing spirituality, an ecclesial praxis that is at the same time individual and social-political. As a propaedeutic to this more sweeping and challenging task, this book undertakes an analysis of how spiritual traditions can have, and indeed have had, an influence on the work of academic theology.

This task is more manageable. For one thing, we have at our disposal the fruits of more than a century of sustained historical scholarship focused on Christianity's spiritual traditions. We have critical editions and excellent secondary works that introduce those past masters who strove to lure men and women into theology as a radically transformative and deeply satisfying way of life. We can and should learn from them, for the works of the Spirit are at once life-givingly new and yet also best perceived from the vantage of the long history of that Spirit's presence in and to history.

It is in part this critical retrieval of spiritual traditions, along with the great interest in spirituality in both academy and surrounding culture today, that has made us so aware over the past several decades of the need to reestablish a living circulation between spirituality and academic theology. Yet the need both to reconfigure the practice and contents of academic theology and to reintegrate spirituality and academic theology have been felt for much longer, even if it was not named in these precise terms. Indeed, confining ourselves to Roman Catholic theology, if we survey the names of some of the theologians of the past century who militated for a richer use of Christianity's spiritual traditions, we find some of the most important figures in the reinvigoration of academic theology: Jean Leclercq, Yves Congar, Marie-Dominique Chenu, Hans Urs von Balthasar, and Karl Rahner, to name a few. This suggests the hypothesis that those theologians who were most successful at reconfiguring academic theology to meet the challenges of late modernity were also most successful at reintegrating spirituality. This in turn prompts the corollary hypothesis that their success in the former can be understood at least in part in terms of their success in the latter. Both hypotheses will be explored in the case studies of chapters 4–6.

The three case studies that form the heart of this book are offered, therefore, in the conviction that as these three theologians struggled to renew academic theology to meet the challenges of these late modern times they turned to a specific spiritual tradition, just as many of the century's other great theologians did. We will consider three Jesuits: Karl Rahner, Ignacio Ellacuría, and Pope Francis (Jorge Mario Bergoglio). The first two, who had extensive philosophical and theological training, and the third, who spent decades of work in ecclesial leadership, all perceived, albeit in different ways, the profound challenges posed to Christian faith and theology by the conditions of late modernity. Rahner responded primarily through the texts that he wrote and the lectures that he presented; Ellacuría responded in his writings, but also by his work at the Universidad Centroamericana José Simeón Cañas (UCA), of which he was rector during the last ten years of his life. Pope Francis has responded primarily through his praxis as a leader within the Society of Jesus, as archbishop of Buenos Aires, and then as bishop of Rome.[7]

They came from different cultures: the edges of the Black Forest in Germany, the Basque Country and Central America, and a megacity in Argentina. They drew on different intellectual resources: neoscholasticism, German idealism, different strands of post-Husserlian phenomenology, and the literature and philosophy of Argentina. What unites them is their common involvement in Ignatian spirituality and their commitment to reformulating theology in response to the challenges they discerned to arise from modernity. I use the term "discerned" (a term from

Ignatian spirituality) intentionally. It was, I suggest, their appropriation of Ignatian spirituality that led them to discern these challenges the way they did. I proceed under the hypothesis that a necessary (if not sufficient) condition for understanding the different ways that these men sought to renew theology is a consideration of how Ignatian spirituality affected the way they perceived the challenges of late modernity, what they thought would constitute an adequate response, and how they drew upon the sources of Christian faith and on conceptual tools to specify that response and elaborate its implications.

Relating theology to spirituality immediately confronts the challenge of definition. Defining theology is as much a subject of debate today as in the past. The term "spirituality" is at once more widespread and more protean. Issues of definition will be tackled in chapter 1, but even then we may be forced to fall back on Bernard McGinn's suggestion (paraphrasing the famous remark of Justice Potter Stewart on pornography) that we may not be able to define spirituality with precision, but we can recognize it when we see it.[8] Ignatian, or Jesuit, spirituality is chosen with this dictum in mind. Whatever definition we give of spirituality, Ignatius's heritage will surely count as a paramount instance. His legacy has the further advantage of clarity and relative ease of delineation. It has a central book, the *Spiritual Exercises*, in which its components and overall structure are carefully elaborated and intercalated, even if it also proves crucial to consider other documents, such as the *Constitutions* of the Society of Jesus, Ignatius's autobiography, his spiritual journal, and his extensive correspondence, to flesh out what is implicit or left open in the *Spiritual Exercises*, and even if, as more recent scholarship insists, we must consider the contributions made by Ignatius's first companions (by Pierre Favre, Diego Lainez, and Jeronimo Nadal, for instance) to the spirituality that bears his name. A final reason to choose Ignatian spirituality is that it is an incipiently "modern" spirituality, not only because it emerged at the dawn of modernity itself, but because it reflects the conditions of modernity and grapples with them in all their ambiguity.

In chapter 1, therefore, I discuss the relationship between spirituality and theology under the conditions of modernity. I argue there that the divide that gave rise to "spirituality" was opened up by the same forces that came together to form what is called "modernity," so that the difficulties in defining the former can be illuminated by considering the difficulties of naming the latter. The spirituality that Ignatius inaugurated shows the marks of modernity quite clearly. Indeed, part of what makes Ignatian spirituality so interesting, and so promising a candidate for case studies on the relationship between spirituality and theology, is its involvement in early modernity. Ignatian spirituality is a prime example of the phenomenon that spiritual traditions are paradoxically characterized both by a greater inertia and also, at the same time, greater ductility, proving themselves more capable of responding to the challenges of a new era. The spirituality created by the Basque nobleman and his companions not only brought together elements from a wide spectrum of late medieval and Renaissance spiritualities, but did so in a way that made the resulting weave powerfully attractive to a broad cross section of Christians in the sixteenth century. Ignatius had an intuitive sense for the difficulties involved in living Christian faith more fully in his time and a genius for configuring a set of practices that would make this possible. Pneumatologically, we would have to say that, just as for any authentic spirituality, Ignatius's was (and continues to be) a gift of the Holy Spirit, a sacramental locus of God's ongoing presence in history.

Chapters 2 and 3 give an initial overview of Ignatian spirituality from this perspective. The focus will be the *Spiritual Exercises*.[9] I choose this focus not only because the *Spiritual Exercises* discloses the heart of Ignatius's spirituality, but also because it is the one document with which all of the Jesuits treated in this book would have been intimately familiar.[10] Other sources for early Jesuit spirituality will be introduced when they help to clarify the elements and dynamism of the *Spiritual Exercises*. My goal is not to break new ground in the understanding of Ignatius, the first Jesuits, or the spirituality they brought to birth and nurtured. Others more qualified for it have done that work, and my debts to them will be noted throughout this book. Neither is it my intention to identify the "Ignatius of history," much less "the" Ignatian theology. The former is as much an idealization and as difficult to construct as for any seminal historical figure, and the latter does not exist, even if the term can be helpfully used to denote a group of family resemblances among theologies inspired by Ignatius. This will become clear from the case studies that make up the second part of this book and will be argued more explicitly in chapter 7.

With this in mind, the overview of Ignatian spirituality has two goals, which are taken up in chapters 2 and 3, respectively. First, it is important to display its openness and multidimensionality. In chapter 2, I highlight the different elements that make Ignatian spirituality so flexible and susceptible to diverse theological receptions and applications. The second goal has to do with the situation in which the spirituality was born and in which it is still received: modernity. A crucial element of Ignatian spirituality is the way it is embedded in the origins of modernity. Spiritualities often act as advance warning systems, detecting dilemmas and resources presented by new historical eras that will not become perceptible in more overtly intellectual genres for some decades, or even centuries. This suggests that we consider Ignatian spirituality in the light of the conditions of modernity that were present at least incipiently in Ignatius's world. This horizon of presentation has the further advantage of setting the stage for the case studies that will follow. If it can be shown that certain features of Ignatian spirituality can be understood as responses to the challenges of modernity, as these were just beginning to show themselves in Western Europe, then the further hypothesis suggests itself that when the Jesuits who inherited that spirituality four centuries later attempted to respond to the same challenges, now greatly magnified, they would gravitate toward just those features.

Chapters 4 through 6 will take up three case studies to explore this hypothesis. The goal cannot be to give exhaustive evaluations and critiques of the work of Rahner, Ellacuría, or Francis. Each has produced a body of work so extensive as to render that goal beyond the scope of a single chapter. The goal, rather, is to show how each Jesuit responded to the challenges of modernity in a way that is uniquely illuminated and nourished by one or more themes and dynamisms immanent to Ignatian spirituality, a complex enough goal in itself. As with any important thinker, there are many avenues into the thought of each of these men. I will not claim that the one I am suggesting here—that of Ignatian spirituality—is the only one or even the best for every purpose. I will claim, however, that a complete evaluation of their theologies benefits from a consideration of the spirituality that structured at a profound level their encounters with God and with the world (the two encounters, of course, being dialectically interrelated). I will suggest, moreover, that their theologies disclose themselves with particular clarity and force when their animating (spirit-giving) source is identified and placed in the foreground.

The theologians treated here do not agree in every detail on the contours of modernity or on the form and goal of the theological endeavor that would respond to it. Perhaps the most prominent and radical disagreement arises in the argument (often polemical) between liberation theology (of which Ellacuría is an important representative and toward which Bergoglio/Pope Francis took up a complex and complexly evolving stance) and European and North American "progressive" or "revisionist" theologies (represented by Rahner).[11] The temptation is to take up an either/or perspective. The problem is that of adjudicating differences between theological positions in a world in which there is no one *theologia perennis*, nor one philosophical system that provides the basic vocabulary and argumentative canons for theology. Neither is there one *place* that provides the authentic context for theology, one *culture* that determinatively, ineluctably, and more or less univocally enfleshes the encounter with God that is the necessary precondition for theology.[12] Here we touch upon the problems of pluralism and inculturation. Various approaches have been suggested for providing the tools for contextualizing theological work in such a way that pseudo-disputes that arise from misunderstanding cultural differences can be avoided, and the real differences brought to the surface and debated in a meaningful and productive way. These approaches exploit philosophies of language, or new cultural anthropologies and ethnographic methodologies that focus on the material, symbolic, and conceptual dimensions of religious belief and practice. Others have emphasized the necessity of continually rooting theology in scripture, as that is variously received by (and, it is important to note, as it variously transforms) different cultural contexts.

I suggest that rooting theological work in underlying spiritual traditions is another fruitful avenue for addressing theological differences. In part it will involve the other techniques, because understanding spiritual traditions requires the painstaking deployment of rigorous linguistic and historical-contextual studies with regard to those traditions, texts, and actors.[13] Second, at least until recently, Christian spiritualities have been characterized by a strong scriptural engagement, so that to understand them or immerse oneself in them one cannot but encounter scripture, particularly as it has functioned as a normative locus of God's revelation. Finally, spiritualities travel easier. They often make the jump across cultures with greater ease than more elaborately articulated doctrinal assertions and theological systems. This is not to say that doctrinal assertion or theological systems are irrelevant, but that they are *actus secundus*. They arise out of spiritualities that are received and lived out in diverse cultural, political, and economic conditions. This suggests that by asking how a common spiritual tradition has been thus received we can make further headway in bringing about an authentic theological dialogue that goes beyond polemical rejection or laissez-faire relativism.

I hope that this suggestion will also be substantiated by the three case studies. By treating these Jesuits together in the light of their common Ignatian heritage, we will see how each in his own way has uncovered a crucial feature of our complex, multidimensional world. Further, I will argue that the best way to achieve an empathetic grasp of each theologian in his differences is through the spirituality that mediates his encounter with the one God, whom we all as Christians long to find, and the one world in which we all, like it or not, must find and be found by that God.

This brings us back to Ignatian spirituality in chapter 7. For if the initial overview discloses Ignatian spirituality in its basic elements and dynamisms, at the end, after seeing its actualization and theological elaboration in these three different cases, we will be prepared to understand it anew as a gift not just to the sixteenth century but to our own. Here we will discover that not only does theology need spirituality as its animating center, but spirituality needs theology, and academic theology at that. If spirituality is a set of spiritual exercises that animates and renews the theological imagination, enabling it to see the world afresh, it is the exercises of academic theology that present the world, so richly explored by other academic disciplines, to that imagination. What is more, it is academic theology, again mediating those other disciplines, that can light up a path toward the concrete realization of the world newly reimagined. If spirituality roots us concretely in the here and now, inviting us to encounter the God who would be found in the world of the everyday (a world at times wonderful, often tedious, at times horrific), it is theology that invites us to expand that vision, to connect our here and now, and the understanding of God we come to therein, with other horizons, separated from us in space and in time. Theology without spirituality runs the risk of devolving into technical jargon, reserved for experts. Spirituality without theology runs the risk of provincialism, vague romanticism, or fanaticism. Theology can continually remind us of the same insight that every spirituality (particularly the mystical members of the family) conveys: the God mediated to us by any spirituality always exceeds its bounds, and is to be found in other spiritual traditions, in other religious traditions, even in the secular world outside the religions (and even in the modern university).

This is an insight that the men whose work we are about to examine also understood well.

This work would not have been possible without sabbatical leaves granted me by the University of Notre Dame and the generous support both of ND and of the Boston College Center for Ignatian Spirituality, where I resided for a year as visiting scholar. I would like to recognize, in particular, Michael Buckley, SJ, who extended the initial invitation to come to Boston College while the Center for Ignatian Spirituality was still only in its formative stages, and Howard Gray, SJ, director of the Center. Without their generosity, encouragement, and sage counsel, this book would not have even gotten off the ground two decades ago. I regret that I was not able to finish the book before they entered eternity, but I hope, in the presence of that which we see only through a glass darkly, they will smile on its completion. As with everything I do, the great liberality of spirit (as Ignatius would put it) and intellectual acuity of my wife, Anselma, inspires and pervades this work. I can never thank her enough. Another debt I can never recognize enough is to my colleagues, both faculty and graduate students, in the Department of Theology at Notre Dame. Their accomplishment in the craft of theology has both humbled me and inspired me.

This book has benefited from critical appraisals, in part or in whole, by a number of receptive and generous readers. I would like, in particular, to thank the following people, who read all or part of this book and made invaluable suggestions: Kevin Burke, Robert Krieg, Brad Hinze, Ernesto Valiente, Andrew Prevot, and Robert Lassalle-Klein. I also am very grateful to the editors and staff at the University of Notre Dame Press, for their patience in waiting for this manuscript to mature, their tenacity in moving it forward during the difficult conditions of the pandemic, and their care and attention to detail in the production of the finished book. Finally, I thank my anonymous reviewers, who alerted me to issues to which I had not attended sufficiently and places where my argument needed greater precision. The opportunity their reviews afforded me to think again and think more deeply was very welcome. Obviously, the responsibility for the book's remaining shortcomings is my own.

Most of all, I would like to thank Kevin Burke, without whose friendship, continual encouragement, and the inspiration of his own example as someone who integrates Ignatian spirituality into theology, making of both together "an art of living," I would never have had the courage to persevere to bring this long project to a close. This book is dedicated to him. I also hope it is not impertinent to dedicate it in a secondary way to the men of the Society of Jesus, particularly its theologians. May this book in some small way encourage them to continue to ask, and help all of us to ask, with all the spiritual depths, intellectual rigor, and self-sacrificing courage that characterized Ignatius of Loyola, his demanding questions: "What have we done for Christ? What are we doing for Christ? What ought we to do for Christ?"

CHAPTER ONE

Haven in a Heartless World or Well of Vision?

Modernity and the Origins of Spirituality

"Spirituality" is a modern phenomenon, and this in two senses. First, the way we use the term today goes back only as far as the origins of modernity itself; second, it is the conditions of modernity that have made it possible, indeed almost inevitable, that we so use it. Spirituality arose as a response to the gradual triumph of that cluster of social, political, and intellectual conditions that is named modernity—first in Western Europe and North America, but increasingly around the world, albeit with varying inflections. It is, however, an ambiguous response, as many of its contemporary observers note. On the one hand, spirituality can end up being nothing but a mirror image of those conditions or a compensatory device for managing their negative consequences; on the other hand, it could become a way to transcend and even transform them. In theological terms, a spirituality could be nothing but an element of, or unreflective reaction to, the world (in the Johannine sense); or, it could be what its etymology suggests: a way of life in conformity to the Spirit of God, a gift of that Spirit to the church for the ongoing evangelization of the world. The purpose of this chapter is to elaborate on this ambiguity, in the course of which I will propose a framework examining the specific Christian spirituality that will be the focus of the rest of the book: Ignatian spirituality.

SPIRITUALITY:
ETYMOLOGICAL HISTORY AND MODERN USAGE

A look at the history of the term "spirituality" provides an initial justification of my claim that it is a child of modernity. What is striking in this regard is how recent the widespread use of the word is. In the United States, for example, the first edition of the *Catholic Encyclopedia*, completed in 1915, has no article with the title "spirituality." The new edition, completed seventy years later, has eight articles that include the word "spirituality" in their title and thirteen references to the word in its index.[1] Ten years later, Liturgical Press published its *New Dictionary of Catholic Spirituality*, with more than 1,000 pages and 600 entries.[2] An internet search today will produce sites in the hundreds of thousands. Where did this word come from and what explains its burgeoning popularity?

It is, to be sure, of distinguished lineage, with ancestors in the Hebrew Bible's expression for the spirit, or breath of God, and, more proximately, in Paul's deployment of the concepts of spirit and living according to the spirit. But the abstract noun—the Latin *spiritualitas*—does not appear until the early fifth century. Even then, it was rare, generally a way of rendering Paul's usage in which living according to the spirit is a way of talking about the whole person living in harmony with God's will. It is only in the High Middle Ages that we begin to find it being used to refer to specific regions of human experience and action. It was, for instance, used in law to express ecclesiastical jurisdiction and those who exercised it (the "lords spiritual," as opposed to the "lords temporal," or even a "spirituality" of bishops). In addition, in a fateful application, it was used by scholastic theology as a contrastive term to materiality or corporeality.[3]

At about this time, *spiritualitas* migrated into the different vernaculars of Europe. By and large these immigrants continued either to carry the more holistic, Pauline usage, or to denote ecclesiastical jurisdiction. But, in a development culminating in the sixteenth and seventeenth centuries, the term gradually came to denote the inner dispositions of the soul. As one seventeenth-century French dictionary put it, spirituality is "everything connected with the interior exercises of the soul free of the senses which seeks only to be perfected in the eyes of God."[4] After something of a golden age in France, however, the word fell out of favor, collateral damage to the condemnations of quietism at the end of the seventeenth century.[5] It was never prominent in the Anglophone world before the nineteenth century. In English-speaking North America, for instance, Jon Alexander notes that none of the titles of the most popular devotional tracts published before 1800 contain the word "spirituality," and in the following century it was far more likely to be found outside of the mainline denominations. Protestants preferred "devotion" and "piety," while Catholics often followed the Italian Jesuit Giovanni Battista Scaramelli for whom these matters were treated under subcategories of moral theology: ascetical and mystical theology.[6] This begins to change in the nineteenth century, even though the change first made itself felt outside the boundaries of the mainline churches.

In his book *Restless Souls*, Leigh Eric Schmidt tells the story of how the various elements that would constellate themselves in the United States to make up the discourse of spirituality in the twentieth century came into being in the nineteenth. Seeking the key to the genealogy of contemporary mania for things spiritual, he ends up with the following thesis: "What really counts in the invention of modern American spirituality? The history that matters most, by far, is the rise and flourishing in the nineteenth century of religious liberalism in all its variety and occasional eccentricity."[7] An assortment of practices from America's Protestant churches were taken up in this invention, including private prayer, diary writing, narration of conversion experiences, and Bible reading. The crucial additional step requisite to their regrouping (and often redefinition) under the umbrella category of spirituality was their extraction from the normative institutional and intellectual frameworks in which they had been carried across the Atlantic. This is what their "re-embedment" in a complex that Schmidt names "religious liberalism" provided.

By "religious liberalism" Schmidt intends a particular foregrounding of a dimension internal to liberalism in general. This dimension is mapped by a desire for individual mystical experience, a preeminence given to solitude and silence, an insistence on the immanence of the sacred, both to the individual and to nature, and an appreciation of religious diversity. This is what makes religious liberalism religious; the broader genus of liberalism is marked by the advocacy of reforms in society and an emphasis on creative self-expression and adventuresome seeking on the part of the individual.[8] It was the American Transcendentalists,

Ralph Waldo Emerson, Theodore Parker, and Amos Bronson Alcott, among others, who began the extraction of elements from New England Protestantism in order to group them together as "spirituality." The crucial steps in the process were their retrieval and renovation of "mysticism," their celebration of solitude and individual interiority as the locus for encountering the transcendent, and their celebration of nature. They also were the first to dabble in Asian religions, and thus opened the path for a fascination with meditation and prepared the way for a stance toward other religions that went beyond toleration to a virtual demand that one must understand and embrace them in some measure. Schmidt also insists—countering critiques of this growing fascination with "spirituality" as individualist, narcissistic, and indifferent to community and the common good—that religious liberalism gave rise to significant impulses toward a more just society:

> The same liberal spirit that led to the critique of conventional Christianity and organizational religion readily energized strenuous activism and self-denying social engagement, including innumerable reform causes from abolition to suffrage, from international relief to workers' rights. Commonly contained within this seeker spirituality was a critical social and political vision; repeatedly, self-reliance and solitary retreat were held in creative and effective tension with a sharply honed social ethics.... The religious and political vision of Martin Luther King Jr. in the 1950's and 1960's gained much from that combined inheritance from Thoreau to Mohandas Gandhi.[9]

On Schmidt's account, in sum, the growth of religious liberalism prepared the ground in the United States for the blossoming of this set of elements into a fascination with "spirituality" in the 1950s and, especially, the 60s, as detailed, for instance, by sociologist Robert Wuthnow.[10]

Given the Catholic Church's oppositional stance toward all things liberal throughout the nineteenth century and most of the twentieth, it is not surprising that the story that Schmidt tells is not characteristic there. The language of spirituality made its own way into Catholic thought and practice. The principal actors in this story were in Europe, at least to begin with. One entry into that story might be provided by considering the rise of interest in mysticism. To be sure, the history of spirituality is not coterminous with the history of mysticism. Nonetheless, if the story of the rise of "spirituality" in Protestant America has as its first chapter the revaluation of "mysticism," the same might be said in Catholic scholarship.[11] Early twentieth-century milestones in the journey toward mysticism's prominence in the Catholic world are given by two texts: *Mysticism*, by the Anglo-Catholic author Evelyn Underhill, and Baron Friedrich von Hügel's masterpiece, *The Mystical Element of Religion as Studied in Saint Catherine of Genoa and her Friends*. Hügel's work provided a pattern in which the historical retrieval of a group of authors (categorized as "mystics") and the insistence on the "mystical" element of religion need not entail a lack of concern for the historical-institutional element of religion or the analytical-speculative element (to give them Hügel's names). This marked a difference, at least in aspiration, between this Catholic approach and the fascination with mysticism in the United States that Schmidt traces. Identifying and acting on the need to maintain a vital circulation between the mystical, or spiritual, element of Christianity and its intellectual element (theology) became a leitmotif of a number of Catholic theologians as the twentieth century progressed, including Hans Urs von Balthasar, Karl Rahner, Henri de Lubac, Yves Congar, Marie-Dominique Chenu, and Jean Daniélou.

The usage of the term "spirituality," which connoted the same "intuitive-emotional" element of Christianity that Hügel had assigned to mysticism, found in the Catholic realm a decisive impetus in French historical scholarship. Evidence for this can be noted in the first fascicule of the massive *Dictionnaire de spiritualité*, published in 1932, or Étienne Gilson's 1943 inaugural lecture for the chair of the history of spirituality at the Institut Catholique de Paris.[12] These represent only the tip of the iceberg of a growing scholarly interest in "spirituality" that gradually made its way over to the United States, particularly after Vatican II. In the United States this migration can be marked, for example, by the inauguration of Paulist Press's Classics of Western Spirituality series in 1978, which currently numbers more than 120 volumes (expanding beyond its original charter so as to include works in Jewish, Muslim, and Native American spirituality).

A full story of how this scholarly interest in spirituality took root among Catholics, both scholars and nonscholars, in the United States has yet to be written.[13] Certainly the "mainstreaming" of Catholicism in the United States in the 1950s and 60s would be a principal element of its plot. As Catholics began to participate more openly in American culture they encountered the strands of religious liberalism, as Schmidt names it, just as these strands were coalescing and growing in strength to challenge the hegemony of mainline Protestant denominations in American culture and politics. Catholics certainly had their own spiritual practices to bring to the table, and could also boast of a long tradition of spiritual teachers and mystics, which was now being brought to light by the historical scholarship just detailed. Over time these practices and texts appear to have undergone the same kind of disembedding from ecclesial structures and theological framing that practices of Protestant provenance had already experienced. By the time sociologists and theologians began studying the category of the "spiritual but not religious," there are few significant differences between those who transitioned to that stance from Catholicism or from other Christian denominations.

Much work needs to be done to fill in the gaps of this brief history, but what seems incontrovertible is that the discourse of spirituality, especially in the frequent and wide-ranging usage it enjoys today, would have been a puzzle to most Christians until well into the modern era. It is certainly true that although the terminology is new, the reality the term denotes has existed from the beginnings of Christianity, indeed, from the beginnings of the human species itself. This is the position taken by various collections of "world spirituality," with entries for New Testament spirituality, Hindu, or Celtic spirituality, and so on.[14] The difference is that these features and practices were not collected and then contrasted with the network of social relations and tradition-defined ritual practices, institutions, and beliefs about the world from which they had been extracted and which now tend to be denoted by "religion." This is a difference that makes a difference, so that even if the particular practice is the same (say, the Jesus prayer), its meaning shifts when it becomes subsumed and practiced under the category of spirituality. In other words, although there is some merit to the argument that human beings have always had and practiced spirituality (or spiritualities), the foregoing history ought to alert us that something different and quite new is going on with "spirituality" as we move into the modern age. This difference and novelty emerge from even a relatively unsystematic sampling of texts that fall in the category of spirituality. Without seeking to be exhaustive, we now turn to such a sampling.

We might start by distinguishing between treatments of spirituality in the academy, along with handbooks or introductions for educated and interested laypersons, and what, for lack of a better term, I would call "popular spirituality." One can find astonishing diversity in the latter category. Over the past twenty or thirty years, the depth of North America's fascination with spirituality has been satisfied by a vast range of topics and genres, virtually defying definition or categorization. From her vantage point as an editor at the publishers' trade journal *Publisher's Weekly*, Phyllis Tickle observed in the 1990s that "what books currently are establishing about our landscape is, first and foremost, a burgeoning and generalized absorption with spirituality and religion in America today."[15] Whether it be the proliferation of New Age techniques or the retrieval of classics of medieval spirituality onto compact disc, the fascination with spirituality, along with its subcategory of mysticism, has spawned a seemingly unending stream of texts, CDs, DVDs, art works, workshops, conferences, and retreats. A random selection of a few texts proves illuminating.

Starting in the 1990s, consider Phil Jackson's book on spirituality and basketball, *Sacred Hoops*.[16] The phenomenally successful former coach of the Chicago Bulls related in this book how he collected and applied a diverse collection of spiritual techniques, drawn primarily from Zen Buddhism and the Lakota Sioux, but not entirely in opposition to his Pentecostal upbringing in North Dakota. According to his enthusiastic reviewers, his spirituality not only helped Jackson lead the Bulls to multiple NBA championships, but also provided "an earnest and refreshing answer to the dollar-driven soullessness of modern professional sports" (and all without sacrificing multimillion-dollar salaries).[17] Spirituality can, evidently, do the same for the world of business, as *The Corporate Mystic* claims. We are told in this book that "if you want to find a genuine mystic, you are more likely to find one in a boardroom than in a monastery or a cathedral."[18] One can find books on the spirituality of quantum physics, such as Diarmuid O'Murchu's *Quantum Theology: Spiritual Implications of the New Physics*, or, weighing in for Jewish spirituality, Daniel Matt's *God and the Big Bang*, which argues for correlations between Jewish kabbalah and the new physics and cosmology.[19]

A striking feature of much of this popular literature on spirituality is the tendency to understand spirituality as a phenomenon separate from, and even opposed to, religion. The authors of *The Corporate*

Mystic, for instance, tell us that "corporate mystics tend to be allergic to dogma, and often remain at a distance from religion in its more structured forms. Rather, they attempt to live their lives from the universal sources of spirituality that underlie differing beliefs. [For the corporate mystics] it is important for business-people to stay out of theology and potentially divisive beliefs about spirituality, and instead to focus on the unifying benefits of spiritual practice."[20]

In his book on the spiritual implications of the new physics, O'Murchu starts by defining spirituality as "the human search for meaning," or "the relational component of lived experience,"[21] before going on to claim that "spirituality is inherent to the human condition . . . ; in my estimation, religion is not."[22] This juxtaposing of spirituality and religion (usually to the detriment of the latter) is widespread. As Robert Wuthnow points out, "growing numbers of Americans say they are spiritual but not religious."[23] Corollary to this is the tendency to assume that at essence spiritualities are one, that "divisive beliefs about spirituality" and religious traditions and institutions that historically have carried spiritualities are epiphenomenal and, finally, dispensable. Anyone familiar with the seventeenth- and eighteenth-century search for a common core to all the religions will recognize this kind of move as a quintessentially modern one: the search for a "natural religion" or "religion of reason" has been reborn, but now under the rubric of spirituality. The recent literature on "spirituality and science" confirms this. An important criterion for determining what belonged to the "natural religion" of previous centuries was agreement with the new science. So too for spirituality today, but now the agreement must obtain not with Newtonian physics, but with the new quantum mechanics, cosmology, and evolution.[24]

A second feature that emerges from much of this literature is the eclectic and individualistic character of spiritualities. If all spiritualities are essentially one, then it makes no difference whether you follow the Buddha, Meister Eckhart, Black Elk, Isaac Luria, or all of them at once. What Robert Bellah and coauthors reported of religion in the United States in the 1980s fits spirituality like a glove. In a description that has become something of a classic, they wrote:

> Today religion in America is as private and diverse as New England colonial religion was public and unified. One person we interviewed actually named her religion (she called it her "faith") after herself. . . . "I

believe in God. I'm not a religious fanatic. I can't remember the last time I went to church. My faith has carried me a long way. It's Sheilaism. Just my own little voice." In defining "my own Sheilaism" she said: "It's just try to love yourself and be gentle with yourself. You know, I guess, take care of each other. I think He would want us to take care of each other."[25]

Sociologist Meredith B. McGuire confirms this trend from her own research on spirituality in North America in the 1990s. This research led her to conclude that the defining parameters of the spiritualities Americans craft for themselves are autonomy, eclecticism, and tolerance.[26] North Americans draw freely from the wide spectrum of spiritual traditions made available by the American culture industry: "In contemporary spirituality, traditional practices become cultural resources—along with cultural resources drawn from other spheres of life such as art—which individuals select and employ with relative autonomy."[27]

A final relevant point about "spirituality" in popular culture is that it is very often presented as a haven in a heartless world, a way of getting by, of creating a pocket of meaning and value in a hostile environment. It is a way of maintaining one's sense of identity and worth in a society that pulls us first this way and then that, in which we must play multiple roles in multiple settings. Often spirituality is presented (in the form of sabbatical programs, for instance) as a way of managing life-passages that are seemingly being forced on us with increasing frequency, and for which there are no longer any fixed traditions that serve to map these passages against a broader, durable, and sustaining landscape. This feature, as Wuthnow notes, connects the popularity of spirituality today with the popularity of small groups.[28]

Linda Mercadante's closer look at the "spiritual but not religious" provides some important nuances to this account.[29] Based on interviews with those in the United States who self-identify as "spiritual but not religious," she argues for the need for a more complex taxonomy than Wuthnow's division between seekers and dwellers.[30] She also argues that the content and coherence of beliefs play a greater role than is commonly granted when it comes to where and how a spiritual-but-not-religious person situates himself or herself within this taxonomy. Having stipulated the complexity and pluriformity of the spiritual but not religious, she does note some common themes that show up in the majority of her interviewees, some of which we have already encountered. First is the insistence that everyone should have the freedom to determine their spiritual practices rather than be compelled to accept them because of external pressures from the social milieu or religious institutions. Second comes an almost universal criticism and rejection of views that are taken to be representative of Western religious traditions, especially any kind of soteriological exclusivism (which sometimes extends even to a rejection of the category of "salvation" itself as inherently exclusionary), and any "thick" ecclesiology that gives soteriological weight to belonging to a particular community, which (in their view) often translates into a problematic externalization of authority in a church hierarchy or canon of texts.[31] Third, they believe that there is some kind of Universal Truth, to which all religions, particularly in their spiritual cores, are limited approximations. All religions (and all spiritualities) are at root the same. Fourth, as a logical consequence of the first and third tenets, the spiritual but not religious believe that hybridity and mixing of traditions is perfectly appropriate and even necessary for an authentic spiritual life. Identifying two further common features that seem particularly American, Mercadante notes that there is no patience for the way that religious believers or institutions fall short of the ideals that they espouse (a further reason that the spiritual but not religious are allergic to institutionalized religions), and finally that they often find in "pristine nature" a privileged locus for the experience of the sacred. Along with Schmidt, she warns against criticizing her interviewees' spirituality as necessarily narcissistic and purely therapeutic, a criticism that often takes its starting point from the least nuanced instances in contemporary culture of the spiritual but not religious.[32]

If we turn to scholarly treatments of spirituality, and to handbooks and popular introductions closely related to them, these characteristics are absent or muted to the extent that the books focus on a particular tradition and thus resist disembedding spirituality from religion, even if the two are still contrasted.[33] The plethora of academic definitions reveal, however, that there is no consensus on how to define it. Starting from the insight that the way one defines spirituality will depend on how and why one is studying it, Bernard McGinn has constructed a typology of three approaches to the study of spirituality.[34] A theological approach will tend to define spirituality using language that is more highly ramified in doctrinal and theological terms: Christologically, for instance, or on Trinitarian grounds, or pneumatologically. Walter Principe, for example, defines spirituality on a first level as "the *real* or *existential* level. This is the quality—the lived quality—of a person. It is the way some person understood and lived, within his or her historical context, a chosen religious ideal in sensitivity to the realm of the spirit or the transcendent. . . . A formulation of this level of spirituality [for Christians] might be the following: spirituality is life in the Spirit as brothers and sisters of Jesus Christ and daughters and sons of the Father."[35] McGinn names the second method the "anthropological approach." With such an approach, a scholar will stress that spirituality has to do with a universal element, or "depth dimension" of human nature and experience.[36] Roger Haight is representative of this approach. Drawing on Paul Tillich's theology of faith as ultimate concern, Haight defines spirituality as *"the logic, or character, or consistent quality of a person's or a group's pattern of living insofar as it is measured before some ultimate reality."* He goes on to observe that "this construal locates it [spirituality] so far down within the depths of a person that it shares in the mystery that personal being is to itself."[37]

Third, and finally, McGinn names the "historical-contextual approach" to spirituality, which focuses on "spirituality as an experience rooted in a particular community's history rather than as a dimension of human existence."[38] It starts with concrete figures and movements and only generalizes to more universal terms after describing them as carefully as possible.

Each approach brings its own challenges. The theological approach runs the danger of distorting spiritual traditions by too quickly placing them within a particular selection of theological concepts and doctrines, which becomes a Procrustean bed inadequate to the complexity of the experience mediated by that spirituality. Anthropological approaches run the danger of defining spirituality so broadly and vaguely that, covering much in general, spirituality defines almost nothing in particular.[39] The historical-contextual approach does best at examining spiritualities in the past; it is less helpful with the present. Moreover, the anthropological and historical-contextual approaches often operate with definitions that have implicit theological dimensions. It is difficult, for instance, to move very far in speaking about "the interior person" or "the deepest core of a person" without using terminology that has a long history within the Christian tradition (even though that tradition has often been elided as a part of the processes of secularization) or, in using them, cedes too much to reductive approaches that rely on the natural and human sciences. A further difficulty concerns normativity. Is it appropriate, for instance, to talk about a "Nazi spirituality"? This question can be emphatically answered in the negative from the theological approach; it is less clear how to draw such a denial from the other two approaches. As McGinn concludes, approaches to spirituality will be most adequate when they are at least aware of this diversity of approach and definition, and in conversation with those that differ.[40] Indeed, on closer analysis, few definitions will end up being a pure instance, but will rather be hybridizations that emphasize one approach more than the other two.

One feature of the more scholarly treatments of spirituality bears further attention. Many definitions of Christian spirituality sound very much like definitions of Christian faith or Christian life in general. That is, in many of these definitions one could easily remove the word "spirituality" and replace it with "Christian faith" or "being a Christian."[41] Why use this word "spirituality" to define the Christian life as a whole? If popular literature often defines "spirituality" in such a way that it is synonymous with being authentically human, scholarly literature seems frequently to define Christian spirituality in such a way that it is synonymous with being a faithful Christian.

There are different strategies to render the definition of spirituality precise enough that it is not coterminous with religion. In the theological approaches to studying spirituality, this is often done by connecting it with pneumatology, reasonable enough given the word's etymology. Alternatively, one can delimit it according to its object: God. McGinn reports that the editors of a volume on early Christian spirituality tried to deal with the issue of definition by asserting that spirituality is distinguished from religious belief or doctrine in that it has to do with "the reaction that faith arouses in religious consciousness and practice," while it differs from Christian ethics in that it deals only with those acts "in which the relation to God is immediate and explicit."[42] This tends to put the focus on particular practices, such as *lectio divina*, meditative and contemplative prayer, participation in liturgical prayer, or activities that are difficult to account for except as more immediate responses to God: self-mortification, religious pilgrimage, veneration of relics, and so on.[43] The first of these two moves (emphasizing the *reaction* that faith arouses in religious consciousness and practice) is instantiated more broadly in those approaches that nuance the definition of spirituality in such a way as to emphasize its existential character. Perusing definitions of spirituality, one will be struck by the frequent occurrence of phrases such as "subjective appropriation," "personal engagement," "lived" or "real" experience of faith, and so on.[44] This emphasis on personal appropriation could well be a manifestation of the hard contrast we moderns tend to make between the individual and the social character of faith, a contrast given classic articulation by Max Weber with his distinction between charism and institution. If so, then it is an important clue, since it directs our attention to the origins of modernity, when the distinction between inner self and outer world, including the outer social world, came into a clearer (and split) focus.

To sum up, in popular literature today "spirituality" is used in such a diversity of ways and contexts as to defy univocal definition, even though one can identify certain general features that most usages have in common. Even in academic treatments there are at least three general categories of approach and definition, with many hybridizations between them. My point is not to discount the value of talking about or studying spirituality because of its resistance to clear definition. My purpose has been, first, to show that the presence of the terminology is pervasive to our culture, and so too, perhaps, the reality to which it refers, however difficult that reference is to identify and specify. Second, and more important, my intent has been to indicate both the ambiguity and also the modernity of this term on so many lips today. It is of course true that Christians, indeed, human beings, have in the past done and reflected on the sorts of things that we today gather under this category. It was only well into Christianity's second millennium that Christians themselves began to organize them into a category separate from, and even opposed to, the institutional and intellectual elements of Christianity. It is in this sense that Augustine, Bernard of Clairvaux, and Aquinas would have been puzzled by the term "spirituality" as we use it and practice its referents.[45] They certainly did not see it as a bag of tools that one picks up from various spiritual traditions so that one can tinker with his or her self, get retooled for life's passages, or make repairs when broken by the hardness of the world. Spirituality, in *this* sense, arose with modernity.

Early Modernity and the Origins of Spirituality

If this argument is persuasive, then the next step is to understand what is going on in the modern phenomenon of spirituality by looking at it in the context of the passage to modernity in the late Middle Ages and early modern era. This was a passage that also marked shifts of meaning for *spiritualitas* and its migration into the vernaculars. Coincidence or succession in time do not in themselves entail causality, to be sure, and a full account of the historical causes of the rise of spirituality would, in any event, exceed the limits of this overview. My strategy is to argue that some major features of the shift from the premodern to modern shed enough light on the particular features that spirituality has taken on today to make a reasonable case that the two phenomena (modernity and spirituality) are closely interlinked.

In the High and late Middle Ages, the growth of cities nourished a growing and literate middle class, which occupied an increasingly diversified matrix of roles in the expanding European economy. The needs of this class and the general increase in complexity in European society explains at least in part the exfoliation of new forms of life that stemmed from the search for an authentic *vita apostolica*, a development that includes the mendicant orders but also "nonorders" such as lay confraternities or the Beguines.[46] Accompanying and feeding this process was a growing interest in individual "spiritual experience," as we would call it today. It is probably too much to say that the Middle Ages discovered the individual in its modern sense, but there is no doubt that there was a growing interest in exploring and describing the individual and his (and, increasingly, her) interior landscape. This interest was increasingly slaked by a growing production of itineraries of the soul, methodologies for prayer, collections of meditations, and autobiographical accounts of visions, and also by the phenomenon of spiritual direction, particularly of the laity.[47]

In a crucial respect, another important development for which we remember the High and late Middle Ages ran parallel to this one and reinforced it in complex ways. The birth and triumph of the university and its theological innovation, scholasticism, in the thirteenth century, meant a growing hegemony of theology as rational science, with its techniques of *lectio*, *quaestio*, and *disputatio*, structured into the *summa*. While it is true that their ultimate goal was to nurture ministry in general, and preaching in particular (theology was, after all, a professional degree), it is the case nonetheless that the genres and techniques of scholasticism could not easily accommodate the burgeoning interest in recounting and elaborating one's personal and interior experiences of God. The alternative techniques and genres that did meet this need developed outside the university, and because of that increasingly outside the boundaries of "theology," as the university was coming increasingly to represent it. Jean Leclercq's classic study *The Love of Learning and the Desire for God* mounts an argument to keep the definitional boundaries of theology in the Middle Ages broad enough to include "monastic theology," even if the latter did not hew to the procedures and genres of scholastic theology. Perhaps, however, "vernacular theology"—as McGinn names it—was even closer to the joys and sorrows of the growing class of literate laity in medieval Europe than monastic theology.[48] It featured genres that were less frequently found in scholasticism or monastic theology, if at all. McGinn describes it thus:

> Given the practical and synthetic nature of much vernacular theology, there is some overlap with monastic genres, though vernacular theology has less room for explicit biblical commentary, especially because technical biblical study was inaccessible to most laymen and to all women. Much vernacular theology was expressed in sermonic form, though of many different kinds. A wide variety of treatises and "little books" were employed, as well as hagiography and letters. Poetry was also of significance.... Of special importance in vernacular theology was the visionary account.[49]

These genres were tailor-made to the needs and capacities of a new, largely lay audience. Vernacular theology also saw the first large-scale emergence of women's voices in Christian writing. These features, along with the greater linguistic fluidity of the vernaculars at this time, help explain its daring innovations. It also helps explain its explosive growth, despite the suspicion of ecclesiastical authorities and of many scholastic theologians, who had been able to monopolize the universities and make themselves the spokespersons for orthodoxy during the thirteenth and fourteenth centuries. The execution of Margaret Porete and the heresy trial of Meister Eckhart are only the most dramatic manifestations of the tensions that resulted. More generally they manifested in a growing split between different genres, with different audiences, different concerns, and different social loci of production. This split would gradually find terminological expression as a split between "theology" and "spirituality."

Many of these developments bespeak the onset of the secularization of European Christendom. We see a growing differentiation of separate spheres of social activity, with correlative institutions, processes, and modes of discourse, which implied and constructed ways of organizing space and time, not around the medieval axes—between this world and the next, and within this world between the sacred and the profane—but around multiple organizing axes, the two most important being the growing capitalist market economy and the increasingly powerful nation-state.[50] A situation was in the offing that many of us can recognize today: men and women, especially in the cities, found their lives divided among multiple roles—citizen, religious believer, consumer (of goods and services, but also of "culture" and of "religious culture," in particular), worker, intellectual, parent—each of which was increasingly associated with distinct and relatively autonomous institutions and different ways of organizing space and time, interlinked by abstract clock-time and by spatial networks less and less confined to or defined by geographical locale (think, for instance, of the expanding financial networks). Rather than being the organizing center of the human city, *Christianitas* had to find room in a city more and more organized around different foci.[51] In this regard, Michel de Certeau's insight about the origins of "mysticism" as an autonomous field of discourse and practice applies to spirituality as a whole: "The One is no longer to be found. 'They have taken him away,' say so many chants of the mystics who inaugurate, with the story of his loss, the history of his returns elsewhere and otherwise, in ways that are the effect rather than the refutation of his absence. While no longer 'living,' this 'dead' one still does not leave the city—which was formed without him—in peace. He haunts our environs."[52]

This sense of absence was exacerbated by the growth of nominalism in the universities, and the traumatic crises that wracked the fourteenth-century institutional Church. There was less and less incentive to look for a unifying presence of God in either place. As Louis Dupré argues, "spiritualities," increasingly located outside of traditional centers of ecclesiastical and academic work, were able to sustain a bit longer the felt synthesis of human, cosmic, and divine, whose disintegration inaugurated the passage to modernity.[53] Even though exiled from the world of the university, as such, and often marginalized by the institutional Church, they still inspired many of the most profound attempts to knit a new intellectual and cultural synthesis, in Nicholas of Cusa, for instance, in the Jesuits, as I shall argue later, or in the distant influence of the Rhineland mystics on German idealism, and even on Martin Heidegger.[54]

Charles Taylor describes the relative autonomy of the human city that came with modernity in terms of a shift to what he names the "immanent frame." On his view, conceptualizing the shift this way provides a more adequate construal of our history than a crude secularization thesis, according to which a scientifically grounded and structured society gradually, inevitably, and "naturally" triumphs over religion:

> The vector which I want to offer in its place, at least for Western society (and that is what my arguments in this book focus on) is more complicated. We have undergone a change in our condition, involving both an alteration of the structures we live within, and our way of imagining these structures. This is something we all share, regardless of our differences in outlook. But this cannot be captured in terms of a decline and marginalization of religion. What we share is what I have been calling "the immanent frame"; the different structures we live in, scientific, social, technological, and so on, constitute such a frame in that they are part of a "natural" or "this-worldly" order which can be understood in its own terms, without reference to the "supernatural" or the "transcendent." But this order of itself leaves the issue open whether, for purposes of ultimate explanation, or spiritual transformation, or final sense-making, we might have to invoke something transcendent.[55]

His point is that *pace* atheistic construals, which insist that the issue *has* been decided, we all live in a space of undecidability regarding the existence, or, more importantly, the presence and significance of something transcendent when it comes to living our lives within the "immanent frame." This undecidability itself produces in many a sense of loss, even in those who have turned away from traditional religions, a sense of loss to which "spirituality" responds. Thomas Moore, author of the best seller *Care of the Soul*, touches on this need in a more recent book:

> I was speaking with a woman recently about the craving for spirituality. I asked her what she thought it was all about. She became quiet for a moment and then slowly and carefully said, "We want more, more than what is." I've heard this response all over the world, and I believe that simple statement about wanting more expresses the need for transcendence. The object of this desire is unknown and open-ended. It isn't described in typical religious language, and yet I think it evokes the very essence of both religion and spirituality.[56]

The descriptor "spiritual" denotes a "something more," even if one, unlike Moore, steadfastly refuses to associate it with the traditional religions, and wants to keep it more firmly bounded by "the immanent frame." Thus, in his introduction to *The Best Spiritual Writing: 2011*, poet laureate and former Catholic Billy Collins writes of how he "came to sense that a spiritual realm could be accessed, not via the recommended roads of religion leading to portals guarded by priests, rabbis, imams, and religious leaders of other stripes, but instead, directly through *actual daily experience*."[57] For him this happened through poetry: "Along the way in my teaching and reading of poetry, I discovered little apertures into something larger. I sensed that these discoveries were 'spiritual' if only by default; that is, I had no other words for them."[58] In his beautiful final book, *Gratitude*, the late neurologist and writer Oliver Sacks, after a family visit, wrote wistfully about his Orthodox Jewish upbringing, which he had definitively left behind for a nonaggressive but resolved atheism: "The peace of Sabbath, of a stopped world, a time outside time, was palpable, infused everything, and I found myself drenched with wistfulness, with something akin to nostalgia, wondering what if: What if A and B and C had been different? What sort of person might I have been? What sort of life might I have lived?"[59]

To be sure, many persons in this space of undecidability are resolutely, even stoically content to reside and find meaning wholly in the immanent frame (as was Sacks). Some are uncomfortable even with Collins's appeal to spirituality "if only by default." Some "nones" are even hesitant to use the descriptor "spiritual," because it strikes them as still too redolent of the inheritance of traditional religions (usually Christianity), and because it still appears to move too far in the direction of invoking some sort of transcendence vis-à-vis everyday human life.[60] For some, identifying themselves with a term that has been reconfigured over the past two centuries to be a contrastive to "religious" is *still* too much of a concession to religion as a point of reference. Thus, if the undecidability that is inherent to life in the immanent frame does not lead to a sense of loss or mourning, it still results for many people in an anxiety or drive to excise the other option (being religious, having faith, or even "being spiritual") to such an extent that it is no longer plotted in one's spiritual-moral universe at all, even as something one rejects.

This brief historical reconnaissance suggests that spirituality—constituted as a specific and relatively distinct field of practices and beliefs that found expression in a particular genre of literature ("vernacular theology")—arose in response to the social and cultural shifts that gave birth to modernity. "Spirituality" responded to very real needs occasioned by this passage into modernity. Yet spirituality also embodied many of the conditions of modernity to which it responded. That is, we can understand some of the common characteristics of spirituality as practiced and spoken about today by looking at them in the light of the passage to modernity.[61] The following sketch does not aim to be an exhaustive account of modernity (if such were possible), nor even a complete account of the ways that spirituality and modernity coimplicate one another. I focus on three aspects of modernity that find clear resonances in the phenomenon of spirituality: (1) modern individualism; (2) the affirmation of everyday life and the deconstruction of hierarchies of human perfection entailed by this affirmation; (3) the accelerating transience of techno-economic, political, and cultural structures.

Perhaps most prominent among the conditions of modernity is our modern individualism, variously evoked in philosophy and sociology by talk about the Cartesian self, the buffered self, utilitarian and aesthetic individualism, or the radical reflexivity of our sense of self. The basic idea is that formerly the human self was situated and constituted within a broader matrix of the cosmos and of the divine, nourished by currents of meaning, truth, and beauty that circulated more or less unimpeded throughout this broader whole. In modernity, the self has construed itself as buffered from any exogenous currents of this sort, and in the process has come to be understood as the exclusive source, even creator, of meaning, truth, ethical obligation, and beauty. These have to be *produced*, and the guarantee of their legitimacy is taken not primarily from their presence in the objects of our cognitive, moral, practical, and aesthetic activity, but in the adequate policing of the intrasubjective activities that produce them.

Often this means that these activities must be placed within the constraints of various methodical canons—hence modernity's emphasis on "method." Moreover, because meaning, value, ethical obligation, and beauty are now taken to be nothing more than projections of the buffered self onto nature, nature is opened up to instrumentalization, even a violent instrumentalization, since it has no intrinsic value or truth that might resist our impositions upon it.[62] In addition, because the divine is an alternative, heteronomous source of truth and meaning, God can be (and increasingly was) construed as a threat to human freedom and creativity. In a further, and ironic development, this process rebounds back on the person allegedly benefited by it, as the razor-sharp scalpel of radical reflexivity turns upon his or her own identity and the site from which this reflexivity is exercised collapses in on itself like some kind of subjective black hole. As Johann Baptist Metz puts it, we have become less and less our own memory (which is to say, persons who are sustained by their presence to a thickly and temporally rendered identity that is to some extent given to them and outside their control) and more and more our infinitely malleable experiment.[63]

What this means for being a self is that we are less and less able to find moorings and sources for our identity by virtue of our involvement in an ordered cosmos or in human communities constituted by substantive and ongoing historical traditions. Everything is always, at least in principle, up for grabs. Anthony Giddens describes how modern therapeutic literature details the work required to become and remain selves under such conditions. "The self," he summarizes, "is seen as a reflexive project, for which the individual is responsible. . . . The self forms a trajectory of development from the past to the anticipated future. The individual appropriates his past by sifting through it in the light of what is anticipated for an (organized) future."[64] What this requires for the "self-actualized" person is continual self-surveillance, all the more so as "what is anticipated for an (organized future)" is itself under the pressure of accelerating rates of change. Moderns have to manage their identities just as rigorously as they manage stock portfolios—and both endeavors are laden with anxiety and risk.

This work is complicated by what Peter Berger has called the pluralization of life-worlds.⁶⁵ Each of us is involved in a variety of contexts, institutions, and processes, pulling us in different directions and requiring different organizations of the elements, practices, and narratives that sustain our sense of continuity as selves. Thus, not only is it meaningful to speak of "lifestyles" in modernity, but "lifestyle sectors," responding to different contexts, and not necessarily fully coherent, one with the others.⁶⁶ It is not just one, relatively integrated and holistic future that I anticipate as I commit and recommit myself to being a self, but a plurality of futures. This pluralization or even fragmentation of life-worlds adds to the work of maintaining "continuity" of identity by continual and reflexive self-surveillance and commitment to just this (or that) constellation of practices. Yet the "self" exercising this surveillance and commitment has become vanishingly small. It was already apparent to Friedrich Nietzsche more than a century ago that modern man has "a small soul." Dupré notes: "It seems an amazing charge to make after four centuries of unparalleled self-emancipation, and yet a justified one. In the process of assuming control over everything else the self has, as Kierkegaard put it, lost sight of its own identity. Separated from that totality which once nurtured it and largely deprived of the interiority which once defined it, it has become an indigent self."⁶⁷

One need not look very far to see how modern spirituality is implicated in these conditions. It was in sixteenth- and seventeenth-century France that spirituality came to be understood precisely in terms of an interiority that buffered the soul from its various modes of external embodiment as surely as the Cartesian *cogito* was intended to buffer reason from threats to its autonomy. Modern manuals of spirituality are replete with methods and practices for exercising precisely the kind of self-surveillance that being a modern self requires. Among the most common practices recommended in contemporary popular literature are meditative centering practices that allow one to "get in touch with where one is at."⁶⁸ But the goal is not, as it was for the ancient Stoics, for example, to achieve that vantage point from which one could perceive and accede to the order that unites one to the cosmos. The point of "being centered" is to access the detached vantage point necessary for planning an internally coherent life-trajectory in the face of a multiplicity of possible futures that have no inherent order or predictable regime of continuity and change. This brings us to another related theme that is very common in this literature: the notion of false self as opposed to true self. *The Corporate Mystic* puts it this way: "Most mystical traditions speak of a clear space at the center of ourselves, whether it is called soul or spirit or essence. It is what some call the higher self and represents who we really are at the core. Corporate Mystics know how to stay focused on this essence in themselves and in their coworkers, and how to bring it forth reliably."[69]

This "essence" is contrasted with a variety of personae that the corporate mystic takes up in the day-to-day execution of his or her work (and the authors use the etymological sense of "mask" in defining persona). The corporate mystic moves easily back and forth between different personae and holds them together by reference to his or her mystical sense of his or her own "essential self" and those of others. Yet this "essential" self is every bit as thin as Husserl's transcendental ego. Little characterizes it except its function of integrating the different roles that the modern business person must play and its appearance in and through "spirituality."[70]

A further feature of spirituality, as conceived in modernity, becomes intelligible in this context: the importance of ongoing attentiveness to one's spirituality and a willingness to augment or change it as needed. I argued above that, at the limit, being a modern self means having an identity that is sustained by continual reevaluation of and recommitment to the various and shifting sets of practices by which one negotiates one's day-to-day life. It is not too much to say that one would need to do this on a daily basis, particularly given the new information about one's context and the diversity of futures made available on one's cell phone that one has to manage. Even short of this limit case, the number of "life-passages" at which we are exhorted to reevaluate and recommit—or commit to something else—is growing: when I graduate from college; when I change jobs or even change tasks within the same job; whenever a personal relationship disappoints me; at the New Year, and so on. It has long been noted that Americans tend to exercise this kind of choice when it comes to denominational affiliation, but what we are seeing in the new prominence of spirituality is a situation in which not even a multidenominational or multireligious culture is flexible enough to allow the necessary mobility of personal commitment. A culture whose members are "spiritual but not religious" is.

The exigency to continual self-surveillance and self-(re)commitment, arising from the constitutive inability of modern selves to rely on and find sustenance in external structures and traditions is, I suggest, also behind the tendency to define spirituality in terms of personal choice and commitment. This is almost the *sine qua non* of spirituality in the popular literature, and, as I argued earlier, it is a common trope in academic definitions of spirituality as "lived religious experience and practice" or "one's subjective response to and living out of a religious tradition." What this language articulates is this sense of the need for ongoing and pervasive evaluation, reevaluation, and commitment that is such a central part of the modern understanding and practice of spirituality.

Taylor has named the second principal feature of being a self in modernity that I highlight as "the affirmation of everyday life."[71] He describes it by limning a contrast. In classical antiquity and beyond, the "excellent life" was defined in terms of certain privileged forms of life: for the Greeks, participation of the citizen in the life of the *polis* or the life of theoretical contemplation. Christians took the latter and made of it a life centered on contemplative prayer. The everyday tasks of sustaining and reproducing life, though not unworthy of the human, did not, nonetheless, provide access to the most worthy life. As we move into the modern era, Taylor argues, we see a momentous transition, "one which upsets these hierarchies, which displaces the locus of the good life from a special range of higher activities and places it within 'life' itself. The human life is now defined in terms of labour and production, on the one hand, and marriage and family life, on the other. At the same time, the previous 'higher' activities come under vigorous criticism."[72] Taylor locates the proximate sources of this transition in the Reformation, but late medieval spirituality preceded the Reformers in this shift.[73] McGinn has argued that in certain strands of medieval and late medieval mysticism we see the seeds of the "democratization" of Christian mysticism, opening it up to all classes of medieval society, including those outside the monastery.[74] Any way of life could be the locus of that particular perfection—union with God—that had previously been reserved to the eremetic, cenobitic, or mendicant orders. This exaltation of the everyday could tread onto perilous ground, since the Church's ethics and soteriological economy had been articulated in close proximity to the hierarchical vision of perfection that Eckhart and others subverted. He never fully evaded—perhaps could not evade—the suspicion of falling into the error of the so-called heresy of the free spirit: namely, that one could make an end run around the Church's ethical teachings and sacramental system, and reach the perfection of mystical union just by grounding oneself in one's own everyday life.[75]

The affirmation of everyday life is nowhere so evident as in today's literature on spirituality. We've seen it in Billy Collins's assertion that we can and should access the spiritual through "actual, everyday experience"; or in the assertion that mystics are more likely to be found in the boardroom than the cloister. Every possible dimension or way of life can lead to spiritual perfection, as can be seen in the proliferation of books on "the spirituality of . . ."or "spirituality and . . ." : spirituality of commerce, spirituality of sexuality, spirituality of the family; spirituality of agriculture, even, as a columnist in *U.S. Catholic* once advocated, a "spirituality of shopping."[76] This proliferation expresses and reinforces the eclecticism of spirituality we have noted, and it reinforces the emphasis on spirituality as *my* way of embracing and living out my religious ideals in my particular context.

Using more overtly theological terms, we could lay out the logic of this usage in the following way. If all Christians are followers of Christ, called to perfection, and if that perfection is equally available to all persons in all walks of life, then Christians need a term to talk about the various and diverse responses to that call, a term, however, that does not compromise the unity of the faith (that is, Christians can all still profess the same faith, but live it out in diverse ways). "Vocation" or "calling" have performed that task in the past in Catholicism, but they have never been able completely to shed their connection to the hierarchical vision that was subverted by the affirmation of everyday life, as is still evident in many homilies preached on "Vocation Sunday." Moreover, these terms imply a demanding commitment over the course of one's life not to renegotiate or change the particular way that one has chosen to incarnate one's following of Christ. This commitment to not changing one's commitment is in tension with the pressures noted above that impinge on maintaining one's identity under the conditions of modernity, in particular the exigency to ongoing renegotiation in a pluriform and rapidly changing world. Spirituality has become a discursive category more congenial to this work.

Third, modernity is characterized by a dramatic sense of transience. Hartmut Rosa contends that "the time structures of modernity stand above all under the sign of acceleration. The acceleration of processes and events is a fundamental principle of modern society."[77] He argues that this acceleration is composed of a mutually reinforcing trio of technological acceleration, acceleration in the tempo of life, and acceleration of rates of social and cultural change.[78] Moderns labor under a growing awareness of ever-accelerating change, and new technologies and social media are untethering our awareness of time and space from local time (defined by seasonal and circadian rhythms) and geographical neighborhood. Events far removed in time and space now impinge directly on our awareness of who we are and the risks that await our attempts to move into the future with the "self" that we have constructed up to this point. All the more reason why our spiritualities have to be portable and adaptable. We have to carry our shrines and sacred places with us, and keeping up with an accelerating modernity, we must travel light. "Spirituality" is coming more and more to indicate what you choose to carry with you in order to cope with the high demands of becoming and remaining a self in late modernity. In the nineteenth century it was the family that was the haven in a heartless world, presided over by the woman as the guardian of virtue, warmth, and humanity. With the family in crisis, we have learned, like turtles, to carry our havens on our backs.[79]

Perhaps my point has been made clearly enough. Spirituality is so popular today because it responds to very human needs in a world characterized by change that is increasingly rapid, both intensive and extensive, and beyond comprehension and prediction even by our legions of experts. This can be brought home by returning to the metaphorical comparison of managing one's identity to managing one's stock portfolio. In a TED Talk for 2011, MIT's Kevin Slavin explains that more and more of the processes and decisions that shape our lives are governed by networks of computer algorithms that operate with little or no human oversight. And very, very fast:[80] "So let me take it back to Wall Street. Because the algorithms of Wall Street are dependent on one quality above all else, which is speed. And they operate on milliseconds and microseconds. And just to give you a sense of what microseconds are, it takes you 500,000 microseconds just to click a mouse. But if you're a Wall Street algorithm and you're five microseconds behind, you're a loser."[81] Spirituality has taken up the powerful, if protean role it has today because it has provided a response to these conditions of dizzying acceleration of change and the need continually to negotiate and renegotiate one's identity in this "runaway world." We do this, moreover, in the awareness that the changes and risks that impinge on this project are being driven by forces far removed from us both temporally and geographically, with less and less direct human oversight, and within an immanent frame characterized by a fundamental and enduring undecidability as to whether there is "anything more." This is a powerful constellation of forces and changes, and the creation of a spirituality represents the selection of just those practices and the beliefs associated with them that can help moderns respond to it, while bracketing (minimally) or rejecting (maximally) those that do not.

Yet, it is an ambiguous response. On the one hand, the contemporary practice and discourse of spirituality shows that even in one of the wealthiest and most advanced of the nations that modernity engendered, our hearts are still restless. Spirituality provides some succor from the more stressful and inhumane features of our late modern world, while also at least hinting that there is a "more" that constitutes a vantage point from which these features can be placed at arm's length and, perhaps, changed. On the other hand, insofar as spirituality mirrors modernity's conditions it can end up being little more than a coping device; it can accustom us to living on the ever-accelerating juggernaut that is our modern world, considering less and less the costs both to ourselves and to those who fall off—or get run over. This point is raised by Wuthnow in *God and Mammon*. Speaking of our economic behavior, he reports:

> When we *are* influenced by our faith, we are more likely to say we feel better about what we do than to do anything differently.... Our spirituality is often little more than a therapeutic device. A relationship to God is a way of making ourselves feel better.... We pray for comfort but do not expect to be challenged. We have domesticated the sacred by stripping it of authoritative wisdom and by looking to it only to make us happy.[82]

Spirituality comes increasingly to be a way of feeling better under conditions over which we feel less and less control.

What makes spirituality so successful also accounts for its ambiguity. Eclectic and individualized, emphasizing the experience of the sacred *within*, spirituality often (but not necessarily and universally, as Schmidt and Mercadante remind) reinforces the tendency to see my world and my society as either inhuman situations to be endured or a neutral stage on which I play out the drama of my individual selfhood.[83]

Separating spirituality from a tradition of beliefs and from theology—or any form of disciplined inquiry, for that matter—makes it more and more difficult to perceive, to think about, and to discuss intelligently the ways one's spirituality could, and should, cohere with other ways of knowing and acting in the world. Spirituality affirms the possibility of encountering the sacred, of finding God in every walk of life and in all of life's activities, but often at the price of atomizing these activities, of covering over the ways our various "lifestyles" and "lifestyle-sectors" are structured into a broader world in which there is widespread suffering. It is all well and good to see one's visits to the mall at Christmastime as a spiritual exercise, embodying generosity and concern for others, but the "others" in this case do not include the workers in sweatshops in Indonesia or El Salvador, whose dehumanizing labor makes possible my spiritual exercises over here. It is not Phil Jackson's statement to his players that "our journey together each year, from the start of training camp to the last whistle in the playoffs, is a sacred quest"[84] that is the problem; it is the tendency to define that "sacred quest" apart from the wasted lives and crushed dreams of those who litter the sidelines, like the young black men in inner-city Chicago, portrayed to devastating effect in the film *Hoop Dreams*.[85]

SPIRITUALITY AND THE WELLS OF VISION

What are theologians to make of this? As contemporary observers from Schmidt to Drescher remind us, it is too easy to dismiss much of this literature as the typically faddish and ephemeral products of U.S. popular culture, and to see the academic literature as yet another interesting arena of scholarly research, fine for historians and perhaps for those interested in contemporary pastoral theology. If it is true that the interest in spirituality is remaking the religious map of North America, then no one who thinks that critical reflection on the situation and praxis of the church is indispensable to theology can overlook this phenomenon.

To reiterate, the modern phenomenon of spirituality is a sign of the times, replete with challenge, but also with hope, requiring an interpretation in the light of the gospel. This interpretation cannot simply have the world "out there" as its object, but must be a self-examination on the part of the church and theology. How has this situation come into being? To what extent has the church and theology played a part in the history outlined above? How can the interest in spirituality be understood as a gift of the Spirit and as an opportunity for carrying forward the evangelization of culture? What changes in self-understanding and in practice would be required of the church and of theology to enable them to take advantage of this opportunity?

Joining a number of theologians from the past one hundred years, we might begin with the assertion that the separation, often even opposition, of academic theology and spirituality needs to be rethought and the two brought into a more fruitful dialogue. As a start, we can ask what contribution spirituality can make to academic theology. A first answer would be that taking the literature of spirituality seriously offers theology a whole new set of materials for investigation. There is much to be learned from John Ruusbroec concerning the Trinity or from Julian of Norwich on soteriology. Spiritual masters often find refreshing and even scandalous ways of naming God and drawing on and reconfiguring scripture, which can reenliven theological discourse that has become too mired in philosophical terminology or too focused on one strand of scripture and tradition.

As important as this level is, I am after a deeper, albeit more elusive one. At a more profound level, a spirituality, when embraced in depth and over time, transforms one's way of seeing the world, God, and oneself. This transformation cannot but have an influence on one's theology. The theology that results certainly needs to be examined according to its adequacy to scripture, its creative fidelity to the tradition, its argumentative coherence, and its credibility to believers and nonbelievers, but it can and should also be understood as an invitation to share in that spiritual transformation. Pierre Hadot makes this argument with respect to the relationship between classical philosophy and its "spiritual exercises." He shows that in classical antiquity philosophy was not primarily a set of propositions knit together into an account of the world, both physical and metaphysical. Philosophy was more fundamentally a way of life that engaged one's entire being and that had to be entered by means of laborious spiritual exercises. For the Stoics, for instance,

> philosophy did not consist in teaching an abstract theory — much less in the exegesis of texts — but rather in the art of living. It is a concrete attitude and determinate life-style, which engages the whole of existence. The philosophical act is not situated merely

on the cognitive level, but on that of the self and of being. . . . It is a conversion which turns our entire life upside down, changing the life of the person who goes through it. It raises the individual from an inauthentic mode of life, darkened by unconsciousness and harassed by worry, to an authentic state of life, in which he attains self-consciousness, an exact vision of the world, inner peace, and freedom.[86]

It was this that the Christian apologists had in mind when they claimed that Christianity was the true philosophy, or, even earlier, what Philo of Alexandria meant in calling Judaism the *patrios philosophia*. The founders of monasticism were making the same point when they called the monastic life *vera philosophia*. Texts produced by the philosophical schools of antiquity, later the monastic rules, and later still classic spiritual texts proposed sets of exercises, concrete practices that would turn one's life upside down, bringing one to "self-consciousness, an exact vision of the world, inner peace, and freedom."

Hadot argues that even the theoretical productions of classical philosophy have to be seen and interpreted in close relationship to the praxis of spiritual exercises.[87] The philosophical schools wanted to bring their initiates into a new way of life, one that included a new way of seeing the world, but this new way of life could not be opened up simply by presenting that vision of the world in an "objective" systematic treatise: "Above all, the [written] work, even if it is apparently theoretical and systematic, is written not so much to inform the reader of a doctrinal content but to form him, to make him traverse a certain itinerary in the course of which he will make spiritual progress. This procedure is clear in the works of Plotinus and Augustine, in which all the detours, starts and stops, and digressions of the work are formative elements."[88] At root, the division between spirituality and academic theology reflects the breakdown of this synthesis of intellectual-theoretical production and spiritual exercises, which Hadot traces to the High Middle Ages.[89] Both theology and philosophy (especially after it gained its independence from theology) came increasingly to be thought of as abstract-theoretical activities, governed by an ahistorical logic and culminating in written texts that would present "the truth" about reality "out there." "Spiritual exercises" continued, indeed flourished, but they were disconnected from, or at best thoroughly subordinated to, the normative truth contained in the texts, which were produced and interpreted in accordance with a different set of scholarly exercises.

To attempt to recover this connection is to understand spirituality as a set of exercises that transform vision, reforming a Christian's way of seeing the world. Theology is about seeing clearly in the light of the tradition and communicating that vision as evocatively as possible in order to meet the needs of the believing community. Those needs, moreover, should not be defined exclusively *ad intra*. The church's ultimate purpose is to proclaim the gospel. As Gustavo Gutiérrez makes clear, theology and spirituality, both individually and in their relationship to one another, are oriented toward evangelization, toward proclaiming a God of love.[90] Theology fails when its vision fails; what spirituality offers to theology is a way of perceiving and being in the world anew, differently, better. When theology is in dire straits, as I have argued it is today, then we need to revisit the "wells of vision," opened up for us by spiritualities, past and present.[91]

All of this is, on the one hand, simply a way of making the quite traditional claim that theology is *actus secundus*, that it presupposes faith. It is, on the other hand, a way of giving flesh to that claim in our modern age. Too often "faith" is reduced to a matter of subjective intention, or it is understood in terms of physical incorporation and participation in an ecclesial body, judged (for Roman Catholics) by adherence to the statements of the hierarchical magisterium, or to some litmus-test claim (rejecting the theory of evolution, for instance, for some evangelical Protestant denominations). These definitions of faith may well be important, but they are too vague and too specific, respectively, for understanding how "faith" affects the "faith seeking understanding" that we call theology. When faith becomes a matter of subjective intention, it is difficult to see what real difference it makes for any academic endeavor, including theology. What difference does it make, for instance, for reading and analyzing scripture or the work of Thomas Aquinas, if I have this subjective quality called "faith"?[92] Defining faith objectively in terms of adherence to certain authoritative propositions falls short because it is not difficult to show that these "dogmas" are already *theological* propositions (that is, they *already* operate at the level of the *actus secundus*), or at least were originally understood and articulated within certain theological systems, with their attendant cultural backgrounds and intellectual conceptualities. This is to collapse faith into theology (and too often to one particular theology) and to commit faith to a particular cultural and intellectual matrix. Christian theologians who are working in other cultures and attempting to understand and to give an account of the hope that is in them, using quite different philosophical conceptualities, are making this point with ever-greater force. This fact does not negate the significance of doctrinal statements, but it does warn against simplistic articulations of that significance. Indeed, this approach often comes back around to the subjectivist interpretation: only those who have faith (as correct subjective intention) can adequately respect and interpret the doctrinal statements that define faith.

If we understand faith as a "way of life," if we see it as the early apologists did, as true philosophy (in the classical sense that Hadot insists upon), then we can define a spirituality as the concrete set of practices that initiates one into that way of life and sustains its ever-more profound embrace, so that it gradually comes to encompass and transform more and more of my activities, including my thinking. We can detect and analyze the presence of "faith" by looking at the specific set of spiritual exercises that perform this function. This approach presupposes, however, that we understand a spirituality not as a random assortment of practices that I pick up for myself from whatever variety of sources I know and like, but something that makes up, or is at least essentially related to, a whole, an integral totality that has a history and that exerts pressure toward certain patterns of theological questioning, reasoning, and communication.

This is perhaps the point at which I should present the working definition of Christian spirituality that governs this book, which arises out of the points just made. *By "spirituality" I mean a classic constellation of practices that forms a mystagogy into a life of Christian discipleship, along with the particular perception of and discourse about God, the cosmos, and human beings that these practices open up and that, in turn, promote and make sense of those practices.* I use the term "constellation" in the sense that Theodor Adorno used it, as a cluster of elements that cannot be reduced to any one of them, but whose essential features come from the complex network of attractions and repulsions that act between them.[93] Such a definition suggests that a spirituality will derive its uniqueness and force not so much from the novelty of its elements but from the particular way it structures those elements into a whole. It also can help explain why the Christian tradition, which contains a large but not infinite number of foundational elements, can generate, has in fact generated, and is still generating an astonishing number of spiritualities, even though not all of them survive their particular time and context to achieve classic status. In defining spirituality as a "classic" constellation, I am limiting myself to those spiritualities that have stood the test of time, that have continued to work for people, that continue to have broad validity and attraction precisely in their particularity.[94] This definition also implies at least a cautious, if not fully critical stance toward the eclecticism of many popular spiritualities. Wrenching practices, images, narratives, and concepts out of their original constellation will inevitably change their meaning and force. It is certainly true that new spiritualities (including Ignatius's) have been born precisely by this sort of selection and recombination. Yet simply pulling different elements from very different traditions and putting them together into a bricolage is like composing a new piece of music by selecting styles and phrases from wildly different musical periods and cultures. A few great masters in the history of music have done this successfully; more often what results is cacophony.

The term "mystagogy" comes from the Church's liturgical year, indicating the time immediately after Easter when the baptized (and, by extension, the whole community) deepen their grasp of the mysteries into which they have been initiated. It is a part of the Church year (for everyone, and not just the newly initiated) for the same reason that Advent and Lent are: to remind us that just as we are not past the time of intense hope and longing for God's salvific intervention in history, or the time of repentance and conversion, neither do we ever completely leave behind the work of deepening our initiation into the mystery of following Christ, in the power of the Spirit, toward the Father. To assert that a set of constellations makes up a mystagogy is to make a number of qualifications about what a spirituality is and is not. First, then, it is to make the point that spiritualities are instrumental; they do not exist for their own sake. Neither do they exist purely for the sake of the selves who practice them. They exist in and for the sake of a communal context, the Church. They will be judged in part by how successfully they enrich that community and orient it toward its own purpose of preaching the gospel ever anew, in word and in deed, both individually and institutionally.[95] Mystagogy is intended to be a limiting term in a second sense. I pointed out earlier that often spirituality is defined in a way that makes it virtually coterminous with authentic human existence, and Christian spirituality such that it is coterminous with Christian faith. Under the definition proposed here, the practices that make up a spirituality have a formational, initiatory function (with the proviso that the depths of Christian faith are such that on some level at least one is always being formed and initiated anew into it). A given spirituality will take up a certain subset of practices involved (at least potentially) in Christian life and configure them together to give them a more focal significance in this ongoing initiation into the mystery of living Christian faith, excluding other practices from that configuration or constellation without thereby anathematizing them altogether. It is important to note that it may be (and often is) the case that the excluded practices are not only practices that are intrinsically valuable for a Christian life, but may indeed even be obligatory. Their inclusion, exclusion, or relative marginalization in a given spirituality is not in itself a statement of their propriety for a fully lived Christian faith, even for the life of the person whose spirituality does not include them. It is, rather, an expression of the particularity of a given spirituality, a particularity that is a reflection of the specific demands that a given cultural-historical situation places on Christians attempting to live out their faith more intensely. To take an example from Roman Catholicism, it is possible to make devotion to the Eucharist a central practice in one spirituality, even though it figures only peripherally in another. Care for the needs of the neighbor, certainly a central, even obligatory practice in Christian faith in general, will figure differently if one adopts an eremetical spirituality as opposed to an apostolic one. In short, the life of Christian faith is more comprehensive than a given spirituality that is intended to enable and promote a mystagogy into that faith. One can and must engage in practices that are mandatory from the perspective of his or her commitment to the faith tradition, but that does not exclude a more intensive engagement with a certain subset of practices, precisely because of their *mystagogical function* within a given context. One reason that spiritualities have histories, that new spiritualities arise and existing spiritualities decline or undergo reformulation, is that the demands of the situation shift. Thus, a certain constellation of practices that served eminently well on mystagogical terms in one situation ceases to do so in another. It will then either die out or it will endure by developing, incorporating new practices (often practices already existing and current), or reconfiguring the relationship between the ones it already includes.[96]

In any event, according to this definition a spirituality is first made up of exercises, things that one does. The "doing" could be a simple being in God's presence (contemplation) and/or a committed action on behalf of others (the action of love). This "doing" makes up the moment of "silence" of which Gutiérrez speaks. But this doing transforms the exercitant in such a way that God, the world, and the person her- or himself are revealed in a particular way, which one will want to share with others or make clearer to oneself. This brings in the second element of spirituality, which can take the form of short aphorisms, poetry, song, visual media, or more straightforward prose. It can take the form of rituals and social arrangements. It may include, or have a close connection to, theological works.[97] Much here depends on how one defines theology, a definitional task perhaps even more daunting and controverted than defining spirituality. Rather than essentializing this activity, the approach taken here is to look at theology as a discipline, or set of exercises in its own right, which has fulfilled a variety of functions throughout Christianity's history. Gutiérrez identifies three: in Christianity's first millennium, theology primarily sought the pursuit of wisdom for promoting the spiritual life; in its second millennium, it took up the quest for rational knowledge, mediating between the knowledge of faith and the knowledge gained by reason. In the last century, for liberation theology, at least, theology came to include critical reflection on Christians' praxis.[98] The first function of theology recalls the second element of a spirituality, as defined above: the particular perception of and discourse about God, the cosmos, and human beings that these practices open up and that, in turn, promote and make sense of those practices. One would expect this to the extent that what we call "spirituality" is so tightly interwoven with "theology" in the early Church. Gutiérrez's second and third functions of theology, taken together, correspond to what I am naming *academic theology* in this book. Its primary place is the university, and it aims at as comprehensive an interpretation as possible of God, the natural world, and human beings in all their dimensions, including social and historical. It does so in the light of the symbols, narratives, and rituals of the Christian tradition, in dialogue with other disciplines in the university that also interpret its subject matter. Its audience includes not just those within a particular spiritual tradition, and not even just Christians, but the academy and society as a whole.[99] It is constituted, at least in part, by the practices and structures of the modern university, as they have evolved over the past eight hundred years. It is under pressure today, in part because that institution has developed in ways that make it more and more difficult for theology to fulfill its task within it. Theology's vision needs to be reanimated to meet this challenge, and reanimation is precisely what "spiritual exercises" have as their goal. How the "scholarly exercises" of academic theology can and should interact with the "spiritual exercises" of the Christian tradition is the subject of this book.

It should be noted that this definition allows considerable variability within a given spirituality. Put another way, it allows for a "school" of spirituality in which specific forms of the spirituality are related closely enough to one another so as to merit a common name, without being identical in every detail. The variability can arise from either element of the definition. For example, a spirituality of depth and complexity will involve a range of specific exercises, which can themselves be chosen selectively or organized in different ways. This is certainly the case with Ignatian spirituality. Some persons virtually identify it with the exercise of "finding God in all things." This aphorism is not explicitly present in the *Spiritual Exercises*. It is, however, implicit to the concluding Contemplation to Attain Love, and those Ignatian spiritualities that focus on this particular exercise at the end of the *Spiritual Exercises* will emphasize the presence of God in all things. As we shall see in the case of Ignacio Ellacuría, on the other hand, it is equally possible to focus on those exercises of the Second Week that center on imitating Jesus and creatively recapitulating (under the impulse of the Spirit) in our histories what happened in his.

Turning to the second aspect in my definition, the practices of a spirituality will also "play out" differently depending on the vision of God, the world, and human beings that complements them. This variability can be creative insofar as it can highlight different features of the spirituality and give it new life. Giving a sense of the variety of contemporary theologies that can and have been used in this way for Ignatian spirituality will be the subject of the three case studies in chapters 4–6. On the other hand, a theology can be deadening. A number of historians have pointed out, for instance, how a too-rigid post-Tridentine theological approach tended to occlude the genuinely mystical element of Ignatius's spirituality, turning it into a strict ascetical regimen that, ironically, suppressed one's imagination and affect. Of course, one might wonder if the trend to emphasize the mystical element in Ignatius's legacy while ignoring the ascetic aspect and the focus on discipline and commitment to the Church is a result of the focus on the individual, on authenticity and the therapeutic—aspects of the modernity we inhabit.

In other words, the definition I propose allows for great variability in a given spirituality. There will certainly be a point at which certain crucial exercises are left out or marginalized: it is hard to imagine an authentically Ignatian spirituality that did not, for instance, include or incorporate in some way a form of the Principle and Foundation, the meditation on the Two Standards or the Contemplation to Attain Love. It could also happen that the theology is so antithetical to the practices that the latter's spirit is diluted or crushed. This will be on the outer periphery of a broad grey area, however, and the judgment about when a given spirituality has ceased to be "Ignatian" or "Franciscan" will always be a relative one. If we think of different spiritualities as different "species," then they are species in the post-Darwinian sense and not in the Aristotelian sense.

Finally, this definition has the advantage of forefronting the relationship between changes in the cultural, political, and techno-economic features of a given historical period and the spiritualities that flourish, evolve, die out, or come into existence during that period. Different sorts of practices are possible, for example, in an age defined by "clock-time" as opposed to natural time.[100] The practice, or perhaps metapractice, of constructing one's "own" spirituality from diverse historical traditions is made possible by the publication and dissemination of sources from those traditions, first in print, and then, with greater impact, through the internet. Other practices come to be seen as archaic and out of step with the times, even though for those who judge the present age more negatively, this may do more to recommend those practices than undermine them.

I conclude this initial discussion of spirituality by noting that, in terms of McGinn's categories, the working definition I am offering here is primarily a "theological" definition. Yet it is framed in such a way as to require careful historical work. To understand a spirituality as a "classic constellation of practices" one must look at the precise configuration of its constituent practices as it was constructed at a particular social place and historical moment, in close contact with other social practices and forms of discourse. It is this "classic" constellation that sets the stage for further development and to which future generations of disciples often return when seeking to reinvigorate their spirituality (as happened for many Roman Catholic religious orders in the twentieth century, particularly after Vatican II). The contribution that this historical labor makes is to lay open the various dynamisms that are made possible by the interactions of the different practices and discourses of a given spirituality. Then, when considering future actualizations of that spirituality, one can, for example, attend to the way that a given individual actualizes one dynamism and not another in relation to the specific situation in which she or he is living out the spirituality. The situation we will consider is that of the academic theologians living and working in the twentieth century, but before we can consider it, we must turn to the classic constellation of practices that provided them the spiritual exercises that transformed their vision. This is the task we shall now take up with regard to Ignatian spirituality.

Chapter Two

Ignatian Spirituality
A Historical Overview

In September 1523, there was a meeting between the provincial of the Franciscans in the Holy Land and a Basque pilgrim, then in his early thirties. The Friars Minor were charged with supervising the holy places in Palestine, and the pilgrim was seeking their permission to remain there so that he could continue visiting the holy places and "be of help to souls." It had already been explained to the pilgrim that such a life would be one of near destitution, one in which the friars would be able to give him no support. This had not deterred him in the least. He asked only the services of a confessor. Although favorably impressed, the provincial ultimately turned him down. Others who had remained in the Holy Land had been killed or taken prisoner, requiring ransom, and the struggling Franciscan community could ill afford the expenditures that these earnest pilgrims cost. Even this did not sway the pilgrim, and the provincial was ultimately forced to order him to leave under pain of excommunication. The pilgrim relented; the next day he began the long, perilous journey back to Christian Europe.

He left in a quandary. Almost from the very beginning of his profound conversion experience, two years earlier, his one overriding goal had been to journey to the Holy Land and live there a life of extreme austerity, doing the (to his recently converted eyes) glorious things that the great saints, such as Francis and Dominic before him, had done. He was absolutely convinced of the authenticity of his intense desire to imitate Jesus as closely as possible; he knew that it came from God. Where could he fulfill this desire more fully than in the land where Jesus himself had taught, worked, suffered, died, and entered into his glory? Moreover, he had resolved to undertake the journey without companion and without any resources, putting his trust in God alone. Having remained true to that resolve, should he not see the successful completion of the dangerous journey to the Holy Land as a sign that his resolve was also the will of God? Yet he had been ordered by one with the authority to speak in the name of the Vicar of Christ. It was not to be. What would he do now? This question was ever on his mind as he made the long sea journey back to Venice, and he came to an important decision: "After the pilgrim realized that it was not God's will that he remain in Jerusalem, he continually pondered within himself what he ought to do; and eventually he was rather inclined to study for some time so he would be able to help souls, and he decided to go to Barcelona."[1] The pilgrim was, of course, Iñigo López de Loyola, who, while studying in Paris seven or eight years later, began calling himself Ignatius, and who, seventeen years further on, would be elected by his companions as the first superior general of the newly founded Society of Jesus.

The decision was a momentous one, for Ignatius's own life, for the future of the Catholic Church, and for that of Europe as a whole. To be sure, it was his 1521 sickbed conversion in Loyola that set his life on a new course. It is also undeniable that the preliminary elements and structure of "Ignatian spirituality" were laid then, to be tested, deepened, and further elaborated during his months of prayer at Manresa, where "God treated him as a schoolmaster treats a child whom he was teaching."[2] He received mystical illuminations that, he reported, exceeded the sum total of all that he would learn in the rest of his life.[3] He worked out "rules for the discernment of spirits," which enabled him to detect, at least to a modest degree, the work of God's Spirit interwoven in the inner movements of his soul. He came to the conviction that God speaks to each individual in his or her heart, a conviction that would ever after form the foundation of his own spirituality and that of the religious order he founded.

But what practical form of life would emerge out of all of this? It was on this issue that his experience in Jerusalem was crucial. Johannes Gerhartz notes:

> It was not the exaltations of Manresa but the failure in Jerusalem that put Ignatius on the road to Rome and led him to the specific ecclesial character of his Order. For the collapse of his life's plan made the pilgrim into a student, brought him from devotion to the holy places to Latin in Barcelona, from a beggar's life to a "common, ordinary life." It turned a pilgrim and a loner into the man who gathered followers around him and founded his community for the service of souls.[4]

In making this decision, Iñigo was not just choosing a different way of fulfilling God's will, which for him would always mean finding the best way "to help souls." He was choosing a different cultural matrix within which to pursue that goal. Up to this point he had operated out of cultures that belonged for the most part to the late Middle Ages, be it the culture defined by the warrior ethic of the Iberian *reconquista* or the culture that revolved around extreme penances, austerity, and pilgrimage, to which he was exposed in reading Jacobus de Voragine's lives of the saints, the *Flos sanctorum*. Now he would move into the world of learning, which would expose him not only to a scholasticism too often reduced to a shadow of its medieval vigor, but also to a burgeoning, self-confident humanism, which set itself determinedly against that scholasticism.

In other words, Ignatius was moving into a distinctively "modern" culture, taking with him a spirituality that was certainly present in embryonic form from his time in Manresa on, but whose potentialities and dynamisms had not yet fully emerged. In the beginning he made the move somewhat tentatively (he was only "rather inclined"), but as he continued to sound out the concrete implications of his spirituality, he became more and more convinced that the college or university was a particularly appropriate place in which to prepare for the form of discipleship he had discovered. Twenty-five years later, eight years after the corporate form of his spirituality—the Society of Jesus—had been approved, and while he was laboring to compose its full constitutions, Ignatius committed the young Society to the task of running colleges. Again, tentative at first, this move blossomed into a form of ministry that would have profound implications for the growth and transformation of the young religious order, in large part because of the way it involved it in the emerging cultures of modernity. As John O'Malley argues,

> Perhaps the most important change the schools wrought within the Society... was the new kind and degree of its members' engagement with culture beyond the traditionally clerical subjects of philosophy and theology.... That engagement was not occasional or incidental, but systemic. It became interwoven with the very fabric of the Jesuits' understanding of their ministry, of their "way of proceeding." Their religious mission remained basic to them, but, especially as a result of the schools, they also began to see themselves as having a cultural mission.[5]

However fortuitous this move seems when considered from the vantage point of Ignatius's early years, or even from that of the first companions debating in 1539 the form their company should take, it is governed by a particular logic. This logic, immanent to the structure and dynamism of Ignatius's spirituality, slowly emerged as Ignatius and the first companions put that spirituality into practice. It is a logic that reemerges whenever that spirituality is fully embraced, even today.

The purpose of chapters 2 and 3 is to search out this logic, focusing on Ignatius's *Spiritual Exercises*. In the course of this examination we will uncover in the *Exercises* an exigency toward engagement with culture: an engagement with *modern* culture carried on in a *modern* (pluralistic, reflexive, and self-conscious) fashion. The logic is not monolithic; it admits of different inflections depending on the precise way that the complex constellation of elements that make up Ignatian spirituality is approached and appropriated. Its pluriformity also derives from the complexity of modernity itself. Modernity is not a monolithic phenomenon either; it has multiple iterations in different cultures, each of which (and all taken together) can be engaged by different avenues, under different evaluative stances, and with correspondingly different goals.

This overview does not pretend to be an exhaustive summary of Ignatian spirituality or even a full introduction. It is composed prospectively, with a view toward illuminating the case studies that follow in chapters 4, 5, and 6. The first step, taken in this chapter, is to lay out the skeleton of Ignatius's *Spiritual Exercises*. Chapter 3 attempts to bring that skeleton to life by showing how it knits together practices and values from the different cultures or subcultures that Ignatius encountered, which were cultures in transformation and which came together in a volatile mixture to produce the early modern period. This approach has the advantage of showing how this spirituality presses its adherent toward an engagement with modern culture in a specifically modern way. This advantage will bring us back to the discussion in chapter 1, which focused on showing "spirituality's" peculiarly modern character. Ignatian spirituality will turn out to be no exception to this rule; indeed, it will emerge as a paradigmatic instance. The results of chapters 2 and 3 will prepare the ground for the case studies in chapters 4–6, which examine three instances of the continuing appropriation of Ignatian spirituality, always by a necessarily selective actualization of some of its immanent dynamisms that aims at a creative engagement with, and transformation of, modern culture.

THE STRUCTURE AND DYNAMISM OF THE *SPIRITUAL EXERCISES*

Ignatius of Loyola's *Spiritual Exercises* was composed over a period of around twenty years.[6] One can trace its most important symbols, images, and concepts back through the history of the Christian tradition, but its proximate sources lie in his own experience during two remarkable years. This period began with the dramatic conversion he underwent at his family's castle in Loyola while he was recuperating from life-threatening wounds sustained in battle at Pamplona on May 20, 1521. During a lengthy and painful convalescence, he resolved to turn his back on his former way of life and travel to Jerusalem, all the while doing the great things that the saints had done in the service of Christ. After an all-night vigil before the Black Virgin of Montserrat, he set off for Jerusalem, stopping for what he originally intended to be a brief stay in the nearby town of Manresa. The brief stay extended to eleven months, during which time he underwent a series of internal struggles and illuminations. It was during this time that he began to act out of his desire to "help souls," particularly by means of "spiritual conversations." To that end he began to write down notes from his own experience, which formed the nucleus and essential substance of what would become the *Spiritual Exercises*. According to Diego Laínez, one of Ignatius's first companions in Paris, by the time Ignatius left Manresa, in February 1523, he had completed the book, "at least in its substance."[7] He modified and augmented it over the ensuing years, in part, no doubt, as he gained experience in giving the Exercises to diverse persons, in part as he encountered other strands in the complex weave of sixteenth-century Catholicism. Written to begin with in Ignatius's native Spanish, it was translated into a rough Latin version (perhaps by Ignatius himself), and then later into a more refined Latin version, which was approved by Pope Paul III in 1548 and became the official version.[8] Thus, the different stages in the formation of the complete text reflect Ignatius's journey through the various cultures of early modern Europe and give the *Exercises* its complexity, flexibility, and power.

As has been often noted, the *Spiritual Exercises* was never intended to be read in the way that, say, *The Imitation of Christ* was. The text is composed of a diverse collection of meditations, contemplations, considerations, directives, maxims, and rules, which one person is to present to another, accommodating the presentation to the needs and capacities of the one who is making them, but with due recognition of the purpose of the *Exercises* as a whole. As John O'Malley puts it, "they are . . . more like a teacher's manual than a student's textbook."[9] The material that the person is to be given in the course of the retreat itself is sandwiched between a collection of introductory explanations at the beginning geared toward helping the director and the retreatant get the most out of the retreat (*SpEx* 1–20),[10] and a number of supplementary materials at the end: on methods of prayer, on discernment of spirits, on distributing alms, on scruples, and on "thinking, judging, and feeling with the Church" (*SpEx* 238–370). These materials, in particular, evolved over time and reflect Ignatius's own experience of growing in the spiritual life, his experience of giving the *Exercises* to others, his education in Paris, and his encounters with opponents and critics of his structured methodology for spiritual conversation.

The definition and purpose of the Spiritual Exercises are given in the first introductory explanation:

> By the term Spiritual Exercises we mean every method of examination of conscience, meditation, contemplation, vocal or mental prayer, and other spiritual activities. . . . For just as taking a walk, traveling on foot, and running are physical exercises, so is the name of spiritual exercises given to any means of preparing and disposing our soul to rid itself of all its disordered affections and then, after their removal, of seeking and finding God's will in the ordering of our life for the salvation of our soul. (*SpEx* 1)

The first part of the goal, "preparing and disposing our soul to rid itself of all its disordered affections," is expressed positively with the observation that in order to achieve the end for which we are created, "it is necessary to make ourselves indifferent to all created things" (*SpEx* 23). Indifference is one of the key concepts in Ignatian spirituality and has a long history in Christian spirituality. Far from a kind of apathy in which one's affective response to the created world is suppressed or ignored, it entails the subsumption of one's desires and aversions within the broader movement of a graced desire to find and embrace God's presence in the created world as creator, redeemer, and sanctifier. That is, authentic indifference is intimately connected not just with the first, but also with the second goal of the Exercises: "seeking and finding God's will in the ordering of our life for the salvation of our soul." This goal has its specific locus in the section on "election" or choice (*SpEx* 169–89). The election could be either a life-determining choice, such as entering a religious order, or the refinement of a way of life that one has already chosen. Whatever its subject, in doing the Spiritual Exercises the election occurs within the context of a set of contemplations on the life of Jesus, combined with more abstract reflections.[11] It is further guided by a method (*SpEx* 169–89, 313–36) by which one can interpret and, as far as possible, influence the complex interactions between the workings of preternatural spirits, one's affectivity, and one's discursive intellect, which need to be harmonized in choosing the various courses of action in which we seek "the salvation of our soul."

These tasks are not the endeavors of a Promethean individual, working out his or her salvation *sui generis*.[12] Neither are they undertaken exclusively within the private I–thou of an interior relationship with God. Rather, this work is done against the backdrop of the history of sin and salvation, a history that originates in the protological events of creation, fall, and compassionate divine response, that finds its culmination in the person, deeds, and fate of Jesus Christ, and that continues through the power of the Holy Spirit manifested in a signal way in the Church. As the materials of the Exercises make clear, the twofold goal of the Spiritual Exercises is only achieved as one places oneself in the context of this history, with all the powers of one's imagination, affectivity, intellect, and will.

This dramatic context structures the Exercises into four sets of exercises that Ignatius names "weeks," even though they need not correspond precisely to that period of time.[13] During the Second and Third

Weeks, one considers the life, passion, and death of Jesus, as presented in the Gospels. The Resurrection is the subject of the Fourth Week. During the First Week one takes up the destructive power of sin in the world, and in one's own life, and God's merciful response. Creation is taken up in a reflection that introduces both the First Week and the *Exercises* as a whole. It is not presented as a historical moment—history begins with sin in the first meditation of the First Week. Rather, creation is given as an ontological principle. All things are created by God: humans to praise, reverence, and serve God; other things to assist them in this.[14] Sin is taken up in its threefold dimension: as a cosmological, prehuman reality (the sin of the angels); as an event at the origins of humanity (the sin of Adam); and as a present reality (the sins of my contemporaries and, of course, my own sins). The compassionate divine response is not yet fully specified, but it is implicitly present, if in no other way than in the form of divine forbearance. This is brought home to the exercitant as he or she becomes aware that he or she has not shared the catastrophic fate of other sinners, despite sins that are just as serious. Given this, Ignatius exhorts one to give forth "an exclamation of wonder and surging emotion, uttered as I reflect on all creatures and wonder how they have allowed me to live and have preserved me in life" (*SpEx* 60). The depth and price of this divine response is indicated in this week also. In the *Exercises*'s first reference to Jesus Christ, he is to be imagined "suspended on the cross before you" because of your sins (*SpEx* 53).

Finally, and most importantly, Ignatius wants the exercitant not just to reflect on God's compassionate response but to *experience* it sacramentally by means of the General Confession of Devotion.[15] This exercise is to take place at the end of the First Week. Its purpose is not so much the juridical one of being absolved of guilt for all of one's sins. Rather, it enables one to reach "a deeper understanding of the reality and malice of one's sins," and to dispose oneself for the reception of the Eucharist, which helps "not only to avoid falling into sin, but also to preserve the increase of grace" (*SpEx* 44).[16] It should also be noted that in this sacramental act the Church becomes explicitly present above and beyond its representative in the person of "the one giving the exercises."

The outcome envisioned for the First Week, then, is not self-recrimination alone, and not just an awareness of the reality and malice of sin, important as these achievements are. These are way stations on the road, but the ultimate destination is a sense of "wonder and surging emotion" that one can be expected to feel upon discovering that, even in the face of the death-dealing power of sin, one is still being offered the opportunity to find salvation. Moreover, this offer is already connected to its historical roots in Jesus's crucifixion and to its present-day locus in the sacramental community of the Church.

With the successful conclusion of the First Week, the retreatant would have attained at least the first goal of the Spiritual Exercises, or, perhaps better, he or she would have been set decisively on a lifelong journey toward it. The broader historical context of that journey, with its protological, christological, and ecclesiological-pneumatological dimensions, would have been laid out, at least embryonically. The importance of the First Week is clear from Ignatius's refusal to allow one to continue into the other weeks without undergoing the conversion that the First Week entailed.[17] What is more, when it came to persons who did not have the time or talents for the full course of the Spiritual Exercises, it was enough that they be given the exercises of the First Week and taught some techniques for prayer, examination of conscience, and so on, so that they could continue along the path cleared by the conversion of the First Week. As O'Malley puts it: "If the purposes of that Week was successfully achieved, the individuals had found a new and happier orientation at the very core of their being and were thus set more firmly than before on the path to salvation. When, for whatever reason, an individual could not continue with the rest of the *Exercises*, the better ordering of his life with which the *Exercises* were concerned had been essentially set in motion."[18]

For those who do go on, the remainder of the Exercises focuses on the second goal, that of "finding God's will in the ordering of our life for the salvation of our soul." In the Society of Jesus's early years, Ignatius and others among the first Jesuits saw in the full course of the Exercises the primary means of attracting young men to the Society and giving them a deeply felt interior knowledge of its "way of proceeding."[19] Thus, in a letter dictated to his secretary, Juan Polanco, Ignatius instructed that "they [the full Exercises] should be given only to very capable subjects, such as some who are suitable for our Society or other persons of importance."[20] The letter continues by asserting that "the majority of the good subjects in the Society today were drawn there from the world, so that if we wish to swell the Society's numbers with good men this would appear to be an excellent means. For married persons and other persons in the world or in religious life the Exercises are likewise extremely valuable, especially the First Week."[21] As the last statement suggests, Ignatius did not necessarily restrict the full Exercises to young men considering a vocation. What would take the place of such an election for these persons? In his own directory for giving the Exercises, he suggests that someone who is already committed to a particular state of life could "be offered one of two things on which they might wish to make a choice": "The first is, where it is equally for God's service and without scandal or harm to neighbor, to desire injuries, opprobrium, and abasement in all things with Christ, in order to be clothed in his livery and imitate him in this aspect of his cross. The other is to be willing to suffer patiently anything of this kind whenever it should befall him for love of Christ our Lord."[22]

In summary, although the primary matter for election presumed for the Second Week is an irrevocable choice of life's vocation, in fact the principles and methodology presented extend naturally not only to *what* state of life one will choose but *how* one will live it. In each case, the horizon against which options are weighed and choices are made is provided by a deep interior knowledge of and love for Jesus, which should issue in a desire to imitate him as closely as possible.[23]

With this end in view, the Second Week comprises a complex weave of different sorts of exercises. First and foremost, it introduces one to the process of contemplating the events of Jesus's life, starting with the Incarnation and continuing through his public ministry. Throughout these exercises, the grace for which the exercitant is to pray is that of "an interior knowledge of our Lord, . . . that I may love him more intensely and follow him more closely" (*SpEx* 104). The devastating impact of sin, which was the focus of the First Week, is reintroduced in the contemplation on the Incarnation. Now, however, the divine response is the focus of attention. One is instructed to imagine the persons of the Trinity "gazing on the whole face and circuit of the earth; and they see all the peoples in such great blindness, and how they are dying and going down to hell" (*SpEx* 106). One is to hear the response: "I will hear what the Divine persons are saying, that is, 'Let us work the redemption of the human race,' and so forth" (*SpEx* 107). This "metahistorical" contemplation is filled out in the exercises that follow by contemplating how the divine response unfolds historically in the life of Jesus of Nazareth and in the key contributions of collaborators, such as Mary and Joseph, and the disciples.

The exercises on the history of Jesus are interspersed with more imaginative, metahistorical exercises, including the Contemplation of the Kingdom of Jesus Christ (*SpEx* 91–100—often called more simply "The Call of the King"), with which the Second Week begins, and the Meditation on the Two Standards (*SpEx* 136–48), which sets the immediate context for the election. In the first exercise, Christ is compared to an earthly king. Just as an earthly king might issue a call to his people to accompany him in "conquer[ing] the whole land of the infidels,"[24] so the retreatant is to imagine "Christ our Lord, the eternal King" making a similar call: "My will is to conquer the whole world and all my enemies, and thus to enter into the glory of my Father. Therefore, whoever wishes to come with me must labor with me, so that through following me in the pain he or she may follow me also in the glory" (*SpEx* 95). The retreatant prays for the grace "not to be deaf to his call, but ready and diligent to accomplish his most holy will" (*SpEx* 91). He or she ends the exercise by observing someone profess a desire to imitate the "eternal Lord of all things" in "bearing all injuries and affronts, and any poverty, actual as well as spiritual" (*SpEx* 98).[25] What this exercise does is to channel the gratitude and generosity that come with the grace of the First Week and make of them the driving force for the process of election in the Second Week. This exercise does not *itself* entail deciding what form this imitation will take. The grace one asks is "not to be deaf to the divine call" when it comes (*SpEx* 91).[26] The actual "hearing" of this call comes later.[27] Contemplating the life of Jesus over the course of the Second Week will flesh out the precise content of this imitation, and the process of election gives the retreatant the occasion to incarnate the offering made here at the outset of this week.

The second contextualizing reflection is traditionally named The Two Standards and occurs on the fourth day of the Second Week, as the exercitant begins the formal process of election (*SpEx*, 136–48). In it, the standard of Lucifer, the enemy of our human nature, is set against that of Christ. One is to ask for insight both into "the deceits of the enemy" and into "the genuine life which the supreme and truthful commander sets forth," and ask for the graces to avoid or escape the first and to imitate Jesus in the second (*SpEx* 139). The enemy is to be envisioned enthroned, "in aspect horrible and terrifying" (*SpEx* 140). He sends devils to every city and every person, enjoining them to tempt persons "to covet riches . . . , so that they may more easily come to vain honor from the world, and finally to surging pride" (*SpEx* 14). Christ is to be envisioned in the opposite fashion, sending persons (not devils) out, once again, to every place and person: "He recommends that they endeavor to aid all persons, by attracting them, first, to the most perfect spiritual poverty, and also, if the Divine Majesty should be served and should wish to choose them for it, even to no less a degree of actual poverty; and second, by attracting them to a desire of reproaches and contempt, since from these results humility."[28] Then one asks to be received under the standard of Christ our Lord, and to be chosen for actual poverty, bearing reproaches and injuries, so "that through them I may imitate him more" (*SpEx* 147).

Together, these two exercises frame the contemplation of the life of Jesus as a historical backdrop against which to make the choice that is "seeking and finding God's will in the ordering of our life for the salvation of our soul." The scripturally based contemplations are complemented in this purpose by two exercises that are more conceptual and discursive: On the Three Classes of Persons and Three Ways of Being Humble. The first recapitulates the notion of indifference laid out in the Principle and Foundation. One imagines three persons, "each typical of a class," who have acquired a certain amount of money, "but not purely or properly for the love of God" (*SpEx* 150). The desired state (that of the third class of persons) is one in which "one strives earnestly not to desire that money or anything else, except when one is motivated solely by the service of God our Lord; in such a way that the desire to be able to serve God our Lord better is what moves one to take or reject any object whatsoever" (*SpEx* 155).

The Three Ways of Being Humble is a "consideration" rather than a meditation. Moreover, it is not the subject of a single period of prayer, but is to be mulled over by the retreatant as she or he enters into and engages the process of election. It develops the matter raised by the meditation on the three classes of persons in a significant manner. In describing the three ways of being humble, it is the *second* way that corresponds most closely to the disposition of indifference. In words that directly echo the formulation of the Principle and Foundation, this second way of being humble is one in which "I do not desire or feel myself strongly attached to having wealth rather than poverty, or honor rather than dishonor, or a long life rather than a short one."[29] In the third way of being humble, however, one goes beyond this level of indifference by adding a further criterion by which to mold one's affective response to created things: radical imitation of Jesus in his actual poverty and humiliations. All other things being equal, I am *not* indifferent to wealth and honor. Rather, "in order to imitate Christ our Lord better and to be more like him here and now, I desire and choose poverty with Christ poor rather than wealth; contempt with Christ laden with it rather than honors."[30] Coming to a deep interior sense of what this imitation would mean and inculcating a desire to adopt it is the purpose of contemplating the history of Jesus's life.

In the treatment of election itself, Ignatius distinguishes three times or ways in which an election can be made. In the first, the person feels himself or herself indubitably and directly moved by God toward a certain course of action. The third time is one in which one does not feel himself or herself moved affectively one way or another when considering the matter of election in itself and proceeds by a rational-imaginative consideration of the options.[31] Ignatius gives three methods for doing this. In the first, the person is to "consider and reason out" the benefits and value, on the one hand, and the disadvantages or dangers, on the other, of a given course of action, always in terms of the end proposed by the Principle and Foundation: "to praise God our Lord and save my soul" (*SpEx* 179). In the second, I am to imagine a person to whom I am giving counsel about the matter at hand, desiring only his or her perfection. I apply to myself the advice that I would give him or her (*SpEx* 185). In the third, I imagine myself on Judgment Day, and reflect on what course of action I will wish that I had taken at that point. These imaginative exercises are ways of confirming and building on the fact that the person finds himself or herself tranquil and affectively neutral with regard to the options, which is the prerequisite for these more intellectual methods of coming to a sound decision. The person's ongoing consideration of the Three Ways of Being Humble serves as a sort of barometer for measuring the degree to which he or she has attained this state.[32] Given this, these imaginative exercises help the one choosing to determine any slight deviation from the *ceteris paribus* condition.

The second time or way of making an election "is present when sufficient clarity and knowledge are received from the experience of consolations and desolations, and from experience in the discernment of various spirits" (*SpEx* 176). This time is associated with Ignatius's Rules for the Discernment of Spirits, which are found at the end of the book.[33] Ignatius first experienced this way of making a decision on his sickbed in Loyola, and went through it again at a deeper and more complex level during the eleven months he stayed in Manresa. It is the predominant type of decision-making that one encounters in the extant fragments of Ignatius's *Spiritual Diary*.

It is for his extremely methodical approach, both to discerning God's will in general and to the specific form that this takes when "discerning spirits," that Ignatius is perhaps most well known.[34] Taken together, the considerations on the three times for making an election and the Rules for Discernment constitute a flexible and nuanced template for modeling and interpreting the ways humans can make decisions of existential import under the influence of divine grace. It should not, however, be forgotten that when it occurs in making the Spiritual Exercises, this whole process is embedded in the work of imaginatively confronting oneself with the divine economy of salvation, historically manifested in the history of Jesus of Nazareth. If the retreatant is truly ready for it (by having successfully experienced the transformative grace of the First Week), and engages it diligently, this work should fire the retreatant's imagination and stir his or her heart with love for Christ, providing ample material for reflection and a context within which, Ignatius is convinced, a person (with the help of a spiritual advisor) will be able to judge whether a given course of action truly represents a historically concrete and specific way in which she or he can continue in his or her life the divine economy of salvation.

Presuming that the election has been made and made well, the second goal of the *Spiritual Exercises* has apparently been attained. Two "weeks" remain, however: the Third Week, in which one contemplates the passion and death of Jesus, and the Fourth, which treats the Resurrection. Hugo Rahner and Hervé Coathelem argue that these weeks continue the process outlined by the Call of the King.[35] There the retreatant asked for the grace to be attentive to the call of Christ to follow him in his work, "so that through following [him] in the pain he or she may follow [him] also in the glory" (*SpEx* 95). Thus, in the Third Week the retreatant follows Jesus in the pain and then in the glory. Moreover, just as the negative future consequent upon a life in rebellion against God was presented to the retreatant in the meditation on hell at the end of the First Week, the future consequences of the life of *imitatio Christi*, to which the retreatant has committed himself or herself in the election of the Second Week, is presented in the Third and Fourth Weeks. In this way, the identification with Christ that formed the background for the election of the Second Week is deepened and the election strengthened or refined.

In his commentary on the *Spiritual Exercises*, Anthony DeMello offers another explanation of the purpose of the Third and Fourth Weeks. For him, their successful outcome is "unselfing the self."[36] This interpretation reads these two weeks in the light of the first purpose of the Exercises, which is for the soul to rid itself of disordered attachments (*SpEx* 1). DeMello observes that the challenge of attaining this end comes not just from the fact the soul itself has this or that attachment to a created reality. Rather, the deeper problem is that the soul is closed in on itself, *curvatus in se*, so that it cannot love the created world, itself included, in the appropriate way. DeMello argues that it is the deep identification of a generous and grateful soul with the suffering and the glorification of Christ that helps it break out of this prison, which makes it truly free. If the election made in the Second Week continues to attract the person as he or she is "unselfed" in this way, and achieves this level of freedom, then one can proceed with even greater confidence that the election was correctly made. Finally, as Dean Brackley suggests, in becoming present to the resistance and suffering that Jesus encountered, one will be ready to encounter that oneself.[37]

This dynamism (of "unselfing the self") can be perceived by considering the colloquies that end the contemplations of the Third Week. Ignatius tells us that here, as elsewhere, the colloquies are periods in which we "ought to converse and beg according to the subject matter; that is, in accordance with whether I find myself tempted or consoled, desire to possess one virtue or another, or to dispose myself in one way or another, or to experience sorrow or joy over the matter I am contemplating. And finally I ought to ask for what I more earnestly desire in regard to some particular matters" (*SpEx* 199). Thus, it is evident that the process of confirming, strengthening, or refining the choice that one has made stretches into the Third Week, and that it does so by continuing to place that choice against the backdrop of God's redemptive response to human sin, incarnated in Jesus.

Indeed, the retreatant's first introduction to God's work in the First Week is recalled in the first exercise of the Third Week. In the First Week, the retreatant prayed for the grace to feel sorrow, shame, and confusion over his or her sinfulness (*SpEx* 48, 55). In the first exercise of the Third Week, a contemplation that follows Christ from Bethany to the Last Supper, one is to pray for the grace of "sorrow, regret, and confusion, because the Lord is going to his Passion for my sin" (*SpEx* 193). Yet there is a difference that supports DeMello's interpretation that the Third and Fourth Weeks are about "unselfing the self." The focal point of the grace for which one asks is not now my own condemnation, but the price paid by Christ to redeem me, even though the latter is present in the First Week, particularly in the colloquy before the cross. The goal of identification with Christ, proper to the Second Week also, becomes more explicit in the following contemplations, in which the goal shifts slightly but decisively to that of experiencing "sorrow with Christ in sorrow; a broken spirit with Christ so broken; tears; and interior suffering because of the great suffering which Christ endured for me" (*SpEx* 203; cf. 206). The first-person pronoun has virtually disappeared. The self is unselfed.

Another angle of view on the same dynamism starts from DeMello's point that the unselfing of the self leads to genuine freedom. The upshot of having achieved (or perhaps better, having been given) this freedom is that one is now prepared to enter into God's redemptive work as a co-worker with Jesus. In the First Week, one is to experience oneself as the *object* of the divine redemptive response and, out of a profound sense of joy and gratitude, be awakened to a state in which the central issue of my life becomes how I ought to respond. Hence the questions: "What have I done for Christ? What am I doing for Christ? What ought I to do for Christ?" (*SpEx* 53). The scope that my answers to those questions ought to have is presented in the Second Week, in which I experience myself not just as the object of the divine redemptive response but its *subject*, called by Christ the King to participate in it, a call to which I respond by committing myself in some specific way with real consequences for my future life (the election). This twofold experience is recapitulated in the Third Week, in which I feel sorrow for what Christ endured *because of* my sin (myself as object of redemption) and sorrow *with* Christ suffering in carrying out that response (myself as subject, laboring *with* Christ).

In the Fourth Week, I am to ask "for the grace to be glad and to rejoice intensely because of the great glory and joy of Christ our Lord" (*SpEx* 221). If the exercises of the Third Week presented us with a Christ laboring in a state of opprobrium and poverty, in which divinity is veiled, the Fourth Week presents the divinity of the risen Christ, "which now appears and manifests itself so miraculously in this holy Resurrection, through its true and most holy effects" (*SpEx* 223). The "true and holy effect" that Ignatius highlights in the very next point is that of consolation (*SpEx* 224). At the end of the Third Week the retreatant is to "consider . . . Our Lady's loneliness along with her deep grief and fatigue; then, on the other hand, the fatigue of the disciples" (*SpEx* 208). In Ignatius's vision, Jesus's first act after rising from his tomb was to visit his mother, and the "office" that he carries out is that of consoler (*SpEx* 219, 224). This is the only work or power of the risen Christ that Ignatius mentions in the Fourth Week. It will be important to remember this christological element when we turn to consider the central Ignatian concept of consolation.[38]

The Fourth Week closes, and with it the Spiritual Exercises, with the remarkable "Contemplation to Attain Love." This prayer recapitulates the logic of the Exercises as a whole in an exercise that follows the wisdom expressed in the First Letter of John: "In this is love, not that we loved God but that he loved us and sent his Son to be the atoning sacrifice for our sins. Beloved, since God loved us so much, we also ought to love one another. No one has ever seen God; if we love one another, God lives in us, and his love is perfected in us" (1 John 4:10–12). The condensed presentation of the logic of the Exercises found in this exercise is enriched by the experience of working through them in their entirety. That is why it is best interpreted not in isolation, but as the end and culmination of a process. The grace to be asked for in the contemplation is "interior knowledge of all the great good I have received, in order that, stirred to profound gratitude, I may become able to love and serve the Divine Majesty in all things" (*SpEx* 233). Praising, reverencing, and serving God were defined at the outset of the Exercises as the end of human existence and the way to salvation (*SpEx* 23). Praise and reverence are now understood to be constituted by love; the import and concrete features of this further precision in the meaning of "praise, reverence and serve" will be vividly present to the one making the exercises after having worked through them (ideally over the course of thirty days) and come to an election. A primary goal of the First Week (particularly in the General Confession of Devotion that completes it) was to awaken in one a sense of gratitude that is the proper motivation for praise, reverence, and service, and this essential link between gratitude and genuine praise and reverence, in which all three are subsumed into the dynamism of love, is found in the Contemplation to Attain Love. The Second and Third Weeks have disclosed the preferred way of praising, reverencing, and serving: as radical as possible an imitation of Jesus of Nazareth. It has also offered one the opportunity to concretize that praise, reverence, and service (in imitation of Jesus) through a specific choice. They thus prepare the retreatant to understand the Contemplation to Attain Love's preliminary observations that "love ought to manifest itself more by deeds than by words" (*SpEx* 230), and "love consists in a mutual sharing of goods" (231).

Four points in the Contemplation drive home the awareness of the goods that God has already shared with us and continues to share with us—how much God first loved us. In the first point one calls to mind the gifts received: "creation, redemption, and other gifts particular to myself" (*SpEx* 234). Having gone through the course of the Exercises, these gifts have been specified and rendered vividly present. There is not just the gift of being saved from out of a world trapped in blindness and death and going down to hell, but also the gift of being called to participate myself in that divine salvific activity, using all the "gifts particular to myself." In the process of the election, the retreatant has worked hard to envisage and commit him- or herself to a life in which he or she uses all of those particular gifts to imitate as closely as possible the person of Jesus, presented in imaginative detail in the contemplations of the Second and Third Weeks.

The second and fourth points draw on traditional ways of understanding and perceiving God's active presence on my behalf. In the second point, one considers how God is present in all things by essence and power, giving them existence and their proper activity. In the fourth, using the classic language of the Christian Neoplatonic tradition, one is told to consider "how all good gifts descend from above . . . just as the rays come down from the sun, or the rains come from their source" (*SpEx* 237). God manifests Godself as active presence, as self-diffusive Good.

Hugo Rahner has argued that the fourth point, with its emphasis on the "from above," maps a regionalization of soteriological space that offers the key to Ignatius's theological vision.[39] The third point can provide an equally important and complementary clue. In that point, one is instructed to "consider how God labors and works [*trabaja y labora*] for me in all the creatures on the face of the earth; that is, he acts in the manner of one who is laboring" (*SpEx* 236). On one level this recapitulates the idea presented in the prior point about God's active presence in all created things, giving them existence and activity. Yet the point is attempting to inculcate in the retreatant not just the fact *that* God is dynamically and constitutively present to all things, but the *way* in which God is so present: "[God] acts in the manner of one who is laboring." This point encodes and refers the retreatant back to the ways that God's ongoing labor for us have been presented with mounting force as the Spiritual Exercises progress. This reference can be seen by considering some instances in which work, labor, or doing are presented at key junctures in the *Exercises*. In the Contemplation on the Kingdom of Christ, the exercise that is liminal between First and Second Weeks, Christ, the eternal King, calls us to participate in the *labor* (*trabajo*) of "conquering the whole world and all my enemies."[40] In the Contemplation on the Incarnation that follows, we hear the divine persons resolve to "work (*hagamos*) the redemption of the human race (*SpEx* 107). This is done by "bringing about" or "working"[41] the Incarnation. In the next contemplation, on the Nativity, in what could count as an anticipatory summary of the Second and Third Weeks as a whole, one contemplates Mary and Joseph, "journeying and toiling [*trabajar*], in order that the Lord may be born in greatest poverty; and that after so many labors [*trabajos*], after hunger, thirst, heat, cold, injuries, and insults, he may die on the cross! And all this for me!"[42] In sum, for someone who has made the full course of the Spiritual Exercises, "how God labors and works for me" recalls to mind the history of salvation that has been presented in the prior weeks, into which the retreatant has inserted him or herself, imaginatively in contemplation and existentially through his or her election.

In this way, the Contemplation to Attain Love brings together the dynamism of the earlier exercises. Each of the points concludes with the retreatant reflecting on himself or herself, in the course of which Ignatius suggests that one make an offering to God, which is commonly referred to by its first word in the Latin: the *Suscipe*:

> I will speak as one making an offering with deep affection and say:
>   Take, Lord, and receive all my liberty, my memory, my understanding, all my will—all that I have and possess. You, Lord, have given all that to me. I now give it back to you, O Lord. All of it is

yours. Dispose of it according to your will. Give me love of yourself along with your grace, for that is enough for me. (*SpEx* 234)

The grateful "colloquy of mercy" of the First Week, which follows upon "an exclamation of wonder and surging emotion" (*SpEx* 60, 61), has now flowered into "an offering with deep affection," an offering of myself for the divine work. Having contemplated the life of Jesus in the Second, Third, and Fourth Weeks, the retreatant will understand this offering as an offer to recapitulate Jesus's life and work by radical imitation.[43] As in the First Letter of John, the proper response to God's love for us is to love others with that same love, to allow that love to be perfected in us, which ultimately means to become united in and through the power of the Holy Spirit, to the God who *is* that love. Thus, although the early Jesuits were correct in categorizing the Fourth Week under the unitive way, the union attained is a union located in the heart of the *vita activa*.[44] Therefore, even though the phrase, "contemplative in action" is never used there, the Contemplation to Attain Love is an appropriate locus for understanding this Ignatian ideal.[45]

Discernment of Spirits

The text of the *Spiritual Exercises* ends with a set of supplementary materials that the one giving the Exercises can use as he or she sees fit, providing them to the one making them according to his or her needs. First, Ignatius lays out three methods of prayer. This is followed by a list of mysteries of the life of Christ to fill out the contemplations done during the Second through Fourth Weeks. Finally, there are five sets of rules or notes: two on discernment of spirits, one governing distribution of alms, some notes for dealing with scruples, and rules for thinking with the Church. The most important of these for our purposes are the rules for discernment and the rules for thinking with the Church.

Rules for the Discernment of Spirits is a condensation of the more cumbersome but accurate title given in the autograph edition of the *Exercises*: "Rules to Aid us Toward Perceiving and Then Understanding, at Least to Some Extent, the Various Motions which are Caused in the Soul: the Good Motions that They May Be Received, and the Bad that They May be Rejected" (*SpEx* 313). One set of rules is labeled as more suitable for the First Week, and the other for the Second Week. These rules stand in a long tradition in Christian spirituality concerning the discernment of spirits.[46] Yet, as Susan Schreiner notes, the late Middle Ages and Reformation saw a growing concern with discerning whether a particular movement, theological idea, or spiritual inspiration was from God. The wave of spiritualism that was occurring throughout Europe caused increasing concern: "Reformers, visionaries, beatas, and mystics all claimed illumination and thereby created suspicion and the need to test the authenticity of their experiences. Added to this phenomenon were the religious controversies that were shattering the unity of Western Christendom, bringing in their wake the crisis of authority, the need for certainty, and the appeals to the Spirit."[47]

According to Michael Buckley's helpful interpretation, the earlier discussion of "times for election" (which pertains to discerning God's will in an election) and these rules (which focus on the second time for making an election) take up three mediations in which Christians have traditionally sought God's guidance: the influence of preternatural spirits, one's own processes of intellection, and the attractions and aversions of one's affectivity.[48] We have encountered these three already in the three times for election. The first time for an election occurs under the immediate influence of the good spirit (Buckley's first mediation); the third depends on rational reflection (Buckley's second), and the second has to do with interpreting the interplay of consolations and desolations (Buckley's third mediation, combined with the first). Ignatius, Buckley notes, was not original in defining these ways of finding God's guidance: "What Ignatius provided was a structure within which each of these finds a significant place; none is dismissed out of hand. A co-ordination among them is established so that they reach an integrity of effect, and one is taught how to recognize and reply to each."[49] The general context is one of struggle between the evil spirit, which Ignatius is wont to call the enemy of our nature, and the good spirit, which could refer to angels or simply to God. Since the struggle is overt and straightforward in the First Week, the rules for this week are correspondingly simple. Regardless of whether a "motion," that is, a change in our soul, originates in thought, affect, or the influence of one or another spirit, it is easy to distinguish the good from the bad. For persons going from one sin to another, the enemy proposes "delights and pleasures of the senses," while the good spirit appeals to reason and "stings their consciences with remorse" (*SpEx* 314). For persons who at least desire to reform their lives (thus, those actually making the exercises of the First Week), the evil spirit will cause anxiety and sadden them, setting up obstacles.[50] A sense of fortitude and confidence in God's assistance will indicate the presence of the good spirit.

In the Second Week, the conflict is more subtle and typically develops gradually over time. It is accordingly more difficult to analyze with clarity, requiring a second, and different, set of rules. The difference between the rules "more appropriate" for the First Week and those for the Second Week is so consequential that Ignatius prescribes that only the rules for the First Week be given to a person who has not yet undergone the conversion that separates the two weeks and is ritualized in the General Confession of Devotion (*SpEx* 9). Even a simple and straightforward case becomes complex. For example, a "consolation without a preceding cause"—that is to say, an affective response to reality that is directly aroused by God—is self-authenticating and compelling in itself.[51] As such it does not require a very sophisticated diagnostic tool to identify and act on it. But that is only the beginning of the story. Ignatius notes that the consolation without preceding cause often gives way to a period in which the enemy can insinuate thoughts, subtly shape resolutions, or bend one's affectivity in such a way that, still lit with the glow of the preceding consolation, these new developments seem to share in its unquestionable authenticity (*SpEx* 336). In other words, a temporal-historical dimension enters the picture, appropriately enough, since the matter for contemplation of the Second Week is itself historical: Jesus's life.[52] One is now advised to keep careful track of the course of a given process of choice and implementation of choice, particularly if it turns out that from a good beginning it devolved into a bad end (*SpEx* 333, 334). Intellectual reflection, aided by the counsel of a confessor or spiritual director, have to go hand in hand with one's accumulated experience of different affective responses to the goods of the world. The central diagnostic concepts in evaluating and reflecting on this experience are spiritual consolation and spiritual desolation. To these concepts we now turn.

Many disciplines have foundational terms that are so fundamental that they resist univocal definition—"religion" for religious studies, "society" for sociology, or "life" for biology. "Consolation" is such a term in Ignatian and Jesuit spirituality. For this reason, and because it is used so broadly, variously, and fundamentally by Ignatius and his first followers, it has been defined in equally various ways. In the Rules for Discernment, Ignatius includes a variety of experiences and modifications in a person's awareness (interior motions of the soul) under this category. Talking of "spiritual consolation" in the third rule (of the rules appropriate to the First Week), he describes it with three paragraphs that take up different forms of consolation. First, it is "that which occurs when some interior motion is caused in the soul through which it comes to be inflamed with love of its Creator and Lord. As a result it can love no created thing on the face of the earth in itself, but only in the Creator of them all." He adds, second, that "this consolation is experienced when the soul sheds tears which move it to love for its Lord—whether they are tears for its own sins, or about the passion of our Lord, or other matters directly ordered to his praise and service."[53] Third, he states that "under the word consolation I include every increase in hope, faith, charity, and every interior joy which attracts one to heavenly things and to the salvation of one's soul by bringing it tranquility and peace in its Creator and Lord" (*SpEx* 316).

This is an expansive list. One interpretive strategy is to interpret it against a similarly expansive horizon; another strategy is to render it more precise. The effect of the former is to make it more difficult to use as a diagnostic category within the process of discernment of spirits in a retreat. On the other hand, the precision achieved by the latter strategy often requires forcing certain readings on the text, or ruling out usages of consolation that make sense within the broader context of the *Spiritual Exercises* (outside of the rules for discernment), or usages that Ignatius himself and his early companions embraced as they worked to form a new religious order. Since the meaning (or at least the scope of possible meanings) of "consolation" in Ignatian spirituality is important for this overview in general, and for considering the three case studies later in the book, in particular, this debate requires some more detailed attention.

The interpretation of Jesús Corella, the Spanish Ignatius scholar, in the *Diccionario de Espiritualidad Ignaciana*, is of the former, more expansive type.[54] In an initial lapidary statement, he contends that "authentic consolation . . . is a sensible sign of the presence of God communicating Godself to the creature. One might say that consolation is the language proper to God."[55] He goes on to argue that the three descriptions of consolation in the third rule (listed above) are "three levels of consolation . . . that are three modalities of God's language."[56] The first is the most episodic and affectively "explosive."[57] The second indicates a gradual process of growing emotion in the soul, which builds more gradually over time, until it "overflows mysteriously through the eyes."[58] This is even truer of the third, which is more ordinary, more indicative of the tone of life, and the stability of experience for someone who is resting quietly in God, "without intermediaries, mediations, or messengers. . . . It is the fullness of consolation, its culminating point."[59] Corella deliberately connects his interpretation of these levels of consolation with other elements of the *Spiritual Exercises*: the Principle and Foundation (with the first modality of consolation) and Contemplation to Attain Love (with the third).[60] Thus, the third modality of consolation is for him the one proper to the "contemplative in action." Contextualizing these levels of consolation in terms of the movement from the Principle and Foundation to the Contemplation to Attain Love mapped out by the *Spiritual Exercises*, he writes:

> Indeed, Ignatian consolation can be defined as a meaningful moment in the process of recovering "things" placed by the creator on the face of the earth, and in us, which were subjected to vanity by their inappropriate use by human beings, but are returned to us in virtue of the resurrection of Jesus (4th Week), as a gift of life (*SpEx* 234), the locus of divine presence (*SpEx* 235–236), and as a real participation in the very being of God (*SpEx* 237). Thanks to being enabled to live in this way, the reign of God grows among us. When we grow in this process of recovery and personal integration we feel consolation.[61]

Brian McDermott, following Jules Toner, argues for a far more restrictive interpretation of Ignatian consolation.[62] On McDermott's reading of the Rules for Discernment, consolation always means *spiritual* consolation for Ignatius (that is, the adjective "spiritual" should be considered to be implied in the subsequent two namings of consolation in the third rule). He argues further that as such it is always for Ignatius a pleasant, delightful, and peaceful experience.[63] In this he disagrees with Michael Buckley, who argues that neither consolation nor desolation map clearly and consistently onto specific affective states.[64] McDermott also argues for a strict distinction between spiritual consolations understood as episodic moments in a person's life of faith, given to help the person make an election (or persevere in an election already made), on the one hand, and other more comprehensive, perhaps deeper, elements of a person's spiritual journey into greater union with God, on the other, such as the deepening of the theological virtues of faith, hope, and love, or gifts of the Spirit, such as fortitude in adversity.[65] He argues against including these other elements of the spiritual journey in the category of "spiritual consolation."

Corella's interpretation has the advantage of connecting the understanding of consolation with the broader movement of the *Spiritual Exercises* as a whole, rather than focusing just on what is stated in the rules themselves, or on commentaries Ignatius gave on their use. Yet, McDermott is on firm ground in arguing that in the actual process of discernment during the second time for election, for which the rules are composed, greater precision is required. On this, McDermott makes telling points on exactly how this process should be understood and how a director can be of assistance in guiding it.

This being granted, however, the arguments from the text itself that spiritual consolation is always a pleasant feeling of joy or peace are suggestive but not conclusive. For instance, McDermott argues that the action of the good spirit described in the first of the rules (*SpEx* 314), in which the good spirit stings one's conscience (certainly unpleasant), should be excluded from an understanding of consolation (*pace* Buckley), because this rule comes *before* the one in which Ignatius defines consolation. This seems to put more evidentiary weight on the ordering of the rules than is warranted, since, after all, all the rules were to be given together. Moreover, Ignatius names the actions of the good spirit in the second rule as "stirring up consolations," which is also prior to his definition of consolation in the third rule, so he appears to have had consolation (and desolation) in mind in composing the rules even before he got around to defining them in the third and fourth rules.

As a second argument, McDermott points out that the tradition of spiritual consolation that Ignatius inherited (say, from *The Imitation of Christ*, and its Book on Interior Consolation) always understood it as a pleasant, peaceful experience, and if Ignatius had meant to innovate in this matter, he would have indicated it.[66] There is some weight to this argument, but Ignatius *was* often an innovator, even when it came to Kempis and the Modern Devotion.[67] In deciding whether it is warranted to expect

Ignatius to specify when and how he was innovating, it is important, once again, to keep the genre of the text in mind. As I have observed before, the *Spiritual Exercises*, including the rules, was not written as a treatise on spiritual consolation (as Kempis's book was), nor on discernment, for that matter. He was providing a set of rough-and-ready guidelines. In the former case, one would expect explanation, or at least an indication, of the sources on which one is drawing and how one is doing it; in the latter, it seems to be asking too much.

McDermott argues that the "tears" mentioned in the second modality of spiritual consolation cannot count as counterevidence. They are, he contends, sweet tears that come with the realization that God loves me, even in my sinfulness.[68] His argument for this is that all the other manifestations listed in this second modality are pleasant and peaceful—again, suggestive but not conclusive. Yet a problem for this interpretation is found in the Third Week, when Ignatius mentions tears in connection with Christ's passion. There, he associates them with grief and sorrow over what Jesus is suffering (*SpEx* 195), *not* sweetness. The grace proper to the Third Week is "sorrow with Christ in sorrow; *a broken spirit* with Christ so broken, *tears*; and *interior suffering* because of the great suffering which Christ endured for me" (*SpEx* 203; emphasis added). Tears, in this context, are indicative of sorrow, brokenness of spirit, and interior sorrow. In fact, in the Third Week, Ignatius admonishes the retreatant to do all he or she can to *resist* joyful thoughts, even if they are good and holy. If the play of consolations and desolations that Ignatius expects to be going on throughout the Exercises is also happening here, it is hard to imagine what the consolation in this week would be were it to be restricted to pleasant feelings, joy, and peace. A broader ambit for what Ignatius had in mind when thinking about consolation seems required.[69]

Finally, with Ignatius's statement that under consolation he includes "every increase in faith, hope and love," McDermott argues that the text should be understood by emendation. He refers to Toner, and Michael Ivens, who contended that in talking about the increase of faith, hope, and charity, Ignatius "unfortunately omitted an important modifier—namely, *experienced*."[70] This seems a dangerous argument to me. If the other arguments from the text for restricting the meaning of spiritual consolation are decisive, then the emendation might be justified. If they are not, then the fact that Ignatius did leave out the modifier should be respected, and the text interpreted as it stands (which is what Corella does).

This is a complicated issue that needs further scholarly work. At present, it seems most prudent to admit that Ignatius is not clear, and that the nature of this text (not a treatise but a manual) makes it difficult to arrive at the kind of precision that we might want. The interpretive conundrum is complicated by the fact that when Ignatius and his followers used the term consolation, they drew not only on the sense we have been looking at in this debate (about spiritual consolation), but also from the tradition of the works and ministries of consolation. This term (*consolar*) has a different, albeit overlapping history of usage in the Christian spiritual tradition.[71] This complication does suggest that it is helpful to make it clear when one is talking about spiritual consolation, and when one intends a broader sense of consolation that incorporates other elements of the experience of Ignatius and his first companions. I shall follow this practice in what follows.

Yet even in doing this one cannot, it seems to me, hermetically separate the two usages, in part because the first Jesuits did not. There is a sort of reciprocal palimpsest of meaning, in which meanings from one usage always shine through the other usage. This is an important feature of what I would argue is an ultimately irreducible internal pluralism of meanings for "consolation" in Ignatian spirituality. I would propose the following as a working hypothesis, which I do not have space to investigate further here. Ignatius's understanding of "spiritual consolation," which he took from the tradition (through reading the *Imitation of Christ*, in particular) evolved and deepened because of his growing conviction that it was characteristic of the way God deals with human beings more generally, and not just during a retreat or an election. This evolution is already evident in his threefold defining of "consolation" (as Corella points out), which is cognate to his treatments of consolation in the whole scope of the history of salvation, as laid out in the four weeks of the *Spiritual Exercises*. Moreover, as Ignatius and his first companions expanded from the focus on "spiritual conversation," for which "spiritual consolation" was the focus and goal, to "helping souls" in the diverse ministries they took up, they evidently believed that the dynamisms and the characteristics of the relationship between God and humans characteristic of "spiritual consolation" still obtained and thus did not hesitate to call what they were after in this broader scope of apostolic activity by that name. This appears to be behind Nadal's commentary on the 1550 Formula of the Institute given in the bull *Exposcit debitum* of Julius III. Commenting on the prescription to attend "especially to the spiritual consolation of Christ's faithful through the hearing of confessions and administering the other sacraments," Nadal observes:

> These words—"especially spiritual consolation"—refer to all the primary ministries of the Society. They at the same time mean that we are not to be content in those ministries only with what is necessary for salvation but pursue beyond it the perfection and consolation of our neighbor. For spiritual consolation is the best index of a person's spiritual progress. The word "especially" means that there are other ends we must pursue, but this one in the first place, as our primary intention and goal. If we do not have time and resources for both this and the others, we should omit doing them, apply all our energies to this one.[72]

Given the diverse usages, even within the *Exercises* themselves, which expanded over time among the first companions as they explored the consequences of their insights into spiritual consolation for the broad range of ministries they came to adopt, space has to be held open for the broader interpretation, of the sort that Corella offers. Given this situation, in what follows I will use "spiritual consolation" when I have in mind the usage on which McDermott helpfully focuses. I will speak (more usually) of "consolation" in reference to the broader, more polysemous usage that, I would argue, is most representative of the way the term came to be used and understood by Ignatius and his followers and that appears prominently in the three Jesuits I analyze later in this book.

After this lengthy but necessary discussion of debates over the meaning of Ignatian consolation in general and spiritual consolation more specifically, we continue the review of the rules. In the fourth rule, Ignatius defines spiritual desolation as the contrary to spiritual consolation, as described in the third rule. It is an event or state that brings turmoil, confusion, and impulsive motions toward low or base things. It afflicts one with tepidity, unhappiness, a sense of alienation from oneself and from God (*SpEx* 317). As the opposite of spiritual consolation, it brings an increase in despair or apathy, rather than hope; doubt and irresolution, as opposed to faith; selfishness and deadening indifference, as opposed to active charity.

Although they are affective states, spiritual consolation and desolation do not map directly and consistently onto happiness or unhappiness, especially in the Second and Third Weeks.[73] There is a further complication that is treated in the rules for the Second Week. When one is experiencing *authentic* spiritual consolation the presupposition is that one is under the influence of the good spirit. Yet Ignatius points out that the evil spirit can "mimic" spiritual consolation, so that one has to reckon with the possibility of inauthentic or misleading spiritual consolation.[74] This possibility is more prominent when one is in the state consonant with the Second Week of the *Exercises*, and this prominence is taken into account in the rules appropriate with that week. Spiritual desolation is simpler: it always indicates the presence of the evil spirit, even though it does not indicate that one has been abandoned by God or is outside the ambit of God's redeeming and sanctifying love.[75]

When one is experiencing spiritual desolation, one should be suspicious of any conclusions one might draw, either about one's present state or about resolutions for the future. It is particularly important that one not change in time of desolation a resolution made in a prior state of spiritual consolation (*SpEx* 318). There are strategies for resisting spiritual desolation and disposing oneself for spiritual consolation: patience, prudently chosen acts of penance, firmness in one's resolutions, and, above all, openness to a confessor or spiritual guide. In Ignatius's anthropology, we are not simply at the mercy of our moods. We can focus our thinking, engage our imagination, and even modify our physical environment in order to mold our affective response to the world.[76]

After this all too brief overview of the rules, it is apparent why the title from the autograph version of the *Exercises*, even though cumbersome, is more accurate. The goal is to perceive and understand various motions caused in the soul—a change in internal disposition or external orientation that can be identified as spiritual consolations or desolations. It is not an exact science, and thus the discernment of spirits must always be open to reassessment and revision. This leads Ignatius to be realistic in his appraisal of the complexity of human choice and modest in his goal: "to perceive and understand, *at least to some extent*." As we have seen, the matter becomes even more complex as one is in the state that corresponds to the Second Week. Yet Ignatius holds out hope that as one progresses, the influence of the two spirits will become more evident from the outset (rather than having to await the full unfolding of the process). In one of his most beautiful passages, Ignatius tells us that

> in the case of those who are going from good to better, the good angel touches the soul gently, lightly, and sweetly, like a drop of water going into a sponge. The evil spirit touches it sharply, with noise and disturbance, like a drop of water falling on a stone.
>
> In the case of those who are going from bad to worse, these spirits touch the souls in the opposite manner. The reason for this is the fact that the disposition of the soul is either similar to or different from the respective spirits who are entering. When the soul is different, they enter with perceptible noise and are quickly noticed. When the soul is similar, they enter silently, like those who go into their own house by an open door. (*SpEx* 335)

In the final analysis, the goal of these rules, along with the methodologies appropriate to the other two "times" for election, subserves that of the *Exercises* as a whole: to grow into a state in which one loves God above all and all things in God, and embraces and conforms one's life to the work of the God thus loved and found in all things. These rules are directly related to the second time of election, and perhaps (for those rules touching the consolation without prior cause) to the first.[77] But even when one is not experiencing the swings of consolation and desolation and makes the decision by rational reflection alone (the third time), one is urged to offer that decision to God and pray that it be confirmed, presumably through consolation, which means that the rules apply for this way of making an election too (*SpEx* 183, 188).[78]

At the root of Ignatius's understanding of consolation and of the methodology for nourishing it and identifying it laid out in the *Spiritual Exercises* was the conviction that God deals directly and personally with each person. This conviction was Ignatius's most profound conclusion from his own experience, beginning with his conversion in 1521. The structure of the *Exercises*, including the rules for discernment, elaborated that insight into a conceptuality and a method that could communicate it to others but also protected it from disintegrating into an arbitrary relativism or subjectivism—the errors of which the sixteenth-century *Alumbrados* were accused, with whom Ignatius, not surprisingly, was often associated, but from whom he adamantly differentiated himself.

Ignatius's refusal to draw from this conviction the conclusion that external authority is irrelevant, superfluous, or even illegitimate is nowhere clearer than in the final set of rules in the *Spiritual Exercises*. Once again, it is good to recall Ignatius's long, if cumbersome, title: "To Have the Genuine Attitude Which We Ought to Maintain in the Church Militant, We Should Observe the Following Rules" (*SpEx* 352). The rules are probably the last substantive material to be added to the text of the *Exercises*, but that does not necessarily mean they represent a deviation from or addition to Ignatius's early sense of the Church and his stance toward those who hold office in the Church. As his behavior in the Holy Land shows, Ignatius believed that legitimate authority in the Church could trump a conclusion or resolution reached by one's own prayer and discernment. Thus, the attitude that these rules represent was Ignatius's from the outset.

Yet, the rules are not a list of propositions intended as a test of orthodoxy. They define a *sentido*, which is translated "attitude," but embraces further meanings such as "inclination" and "thinking."[79] As Avery Dulles puts it, what Ignatius has in mind is "a kind of instinct or taste that disposes one to accept what is suitable [and] to reject what is unsuitable."[80] The specific issues that the rules do take up reflect the situation in Paris while Ignatius was a student there, and then problems he encountered in Italy, which is one reason for dating them toward the end of the period of composition of the *Spiritual Exercises*.[81] A first set of eleven issues is framed by two paragraphs that contain Ignatius's ecclesiological vision. We are to be ever ready to put our own judgment aside and be obedient to the Church, which Ignatius gives the titles "true Spouse of Christ," "holy Mother," and "hierarchical."[82] In one of his most famous statements, Ignatius urges one to act on the principle that "what appears to me to be white, I will believe to be black if the hierarchical Church thus determines it" (*SpEx* 365). It should at least be noted that this statement is not untypical of Ignatius's time. Further context can be provided by recalling Ignatius's warning that the evil angel can appear as an angel of light (*SpEx* 332). That is, it can appear to me to be for the good, even though its ultimate aim is evil. In this context, then, Ignatius is proposing that the Church should stand in a position analogous to that of the confessor or director, guarding us from self-deception.

When Ignatius does single out particular issues, the ones he cites are those that were most controversial during his student days in Paris. He defends practices criticized by reformers, both Protestant and Catholic:

veneration of relics, fasting and abstinence, institutions of religious life, priestly celibacy, and so on (*SpEx* 358, 359, 356–57). One is not to criticize the behavior of one's superiors publicly, whether they are religious or ecclesial, since this would give rise to scandal and divide the Church.[83]

In a telling passage, Ignatius tells us that "we ought to praise both positive theology and scholastic theology (*SpEx* 363). The latter — Ignatius names Thomas, Bonaventure, and Peter Lombard — is particularly apt for defining and explaining what is necessary for salvation, and for exposing and refuting heresy. But, his description of the former, by which he means patristic theology, betrays his preference for their approach. The Fathers "stir up our affections toward loving and serving God our Lord in all things" (*SpEx* 363). Stirring up one's affections toward loving and serving God is of course the primary means toward the goals of the Spiritual Exercises themselves, the purpose that Ignatius sought in his spiritual conversations with others, and the ultimate goal and culmination of any authentically Ignatian labor to "help souls." In this, Ignatius and the early Jesuits agreed with the censures that the *Imitation of Christ* levels at much of what passed for scholastic theology at that time. The difference was that, offering no real alternative to the scholasticism it rejected, the Modern Devotion's most well-known work could be read to oppose any sort of theology or intellectual reflection. Ignatius and the early Jesuits, in contrast, refused to reject scholasticism tout court, but believed that it could be augmented and transformed to bring about the goal proper to their way of proceeding.[84]

In a second set of rules, Ignatius lays down some prudential guidelines for dealing with some of the most hotly contested issues of the day: predestination, the relationship between faith and works, and the relationship between fear of God and filial love of God. Here the rules did not try to solve these complex doctrinal issues but attempted to lay out a reserved and prudent approach to what one said and preached.

Much has been made of these rules, often starting from one of the least successful attempts to give them a summary title as "Rules for Orthodoxy." In fact, as O'Malley points out, "the relatively little comment and controversy aroused in the sixteenth century by the 'Rules for Thinking with the Church' indicate that they should not be invested with the exaggerated orthodoxy they were often later made to represent."[85] What the rules do show, however, is that just as the background against which the Call of the King is to be perceived and pondered has a specific and concrete historical locus—the life of Jesus of Nazareth—it also has a specific and concrete locus within which it is to be received and answered: the Church militant, struggling in the present to continue the work, guided by "the same Spirit that guides us and governs us for the salvation of our souls" (the "Thirteenth Rule," *SpEx* 365).

The Place of the *Spiritual Exercises* in Ignatius's Spirituality

Are we at a stage to develop a summary or synthetic overview of Ignatian spirituality? There are compelling reasons to defer such an ambition at this point. For one thing, I have dealt only with Ignatius's *Spiritual Exercises*. Ignatius lived for more than three decades after he wrote down the essentials of the *Exercises* at Manresa. As the fruit of those decades he left not only the *Spiritual Exercises* but an autobiography and fragments of his spiritual diary.[86] With the help of Juan Polanco he composed the *Constitutions* of the Society of Jesus.[87] This unique form of rule describes the kind of person best fitted to join the Society of Jesus, follows this person through his training, outlining the kinds of ministries he might engage in, and concludes by describing his apotheosis in the figure of the superior general. This structure makes the *Constitutions* an essential source for understanding Ignatian spirituality as lived out corporately in the Society of Jesus. Finally, Ignatius left almost seven thousand letters, the largest extant body of correspondence of any figure from the sixteenth century. Surely a complete picture of Ignatian spirituality would have to take these sources into account.[88]

This notwithstanding, I shall not go on to consider these materials in detail, both for strategic reasons and for more principled ones. On the one hand, it has not been the goal here to give an exhaustive summary of Ignatian spirituality. If possible, this task would require a book in itself, if not several.[89] What is more, the purpose of the overview provided by this chapter and the one that follows is to understand the impact of Ignatian spirituality on the reconfiguration of academic theology, exemplified in three twentieth- and twenty-first-century Jesuit theologians. For them, I contend, it is necessary and sufficient to use the *Spiritual Exercises* as the "classic" that defines Ignatian spirituality. To repeat the reasoning given in the introduction, this status of the *Exercises* obtains as a matter of historical fact for these men, given the time when they were formed as Jesuits. The *Spiritual Exercises* was *the* book that formed each of them into Ignatian spirituality. With a few caveats, to be considered in the relevant chapters, it can be said that none of the other sources for Ignatian spirituality played anywhere near as important a role as the *Exercises*. Even if one factors in periodic study of foundational documents during, for instance, the final period of formal training (so-called Tertianship),[90] the fact remains that the book to which each would have returned yearly, at least, was the *Spiritual Exercises*.[91]

There are also more principled reasons for using the *Spiritual Exercises* to obtain a first approximation—and an extremely accurate one at that—of Ignatian spirituality. Ignatius himself clearly considered this book to be the distillation and foundation of his spiritual experience. When justifying a decision he made as superior general, he often traced it back to "something that happened at Manresa."[92] The first Jesuits agreed with him. Polanco, for instance, considered this book a compendium of all the means that Jesuits had for helping souls.[93] At first the *Spiritual Exercises* were seen as a means for identifying promising recruits and bringing them into the Society of Jesus. As time passed, it was increasingly seen as a means of inculcating "their way of proceeding" into Jesuits at all stages of spiritual progress. Thus, within a generation most Jesuits had adopted the practice of undergoing an abbreviated version of the Exercises every year.[94]

It is true that much of what is taken as essential to Ignatian spirituality is only found explicitly outside the *Spiritual Exercises*. The well-known motto "contemplation (or "contemplative") in action" was coined by Jerome Nadal, Ignatius's trusted advisor.[95] The phrase "finding God in all things" is found, albeit somewhat obliquely, in the Contemplation to Attain Love, but far more frequently in Ignatius's letters. Moreover, there are clearly significant differences between the way Ignatius lived his spirituality in his final fifteen years as general as opposed to his early years as "the pilgrim." As Peter Schineller has argued, over the course of Ignatius's life and writings there is a shift of key metaphors that determine the center of gravity of his spirituality: from soldier and pilgrim to laborer in the vineyards of the Lord.[96]

Yet, does this justify Schineller's claim that "while the text of the *Exercises* remains a classic, if one wants to be faithful to the mature spirituality of Ignatius there is a legitimate need to interpret and supplement the exercises,"[97] or Juan Luis Segundo's even more provocative contention that the spirituality and theology of the *Spiritual Exercises* are separated from the views articulated in the *Constitutions* and Ignatius's correspondence by "a theological quantum leap"?[98] I argue that it does not. A brief consideration of their positions, and my objections, will serve to clarify my own position on the place of the *Spiritual Exercises* in Ignatian spirituality and the legitimacy of taking it as a touchstone for considering the relationship between Ignatian spirituality and contemporary theology.[99]

First Segundo. He argues that later in life, in his work as founder and governor of a new apostolic religious order, "Ignatius's spirituality simply reflects a different experience of God than that of Manresa, an experience that becomes more and more a part of his life: that of a God revealed in the historical challenges posed to human liberty, and in the realistic projects that arise from those challenges."[100] The "early Ignatius," he contends, operated in terms of a spirituality that values human activity in this world (the praise, reverence, and service spoken of in the Principle and Foundation) only in terms of its expected outcome in the next life: eternal salvation. In contrast to this "trial spirituality," which views this life as something like an admission examination for the next, the "later Ignatius" held what Segundo calls a project spirituality. A "project spirituality" looks at human history as subject to a divine plan, a plan whose inner-historical execution is vital for human fulfillment and that requires human collaborators if it is to succeed.[101] As a consequence, the successful historical execution of this project (judged by inner-historical criteria) is the sign and, at least in part, the substance of human salvation.

Continuing his argument, Segundo maintains that whereas for "trial spirituality" imitating Christ means mimicking him, or at least mimicking those elements of his activity that he prescribes as the test that one must pass in order to gain heaven, for the project approach imitation means following-with, it means accompanying and aiding Christ in bringing about a certain historical outcome. Segundo argues that Ignatius came to appreciate this latter sense of imitation only after he founded and began governing the Society of Jesus. As superior general he comes to have a "passion for what happens in history" and a "conviction that all of it [what happens in history] bears profoundly on the service of God that is the duty of human freedom."[102] This passion and conviction is most strongly evinced in Ignatius's vast correspondence, but it is also, on Segundo's reading, the key principle in the composition of the *Constitutions*. For example, in contrast to the attitudes urged in the *Exercises*, the relevant passages in the *Constitutions* show an Ignatius who did not accept insults and contempt when they compromised the reputation of the Society, and consequently the Society's effectiveness as a social-historical force. He fought back with all of the formidable political skills gained from his youthful training in the courts of Spain.

The cornerstone of Segundo's argument is his contention that the "praise," "reverence," and "service" of the Principle and Foundation are not just left undefined in the *Exercises*, but are defined in terms of a world-denying asceticism. Such asceticism is the hallmark of "trial spirituality." This is true, on his reading, even of the Call of the King and the Third Way of Being Humble. The latter, he maintains, is particularly dangerous because it defines extreme elements of Jesus's life and death as the extraordinary actions by which one distinguishes oneself, or, to put it somewhat colloquially, gets an A on the exam.[103] Nowhere, he contends, is the true character of the *Spiritual Exercises* more clearly revealed than in the First Week, in which one meditates on how a person is condemned for a single mortal sin. The entire emphasis is on one's state vis-à-vis the terms of the trial at the end of one's life, rather than on how one's life as a whole has contributed to an inner-historical project. Finally, both the Principle and Foundation at the beginning of the *Exercises*, and the Meditation to Attain Love at the end, operate under the assumption that the created world is a finished product, and as such is a morally and soteriologically neutral "stage" on which one takes one's test. As a result, the criteria for the enjoyment and use of elements of the created world will not depend on any project within the world that might complete or heal it, but on the terms of a trial, which is set and evaluated outside of the created world and its history, and for which the world is only an arena.[104] If Segundo is correct, then using *Spiritual Exercises* as the sole, or even primary, touchstone for understanding Ignatian spirituality is profoundly mistaken.

There is no doubt that Ignatius uses imagery and theological concepts that can (and often did) lead to an overly Pelagian soteriology, which is hostile to the world and to working within history. It would be unfair, however, to expect of Ignatius our own quite modern view of history as a process in which the really new can come into being and augment or complete what existed before, and in which our first impulse is to find rationales and desiderata for acting in history in terms of this process itself without reference to what is outside of history. We live in "the immanent frame," as Taylor puts it; Ignatius did not. Yet does that mean that we should interpret and prune Ignatius's spirituality so that it "fits" the immanent frame? It might be better to follow Johann Baptist Metz's advice that we exercise a "productive noncontemporaneity" and tarry, at least for a few moments longer, with elements of Ignatius's vision that do not seem to fit our own age. In addition, Segundo's interpretation is flawed even on textual terms. For example, he can only assert that the Contemplation to Attain Love presents the created world as a finished product by ignoring the third point, which presents God as one who acts in the world "in the manner of one who labors," which indicates the opposite. It is not finished, which is why God is still laboring.

Segundo's more serious error, however, is to mistake the genre of the *Spiritual Exercises*. To state it once again, it is not in itself a work in theology. It describes a set of spiritual exercises, exercises that draw in a far wider ambit of material than the written text bound within the covers of the book itself. For example, it involves the exercitant deeply in the Gospel portraits of Jesus.[105] Furthermore, it is not a set of propositions or claims about Jesus and the God of Jesus, but rather a process, a set of exercises that presses one through a successive and cumulative series of conversions or, to use Lonerganian terms, expansions of one's horizon. Each part must be interpreted in terms of how it fits into the dynamism of the whole. Thus, to criticize the Principle and Foundation or the First Week for a lack of explicit reference to Jesus is to assume that these are stand-alone units that collect discursive claims about creation, anthropology, and soteriology, rather than a series of exercises that one *does* and which unfold dynamically and dialectically into other exercises. The purpose of the earlier material is to prepare the exercitant to meet Jesus in the Second Week in a way that will bring the greatest fruit. Indeed, if one were *not* to experience and follow this dynamic, then Ignatius will not allow one to continue on to that second-week encounter with Jesus and the election. Given this, it is perfectly legitimate, indeed requisite, to interpret the earlier materials prospectively, in the light of how they are transformed-by-being-complemented by the later.[106] The same point is true a fortiori of the closing Contemplation to Attain Love.

It is true that "service" and "praise" are abstract, and can be rendered in the ways that Segundo portrays. Furthermore, if one focuses only on the many instances in which Ignatius does speak in terms of "what is conducive to the salvation of one's soul," then Segundo's point about a "trial spirituality" seems compelling enough. Yet, the grace of the Second (and central) Week of the *Exercises* is the grace of knowing and loving Jesus more intimately so as to follow him more faithfully. Effectively, then, when considered in terms of the impact of performing the exercises of the Second Week, the salvation of one's soul, and the way that one praises, reverences, and serves God, is defined in terms of discipleship. And how does Ignatius wish that this term, "discipleship," be made concrete for the one making the Exercises? Is it not clear that for a person who is contemplating (particularly during the Second Week) the work of Jesus, "service" and "praise" are quite concretely presented in terms of what Jesus is portrayed as doing in the New Testament, particularly in the Synoptic Gospels? That there we find a man deeply concerned about others? That Ignatius presents even the risen Christ as first and foremost concerned with consoling his heartbroken mother?

This "content" of the *Exercises*, far more important because the exercitant engages it for multiple hours on successive days,[107] and on the deepest, most existential level, presents a potent counterweight to any spirituality that would see this world, and the needs of persons in it, is ultimately of only indirect significance. This content is, perhaps, easy to overlook since it is merely indicated in the actual text of the *Spiritual Exercises* and can only be fully fleshed out and have its proper effect in the exercitant's labor of performing the exercises and making the election. Yet it is crucial for any adequate interpretation of the *Spiritual Exercises*, and consequently, of Ignatian spirituality (early or late). In short, Segundo misses the mark in his interpretation to the extent that he analyzes the work as a text in (modern, academic) theology, rather than a work in spirituality, defined first and foremost as a set of exercises designed to bring about a certain transformation in a person. Because of this, his heuristic device of "trial spirituality" and "project spirituality" provides too open a net to capture the nuances of Ignatian spirituality.

Schineller's argument is more nuanced than Segundo's and correspondingly more successful.[108] The textual evidence that he adduces clearly indicates the shift in metaphor from the more military imagery in the *Exercises* to the imagery of fruitfulness and laboring in the vineyards of the Lord in the *Constitutions*. Yet it is not immediately clear that the latter represents a "mature" Ignatian spirituality. It certainly represents the way that Ignatius himself worked out the dynamisms of the *Exercises* as the founder of a religious order under the specific conditions of mid-sixteenth-century Europe and in his grappling with the ecclesial politics in Rome. Ignatius followed his own persistent admonitions to others that the spirituality mapped out by the *Spiritual Exercises* had to be accommodated to the situation of the one (or ones) living it. So, under the dramatically shifting circumstances that followed the foundation of a growing religious order, and even more, late in Ignatius's generalate, the embrace of the apostolate of education, there were significant adaptations in the concrete ways that Ignatian spirituality would be lived out. Schineller suggests that this adaptation reflects a changing vision of the world: from a stark battlefield between good and evil (hence the military imagery) to a place where we are to put down roots, to labor and cultivate over the long term (thus, the imagery of laboring in the Lord's vineyards).[109] Yet, if situations were to change, if persons found themselves in a place where evil was more overt, where the apocalyptic imagery of a direct confrontation between a God of life and the idols of death is more appropriate, would an Ignatian spirituality that reverted to the military or apocalyptic imagery be less mature when measured against Ignatius's usage in the *Constitutions*?[110] On the contrary. Such a move would represent an authentic engagement with Ignatian spirituality as presented by the *Spiritual Exercises*, and a shift in metaphor driven not by a slavish fidelity to the letter of the text of the book, but by a fidelity to the dynamism structured by the book's exercises, as that dynamism molds and is molded by one's concrete conditions. It would, I contend, be equally mature and complete. The key question to ask would be whether, or the way in which, such a shift represented a genuine engagement with the *Spiritual Exercises*. They are the key.

The Open-endedness of Ignatian Spirituality

What follows is that there is something open-ended about the *Exercises*, and this is its virtue, not a weakness. Any interpretation of the spirituality that a person or group of persons lives as a result of embracing the

Exercises will necessarily entail some further elements. A strong argument can be made that a priority should be given to Ignatius's own lifelong process of living that spirituality and continually adapting it as he lived it in the context of founding and nurturing a new religious order. This principle is obviously exigent for those who live Ignatian spirituality within the Society of Jesus, and insofar as one of the characteristics of the early Society was the desire of the first Jesuits to share their ministries with laypersons, its validity extends beyond the boundaries of the Society. However, the *Exercises* still constitute the deepest source for the dynamism animated and structured by Ignatian spirituality. The open-endedness of the *Spiritual Exercises* is not an incompleteness that requires further augmentation in order for Ignatian spirituality to be unleashed, but an important feature of that spirituality itself. It is the interaction of the practices that the Exercises proposes with the specific situation of the individual, or group of individuals, along with other "practices" (among them, academic practices of scholars in the modern university) in which they are involved, including the vision of the world entailed by those practices, that gives rise to a diverse set of Ignatian spiritualities. All of them can claim to be Ignatian to the extent that they respond creatively, transformatively, indeed, evangelically, out of the spirit of the *Spiritual Exercises*, to those specific situations.[111]

For this reason, rather than delving into a further investigation of the other important texts in the history of Ignatius and the first Jesuits, the purposes of this overview of Ignatian spirituality will be better served by considering how this spirituality was such a transformative, evangelical force in sixteenth-century Europe. This will in fact require some attention to these texts, especially to the *Constitutions* and to the correspondence of the first Jesuits. But, the emphasis will shift to look at how these documents outline the influence of Ignatian spirituality in that time. This will set the stage for a consideration of how Ignatian spirituality has again been such a force in the ambit of professional theological production in our own late modern times, when many of the tendencies, opportunities, and challenges faced by the first adherents to Ignatian spirituality attained maturity.

CHAPTER THREE

Ignatian Spirituality and the Limits of Modernity

In chapter 1, I argued that spirituality is a modern phenomenon, in the sense that the same forces that came together to produce the conditions that we name "modernity" in Western Europe also brought modern persons in Europe and across the Atlantic to think about and engage in "spirituality" as a set of techniques and beliefs conceived independently from, and often in conflict with, both the beliefs and doctrines handed down by historical traditions and the practices and structures of institutional religion that conserved and passed on those beliefs and doctrines. This suggests that "spirituality" is, in some measure, a response to modernity; it is a way of dealing with the opportunities and challenges of living and thriving under its conditions. As these conditions have become more demanding in late modernity, spirituality has become a more widespread phenomenon.

I also maintained that it is an ambiguous response. Spirituality can, on the one hand, be an enlivening force; it can be an authentic force for evangelization, bringing the good news to modernity and giving it flesh, so that it is a real option for modern men and women. On the other hand, spirituality can be little more than a coping device, a way of accommodating ourselves to the conditions of modernity rather than holding them up to the prophetic and transformative power of the gospel. Thus, a key question for a theological reading of this sign of the times is whether spirituality is truly a well of vision, renewing our presence in and to the world, or a haven in a heartless world, sealing us off from it. The purpose of this chapter is to pose this question with respect to Ignatian spirituality. Answering this question will also complement the overview of Ignatian spirituality, based on its historical source in the *Spiritual Exercises*, offered in chapter 2. If, as Pierre Hadot asserts, the real purpose and import of "spiritual exercises" is not so much to inform as to transform, then a fuller understanding of the exercises that make up Ignatian spirituality will follow from an investigation of the sort of transformations it has brought about in persons embracing it under the conditions of modernity. Finally, this will make it possible to treat, albeit in a more cursory fashion, some other important documents for understanding early Jesuit spirituality.

Because of their pervasive presence to almost every institution in modern society, and especially because of their schools, colleges, and universities, Jesuits have had a significant influence on the modern world, in general, and on the way that Catholics, in particular, understand their presence in it. This has been true almost from the moment that Ignatius and his first companions banded together as a religious order with papal approval in 1540. They have been as controversial as they have been influential. The consolidating nation-states of Europe perceived the Society as a principal means by which the papacy attempted to match them in becoming centralized, modern political entities. What many moderns have found most odious about the Society of Jesus are precisely those features that have made conditions of modernity so productive for those who embrace them: a mobility and adaptability that bridges geographical distance and transcends cultural differences; a single-minded search for the most effective means to bring about desired ends; an ability and determination to meet persons on their own ground, to go in their door in order to bring them out one's own.[1] In short, Jesuits confronted, and continue to confront, modernity on its own grounds. What is it about their spirituality that impelled and empowered them to do this?

This chapter thus attempts to provide an outline of the relationship of Ignatian spirituality to modernity. This cannot but be a provisional one. Indeed, just as the case studies in chapters 4–6 will reveal that there is no one Ignatian theology, they will also show that there is no one monological relationship between Ignatian spirituality and the complex weave of social forces and cultural forms that come together to make up this thing we call modernity, or, perhaps, multiple modernities.² Ignatian spirituality and modernity intersect along a number of axes, and the way that someone shaped by Ignatian spirituality engages modernity will depend on which of the axes predominates.³ I will, therefore, construct the outline by identifying some of those axes, building on the overview of Ignatian spirituality from chapter 2. Some of the axes can be located by placing Ignatian spirituality within the tumultuous passage to modernity already underway by the middle of the sixteenth century. Then we can return to the discussion of those features of modernity that are most reflected in the modern phenomenon of spirituality and ask how those features show up in Ignatian spirituality. This will allow us to see why and how Ignatian spirituality presses its adherents toward an engagement with modernity and will help us to make some preliminary conclusions as to how that engagement might turn out. This prepares the ground for an examination in depth of that engagement in the Jesuit theologians to be studied in chapters 4–6.

IGNATIUS AND THE CULTURES OF EARLY MODERNITY

When Ignatius dictated his life's story to Gonçalves da Câmara, the name he gave himself was "the pilgrim," not just during the time he spent going to and from the Holy Land, but for the whole of his life up to 1538 (the point at which his autobiographical musings end).⁴ This title is emblematic of a restless longing that kept him continually on the move. Like the Protestant Reformers, Ignatius expressed that longing for God that was so characteristic of late medieval and early modern Europe, a longing for the *vita evangelica* that the institutions of Church and academy struggled to meet. Ignatius the pilgrim was able to develop an instrument that did not so much assuage this longing as enable one to structure one's life around it.

Yet Ignatius was also a pilgrim in the more literal sense that, up until the time he settled in Rome in 1540, he lived a mobile life. He not only covered great geographical distances but moved through the various cultures or strands of culture that were, on the one hand, fragments of late medieval culture, and, on the other hand, were coalescing into that cultural matrix that would make up modern Europe.

Part of the appeal and power of the *Spiritual Exercises* lies in the way the pilgrim forged in his handbook a unique synthesis of these cultural elements. It has often been noted that Ignatian spirituality is able to bring off a synthesis of elements that, when articulated in theological systems, are often separated or even opposed to one another. Avery Dulles takes this tack in his reflections on the relationship between Ignatian spirituality and theology: "Ignatian spirituality is a unique combination of world affirmation and world denial, reserve and commitment, personal creativity and obedient submission. It finds the sacred in the secular, God in creatures, grace in nature, contemplation in action, freedom in obedience, and, ultimately, life in death."[5]

As the polemical debates of the Reformation intensified, it was becoming increasingly difficult to hold these sorts of dialectical tensions together creatively. Yet there was more going on here than intra-Christian debates. These debates and the hardening of positions that they manifested evince a deeper shift in the tectonic plates of Western Culture. However difficult it is fully to specify the nature of these changes, *something* was happening in Western Europe that was making a synthesis between elements like the ones that Dulles names more and more difficult to sustain. This happening is frequently denoted by talk about modernity and its beginnings. Our inability to decide precisely what this thing is, how and when to date its beginnings, and whether we are still "in" it, or have passed on to "postmodernity," derive in part from its bewildering effect on our sense of who we are and how we relate (or feel we ought to relate) to our world.

A standard account, constructed by proponents and opponents alike, has it that modernity begins in the mid-seventeenth century and identifies its archpriest (or archvillain) as René Descartes (with Galileo Galilei, as the "father" of modern science, running a close second). A number of studies have, however, urged us to look earlier, at the breakup of the medieval synthesis in the fourteenth century and the advance of a new, albeit provisional, synthesis in the fifteenth and sixteenth centuries.[6] If we accept this account, Ignatius forged his distinctive spirituality at the dawn of modernity. In the next section, I shall follow up on this clue. Before those more abstract considerations, however, it will be helpful to consider how Ignatius's spirituality gathered together numerous strands of late medieval and early modern culture. These strands were starting to come apart in the tumultuous passage to modernity. What Ignatius's spirituality was able to do was to reweave them into a new synthesis with the potential tentatively to reassemble the dynamic synthesis of the divine, the cosmos, and the human, which had been the bedrock of ancient and medieval culture.[7]

Even the most cursory survey of Ignatius's biography reveals a man formed through and through by feudal society. Ignatius's family was deeply involved in the feudal power structure of the Basque Country and had distinguished itself in the service of the crown of Castile, receiving substantial rewards in return.[8] As a youth, Iñigo was attached to the household of a distinguished Castillian nobleman, Juan Velásquez de Cuéllar, where he received a thorough courtly education. When Velásquez was cashiered as treasurer in 1517 by Charles II, Iñigo was received into the service of the Duke of Nájera, recently appointed viceroy of Navarre. As a *gentilhombre* in the duke's court, Iñigo showed the skills (and the vices) of such a gentleman, as a courtesan, as a diplomat, and as a soldier. He proved himself both loyal and stubborn as a soldier at the siege of Pamplona, where the Spanish resistance lasted only as long as the young Loyola's own.

Ignatius later dismissed these formative years: "Up to the age of twenty-six he was a man given to the vanities of the world; and what he enjoyed most was warlike sport, with a great and foolish desire to win fame."[9] Yet there is no doubt that his outlook on the world, and thereby his spirituality was deeply formed by this chivalric culture.[10] The Call of King at the beginning of the Second Week has strong echoes of the recent successful conclusion of the Iberian *reconquista* and of the still-vibrant crusade ideal.[11] In that exercise, the retreatants are to model themselves after medieval knights: "Those who desire to show greater devotion and to distinguish themselves in total service to their eternal king and Lord will not only offer their persons for the labor, but go further still."[12] Earlier, in the Introductory Explanations to the *Exercises*, we are told that those making the Exercises should enter into them with the "great spirit and generosity" (*grande ánima y liberalidad*) that was the hallmark of the medieval *gentilhombre*. Thus, for Ignatius the service of God, which the Principle and Foundation defines as the end for which we are created, is modeled on the service a liege is to give his lord.[13]

Ignatius's exposure to medieval culture did not end at Pamplona, however. His conversion was shaped by important devotional works from the High and late Middle Ages. When he asked for some courtly romances to read while recuperating from the grizzly surgeries on his wounded leg, none were found in the castle at Loyola. Instead he was given two books, both in Castilian translation, which were among the most popular works of late medieval spirituality. One was Jacopo de Voragine's *Golden Legend*. This collection presented the saints to Ignatius as knights of Christ. For example, in his introduction to the Castilian translation, Guaberto Vagad exhorted his readers "to take the crucifix in hand as the royal, powerful, and always victorious standard of the knights of God who are the saints."[14] Thus, the book showed Ignatius the way to translate the ethos of a knight of the *reconquista* into that of a heroic knight of God. It led him to take up the more spectacular penances and abnegations that characterized his first few months at Manresa.[15] If he later gave up these more outward signs of his resolve to live a life of greater distinction in the service of God, it was only because he had come to think of this distinction as an ever-more radical imitation of Jesus, who for his part placed himself utterly at the disposal of God's saving will for humanity.

The *Life of Christ* that Ignatius read and meditated on was written in the first half of the fourteenth century by Ludolph of Saxony, a Dominican-turned-Carthusian. It drew heavily on the *Meditationes vitae Christi*, once attributed to Bonaventure, but in fact written by a fourteenth-century Franciscan named John of Choux. These echoed Bonaventure's own *Tree of Life*, itself a series of meditations on the life of Christ. Specific contents from this book found their way into Ignatius's *Spiritual Exercises*, but more important is the way it instructed Ignatius on how to contemplate the life of Christ.[16] Its meditations and contemplations are all intensely scriptural, placing the work in the long medieval tradition of *lectio divina*. Yet there is a crucial difference in the way that the *lectio* opens out into a mystical encounter with God, a difference denoted by Ewert Cousins, using a term he coined: "the mysticism of the historical event."[17]

Cousins traces the lineage of this feature of Ignatius's spirituality back through Ludolph's work to John of Choux and Bonaventure. Bonaventure was, of course, passing on the spiritual patrimony of the founder of his order, Francis of Assisi.[18] What unifies this tradition, Cousins argues, is a devotion to the humanity of Christ, exemplified in Francis's erection of a crèche for Christmas 1223 midnight Mass at Greccio. Cousins points out that more is at stake in these sorts of practices than flights of imagination, embroiderment of doctrine for simple folk, or preparation for "true," apophatic mystical prayer:

> I believe that it [this new form of prayer] is rooted in the very historicity of human existence and that it activates that level of the psyche whereby we draw out the spiritual energy of a past event. I have called this elsewhere "the mysticism of the historical event." By that I mean that it constitutes a distinct category of mystical consciousness. . . . Just as in nature mysticism we feel united to the material world, so in this form of mysticism we feel part of the historical even—as if we were there, as eye-witnesses, participating in the action, absorbing its energy.[19]

Cousins argues that this form of mysticism emerged in the Middle Ages as a counterpart to the Neoplatonic mystical tradition, with its penchant for the risen, glorified Christ, and its tendency to find in historical events allegories propelling the mystic out of history and into the timeless.[20] Bonaventure's contribution, in Cousins's view, is his ambitious integration of "Francis's innovative, visionary, Christ-centered mysticism into the classical Christian speculative wisdom derived from Neoplatonism."[21] This integration not only gave conceptual articulation to Francis's spirituality, but also effected a fundamental shift, "Franciscanizing" the foundations of the Neoplatonic theological structure. Cousins concludes by wondering whether Ignatius has had a "Bonaventure" of his own to integrate his spiritual vision into the broader stream of Christian spirituality, and to situate it within a comprehensive theological vision.[22]

In sum, Cousins alerts us to the fact that Ignatius had learned (and then formulated, particularly in the contemplations of the Second Week) a different way of praying on scripture than the allegorical methods of reading scripture so central to Christian Neoplatonism and the Dionysian mainstream of Christian mysticism. Christian Neoplatonism did not ignore the immanence of God any more than the mysticism of the historical event ignores God's transcendence—after all, both must be accommodated by any spiritual or theological tradition that is faithful to the reality of the Incarnation. But they make this joint accommodation in different ways. Speaking, admittedly, in broad strokes, in the Christian Neoplatonic tradition, the mystical power of the text is unleashed by freeing it from its historical context, finding in the text mythical or cosmic archetypes that elevate one to the God above and outside of the vicissitudes of history. The world is deeply physical, but deeply symbolic too, and it is the symbolic on which this tradition focuses.

In Ludolph's book, and in the *Spiritual Exercises*, things are different. The divine is found within the movements of history. One is not to use the narratives as a springboard propelling one out of history, but is to enter into the history recounted, making oneself a contemporary, an actor within the drama.[23] This energizes discipleship, *imitatio*. Thus, in Ludolph's introduction to *The Life of Christ* he tells the reader: "Let him more often return to the principal mysteries of Christ, namely, the Incarnation, the Nativity, the Circumcision, the Epiphany, . . . which are all topics for special recall, exercise, spiritual remembrance, and consolation. Let him read the life of Christ in such a manner that he endeavors to imitate him as far as he can. For it profits him little to read unless he also imitates."[24] These features—attention to the historical detail of Jesus's life, a hesitancy to move too quickly to allegorical readings, and the emphasis on imitation as the goal of *lectio*—are pivotal elements of Ignatian spirituality, as can be clearly seen from, for example, the contemplations of the Second Week and the Rules for Eating given in the Third.[25]

With his exposure to Ludolph's work, Ignatius's spirituality continued and deepened a current in medieval spirituality that began with Bernard of Clairvaux and, above all, Francis of Assisi, and emphasizes more the historical Jesus than the risen Lord, and that, partakes of the growing medieval sensitivity to history.[26] Of course, one of the hallmarks of modernity as a whole is the birth and maturation of "historical consciousness." As Gillespie puts it, "to think of oneself as modern is to think of one's being in terms of time."[27] Charles Taylor argues that distinctive of the temporal dimension of modern self-awareness is the way we have come more and more to bracket or suppress any sense of "higher time," which previously had encompassed, grounded, and, on occasion, interrupted "secular" time.[28] As with so many of its other features, this modern awareness of history has roots in the Middle Ages, carried by one strand of the complex weave of medieval culture. This sense for time and history had not yet, however, broken free of the constraints placed by a timeless metaphysical framework and a static economic, political, and ecclesial social matrix, all of which were ritually enacted and reinforced, and which taken together tended to make historical particularity irrelevant, accidental, or even heretically deviant. This sense for time and history found its way into modernity, and into the *Spiritual Exercises*, but in a way that emphasized a transcendence and a transformative power immanent to the historical event itself. Running against the grain of modernity's flattening out of time, the latter emphasis had the capacity to make present a "more," a surplus of meaning within history that previously had been accessed by leaving history behind.

The two books that Ignatius read during his conversion at Loyola initiated him into this more historically focused tradition, with its Franciscan roots, but they also exposed him to the broader scope of patristic and medieval spirituality. In its more than 700 folio pages, Ludolph's book is shot through with thousands of quotes from the Fathers of the Church, giving Ignatius his initial exposure to the "positive theology" that he came to value so highly (*SpEx* 363). What is more, Ignatius also came early into contact with another important spirituality of the late Middle Ages: the Modern Devotion. He would have first encountered it at the monastery at Montserrat, a center of enthusiasm in Spain for the Modern Devotion. He would have also encountered it in what was, with the exception of the Bible, his favorite book: the *Imitation of Christ*. The title of this book captured one of the central themes of the Modern Devotion, echoing the centrality of *imitatio* in Ludolph of Saxony's work. However, for the Modern Devotion, including its most well-known text, imitation shows a subtle but crucial difference. In Kempis's masterwork, imitation of Christ means following the way of the cross, and this in turn means exercising self-knowledge, self-mortification, humility, and obedience, rejecting the world without, and entering with all one's strength into the battle against one's vices within. Thus, what Ignatius found in the *Imitation of Christ* was in fact a repristinated medieval monastic spirituality.[29] It was the focus on interiority and single-minded struggle against one's vices that attracted Ignatius, yet he did not share the movement's disdain for labor in the world outside the cloister.[30] So, if we find themes from the Modern Devotion in the *Spiritual Exercises*, we find them reconfigured and incorporated into a broader spirituality that sought imitation of Jesus at work in the world.

Other common themes from medieval spirituality are also woven into Ignatius's spirituality. Mystical themes common to the Christian Neoplatonic tradition figure prominently in the Contemplation to Attain Love. The Ignatian spiritual disposition of indifference has strong affinities to the key mystical stance of "*Gelassenheit*," elaborated in Rhineland mystics such as Meister Eckhart. Indeed, the entire Ignatian tradition of "finding God in all things" unfolds in a way that is so uncannily akin to the Eckhartian mystical tradition that Hugo Rahner, unable precisely to locate the historical lines of continuity between the two, postulated "metahistorical continuities" as an explanation.[31] Connecting Ignatius with a long and rich Christian tradition, with both theological and mystical resources, this continuity opens up a powerful way of articulating and interpreting Ignatian spirituality, as we shall see in chapter 4 in our study of Karl Rahner. It also can disclose a key point of contact between Ignatian spirituality and modernity.

If the mysticism of the historical event helped to initiate the modern turn to history, the Rhineland mystical tradition provided a potent contribution to another feature of modernity I discussed in chapter 1: the affirmation of everyday life. Eckhart emphasized that union with God could and should be sought in the everyday work of service — Martha's part. He complemented this with the novel and radical claim that the contemplative life — Mary's part — is only the initial stage in the Christian mystical journey. This was a potent message in an age convinced that the life of laypersons came in a distant second (or third) in the quest for the perfection of the *vita evangelica*, well behind the eremetic and cenobitic lives. It was a message well suited for the burghers and Beguines who received it, but one in tension with the hierarchical vision of the medieval Church. Eckhart never denied the importance of the Church's sacramental mediations or the binding character of its ethical teachings, but many believed that his ideas tended in that direction, as the similar teachings of Marguerite Porete manifestly did. The tradition was carried on, albeit with modifications, in the work of Eckhart's disciples Johannes Tauler and Heinrich Suso, and in the *Theologia Germanica*, attributed to Tauler, which influenced both magisterial Reformers such as Martin Luther and radical Reformers such as Thomas Müntzer and Menno Simons. The latter went even further in rejecting the Church's hierarchical vision in favor of an immediate union with God possible within the everyday.[32]

Some of these tensions are found in Ignatius's own work. One of the early objections to the *Spiritual Exercises* was that it did not recommend religious life highly enough. It is true that the Rules for Thinking with the Church instruct one to "praise the vows of religion."[33] However, in the introductory explanations, the director is charged *not* to recommend the evangelical counsels during the course of the Exercises, nor to encourage an inclination in the exercitant toward such a life that comes in a period of consolation.[34] The reason for this could never be for Ignatius a hesitation to aid another person to seek and find a life of ever-greater praise and service of God (which religious life represented for him and his companions). Rather, it is a matter of how to go about doing that. For Ignatius—as for Eckhart—God is dynamically present in all things, and particularly in the depths of the soul. Hence, authentic perfection is attained by attending to that dynamic presence and allowing that presence to inform the way that one lives one's everyday life, in whatever state. Helping another find and attend to this presence for him- or herself would, in Ignatius's view, be far more likely to yield a lasting and fruitful commitment than any urgings from without.

The affirmation of everyday life, with its tendency to pull down hierarchies of life-states, is in tension with the other strand we found in Ignatian spirituality: the mysticism of the historical event. For if, on the one hand, it is Ignatian spirituality's focus on God's dynamic presence to the individual person that "trumps" the normativity of hierarchical orderings of states of life, it is also true, on the other, that God's dynamic presence is best disclosed and interpreted against the backdrop constructed by prolonged and intensive contemplation of the history of Jesus. One makes oneself contemporaneous with his life, or, perhaps better, sees one's own history as a recapitulation or extension of his. A new ideal, a new "hypergood," to use Charles Taylor's language,[35] enters in: a life of radical imitation of Jesus, in his concrete historical reality, as one who labors in poverty and often in opprobrium on the behalf of human beings. Ignatius no doubt believed that this way of finding God's presence would move many to imitate this Christ within one of the approved religious orders, but, as we've seen, he was also ready to believe that this movement could take place by transforming states—religious, clerical, or lay—to which a person was already committed.[36]

In summary, therefore, Ignatius drew on at least two important streams in medieval spirituality: Christian Neoplatonism and the mysticism of the historical event. The two stand in some tension with one another, as Cousins points out.[37] In fact, as Cousins also shows, the work of important medieval theologians such as Bonaventure can be seen as an attempt to bring the two together into a theology, in part (for Bonaventure, at any rate) to legitimate the legacy of Francis of Assisi and protect it from the radicalizing tendencies and millenarian conclusions of the Spiritual Franciscans.[38] Ignatius's spirituality spans the same tension.

Thus far we have seen the influence of feudal political culture and of medieval and late medieval devotional literature. We have yet to consider another important medieval current: scholasticism. Here one finds that although "the pilgrim" spent considerable time in the world of scholasticism, its influence needs to be assessed soberly. His spirituality was substantially complete by the time he came to Paris in 1528. Furthermore, Ignatius did not take the doctorate in theology, although he did attend lectures in theology during his final year in Paris, after he had received his Master of Arts degree in 1534. He proved competent enough in the liberal arts (philosophy), but he was not interested in pursuing scholasticism as a theological discipline, and when its more formal conceptuality appears in his writings (in the *Constitutions* or in his correspondence), it is often the work of his secretary, Juan Polanco, to whom Ignatius entrusted such theological labor, and who did have formal theological training from the University of Padua.

This is not necessarily to deny Outram Evennett's thesis that Ignatius found in Aquinas's understanding of nature and grace an intellectual basis that illuminated his profound experience of God's presence in the world.[39] It is certainly true that the more precise philosophical formulations of the Principle and Foundation, and of the Rules for Thinking with the Church, betray scholasticism's influence.[40] Yet, if Ignatius and the first Jesuits were attracted to the precision and proven orthodoxy of the scholasticism they learned at Paris, the way that the theologians at Paris carried on their discipline was at odds with their own *modus procedendi*. O'Malley observes that for the first Jesuits,

> the theologians of Paris lived in their heads, not in their hearts, and they practiced their discipline for the sake of their colleagues not for the Lord's flock. In other words, they divorced theology from both spirituality and from the practice of ministry. Others had earlier pointed out these two divorces, for the *Devotio* had implicitly given voice to the first, and Erasmus and other humanists explicitly to both. They had all as a result repudiated scholastic theology, whereas the Jesuits hoped to reshape it, at least for themselves.[41]

This attitude is evident in the Rules for Thinking with the Church, in which scholasticism is praised.[42] We've seen that although Ignatius there praises both scholastic theology and positive (patristic) theology, it is the latter that defines an approach to the things of God that is more consonant with that of the *Exercises*. Furthermore, in the Introductory

Explanations, Ignatius evinces an attitude toward learning that calls to mind the critiques of scholasticism leveled by the Modern Devotion and Christian humanists alike: "What fills and satisfies the soul consists, not in knowing much, but in our understanding the realities profoundly and in savoring them interiorly."[43] Ignatius's spirituality was not opposed to "knowing much," but it subordinated it to the goal of the *Spiritual Exercises*: rousing oneself to answer the call of the divine king and helping others to do the same.

The similarity between Ignatius's understanding of the place of knowledge in the human journey and that of the Renaissance humanists brings us to that important and more clearly nonmedieval strand of early modern Europe. The relationship of the early Jesuits to the culture of Renaissance humanism is still a matter of debate and need not concern us overmuch here.[44] Ignatius would have encountered this movement during his time at the newly founded University of Alcalá, which was a center of enthusiasm for Erasmus's writings. By the time he arrived at the University of Paris, humanism was a focus of both enthusiasm and also vitriolic debate, and Ignatius may have picked up some of his reservations about the movement as a whole, and about Erasmus in particular, while he was there.[45] Whatever Ignatius's specific attitudes toward Erasmus, however, his *Spiritual Exercises* manifestly shares with Erasmus and other humanists a key feature: a turn to rhetoric.[46] Implicit to the *Spiritual Exercises* is the central claim made by the humanists in arguing for a retrieval of classical rhetoric: in the quest for and communication of truth and wisdom a person's imagination and affect have to be engaged as much as, if not more than, her or his discursive-conceptual reason. The goal of learning and teaching must be not just, nor even primarily, apodictic demonstration or proof, but *persuasion*, bringing oneself and others to a profound understanding and savoring of the truth, so that it is integrated into one's whole way of thinking, feeling, and acting. The humanists were convinced that scholasticism had failed in this; though Ignatius would never issue such a sweeping condemnation, he and the first Jesuits did seek the reform of scholasticism so that it might serve such a goal.

There are two features of this turn to rhetoric that bear further comment. First, it provides a larger context within which to understand the dictum that the one giving the Exercises should accommodate their structure and content to the person to whom they are being given.[47] If the goal is not to communicate timeless truths in an apodictic fashion, but to persuade concrete persons situated in specific contexts, then the approach must be tailored to those specific persons and contexts, as is the case for classical rhetoric. Second, classical rhetoric was oriented toward the public sphere. Its purpose was to engage other persons in matters of import in the polis in order to bring them around to one's own position. In this light, the Meditation on the Two Standards enjoins a quintessentially rhetorical task on those who would serve under the banner of Christ. Christ sends these persons "to spread his doctrine among people of every state and condition," but they are to do so *"by attracting them"* to his particular strategy for living in the world.[48] This exigency of persuading and attracting persons of every state and condition is one of the tacit pressures that moves someone who has been shaped by Ignatius's spirituality into an engagement with culture, since it is precisely by that engagement that one gains the tools requisite to such work.[49]

Ignatius and the first Jesuits are perhaps most known (or notorious) for their involvement in one final strand of early modern European culture: the Counter-Reformation.[50] One of the most common and misleading stereotypes of the early Jesuits is that they were the pope's elite soldiers, gathered into a military company to turn back Protestant reformers and to spearhead the reform of the Church prescribed by the Council of Trent. This picture was not just the fabrication of Protestant attacks, such as by Martin Chemnitz, but was propounded by the early Jesuits themselves. Not long after Ignatius's death, following the lead of Jerónimo Nadal, they took to paralleling his life with Martin Luther's, presenting Ignatius as a providential counterweight to the German Reformer.[51] Admittedly, when the Society of Jesus became active in northern Europe, confronting the Protestant reformers quickly became a primary focus around which Jesuits practiced their *consueta ministeria*. It is hard to conceive how it could have been otherwise. Yet, it is important to remember that combating the Reformers was less a focus near the Mediterranean, and even less so in the distant missionary territories.[52]

Ignatius himself was relatively unconcerned with the Reformation in the first years after his conversion. It was not Wittenberg, or even Rome, that was the focus of Ignatius's ecclesial-ministerial imagination during those early years. It was Jerusalem. Reading his account of the Paris years, one is struck by the almost total lack of reference to the tumultuous events that were transpiring there, reflecting the growing storm of the Reformation. Later, when the first companions submitted the results of their original deliberations to Paul III for approval in 1539 (the so-called *Quinque capitula*), neither the defense of the faith nor the reform of the Church was mentioned. It was only when papal approbation was confirmed by Julius III a decade later that "defense of the faith" was inserted into the Formula of the Institute. Finally, even when the seriousness of the challenge presented by the Reformers became apparent to the early Jesuits, "reform" was not the primary category by which they understood their response. When they did use the term they did not mean, as most prelates did, the institutional reform of the Church. They approached the problem from the base that was already established in the spirituality Ignatius gave them. Reform would be best achieved by bringing each person to lead a more intensely devout Christian life. This was, of course, already their goal: the salvation and perfection of souls. Thus, if they threw themselves energetically into the challenge of answering the Protestant Reformers, it was because they understood it to be consonant with their way of proceeding, and because, thus understood, they felt themselves particularly well equipped to do so, above all with the instrument of the *Spiritual Exercises*.[53] This meant, however, that they entered the task on their own terms, and according to their own particular way of proceeding.

We need not dwell too long on the complicated issues surrounding the question of the Jesuits' role in Reformation and Catholic Counter-Reformation (including the problem of the adequacy of those historical labels).[54] Ignatian spirituality would be swept up in the heated, and often tragic, religious conflicts of the late sixteenth and seventeenth centuries because it arose out of the same milieu that produced those storms. In retrospect, it is not difficult to see how elements of the *Exercises* would lend themselves to a militantly anti-Protestant application. The Two Standards, for example, does present the world as a field of struggle, but it is important to note that the struggle is not between two groups of human beings, but between demons, on the one hand (who are present to *everyone*, Protestants and Catholics alike), and persons sent by Christ, on the other. That meditation, along with the Call of the King, clearly depicts the Christian's response as a *corporate* response, so that the well-being of the body within which that response was incarnated—the Church—is of vital concern. The Rules for Thinking with the Church present a full-fledged and well-developed articulation of that concern. Finally, the special vow of obedience to the pope regarding missions bound the young Society to the pope and the institution of the papacy in a special way. This relationship to an institution that was under attack by Protestants, and that was controversial even for many Catholics, brought the Jesuits both advantages and tribulations.

Nonetheless, in all of this it should not be forgotten that Ignatius himself did not descend to name-calling in dealing with the Reformers, an example followed by other Jesuits at least up until his death. The "Presupposition" of the *Exercises* is that one should "put a good interpretation" on another's statements (*SpEx* 22). This dictum undergirds a response to disagreement and even error that is anything but polemical and militant. To be sure, when required, Ignatius insisted that doctrinal error (particularly when propounded from the pulpit) be confronted and corrected; yet, in the realm of "spiritual conversations" where Ignatius was most truly at home, his deepest conviction was that persuasion and attraction, not confrontation and polemic, would produce the most fruit.[55]

In summary, five different elements or cultures within the broader mix of early modern Europe either had an influence on the initial formulation of Ignatius's spirituality or provided a context for its early development. In more or less decreasing order of importance (particularly for the composition of the *Exercises*) they are (1) medieval spiritualities, (2) feudal political culture, (3) Renaissance humanism, (4) scholasticism, and (5) the confrontational culture of the Reformation. There seemed to be something for everyone in Ignatian spirituality, and the principles of adaptation and accommodation made it possible to exploit this capaciousness to the full. This open eclecticism, as opposed to the more conservative tendency of, say, the Modern Devotion, is part of what makes Ignatius's a genuinely modern spirituality. But, there is more to it than that. Ignatian spirituality is "modern" because it includes so many themes that would become characteristic of modernity. He picked up various strands of the late medieval world, which were fast unraveling, and wove them together. But the result was not an *intellectual* synthesis; the accelerating modernization of Western European culture and the fragmentation of the necessary cultural background for such a synthesis made that well-nigh impossible. What Ignatius produced was a *spirituality*, in the sense we have defined it, as a set of exercises or practices that would initiate one into the mystery of discipleship, one that could and did appeal to a very broad spectrum of Christians in early modern Europe precisely because it exhibited an eclecticism that was more than mere bricolage. Indeed, the time was now ripe for Ignatius's achievement to be perceived and experienced *as a spirituality*, as a response to the conditions of modernity. The question then is what kind of response it is. Is it only a reflection or coping device for modernity? Or, alternatively, does it make possible and even exigent a transformative encounter with the cultures of modernity that leaves neither the practitioner of Ignatian spirituality nor the particular modern context that she brings to that practice untransformed? To this issue we now turn.

Ignatian Spirituality and the Conditions of Modernity

In chapter 1, I argued that spirituality as it is thought of and practiced today emerged as a part of the general transformation of European society and culture that began in the late Middle Ages. It was made possible—and in some senses necessary—by the growing dominance of a number of pivotal conditions of modernity that define the task and challenges of forging and sustaining a coherent and stable sense of personal identity. The three main conditions I identified there were (1) modern individualism, which brings with it the need for ongoing and intensive self-surveillance and self-management; (2) the affirmation of everyday life with its displacement of traditional hierarchies of lifestyle choices; and (3) the dramatic and accelerating sense of transience and rootlessness of modern life, driven in part by the disembedding of social processes from circadian time and local space. Ignatian spirituality already reflects these three conditions.

After even a brief perusal of Ignatius's spiritual diary of 1544 and 1545, the reader will be struck by how painstakingly he scrutinized his internal life.[56] Of course, the need for continual self-surveillance is present in the *Imitation of Christ*. What Ignatius added was a structure and method of unprecedented thoroughness. Thus, a century before one of the Jesuits' most famous pupils, René Descartes, established "method" as the defining mark of modern philosophy, Ignatius established it in a spirituality. He formulated intricate "rules for the discernment of spirits" to probe one's inner experience. He advocated a daily examination of conscience and periodic "inventories" of one's state, formalized in the general confession of devotion. With the aid of the book that lays out this structure, *Spiritual Exercises*, the early Jesuits virtually invented the modern institution of the "retreat" as a methodically organized time away from the hustle and bustle of modern life.

Ignatius's spirituality also reflects the affirmation of everyday life. We've seen that Ignatius enjoins the one giving the *Spiritual Exercises* not to urge the life of the vows on the retreatant, even if, in the first blush of consolation, he or she wants to embrace it.[57] This does not mean that the early Jesuits did not think that religious life embodied evangelical perfection. They did. But this attitude coexisted with another. They did not see the election of religious life as the only authentic outcome of making the *Spiritual Exercises*, and did not give them only to those persons whom they thought would make such an election. Their habit of giving the *Exercises* in modified form to men and women of almost every class and state in European society reflected their belief that the evangelical perfection of being absolutely open to the will of God and engaged in God's work of "helping souls" was available to all persons. Since helping souls entailed responding to the physical and cultural needs of embodied souls, in addition to their spiritual needs, the various this-worldly works of creating, sustaining, and enriching life were not excluded from this way to perfection. These convictions were reflected both in the early Jesuits' broad understanding of cultural endeavors and institutions that lay within the ambit of their vocation and in their practice of training lay helpers and founding confraternities for almost every nonsacramental form of ministry they undertook. This feature of their "way of proceeding" (as they called it) can be seen in a book written by the Spanish Jesuit Luis de la Puente a century after Ignatius. His four-volume *De la perfección del christiano en todos sus estados* was the first work of such breadth that attempted to work out the meaning and practice of "Christian perfection" for all the different states of life, including for the laity.[58]

This is not to say that Ignatius and his earlier followers did not advocate a strongly disciplined and ascetic style of life. They did. But it was an asceticism geared toward a fuller involvement in the work of the everyday world by means of breaking through to the pulse of divine life that flowed in it. As John O'Malley notes, Ignatius conceived of a form of life of utmost rigor and asceticism, but this was not a life in which one disciplined the desires and passions whereby we are involved in everyday life, so as then to attain to a contemplative union with God that removes us from that life. Rather, "A new asceticism begins to emerge that is not dependent for its practice on self-imposed austerities to curb one's own disordered tendencies, but on the rigors and hardships imposed by total dedication to an ideal of ministry in the world of ordinary people, with their often undisciplined needs and demands."[59] This was a "this-wordly" asceticism and vision of perfection, one open to all, and the Jesuits strove to convey it as such. In a sense, though, this shift required the kind of ongoing self-surveillance that is served by the *Spiritual Exercises*. The scale of less perfect to more fully perfect (or evangelical) is no longer mapped hierarchically and institutionally in terms of different states of life. Rather it is traversed according to the degree to which one incarnates a more radical imitation of Christ within the specific role one plays in society, whatever it be. This radicality is empowered in turn by the kinds of internal dispositions on which the Exercises focus and for which the exercitant is to pray (indifference, compunction, gratitude, familiarity with and love of Christ). This being so, one's focus must be there. This could lead to a deeply rooted anxiety and desire for certitude about the kind of life one had chosen and the way that she or he was living it.[60]

A final condition of modernity is the disembedding of social processes and institutions from local time and geographical vicinity and their realignment over large and continually shifting domains of time and space. This result of modernity has been contingent upon the flattening out or the homogenization of time, as Taylor argues, and techniques of communication that intimately tied distant regions together and led to an ever-intensifying social acceleration, as Rosa argues. We've seen that this condition has found its reflection in the requirement that modern spiritualities be portable, highly malleable, and adaptable to rapidly changing conditions. This condition can be seen in Ignatius's often stated exhortation to accommodate the spirituality of the Exercises to the needs of particular persons or groups. In addition, the early Jesuits lived through and lived out the temporal and spatial reconfiguring of the modern world. It is not just that they were uncommonly mobile, so that within Ignatius's own lifetime Jesuits were active in the Americas and in the Far East. Even more, as superior general, Ignatius developed, indeed insisted upon, far-reaching networks of correspondence that would arc across and link these very different locales and cultures. Perhaps most emblematic—and controversial, at the time—of their embrace of this modern characteristic was the disembedding of Jesuit religious life from the geographical locale of the cloister and the temporal rhythm of communal prayer of the Divine Office (which for its part reflected nature's circadian and seasonal rhythms). Nadal gave classic expression to this in speaking about the "fourth kind of house" (besides novitiates, colleges, and professed houses) in which Jesuits would live:

> That [fourth house] is altogether the most ample place and reaches as far as the globe itself. For wherever they can be sent in ministry to help souls, that is the most glorious and longed-for "house" for those theologians. . . . [T]hey consider that they are in the most peaceful and pleasant house when they are on the move, when they travel throughout the earth, when they have no place to call their own, when they are always in need, always in want—only let them strive in some small way to imitate Christ Jesus, who had nowhere on which to lay his head and who spent all his years of preaching in journey.[61]

If we use these three themes characteristic of modernity as a diagnostic, therefore, we can see Ignatian spirituality is at least incipiently, a modern spirituality.[62] Is it anything more than modern?

Followers of Ignatius have been accused of this, perhaps rightly so in some cases. Like any modern spirituality, Ignatius's can lose its critical, spirited edge. Closer examination reveals, however, that in each of these three conditions of modernity, Ignatian spirituality both mirrors it and also constrains it by contextualizing it in a broader frame. Starting with modern individualism, even though Ignatius's spirituality, particularly in the *Spiritual Exercises*, is directed at the individual, intended to promote self-reflection and ever-deeper personal commitment, it places this individual task within a communal context—the Church—and a transpersonal history, the history of salvation.

That Ignatius's theological anthropology has resources to resist modernity's individualism can be seen from the rules for discernment of spirits. They do not presume what Taylor in his later work calls "the buffered self." Developing a buffered self is a crucial element, on his account, in the construction of a modern identity, which is individualized, abstracted from social networks, and thus capable of taking a neutral, disengaged stance toward the external world and even (via a strong mind/body distinction) toward its own embodiment. This is all in contrast to the premodern, "porous" self, for which currents of meaning and value originate outside of the self and impinge decisively, and at times destructively, on the self:

> For the modern, buffered self, the possibility exists of taking a distance from, disengaging from everything outside the mind. My ultimate purposes are those which arise within me, the crucial meanings of things are those defined by my responses to them.... This is not to say that the buffered understanding necessitates your taking this stance. It is just that it allows it as a possibility, whereas the porous self does not. By definition for the porous self, the sources of its most powerful and important emotions are outside the "mind"; or better put, the very notion that there is a clear boundary, allowing us to define an inner base area, grounded in which we can disengage from the rest, has no sense.[63]

Ignatius's rules for discernment clearly presuppose a porous self; moreover, they do not envision or aspire to overcoming that condition so as to attain a fully buffered self. Whatever "indifference" is, it is not the neutral, disengaged stance of the buffered self. Ignatius's rules do involve careful scrutiny of "the various motions which are caused in the soul," including those caused by "the good spirit" and by "the enemy of our human nature." However, the degree and depth of perception, understanding, and manipulation of these preternatural influences rises only to the level of "to some extent" (*SpEx* 313). Complete disengagement (and the completely disenchanted world corollary to it) is impossible; relative disengagement depends on the traversal of the Spiritual Exercises that culminates in an election. And this election entails an *engagement* in God's work in history, a work that is constitutive of that history's creation, redemption, and sanctification.[64]

Ignatius certainly did not divorce spirituality from religion, which for him meant the institutional Roman Catholic Church. The rules for discernment of spirit are central to the *Exercises*, but we cannot dismiss the Rules for Thinking with the Church as a mere afterthought. Ignatius had the utmost respect for the individual's inner experience of God, yet he was also convinced that the same God at work within is also at work without, particularly in the Church founded by God's son and guided by the Holy Spirit. This was by no means a naïve and untested conviction on his part nor an easy balance to maintain. It was tested in Ignatius's dealings with Gian Pietro Carafa, Pope Paul IV, at whose election an observer reported of Ignatius that "all the bones in his body began to shake."[65] But it was central to his spirituality.

Second, the early Jesuits certainly contributed, decisively, to the "affirmation of everyday life" insofar as the spirituality they initiated increasingly found—and encouraged others to find—God's presence in every licit way of life and profession, no matter how quotidian. Yet their spirituality did not, in the process, lose sight of a vision of the whole, a very demanding vision, laid out in exercises such as the Call of the King, and given depth and personal appeal by contemplating its normative exemplification in the person of Jesus. Ignatius's spirituality has the resources to elevate the everyday callings of the reproduction and sustenance of life and find in them, as much as in the callings of religious life or ministerial priesthood, the materials for a genuine and transformative union with God, but it also holds *every* way of life up to the rigorous standard of the radical imitation of Christ, as the third way of being humble makes clear (*SpEx* 167).

Finally, the mobility and consciously chosen rootlessness of Ignatian spirituality did not lead necessarily to fragmentation and inability to grasp broader wholes that threaten our "runaway world" (Giddens). In the *Spiritual Exercises*, the ordering irruption of "higher time" (Taylor) into secular time is foundationally present in the Contemplation on the Incarnation, in which one participates both in secular time (one's own, and the time of Jesus's life on earth) and in the Trinitarianly grounded time of salvation history.[66] In the *Constitutions*, Ignatius devoted an entire section to the union of its members, recognizing how difficult that would be to sustain once traditional structures such as monastic stability, common recitation of the Office, or ecclesial benefice were abandoned. This explains in part why Ignatius insisted that Jesuits should excel at the vow of obedience, rather than poverty (as one might expect from the Meditation on the Two Standards in the *Spiritual Exercises*). It is also gives part of the reason for the global networks of correspondence that the Jesuits created. They existed not so much so that the general could supervise and micromanage the affairs of local communities of Jesuits; the slowness and unreliability of the mails made that impossible. Rather, the correspondence was to reinforce the Jesuits' sense of belonging to a larger body, called by God to labor in the vineyard of the Lord. Ultimately, in the *Constitutions*, as in the *Spiritual Exercises*, the one thing necessary is consolation, everything that conduces to the love of God: "The chief bond to cement the union of the members among themselves and with their head is, on both sides, the love of God our Lord. For when the superior and the subjects are closely united to His Divine and Supreme Goodness, they will very easily be united among themselves, through that same love which will descend from the Divine Goodness and spread to all other men, and particularly to the body of the Society."[67]

The *Spiritual Exercises* gives the one who makes its exercises faithfully and regularly a method of coming to a deep awareness of that unifying love, descending from the Divine Goodness (see *SpEx* 237). It exposes him or her to the concrete form of that love in the life, deeds, and fate of Jesus the Christ. It presses him or her not just to experience oneself as the *object* of that love (important as that is), but as one called to participate in and with it. It is this vision and sense of belonging that constrains the dizzying and atomizing effects of the ever-accelerating transience and globalization of social processes in modernity.

In short, forged at the beginning of the passage to modernity, and in the midst of the fragmentation of the various elements of the classical and medieval synthesis, Ignatian spirituality aims to enact a holding-together of those various elements. This is an ambitious claim. I repeat that it is not an exclusive claim: other spiritualities, especially the classic ones that have proven their worth over time, can do the same, if embraced deeply enough, even (perhaps especially) in those elements that seem "out of step" with our times. And some are more apt on some matters. The great sixteenth-century Carmelites Teresa of Avila and John of the Cross, for example, move in a more penetrating way into the complexity of the interior spiritual journey under the conditions of modernity.

To complete my argument, something like a meditation on one of the central themes of the *Spiritual Exercises*, at least as read in the light of the story I have been telling, might be able to suggest that inner dynamism that enables Ignatian spirituality to be more than just a haven in a heartless world.

The theme is that of work. *Labor.* If there is one word that would serve as a metaphorical summation of the conditions of modernity, this would be it. It was there at the beginnings of modernity. The Renaissance humanists, so influential, at least indirectly, on the early Jesuits, emphasized a creative self that, in the *work* of metaphor, rhetoric, art, and poetry, is able not just to grasp and reflect what is but to *bring forth*, to *produce*, the new. Initially, at least, this was understood to be a likeness to or participation in the work of divine speech in producing *ex nihilo.* It was, again initially, production in the etymological sense of *pro-ducere*, "to lead forth" the new from the old. Gradually, however, the creative self was divorced from the primordial architect, and what was initially seen as a participation in the divine work came to be seen as competition and supplantation. It was only as moderns came to see less and less "at work" in nature than a blind interplay of randomly configured forces that the now-isolated, fragmented "work" of being a self took on the disorienting and alienated features that modern existentialists so tellingly describe. It is no accident that Karl Marx, drawing on Hegel before him, seized on work, labor, and production as key metaphors for understanding both the dignity and the dilemma of the human self in modernity. To be a self under the conditions of modernity is to be at work. It is hard work! In its most extreme forms, the modern self is presented as existing almost *sui generis*; the self *is* its own work. *Laboro ergo sum.* But when work exhaustively defines what the self is, and the self alone is at work in a soulless nature in which God is dead, then work exhausts the self.

In chapter 2 we saw how important the theme of work is to the *Spiritual Exercises.*[68] It shows up at key junctures: in the Call of the King, in the Contemplations on the Incarnation and the Nativity, and in the Contemplation to Attain Love. What becomes vividly present to the retreatant in the course of the Exercises is that God is Godself at work, not just in creating and sustaining, but in the work of redemption that flows from God's compassionate response to a world mired in blindness and death. In the course of the Second Week of the Exercises, the retreatant follows Jesus in his work and is challenged to place his or her own work in this context. It is a context that is as expansive as the whole face of the globe, which I survey in making the Contemplation on the Incarnation, and as local and particular as a small house in "the city of Nazareth in the Province of Galilee," where Mary is addressed by the angel; or again as particular as my own place. Thus, the Exercises' "composition of place" is an intercalation of the local and global so typical of modernity and of Ignatian spirituality. But it does not result either in the dissolution of the local into the global or the fragmentation of the local, in which persons cannot but flee the global context, overwhelmed by its risks and demands. Rather, these contexts are united, and that union forms the context of the person's own work.

What unites them? The work of a God who "acts in the manner of one who is laboring" (*SpEx* 236). It is a work of compassion, responding to the suffering and blindness of a world groaning under the power of death. And the good news? Not only is the individual person the object of God's work (this has been established in the First Week), but he or she is invited to participate in God's work. And none of the human powers to know and to create (that is, to work), none of the human powers developed and so rightly celebrated by Renaissance humanism, by the scientific revolution, by the technological revolution, and all of modernity's other children, are outside the ambit of that invitation. But neither is any human activity, no matter how humble and quotidian, unworthy of it.

This is a grand vision of the ultimate "place" of human work, one that reconnects on modern terms person, cosmos, and God. It exhilarated Ignatius and his first companions, it caught the imagination of many in early modern Catholic Europe, and it continues to transform the lives of modern persons to this day. But one must take care. If one allows oneself to be filled with enthusiasm and gratitude for the work that God is about in the world, if, consequently, one lets oneself get swept up in that work, then this majestic celebration, indeed, divinization of human work, has its price. Nothing less than the prayer at the end of the *Exercises*: "Take Lord, and receive all my liberty, my memory, my understanding, and all my will—all that I have and possess. You, Lord, have given all that to me. I now give it back to you, O Lord. All of it is yours. Dispose of it according to your will. Give me love of yourself and your grace, for that is enough for me" (*SpEx* 234). This uniting of the exhilarating yet precarious work of being a person in our modern age to the work of a compassionate, loving God is what makes Ignatian spirituality at once thoroughly modern and yet, at its best, anything but a "haven in a heartless world."

Ignatius the Theologian

In 1561, Jerónimo Nadal sent an instruction to the Jesuits working at the college in Alcalá concerning the program of studies in the Society. In it he spoke of Ignatius as "our father, the theologian."[69] He did not, of course, mean that Ignatius was a "professional" theologian. Ignatius did not take a doctoral degree in theology at Paris, and he did not write theological works. He left that labor to others, Juan Polanco in particular. He did, however, have a compelling vision of who God is, and how this Triune God acts decisively in the person of Jesus in order to bring about the salvation and perfection of embodied souls. In chapter 1, I argued that a spirituality is primarily a set of practices, but that it is accompanied by "a particular perception of and discourse about God, the cosmos and human beings that these practices open up and that, in turn, promote and make sense of those practices."[70] This perception has not always taken the form of a uniform systematic interpretation of God, cosmos, and human beings in dialogue with other academic disciplines. Indeed, the case studies in the next three chapters show that different systematic interpretations of this sort can equally claim to be coherent with this perception and claim the title "Ignatian."

It is certainly true that a number of important general claims about God and the human person emerge as indispensable for Ignatian spirituality. Among them would be the following: (1) At certain points persons are called to make choices on which the fulfillment of their lives as Christians (that is, the salvations of their souls) turns, and which are not fully determined by ethical norms or ecclesial guidelines. Thus, there is need for a methodology such as that given in the *Spiritual Exercises* to help persons make these choices well. (2) God deals immediately with the individual person in the making of such choices, and therefore, by extension, in his or her full living out of the Christian vocation. So, Ignatius's preferred title for the "director" of the Exercises, "the one giving the Exercises," is more precise, insofar as it indicates that the role of this person is not so much to "direct" as it is to serve as a catalyst in which *God*'s direction will become clearer to the one making the Exercises. (3) Such immediacy does not rule out but complements and works through various mediations of God's will. (4) These mediations include elements of the person's own psychic makeup, such as his or her affectivity and intellect. They also include elements of his or her embeddedness in social structures (most importantly in the Church), and in the natural world, so much so that these realities that are "external" to the self are in decisive ways internal to and operative upon the self (Ignatius's is a "porous" and not a "buffered" self). Thus the importance of composing one's place physically and also imaginatively, of making use of light and darkness, and so on. (5) God's grace is primary. Everything in the *Exercises* depends on coming to an awareness of the utter gratuity and prevenience of God's saving love. This is why the most important affective-spiritual work to be done in undergoing the Spiritual Exercises is that of moving (a movement never completed once for all) from genuine contrition and sorrow for the ways that one has been a part of the sin that opposes God to the grateful love that comes from the realization that God has taken the initiative not only to forgive one for this opposition but to invite one to be a part of the divine salvific work that overcomes it in oneself and in history as a whole.[71] (6) The relationship of "mediated immediacy" to God, far from being a private affair between the individual and God, is embedded in a comprehensive history. This is most evident in the fact that the most important conceptual and imaginative work for the person making a good election is that of imagining him- or herself a part of God's broader work in history, particularly as this work was definitively manifested in Jesus of Nazareth.

The point to insist on here is that these are general claims, and certainly not unique to Ignatius. They are proper to any thoughtful Christian theology, and a spirituality that denied them would do so at risk of losing its ties to scripture and tradition. The themes reflect how broadly he drew from theological and spiritual currents in sixteenth-century Europe. To reiterate, Ignatius's genius did not lie in particular theological insights, rather, the uniqueness of his spirituality derives from the particular way that these claims are actualized by the highly structured yet flexible lattice of particular exercises that make up the book. It is at this level that we should locate what is most uniquely Ignatian about Ignatian spirituality, rather than at the level of theological assertion. The issue of how this unique character shows itself in speculative, conceptually focused theologies remains to be explored.

In sum, therefore, Ignatian spirituality exemplifies the definition of spirituality given in chapter 1. It is first and foremost a constellation of practices that forms a mystagogy into a life of Christian discipleship.

It opens up a certain vision of God, the world, and human beings that makes sense of these practices. In all of this, it invites one and initiates one into an "art of living" that is Christian, but also responds to the challenges and resources posed by the conditions of our modern world. That it is a "classic," in the sense that David Tracy uses the term, is attested by its enduring power and remarkable adaptability across historical periods and cultures. Yet it is a specifically modern classic. It has an emphasis on going out into the world, in imitation of the *vita apostolica*.

This emphasis combines with a feel for persons as embodied, as possessed of and moved not just by the intellect, but by affectivity, by imagination, by taste, in short, by all of those things that find communal expression in culture. Thus, the Jesuits were the first religious order explicitly to understand their religious mission to include engaging a particular culture on its own terms, in part because the possibility of recognizing culture as such an object of evangelical labor itself rests on crucial conditions of modernity.[72] Ignatian spirituality has a deep sense of the importance of the everyday combined with an emphasis on method and effectiveness. Finally, its feel for the particularity of the historical Jesus could nurture a similar feel and appreciation for the particularity of contemporary persons in their different cultural locales. All of these elements could and did lead Jesuits to engage modern culture across its whole spectrum, and to do so in quite modern ways. Yet not purely so, for there are ways in which Ignatian spirituality cuts across the grain of modernity. It is the bewitching, often troubling alloy of contemporaneity and noncontemporaneity that gives any classic its enduring power, a feature eminently true of Ignatian spirituality.

Of course, none of this happens automatically. A spirituality is a set of practices. It can be taken up partially or it can be taken up in combination with another set of practices or in terms of a different vision, thereby blunting its edge, or diverting it in another direction. It can be misconstrued or mishandled. There have been plenty of its proponents who have interpreted and lived Ignatian spirituality exclusively as a locus of *resistance* to modernity, and who correspondingly see Ignatius as the last of the medievals. It is just as possible to deprive this spirituality of its "unmodern edge," to turn it into another technique for surviving and flourishing under the conditions of modernity, without pressing on to the evangelization and transformation of modernity. The interpretation I have argued for would brand both of these tendencies as false to the core of Ignatius's spirituality. Further evidence for this judgment will be provided by the case studies in the next three chapters.

In any event, it is no surprise that in the histories of Christianity's classic spiritual traditions (including Ignatius's) one finds periodic calls for renewal, for a return to the spirituality in its original and integral vitality, usually personified in its founder. Alternatively, the situation within which one lives a certain spirituality may change radically enough that one is forced to "start from scratch," to reevaluate the ways that the practices of one's spirituality fit, or creatively misfit, one's other individual and cultural practices. Something like the latter has happened on several occasions in the history of the Society of Jesus.[73] Within fifty years of Ignatius's death, for instance, the Society had to deal with its own explosive growth, its growing commitments to diverse and demanding institutions (especially the schools), and the changing face of Europe itself. Under the generalates of Mercurian, Acquaviva, and Vitelleschi, the Jesuits followed a trajectory that paralleled the general shift going on in Europe as a whole. Emphasizing the methodical side of Ignatian spirituality, they produced collection upon collection of specific rules for determining what was proper to their "way of proceeding." What was often lost in the process was the emphasis on accommodation and attention to the particularity of persons and situations.

What was also too often lost was the emphasis (not just asserted but lived) that it is finally the love of God, marked by the experience of consolation ("spiritual consolation," in particular, focused exercises of discernment of spirits, but also the broader movements of consolation the early Jesuits encouraged and looked for among those to whom they ministered), which provides coherence and unity to the diverse practices of this spirituality, the works in the wider culture it inspired, and the persons who carry out those works. This emphasis aligned Ignatian spirituality more closely with the movement toward the modern, disengaged self, charted by Taylor. It also made it more congenial to the disenchanted world that reached a certain apotheosis in the vision of God, cosmos, and persons presented by the mechanized cosmos of the seventeenth century, its remote designer-God, and human beings rendered godlike by their science and technology.

As Stephen Toulmin points out, in the fifty or so years that separate Montaigne from Descartes, European philosophy executed a similar shift: from the oral (rhetoric) to the written (logic); from considering particular cases to looking for universal principles; from an appreciation of concrete diversity to a search for abstract axioms; from an appreciation of the timeliness of judgments and decisions to an emphasis on the permanently and uniformly valid.[74] Ignatian spirituality was not exempt from this broader culture shift. There was thus an emphasis on the ascetic and rigorist side of Ignatius, downplaying his mystical side, and his insistence that a person come to experience and relish the presence and work of God within his or her own soul in order to find that same presence in the world.

There were, to be sure, individual exceptions. But, these tendencies predominated, particularly in the eighteenth century (toward the end of which the Society of Jesus was finally suppressed under the pressure exerted by its enemies in the Bourbon courts of Europe) and in the nineteenth, when the reestablished Society struggled to regain its identity. And perhaps necessarily so. The point of making a distinction between an ascetic "spin" of Ignatian spirituality and a "mystical" spin is not to brand one as "truly Ignatian" and the other as not. The degree to which emphasizing one or the other is an appropriate application of Ignatian spirituality (or Jesuit spirituality, if we are speaking of Jesuits alone) requires careful attention to the specific historical context. And, indeed, the mysticism represented by "contemplation in action" certainly entails an asceticism of its own.

In part because of the renaissance in historical work that began at the end of the nineteenth century and blossomed in the twentieth, with the concomitant recovery and dissemination of Ignatian spirituality in its original sources, and in part because of the Jesuits' response to Vatican II's charge to religious orders to recover the charisms of their founders, there was, over the course of the twentieth century a reevaluation of the first sort mentioned above: an attempt to return to the practice of Ignatian spirituality in its original integrity and vitality.[75] Thus, in recent decades there has been a renewed emphasis on making the individually directed Ignatian Spiritual Exercises, on the validity and necessity of accommodating them to diverse groups of persons, and, above all, on the "mystical" side of Ignatian spirituality. The Jesuits we shall consider in the next three chapters had mostly completed their formation before these shifts were complete, but they certainly lived through them and were variously involved in them. Our task now is to see how these men continued the very Ignatian engagement with modernity as theologians.

Chapter Four

Karl Rahner
Theology in a Secularized World

I do think that in comparison with other philosophy and theology that influenced me, Ignatian spirituality was indeed more significant and important. There, too, to be honest, I cannot say that individual Jesuits, spiritual directors, retreat masters, and so forth made an overpowering impression on me.... But I think that the spirituality of Ignatius himself, which one learned through the practice of prayer and religious formation, was more significant for me than all learned philosophy and theology inside and outside the order [the Society of Jesus].[1]

THE ARGUMENT THUS FAR AND ITS APPLICATION TO KARL RAHNER

Up to this point I have argued that a spirituality, taken as a classic constellation of practices and a cognate perception of God, the cosmos, and human beings can and should exist in a mutually fructifying relationship with theology, understood as the conceptual-argumentative work of interpreting as comprehensively and systematically as possible self, cosmos, and God in the light of the fundamental symbols of Christian faith and in dialogue with other conceptual-argumentative disciplines through which we interpret the world. I have suggested that spiritualities exhibit greater relative freedom and flexibility than do academic theologies in responding to shifts in cultural conditions that require a creative reenvisioning of Christian faith. Focusing on one particular spirituality, I have argued that Ignatian spirituality has had and continues to have its distinctive power and appeal because it responds in a positive yet critically creative way to precisely such a shift: the shift to modernity. If this is so, then we may reasonably expect that at least some theologians committed to this spirituality would have exploited it in their own grappling with modernity.

This hypothesis will be tested in this chapter with respect to Karl Rahner. I will proceed in three stages, considering (1) that and how he engaged the particulars of Ignatian spirituality; (2) that and how he perceived "modernity" to be a challenge to the practice of Christian faith in general and to academic theology in particular; (3) that there are strong positive correlations between how he responded to the latter challenge, on the one hand, and themes and motifs from Ignatian spirituality drawn from his engagement with it, on the other. The first two of these steps can be taken care of more briefly, with the third one engaging the majority of the argument of this chapter

RAHNER'S ENGAGEMENT WITH IGNATIAN SPIRITUALITY: AN OVERVIEW

Since he spent more than sixty years as a Jesuit, we can presume that Rahner (1904–84) had at least some exposure to the spirituality of Ignatius of Loyola. Beyond this biographical datum, moreover, there is ample textual evidence for his interest in spirituality, in general, and in Ignatian spirituality, in particular.[2] This literature can be conveniently divided into three phases. In a first, early phase, roughly the 1920s and 30s, Rahner's writings evince a strong interest in classics of Christian spirituality in general and an interest in locating Ignatius within the history mapped out by those classics. In a second phase, the 1950s, we find Rahner confronting the theological mechanics that he had developed in his fundamental works in philosophical and doctrinal theology in the 1930s with key themes from the *Spiritual Exercises*. In a third phase, the 1970s, Rahner wrote essays on Ignatius that show his own growing insistence on the centrality of Ignatius for his theological itinerary. Let us consider these three phases in somewhat greater detail.

We know that Rahner had an early interest in classic authors in the history of Christian spirituality.³ Some of his first writings dealt with the doctrine of the spiritual senses in early and medieval Christian spirituality.⁴ These writings were not less important for his thought than works he began later that were more focused on philosophical and systematic theology. Indeed, looking back over his writings, Rahner himself insisted that his pastoral and spiritual works (as we would today call them) were just as important as his works in speculative theology, more narrowly defined:

> I would say that though I didn't have an explicit plan in mind, I was theologically concerned from the very beginning with questions dealing with pastoral, ecclesial, and personal religious life. In my early years, at least, I preached a lot; in Innsbruck almost every Sunday for ten years. I have given Ignatius's Spiritual Exercises rather frequently.... Might I say that I regard my devotional works, *The Eternal Year*, *Encounters with Silence*, *On Prayer*, *Spiritual Exercises*, and many similar works, not as secondary by-products of a theology that is sort of an art for art's sake, but at least as important as my specifically theological works.⁵

Besides his general interest in spirituality, there are several indicators of a more specific engagement with Ignatian spirituality. In 1922, Rahner's brother Hugo produced a catalogue of primary sources concerning Ignatius and other early Jesuits, which Karl expanded in 1925.⁶ This collection shows a preference on the part of both brothers for Nadal's interpretation of Ignatian and Jesuit spirituality: that is, they had an antipathy toward the interpretation of Ignatius's spirituality that sees it as a severely ascetic and disciplined regimen, and thus had a correspondingly emphasis on the mystical element of Ignatius's spirituality. Reflecting back on their early years in the Society of Jesus, Rahner said of himself and Hugo that "for us Ignatius was first of all a mystic, a man who was bound up with God in a mysterious and radical way, a man who experienced a mystical immediacy with God, and shaped his life in this immediacy, from out of the depths of this kind of encounter with God, the absolute mystery."⁷ This emphasis on the *mystical* dimension of Ignatius's life and legacy and the attendant impatience with definitions of mysticism and readings of Ignatius that would prevent one from speaking of Ignatius in these terms surface repeatedly in his writings.

During his theological training in Valkenburg, Rahner continued this interest in Ignatian spirituality. Moreover, he integrated, or at least desired to integrate, this interest with his study of dogmatic theology. Later, in 1936, while Rahner was already in Innsbruck working on his *Habilitationsschrift*, he received a communication from one of the teachers at Valkenburg, Emmerich Raitz von Frentz, who led seminars on the *Spiritual Exercises* and had taken on responsibility for revising the standard German translation of that text. Frentz intended for his revision to include a critical commentary. He invited Rahner to contribute a piece from the perspective of systematic theology. "Since even back then," wrote Frentz, speaking of Rahner's time at Valkenburg, "you were already of the view that we still basically lack a systematic theology of the Exercises, I should like to ask you to undertake one or more chapters on the subject."[8] Rahner's concern, first evidenced here, that systematic theology did not have at its disposal the conceptual tools to do justice to the encounter with God facilitated by the Spiritual Exercises emerged with great clarity in the mid-1950s and then again in the 1970s.

Rahner never produced an extended monograph on the *Spiritual Exercises* of the order, for instance, of Erich Przywara's massive, theological commentary.[9] He did nonetheless write a number of significant essays on various elements of Ignatian spirituality.[10] The first lecture to be publicly presented and then published was "The Ignatian Mysticism of Joy in the World," delivered in February 1937 to an adult education group in Vienna.[11] A number of crucial essays were occasioned by the 400th anniversary of Ignatius's death (1956). The most important (if also controversial) of these was a long essay on the theological logic behind Ignatius's rules for discernment of spirits, which first appeared in a collection of essays on Ignatius and which Rahner later included in a trio of essays devoted to the relationship between the dynamic, changing elements of the Church and its permanent structures.[12] This text marks a pivotal emergence of key themes in Rahner's appropriation of Ignatian spirituality and has given rise to no little controversy among students of Rahner's thought, as we shall see. Along with some published exhortations related to Ignatian spirituality, we also have a record of "preached retreats" that Rahner gave during these years.[13] Those who heard him give these lectures on the elements of the *Spiritual Exercises* pooled their transcripts in order to produce a volume of reflections, which thus give a broad overview of how Rahner approached the *Spiritual Exercises*.[14] In 1961, he gave a retreat for Jesuits about to be ordained following the structure of the *Spiritual Exercises*.[15]

During the 1960s, he was relatively silent on the subject of Ignatian spirituality. A final cluster of essays dates from 1974 to 1978. It is during this period that he began openly asserting the importance of Ignatian spirituality to his theology. The most important of these is an essay that he originally wrote to accompany another book on Ignatius.[16] He later called this "a sort of last will and testament" for his theological career.[17]

Thus, we have ample textual evidence for Rahner's interest in Ignatian spirituality. Moreover, Rahner shows a strong concern to rescue Ignatian spirituality from an overly ascetic interpretation. To render Ignatian spirituality thereby "more mystical" required rescuing it in turn from a narrow understanding of what would constitute mysticism and mystical experience. In a related vein, he also frequently asserts that philosophical and systematic theology has not adequately utilized the resources offered by Ignatius's heritage, which provides good reason to believe that at least a part of his own theological writing on Ignatius was meant to remedy this situation. As a consequence, it is also reasonable to believe that at least one of the desiderata that guided Rahner as he developed his theology was that it be conducive to this end.

Rahner's Perception of Modernity's Challenge to Theology

Rahner believed that the modern age presented a unique set of challenges to Christian faith and theology. William Dych argues that Rahner construed and responded to a twofold challenge to Christian faith and theology in modernity: "The task was, first, to make theology intellectually respectable in the modern world by honestly confronting the difficulties posed by modern philosophy and science, and, second, to place theology at the service of larger concerns of Christian faith and life. The principle governing both is that they must be done together, that the success of one depends on the success of the other."[18] This is not the place for an account of Rahner's theology as a whole; a precis that highlights its principal concerns and approach must suffice.[19] With that purpose in view, it may be said that from the early 1930s until the time of Vatican II (1962–65), the first task that Dych names entailed for Rahner a reentry into the conversation with modern philosophy largely suspended and suppressed during the hegemony of the neoscholastic paradigm in Roman Catholic theology. After the council, Rahner focused increasingly on the difficulty of doing theology in an intellectually responsible way in the midst of a growing pluralism in philosophy and a "knowledge explosion" in all realms of human knowledge. As Dych suggests, however, these intellectual challenges and tasks were never simply academic matters for Rahner. Rather, he understood them to reflect a situation of growing secularization and pluralism, which rendered increasingly ineffectual the ways that theology had served the institutional Church and the faith of individual believers for the prior century.

Rahner's early understanding of the conceptual-argumentative challenges facing Catholic theology is, of course, determined by the context of his training as a theologian. This context was set by the ascendancy of the neoscholastic paradigm in the final third of the nineteenth century and into the twentieth.[20] A substantial part of its agenda, explicitly endorsed and implemented under the pontificates of Pius IX and Leo XIII, entailed the rejection of modern philosophy because of its alleged incapacity to articulate properly the foundations of Christian faith (in particular, the relationship between nature and grace, and reason and revelation). Neoscholasticism understood itself to be a necessary counterdiscourse in philosophy and theology. According to Jesuits Matteo Libertore and Joseph Kleutgen, the most vigorous proponents of this counterdiscourse, it amounted to nothing other than the "scholasticism" that had, they contended, been the common philosophical parlance of the thirteenth century and had gathered up everything of importance in the Catholic tradition up to that time. On their view, only a shift in the Catholic philosophical and theological world back to this tradition would enable it adequately to express and argue the foundations of Catholic doctrine. Such a move, moreover, was not just a move away from modern philosophical currents. It also entailed a move away from other intellectual disciplines (especially the natural and historical sciences), which in one way or another were committed to some or all of the fundamental premises posited in modern philosophy concerning the cosmos and human beings' place in it. This shift was authoritatively promulgated in Leo XIII's 1879 encyclical *Aeterni Patris* and vigorously enforced as a part of the antimodernist "crusade" of the first two decades of the twentieth century.

In his early philosophical and theological education as a Jesuit, Rahner was initiated into this theological paradigm, as *Aeterni Patris* required.[21] He never rejected his early intellectual formation tout court (and even compared it favorably with later theological curricula for the way it introduced students to the history of Catholic theology), but it did not catch his imagination or feed his theological hunger.[22] His immediate attraction to, indeed captivation by, Joseph Maréchal's *Le point de départ de la métaphysique* shows his openness to alternatives that would reenter a lively conversation with modern philosophy. As commonly recognized, Maréchal exercised a decisive influence on Rahner's development of his own version of "transcendental Thomism," laid out in his two major works from the 1930s.[23] Giving adequate conceptual formulation to the relationship of nature and grace, along with the cognate pair of reason and revelation, had become the touchstone for an adequate Catholic philosophical theology, as the decrees and canons of Vatican I made clear. It is thus no surprise that these were the focal points of Rahner's scholarly endeavors during this time. The latter pair—revelation and reason—was the specific focus of his second major work in philosophical theology, *Hearer of the Word*.[24]

After the interruption of the war years, Rahner continued this project, turning to the relationship between nature and grace and working out more explicitly the other doctrinal lattices of the system he was seeking. The late 1940s and 1950s saw much of his most creative work, elicited by his partnership with Hugo, as the two labored together to re-create and reinvigorate theological education at Innsbruck, reopened after the end of World War II. The major conceptual pieces of Rahner's system (the notion of the supernatural existential, his understanding of the Trinity, the conception of God as Holy Mystery, the philosophy and theology of the real symbol, and so on) took final form during this period. At the same time, Rahner began to turn increasingly toward an interpretation of the social-cultural milieu in which theology was required to do its work.

The 1960s was the decade of Vatican II, and Rahner's research and writing clearly mirrors his involvement in the council and in initiating its dual program of *ressourcement* and *aggiornamento*.²⁵ During this time his understanding of what it would mean for a Catholic theology to be intellectually responsible shifted. He came to see the principal challenges facing such a theology to be, first, an irreducible philosophical pluralism, such that conversance in a particular philosophical system could no longer in itself confer intellectual credibility on one's theology. This challenge came, second, with a "knowledge explosion" in the sciences (natural and social), such that theology could no longer deal with them exclusively through the mediation of philosophy. The resultant situation, Rahner maintained, is one in which "all of us with all our theological study are and remain unavoidably *rudes* in a certain sense," a condition that "we ought to admit . . . to ourselves and also to the world frankly and courageously."²⁶ To continue a "traditional" approach to fundamental theology that would first secure the credibility of doctrines by means of a prior philosophical defense of the act of faith, and then defend the authority of revelation by appeal to external criteria (attestation by miracles and fulfilled prophecies), would be to ignore these changes in the situation, with debilitating results.²⁷ Rahner argued that the proper approach was an articulation and defense of Christian faith on a "first level of reflection,"²⁸ which meant providing an initial defense of the credibility and meaningfulness of Christian faith in terms of some fundamental account of the human person. This "new fundamental theology" would transgress the traditional (neoscholastic) division between fundamental and dogmatic theology. For the earlier approach, the credibility of the system as a whole was first established by fundamental theology (or philosophical theology) independent of the actual content of that system, subsequent to which the meaning of the different contents would be drawn out and elaborated by dogmatic theology. Now, fundamental theology would itself elaborate doctrinal contents to the extent necessary to disclose how they could cohere with, bring to words, and thus thematize the modern person's experience of his or her identity, especially as it is threatened by guilt, and by the final, always imminent limit-situation of death. The older approach had depended on the apodictic force of the philosophical demonstrations, but just as much, albeit tacitly (on Rahner's view), on the formative influence of a uniform Christian cultural milieu, which shaped persons before they came to theology and gave them an at least tacit sense of the meaningfulness and coherence of Christian faith. Rahner's alternative requires conceptual clarity and argumentative rigor, but also depends for its persuasive power on its ability to illumine and empower the life of everyday Christians in a secularized milieu by grounding that life in the mystery of God's presence in the world.[29]

There is more going on with this proposed reform than an appraisal of the demands placed on Catholic theology by the changing intellectual scene of late modernity. Over the course of the 1950s, Rahner became more and more convinced that this scene was comprehended by the broader drama of the growing secularization of European society. This secularization was vitiating the homogenous Catholic (or Lutheran, or Reformed, for that matter) social and cultural milieus that, with their taken-for-granted sacred ontologies, had provided a vital formation system into the life world of Christian practices, intuitions, and convictions.[30] Neoscholasticism's intellectually sophisticated but abstract systems could not compensate for the loss of this formation system. Its loss, therefore, posed an urgent problem for catechesis and theology alike. Thus, as Dych avers, Rahner's effort to show that modern philosophy (in the lineage of Kant and German idealism) could indeed be mined for ways of making Catholic theology more intellectually credible was at the same time an attempt to grapple with the problems of grounding the credibility of faith in a secularized milieu. This connection is presented in condensed form in Rahner's thesis that theology had to become a form of mystagogy. No longer being able to delegate to a religiously homogenous cultural milieu the task of conferring a fundamental sense of the meaningfulness of Christian faith, theology would itself have to take on this work, primarily by engaging the individual at those points where he or she encountered the mystery of his or her existence and was thus most open to a correlation of the experience of this mystery with the Christian message.[31]

Therefore we can say with confidence that Rahner was vitally engaged with Ignatian spirituality and that he also believed that academic theology needed to be reformed so that it could better discharge its distinctive responsibilities. Moreover, there is evidence that these tasks were related in Rahner's mind, at least to the extent that he was convinced that the theology in which he was trained was not up to the challenge of retrieving and deploying the resources of Ignatian spirituality, so that a reform of academic theology was of vital interest to those concerned with interpreting and promoting Ignatian spirituality in a new cultural situation.³² It is also the case that Rahner's commitment to the reform of academic theology implied a certain diagnosis of "the modern condition," with its opportunities and challenges to faith. These challenges, moreover, were not just of the conceptual-argumentative order. It would not be enough to construct a more conceptually rigorous proof of the existence of God or more sophisticated Trinitarian theologies that were both faithful to the tradition and more resistant to modern philosophical attacks. What was at stake for theologians, as "rudes," along with everyone else, was an account of Christian faith that could help Christians *live it* under the demanding conditions of modernity—and this is where the approach and resources of Christian spirituality had, on Rahner's view, much to say. It is a two-way street: reformulating theology to make it a more apt tool for interpreting Christian (Ignatian) spirituality and deploying the resources of Christian (Ignatian) spirituality for the sake of theology's ecclesial-existential work under the conditions of secularized modernity. This brings us to the third and most important of the three tests for this chapter's hypothesis: disclosing positive correlations between how Rahner responded to the challenges he saw from the modern age, on the one hand, and themes and motifs from his engagement with Ignatian spirituality, on the other.

Early Engagement with Ignatian Spirituality: "Ignatian Mysticism of Joy in the World"

In February 1937, Rahner gave a lecture in Vienna to an adult education group, the Logos-Verein, entitled "The Ignatian Mysticism of Joy in the World."³³ He was at a transition point in his life. He had completed two years of study with Martin Heidegger and was in the middle of a protracted and ultimately unsuccessful negotiation with his thesis director, Martin Honecker, to win approval for his dissertation in philosophy.³⁴ The negative outcome did not really matter in one sense, since Rahner's Jesuit superiors had already reassigned him to teach theology rather than philosophy. For that he needed a dissertation in theology, which he completed in December 1936, and a *Habilitationsschrift*, on which he was working during the first half of 1937. Subsequently, he assumed a position as professor of fundamental theology in the Jesuit theological faculty in Innsbruck. He would hold it for less than a year, however, because the Nazis closed the faculty and expelled its members soon after the *Anschluß* in 1938. While working on the dissertation and *Habilitationsschrift*, he gave a number of lectures on different topics (including the one to the Logos-Verein). The most well known, eventually, was a series of lectures in Salzburg during the summer of 1937, which were collected and published four years later as *Hörer des Wortes*.[35] Thus, this lecture took place in the midst of Rahner's formal movement into a career as a theologian that would last for almost five decades. It shows features that would become standard in Rahner's theological production and concerns that continued to shape his engagement with Ignatian spirituality.

Rahner begins his lecture on Ignatian mysticism by noting that in their everyday usages "mysticism" and "joy in the world" appear to be opposed to one another. The question of their relationship needs to be rethought. By the end of the lecture it emerges that this rethinking is best done by considering the cognates of "mysticism" and "joy in the world" to be found in Ignatian spirituality: "indifference" and "finding God in all things."[36] Rahner constructs an interpretation of the latter pair—one of which entails distance and reserve with respect to the world, and the other an engagement and affirmation of the world—such that they are two elements of the one dynamism of the graced human spirit. Those familiar with Rahner's method will recognize it at play. One begins with a given actualization of Christian life (something that Christians in fact do or have done) and seeks to understand it by working back to those structures of human being that must be posited in order to make sense of that activity (the "conditions for the possibility" of its actualization, to use the Kantian terminology). These structures provide an interpretive framework for understanding the phenomenon anew: in its distinctively Christian character, in its relationship to other facets of Christian belief and practice, and in its significance for human fulfillment.

The activity, then, is the activity in the world characteristic of the first generations of Jesuits: their embrace of the culture and works of Renaissance humanism (Rahner mentions the building of extravagantly luxuriant baroque churches), but also the self-denial evident in their embrace of the sufferings of the foreign missions ("the boiling fountains of Japan or the bamboo cages of Tonkin").[37] If this is not (as Rahner will argue) the result of two dispositions toward the world, but *one* spirit, then the genuinely Ignatian form of affirming the world must be distinguished just as much from a blanket rejection of the world as from a naïve absorption in it. To show how this might be possible, Rahner begins with one side of the polarity and derives its ground (the condition for its possibility) from the existential structure of the person caught up in the divine work of redemption. This ground then makes it clear in turn how the other side of the polarity is both possible and can be a reflection or manifestation of the first.[38]

Rahner thus begins with the claim that Ignatian spirituality is a spirituality of the cross, of distance from the world. It is a "monastic piety," a piety of the *fuga saeculi*. As evidence he observes that Ignatius and his companions bound themselves under traditional monastic vows (not strictly correct, since they did not take a vow of stability), and quotes at length a well-known passage from the General Examen of the Jesuit *Constitutions*, recommending to an aspiring candidate for membership in the Society of Jesus that he understand how much growth in the spiritual life depends on rejecting the world and loving what Christ loved, accepting, indeed even preferring, insults and injustice (provided the Divine Majesty be not offended).[39] This dictum of Ignatius's articulates one side of the polarity so forcefully that it is hard to see how one could arrive at an affirmation of the world of any sort. Rahner's strategy is to move to the metaphysical ground or reason (Grund) for the flight from the world. This is, he asserts, integrally related to a second key feature of Ignatian spirituality and constitutes "the inner possibility of Ignatian acceptance of the world."[40]

This ground is found in the particular relationship that obtains between God and the world, a relationship that is constitutive of the world. God is both the God who is the absolutely transcendent ground of the world and the God who, in Jesus Christ, has freely and irrevocably revealed Godself in that world. To say that God is the absolutely transcendent ground of the world plays on the unique relationship of God to the world as its creator *ex nihilo*. That the world is grounded in a God who absolutely transcends it entails a radical relativization of the world, since nothing in the world can be taken as absolute and ungrounded in itself. It also means that the most that unaided reason can discern within the world is its groundedness in a ground that is beyond reason's reach, since that ground transcends the world absolutely and in principle. Such a rational insight into the ungroundedness of the world would not in itself necessitate a flight from the world, even as a world radically relativized; one would be justified in living with whatever sober reserve and existential honesty one could muster within the confines of this relativized world.[41] However, the second part of the God–world relationship (that God has also revealed Godself freely *in* the world) means that we cannot rest (with any degree of existential reserve and honesty) in that relativized world, but must orient our existence by that God who reveals Godself into that world. This enables, indeed necessitates, a particular "spiritual" stance in and toward the world:

> In this way . . . a sacrifice of the world, a renunciation, a flight from the world, an abandonment of its goods and values becomes possible, which goes essentially further than one that would be thinkable in any meaningful way if these goods and values in a merely natural order constituted the highest fulfillment of the existential task demanded of man. . . . A flight from the world of this kind becomes necessary because the need to take into account the possibility of a free act of revelation on the part of the personal God, which is a fundamental constitutive character of a finite spirit in any hypothesis, is transformed by the actual fact of such a revelation into the duty of living existentially the need of obedience *vis-à-vis* the God of revelation.[42]

This brings us to what Rahner takes to be the second key feature of Ignatian spirituality: "The God of Ignatian piety is the God of supramundane grace who deals with man freely and personally, and 'historically.'"[43] If, on the side of the human subject, the reality of revelation entails a decentering of human existence in the world, on the side of God it defines the particular character of how God does in fact deal with human beings: not primarily as mediated by God's effects on and in creation (including that "effect" of conferring existence *ex nihilo*), but rather through free, unmerited acts of self-revelation to us as persons: "Only his [God's] free action in history can reveal to us what he is in himself and how he wills to be related to men."[44]

If the earlier feature finds expression in the spiritual tradition of *fuga saeculi*, a tradition in which Ignatian spirituality participates, this one also finds concrete expressions in Ignatian spirituality. As evidence, Rahner adduces the historical character of the meditations in the *Spiritual Exercises*. We grasp the nature of sin and God's response to sin, for instance, not by a metaphysical consideration but by considering the *story* (the history, *Geschichte*) of the fall of the angels or Adam and

Eve.⁴⁵ We understand who God is by meditating on the history of Jesus. Finally, and significantly, Rahner points to the process of discernment of spirits at the core of the *Spiritual Exercises*: "All the discernment of spirits—*that most important part of the Exercises*—is ultimately based on it [this understanding of how God relates to human beings]: in the last analysis it is not a discernment of the impulses of one's own heart on the basis of general moral criteria, but a listening to the word of command from God, the seeking and finding of the free decrees of the will of the personal God for man in his concrete situation."⁴⁶

How should we analyze these two features in order to come to the fullest understanding of the way in which Ignatian spirituality affirms the world? The key, Rahner argues, lies in correctly understanding the import of the ground of an authentically *Christian* flight from the world. It does not arise simply from the always only relative value of the world and its constituent elements. That takes into account only the first of the two virtues. Nor is it a response to the presence of disvalue or evil in the world. The Christian flight from the world cannot be understood in a rather crude spatially rendered representation of the God–world relationship, according to which one would have to "leave" the world in order to "get to" God.⁴⁷ The *fuga saeculi* is authorized and made possible by the combination of both the relativity of the world, its radical deficiency as the grounding center of our existence, and God's free entry into the world as an offer of Godself as our center. Together these two realities make meaningful a search for a fullness *in* the world that no inner-worldly reality can offer (which thus always requires the distance from every element in the world, which is the reason for a *fuga saeculi*). The second of these elements modulates the first in a crucial way. Focusing on the importance of the liberality of God's revelatory entry into the world, and not on the world's relativity, means that it is possible for this fullness of God's presence to be encountered once again *within* the world:

> Since, however, the grace of God is in this sense free, the Christian knows . . . that the free God can bless and allow to become a step forward into his presence even those actions of men which do not of themselves already bear such a significance, as does the dying flight from the world, which [flight] is only meaningful when it is a dying into the new life of God. Provided that man has once submitted himself in faith to the claim of God revealing himself,

God can accept in grace also his [man's] service of the world, so that man encounters the absolute God not only in a radical opposition to the world, but also *in* the world.[48]

Ignatian indifference, understood in terms of Rahner's theological anthropology, authorizes, indeed prescribes the "finding God in all things" for which Ignatian spirituality is also so famous. This indifference is what is most characteristic of and specific to Ignatian spirituality, according to Rahner. It names for him a basic structure of human (graced) existence in the world, which, if embraced and actualized, blossoms into a finding of God in one's actions in the world. This is why for Ignatian spirituality a life of radical discipleship, traditionally defined in terms of the self- and world-denying embrace of the cross, can be lived out in a life that embraces the world and activity in the world, since it is not the denial of the world *per se* that grounds this radicality, but indifference—the centering on the God who both radically transcends the world and yet freely and radically makes Godself present in the world:

> *Indiferençia* is possible only where the will to a *fuga saeculi* is alive, and yet this *indiferençia* in its turn disguises that love for the foolishness of the Cross into the daily *moderation* of a *normal style of life* marked by *good sense*. Filled with such *indiferençia*, Ignatius can even forgo manifestations of mystical graces—after all God is beyond even the world of experience of the mystic—he can forgo the mystical gift of tears because the physician wanted it—Saint Francis had angrily rejected precisely the same remonstrances of the physician.[49]

In this sense, Ignatian mysticism of joy in the world constitutes an *Aufhebung* (in the Hegelian sense, Rahner writes) of the traditional opposition of a mystical piety of flight from the world and the prophetic piety of divinely commissioned work in the world, an *Aufhebung* that is articulated in the Jesuit motto of "contemplation in action."[50]

Several features of the argument of this lecture will help us understand Rahner's appropriation of Ignatian spirituality. First of all, Rahner approached Ignatian spirituality as a locus and source for theological reflection; he applies to it the same theological apparatus that he applies to more traditional theological loci (revelation, Jesus Christ, grace, etc.). This can be seen by comparing this lecture with the roughly contemporaneous *Hearer of the Word*. In that text, Rahner starts with the reality, known a posteriori, that humanity has in fact been addressed in history by God, and then asks what must be presumed about the structures of human existence such that we can be and are "hearers" of such a word of address.[51] In "Ignatian Mysticism of Joy in the World," Rahner begins with the Jesuits' characteristic stance toward the world (as evidenced particularly in the first generations of Ignatius's followers), and he inquires into its ground in a more universal and primordial structure of our human way of being in and toward the world. The paradoxical character of the world, according to which it both points toward its ground and yet is ultimately opaque to that ground, is homologous to a similar polarity in *Hearer of the Word*. There Rahner argues that our engagement with the world makes it *possible* for us to "ask about being," despite the fact that being is ultimately transcendent to beings. Yet, on the other hand, we can only relate to being as something *always to be asked about* and never as something we exhaustively and definitively possess, no matter how many individual beings we understand. Both approaches show the influence of Rahner's study with Heidegger, who unveiled Dasein's paradoxically ungrounded groundedness in being in *Being and Time*.

This comparison enables us to identify an element of Ignatian spirituality that will become increasingly important for Rahner, not only for his interpretation of Ignatius but for his theological project as a whole. Rahner's philosophical-theological anthropology in *Hearer of the Word* takes its starting point and justification in the historically established fact of God's self-communication in Jesus. This historical fact appears at the crucial juncture of the 1937 lecture on Ignatius.[52] However, in this lecture Rahner alludes to another historical-experiential "ground" or "warrant" for the argument: the experience of discernment.[53] Here too, Rahner suggests, we have an actualization of the free, personal address of God to the person. The Ignatian account of discernment is thus more than just an incidental feature of one particular spirituality. It takes on evidentiary power for Rahner's theology, to the extent that it maps out a type of experience available to all persons and is also open to phenomenological analysis, one that complements the historically remote (albeit still potent to the extent that it is appropriated in faith) event of the Incarnation.[54] For it to do this, however, it must be possible, indeed necessary, to articulate this experience in a particular way, just as a particular articulation of the person/event of Jesus Christ is essential for Rahner's appeal to Christ in his transcendental anthropology. It is giving this account that makes up the core of Rahner's longest essay on Ignatian spirituality, to which we will soon turn.

Before doing this, two further observations about this lecture will help underscore further features of Rahner's approach to Ignatian spirituality. First of all, one is struck by its timelessness. There is a concluding mention of the persecutions endured by Clement of Alexandria and the possibility that "the sun is setting in the Occident," which may or may not be an allusion to the darkness descending on Europe as Rahner composed and delivered this lecture.[55] Otherwise, however, the lecture presents itself as a timeless reflection on human existence in Christ. Ignatius is portrayed as a representative of monastic piety, but there is nothing to suggest that his legacy is anything other than a presentation of an eternally valid and applicable spirituality. This will change in the 1950s.

Second, Rahner evinces a certain discomfort in talking about "mysticism" in connection with Ignatius. He points out that the word is so protean that it can cover everything from the Upanishads, to Gregory of Nyssa, to Goethe.[56] He also seems aware of the fact that, measured by his great Carmelite near-contemporaries Teresa of Avila and John of the Cross, Ignatius's credentials as a mystic were often overlooked.[57] Rahner's response in the original lecture was to define Christian mysticism in the following terms: "the experience of unmediated interaction between the personal God and man. . . . Wherever the living God of Jesus Christ himself deals with the soul (which does not necessarily mean the *visio beatifica* in the theological sense), there we have Christian mysticism."[58] Rahner does not cite it here, but this definition echoes one of Rahner's favorite and most-cited passages from the *Spiritual Exercises*, in which Ignatius instructs the one giving the Exercises that he or she ought "to allow the Creator to deal immediately with the creature and the creature with its Creator and Lord" (*SpEx* 15).

In his later reediting for publication in *Schriften zur Theologie*, Rahner rewrote this paragraph. Rather than including Ignatius among the mystics by a definitional *fiat*, he dropped the definition of mysticism and replaced it with a series of questions that would have to be resolved in order to deal adequately with the phenomenon of mysticism. Among these are the questions of whether or not there is such a thing as "natural" mysticism and whether supernatural mysticism can be found outside Christianity. Significantly, he also asks

> whether the experimental contact with grace in infused contemplation (which one likes to regard as the essence of mysticism) is compatible with the theological data concerning the nature of grace, whether, in other words, a true experiencing of grace, where it is really entitatively supernatural, in the strict sense of a grasping of the experienced reality in its proper intelligibility and its own being, is reconcilable with the fact that grace is necessarily and invariably also uncreated grace and whether such an experience would not be conceptually identical with the Beatific Vision. Theologically, therefore, the question would have to be posed, whether and how there can be any middle term between faith and immediate vision of God, and if not, how then mystical experience should be conceived so that it remains really genuine and yet falls unmistakably into the sphere of faith.[59]

These caveats indicate that early on Rahner was less than happy with the current senses of the term "mysticism," both in its popular and more technical usage.[60] The 1956 rewrite shows that he had come to see the problem as one that needed to be solved on a theological level.[61] In particular, it needed to be worked out in the sphere of the theology of grace.

This points to a significant tie between Rahner's theology of Ignatian spirituality and his theology of grace, a connection well documented by Philip Endean.[62] From interviews late in his life, we know that during these early years Rahner understood himself to have been working out an alternative to the prevailing Jesuit theology of grace (which he had learned at Valkenburg). According to this theology, one cannot experience directly the presence of grace in one's life.[63] Rahner's alternative entailed the elaboration and defense of a counterposition in epistemology and anthropology to one that "wrongly supposes that everything conscious can become, through reflection, an object objectively represented as such in itself."[64] With such a counterposition established, one could identify and analyze a transcendental apprehension of the totality of being as an always concomitant — but real nonetheless — element of our experience of finite beings. It would also be possible to speak of an "experience" of grace, that is, a mystical presence to God, that would be distinct from the experience of specific entities, and also distinct from that experience proper to our final salvation (the *visio beatifica*, as Rahner mentions). As Endean, and also Arno Zahlauer show, executing this project was at issue in Rahner's investigation of "the spiritual senses" in Origen and the "spiritual touch" in Bonaventure, and also, on the level of fundamental ontology and epistemology, in *Spirit in the World* and *Hearer of the Word*.[65]

It is clear then, minimally, that there was an important cross-fertilization between Rahner's early (from 1924) interest in a classic tradition in Christian spirituality, which he traced from Origen through Bonaventure to Ignatius, and his somewhat later immersion in philosophy and fundamental theology, first in Freiburg and then in Innsbruck. The experiential ground in which this cross-fertilization bore fruit was "indifference," interpreted as the key feature of Ignatian spirituality. For Rahner it specified the authentic relationship between human experience of the concrete and particular, on the one hand, and of the reality of God, on the other—a God who is at the same time utterly transcendent and yet is also not only the ground to the concrete (as creator), but also the one who has willed to reveal Godself "personally" and "historically" in the concrete and the particular. This God can be experienced as such, provided that one's understanding of what it means "to experience" is sufficiently broad and nuanced. This suggests that the relationship between theology and spirituality in Rahner goes from the former to the latter: that is, that he used a conceptual framework developed in philosophy and theology to articulate what is at stake in the Ignatian experience of finding God in all things, fundamentally grounded in the graced disposition of indifference. Yet, given Rahner's method, it can equally be argued that these "Ignatian experiences" play a more important role, particularly given the provenance of Rahner's theology in the tradition of Kant and Kant's transcendental method. That is, just as the "scientific experience" of the world and its self-evident authority (to Kant's generation, at any rate), paradigmatically represented by Isaac Newton, formed both the starting point and the warrant for Kant's analysis in his *Critique of Pure Reason*, one can argue that the experience of God's presence to the person articulated in the paired concepts of indifference and finding God in all things formed an important starting point and warrant for the young Rahner as he attempted to work through fundamental questions in philosophical and systematic theology.[66] This in fact becomes more apparent in the crucial years of 1955 and 1956. In addition, during these years a new element enters: a pointed and increasingly central awareness on Rahner's part of the historical location of Ignatius at the threshold of modernity.

THE 1950S: IGNATIUS AS A PROPHET FOR THE END OF THE MODERN WORLD

Romano Guardini's Diagnosis of the End of the Modern World and Rahner's Interpretation of Indifference

During the winter session of 1947–48 in Tübingen and then during summer session of 1949 in Munich, Romano Guardini gave three lectures that were subsequently published under the title *The End of the Modern World: A Search for Orientation*.[67] In it he argued that the modernity that emerged subsequent to the dissolution of the medieval world is now giving way in turn to a new world, and that this transition is already manifest in dramatic shifts in our general sense of the natural world, the identity of the human subject, the nature of human culture, and, as a consequence of all of this, the role of religion. Guardini insisted that he desired to engage neither in Spengleresque *Schadenfreude* nor in nostalgic longing for the Middle Ages. His aim, rather, was to gain a clearer understanding of the new world that is coming into existence, in order better to understand the opportunities and challenges it presents to the Church that is called to live and evangelize in it.[68]

This was not Guardini's first attempt to grapple with the dramatic changes so evident in early and mid-twentieth-century Europe.[69] Neither, of course, was he the only one to conclude that these cultural, economic, and political convulsions were signs that "modernity" was coming to an end. Guardini's work is significant, however, as an instance of a general shift in Catholic theology, which was making history and historical reflection a crucial element internal to the work of systematic theology itself. This shift was most controversially felt in France, with the so-called *nouvelle théologie*, but it was also present in Germany. Not without resistance, this turn to history initiated a process that led ultimately to the formal recognition of the necessity of this sort of reflection at Vatican II.

Guardini's reflections on "the end of modernity" had a particular influence on Rahner's theological work (no doubt reinforced by memories of the grim landscape of Munich's bombed-out ruins, where Rahner spent the immediate postwar years), leading him to reflect far more explicitly on the historical situation and how it determines the work of theology. Guardini's *Ende der Neuzeit* appears frequently in Rahner's reflections on this theme, including in his work on Ignatian spirituality.[70] As he became more historically self-reflective, Rahner became increasingly persuaded that the work in which he had been engaged for more than two decades was not just a matter of correcting, augmenting, or polishing up a timeless theological system, but it rather involved accommodating theology to dramatically changed circumstances. In the process he began to understand Ignatius of Loyola as an indispensable resource for that task.

This shift did not, to be sure, change Rahner's conviction about the essential elements of Ignatius's spirituality, but it did inflect the way that he expressed those elements. Indifference still counted as the most important pillar of Ignatian spirituality. For example, in a series of lectures on the relationship between Ignatian spirituality and devotion to the Sacred Heart, which he gave to the seminarians at Innsbruck, he still lists indifference first among the essential features of Ignatian spirituality.[71] He lists two others—"existentiality" and "ecclesial character"—but relates or even derives them from this first one. What is new is that he does not relate indifference to purportedly perennial themes, such as a spirituality of the cross and the *fuga saeculi*, as he had done in his 1937 lecture on Ignatian spirituality. Indeed, he seems at this point more concerned to highlight what is *unique* about Ignatian indifference than he is to stress its exemplarity of traditional themes in spiritual theology. Indifference is, he maintains, more than a readiness to detach oneself from some good in order to attend to God's will; otherwise, it would not be characteristic of Ignatian spirituality alone, but would be common to any genuinely Christian spirituality (a possibility that he did not find objectionable in his 1937 lecture on Ignatius). Rather, *Ignatian* indifference entails an almost painful sensitivity to the utter provisionality of all inner-worldly realities, including even those identified as "religious."[72] It is not difficult, to be sure, to square this claim with his approach in the 1937 lecture, and Rahner adduces once again the different reactions of Francis of Assisi and Ignatius to the gift of tears in order to mark the uniquely Ignatian form of indifference. Yet, in 1937 Rahner did not emphasize the difficult situation into which this experience of provisionality thrust the person of faith, as he would two decades later. Rahner is now after a further dimension of this indifference, a dimension that renders Ignatian spirituality more novel and specific to a particular time period.

What this dimension is becomes evident when he goes on to name the second feature of Ignatian spirituality: its existentiality, or existential character. When he describes it, it seems to recapitulate much of his description of indifference:

> This attitude of disillusionment, of regarding things as interim and provisional, this faint skepticism, this pressing into service of everything that is not God himself, and along with this the readiness to meet each unique, fresh situation and the fresh summons ever being made in it—uniqueness experienced not as riches but as service, as a responsibility that cannot be evaded by fleeing into the commonplace nor perverted into an enjoyment of one's own special richness—all this is what I want to call the existential quality. To my mind this is so characteristic of Ignatius that I dare to think, on this ground, that he belongs to the future, not to an age now coming to an end; that this is a character not of the modern age now ending but of the age to come.[73]

What is added that is not found in the portrait of indifference is a contrast between a kind of individuality that, following Guardini, Rahner ascribes to the Renaissance, and thus to "the modern world," and the kind of individuality he ascribes to Ignatius. Guardini had described the experience of subjectivity typical of the modern age using the concept of "personality":

> Subjectivity revealed itself most distinctly in the concept of "personality." Conceived as that which most expressed the human, as flowering from roots intrinsic to itself, as shaped in its destiny through its own initiative, personality became . . . something primary and absolute which could not be questioned or doubted. The great personality

was looked upon as a man who had to be taken inevitably upon his own terms. Only in the light of his own unique "personality" might one dare to justify the actions of a man. Ethical standards seemed relative when compared with those which genius deserved.[74]

Guardini associates this understanding of subjectivity most strongly with Goethe and German Romanticism.[75] Other analysts of modernity have made similar claims. For example, this description is recognizable in what Robert Bellah and his coauthors named "aesthetic individualism," and is well known in England and the United States, exemplified in figures such as Ralph Waldo Emerson and Samuel Coleridge.[76] Charles Taylor also identifies it in *Sources of the Self* as an "expressivist turn" against disengaged Enlightenment rationalism.[77] On Guardini's reading, our own age, the age of modernity's dissolution, is witnessing the end of the "genius" and the "Great Individual," with his unique "personality," which serves him as a *norma normans non normata*. Ours is, instead, the age of "technological man," "mass man," and "organization man."[78] The Renaissance/modern ideal of "personality," of glorying in and resolutely cultivating one's uniqueness and differentiation from others, is inimical to "mass man." Guardini does not fully mourn that ideal's passing.[79] He argues that insofar as the subject's authentic personhood (which he speaks of in terms of being a *person* as opposed to a *personality*) comes not from the capacity to be a refined individual cultivating his or her unique personality but from being called forth into existence by God and held responsible before God; *that* ideal (personhood) can survive the end of modernity. Guardini worries, nonetheless, that the individual subject, oriented by the authentic ideal of personhood, will be submerged and swallowed up into the crowd.[80] As a consequence, the age now coming into existence presents unparalleled challenges for Christian faith. He closes in an air of what he calls "true and valid pessimism," which measures the dangers to be faced realistically in order to muster the necessary resolve to find and implement the resources for meeting them.

In the light of this brief overview of Guardini's position on modernity and its dissolution, much of what Rahner says in the 1950s about Ignatius and Ignatian spirituality comes into clearer focus. It helps us understand, for instance, Rahner's frequent insistence that Ignatius's legacy should be distinguished from the inheritance of the Renaissance: "Ignatius has not, at bottom, much connection with the Renaissance, frequent as have been attempts to explain him in terms of it."[81] In a clear evocation of Guardini's analysis, he calls Ignatius "the individualist not of *personality* but of *person*, . . . the person who knows his vocation to come from the immediate will of God."[82] In the definition of Ignatian "existentiality," quoted above, in which Rahner cites the exigency to "uniqueness" that characterizes Ignatian spirituality, he qualifies it in terms that unmistakably echo Guardini's distinction between "personality" and "personhood": "uniqueness experienced not as riches but as service, as a responsibility that cannot be evaded by fleeing into the commonplace nor perverted into an enjoyment of one's own special richness." He proceeds to argue that the properly Ignatian form of existentiality makes Ignatius a figure "who belongs to the future, not to an age now coming to an end; that this [existential character] is a character not of the modern age now ending but of the age to come, though it remains to be seen whether those who, historically, call themselves his disciples and pupils will be the ones who really represent this spirit in the future."[83]

This is an instance of how when Rahner began to think more historically in the course of the 1950s he began to qualify his earlier judgment that Ignatius was a man wholly of the Middle Ages, who had merely recapitulated classic themes from the Fathers and from Bonaventure. Yet, neither is he ready to assign Ignatius fully to modernity. Indeed, if we contextualize Rahner's historical placement of Ignatius against the backdrop of Guardini's remarks on the end of modernity, it becomes evident that, for Rahner, Ignatius, living during the Renaissance and on the threshold of the scientific revolution (two key markers for Guardini of the modern age's maturation), had already grasped intuitively the problem with the new ideal of subjectivity that was arising at that time ("personality") and had articulated a spirituality that grounded a counterideal ("person"). This counterideal offers a resource for dealing with modernity's disintegration today, which threatens to be not just the end of the ideal of "personality" but the end of the ideal of responsible subjectivity before God and other human beings, an ideal that both Guardini and Rahner took to be an indispensable entailment of Christian faith. Indifference, the key to Ignatian spirituality, is now therefore distinctly modern at least in the sense that it arose in response to a modern dilemma. Rahner's critique of his fellow Jesuits—to the effect that they have thus far failed to appropriate and apply this crucial resource—suggests not only that he shared Guardini's concern over what kind of Christianity could survive the dissolution of modernity, but that he saw Ignatian spirituality as a crucial resource for responding to that concern.

Making this resource available locates the hermeneutical vantage point from which Rahner read Ignatius at this time, and defines an interpretive strategy to which some have taken exception, as we shall see when we come to his essay on discernment in the next section. But it must be stated from the outset that Rahner did not consider himself to be an exegete of "the Ignatius of history," as important as he thought that work was. His way of reading Ignatius was not unlike the way he had read Thomas Aquinas in *Spirit in the World*. In his preface to the second edition of that work, he wrote:

> However much this inquiry into the teaching of Thomas is a historical investigation, it is also meant to be philosophical. Our concern, then, is not with the Thomas who was conditioned by his times and dependent on Aristotle, Augustine, and the philosophy of his day.... [T]he primary concern of this historical work is not to be "history," but philosophy itself. And if what matters is to grasp the really philosophical in a philosopher, this can only be done if one joins him in looking at the matter itself. It is only then that you can understand what he means.[84]

One might therefore say that Rahner's intent in approaching Ignatius is to be "really theological," and he did this by joining Ignatius in looking at "the matter itself." Agreeing with Guardini, he thought that the matter itself was a serious one indeed, having to do with whether Christian faith would have a future after "the end of the modern age." Historical accuracy matters (and Rahner is vulnerable on that count, as we shall see), but it is not everything. Writing, once again, about his reading of Aquinas, Rahner further maintains that "a work that is historical in this sense, a work which does not merely want to 'narrate' what Thomas said, but tries to relive the philosophical event itself in Thomas, is naturally more dependent on what its author himself was able to understand of metaphysics than a 'strictly' historical work would be. Not as though it were a question here of the author's own view, as though consciously or unconsciously he wanted to read his own opinions into Thomas."[85] What governs the "objectivity" of this kind of reading, Rahner avers, is its capacity to bring about a "reliving" of its subject matter, precisely in relation to a contemporary problematic. I suggest that this approach, which he first tried out in writing on Aquinas, governs the way he reads Ignatius too. When Rahner writes on Ignatius, he will try to construct an argument that "relives" the philosophical-theological event that gave expression five-hundred years ago to Ignatius's spirituality, but do it in response to a contemporary problematic (the end of the modern age), a problematic that Rahner believed Ignatius had already sensed. Without taking this risk, the resource that Ignatius provides for contemporary Christian faith would remain "unmined."

Another text that displays the same interpretive position toward Ignatius comes from a lecture that Rahner gave five years later on the Ignatian motto of *Ad maiorem Dei gloriam* ("to the greater glory of God"), this time to a specifically Jesuit audience.[86] He begins by laying out a number of challenges that a successful interpretation of the motto must overcome. His argumentative strategy for doing so shifts in a telling direction vis-á-vis his earlier lecture on "Ignatian Mysticism of Joy in the World." Rather than resolve the difficulties by a more or less ahistorical transcendental argument, as he had in 1937, he does so twenty-two years later by placing Ignatian spirituality in its historical context. Now, moreover, Rahner is quite clear that this context is the transition from the church of antiquity into the church of modernity.[87]

In his opening discussion, Rahner gives five difficulties for interpreting the motto, which he will use to frame his own reading. In the second and third, he records the worries that the motto foments tacit or overt hubris among those who would adopt it, not to say Pelagianism. In the fourth, related point, he lays out the objection that, from a biblical perspective, we humans can only aspire to be the recipients and percipients of God's greater glory, not its augmenters.[88] The first and fifth objections are of a different sort. In the first, he asks whether it is really permissible to speak of "AMDG" as specific to Ignatius or to the Jesuits, insofar as it articulates an ideal incumbent on all Christians. In the fifth, he takes the opposite tack and asks whether or not the motto is not tellingly (and damningly) modern. Does it not reflect too much of a Promethean humanism, the motto of a man who thinks that he is the perfecter of the world, ushering in the kingdom of God by his own efforts? In addition, insofar as the world *is* becoming more and more the product of human labor, is it not becoming increasingly profane and ambiguous? Can we really assume that men and women living at the "end of the modern world" (Rahner puts Guardini's catchphrase in quotes) will find in all this work God's greater glory, or that they can discern so easily what element of their work is in fact tending toward that greater glory?[89] In these two objections, then, the issue is, on the one hand, whether the motto is so general and ahistorical that it should not be applied to Ignatian spirituality in particular, but rather to Christian faith as a whole; and, on the other, whether it is so historically particular, so proper to "the modern age," that linking it to Ignatian spirituality would render that spirituality as moribund as modernity itself. In short, the issue is how properly to evaluate the historicity of Ignatian spirituality.

That this is the pivotal issue becomes clear as Rahner goes on to argue that the birth of every human idea, attitude, and intellectual or spiritual form is governed by the temporally conditioned situation in which it arose. Yet, however much a *novum* arises at a particular moment in human history that delimits it, it can outlast that moment, contributing something lasting. This is as true of the Egyptian monasticism of late antiquity and the Franciscanism of the High Middle Ages as it is of Ignatius. Thus, although Rahner now contends that Ignatius is "ultimately speaking, . . . still, in a true sense, a man of the New Age (*Neuzeit*)" and agrees with Guardini that this age is indeed passing away in one sense, the anthropocentricity that became the hallmark of the modern age is *not* passing away. The emphasis on rational planning and technical control, which places the human at the center of both cultural and natural processes, will be lasting. The centrality of the subjectivity of the individual, his or her right and absolute responsibility to dispose of him- or herself in a process that cannot ultimately be deferred or delegated, will continue to characterize our "being-in-the-world." Ignatius was there at the epicenter when this earthquake began reshaping the historical situation that is so pervasively and inescapably a part of our modern life, and he was able to make a decisive contribution to the extent that he appropriated it in such a way that it can be of lasting value to the Church. This is the context within which to interpret the significance of *Ad maiorem Dei gloriam*. It is the historicity of Ignatian spirituality that makes it (and the motto) something new in Christianity; it is Ignatius's genius in appropriating modernity critically that makes the spirituality he founded greater and more lasting than the historical condition that gave birth to it.

What is it, precisely, about the spiritual stance entailed by the motto that marks it as both distinctively modern and yet also enables it to transcend and point beyond modernity? Rahner claims that it is the particular sense of human subjectivity that, though always a possibility for human existence, and perhaps incipiently present in other historical eras, (1) has really only become explicitly thematized in modernity, (2) was prepared and made possible by Christianity, and, finally, (3) makes possible a new concretization of Christian life in which *Ad maiorem Dei gloriam* becomes meaningful in a way that it could not have been before.[90] Rahner gets at this sense of subjectivity by analyzing what is entailed by any successful attempt to live "for the greater glory of God in all things." As in the 1937 lecture, there are two elements in tension with one another. On the one hand, living out this motto entails placing one's freedom at the service of God, of disposing oneself for the greater glory of God, which, of course, is only possible if one has a deep sense of one's capacity in freedom to dispose oneself.[91] This is a major element of the "modern" experience of human subjectivity. Yet there is another equally crucial realization: in so many ways we are already disposed by God even before we dispose ourselves in God's service "for God's greater glory." That is, we do not have the kind of pure and absolute freedom that the motto seems to imply that we have. This complicates what might otherwise appear to be a quite straightforward motto:

> Obedience does not in the least mean that we have to work out a plan on the grand scale once and for all by some abstract principle.... 'Ad majorem Dei gloriam,' therefore does not by any means imply—at any rate in any adequate sense—that man can map out the course of his life once and for all using the *a priori* principle of the greater glory of God. It means that in essence he is not so much the author of projects [*der Entwerfende*] as the one who has been "projected" [*der Geworfene*], one whom God has already made dispositions for, and who is always only partially in a position to make fresh dispositions on his own account.[92]

Yet, Rahner goes on to argue, this is not to deny that

> man is capable ... of perceiving, realizing, taking into his calculations in an extremely impressive way, the fact that this state of being subject

to prior dispositions and the changeableness of such dispositions is under the greater, broader power of God to dispose of things—and at the same time in man's own power.... In other words in the concept of "major Dei gloria" the explicit reflexive conscious planning of life really is included, even though man is, and necessarily must be, the one who submits to being disposed of, one who accepts, and in a certain sense, who is not capable of planning.[93]

Rahner's language is revealing here, as both *"der Geworfene"* and *"der Entwerfende"* are terms of art in Heidegger's early masterwork, *Being and Time*.[94] In Heidegger's phenomenological uncovering of the being of Dasein, *"Geworfenheit"* (thrownness) denotes the simple, brute "thereness" of Dasein in a particular situation over which it has no control, but which decisively shapes it, for good or for ill.[95] According to Heidegger, we are "thrown" into existence in a way that is veiled from us but that profoundly "inflects" (*stimmt*) the way we are in and toward the world. On the other hand, we also are always "projecting" ourselves (*sich entwerfen*) into the future. We are always present to ourselves and comprehend ourselves in terms of the possibilities for the future that give our present world its meaning and value: "Any Dasein has, as Dasein, already projected itself; and as long as it is, it is projecting. As long as it is, Dasein always has understood itself and always will understand itself in terms of possibilities.... Because of the kind of Being which is constituted by the *existentiale* of projection, Dasein is constantly 'more' than it factually is."[96]

In other words, Dasein is always at the same time inescapably rooted in the past and present into which it has always, at any given moment in time, been "thrown," and also more than that, more than it is, because what it is now is always ahead of itself, "projecting" and transcending itself into the possibilities available in an as-yet indeterminate future. This structure leads Heidegger to characterize Dasein's being as the sheer transience and provisionality of temporality, a temporality that is oriented by and toward the nothingness (which is to say, indeterminateness, neither this nor that) of sheer possibility.

Rahner took up this phenomenological articulation of human subjectivity, but now, of course, the whence and whither of our "thrownness" and our future-directedness has a name: God and God's greater glory. Rahner's point, implicit in his use of the Heideggerian account of subjectivity, but explicit in his insistence that modernity is characterized by just these kinds of thematically self-reflective articulation of the "subjecthood" of the subject, is that it is precisely because the subjectivity of the subject has become thematic in the particular way it has in modernity (which, of course, is more than just an event in modernity's intellectual history, but a defining shift in all of its dimensions: social, cultural, and perhaps even ontological) that this motto can be articulated, experienced, and actualized with a previously unknown depth of meaning, however much, once expressed, it is recognized as a possibility inherent to Christianity all along:

> But just as it is not until modernity that this sense of the self as subject is arrived at, so too this saying "ad majorem Dei gloriam," intended in the same sense and with the same depth of meaning, is likewise only arrived at in modernity, and in fact only from Ignatius onwards. This "selfhood" of the subject was not always a theme of investigation for the subject himself in the sense in which it has come to be so in modernity. And therefore the wider range of possibilities over and above the conditions actually prevailing in the concrete here and now and ordained by God was not always a theme of investigation for the Christian considered as a subject in this sense.[97]

It is only on the basis of this fundamental recognition of the possibilities and challenges of being a (Christian) subject that it makes sense for a Christian to ask what is "for the greater glory of God."

One can and must both plan for the future and realize that one's action always arises out of a past over which one has had only a modicum of control (if any), and is oriented toward a future field of possibilities that will always exceed one's capacity to plan. In the case of the future, this is not just because this field exceeds the range of possibilities that one has realized to this point, but because it is in principle greater than *any* range of possibilities that one can take into account in his or her process of planning out possible courses of action and ways of life, now and in the future. This is because ultimately this field of possibilities is coterminous with the infinitude of the actuality that is God. Rahner points out, thus, that the motto, correctly understood, is framed dynamically: *toward* the greater glory of God. The glory of God is not so much a concrete achievement that one realizes once and for all as it is an ever-receding horizon against which any finite goal is placed, perceived, and embraced, but at the same time always relativized, even in the moment at which one conceives of it and commits oneself to it. This entails a subject who, aware of all the complex factors involved in his or her decision (including the ultimacy of God), "draws back from them in a special way for which there is no precedent."[98] The "drawing back from" clearly intends "indifference," which is still, on Rahner's view, central to Ignatius's contribution. In the 1950s, however, Rahner comes to insist that it "has no precedent." Moreover, if the doctrinal locus for defining this "drawing back" was the doctrine of creation in 1937, now it is eschatology; not protology, but futurology.

That such a form of subjectivity is possible and actual is a matter of empirical fact for Rahner: "This peculiar attitude of choice, this withdrawal of one's self to an absolute point in order from *there* to reflect and to test what is to be done, does exist. And this existential structure involved in the act of choice does exist in the case of St. Ignatius in a degree which the moral theologians right to the present day have probably not yet sufficiently grasped."[99] This existential attitude (or spirituality, looked at from the perspective of its appropriation into the entirety of one's lived Christian faith, as suggested by Ignatius) has its dangers, as Rahner admits in both essays from the 1950s that we have studied thus far.[100] Rahner names a potentially paralyzing overscrupulosity that comes from feeling overwhelmed by this stance of continual evaluation and reevaluation. This feeling can arise from the insight that one's "thrownness" by God is ever changing and that the field of possibilities illuminated by the horizon of God's greater glory is always calling for a "re-projection" of our life-trajectory into the future. One can freeze, as it were, in a sort of experience of existential vertigo. There is, second, a relativization of fixed hierarchies of goods (including religious goods) that comes from the stance of indifference and the orientation toward an "ever-greater" God that exceeds exhaustive structuring by any possible finite order, no matter how sacred. This can cause a skeptical, even cynical detachment, resulting in a refusal to commit oneself wholeheartedly to any innerworldly good or project. Paradoxically, this destabilization (perhaps one might even say "deconstruction") of secular and religious hierarchies of goods can also lead to a kind of anxiety that drives one to assert and embrace an absolute value and normativity of these hierarchies in a decisionist way.[101]

Rahner identifies these as very real dangers, which have confronted Ignatius's followers in the past and continue to do so today. But they are modernity's temptations too: skeptical rationalism; an alienating loss of a sense of the meaningfulness of social structures and cultural symbol-systems; enervated withdrawal from sustained personal commitment to the grand ideals of the past, either on the personal or public level; ideological decisionism, with the totalitarianism that is its political concomitant. These dangers will not be avoided by rejecting the Ignatian ideal, since they are rooted in the deeper and now irreversible shift in our sense for what it means to be human. However, a Christian appropriation is possible, as can be verified in the life of Ignatius. As Rahner points out in his early assessment of Heidegger's work, the sense of subjectivity uncovered by Heidegger's fundamental ontology could be the source of the most radical atheism, but it could also be the root of an equally profound *religiosity*.[102] Tipping the balance in the latter direction requires identifying, describing, and providing a legitimation for the realized possibility that men and women are capable of "perceiving, realizing, taking into [their] calculations in an extremely impressive way" this condition, at once radically liberative and profoundly disorienting.

Ignatian Discernment and the Hermeneutical Circle of Spiritual Practice and Theological Analysis

This brings us to the longest essay from this period; indeed, it is the longest single essay that Rahner wrote on Ignatian spirituality: "The Logic of Concrete Individual Knowledge in Ignatius of Loyola."[103] It is not only Rahner's longest text on Ignatian spirituality, but has also generated the most commentary, a good deal of it critical.[104] Space precludes an exhaustive treatment of the philosophical and hermeneutical complexities of Rahner's text. A brief recap of the argument thus far will set the parameters of my treatment here. I have argued that in the 1950s Rahner began to think explicitly in terms of the challenges facing the church and theology caught up in "the end of the modern world." Guardini's reflections and Heidegger's philosophy were the primary sources for an account of what Rahner took to be the situation of the modern subject, and his treatments of Ignatian spirituality began to reflect a conviction that Ignatius had worked out a spirituality that provided crucial resources for dealing creatively with this situation. This is particularly the case with the disorienting sense of groundlessness that defines the modern subject, who must take up far more fully and explicitly than ever before the task of mapping out and planning his or her life-project into an open future, while reckoning at the same time with having been "thrown" into this situation in such a way that he or she cannot enlist for this planning either some universal, fixed ethical framework or a scientifically complete account of human nature. Lacking a more serious investigation and deployment of such resources, Christianity and "the coming age" face serious threats. Specifically, the "postmodern" sense of the subject, which is undermining and replacing the modern sense of the subject as "personality" and which cannot be undone or augmented by an ad hoc regression to the medieval ideal, will fatally infect and debilitate that sense of responsible subjectivity that is a crucial prerequisite for Christian faith, if not for the continued flourishing of Western culture as a whole. In order to mine these resources, Rahner took up a way of reading Ignatius, like the one he had used to read Aquinas, joining Ignatius to look at this contemporary "matter itself," in all its seriousness, in the conviction that only in this way, and not by a simple recounting of what Ignatius wrote or did, can one bring his contributions effectively into play.

This way of framing the matter leads us to expect Rahner to take up at least two tasks in order to find a way through the problem of "the end of modernity." On the one hand, it would need to be shown that the dizzying breadth of possibilities that opens up before us as we project our life-careers into the future is not the nothingness of pure possibility, but the fullness of actuality that is "the ever greater God." In his early essay on Heidegger, Rahner argues that the former conclusion only follows if one takes as fundamental and unavoidable the pervasive modern "mood" of *angst*, the anxiety that ineluctably attends Dasein's necessary work of taking possession of both its opaque "thrownness" and its "projection" into the ever-open future (or even attends the deferral of this work to "das Mann," to "what 'they' say").[105] Thus, it would follow that Rahner needs to make available a "countermood" to anxiety, a realm or dimension of experience that can attend the same work, but would disclose a "thrownness" whose whence and whither is the ever-greater God. Second, Rahner would need to show how it is possible in the concrete for the person "at the end of the modern age," with his or her sense of subjectivity both endangered but also inflected in the positive sense just named, still to experience and respond effectively to a sense of responsibility before God, and to make decisions out of that sense of responsibility, which, though not fully governed by the stable hierarchies (both sacred and profane) that have lost their grounding as modernity passes away, can still be more than Promethean-Dionysian self-assertion, or a passive acceptance of "whatever God sends."

The latter task is precisely what Rahner has in mind when he talks about a logic of "existentiel insight."[106] He frames the issue in traditional terms. He starts with the claim that the individual is more than simply a specific instance of a universal, such that the nature, *telos*, and good for that individual can be attained by a science of that universal. This raises a challenge for ethics in general and moral theology in particular. Rahner lays this challenge out in a contemporaneous essay on ethics.[107] In that essay, and in the one we are considering here, he is at great pains to distance himself from "situation ethics," which he was accused of advocating, but which would, on his reading, represent a "massive nominalism" denying the validity of any universal knowledge about human beings on which to ground ethical norms.[108] He does maintain that as created, embodied beings we share a universal nature or essence from which substantive norms for a material universal ethics can be derived, what he calls an "essence ethics" (*Essenzethik*). Yet we are free, rational agents who shape our individuality over and above those features that characterize us as members of a universal class, and do so in ways that need to be accounted for by going beyond or augmenting what an essence ethics can do. But there is more at stake than this. He also argues that we are destined as unique *individuals*—and not just as instances of a species—to share in the life of God. This being so, our choices as individuals have a moral weight that needs to be taken into account, but that cannot by definition be fully analyzed using norms drawn from reflection on our common human nature. In short, God has a will for those decisions, insofar as they orient us toward that particular union with God for which God created us as unique individuals.[109]

Rahner is not denying the legitimacy of universal material norms. His point, rather, is that at least some of our choices are underdetermined by those norms. We may have several equally permissible options, or we may have several ways of effecting the same normed action.[110] What then? Following the Kantian maxim, "If one *ought* to do something, then one must *be able* to do so," Rahner concludes that there must be a "logic" for this type of decision. Or, using an alternate terminology that comes to the same thing, there must be a "formal existential ethics": "In so far as there is a moral reality in an existential-ethic sense and of a binding kind which nevertheless cannot (in the very nature of things) be translated into universal propositions of material content—there must be an existential ethics of a formal kind, i.e., an ethics which treats of the basic elements, the formal structures and the basic manner of perceiving such an existential-ethic reality."[111] He goes on to assert that "there must be some function of conscience which . . . grasps also what has not been made absolutely clear by the situation and the universal norms, and which is precisely and as such what has to be done by me individually."[112] Yet he pleads limitations of space when it comes to working out in greater detail what precisely this formal existential ethics would look like, or how this "function of conscience" would disclose itself in human beings' day-to-day lives. He does, however, give a significant hint, asking (rather rhetorically) whether "we could not understand the whole teaching on election in the *Spiritual Exercises* of St. Ignatius much more profoundly and exactly if we were clearly aware of such an existential ethics and the way of finding an ethical existential-imperative."[113]

This is the hint that Rahner expands at length in his essay on existentiel insight in Ignatius of Loyola. There he begins by arguing that "Ignatius tacitly presupposes a philosophy of human existence in which a moral decision in its individuality is not merely an instance of general ethical normative principles."[114] In other words, Ignatius was a man who intuitively grasped the validity and exigency of an "existential ethics" and responded to it with his *Spiritual Exercises*. This makes Ignatius a man for our times, even if the only *tacit* nature of his sense for the characteristic feature of modern (or "postmodern") subjectivity means that we should not expect from him the *explicit* philosophy and theology that will secure this accomplishment and make it available for further examination and development, or translation from its still, in many respects, medieval idiom into one for the end of the modern age. This is the duty that falls to theology. It is a duty, however, which Rahner is convinced has not been adequately discharged, in part because of a tendency to trivialize or dismiss the figure of the saint and the genre of "spiritual literature" as a locus for theological reflection.[115] To remedy this problem, theology has to expose itself to the questions raised by texts in spirituality, and it is this self-conscious engagement with the saint that Rahner cites as the purpose of his essay on Ignatius.

The principal argument Rahner gives for Ignatius's tacit articulation of an existential ethics revolves around what Rahner takes to be Ignatius's emphasis on the "second way of making an election."[116] Recall that the second way of making an election is neither the response to the experience of a self-authenticating divine illumination of the soul (the first way) nor the deliberative weighing of reasons for and against a given choice and its future consequences (the third way). The second way occurs in a time when one experiences contrary, sometimes powerful, affective movements pushing one in different directions with regard to the choice at hand. By means of the rules for discernment of spirits, Ignatius proposes that one can decide which of these movements is in fact from God in order to cooperate with it and resist the others. Rahner not only argues that Ignatius stresses this "way" of making a choice, but that he took it to be the normal way an election happens:

> Ignatius regards as the normal case of his Election a decision whose content is not simply and solely a deduction from general principles of reason and faith with the help of an analysis of the particular case concerned. Rather is he convinced that in the normal case God in a kind of individual "inspiration" ... makes known his will, which, while falling within the domain of general revelation, the Church and reason, nevertheless in its concrete particulars can only be known through this supplementary motion from God.[117]

Rahner goes on to claim that the first way of making an election is an extraordinary, intensified "limit case" of the second, and that the third is "a deficient modality of the one identical kind of Election, the genuine nature of which appears in its pure and fully developed form in the first two."[118] Few commentators would deny that Ignatius's distinctive contribution lies in his development of "rules" governing the second way of making an election; but some have bristled at Rahner's assertion that the third way is a "deficient modality" of the second.[119] It has been objected that Rahner is going beyond the textual evidence, that in fact Ignatius did use the third method of making an election, and never denigrated it in comparison to the others. We shall have to return to these objections later, since they call into question whether one can really say that Rahner's theology is inspired by Ignatian spirituality or, at least, whether it is inspired by a correct reading of that. But to move ahead, and in anticipation of the more explicit engagement with Rahner's critics, it will help to clarify what Rahner himself thought he was doing with this essay.

Rahner was convinced that Ignatius had arrived at (or, more precisely, been inspired to have) a profound insight into how God deals with human beings. As he had suggested in his essays on the devotion to the Sacred Heart, and on the ever-greater God, this was an insight that could only have surfaced in the context of a dramatic shift in the lived experience (and subsequently, conceptual articulation) of human subjectivity. It is now more necessary than ever as the social and cultural world to which that shift gave rise disintegrates. Yet how can theology make use of this insight? It must sift, as it were, the data of Ignatius's writings and learn to ask questions that it had not been accustomed to ask under the conditions of modernity, and to problematize tacit answers it had accepted all too unreflectively. Subsequently, however, theology has its own constructive task of elaborating the insight that the new questions elicit when we read Ignatius, rendering a framework that is not simply the repristination of the Ignatius of the sixteenth century, but an Ignatius made productive for ours. In this sense, theology goes beyond the spirituality, or an historical exegesis of it, narrowly construed. It was the same sense in which he had taken up Aquinas in *Spirit in the World*.

In sum, although Rahner states at the beginning and the end of the essay that he is only allowing Ignatian spirituality to confront and question contemporary systematic theology,[120] in fact the process is a two-way one, as he makes clear in the middle of the essay: "Only fragments, obviously, can be offered here on this method of an individual, concrete [*existentiellen*] ethics of the discovery of that particular will of God which cannot fully be resolved into general principles. They will consist of a free movement alternating between the text of the Exercises and theological observations, in which each party by turns questions or answers."[121] One might reconstruct Rahner's alternations in the mutual interrogation between spirituality and theology in this way. Neoscholasticism's account of how God's will becomes available to human persons has two categories. On the one hand, God deals with creatures via miraculous interventions—Rahner clearly has the understanding of divine inspiration of scripture in mind—that come self-authorized, as it were, and that can lead to norms either directly (say, the Ten Commandments) or by means of authoritative elaboration (by the Church's magisterium in defining, say, the Easter duty). On the other hand, God's will is mediated by creation, as primary cause working "underneath," "in," and "through" secondary causes. This way can lead to norms by way of reason's deliberation on the intelligible order of creation.

If Ignatius is right that God also commonly deals with individual persons directly, then this way of dealing with persons will not fit into either category. It is not the miraculous, self-authenticating "intervention" of the first category, insofar as it requires deliberation and discernment.[122] Neither is it the mediated presence of the divine will immanent to creation. It is no wonder, then, that traditional theology has failed to capture what is distinctive about Ignatian spirituality. It lacks the category necessary to understand what is unique in it. Or almost. In a telling first hint, Rahner suggests that there are possibilities in this direction to be found in the Thomistic doctrine of God being the "formal object" of experience by virtue of God's sanctifying grace. This is a direct divine action in the sense that it is "uncreated grace," the gift of God's very self. Only because of grace, only because human being comes to participate immediately (without mediation) in God's own being is human consciousness placed within a "broader," divinized horizon, as it were, against which objects of our experience show up to us in a new way.[123] The problem, here, however, is that this modulation of our human knowing is not a material object such that we can separate it out and identify it in order to use it as an "anchor" or "marker" for discerning specific elements of our experience as being from God in a special way.[124]

Thus far spirituality has been framing the questions. It has been Ignatian spirituality, with its claim that God deals directly with persons in revealing an individual will for them, that has been driving the inquiry, interrogating systematic theology, and demonstrating its lack. The result has been the emergence of a requirement that traditional theology be changed or emended in order to do justice to this reality. Yet the hint (formal causality) already indicates that theology could take, and perhaps is about to take, the lead in the conversation. First, however, Rahner further specifies the issue by locating the precise point in Ignatius's rules for discernment where the immediacy of God's action on the individual is most clearly evident: the consolation without prior cause.[125] Ignatius asserts that "only God our Lord can give the soul consolation without a preceding cause," and "when the consolation is without preceding cause, no deception can be present in it, since it is coming only from God our Lord" (*SpEx* 330, 336). It is not itself subject to the testing process governed by the rules for discernment of spirits (since "no deception can be present in it"). Rahner infers from this that it should be thought of as a touchstone in comparison with which other movements in the soul are evaluated, since it manifests in pure form the sort of unmediated action of God on the soul that one is to look for elsewhere in "mixed form," in alloy, that is, with other movements of the soul and one's own reflections concerning the options among which one is making a decisive choice. If theology can give an account of this "experience," then it can be confident that it has opened up the categories and discursive strategies necessary for working out the broader structures of Ignatian discernment and the "logic of existential insight" that follows therefrom (a task that, Rahner admits, he does not take up in this essay).

At this point in the argument, it is a theological system that begins to structure the inquiry; the direction of the mutual interrogation has shifted. Rahner concedes that "it is not easy to say what Ignatius means by this first kind of divine movement."[126] Rahner proposes what he takes to be an essential and unavoidable clarification of Ignatius's account: when Ignatius speaks of the "cause" of a consolation (or the lack of a cause), he cannot have in mind a temporally prior object stimulating a subsequent train of reactions and reflections. He argues this by reference to Ignatius's contrasting point that the good and evil spirits can console "*con causa*" (with cause). If one interprets statements like this into a temporal framework, so that it would mean that the spirits do so by means of "inserting" contents of experience or ideas into consciousness "prior" to the intended consolation, then where would they find the temporal space or gap in our stream of consciousness to do so? It is evident here, and elsewhere, that Rahner is arguing for a "noninterventionist" account of preternatural (including divine) agency.[127] The "cause," on his reading, has to be thought of as the object of consciousness that accompanies the subjective stance (of consolation) of the one experiencing it:

> *Consolación* signifies the inner frame of mind that follows from the object, things that Ignatius designates as *paz, tranquilidad, quietud,* etc. (peace, tranquility and quiet). The *causa* is simply the consoling object present in the actual occurrence of consolation itself. At

most it precedes the consolation (instead of being merely logically antecedent to it) to the extent that by the nature of the case there is normally an interval of time before a person responds to the object and is consoled.[128]

With this clarification established, he goes on to assert that one now must say that the consolation without "prior" cause is a consolation that has no object associated with it. Rahner is well aware of possible objections to what he is suggesting. What sense can it make to talk of a human subjective state that transpires without any object being present to consciousness, but of which one can not only be aware, but be aware in the modality of knowledge? Both Kant and Aquinas (who figure strongly in Rahner's philosophical genealogy) had asserted in different ways that human knowledge can only arise with the concomitant presence of an object to the knower, and Rahner's first systematic work, *Spirit in the World*, focused on the indispensability of the "turn to the phantasm," to the image, in human knowing. Present-day critics have objected that Rahner is here proposing a form of "nonlinguistic" experience that cannot be sustained after philosophy's "linguistic turn."[129] Even as sympathetic an interpreter as Endean objects that Rahner's rhetoric at times "loses touch with reality."[130]

In a particularly important footnote, Rahner attempts to forestall these kinds of objection. He argues that one should not reject his proposal out of hand, since there are in the history of the tradition instances of this kind of experience.[131] He names Bonaventure, and cites his own work on the doctrine of the "spiritual touch" in Bonaventure, which dates from the 1930s. There is also, he argues, "at least one awareness which is not consciousness of an *object*: the concomitant awareness of oneself in every act of the mind when it is directed to any object." Rahner goes on to suggest that

> the question can, therefore, only be whether there can be an awareness unrelated to an object [*ungegenständliche*] with respect to other realities besides one's own "I." If an affirmative answer can be given with respect to God, then (quite independently of the question as to whether or not an experience of this sort could happen only within the sphere of mysticism but also outside of it as well) it would be possible to formulate the concept of an experience that, in being

completely taken hold of by the love of God, is an experience of God that is "unrelated to any object." All of this, however, must be worked out as far as possible in greater detail using Ignatius himself.[132]

Rahner invokes thus his early work on Christian mysticism and his work on the ontology of human cognition, and links them in gesturing toward the possibility of conceiving what a "consolation without prior cause" could be. At this point he returns to the hint he gave earlier. One way in which a conception of this experience could be worked out would be to start with the experience of transcendence that is concomitantly present with any act of human knowing or willing, to the extent that these acts are already placed against the horizon of being as such, which is always beyond the grasp of our conceptualized knowledge of any particular object that is the subject of our knowing and willing. As a consequence, we have a sort of reaching forward (*Vorgriff*) beyond the objects of these specific acts, which, even though it cannot be grasped in a concept (*Begriff*), nonetheless counts as a mode of being aware, and can, with the proper reflection, provide insight (that is, it can become known). Thus far, Rahner is trading on arguments from his early work, from *Spirit in the World*. Even more, however, "such a transcendence is the synthesis of the intrinsic ordination of mind to being in general, and of grace which supervenes to mould this natural unlimited openness and make of it a dynamic orientation in the life of God himself."[133] Thinking of it as an instance of "formal causality" (or, as Rahner more cautiously puts it, "quasi-formal causality") means thinking of our ability to perceive all the elements of our experience in their modality as manifestations of God's presence to us, instances of God's offer to us of intimate communion, which, if embraced as such, will lead to (or better, in grace will carry us into) that communion.[134]

In most human acts of knowing and willing this transcendence is present in awareness in a tacit way. Rahner postulates that this element of experience, this dynamism, can become itself more and more the focus of awareness, the object virtually disappearing from awareness. An analogy might be useful. In experiencing our world (particularly in and through art) the "formal object" of color is usually present to us only in the experience of "colored objects," yet there are experiences in which the power of the interplay of color and form so overtakes us that it transcends and even eclipses our awareness of the particular objects that mediate its presence to me—a sunset, a particular work of art. We verge on an experience of "color" itself, almost untethered from the experience of the colored object. Something similar to this, I suggest, is what Rahner is proposing can happen with the experience of God's presence to us as we contemplate our world as an object of reflection, appreciation, love, and choice.[135] It is not necessary, I believe, to deny that there is still an object present along with the experience of consolation, but the force and power of the consolation has become so powerful and "detached," as it were from the experiential moments related to the perception of the object itself, that it is appropriate to say that it is unrelated to the object.

On Rahner's reading, this interpretation of the consolation without prior cause can account for the certitude that it bears. Since it thematizes the graced opening outward to God that is occasioned by God's self-gift to us, nothing is present in it but God. It is an emergence into awareness of the graced transcendence of the person that is already present to God as its ground (in quasi-formal causality) and term. It should be noted that no statement about God (or God's will) is intrinsic to, entailed by, or warranted by this experience. In asserting that the experience cannot deceive, Rahner does *not* mean that it directly grounds, without possibility of deception, some conceptual assertion. What we are not deceived about, I contend, is the basis and telos of the fundamental ground and orientation of our being, not in and toward the sheer possibility-not-to-be of death (Heidegger), but the fullness of being that also graciously reaches out and gives of itself to us, intimately and in the absolute specificity of our individual existence.

This responds to the first of two tasks that I noted at the beginning of this section for interpreting this essay as a response, based in Ignatian spirituality, to the modern (or postmodern) dilemma of the self. In consolation without prior cause Rahner has identified the kind of "experience" he needs in order to counter a Heideggerian interpretation of *Dasein* at the end of the modern age. Insofar as this experience forefronts a presence to the God who is in fact beyond all finite assertions, it is rendering that inexpressible mystery of God present that gives meaning to the true affirmations we can make about God, even though they are only true as they are circumscribed by negations.[136]

It is also evident why discernment proper only begins in the aftermath of the consolation without prior cause, since it is only then that "objects" are once again focally present in consciousness so as to be subject to discernment. Finally, it is not hard to see why the signals of this consolation are peace, joy, and tranquility, since it represents the fulfillment of the most essential dynamism of the graced person: it is an intense realization of the presence and centrality of "the end for which we are created."

Rahner does not deny that the consolation without prior cause can take "varied and higher and profounder forms."[137] But developing it at this simplest, most spare level has the advantage that he can now connect it with "finding God in all things." Since the structure of human subjectivity that is involved in consolation is the actualization of a self-transcendence that is also always present in human knowing and acting in the world in general, and since consolation is not a particular object-oriented experience that would be unavailable were one to be experiencing (in knowledge and choice) other objects, then the particular presence to God that is represented by consolation without prior cause can be extended to serve as a criterion to construct a backdrop or framework within which all my acts of knowing and choosing, regardless of the object, are placed:

> The particular that is met with or that must be chosen, done or undergone, is placed within this pure openness and receptivity of the consciously experienced transcendence towards God, and kept there. No wonder then that everything then becomes transparent in relation to God, that everything is found in God and God in everything, for everything is seen in the ever-open supernatural transcendence founded on the theological virtues and no longer obstructed by the particular object.[138]

This also provides an indication of how the consolation without prior cause becomes a touchstone for discernment, to the extent that what is at stake in that consolation is the unconditional and unlimited openness to God that is the innermost ground/dynamism of the graced person. The process of discernment during "the second time" depends on observing a correlation (positive, neutral, or negative) over time between the root experience of consolation and the options among which one is choosing: "By frequently confronting the object of Election with the fundamental consolation, the experimental test is made whether the two phenomena are in harmony, mutually cohere, whether the will to the object of Election under scrutiny leaves intact that pure openness to God in the supernatural experience of transcendence and even supports and augments it or weakens and obscures it."[139]

One will come to find God more in some things than in others, so to speak, not because of any inherent value or dis-value in the thing itself (anything inherently sinful has already been excluded before one begins the process of election), but because it is God's will for me as an individual, it is the way given to me by God in God's creating me, "disposing of me" (to return to the essay on the greater glory of God), to reach that unique, individually tailored, if you will, union with God that is God's desire and gift for me.[140] My fundamental graced orientation and movement toward God, which is nothing other than a sharing in God's own being, is most clearly present to me and integrative of my life as the "North Pole" of my movement through life, in *this* (and not *that*) otherwise valuable option for engaging with a specific range of realities in the world in which I find myself. This process obviously takes time, and will not have the conviction of the indubitable illumination described by the first time; neither does it have the syllogistic certainty that comes from subsuming a particular case under a universal norm, which is what Rahner takes to be the "logic" of decision-making in the third time. However, it can, in Rahner's view, be a way in which the innermost core of the person, her individual self-transcendence toward God, comes to permeate the concrete details of the actualization of her life in time. It will thus represent God's will for that person, and have the corresponding ethical-spiritual exigency.

Rahner concedes that at this point one would need to go into further detail about how Ignatius provides tools for analyzing one's experiences in order to determine if the sort of synthesis or harmonization described above in fact obtains. That is, one would need to proceed to an exegesis of the rules in themselves. He does not do this. What *has* he achieved in this lengthy and difficult essay? He has, as I have suggested, shown that there is a "countermood" to the angst of Heidegger and other existential philosophers. It is consolation, present in "pure form," as it were in consolation without prior cause, which is an emergence into awareness of the fundamental dynamism of my being, *not* as a being toward nothingness and death, but as a graced being-carried towards the fullness of being and love that is God. Second, he has shown (but only with a very rough sketch) that such a fundamental mood or inflection of my experience of myself can serve as a touchstone for making meaningful decisions in our situation "at the end of the modern age," rather than falling victim to the various pathologies of modernity that he indicates in his essay on the ever-greater glory of God.

But, has he succeeded? Critics of his interpretation of Ignatius on consolation argue that its reading is overdetermined by Rahner's philosophical-theological presuppositions, a flaw further compounded by exegetical errors in his reading of the Ignatian texts (some of which came from his reliance on Hugo Rahner's translations). There is no evidence in Ignatius's writings or practice that he thought that the "first time" for making an election was always an instance of consolation without prior cause, and it is clear from his *Spiritual Diary* that he used both the methodology of the second time and of the third time to arrive at decisions, often using one to confirm the other. It could be here that Rahner is forcing the sorts of practical distinctions that Ignatius had in mind in identifying these three times to carry more speculative weight than they can bear. I observed in chapter 2 that the *Spiritual Exercises* is not a theology, and not even a "spiritual theology," but a set of practical guidelines for the one who would give them; it is a spirituality, not a theology.

Yet, this feature can be adduced in favor or Rahner's interpretation as much as in condemnation of it. Rahner's claim, which is persuasive, is that more than ever theology must mine the resources of the saints, or past spiritualities, and bring to the fore their potentialities to address the sorts of challenges to a life of faith that Guardini and others were increasingly recognizing in the middle of the last century. Yet, even more so than with other classic texts of the past, in order to do this for Ignatius's *Spiritual Exercises* one will have to bring a theological system to bear in interpreting it that cannot be fully and apodictically derived internally from the text itself in any straightforward way. The questions that are foremost in Rahner's mind are, first, whether the theology is adequate to the sorts of experience that Ignatius believed would be educed (with God's grace, to be sure) by these exercises, however cryptically and elusively they are described, and, second, whether the theology can make these experiences a resource for us today, in a different context than Ignatius's. Rahner was convinced that the regnant theologies of his day were not up to this work. Making the paradigm shift needed to mend this problem required the kind of innovative reading of Ignatius that Rahner had carried out with respect to Aquinas. This does not give a license for ignoring the historical details altogether, and if one's grasp of the details is flawed, that will destabilize the interpretation, but it nonetheless remains that a reading of this sort will necessarily "go beyond" what a construction of "the Ignatius of history" will allow.

However, Endean seems to me correct in asserting that Rahner did not need to make some of these claims (rendered dubious by closer attention to the texts) in order to make his basic point.[141] Rahner's point is that there are moments in experience when the object, the material content of what I grasp in knowledge and freedom as I commit myself to a particular option, recedes into the background, and what one feels most powerfully—and in a way that cannot be explained by an affective response proportional to that option itself—is the "more" that is drawing one forward, carrying one toward an ineffable but fulfilling horizon. Furthermore, with time and practice, and sage counsel, one can learn to detect this root experience as it is present in less dramatic forms, when the goodness or "fitness" of the particular choice is more prominent but still does not completely explain why one is drawn to it. This gives Rahner what he needs to present resources to a Christianity that was facing "the end of the modern age," so that it can continue to present the gospel. And Ignatius was for him the indispensable resource for doing so.

The Dependence on Ignatian Spirituality Thematized

In the 1960s, Rahner's energies were taken up with helping to implement in theology the new vision of the Church and of Christian life in the world that had been the great accomplishment of Vatican II. Much of his time was taken in editing several major encyclopedias and dictionaries of theology, not to mention writing many of their entries. He deepened his views on the historicity of the church and of theology, in part because of his dialogue with Marxism and its philosophy of history. He did take up themes in spirituality, broadly considered. Yet he did not write as focally on Ignatian spirituality.[142] In the mid-1970s, he returned to Ignatian spirituality. It was at this time that he made the claim for the preeminent significance in his thought of "the spirituality of Ignatius himself." It seems plausible to speculate that as he neared the end of his life, Rahner naturally felt the need to make some sense of five decades of intense yet also wide-ranging theological labors. Perhaps he also wanted to have some control over how his thought was received after his death. Rahner never doubted his own vocation to the Society of Jesus, and so it is no surprise too that he would connect the two features that together so defined his life, from early adulthood on: being a Jesuit and being a theologian. Finally, he may also have been responding positively to the claim made by some of his students that Ignatian spirituality offered a key to his work.[143]

Whatever the reason, Rahner returned to Ignatian spirituality in the 1970s. The primary development one notices is an even tighter linking of concerns and investigations that had engaged Rahner's energies from the 1920s into the 50s. First, Rahner becomes more emphatic and overt in using mystical, indeed apophatic, discourse to describe the core of Ignatian spirituality. There is, second, an even stronger reassertion of the importance of the "root experiences" of Ignatian spirituality—rendered apophatically, as it were—to Rahner's theological proposal for a way forward under the increasingly difficult conditions of late modernity. Finally, as the one new feature in his late reflections on Ignatius, Rahner comes to assert the necessity in and for the Society of Jesus of a more radical and literal imitation of the poor and humble Jesus.

The Immediate Experience of God

In his later work, Rahner came to stress more and more strongly that the distinctive feature of Ignatian spirituality was the "direct (that is, unmediated) experience of God." This is *the* theme in the essay that Rahner called his "theological legacy": "Saint Ignatius of Loyola Speaks to a Jesuit Today." Over and over again Rahner has Ignatius say to contemporary Jesuits: "I was convinced that I had experienced God immediately."[144] Rahner has Ignatius insist that bringing men and women to this kind of experience is the core of their mission as Jesuits. Moreover, when he describes this experience his language is strikingly apophatic. Take this passage, for instance:

> If you were not to help [men and women] finally to let go of every conceptual certainty and particular insight, in a trusting fall into that inconceivability in which there are no longer any paths, if you were not to help bring this about in the deepest, most frightening hopelessness of life, as well as in the measurelessness of love and of joy, and then radically and definitively in death (with the Jesus dying forsaken by God), then in all of your so-called pastoral work

and missionary tasks you would have forgotten or betrayed my "spirituality."[145]

In a somewhat later essay titled "Christmas in the Light of the Exercises," Rahner begins with indifference, as he almost always did when giving the essential elements of Ignatian spirituality. Then he moves rapidly to define it in terms of another description of the "immediate experience of God," one that is robustly apophatic:

> Indifference and freedom, as one and the same thing, describe that infinite and open space in which God Godself, not represented by anything finite, becomes the event of our existence. To be sure, this still happens in emptiness and darkness, in the muteness and silent adoration of that ineffable mystery which shelters us namelessly in its infinitude without giving us a place from which we would be able to settle down to survey the whole.[146]

Rahner goes on here to cite two well-known essays that he wrote toward the end of his life having to do with the incomprehensibility of God.[147] A number of Rahner scholars have noted that toward the end of his life he turned increasingly to apophatic images and strategies for naming God.[148] As valid as this observation is, it should not be forgotten that he had begun his theological career with studies in mystical theology. This work culminated with a study of "spiritual touch" in Bonaventure, which Rahner argued was another name for "ecstasy."[149] Rahner was concerned to distinguish "ecstasy" in Bonaventure, as the highest point of mystical experience, from the unmediated vision of God that is confined to the afterlife, on the one hand, and from the mediated experience of God through God's effects (including the effects of grace within the soul), on the other.[150] Rahner's reading of Bonaventure from the 1920s and 30s was that the Seraphic Doctor held a view of ecstasy that entailed a union with God at a point that Bonaventure called the *apex affectus* and that Rahner describes as a "ground of the soul" that is prior to the intellect and the will, but from which intellect and will proceed as the soul's actualizations. With that anthropological precision established, Rahner concludes that "ecstasy does not involve the intellect at all. This explains why mystical union is an entry into darkness, into a divine obscurity."[151] Rahner argues that this teaching of Bonaventure's influenced the German mystics (he names Eckhart), and that it was known at least to Ignatius's early companions, even if one cannot demonstrate its presence in Ignatius himself.[152]

Toward the end of his life, then, Rahner was continuing to take up language first forged in his early work on patristic and medieval Christian mysticism. But now the philosophical and theological anthropology that he had worked on in tandem with his work in the history of spirituality had come to maturation, and provided warrants for the claim that this sort of presence of God to the ground of the soul was not a relatively rare phenomenon reserved to a select few, but a constitutive (if tacit and usually unnoted) feature of graced human existence as such. Moreover, in his early work Rahner had associated Ignatian spiritual experience with this mystical tradition. In the 1950s, he came to see Ignatius thus contextualized as a resource for the church at the end of the modern age. As we have seen, he went on to elaborate the Ignatian variant of this mystical tradition further in terms of Ignatius's teachings on discernment. It is in negotiating those decisions and dealings with the world that most matter to us, and for which standard modes of ethical deliberation fall short, that we can and should (with Ignatius's help) rely on and experience the sort of presence to God that the earlier tradition had tended to reserve to those who strove as far as possible to remove themselves from the distracting concerns of "Martha's part" in order to find "the one thing necessary" with Mary (Luke 10:41–42). This had been Ignatius's core insight, on Rahner's reading, and the purpose of the *Spiritual Exercises*. Ignatius was a mystic of everyday life. Rahner's insistence on both parts of this claim, that Ignatius really was a *mystic* and that his was a mysticism available in *everyday* life, particularly as this everyday life is fraught with distinctively modern dilemmas for the Christian subject,[153] makes Rahner one of the premier "democratizers of mysticism" in the twentieth century.

Ignatius as Paradigm and as Warrant for Theology

At several points in the 1970s, Rahner reaffirmed the relevance of Ignatian spirituality for our times, now not only for the construction of an "existentiel ethics," but for the work of fundamental theology and, even more, for the viability of Christian faith as such. In an interview in 1978,

Rahner was asked about meaning and significance of the "immediate experience of God" mediated by the Spiritual Exercises. He responded as follows:

> I am convinced that immediacy of this kind between God and the person is more important today than ever. In this secularized and pluralistic society, all of the social supports for religion have ceased; they have withered away. If there is nonetheless to be genuine piety, then it cannot keep itself healthy and strong by means of external aids, not even those proper to the church, not even of a sacramental sort—taken directly and exclusively in themselves. Rather, this can only happen by means of a final, unmediated encounter of the person with God.[154]

He goes on to repeat his oft-quoted assertion: "The Christian of the future will be a mystic or there won't be any."[155] Rahner was not given to hyperbole; thus, his statement that this kind of experience cannot be provided even by the sacraments on their own betokens the unparalleled significance with which he had come to invest it. He does not discount sacraments or other mediations of the institutional Church. He compares them to an external irrigation system for delivering water to the soil of the heart; he likens the immediate experience of God to a deep well, from which water wells up "from within."[156] The two are mutually complementary; each needs the other:

> Obviously these two realities mutually determine one another. Every call from the outside in the name of God (another image) only aims at making the inner self-address of God clearer. The latter, in turn, needs that call to be made in some sort of earthly form, even if this can be much more varied and more modest than your theologians have been accustomed to allow, even if this kind of call from without, a call to responsibility, to love and fidelity, to selfless commitment for freedom and justice in society, would probably sound a lot more worldly than your theologians would like. But I will stubbornly insist again and again on this point: this kind of external indoctrination and imperative, these kinds of external conductors of grace, are finally only useful when they meet up with the ultimate grace from within.[157]

The modern condition, defined by atheism, secularization, and pluralism, makes it more essential than ever that the mediation of grace provided by institutional structures of religion be complemented by the inner, unmediated experience of grace. Rahner makes it clear that, when accompanied by this experience, even the deathly stillness being disseminated by atheism can be recognized as a stillness that "speaks of God once again."[158] This recalls the option he had identified in the essay on Heidegger, and which Guardini had identified in his own reflections on faith's prospects: the coming age of modern humankind can be the occasion either of the most profound godlessness or of the most radical religiosity. The key, in Rahner's view, is the kind of experience found at the core of Ignatian spirituality.

If the viability of Christian faith in the future depends on Christians becoming mystics (in the specific way that Rahner had elaborated from his work on Ignatius), then this could not but have consequences for theology. In the 1950s, Rahner had argued that theological ethics needed to turn to saints such as Ignatius of Loyola in order to create an ethics adequate to the modern age. In an essay published in 1972, he argued in a similar vein with respect to fundamental theology.[159] Fundamental theology is charged with reflecting systematically on the grounds on which Christian faith can be credible and can make claims on us (precisely as rational and free beings, and not otherwise). Yet, in Rahner's view, it had become chronically evident in modernity that any possible evidence and arguments that reason could marshal fell far short of the evidentiary force required to justify a commitment with the scope and gravity of the act of faith. Or, perhaps more accurately, the degree to which they fell short (and perhaps finally cannot but fall short) was being felt far more acutely than in the past. Fundamental theology can no longer rely tacitly (as it had in the past) on the more or less taken-for-granted meaningfulness of Christianity conferred on it by the institutions, social practices, and worldview of a culturally homogenous "Christian" society. Nor can any one theologian master all of the disciplines that would be necessary to respond on a case-by-case basis to the vast array of challenges that the modern situation raises for Christian faith: from the challenge of historical-critical methodology to New Testament accounts of Jesus, to the problems raised by modern cosmology and evolutionary biology and psychology, to philosophical attacks raised now from diverse points within a multitude of philosophical frameworks, to the challenges raised by the other world religions. What is the way forward?

Rahner is certainly comfortable with an approach that would focus far more than previously on the role of grace and the illumination of the Holy Spirit in the decision of faith, but he maintains that it is still incumbent on such an approach to provide criteria for determining when one can assert that these are present in one's experience and give an account of how they interact with the structures of the knowing, willing subject in such a way that the decision of faith is not an abrogation or end run around these structures, but their fulfillment. This was precisely the sort of dilemma in response to which Rahner had adduced Ignatian discernment in the 1950s: how to approach a decision of great moment for a person that was at the same time underdetermined by the canons of a rationally deductive method. Expanding or extending the purview of the authority of Ignatius for theology, Rahner contends that what is required of fundamental theology is that it attend more carefully to those saints (and Ignatius clearly ranks highly among them) who explored this kind of experience and reflected methodologically on it (even if "practically," that is, with a view to providing exercises that would inculcate it and help one draw on it for one's faith life). Such theological appropriation can provide crucial starting points for fundamental theology's "new task" in a post-Christian world.

Rahner complains once again that Jesuit theologians have not picked up on this.[160] The problem is that Jesuit theologians (and others too, presumably) have at most looked upon Ignatius as a holy man and an important figure in the history of the Church, but not as "a central figure in the intellectual history [*Geistesgeschichte*] at the beginnings of modernity."[161] This brings us back to Rahner's evaluation of Ignatius's place and importance in history.

Ignatius and Modernity—and Beyond

In the 1970s, Rahner becomes quite unequivocal about the place of Ignatius at the origins of modernity: "Saint Ignatius' Exercises are a decisive co-cause and a fundamental document of the church's modern age, which corresponds to the modern age of the West even if it has its own specific character. The Exercises have helped to bring something really new into the church, something that, in our situation at 'the end of the modern age,' has both passed away in a specific way while at the same time continued on."[162]

Again we have the talk of "the end of the modern age." Rahner's discussion of modernity and its ending is still heavily indebted to Guardini's reflections. The discovery of the individual is integral to the modern age. What the *Spiritual Exercises* facilitated was a Christian, ecclesial recognition of the uniqueness and autonomy of the subject, a recognition that was gaining momentum in European culture at the time, and which was already beginning to destabilize the taken-for-granted sacred and secular hierarchies of the medieval synthesis. This was done, in Rahner's view, by tacitly identifying this subjectivity with "a transcendental subjectivity, which is also—as we of course have to add—elevated and radicalized by grace, where grace has to be understood as anything but something simply universal, but rather must be understood as the immediacy of God to the always-unique subject as such."[163] This allows the Church to affirm and appropriate the modern "turn to the subject," but to do so on its own terms (with a tradition that, as we have seen, Rahner believed could be traced back not just to Aquinas but also to Bonaventure and through him into the patristic period). What this set of claims indicates is that Rahner's theology can be described in terms of the "turn to the subject" only if we recognize that it is a "turn" against a theory and praxis of subjectivity that is closed in on itself. Ignatian spirituality is the crucial resource for Rahner's appropriation by transformation or even transgression of the modern subject.

Like Guardini, Rahner believed that modernity was coming to a close. As symptoms of this he cited (again, echoing Guardini) the ascendancy of "mass man." The "postmodern" age coming into existence was characterized by a search for "higher forms for the socialization of human beings, in which the dignity and value of the individual are reconciled both with his or her sociality and with those necessities which human survival, today and tomorrow, lays upon them."[164] He adverts to a historical struggle over which form this "new sociality" will take, probably with the Cold War and the conflict between communism and neoliberalism in mind. He worries (as had Guardini) that these new social forms will submerge the individual, and he promotes the *Spiritual Exercises* as a way of preserving, in an authentically and indispensably Christian form, the novel modern discovery of the subject, suitably circumscribed, of course. This explains, perhaps, his general lack of enthusiasm for modifications of the Exercises, particularly those that did away with the element of solitary prayer in the Ignatian retreat.[165]

Does this mean that Ignatian spirituality can be at most a vehicle for preserving an indispensable achievement of Western culture and the church in an age that has more or less come to an end? In an intriguing line of argument that he does not develop in detail, Rahner gestures in a new direction. As we have seen, for Rahner the new age being born is one characterized by a search "for higher forms of social structure" that seek to reconcile on a global scale the dignity of the individual and human beings' essentially social character.[166] This is reflected in the Church by the increasingly insistent demand for new ways of thinking and acting in the Church that articulate its normative social character, not just in the institutional hierarchy but in other forms of communal life. Rahner mentions the base Christian community movement in Latin America and movements seeking more democracy in the Church.[167] He sees in this general movement a way of contextualizing and evaluating innovative approaches toward giving the Spiritual Exercises in and for groups, approaches about which he otherwise showed himself to be rather skeptical. He notes that Ignatius was not just the individual author of the *Spiritual Exercises*, but the founder of a religious order, in community with his other early companions. "He knew and practised the 'deliberatio communitaria' with his companions (deliberations not only *in* the group but *of* the group), where the logic of existential choice was to apply and operate for the group as a whole."[168] Rahner extrapolates from this to suggest that Ignatius might offer a way for local communities to address important decisions facing them, a way that would involve a logic that "is basically 'mystical' and leads therefore to the self-realization of a Christian community and thus to the self-realization of the Church. We would hold that an entirely new form of ecclesial self-realization is here being proposed, but that despite its novelty it is just as legitimate as the self-realization of the Church in the activities of the hierarchy or in the liturgical community."[169]

The analogy Rahner is deploying would seem to run something like this. The "modern age" was defined by the emergence of the autonomy of the individual with unparalleled depth and force. This brought with it the challenge of securing a meaningful framework and methodology for life-defining individual choices once the taken-for-granted normativity of social-cultural institutions and the hierarchies of values they represent had been relativized by the "turn to the subject." Ignatius offered a way for the Church to respond creatively to this development, appropriating the "existentiality" of the modern subject as another mode in which the grace of God's self-gift could be experienced. With the modern age coming to an end, it is the sociality of the person that is coming increasingly to the fore, with the concomitant search for social structures in society and Church that respect and give full play to this sociality. One challenge this represents (as Guardini had already noted) is that the inalienable responsibility of the individual, before his or her fellow humans and, ultimately, before God, is being attenuated by the rise of "mass man." For this reason Rahner insists to the end of his life that the sort of solitary encounter articulated by Ignatius, in which God deals "directly" with the individual person, is a permanent and indispensable achievement that Ignatian spirituality has bequeathed to the Church. A second challenge comes when the local ecclesial community takes seriously its responsibility to actualize the Church in its specific time and place, particularly in the choices it makes. It cannot simply follow directives from the hierarchy above it, because of the underivable specificity of its situation, and it is thus in the same situation vis-á-vis normative traditions as the modern subject. Rahner suggests that, *mutatis mutandis*, the same sort of presence of God to the individual making a choice could be available to the community. Moreover, just as the individual would actualize his or her innermost essence and telos for graced union with God in the dynamics of Ignatian discernment, particularly as these structured a stance of "finding God in all things" with regard to all of creation, so the local community would actualize its innermost essence and telos: in this kind of *deliberatio communitaria* it would "be" and "become" church in a way that is different from but not inferior to its self-actualization in the Eucharist. This "both/and" of external markers and supports for ecclesial self-realization, on the one hand, and mystical ones that appeal to a kind of "communal interiority," on the other, is similar to the complementarity already noted in Rahner's positing of the "external irrigation systems" of sacrament and catechesis, on the one hand, and the interior-spiritual well of grace, on the other.[170] He hints, finally, that Ignatius himself was aware of this, particularly in his dealings with the nascent Society of Jesus. This direction would constitute a contribution of Ignatian spirituality to "postmodernity," and would apparently warrant some innovations (while never discounting the ongoing validity of the "traditional" Ignatian retreat and the needs to which it responds).

This clearly takes us into Rahner's ecclesiology, the exploration of which goes beyond the scope of this chapter. His suggestion that there could be another form of the Church's self-actualization alongside the Eucharist is clearly a radical one, but it just as clearly parallels his equally radical position that the individual union with God facilitated by the Exercises is just as important as that union instantiated in the sacraments, including the Eucharist. It is also clear that the "*mutatis mutandis*" gestures toward an expansive terrain that Rahner leaves virtually unexplored. As we have seen, on Rahner's reading, theology has the task of providing a structure within which to identify, investigate, and integrate into broader philosophical and theological discourses the fundamental principles of the kind of experience that "the saint" makes available, a task that had occupied a large part of his work with regard to the "experiences" of Ignatian indifference, discernment, and finding God in all things. To the extent, however, that he worked this out in the context of the irreducibly unique individual and his or her graced transcendence unto God, it is not immediately evident how he could extend that treatment in order to determine a "first principle" of the kind of communal discernment that he seems to be reaching for here. The unmediated experience of God that is at the core of discernment, consolation, and finding God in all things is finally incommunicable and nontransferable; at best one can lead another toward it, always ready, like a good director of the Spiritual Exercises, to leave the individual and God to their unmediated communion, as the fifteenth annotation of the *Exercises* states. The penultimate status of human historicity and sociality, noted by Johann Baptist Metz and Philip Endean, among others, makes it difficult to see how Rahner could make good on this *mutatis mutandis*.

Leaving aside the issue of whether or how this move toward communal discernment could be legitimated, it does bring us to one final theme in Rahner's appropriation of Ignatian spirituality. In a homily on Ignatius that Rahner gave to the Jesuit community in Innsbruck on July 31, 1978 (the saint's feast day), he argues that the contemporary Society of Jesus has lost sight of Ignatius's desire that his followers be materially poor and, perhaps, more important or more comprehensive, that they be "marginal," particularly with respect to the official Church.[171] This point is also found in the contemporaneous essay "Ignatius of Loyola Speaks to a Jesuit Today."[172] On the one hand, Rahner connects this "will to marginality" with the homelessness and sense of detachment from inner-worldly structures of power and value (even ecclesial ones) that come with Ignatian indifference—a motif that goes all the way back to the 1937 essay.[173] On the other hand, he seems to suggest that it should be a particular trait of the Society of Jesus, as an inner-ecclesial community, part of whose function is to "institutionalize" marginality within the institution, with all the paradoxes this brings. Rahner also mentions here an embrace of material poverty and marginality that comes from a love of Jesus and a desire to be in union with him even in the concrete conditions of his life, a motif that is not as present in the earlier works.[174] This pulls Rahner away from the meditations that center directly on indifference or discernment, and into the substance of the Second Week meditations, in which one prays precisely for this kind of desire simply to know Jesus and imitate him.

It may be here that Rahner was responding to the writings of his student, friend, and younger colleague Johann Baptist Metz, who advocated this kind of marginality and a radical, "foolish" imitation of Jesus, as the key contribution and mission of religious life today.[175] Rahner may have also been reacting to the call of the Jesuits' 32nd General Congregation (1975–76), which reoriented Jesuit apostolates toward the service of justice and called Jesuits to a deeper commitment to the marginalized.[176] This was a decision that brought no little controversy within the Society and critique from the outside.[177] It is intriguing to speculate that the drama of this *corporate* decision on the part of the Jesuits explains in part Rahner's move into discussing the resources that Ignatian spirituality might offer for corporate decision-making, as we just discussed. In any event, Rahner clearly supports this decision for marginality, but he does so ultimately as arising from a foolish love for Jesus, rather than from any sociopolitical agenda.[178] Minimally, then, Rahner was complementing the "ontic marginality" that follows naturally from the "ontological marginality" that he had first explored with his reflections in the 1930s with a marginality that comes from a radical love and imitation of the Jesus whose career was in fact marked by marginality and a commitment to the marginalized. These two motifs run in parallel in these later essays, and Rahner does not connect them in a more systematic way, leaving only tantalizing hints for how that might be done, if at all.

Finding God in All Things in a Secularized World

"I think that the spirituality of Ignatius himself, which one learned through the practice of prayer and religious formation, was more significant for me than all learned philosophy and theology inside and outside the order."[179] On any objective measure, Rahner did not write a great deal on Ignatius (say, in comparison with his writings that center on Aquinas). Often what he says about Ignatius seems to reflect more his analysis of the mystical tradition that culminates in Bonaventure. If we take Rahner at his word, what could this statement uttered at the end of his life mean? My argument has been that, these reservations notwithstanding, the relationship between theology and spirituality that emerges from the foregoing story is complex, to be sure, but forefronts the centrality of Ignatian spirituality for understanding Rahner's thought. Perhaps we could say that Ignatian spirituality was causal more in the way of being a "final causal" than as a material or effective cause. Rahner did not center his career on writing about Ignatius; neither was every essay directly "caused" by some concern in Ignatian spirituality (even though some were). My argument, rather, has been that a theology adequate to what Rahner took to be the essence of Ignatian spirituality—mapped by the concepts of indifference, discernment, and finding God in all things—was always a crucial telos for Rahner's work. And though we cannot know the degree to which this teleological attraction was fed by Rahner's own spiritual experience, we *can* say that it was nourished by Rahner's growing conviction that Ignatius offered something crucial to the church "at the end of the modern age."

This account offers an important corrective to a common narrative of Rahner's intellectual development, one that begins by recounting his philosophical work in *Spirit in the World*, but fails to give due weight to his work on patristic and medieval spirituality. As recent work by Zahlauer and Endean, among others, has made clear, his early research in both philosophical theology and the history of spirituality was characterized by a concern to give a more adequate account of human subjectivity and our presence to the world and to God than was possible with the categories of neoscholastic philosophy and theology. The two sides of this search were mutually fructifying. The work in the history and theology of mysticism provided precedents and warrants; the work in fundamental theology provided a possible conceptuality for translating those precedents to make them productive today. If, in other words, the transcendental Thomism worked out by Rousellot and Maréchal, together with key motifs from Heidegger's existential phenomenology, provided categories and argumentative strategies out of which Rahner constructed his theology, it was the "experience of grace" that defined the kind of experience, the particular actualization of human subjectivity, that Rahner took to be the ultimate test case for the adequacy of the account he was looking for, and thus led him to nuance or even (in Heidegger's case, and to some extent, Maréchal too) to disagree with these sources.

It is also evident that Rahner believed Ignatius to stand in continuity with the tradition of "spiritual touch" that he had worked on in patristic and medieval mystical theology. Karl and Hugo Rahner were a part of a broader movement of Jesuit historians and theologians who were just beginning to make the case for Ignatius the mystic, which meant locating him in the great strands of Christian mystical prayer and theology. Moreover, in Rahner's view an important part of making that case was giving an alternative account of mystical experience.[180] That he saw this task to be connected with the other (giving a more adequate account of the "experience of grace") is evident from his emendation of the 1937 essay on Ignatius for republication in 1956. By that time, too, he had discovered the historicity of Ignatian spirituality, and had become even more convinced of its importance for the church, and European culture as a whole, facing "the end of the modern age." The mutual interrogation of Ignatian spirituality and transcendental theology are evident in the essays from the 1950s, particularly as Rahner stretched his theological epistemology and anthropology to the breaking point to talk about the "consolation without prior cause." This "stretch" was a necessary part of Rahner's project of confronting the conditions of modernity as they had been articulated in different ways by Heidegger and Guardini, in particular. It was, in other words, his way of conducting what Johann Baptist Metz has described as Rahner's signal contribution to modern theology: "the attempt to appropriate the heritage of the classical patristic and scholastic traditions precisely by means of a productive and aggressive dialogue with the challenges of the modern European world: the discovery of subjectivity as a crisis for classical metaphysics, and the critical-productive confrontation with Kant, German Idealism and Existentialism, on the one hand, and with the processes of secularization and scientific civilization, on the other."[181]

For Rahner, Ignatius's life and the spiritual exercises he left behind at modernity's beginnings were evidence that it was possible to *live* this dialogue in modernity's twilight and beyond. But this requires that theologians now *think* the dialogue out more radically and thoroughly than they had in the past. Thinking through Ignatius's way theologically meant nuancing or discarding categories and arguments that prevented him from appearing as both the mystic and the pivotal figure in European intellectual history that, by the 1970s, Rahner had become convinced he was. For Rahner, then, Ignatius not only offered *encouragement* that it is possible to live faithfully and to think theologically on modernity's terrain but also some direction on how to do so both productively and aggressively, neither rejecting modernity tout court nor capitulating to it.

The primary front on which Rahner carried on this engagement with modernity concerned the radical reflexivity of the modern experience of subjectivity, which had destabilized taken-for-granted hierarchies of the sacred and frameworks for ascertaining the presence of the traditional transcendentals: the true, the good, and the beautiful. As I argued in chapter 1, using Charles Taylor's work, this shift made possible the "affirmation of everyday life." This is surely one of modernity's gains, but it also necessitates the kind of continual self-surveillance and ongoing construction and maintenance of identity that has made late modernity not only an age of anxiety but also such a ready market for "spirituality." This is a more ambivalent heritage. Rahner reconfigured this modern sense of subjectivity within a framework that complemented "indifference" with its flowering in "finding (the always ever-greater) God in all things." This framework is worked out and warranted by assertions about the relationship between God and the world drawn from a theology of creation, grace, and revelation. Yet, it is also warranted by the experience of God's dealings with the person "without mediation," which Rahner understood to be at the heart of Ignatian spirituality. One can look at this experience, which is the experience of consolation, as occupying the same place in Rahner's system as "anxiety" in the early Heidegger. It discloses a world "re-sacramentalized," as always already potentially transparent to the God who is its ground and, even more, gives Godself radically into and in this world, in a way unique to each individual. This "re-sacramentalization" can be achieved (or, better, perceived and received) even in an age that is witnessing the deconstruction or destabilization of the social and cultural institutions of a homogenous Christian milieu by modern processes of secularization.

Toward the end of his life, Rahner began to gesture toward other possible contributions of Ignatian spirituality to modern faith and theology, particularly in enabling different *corporate* actualizations of Christian faith in local ecclesial communities. There are also hints that he realized that one would have to broaden the field of view of Ignatian spirituality in order to work these out: moving beyond the *Spiritual Exercises* or perhaps looking at them in a different light. Indeed, when one looks at the elements of Ignatian spirituality on which Rahner builds, one is struck by how much they come from its Neoplatonic roots. Rahner constructs his interpretation of Ignatian spirituality as a dialogue-partner for theology from three major components of the *Spiritual Exercises*: the Principle and Foundation, the Rules for the Discernment of Spirit, and the Contemplation to Attain Love. He early made a connection between Ignatian spirituality and Christian Neoplatonism, as represented by the tradition that culminates in Bonaventure, in particular. This also opened a path for him when he became more explicit and focused on the centrality of the apophatic element of Christian faith and theology. As he made this move in his theology, he emphasized the Neoplatonic elements in Ignatian spirituality even more, another instance of how Rahner's theological development goes hand in hand with his understanding of Ignatian spirituality.

What is *not* present in Rahner's interpretation of Ignatius is the other important medieval stream identified in chapter 3: the "mysticism of the historical event." Rahner is certainly aware of the historical character of many of the exercises. In his 1937 essay, Rahner takes as one of the two fundamental characteristics of Ignatian spirituality that "the God of Ignatian piety is the God of supramundane grace who deals with man freely and personally, and 'historically.'"[182] Yet, as the argument unfolds, it is clear that "historically" adds little to "freely" and "personally."[183] It is another way of distinguishing a mode of God's interaction with the individual from that mode mediated by God's effects in the created order. The meditations on Jesus's life are mentioned, but the center of gravity remains the "direct" dealing of God with the person, and its priority over those dealings mediated by creation and the concrete events in history (including the events of Jesus's life in first-century Galilee and Judaea). This repeats itself in Rahner's lectures on the *Spiritual Exercises*, even though he evinces here an awareness of a greater potential in focusing on the Christocentric, indeed, "Jesucentric," meditations of the Second Week. Rahner tells his listeners that "I can only meet Him [the Lord] when I know by means of a real anamnesis of an ecclesial-sacramental and contemplative-existential kind that He is the one Who lived in Palestine in his own age."[184] Earlier, talking of the Call of the King, Rahner states that "God's relationship to the world is not a reign that absolutely transcends metaphysical time and space, so to speak; rather it is history, in which God participates through his Son, who has become human."[185] Rahner asserts, correctly, that the following of Christ that Ignatius has in mind is not a matter of making oneself a clone of the first-century Nazarean, but of "allowing the inner structure of His life to work itself out in new and different personal situations."[186] There are certainly, on Rahner's reading, some "basic traits" or "universally valid principles" that have to be taken into account for one who wants to follow Christ, yet, when Rahner enumerates these, he works for the most part from principles he had already worked out in interpreting the Principle and Foundation and the fundamental anthropological-mystical structure of indifference, rather than from an examination of the Jesus disclosed by the scripturally framed meditations of the Second Week.[187] It is true that Rahner gestures toward a more Christologically rooted understanding of "contemplation in action," in which one is called and empowered to recapitulate in one's own circumstances what happened in Jesus. Yet, on balance, it must be said that these gestures are not integrated into the more fully elaborated account of discernment and finding God in all things that is based on principles drawn from Rahner's theology of revelation and of grace. Neither do they appear in any substantive way after the mid-1950s.[188]

If Rahner was aware on some level of the elements of Ignatian spirituality that I have discussed under the rubric of the "mysticism of the historical event," he did not follow them very far. He was predisposed by his study of Neoplatonic streams within patristic and medieval spirituality to understand Ignatius on those terms, and the philosophical conceptuality he learned from Rousselot, Maréchal, and Heidegger, with its own very strong affinities with the Christian Neoplatonic mystical tradition, did not induce him to do otherwise.[189] It may be that toward the end of his life he became aware of the need for a retrieval of Ignatian spirituality that would attend more to different resources, particularly for making a communal decision, and for taking Jesus's "marginality" in history (as a social category) more seriously than his "everydayness" and "unremarkableness." He himself did not embark on that retrieval. Whether or how his approach could be emended or expanded to achieve it remains an open question.

What I have tried to show in this chapter is that one cannot understand Rahner's theological itinerary without taking into account the role that Ignatian spirituality played for him as a kind of "final cause" for his theological labors. Arno Zahlauer has aptly called Ignatius a "productive exemplar" for Rahner's thought.[190] I have argued that when Rahner says that "the spirituality of Ignatius himself, which one learned through the practice of prayer and religious formation, was more significant for me than all learned philosophy and theology inside and outside the order,"[191] it is because Ignatius and the spirituality he crafted gave for Rahner an example of and warrant for Christian life under the unique and uniquely challenging conditions of late modernity. Corresponding to this life—which must necessarily be a life empowered by the presence of the God of Jesus, experienced and embraced in the world—is a way of thinking, of doing theology, which depends upon and exploits the particular way that this presence is manifest. The particular way this presence was manifest for Rahner was defined by Ignatius, and the sense of presence, thus structured, formed the root and wellspring of Rahner's theological imagination. This experience was so vital for Rahner that he became convinced that there could only continue to be Christians in the modern, or "postmodern" world, if they had something like this experience, even if it were not articulated in explicitly Ignatian terms—that is, if they became mystics, in an Ignatian register. One suspects that on Rahner's reading, lacking this re-sacramentalization of a world become secular, enabled by something like the Ignatian practices of indifference and finding God in all things, the formal-institutional structures (including the formal sacraments) by which the Church in the past actualized this more primordial sacramentality, would increasingly wither and die away.

This does not mean that Rahner thought that everyone should become Jesuits or be formed by Ignatian spirituality.[192] Far from it. Yet, he clearly thought that Ignatian spirituality isolated and transmitted a way of experiencing God that was particularly important for a world that, however "postmodern" it became, would continue to move in the ambit of modernity's "*Wirkungsgeschichte*," would continue to be a history as markedly formed by modernity as it is by the Greeks and by the patristic and medieval synthesis of the Jewish-Christian and Greek spirits. In the light of this experience, one could continue to live with integrity and hope in a world that in so many ways appeared to be godforsaken and God-forsaking. It is this that informs Rahner's "optimism" about the modern world and his openness to dialogue with it.[193] He sought to reformulate theology to conform with that optimism. It is in this way that Rahner carried on as a theologian the creative encounter with culture—in this case, primarily the intellectual culture of late modernity—that was a hallmark of the first generations of Jesuits, and that has its roots in Ignatian spirituality. It is also this that warrants the judgment that Rahner must be counted among the most creative and influential "Ignatian theologians" of the twentieth century.

CHAPTER FIVE

Ignacio Ellacuría
Theology under the Standard of Christ

Introduction: Making Theology Latin American and Ignatian

In early December 1969, a thirty-nine-year-old Jesuit named Ignacio Ellacuría delivered a series of talks to the members of the Society of Jesus in Central America in what would be a defining moment for him and for the Central American Vice Province.[1] He argued two complementary claims. First, he asserted that the institutions and programs of the Central American Jesuits should be reshaped in order to respond directly to the social and political challenges in Latin America. This was, he contended, not a deviation from their charism as Jesuits, but the most apt way of rediscovering and incarnating its heart, as defined by the *Spiritual Exercises*. "The Third World," he said, "demands that we incarnate the experience of the *Exercises* right now, and it offers us the best conditions for doing so."[2] If the First Week would have Jesuits attend to the scandal of sin, then what more scandalous instance of sin than the dehumanizing poverty and injustice so prevalent in the Third World? If the Second Week is meant to build on a natural human disposition to commit oneself to a great cause, then what greater cause than helping the people of the Third World in their struggle for liberation from the inhuman living conditions suffered by the vast majority of its peoples and the endemic injustice and violence to which they so often fall victim?[3] Would not this commitment, construed through the lens of the *Exercises*, provide the essential link (essential in particular for a religious order such as the Society of Jesus, committed to working in the world) between a "spiritual" stance oriented toward the transcendent and a "secular" stance oriented toward achieving a better world now?

Second, Ellacuría argued that reconfiguring their commitment in this way would make of the spirit of the *Spiritual Exercises* a vital contribution to Central and South America, where the Society of Jesus had labored for more than four centuries.[4] Would not a witness to the Standard of Christ and the Third Degree of Humility that is concretized socially/institutionally (and not just individually/devotionally) offer to the Third World a desperately needed model for building a more humane society? Would this not fill the need for an alternative to the ultimately unworkable model offered by advocates of "development," with its tacit assumption that the First World is the only or best model? Was not this, finally, the Society of Jesus's proper way of assisting the Church in its mission to the world?[5]

The impact of these talks by Ellacuría, along with the presentations by Miguel Elizondo, Florentino Idoate, and Ricardo Falla, was immediate and dramatic. The Central American Jesuits had been divided over how to respond to the difficult and painful transformation going on in the Latin American Church as a whole in the 1960s. This transformation had been embraced and affirmed at the Second General Meeting of Latin American Bishops at Medellín fifteen months earlier.[6] Just before that, the Jesuit provincials of Latin America had themselves decided to give "absolute priority in our apostolic strategy" to what they called "the social problem of Latin America." Indeed, they pledged "to orient our whole apostolate around it."[7] The younger members of the Society had generally responded with enthusiasm to this call to action. They also reacted with growing impatience to individuals, communities, and institutions that they felt were too slow to change. Older Jesuits, on the other hand, were quick to reject what they perceived as a misplaced zeal that would vitiate what was distinctive to religious life and destroy the work of generations of Jesuits in Latin America. They pointed to the Society's already alarming hemorrhage of membership in the late sixties, and to what they took to be the scandalous secularism infecting the lifestyles of younger Jesuits. These divisions had placed many communities across the continent in virtually open warfare, and the Central American Jesuits were no exception (we turn to Argentina in the next chapter). This was the situation that brought the embattled provincial, Segundo Azcue, to charge Ellacuría and Javier Llasera, a member of the province staff, with planning a province retreat to help heal divisions and chart a path into the future. Ellacuría recruited Miguel Elizondo, who had served at one time or another as novice master, provincial, and trusted spiritual director to the Jesuits of Central America. Their plan was simple and dramatic: to re-create on a modest scale the group discernment of Ignatius and his followers that led to their decision to present themselves to the pope as a religious community.[8]

They succeeded in bringing the assembled Jesuits to chart a bold path, even if resistance and divisions persisted. The group of Jesuits present at this retreat committed themselves to the "redemption and liberation" of Central America, to strengthening mutual respect and simplicity of lifestyle in the province, and to deepening a spirit of willingness to put themselves and their institutions at the service of the poor.[9] At a later meeting, in September 1970, the provincial leadership discussed a sociological self-study of the Central American Jesuits and various recommendations for action. It was decided that "our apostolates... should foment attitudes of commitment to the social liberation of our peoples, giving the latter the theological depth of being viewed as an integral part of the redemptive liberation of Jesus Christ."[10] Despite continued resistance on the part of some of the older generation, changes were soon forthcoming in the Jesuits' universities, high schools, and parishes.[11] The backlash was not long in coming. It came from within the Society of Jesus in Central America, from within the Church, and from the Salvadoran ruling elites. It was in the last arena that the reaction most fulfilled Ricardo Falla's warning in 1969 (but perhaps not in the metaphorical sense that he had in mind) that if the Jesuits were to make the option for the poor, they would experience "death and resurrection."[12]

A new novice master, Juan Ramón Moreno, began changing the way young Jesuits were trained, with a greater emphasis on immersion in the particularity of the Central American context, especially among the poor. This shift was supported and deepened by Ellacuría himself, who was put in charge of the program of training Jesuits from novitiate to the pronouncement of final vows.[13] Similar changes were brought to the

Salvadoran major seminary, which was jointly sponsored by the five Salvadoran dioceses, located in the capital of San Salvador, and run by the Jesuits. Rutilio Grande, who was in charge of the spiritual formation and pastoral training of the seminarians, instituted working visits to parishes, emphasizing awareness of the social context of the people there as an integral part of promoting their growth in the faith.[14] This change in an institution that had long resembled a cloister drew criticism from some of the bishops, including the then auxiliary bishop of San Salvador, Oscar Romero. In 1972, the bishops took direction of the seminary away from the Jesuits.[15] In the same year, Romero had written a fiery denunciation in the archdiocesan newspaper of the changes in the curriculum at the Jesuit high school, Externado San José. This led to a painful confrontation with some of the parents and the threat of government investigation. The investigation was averted by a determined effort by Jesuits from both the Externado and from the Jesuit university in San Salvador to defend these changes. The affair died down after a commission appointed by Archbishop Chávez y González exonerated the Jesuits of the charges of Marxist indoctrination and when a vote of all the parents showed overwhelming support.[16]

It was perhaps the changes made at the Jesuit university that brought the most violent response. Founded in the late sixties, the Universidad Centroamericana José Simeon Cañas (UCA) was originally supported by wealthy families in El Salvador horrified by what they saw as the pervasive Marxism of the national university, Universidad de El Salvador. It changed rapidly, not without divisions and vigorous debate, under the influence of a remarkable series of rectors: Luis Achaerandio, SJ (1969–75); Ramón Mayorga, a layman (1975–79); and Ellacuría himself (1979–89). Other important figures included Jesuits Jon Sobrino, Segundo Montes (who came to the UCA after teaching and administration at the Externado San José, a veteran of the 1972 imbroglio there), Francisco Ibisate, and Ignacio Martín Baro, and laypersons such as Italo López Vallecillo, Axel Soderberg, and Guillermo Ungo.[17] Under Ellacuría's editorial leadership from 1976 on, the university's premier journal, *Estudios Centroamericanos* (*ECA*), focused on analyzing the social, economic, and political realities of El Salvador, with authoritative essays by faculty across the university often critical of governmental policy. In 1984, Ellacuría initiated publication of a theological journal to add theological analyses to those provided by *ECA*: the *Revista Latinoamericana de*

Teología. In 1985, a human rights institute (IDHUCA) was founded under Montes's directorship. A year later it was joined by an Institute of Public Opinion (IUDOP), founded and directed by Martín Baró, which produced public opinion surveys pioneering new methods for accurately surveying refugee populations. The high standards of objectivity that these surveys maintained is perhaps indicated by the fact that IUDOP was alternately accused of being a tool of the right and of the left, even though both the right and the left relied on its data![18]

The first bombing came in early 1976, the result, it was thought, of an article in *ECA* by liberation theologian Jon Sobrino, "The Historical Jesus." A more violent bombing came at the end of the year in response to a savage editorial penned by Ellacuría criticizing the government's abandonment of a very modest agrarian reform program in the face of resistance from the wealthy landholding elite.[19] Death threats and violence quickly became a fact of life for the personnel of the UCA, as it did for Jesuits throughout the country.[20]

The first political murder of a Jesuit, however, came not at the UCA but in the parish of Aguilares, to the north of San Salvador. Its pastor, the former seminary professor and spiritual formator Rutilio Grande, had implemented a pastoral plan based on the documents of Medellín and the new directions the Jesuits had set for themselves in 1969. Grande worked very hard to avoid the politicization of parish activities, but he also supported the right of the desperately poor farm laborers of the region to organize and demand more humane working conditions and a living wage from the owners of the region's large sugarcane plantations.[21] He was murdered in March 1977, the first of many priests to be murdered over the coming decades. To these assassinations must be added the murders of hundreds, if not thousands, of lay pastoral workers, and religious women and men, including Archbishop Oscar Romero in March 1980, and four North American women missionaries nine months later.[22]

Throughout the civil war that ignited after Romero's murder, Ellacuría worked tirelessly for a peace with justice, and he made the UCA a platform for producing and disseminating social research and analysis. The UCA made the case that the only solution to the war would be negotiations that addressed the systemic roots of the war. This, Ellacuría contended, was how the university was to make an option for the poor "in a university way."[23] He had begun insisting even earlier that systemic violence traceable to Salvadoran society's gaping economic and political inequalities was the underlying root of both the insurrectionary violence from the left and the retaliatory violence from the right. It was so provocative, indeed dangerous, to say these kinds of things publicly that Ellacuría was twice forced into exile. The first exile lasted from 1977 to 1978, after being refused reentry into the country; the second was from 1980 to 1982, in response to a credible death threat that came not long after Romero's assassination. He was out of the country when the insurgency launched an offensive focused on the capital city in November 1989, which led to military occupation of the UCA. Ellacuría was warned by friends to stay away. He disregarded these warnings in what proved to be a fatal miscalculation of what the Salvadoran military was capable of. In the early hours of November 16, an elite battalion of the Salvadoran defense forces entered the campus and assassinated him along with seven others: Jesuits Ignacio Martín Baró, Segundo Montes, Amando López, Juan Ramón Moreno, Joaquín López y López, and laywomen Elba Ramos and her daughter Celina Ramos. This was the culmination of the decisions made in 1969, following the grim logic that has replayed itself many times in many Latin American countries over the past seven decades.

This brief sketch of two amazing decades in the history of the Jesuits in El Salvador suggests the difference in context between Central Europe, where Karl Rahner spent his career, and Central America. It also reveals in Ellacuría a man passionately committed to social change and a man persuaded that Ignatian spirituality required a change in direction of the Society of Jesus in Latin America. To this change in direction Ellacuría brought formidable intellectual, administrative, and political gifts, which have been investigated elsewhere.[24] The argument of this chapter is that demonstrating the truth of the claims he made at San José de las Montañas Seminary in 1969 was one of the defining foci of Ellacuría's intellectual output during the two decades that followed.

In Ellacuría's efforts to find and legitimate a form of Christian life and theology adequate to the situation he perceived in El Salvador, the *Spiritual Exercises* became a vital resource. In a way that, despite difference in context, bears striking similarities to the development of Rahner's thought, the *Exercises* for Ellacuría came to disclose and frame a form of experience, and outlined a methodology for mining that experience, that was indispensable for the kind of Christian response to "modernity" for which he was searching.

In contrast to Rahner, however, for Ellacuría the feature of modernity that posed the greatest threat to Christian faith (indeed to humanity itself) was modernity's horrific capacity to generate unprecedented levels of systemic injustice, oppression, and suffering. It was modernity's propensity to create entire "crucified peoples," in the terminology that Ellacuría coined to describe them, and this in dialectical opposition to modernity's own self-professed *telos* of freedom, equality, and fraternity among all persons. To the extent that this is a historical phenomenon that entails the dialectical interplay of human freedom and social structures, its analysis (in order to overcome it), whether in philosophy, social theory, or theology, demands a conceptual apparatus that can identify and analyze the character of social and historical processes. It was this, on Ellacuría's reading, that was lacking in Western thought before the birth and development of historical consciousness, itself one of modernity's hallmarks. Ellacuría found in the *Spiritual Exercises* a spirituality with important resources for overcoming this lack.

There are no texts on Ignatius among Ellacuría's early writings, as there are for Rahner, but there is abundant evidence for his engagement with Ignatian spirituality. Indeed, he belongs to the generation of Jesuits who began to reap the fruit of the labors of Rahner's generation to retrieve Ignatian spirituality in its original documents and practices. Thus, his choice to use the *Spiritual Exercises* in 1969 for the province meeting was much more than a strategic decision to enlist Ignatian spirituality in order to generate the consensus around the agenda he and other younger Jesuits were promoting. Our first task is to chart his early development, not only as a Jesuit but as an intellectual who fully embraced philosophy "as a way of life."[25]

After we have established Ellacuría's Jesuit character and provided an overview of his philosophical response to the Salvadoran reality, the next task is to analyze the particular reading of Ignatian spirituality that emerged when he applied this philosophy to Ignatian spirituality. In the course of elucidating this philosophical reading of Ignatian spirituality, however, it will become clear that the interpretive influence goes the other direction too. That is, it is not only the case that Ellacuría's philosophy provides a key to understanding his appropriation and application of Ignatian spirituality, but also that Ignatian spirituality provides an important key for understanding Ellacuría's philosophy and theology. This will be argued in a concluding section.

The Formation of a Contemplative in Action for Justice

A number of biographical facts strongly suggest that Ellacuría was deeply formed, both personally and intellectually, by Ignatian spirituality.[26] He was born in the Basque Country of northeast Spain in 1930. He was schooled by the Jesuits and entered the Society of Jesus in 1947. The next year he was sent to El Salvador with several others in order to start a novitiate there. Their novice master was a remarkable Jesuit named Miguel Elizondo, whom we have already encountered as the man Ellacuría recruited twenty years later to help him with the 1969 province retreat.[27] Ellacuría was later to remark that the foundations of his spirituality were laid by Elizondo.[28]

The young Spaniards had to find their way in a new land and culture, and Elizondo insisted that they adapt to the new rather than cling to the old. This dictum extended to the many details of the highly regimented daily life typical of a religious in Spain but difficult to live out in Central America. When one or another of his charges would recall their prior year in the novitiate in Loyola, with "but in Spain we . . . ," Elizondo's response was "none of that, none of that. We're not in Spain now. Just because something is one way in Spain, it does not have to be the same in El Salvador."[29] Focusing on the foundational documents, the *Spiritual Exercises* and the *Constitutions*, Elizondo laid greater stress on getting to what was essential in Ignatian spirituality than on observing the external details of a particular regional (Iberian) way of living it. Whitfield's closing description of this remarkable novice master and the novitiate he created for the young Jesuits (including Ellacuría) is worth quoting in full:

> Elizondo knew his novices well and set high standards for them. Forty years later he would remember: "I wanted to prepare in them the openness that is necessary for what the future will bring, without ever knowing what the future may be." One of Elizondo's novices— and one who, as a future provincial in Central America, would have reason to appreciate the value of the lesson—would remark that, quite simply, "he taught us not to be afraid."[30]

In sum, the young Basques and Spaniards were not to re-create the Iberian Peninsula in their little house in Santa Tecla. Rather, they were to be attentive to the culture in which they were now living and working. Knowing and appreciating that culture, they were to accommodate their spiritual lives and apostolic practices to its resources and needs. This engagement with the particularities of culture is one of the hallmarks of early Jesuit spirituality, and Elizondo's charges were thoroughly initiated into it.

If his passion for El Salvador and his conviction that spiritual and intellectual practice must be inculturated to that region were born during these initial years, his passion for the world of the mind was awakened during nine years of study, first in Quito, Ecuador (1950–55), and then at Innsbruck (1958–62). From Quito, Ellacuría remembered first and foremost his teacher, Aurelio Espinoza Pólit. Espinoza initiated Ellacuría into the practice of appreciating and engaging a specific cultural reality in its details. Espinoza's teaching was a powerful introduction to the textual articulation of this practice in the humanistic classics of Western culture. The passionate way Espinoza read and taught texts, rooted in his conviction that grappling with classics of the humanistic tradition could disclose the full depths of the human drama, made a lasting impression on Ellacuría. Ellacuría was surely thinking back to his experience in Espinoza's classroom when he (Ellacuría) impatiently dismissed objections from young Jesuits in the 1970s that the life of the mind was irrelevant to the dramatic struggles for liberation transpiring during that violent decade.

The strand of continuity that binds these two phases of Ellacuría's formation is the same humanistic tradition that was so formative for Ignatius and his first companions.[31] As a consequence we will not be surprised to see in Ellacuría's appropriation of Ignatian spirituality the insistence, so typical of the first Jesuits, on moving not just the intellect, but the heart and imagination too. More precisely, for Ellacuría, this developed into an obstinate but intricately elaborated refusal to separate mind from heart, affect from intellect. This refusal was one of the driving motivations behind Ellacuría's intellectual development, one that would fully emerge in his philosophical anthropology and epistemology, developed under the influence of the fourth of Ellacuría's great teachers: Xavier Zubiri.

This philosophical apprenticeship lay seven years in the future, however. In the interim, Ellacuría returned from Quito to teach for three years in the seminary in San Salvador. Subsequently, he was sent to Innsbruck in 1958 for theological training preparatory to ordination. There he studied theology during the exciting years leading up to Vatican II. He identified Rahner as one of the most important teachers and mentors from those years, an important detail for the thesis of this chapter given Rahner's own conviction about the importance of the *Spiritual Exercises* for Christian faith and theology in modernity. Martin Maier has identified three major themes that Ellacuría learned from Rahner and that are pervasive in his later work.[32] First is Rahner's understanding of the relationship between nature and grace. According to Rahner, human beings are by nature constituted with an unrestricted openness to the transcendent that makes them possible recipients of God's self-communication. With the graced elevation of this openness, human experience becomes the place for divine revelation. As Maier shows, this theme is taken up by Ellacuría, but applied within the domain of history. For example, in a late unpublished essay, in which the connection to Rahner is explicit, Ellacuría asserts that

> history is, in fact, that which is transcendentally open, because it encompasses the dual openness, united into one, of intelligence and of will, of apprehending and of making commitments. This openness, which, in each individual is the transcendentally elevated openness of the "supernatural existential" (Rahner), is, in history taken as a whole, a transcendentally elevated openness of a graced historicity.... History is in itself transcendentally open, and God's presence is already there, at least inchoately, in this transcendentality.[33]

A second important theme revolves around Rahner's reflections on the logic of existential knowledge, with the formal existential ethics (and fundamental theology) it implies and the method of discernment it requires. As we saw in chapter 4, Rahner argued that God's self-revelation is uniquely offered to each individual in terms of a call to a way of life that is authoritative for the individual, and this way of life cannot be fully deduced from any set of universal ethical principles, whether those principles be grounded in nature or in revelation. Once again, Maier argues, Ellacuría transposes this theme into a historical key. This is the point of Ellacuría's reflections on the necessity of discerning "the signs of the times." Briefly, Ellacuría argues that God's revelation is not over and done with in any one historical moment; as a consequence it cannot be exhausted or encapsulated in any ahistorical collection of theses. Rather, the word of God "contains real possibilities that can only be actualized according to the various new necessities of historical events."[34] Thus, the presence of God, which is already located, however inchoately, as the ground and referent of history's transcendental openness, becomes thematic in terms of possibilities and exigencies that develop historically, in a way that cannot be rationally calculated out in advance. The Church's evangelizing mission requires that it identify these possibilities and exigencies, and reconfigure its evangelizing mission with them in mind. This is what it means to "read the signs of the times." For Ellacuría, Vatican II initiated this process, but it was fully carried out at Medellín for the Latin American Church in particular, albeit not without import for the Church worldwide. This is what Ellacuría was calling his fellow Central American Jesuits to do in the 1969 retreat.

The final theme Maier identifies concerns the radical mystery of God. Rahner became more and more insistent over time that God is a God of Absolute Mystery, who comes close to us without losing God's character as mystery. One does not find this theme so explicitly or pervasively present in Ellacuría's writings, but it can be discerned in his reflections on the two men who most influenced him after he completed his studies and took up his work in El Salvador: Pedro Arrupe and Oscar Romero.

Ellacuría had many dealings with Arrupe, superior general of the Society of Jesus from 1965 to 1981. This was in large measure because of the positions of responsibility that Ellacuría held. He was in charge of the formation of young Jesuits in Central America from 1970 to 1974, and in charge of a major Jesuit institution, the UCA, from 1979 until his death in 1989. These dealings were not always untroubled, as Ellacuría himself admits, but he asserted that over time he and Arrupe achieved a growing consensus concerning what was necessary in El Salvador.[35] Ellacuría had great admiration for his superior, seeing in him a passion for religious life in general and the Society of Jesus in particular, coupled with a deep desire to make of religious life an evangelical force in the world. Above all, what Ellacuría saw in Arrupe was an immense love of God. In Ellacuría's judgment, this love for God as *semper maior* was precisely what made Arrupe open to the signs of the times in history and willing to recommit the Society of Jesus in the light of those signs, no matter what the cost. In a passage that is perhaps as much autobiographical as biographical, Ellacuría writes the following of Arrupe:

Arrupe was a man of God, above all else, and he wanted the Jesuits to be truly men of God. This "truly" means that God was the one that he sought, and not anything else that might be passed off for God, even in religious and ecclesiastical milieus. He never substituted anything else for God, a God who is greater than human beings, a God who is greater than the *Constitutions* and the historical structure of the Society of Jesus, a God who is greater than the church and all of its hierarchy, a *Deus semper maior et semper novus*, who remains always the same but never repeats Godself, who must necessarily be expressed in dogmatic formulas, but who is never exhausted by them. A God, in short, who cannot be predicted in advance, on the one hand, and cannot be manipulated, on the other.[36]

Ellacuría notes that this God was mediated to Arrupe by Ignatian spirituality, but that Arrupe was not so much a follower of this spirituality as he was a man whose life centered on a God who always remained for him the *Deus semper maior et semper novus*. This is, he asserts, why Arrupe was able to be so perceptive and flexible about new movements in history, and so insistent that the Society respond to them. "From this solid base," Ellacuría writes, "which is never gained once for all, but rather by the nature of the case has to be renewed day by day, Arrupe lived *open to history and in history as someone open to the signs of the times.* . . . In large measure he perceived the novelty of God in the novelty of history."[37]

Ellacuría wrote less on Romero than on Arrupe, but this seems, paradoxically, to indicate an effect at an even greater depth, touching the very roots of Ellacuría's spirituality. Jon Sobrino makes the remarkable observation that Ellacuría, a man who never hesitated to criticize even his friends and closest colleagues, never once spoke critically of Romero during his three years as archbishop.[38] If with his other mentors Ellacuría came eventually to see himself as a colleague and cotraveler, with Romero he always understood himself to be the disciple, the follower. As Kevin Burke states, if others were more important in the development of Ellacuría's head, his theory, and his theology, during those three short years from 1977 to 1980, Romero played a different role: "*maestro* of Ellacuría's heart, praxis and spirituality, his legacy to Ellacuría was the gift of his own faith."[39] As Sobrino puts it:

> I have no doubt that Ellacuría was really and existentially affected by Monseñor Romero, but in a way that differed from a Rahner or a

Zubiri. Monseñor's prophecy and mercy, his sense of utopia and freedom, left clear footprints on him. But in my opinion, the deepest and most specific influence was something else: Monseñor Romero's profound faith in the mystery of God, about which he spoke unaffectedly and naturally, and which he embodied in his person.[40]

Ellacuría often would say that Romero "has already gone ahead of us."[41] Yet, it was an already developed philosophical and theological framework that identified for Ellacuría where that "ahead" was and what made it ahead. Romero's life both confirmed and deepened Ellacuría's vision of Christian faith and life, lived in the presence of the interwoven, albeit asymmetrical, mysteries of human iniquity, on the one hand, and divine love and compassion, on the other. Indeed, Romero fulfilled for Ellacuría the function of a saint or spiritual master, as set forth in the classic essay "Logic" by Rahner that we investigated in chapter 4: "a 'creative' original assimilation of God's revelation *in Christo*. . . . a creative prototype in accord with historical circumstances, and by way of example, as a new gift by God's Spirit of the ancient Christianity to a new age."[42]

Ellacuría's Intellectual Project: A Philosophy and Theology of Historical Reality

Continuing to develop over the ensuing decades, Ellacuría's intellectual vision reached maturity during his studies in Spain, where he returned in 1962 to study with the philosopher Xavier Zubiri (1898–1983). He became not only Zubiri's student, but also one of his most important interpreters and collaborators. Moreover, Ellacuría carried on his own innovative continuation of Zubiri's philosophy. One of the most important philosophers of the twentieth century, Zubiri's thought is not easily summarized.[43] Here we confine ourselves to those features of his thought that are most important for understanding Ellacuría's theological project.

Philosophical Underpinnings

Like so many philosophers of late modernity, Zubiri sought to close or at least bridge the breaches and dualisms that had opened up in modern philosophy (reflecting cognate rifts in modern life and culture itself).

Again, as with many, he was convinced that a crucial wrong turn had been made early in the history of Western philosophy. He identified this wrong turn in terms of two mutually implicatory reductions. The first, the "logification of intelligence," reduces human intelligence to the apprehension of the logos of things, such that it is only after and by means of this act that intelligence encounters reality. The second is the "entification of reality," in which "being and entities have displaced reality in philosophy, with which philosophy has ceased to be what it ought to be and human beings are detoured away from the exigencies of reality and toward the illusions of being that are possible when being is not rooted in reality."[44] Zubiri argued that this dual reduction set the stage for an irresolvable conflict between idealism and materialism, in which not even the latter is able to affirm fully the materiality of human knowing and acting, since it cannot offer an adequate account of the transcendence that characterizes these specifically human activities *as* material. Overcoming this cluster of problems is the goal of Zubiri's "open materialist realism," to use Ellacuría's name for it.[45]

The solution, worked out elaborately and at length throughout Zubiri's opus, entailed most fundamentally a thoroughgoing prioritization of "reality" over "being" or "meaning." Reality, as the "ultimate," is taken to be the object of philosophy. It is to be approached by means of an investigation of human subjectivity, which is the privileged place where philosophy can gain access to its object. But the focus has to be kept resolutely on *reality*. What is most primordially made present in human intelligence is reality, such that the disclosure of meaning, being, or what have you, is dependent on this prior and more basic confrontation and engagement with reality. This engagement with reality is also what makes human intelligence what it is.

To avoid the twofold reduction that Zubiri discerned in other correlations of "the absolute" and human subjectivity (whether it be in Kant, Hegel, Schelling, or even in contemporary figures such as Husserl or Heidegger), Zubiri worked out a theory of human intelligence as *sentient* intelligence. What is most at stake in this definition is the claim that intelligence is rooted in the senses in every phase of its actualization, as opposed, for instance, to a Kantian schema in which the senses only provide the material (already formed, to be sure) for subsequent processing by a reason separable from the senses. Human sensation and intelligence form an indivisible unity, and it is in and through the actualization of that unity that reality is manifested. Consequently, if it is the case (as Zubiri and Ellacuría insist it is) that human intelligence entails self-transcendence, then this is not a transcendence that occurs by leaving the senses behind, along with the materiality in which the senses embed human beings. Rather, transcendence happens precisely to the extent that sentient intelligence apprehends-by-actualizing a transcendence, a power that is immanent to and constitutive of reality, by which reality is able to "give more of itself" (*da mas de si*).[46]

Not to apprehend this feature of reality is not to apprehend intelligently; apprehending it entails nothing less than its actualization in the one who apprehends.[47] An analogy with Thomistic epistemology will bring out an important consequence. For Aquinas, knowing something means becoming that thing in an important sense; the form or essence that is actual in the individual thing that is known (such that it exists as the particular thing it is) also becomes actual in the intellect of the knower. The same is true in Zubiri's epistemology, *mutatis mutandis* according to the Zubirian "turn" to reality. As Samour puts it: "Apprehending intelligently is the actualization of reality in intelligence; it is the physical turning [*remisión*] of intelligence to reality as a *prius* to its presentation by the very power of reality. And this is prior to any judgment or concept, without it being understood as the mind being affected by some presumed impressed species."[48]

The reality that emerges when one investigates it in terms of its presence in and to sentient intelligence, is dynamic and multileveled. Minimally one can speak of physical, biological, sentient, and (sentiently) intelligent levels on which reality manifests itself, with the "higher" levels made possible by embracing, and continually making present, structures, interrelationships, and dynamisms proper to the lower levels. On the other hand, the higher levels "liberate" new possibilities in which reality "gives more of itself" or transcends itself. To apprehend intelligently is most primordially a recapitulation in sentient intelligence of the real, including the dynamism of the real, in its process character, but in a way appropriate to the human.

To take the next step in this analysis, we determine what this appropriateness entails, by starting from the claim that human beings are free. They manifest most fully an openness and self-transcendence that is characteristic of reality as a whole, made possible once the dynamism of reality-as-process (by which Zubiri and Ellacuría have evolution in mind) has produced human beings. In order for reality to be actualized in human intelligence, the dynamic and interrelated character of reality has to "happen" in human beings. This happens to the extent that human beings fully engage the reality they are apprehending, position themselves axiologically within its complex network of interrelations and dynamisms, and make a commitment within this network, thus continuing reality's own process of giving more of itself. In short, in addition to conceptualizing and grasping meaning, Zubiri's position compels the conclusion that acting, human praxis, is an integral part of intelligence, rather than just an act subsequent to an already completed act of knowing. Lacking that, human intelligence is cut short, and is not most fully and adequately what it should be.

This philosophical vision is clearly manifest in an article in which Ellacuría attempts to lay out philosophical foundations for a Latin American theology.[49] There he asserts that the structure and function of intelligence "is not that of comprehending being or capturing meaning, but rather the structure of apprehending reality and engaging it [or confronting oneself with it: *'enfrentarse con ella'*]" and that intelligence does this as a biological activity; that is, its orientation and goal is the service of life.[50] He elaborates what apprehending and engaging reality means by laying out a view of intelligence with noetic, ethical, and praxical moments:

> Engaging real things in their reality has a threefold dimension: *becoming aware of the weight of reality* [*el hacerse cargo de la realidad*], which entails being in the reality of things (and not merely being present before the idea of things or being in touch with their meanings), being "real" in the reality of things, which in its active character of being is exactly the opposite of being thing-like and inert, and implies being among them through their material and active mediations; *shouldering the weight of reality* [*el cargar con la realidad*], an expression that points to the fundamentally ethical character of intelligence, which has not been given to us so that we could evade our real commitments, but rather to take upon ourselves what things really are and what they really demand; *taking charge of the weight of reality* [*el encargarse de la realidad*], an expression which points to the praxical character of intelligence which only fulfills its function, including its character of knowing reality and comprehending its meaning, when it assumes as its burden doing something real.[51]

The full actualization of human intelligence is thus not an observation and description of realities from the outside, or an abstraction of an essential form from what is known, or even an encounter with the being of what is known. It is, rather, "a being present in the reality of things, . . . which, in its active character of existing, is the opposite of being thing-like and inert."[52] To know reality is to find our place in reality. As such it necessarily includes an ethical moment, in which human intelligence grasps the demands that reality places upon us as that species that self-consciously participates in the ongoing history of created being. Finally, human intelligence is short-circuited if it stops short of corresponding to the "active character" of that which it apprehends, and if it fails to act on that ethical imperative; in short, if it does not lead to transformative action that participates in and contributes to the ongoing history of reality.

Given all this, the work (in its most literal sense) of human, sentient intelligence turns out to be a crucial locus for the self-actualization and self-transcendence of reality itself. It also must not be forgotten that human existence is fundamentally and irreducibly social, so that human intelligence always happens in society and in terms of the ways that this society has been shaped historically.[53] This means for Ellacuría that it is not just reality that is the ultimate, and as such the object of philosophy. It is *historical* reality.[54] It is the level of historical reality that most comprehends and integrates the other levels of reality, so that a full and adequately nuanced account of reality can only be achieved from that vantage point. This is not to deny the relative autonomy of other levels. It is not, for instance, to deny the relative autonomy of the individual person, collapsing her or him into a social-historical collective. It *is* to claim that the fullest account of this individuality, even one that gives due weight to the individual's freedom, will only be gained from the perspective of society and history, rather than from, say, physical reality or from the level of individual human subjectivity.[55]

It is in history itself, then, that the fullest actuality of the transcendental opening outward (*apertura*) and realization of reality is to be located. This happens through and because of human praxis, and what this praxis can create in history, by means of appropriating and actualizing possibilities available at a given time and place in history.[56] In his posthumously published book, *Filosofía de la realidad histórica*, Ellacuría names this constitutive dimension of human praxis "historicization." It indicates the transformative power that human beings can and should exercise over the natural levels of dimensions of reality, as they already have been previously transformed (or previously historicized) by human praxis and presented to a new generation. "The historicization of nature," Ellacuría writes, "consists . . . in the fact that humanity makes history on the basis of [*desde*] nature and with nature."[57] On this view, then, history and the human praxis that is constitutive of history move more centrally into the "ontological foreground" than they do against prior philosophical horizons: be it the horizon found in Greek philosophy, which is projected in terms of a fundamentally atemporal cosmos or the horizon of individual human subjectivity, which determined Enlightenment and post-Enlightenment philosophy. Making this shift in horizon is what Ellacuría has in mind when he calls for a historical logos for philosophical and theological investigation, as opposed to a Greek logos.

If this shift is made, then a primary feature of philosophical method will be the "historicization" of concepts and practices. This is a reflection, or derivation, as it were, of the more primordial sense of historicization we noted above.[58] It indicates the proper intellectual methodology for philosophy and theology (but not just for them) given the historical character of their object and the dynamism of historicization (just described) that is the proper way in which human beings participate in that object (that is, in historical reality). As we have seen, Ellacuría's position was that all concepts and practices emerge through the ongoing historical engagement with reality on the part of human beings, which is the hallmark of human sentient intelligence. Thus, they can only be fully understood in terms of how they arose in that history and continue to function in that history, either positively or negatively. They function positively if they open further possibilities for engaging reality, socially and culturally, so that it "gives more of itself," and in so doing approximates a more fully human history. They function negatively if they occlude or stall this history, closing down further possibilities. A principal way in which the latter can happen is by the assertion of some ahistorical standards or criteria for judging history, abstracted from one particular history within the broader weave of historical reality. This indicates the presence of ideology, in the pejorative sense.[59]

For Ellacuría to understand how any complex of human concepts functions in a specific social location, shaped by a unique constellation of historical forces, is to "historicize" those concepts: "*Demonstrating the impact of certain concepts within a particular context is what is understood here as their historicization.* Hence, historicization is a principle of de-ideologization."⁶⁰ For instance, in the article from which this definition is taken, Ellacuría points out that in the particular historical context of El Salvador, the defense of private property as a basic human right serves in fact to disguise and legitimize a system that attacks human dignity, in general, and denies in practice and systematically the right to own property to the majority of its people.

According to Ellacuría, appeals to concepts such as the right to private property, or even "human rights" in general, stand in urgent need of a historicization. I would sum up this discussion by describing historicization as a critical historical contextualization.⁶¹ First, historicization is a *contextualization*; it discovers the meaning of a concept in terms of the context within which it is used. Second, it is a *historical* contextualization insofar as the context is not nature, but history—the realm of human freedom and responsibility, the realm of praxis.⁶² This means that the interpreter must reckon with the fact that the meaning of concepts will change with their historical setting because of decisions that human beings make. More importantly, the interpreter must take responsibility for the way that his or her interpretation itself contributes to the historical process within which ultimately this interpretation, too, finds its context of meaning. Finally, this is a *critical* process. It operates out of a hermeneutics of suspicion, deeply aware of the ways that concepts are used to hide reality or distort our apprehension of it.⁶³ The example of property rights is taken from political discourse; yet, insofar as dogmatic and theological concepts (sin, salvation, or the Reign of God) are historically conditioned human creations, Ellacuría refused to exempt them from the danger of distortion and manipulation and thus from the need for an ongoing critical historical contextualization.

It should be noted in conclusion, however, that to historicize particular concepts and practices, and other products of human intellection (empirical analysis, interpretation of texts, etc.), is not only a negative, as it were "deconstructive" task. It also opens up possible avenues for modifying thinking so that it more closely approximates the kind of creative engagement with reality that is required if history is to move forward and human beings, as sentiently intelligent beings, are to flourish. It is this work that gives philosophy its rigorously demanding character as thinking; it also defines its indispensable task in human life. Ellacuría expressed this insight in an essay on the role of philosophy in El Salvador:

It is certain that our peoples need transformation, but a transformation filled with truth. As things stand, we are not going toward human liberation but toward human alienation. Philosophy as the search for the fullness of truth—not the mere absence of error but the full presence of reality—is thus an indispensable element in the integral liberation of our peoples. When these peoples count on the real possibility of thinking for themselves in all the orders of thought, they will take the path of liberty and of full possession of themselves. *That* is what philosophy is for.[64]

Theological Consequences

Xavier Zubiri was primarily a philosopher, yet he did think of himself as a theologian too, at least in some dimensions of his work, and his philosophical concepts had, even for him, theological resonances and applicability.[65] Constitutive to his account of reality was something he called its "theologal dimension," a concept that Ellacuría took over. Their articulation of this dimension turns on a strongly Trinitarian understanding of God. We can explore this dimension by considering another of Ellacuría's most important foundational essays: "The Historicity of Christian Salvation."[66] In examining the general problem of the historical character of Christian salvation, Ellacuría focuses his investigation on "the salvific character of historical acts." To examine this is to ask "which historical acts bring salvation and which bring condemnation, which acts make God more present, and how that presence is actualized and made effective in them."[67] Ellacuría wrote this essay with the 1977 statement of the International Theological Commission in mind.[68] One of the most frequent and insistent charges leveled by this and other critiques was that liberation theology reduced salvation to a this-worldly process that could and should be described exclusively in terms of cultural, political, and economic transformation, thus virtually excluding a priori any transcendent dimension that could be ascribed to God's supernatural activity.

Ellacuría's response is that this critique follows from an unreflective application of analytical categories of "natural" and "supernatural" to the understanding of history. This flawed categorization maps liberation theology onto a distinction between profane history and salvation history that leads ineluctably to misunderstanding and distortion. Not only does such an approach fail to do justice to liberation theology's understanding of history, it is itself unable to structure an adequate understanding of history.[69] Echoing Rahner, whom he cites, Ellacuría argues that there are not two histories, the history of salvation and profane history, whose connection has then subsequently to be worked out. Rather, "salvation history and so-called profane history are encompassed by a single history, which they subserve. This history is God's history: the history of what God has done with nature as a whole, what God is doing in human history, and what God desires to result from God's on-going self-gift."[70] This is not to claim that there is yet a *third* history alongside salvation history and profane history. Rather, to speak of God's history is to speak of salvation history and profane history as a unity that, at the level of human history, forms "a single historical reality in which both God and human beings intervene, so that God's intervention does not occur without some form of human participation, and human intervention does not occur without God's presence in some form."[71]

With this in view, Ellacuría argues that the fundamental distinction to be made is not between the natural and the supernatural, between worldly history and salvation history, but between the contexts of sin and of grace. The ways that the divine and human involvements in historical reality transpire and interrelate with one another differ fundamentally depending on whether the context is one of sin or one of grace.[72] In a context of sin, one would talk of nature and profane history in terms of human rebellion; divine intervention would be located in prophetic denunciation of sin, annunciation of hope, and bearing of sin. In a context of grace, one would talk of nature and profane history in terms of human flourishing; God's mode of presence would be an affirming expression and shaping *ad extra* of the divine, Trinitarian life within that human flourishing. In either case, historical reality would be pressed toward a "more," instantiating a dynamic transcendence that does not leave history behind, but causes it to "give more of itself," or fail to do so, to the extent that it becomes more or less the site of an enlivening divine presence.[73]

Properly articulating this conceptual scheme demands a painstakingly careful understanding of the doctrine of creation. Ellacuría agrees with many in insisting that creation should not be understood as an event in which God acts as an "efficient cause" to bring about an effect separate from God.[74] Rather, creation should be understood as "a giving-shape *ad extra* of the Trinitarian life itself, a giving shape that is freely willed, but of the Trinitarian life itself."[75] In this view, creation would not happen according to an exemplary, idealist causality, but would be a "communicative and self-donative action of the Trinitarian life itself."[76] This giving-shape of the Trinitarian life *ad extra* manifests itself in a long process, in which are found "the purely material form of creation, the form of life in its different phases, and finally, the form of humanity and its history. The human being . . . and history are the realities where this giving-shape of the Trinitarian life can be more and more present, although always in a limited form, limited, but open."[77] This grounding of all things in and by the self-communication of the Triune God in creation constitutes the "theologal character" of all things, including human beings and of human history. This theologal dimension is the condition for the possibility for any talk of an "experience" of God, of revelation, and, hence, of theology:

> It would not be simply that God is in all things, according to each one's character, through God's essence, presence, and power; it would be that all things, each in its own way, have been given shape according to the Trinitarian life, would be essentially referred to it. The theologal dimension of the created world (which should not be confused with the theological dimension) would stem from this presence of the Trinitarian life, which is intrinsic to all things, but can be grasped in the human being as something real and as the principle of personality. There is an experience, in the strict sense, of this theologal dimension, and through it, a personal, social and historical experience, in the strict sense, of God. This experience will happen to different degrees and in different forms, but whenever it is a genuine experience of the real theologal dimension of the human being, of society, and, to a different degree, of purely material things, then it will be a physical experience, a physical proof [*probación*] of the Trinitarian life itself, however mediated, incarnated and historicized.[78]

Things continually come to be, in the different ways that they exist, insofar as they are expressions of the Trinitarian life. Human beings are "tied back" in a unique way to this foundational self-expressive and self-donative presence of the Trinity to creation, a presence that makes each created thing to be in its own particular way within the field of historical reality.[79] It is this "being-tied-back" that enables human beings to apprehend and affirm intelligently (with the three dimensions we detailed earlier) a "more" to the historical reality in which they are embedded, a "more" whose "whence" can be named God. It is this general openness that makes it possible for human beings to receive in history a particular revelation. In other words, this historical-anthropological framework does the same work, as it were, in Ellacuría's thought, as the one that Rahner developed in *Hearer of the Word*, in which he asked after the conditions for the possibility that human beings be the recipients of a Word of revelation if it were to be freely proffered. A crucial difference in Ellacuría's construction is that this apprehension and affirmation occur in and through an engagement with historical reality that is not complete without a commitment to history, a commitment that can be understood as a participation by human beings in the ongoing Trinitarian *"plasmación"* of creation.

On this view, the most fundamental rebellion against God, sin formally defined, would not be the denial of God's existence "in theory" (atheism); nor would it be individual infractions of a revealed moral code. It would be refusing the call to participate freely (as appropriate for the human) in the ongoing self-transcendence of historical reality, by which it becomes more what it already is at root: the *plasmación* of the divine life. This refusal, this negation, always occurs in and through an avowal, asserting something positive: to be specific, as an absolutization of some inner-historical reality, setting limits, frustrating, and subverting the open-ended movement of history that marks it as the *plasmación* of the Triune life of God. In other words, looked at in terms of what it affirms rather than what it denies, the primordial sin is idolatry.[80]

Thus, to reiterate, the most basic distinction to be made is not between profane history and salvation history, but between sin and grace within the one history that is a structurally interwoven union of worldly history and salvation history (and as thus interwoven must be named "God's history"). The task all of this sets to Christian theology is that of "discern[ing] what there is of sin and of grace in a specific historical situation. We must ask with all rigor what the sin of the world is today or in what forms the sin of the world appears today."[81] This, however, requires looking at history, using those "secular" disciplines appropriate for analyzing history. Lest the claim of "reductionism" be leveled again, Ellacuría insists, speaking of the realities of poverty and injustice, which certainly call out for empirical analysis, that "the very same phenomena [of history] appear in the light of faith as a fundamental event in the history of God with humanity."[82] Unjust poverty and the death that it brings in and through concrete social and political structures thus come to light as a "fundamental event" in God's history with humanity, as sin. This tenet explains Ellacuría's dual characterization and analysis of the situation of the poor. On the one hand, he analyzed this reality in multiple essays in *ECA*, using the tools of economics, sociology, and political science.[83] On the other hand, he described it in thickly contextualized theological language, most strikingly in the essays in which he described the poor as "the Crucified People."[84] These modes of analysis were neither mere paraphrases of one another, saying the same things in different terms, nor opposed to one another, nor simply juxtaposed without any internal connection. Both describe the *totality* of a historical reality — that of the poor — and neither is complete without the other.

Following the threefold characterization of human sentient intelligence we discussed above (becoming aware of the weight of reality, taking charge of the weight of reality, and shouldering the weight of reality) one might say that human beings are called to become aware of the stranglehold that unjustly inflicted poverty has on human history, to take upon themselves the ethical challenge that is integral to this realization, and to take responsibility for eliminating it. Christians do this, illuminated and empowered by the history of revelation, by "making God's power present [in history], but the power of God that is revealed in Jesus, and in the ways it is revealed in him."[85] This means proclaiming the Kingdom of God, making it present in one's own life and setting it in motion through one's own actions vis-à-vis society. It also means embracing the scheme of cross and resurrection, as Ellacuría had noted as early as 1969.[86]

Ellacuría concludes this long, programmatic essay with a discussion of spirituality, which has as its theme "a personal encounter with that Christian historical transcendence" that had been under discussion throughout the essay.[87] He takes up the Ignatian motto of "contemplation in action" to describe the necessary characteristics of this personal encounter: "Contemplation in action can only mean the contemplation that can be done and should be done when one is acting. This does not only mean contemplating the action one has taken but transforming one's past actions or future intended actions into what is contemplation strictly speaking, an encounter with what there is of God in things, and an encounter with God in the things."⁸⁸ We shall examine this description in detail in what follows, uncovering the many Ignatian themes woven into it. Before we do so, however, it will be helpful to conclude this long section by summarizing some of the key elements of Ellacuría's understanding of the nature and task of theology.

1. Christian theology has as its object historical reality. Historical reality is an integrated totality of diverse structures and dynamisms, operating on different levels, each with its own relative autonomy. Its ultimate *telos*, the term of history's ongoing process of self-transcendence, is to be the outward giving-shape by and of the Trinitarian life of God. To the extent that this *telos* is attained, all things in historical reality will be, in accordance with each thing's specific features, an instantiation, however limited, of the real presence of the divine. This process of self-transcendence finds its richest (but also most imperiled) actuality at the level of human history. At this level, the frustration of history's movement toward its *telos* is manifest as the presence of sin. Grace, however, equally present, is ultimately more comprehensive and more efficacious.

2. Christian theology necessarily takes up its object, historical reality, from a particular historical place and the dynamisms that characterize historical reality there. It takes this object up as the action of a particular historical subject: the church as the people of God. Since no description of historical reality is complete without a full characterization of all of reality's dimensions, theology must necessarily attend to those descriptions and analyses of reality that come from other disciplines, especially the social sciences. Its task in so doing should be described as "reading the signs of the times," which is the discernment of the mode of God's presence in things at a particular point within historical reality. This mode of presence will differ depending on whether the context presents itself primarily as one of grace or one that is, in the first instance, one of sin.⁸⁹

3. As with any intelligent apprehension of reality, the church must have the threefold structure of realizing the weight of historical reality, shouldering that weight, and taking charge of it. Praxis is an integral part of the church's discernment of God's salvific presence, and thus of theology's work also. To say the same thing using more explicitly theological language, the church continues the work of Jesus Christ: announcing the Reign of God, denouncing the sin of the world that opposes it, making that reign present in historical signs, and releasing the power of the scheme

of cross and resurrection to renew a history marred by sin. Theology represents the methodical, self-critical reflection on how the church is doing in this, its task.

4. Given its task and character, theology must situate itself at that place in historical reality at which God's presence is most fully manifest. This means the point at which the historical salvation that God offers is given in its densest, most powerful form. This will in turn be the point at which historical reality is most threatened by the power of sin, distorting historical reality and diverting it from its *telos*. It is here that God's power will be most fully manifest, even though it will be the kind of power disclosed in the paschal mystery. This place, Ellacuría argues, can be none other than the place of the poor and marginalized, those who, as Gustavo Gutiérrez so succinctly puts it, die unjustly before their time.[90] In short, the church and theology must make a preferential option for the poor, even and precisely for the sake of the integrity of its theoretical work, which is, let it be stated again, inseparable from historical action.

5. Theology, on this view, will take up all the tasks traditionally ascribed to it, albeit with different accents and aims. Like any form of theoretical investigation, theology will have to carry on the task of historicization, a critical historical contextualization of the empirical investigations, hermeneutical interpretations, scientific conceptualizations, and practical applications that shape and direct human culture.[91] Historicization is a form of de-ideologization. This kind of "ideology critique" is particularly important in societies such as that of El Salvador, but to the extent that El Salvador is symptomatic of broader global dysfunction, the indispensability of ideology critique obtains elsewhere also.[92] To the extent that theory is separated from praxis, constellations of ideas and theories can become historically "frozen," abstracted from the original historical context in which they arose and were operative. Then they frequently obscure rather than enlighten historical reality; indeed, they can come to legitimate unjust social and economic strictures. They become ideologies in the pejorative sense. They facilitate not a full realization of the weight of reality, but a rejection or evasion of that (often painful) burden; they do not call us to shoulder the weight of that reality, but make it easier for us to assign that work to others, or to put it off to the indefinite future; they prove not to be instructive in how to take charge of the weight of our historical reality, but to provide an easy out, perhaps an apparently more "realistic" alternative than the hard work of

changing social structures so that they conduce more to a history worthy of human beings, indeed, a history in which it is possible to be a human being in solidarity with others. In terms more specifically Christian, they make it more difficult to follow Jesus, which means following him by continuing what his life was about.

These points do not necessarily define all that theology is and should do for Ellacuría, but they do define an essential framework of tasks within which other tasks (scriptural exegesis, historical research, elaboration of a systematic dogmatic theology, moral analysis of particular cases, discernment and implementation of pastoral strategies) find their appropriate interrelations and goal. They also provided the framework within which Ellacuría interpreted the meaning and contribution of Ignatian spirituality, to which we now turn.

Ellacuría Interprets Ignatius: The *Spiritual Exercises*

In 1974, Ellacuría gave a series of lectures on the *Spiritual Exercises*, for which we have detailed outlines.[93] After some introductory remarks, Ellacuría presents the guiding thesis for his interpretation of the *Exercises* in a section entitled "St. Ignatius's *Spiritual Exercises* as the Theological Place [*Lugar*] for Historicization."[94] The thesis centers on the programmatic claim that "Saint Ignatius' *Exercises* use what is fundamentally an historical method, one that is very effective theologically for historicizing Christian faith and praxis."[95] In fact, on Ellacuría's reading, the *Exercises* has precisely the "historical logos" that he contended was necessary for all theological reflection.[96] After considering his arguments for this claim, I turn to the centerpiece of his interpretation: the contemplations on the life of Jesus and the meditation on the Two Standards from the Second Week of the *Spiritual Exercises*. Then I analyze how Ellacuría takes up the Contemplation to Attain Love in order to provide his own distinctive rendering of the Ignatian motto of "contemplation in action."

First I take up his argument that the *Spiritual Exercises* operates according to an "historical logos." Ellacuría identified three related features of the *Exercises* that mark its logos as a "historical logos," and make of it a theological locus for historicization. First, "to the extent that they have a personal encounter with God's will as their goal, Saint Ignatius's

Spiritual Exercises are already a principle of historicization."[97] The argument here is that the point of the Exercises is not to gain new information about God, or even about God's will in general, but to *encounter* God and God's will in the concrete, to be confronted with God's will in such a way that one responds to it here and now. This certainly entails securing a knowledge of God's will, but goes beyond that to achieving a *sense of the obligation* incumbent on us as a result of this knowledge, and a willingness to take up the *mission* it maps for us. In other words, the way the *Spiritual Exercises* instantiates a historical logos that can be parsed in terms of the threefold structure of human sentient intelligence we described in the section on Ellacuría's philosophical underpinnings.

Second, Ellacuría notes that the Exercises "historicize this word of God insofar as they turn to historical, personal and circumstantial signs in order to enable that word to be discovered in the concrete."[98] Third, Ellacuría explicitly appropriates a Rahnerian principle from the 1956 essay on discernment, "The Logic of Concrete Individual Knowledge in Ignatius of Loyola." Ellacuría observes that the *Exercises* intends an encounter with God that has as its goal an understanding of the world and of one's mission in the world that "cannot be deduced from universal principles."[99] Recall that Rahner had argued that there are concrete particulars of an individual's biography and of the particular will of God for that individual that cannot be evaluated solely by determining their fit or lack of fit with universal doctrinal and ethical principles. They thus call for a different sort of evaluation, one provided, Rahner contended, by Ignatius's Rules for Discernment. For Ellacuría, they offer a similar resource to the Latin American Church, which faces a situation that cannot be adequately met simply by the application of ecclesiological principles derived in the abstract or from different historical and cultural contexts. Recognizing the exigency imposed by this situation was a major theme of Ellacuría's work and a concern of the Latin American bishops at their meeting at Medellín. That he saw a connection between Rahner's theology and this task is evident from his choice of precisely this topic for his contribution to a Rahner festschrift that appeared in Spain: "Theses on the Possibility, Necessity and Meaning of a Latin American Theology."[100] In this long essay, Ellacuría elaborates at length the claim made in his introductory lecture on the Exercises: that "comprehending and realizing the history of salvation in a specifically Latin American situation" is the most important task facing Church and theology on that continent.[101]

In short, the *Spiritual Exercises* lays out and structures a set of practices that allow Latin American theologians and church leaders to "historicize" Christian faith and practice in their particular context. The thesis stated, Ellacuría recognizes at least one problem associated with these claims about the *Spiritual Exercises*. The *Spiritual Exercises* was composed primarily with the individual in mind, and not a community. This challenges his interpretation, since if the *Exercises* is to provide a method of historicization, then it must apply not only to individuals but to a group. His response is to note that although it is true that the *Exercises* was composed primarily with the individual in mind, it is not closed to the possibility of application by and for a community. In support of this, Ellacuría observes that Ignatius himself appropriated it in precisely this way as the inspiration and guide for founding the Society of Jesus.[102] This conviction had guided Ellacuría's own use of the *Exercises* in the "province retreat" of 1969.

Ellacuría summarized his position by asserting that the Spiritual Exercises construct a theological place for a historical contextualization of our understanding of God's will because they "try to posit one's own history as the hermeneutical place [for interpreting] who one is and what God's will is for oneself."[103] In other words, "they make the historical into the essential part of the structure of the Christian encounter with God."[104] The most important element that enables them to do this is "the primacy of the historical Jesus."[105] This locates the part of the *Spiritual Exercises* that Ellacuría took to be the heart of the *Exercises*, and hence the focal point for its interpretation. This focal point lies in the Second Week of the *Exercises*, with its contemplations on the life of Jesus and the election of a way of life that more radically re-presents that life today (which is to say, historicizes it). Before moving to his discussion of the Second Week, in the fourth, fifth, and sixth lectures, I turn briefly to his commentary on the Principle and Foundation and on the First Week.

The ahistorical formulation of the Principle and Foundation presents another challenge to Ellacuría's interpretation. In recognizing this challenge Ellacuría does not frame his critique as strongly as Juan Luis Segundo, but he does maintain that the Principle and Foundation must be interpreted by the core of the *Exercises* (for him, the Second Week) and not the reverse. To take the Principle and Foundation as the key to the *Exercises* and a guide to life would be "to convert life into an exercise of rationalism and Pelagian stoicism."[106] This relativization of the Principle and Foundation is not, however, an excision. Ellacuría suggests that it be interpreted as the statement of a problem and the posing of a question, rather than the presentation of a solution. Though it does frame an account of what human life is and its goal, Ellacuría contends that the substance of that account, particularly as specified by key terms—*man, God, service, salvation*—is left indeterminate. These terms are only given content in the course of doing the exercises that follow.[107] Thus, the Principle and Foundation expresses or urges on one a desire for salvation and an initial stance toward God and toward one's own existence. In framing that stance in terms of "maximality," however (what is *more* conducive to the end for which we are created—*SpEx* 23), it already suggests that an Ignatian response will continually transgress any sober, rational limits we might place on our response to God, opening us instead to the radical response of discipleship.

It is in the First Week, with the meditations on sin, that the substantive process of the *Exercises* gets underway. Ellacuría points out that even though Ignatius accepts the *prius* of creation in a formal way with his reflections in the Principle and Foundation, this *prius* is immediately contextualized against a horizon of sinful rebellion. That is, there is no moment in the history of creation in which sin is not present, however much history is founded on God's good, creative act and the telos of history (laid out in the Principle and Foundation) that should be derived from that foundation.[108] The theological implication of this structure is that we cannot conceive of salvation history solely as development toward a *telos* already present in creation, or as a process overlaid on a substrata of creation (or "nature") that is itself neutral regarding salvation; rather we must also conceive of it as a dialectical reversal, a negation of and liberation from a sin that is always already there determining history.[109]

Ellacuría's comments on the First Week are confined almost exclusively to its first exercise, on "the first, second, and third sins."[110] This division into the fall of the angels (first sin), the sin of Adam and Eve (second sin), and the sin of a man condemned to hell for one mortal sin (third sin) indicates, on Ellacuría's reading, that sin for Ignatius is a *historical* reality. It has a temporal structure of past, present, and future. The past is the "always-already-there-ness" of sin, represented by the sin of the angels and the first humans. Yet sin is a present reality, a product of human freedom here and now. Moreover, it has deadly consequences. It calls for conversion now, but this is a conversion that intends transformation, opening outward into a lifelong process (hence Ignatius's insistence on the examen and other ascetic works). Finally, sin has a futural dimension. It has to be understood in terms of the future toward which it tends (if unchecked): a future of ever-greater death-dealing power over human beings (hell) and one that negates the coming of God's reign.

Considering the colloquy that ends this meditation, in which one imagines oneself before Christ crucified, Ellacuría concludes that for Ignatius sin is only fully understood from the perspective of the cross, which is first and always a historical event. In other words, what sin is about cannot be fully deduced from the Principle and Foundation alone. Sin is the negation of *this* individual, Jesus, and of what he was about: showing us a God who is Father, and doing so by quite specific words and deeds placed in a particular way in his historical reality. Overcoming sin will thus have to be something historical too, even if it will refer to and make present something that exceeds history at any given moment.[111]

In his fourth lecture, Ellacuría repeatedly emphasizes the centrality of the Second Week: "Saint Ignatius gives his interpretation of the key to Christianity in the Second Week"; "the Second Week contains those texts that are most original to Saint Ignatius"; and, finally, "[the Second Week] opens up the mode of life 'for' carrying through all the rest [of the Exercises]."[112] It is in the two lectures on the Second Week that Ellacuría most fully deploys his philosophical and theological foundations in order to interpret the significance of the *Spiritual Exercises*. At the center is the concept of discipleship, following Jesus. Ellacuría asserts that Ignatius presents what is essential to Christian life in terms of following Jesus. As such, Ignatius's masterwork is both "profoundly Christian" and "very useful to a Latin American theology and pastoral practice."[113] The warrants for both these claims are elaborated in terms of fundamental principles of Ellacuría's theology.

First, the *Spiritual Exercises* is profoundly Christian because it presumes a God who is only fully encountered in history, indeed, in historical action: "A human presence and an historical action is always necessary to make God present."[114] This "making-present" is precisely what happened in Jesus of Nazareth, and it is what the Exercises render possible again for the person who makes and is given the graces for which the Exercises are designed to dispose one. This claim follows from Ellacuría's philosophy and theology of historical reality, according to which it is at the level of historical reality that reality is most fully and dynamically real. Considering reality's constitutive "theologal dimension," this means also that it is in historical reality (as the *plasmación ad extra* of the Trinitarian life) that the presence of God is most fully to be found. Yet, reality is a complex constellation of interrelated levels and dynamisms, which must be considered as an integral whole, however much the different dimensions and aspects have their proper relative autonomies, and at times even "pull" in different directions. With the powerful and destructive presence of sin in history and the (more than) equally powerful divine response, further complexity accrues. This complexity is reflected with precision in the *Spiritual Exercises*: "Saint Ignatius's *Exercises*, like Christian faith and Christian life, make up a totality that includes as a unity, but in permanent tension, distinct parts and aspects. In an historical process that is perennially recapitulated, they display sin, the life of Jesus, his death, and his resurrection, situated between the 'Principle and Foundation' and the 'Contemplation to Attain Love.'"[115] The parts build mutually on one another, and the exclusion of any one of them results in the distortion of the whole, and therefore of the other parts. For example, a consideration of sin that prescinds from the historical circumstances of Jesus's death is dangerously abstract, as is a focus on Jesus's resurrection that elides his life and passion. And both must be understood in relationship to the mission that Jesus took upon himself, which is presented in the Second Week contemplations of his life. These parts cannot be once and for all encompassed and related in any conceptual system. Only by following Jesus can a Christian (including the Christian theologian) be so placed that he or she avoids dangerous abstractions and one-sided interpretations such as these, and, more importantly, avoids acting upon them.[116]

Given this, the disposition that provides the interpretive key to the *Spiritual Exercises*, and discloses the way of life in terms of which the totality of Christian life is to be lived out, is discipleship.[117] Following Jesus, however, is not a matter of imitating an ahistorical ideal, but of effecting a historical continuation—Ellacuría tellingly names it a "progressive historicization"—governed by "the spirit of Christ who animates those who follow him."[118] To follow Jesus is at the same time and essentially to continue who Jesus was and what he did.[119] To the extent that the *Spiritual Exercises* centers on this in the core exercises of the Second Week, and offers a methodology for doing this, it is important for Latin American Christianity. It reinforces the insight that the Latin American Church must work out a way to fulfill its evangelical task that is fitted to its particular historical circumstances. It also points to the spiritual work of following Jesus as articulating a way of doing this that neither takes this exigency to be merely (and superficially) a top-down application of universal norms derived elsewhere, nor a knee-jerk reaction to the concrete demands of the social-political situation, as this might be articulated, say, by Marxist analysis.[120]

Ellacuría closes his first lecture on the Second Week with the observation that this work requires "an historical discernment of spirits."[121] Yet he does not go on in the next lecture, as one might expect, to describe and interpret Ignatius's rules for discernment of spirits. Instead he focuses an entire lecture on the Meditation on the Two Standards. Why does he do this? One possible explanation begins by noting that the Meditation on the Two Standards is the meditation that frames the part of the Second Week devoted to the Election. Ellacuría, reasonably enough, takes it as providing the setting within which the discernment, including the "historical" discernment he advocates, should go forward.[122] A second reason comes from Ellacuría's interest in the social and the historical contexts of Christian action and theology. Ellacuría stresses those parts of the meditation on the Two Standards that point toward a social context, above and beyond the individual context that heavily predominates the section of rules for discernment. Devils are sent out, he notes, to tempt individuals to follow the logic of the standard of Lucifer, but, what is more, they are sent to *cities, provinces, places*. Ellacuría draws from this the conclusion that "'place' is just as capable of being demonized [as persons]," or that a particular devil "acts differently according to the place, which is tantamount to the same thing."[123] Ellacuría also stresses the meditation's collective, communal language. What is at issue in the meditation is not so much one person's choice but "bringing many people together under the same standard."[124] The three principles that define each standard "give a certain shape to society as much as they do to individuals."[125] This emphasis links to his fourth lecture in which he had asserted that the kind of following that Ignatius had in mind would naturally create or apply to a group of followers, who act together to "follow by continuing" what Jesus was about.[126] In short, using this meditation to frame the discussion of discernment provides the more natural avenue for producing an interpretation of the *Spiritual Exercises* that emphasizes its power as an instrument for "historicizing" Christian faith on a social, corporate level.

Neither is it difficult to understand why Ellacuría, the liberation theologian, will not fail to exploit Ignatius's naming of the particular principles proposed under the standard of Satan, in the precise order in which they are proposed: wealth, honor, and pride. The significance of wealth is self-evident. Ellacuría interprets the quest for honor as a desire to be higher than anyone, and thus is a principle of alienation from others. Pride is connected with the will to domination.[127] Ellacuría does not reflect as explicitly on the principles of poverty, insults, and humility, which Ignatius counterposes under the standard of Christ. He connects them with Jesus's responses to Satan's promptings in Matthew's and Luke's account of the temptations in the desert.[128] Elsewhere he prefers to draw on the Beatitudes for the principles that define a Christian worldview.[129] It may be that Ellacuría found the principles of Christ's standard too resolutely individualistic in their application, and too reminiscent of an asceticism opposed to working in the world. It is possible that he was both attracted to and provoked by Segundo's critique of the *Spiritual Exercises* as laying out a "test" spirituality, and so wanted to interpret it in terms of other elements that parry that accusation.

What he does insist on is that the principles of Christ's standard have to be instantiated just as objectively and universally as those of Satan's. Moreover, he emphasizes their diametrical opposition. Together with the values of Lucifer's standard, "they present two interpretations of human existence, both of which claim to put themselves forward as religious (Christ and Lucifer) interpretations of what human history is and what its salvific fullness is."[130] Finally, he points out that if one were to ask under which "standard" we should locate the political and economic principles that have normed the development of the modern world, then the answer would have to be the standard of "the mortal enemy of our human nature." Resisting the hegemony of these principles and working to objectify and institutionalize an alternative vision is not "just" a social-political project, but is at the core of the living out of Christian faith; it is, a thoroughly "spiritual" work.[131] Using his concepts of the "theologal" and the "historical," Ellacuría states this in the following way: "The struggle, being theologal, becomes in this way an historical one. The struggle, being historical, and without ceasing for a moment to be historical, becomes a theologal one precisely due to the objectifications of sin that the Gospel propounds and which Saint Ignatius magisterially sums up."[132]

To call this a "theologal struggle" is to call it a struggle in which one is involved in that dimension of historical reality in which God is most densely and foundationally present. This dimension, Ellacuría reads Ignatius's *Spiritual Exercises* as asserting, is one in which two mutually exclusive sets of core, history-forming values compete to define the direction in which human history should move. Whatever rationale might be given for a particular social, institutional implementation of "the standard of Christ" from political theory, economics, or moral philosophy, a Christian will choose it, and choose it most radically, because of the desire to imitate (which means, recall, "to follow by continuing forward") the "historical Jesus." This will not contradict the former rationales, any more than the "third way of being humble" contradicts the first two; it will supplement them by going beyond them. If the resulting strategy appears imprudent, risking the violent destruction of personnel and institutions, or the accusation of being unrealistically, indeed foolishly, utopian, then this is the madness of Jesus, for which he too was accounted a fool. It is "an historical madness when confronted by an historical world whose values are those of the first standard."[133]

This, on Ellacuría's reading, is the fundamental backdrop that sets the stage for an Ignatian discernment. At what sort of evaluation of the world in which it is living would the Latin American Church arrive by doing a "historical discernment" from this perspective? Ellacuría elaborates the answer in his sixth lecture: "The Third World as the Christian Place for Overcoming the Antinomy between the World and the Following of the Historical Jesus."[134] The Third World is the "world of the poor." By world of the poor, Ellacuría means a world that results from the adoption of the values of the standard of Lucifer. He insists that this is a *theological* conceptualization of the world of the poor, not an economic or political one, but it is important to recall here the complex relationship between these different ways of interpreting historical reality, as laid out in his essay on the historicity of salvation, which we analyzed earlier. The theological conceptualization is complementary to the other two, neither independent of them nor reducible to them. This relative autonomy enables it to offer the church a way to act in the world without being assimilated completely to some purely secular constellation of dynamisms and institutions. The church's action will be based on its own proper sources: the actions and deeds of the "historical Jesus." It is, after all, ultimately the example of this Jesus, made concrete via the exercises of the Second Week of the *Spiritual Exercises*, that underwrites the distinction between two sets of values for structuring the world—the two standards. Furthermore, the historical Jesus is made available to the church by means of a set of "spiritual exercises": a creative, imaginative methodology that involves connecting the Jesus of the Gospels with the world in which the church is called to follow him, thereby continuing his message and work. Finally, in the meditations on the Call of the King and the Two Standards, the *Spiritual Exercises* presents "the world of the poor" not solely as an object for objective observation, but as a challenge and a spur to action. This is what a *theological* interpretation of the world adds to a purely economic and political one: "It is important that it not be turned into a purely sociological category; rather, it ought to be seen as a reality that one has to come into contact with, above all in the form of historical praxis. But neither is it a purely empirical category. Rather, it is something that ought to be transcended from the perspective of its profound, real meaning and from the perspective of a theological appreciation."[135]

If there are specifically Christian sources for an evaluation of the world in which the Latin American Church is working, then its labor there can and ought to be specifically Christian, and thus irreducible to "secular" work for liberation. To this extent, "redemptive liberation is not an action that is purely secular; rather, it is a Christian action in the strict sense: a purely secular action ends up truncating the task, abandoning it, or using dehumanizing means."[136] The sixth lecture, in sum, constitutes Ellacuría's proposal for the result of a "historical discernment of spirits" for the Latin American Church.

In the seventh lecture, Ellacuría treats the Third and Fourth Weeks together, reflecting the theological principle that the meanings of the cross and of the Resurrection have to be established conjointly. For the Third Week, he emphasizes that the "the 'mystery' of the passion is totally historicized" by the ways that Ignatius has one focus on visualizing and imagining the concrete historical places and details.[137] Ellacuría is particularly concerned to foreclose an overly aestheticized and emotionalized approach to the Passion, which could result from following Ignatius's dictum that we feel sorrow, regret, and confusion over the Passion to the detriment of cultivating the imaginative grasp of the Passion's historical causes that comes from keeping it connected to the rest of Jesus's life. Neither should the Resurrection be disconnected from history or exempted from the general principle that one comes to know Jesus by following him, which requires continuing now what his life (including the Resurrection) made present in first-century Palestine.[138]

Together, death and resurrection make up the fundamental schema for a Christian life. The negation that is the cross discloses that there is sin in the world, and it discloses this sin as a negation of God that occurs in and by means of the negation of this human being and what his life was about. At the same time, it shows sin to be the negation of this human being that proceeds by negating the center of his life: a life of making this God present, especially for those most crushed by the power of sin. Jesus died because of our sins; he died because of the sin that dominates the world, the sin that structures a world that ineluctably works to obscure and destroy God's presence. This domination manifested itself, and continues to manifest itself, in specific historical structures and actions. Thus, "historically, Jesus was executed for political reasons, and theologically, he died for our sins; instead of excluding one another, these two affirmations give a concrete explanation of the historical mode of the theologal redemption."[139]

The Christian who follows Jesus should expect an analogous fate: "Danger is thus the criterion of the authenticity of faith and of the promise of the resurrection." Yet she or he should also expect to experience the Resurrection, which is the negation of Jesus's death, as equally a historical reality. It will not be an experience of the final, definitive triumph of the God of life, but an experience of "the new Easter spirit [as] the definitive setting in motion of the new human being in the new earth, albeit in a history of the old human beings and of the earth dominated by sin."[140]

Ellacuría does not give further detail as to what this life lived in the "new Easter spirit" would look like, leaving it as an unanswered or underanswered question at the end of the seventh lecture. Yet, the structure of the lectures suggests that Ellacuría intended the final lecture, devoted to the Contemplation to Attain Love, as a gloss on precisely this theme.[141] He tells us that "the contemplation to attain love shows—from the perspective of faith—the real possibility of finding God in creation and the possibility of recovering creation as the presence of God."[142] But this is precisely the meaning of the Resurrection: "The resurrection of Christ is the proclamation of the triumph over sin and of the reconciliation of all of creation with itself and with God."[143]

This is not to deny the continuing presence of sin in the world, which disfigures the forms of God's presence.[144] Rather, the point is that sin cannot fully negate that presence, even now, so that the task of recovering creation as the mediation of God is still an open possibility and an obligatory work. Resurrection is the sign of that triumph over sin, of that reconciliation of creation present now, and it is also the pledge of that reconciliation's ultimate victory. No less so than the other moments of Jesus's life, the Resurrection's presence is ongoing; it should be expected at any point where the power of God confronts sin, but the precise form that it will take will vary according to the historical context. Its presence, moreover, will be incarnated, "historicized," in those who follow Jesus.

Their lives will be characterized by the kind of love that was manifest in Jesus and that discloses the love that defines God's relationship to a world created good (as the Principle and Foundation defines it), but disfigured by sin. Ellacuría points out that for the Contemplation to Attain Love, it is a love "that ought to show itself more in actions than in words," and a love that consists in giving of what one has to the one whom one loves.[145] Most preeminently, this will be the giving of one's own life for the other. Moreover, this love is the result and manifestation of labor extended through time. Ellacuría comments extensively on the third point of the exercise, starting with a quote from Ignatius's text:

> "Consider how God labors and works for me in all the creatures on the face of the earth; that is, God acts in the manner of one who is laboring. For example, God is working in the heavens, elements, plants, fruits, cattle, and all the rest" (no. 236). Here we have a work of God, a labor of God, which incites one to continue this same divine work in the development of nature. The problem comes if this work is developed based on sin and for sin. Here, sin would lie in the negation of love, in a development that is not a communication. Sin would lie in domination, counterpoised to service, as the historical Jesus showed it to us.[146]

Laboring this way, one comes into the presence of the God who is already at work there. "The historical," understood as that dimension in which I experience myself as freely active to shape history in and for the good of others, "appears once again as the privileged place of God's presence."[147] This is a different way of thinking of union with God than the traditional articulation of contemplative union of God in moments of quiet repose, but Ellacuría proposes it as a no less fundamental and authentically Christian way.

This is how Ellacuría offers his own interpretation of the well-known Ignatian formula of "finding God in all things."[148] For him it is a dynamic process, "a contemplation of God in things that is going to give way to a contemplation in action with things."[149] In a dense elaboration of this, Ellacuría asserts that "God becomes present to the person acting, and the person makes God present and becomes present to a God acting." The Spanish original binds these moments—God becoming (*hacerse*), or making Godself present; the person acting; the person making God present; God acting—more tightly together insofar as it deploys the same verb, *hacer*, here translated alternately as "becomes," "act," and "make," to render the way in which God and the person act in such a way that God becomes present to the person and to the world in the same multifaceted process.[150] Prayer and action are not to be counterposed, the first as a passive moment in which the union with God becomes present to the person and the second as an active one that is either preparatory to union or an outflow from it. Prayer and action are both elements in a more comprehensive, and distinctively human, graced, mode of being active, within which the multiple "presencings" of God, person, and world take place. Prayer is that part or element in which the presence of God in the whole is grasped reflexively, but it is not the exclusive locus of that presence.

Ellacuría insists once again that it is action in history that is the most comprehensive ambit within which to map out this relationship between God and persons. As we have seen, this follows from his philosophical and theological ontology, in which historical reality is the fullest, densest actualization of the God–creation relationship. The same insight is pressed by holding the Contemplation to Attain Love in relationship to the rest of the Exercises, particularly with the Second, Third, and Fourth Weeks, with their central positioning of "the historical Jesus" and their goal of opening one to a union with this Jesus that comes from a relationship of following. It is the historical life of Jesus, framed within a broader context of historical reality and actions, that is the historical action par excellence that makes God present. It is in following Jesus that the believer recapitulates this "making-present" in the most authentically

Christian way. Therefore, "it is in the historical following of the historical life of Jesus that the genuine Christian contemplation in action is going to be present."[151] In another essay on the same theme, Ellacuría puts it this way:

> It is not so much a matter of finding God in all things, as if God were present in the same form in all things or in the same mode; clearly, God is not in the Athenian Parthenon and in Jesus of Nazareth in the same way, and God is not in domination in the same way as in oppression. . . . Scripture shows us that the true God and the true encounter with God are two different things; it is not enough to "acknowledge" the former in order for the latter to happen. Consequently, contemplation—that is, the moment of faith—will not be true unless it is realized within that action that is really demanded by the historical following of the historical Jesus.[152]

In these terms, the power of the *Spiritual Exercises* is first that they focus precisely on a true encounter with God and God's will. Second, it is that they place this encounter within the framework of actions, properly discerned, that might otherwise be considered "secular." The only proviso, albeit a crucial one, is that this action be a "historicization" of the God quintessentially present in the historical life of Jesus, a life structured as one that overcomes sin (First Week), through a vocation formed by discerning and responding to a call to mission (Second Week), passing through the paschal mystery (Third and Fourth Weeks). When one attains this love of God, then one will be following the risen Jesus, experiencing "the new Easter spirit [as] the definitive setting in motion of the new human being in the new earth, albeit in a history of the old human beings and of the earth dominated by sin."[153]

Ignatian Spirituality Interprets Ellacuría

The foregoing discussion shows how Ellacuría used technical terms such as "historicization" and "theologal" to work out a particular interpretation of the *Spiritual Exercises*. Yet, one can also argue in the opposite direction that Ellacuría's appropriation of Ignatian spirituality profoundly shaped the way he used these particular terms. That is, the spirituality mapped out in the *Spiritual Exercises* serves as an important context for interpreting Ellacuría's philosophical and theological work, and for elaborating on some of its most important themes. The biographical details of Ellacuría's spiritual intellectual journey already make this a highly likely claim. I add here three additional case studies that show the fruitfulness of using Ignatian spirituality to interpret Ellacuría's theological work and life. They move from the particular to the general: first, such an interpretive stance illuminates how Ellacuría makes use of scripture and "the historical Jesus"; second, it highlights Ellacuría's theology as grounded in and oriented toward a transformed Christian social imagination; third, it helps us understand the importance of the encounter with Jesus Christ, especially today, for understanding Ellacuría.

The Historical Jesus through the Lens of the Spiritual Exercises

At several points we have run across Ellacuría's advertence to the importance of "the historical Jesus," but we have deferred a closer examination of what he means by this freighted term in nineteenth- and twentieth-century theology. Ellacuría's claim that the *Spiritual Exercises* is structured according to the primacy of the historical Jesus touches on a neuralgic point for many scripture scholars. John Meier spoke for many in criticizing the penchant of liberation theologians to appeal to "the historical Jesus" to legitimate theological claims. Analyzing Sobrino's early Christology, Meier concluded that "in the end, Sobrino substitutes unsubstantiated generalizations for the hard work of Jesus-research. The basic problem is never really engaged, and one is left wondering how, if at all, the Bible has really been a source of theology for Sobrino—or for liberation theology in general."[154]

On the hypothesis suggested above, an adequate response to this challenge (at least for Ellacuría's way of doing liberation theology, and, I would argue, for Sobrino's too) will draw on his interpretation of the *Spiritual Exercises*. As a beginning, let us take up once again Ellacuría's definition of liberation theology:

> The theology of liberation understands itself as a reflection from faith on the historical reality and action of the people of God, who follow the work of Jesus in announcing and fulfilling the Kingdom. It understands itself as an action by the people of God in following

the work of Jesus and, as Jesus did, it tries to establish a living connection between the world of God and the human world.... It is, thus, a theology that begins with historical acts and seeks to lead to historical acts, and therefore it is not satisfied with being a purely interpretive reflection; it is nourished by faithful belief in the presence of God within history, an operative presence that, although it must be grasped in grateful faith, remains an historical action. There is no room here for faith without works; rather, that faith draws the believer into the very force of God that operates in history, so that we are converted into new historical forms of that operative and salvific presence of God in humanity.[155]

In this formulation, theology does not draw directly on the Bible. Rather, it reflects on the people of God as they attempt to follow the work of Jesus. They grasp "in grateful faith" the presence of God in history, which also means being grasped by the power of God at work in history and swept up into it. With telling echoes of the language he used to interpret the *Spiritual Exercises*, Ellacuría goes on to say that the church is "that people of God who continue [*prosigue*] in history that which Jesus definitively marked out as the presence of God among men and women."[156]

If theology does not reflect *directly* on scripture, augmenting this definition of theology with Ellacuría's interpretation of the *Spiritual Exercises* discloses the uniquely determinative *indirect* import of scripture. As we have seen, Ellacuría interpreted the Spiritual Exercises as constructing a "place" from which the Latin American Church could grasp and embody the salvific work of God in its own historical context. The focal point lies in the Second Week, in which scripture mediates an encounter with a Jesus who, through the power of the Holy Spirit, is still at work in history, and invites disciples to join in that work. Scripture is, therefore, the place where the Church encounters the Jesus whose history it seeks to continue by following (*proseguir por seguir*). This draws our attention to the contemplations of the Second Week.

In a chapter on the need for a new Christology from a book from the early 1970s, Ellacuría made another illuminating reference to the role of contemplating the life of Jesus:

> This new Christology ought to accord full revelatory status to the flesh of Jesus, that is, to his history. Today nothing would be more ridiculous than to try to construct a Christology in which the

historical realization of Jesus' life did not have decisive significance. What has heretofore been dealt with—and much less so today—under the rubric of "the mysteries of the life of Jesus," as something peripheral and ascetical, must now regain its full meaning. Of course, this presupposes an historical-exegetical reading of what the life of Jesus really was. *What is necessary is a transition to an historical logos, without which every other logos is merely speculative and idealist.* This historical logos would have to start with the fact, incontrovertible to the eyes of faith, that the historical life of Jesus is the fullest revelation of the Christian God, and it would have to be practiced as a logos of history that subsumes and transcends the logos of nature.[157]

The language here utilizes language from "spiritual theology," as Ellacuría would have learned it in the 1950s and 60s. "The mysteries of Jesus' life" refer to events in Jesus's life insofar as they are the subject of Christian meditation and contemplation, as they are in the *Spiritual Exercises*.[158] Ellacuría's comment on their peripheral status in theology refers to the gulf that separated dogmatic and spiritual theology in the decades leading up to Vatican II. Spiritual theology dealt with the journey of the individual Christian to perfection, through the purgative, illuminative, and unitive ways. It was a subdivision of moral theology, and augmented (secondarily) what was really important, which was that individuals conform to universal ethical precepts derived by dogmatic and moral theology. "Ascetical theology" was a further subdivision of spiritual theology. It concerned everyday practices of Christian life, such as fasting but also daily prayer, including prayer on the mysteries of the life of Jesus.[159] This background helps us understand the novelty of what Ellacuría was proposing. Rather than seeing the spiritual exercises formulated by Ignatius—which mediate an encounter with Jesus—as derivative and peri-pheral to conclusions of theology (dogmatic and moral, as it was categorized in the neoscholastic system), he is arguing that they must be central to theology's task. This is of a piece with the claim in his lectures on the *Spiritual Exercises* that the Exercises in general, and the Second Week in particular (which give us Ignatius's "interpretation of the key to Christianity"160), offer an indispensable "place" for the theological work of the Latin American Church.

My conclusion is that in Ellacuría's view, theology does not draw directly on the Bible *simpliciter*. Rather, it reflects on the Bible as a text that has been and is being used by the church, guided by the Spirit, to mediate an encounter with Jesus now, in order to continue in history the salvation that his life both announced and initiated, by enacting it and so making it real (in the dynamic field of "historical reality"). This way of thinking about how theology draws on the Bible requires that theology be vitally concerned with all the diverse means by which Christians have used the Bible in this way and for this end throughout history, ways that in modernity have been collected and too often segregated under the category of "spirituality." One particular set of such means, those that constitute Ignatian spirituality, were, in fact, of vital significance to Ellacuría as a Jesuit, but also as a philosopher and a theologian.

What is the relation of these exercises to the "academic exercises" of the researcher constructing a portrait of the historical Jesus according to the canons of the modern historical-critical analysis of scripture? Here, the underlying philosophical presuppositions are crucial, and Ellacuría can be joined to many others, beginning as early as Maurice Blondel, who criticized the presuppositions underwriting the claim that historical-critical method, as it has evolved over the past two centuries, exhausts the ways human beings know historically and provides the only "objective" access to the person of Jesus.[161] Ellacuría connects his own claim for the need to reappropriate the "mysteries" of Jesus's life for theology, and not "just" for spirituality, with an assertion of the need for the shift to a "historical logos," which is the prerequisite to "a historical-exegetical reading of what the life of Jesus really was." He spent at least two decades working out the philosophy and theology that corresponded to this "historical logos." A crucial element of this project was the understanding of human sentient intelligence as an integrated process with three elements: realizing the weight of reality, shouldering the weight of reality, and taking charge of the weight of reality. Ellacuría's insistence on the need to bring together attention to the mysteries of Jesus's life (segregated earlier into the domain of "spiritual theology") and theology's substantive and normative claims (that is, the products of dogmatic and moral theology) reflects his principle that the first of the three elements of sentient intelligence is not complete and cannot succeed unless it is thoroughly integrated with the other two.

If this is the essential structure of human knowing, what would it mean to "know" Jesus, to apprehend and engage him fully? Would it not be the case that the kind of exercises that Ignatius offers in the Second Week cultivate knowledge in this fuller sense? To be sure, the academic exercises that seek to reconstruct the "historical Jesus" can enrich the first moment of knowing, to the extent that they can "bring Jesus to life" as a historical person, dynamically related to his own context.¹⁶² They can correct and deepen the compositions of place that begin Ignatius's contemplations and that are crucial for "putting ourselves in touch with" the reality of Jesus. They are, however, corrective, not constitutive. If they do not augment and unfold into further exercises that bring us not only to put ourselves in touch with Jesus, but also to take upon ourselves what the reality of Jesus truly is and what it demands of us, and finally to take up an active stance (*pro* or *con*) toward the reality of Jesus, then they cut off rather than open up full knowledge of Jesus. In short, it can be agreed that the "real Jesus" cannot be retrieved by the scholarly exercises of the historical Jesus research program, but this does not demonstrate the inaccessibility of the former but the limited (albeit important) cognitive function and value of the latter.¹⁶³ In his philosophical and theological work, Ellacuría labored to work out the shift to a "historical logos" that would make this evident and would clarify, at least to some extent, how a full knowledge of Jesus, that is, a properly *historicized* knowledge, can be approached. For this, the *Spiritual Exercises* provided an important resource, as a classic example from the Church's tradition of this kind of process, underutilized in academic theology (as Rahner agreed, in his own way). This being the case, one cannot understand the depth and sophistication of Ellacuría's theological position without interpreting it through the lens of Ignatian spirituality.

The Spiritual Exercises *and Healing the Social Imagination*

Using this lens can also alert us to another important feature of Ellacuría's theological performance. This feature points toward a preliminary, or preparatory work, having to do with construing the different data he saw around him in Latin America and the different sources in the Western theological and philosophical tradition for his theoretical production. This preparatory work has to do with the importance of the imagination. To explain what I mean I will start by appealing to another Jesuit, Roger Haight, and what he has written on the importance of imagination for theology:

A first element in theological construction consists in the role of the imagination. Although imagination is difficult to define in itself, people know what it is by its function, by what it does. The imagination imagines: it seeks, produces, and then finds meaning; it projects new forms of unity on the data and construes it in this way or that. The imagination is active and creative. But the theological imagination at this point is not mere fancy. It is already laden with the experience of transcendence mediated by religious symbols, shaped by them, and in possession of the salvific point communicated through them. Moreover the imagination has many sources to work with: the data of traditional symbols themselves, the traditional language of the church, the history of theological portrayals, the spontaneous or strained beliefs of the community, other disciplines which find new leverage for understanding the work of other theologians.[164]

Imagination is vital not only to the activity of Christian theology, but also to the performance of Christian life. This is clear from Ellacuría's own history. When the Jesuit novices came to Santa Tecla in 1948, they had a difficult labor to imagine what religious life could and should look like in this new situation, and Miguel Elizondo interwove this labor with that of appropriating the spirituality of their order's founder. As Sobrino has pointed out, a similar work of reimagination was needed by those who brought their European theological training to bear in Latin America. Without denying the value of the intellectual conversion brought about by his studies in Germany, Sobrino maintains that "it was insufficiently radical and, from a Third World point of view, it was superficial. For me, the world continued to be the First World, the church continued to be the European church of Vatican II, theology continued to be German theology, and utopia continued to mean that in some way the countries of the south would become like those of the north."[165] To be sure, as Sobrino insists, it was the encounter with the poor that brought about a more profound intellectual (and affective, and spiritual) conversion. I return to this point momentarily. Yet, others had this encounter. Such an encounter succeeds to the extent that one's imagination is opened to it, transformed by it. It is the imagination that brings about a creative leap, a "paradigm shift," that "projects new forms of unity on the data," and, even more importantly, considers a different world (the world of the poor, in the case of Ellacuría, Sobrino, and other liberation theologians) to provide significant data in the first place. Theological conceptualization, which "draws the work of the imagination into itself, builds on it, preserves it," comes later.[166]

Yet, the imagination requires not only animation but healing. It is not just a matter of mustering the powers of the imagination to re-remember and reconfigure the world in the light of new experiences and data, but of healing it from constriction, scotosis, and distortion. Willie Jennings captures this exigency with great precision in *The Christian Imagination: Theology and the Origins of Race*. "There is within Christianity," he writes, "a breathtakingly powerful way to imagine and enact the social, to imagine and enact connection and belonging."[167] Yet it has been underutilized and undercultivated, and even when it is operative it fails, in part because it is systemically distorted. This distortion comes to the fore in Jennings's book in considering the reality of race.

Jennings speaks of his own aspirations, and those of his generation of young black men in the 1960s and 70s "who were poised to imagine our belonging in ways unanticipated by our parents and grandparents who had fled the hateful South. Both those imaginative possibilities desperately needed guidance. They needed theological voices that would have drawn us beyond the cultural nationalism, or the conservative theo-political ideologies, or the crass materialism that would beckon in the coming decades."[168] But, he goes on to lament, theology does not recognize its responsibility to social imagination or its dependency on one that is systemically distorted:

> Christianity in the Western world lives and moves within a diseased social imagination. I think most Christians sense that something about Christians' social imagination is ill, but the analyses of this condition often don't get to the heart of the constellation of generative forces that have rendered people's social performances of their Christian life collectively anemic.... And, on the other side, theology now operates within this diseased social imagination without the ability to discern how its intellectual and pedagogical performances reflect and fuel the problem, further crippling the communities it serves.[169]

The social imagination needs healing, but this healing is not a matter of filling conceptual gaps, of theoretical reconfigurations of the relationship between theory and praxis, doctrinal and pastoral disciplines, or orthodoxy and orthopraxis. Jennings proposes a healing that operates narratively and by encountering people who illumine the problem and challenge us to imagine differently, and, in the light of that reimagining, to do theology differently.

To repeat: the imagination (both individual and social) needs both to be animated (enspirited) and healed and liberated from sin and dysfunction.[170] Ellacuría did not speak of the social imagination per se, but he did speak of the necessary relationship between a Christian utopianism that imagines a better, different future (even when, in a negative modality, it imagines that future as gained by fleeing a contemporary history perceived as virtually irredeemable) and a propheticism that is "the critical contrasting of the proclamation of the fullness of the reign of God with a specific historical situation."[171]

If we read Ellacuría and Jennings together, we conclude that propheticism delves to the roots of the diseased social imagination in order to liberate it to imagine, in a concrete, realizable way, specific to one's moment in history, "a new human being, a new earth and a new heaven."[172] The two need one another: "Thanks to propheticism, utopia does not fail to be efficacious in history, even though it is not fully realizable in history, as is the case with Christian utopia."[173] But, on the other hand, Christian propheticism will not "be really Christian without the animation of utopia. Christian propheticism lives by Christian utopia, which, as utopia, lives more and is nourished by the intercession that the Spirit makes throughout history."[174] Ellacuría imagined the Christian university as a place precisely to scrutinize prophetically and animate utopically the social imagination that underlay the national reality of El Salvador.[175] And it is no accident that this reimagining of the university followed and built upon his work to reconfigure the corporate imagination of the Jesuits of Central America at the 1969 retreat.[176] How can his reliance on Ignatian spirituality in the latter work help us understand the former reimagining of the university and of Christian life in general?

If, on Ellacuría's reading, the authentically Christian, life-giving, and salvific constellating of propheticism and utopia (or, in the terms suggested by Jennings, the healing and animation of the social imagination) is an urgent theological task, and if it must also take place in and from a particular historical place and time, then his claim beginning in the late 1960s that the Spiritual Exercises constituted or created a "place" for precisely this kind of historicization of Christian faith, practice, and theology takes on a new significance. On the one hand (moving from Ellacuría's practice as a theologian toward an interpretation of the *Exercises*), it reminds us that Ignatian spirituality is about the transformation—including the healing—of one's imagination. Ellacuría's theology provides a framework for elaborating the *Spiritual Exercises* as a methodology oriented by the healing of the social imagination (which is ultimately, to be sure, the work of the Holy Spirit). The Second Week in particular (which, recall, Ellacuría identifies as the heart of the Exercises) has as its goal a way of imagining one's future that is open to God's will. The rules for discernment help one navigate that imagining by tracking how one responds to it (consolations and desolations) in order to discern what in it is from God.[177]

However, as I argued earlier, the rules for discernment are not applied in a vacuum, but within the context of the contemplations of the life of Jesus, which is richly imaginative. One's imagination is transformed by the creative, imaginative remembering of the life of Jesus, and it is this transformed imagination that generates our imagining of the possible futures among which I am discerning. Moreover, the Exercises begin with an imaginative (and imagination-transforming) confrontation with sin in the First Week, continue through the Second Week with the transformation of the imagination in the encounter with Christ, and end with an extraordinarily utopian exercise, the Contemplation to Attain Love, which, as Ellacuría maintains, imagines nothing less than creation and history as transparent to the love of God.[178] In other words, reading the *Spiritual Exercises* from the perspective of Ellacuría's theology forefronts its possibilities for transforming imagination, and, insofar as Ellacuría understood it as efficacious not just for individuals, but for groups (viz., the Society of Jesus or the Church as a whole in Latin America), its possibilities for healing the *social* imagination in particular.

On the other hand, using the *Spiritual Exercises* as an interpretive key for Ellacuría's work allows us to understand Ellacuría's theology and Christian social practice as a response to the exigency that Jennings identifies: to address a diseased social imagination, first by taking imagination seriously and giving it theological voice, and second by putting a spirituality in play that can open people, individually and corporately, to its healing. It might well seem counterintuitive at first blush to think of Ellacuría as a theologian of the imagination. His dense and densely argued philosophical and theological texts can strike one as exceedingly abstract and intellectual.[179] His imagination was, however, impressively on display as a university administrator and as a public intellectual in a national situation in which the social imagination was being strangled by the dominance of ideologies of nationalism and militarism. If we take seriously his own insistence on the importance of the Spiritual Exercises as constructing a place within which to "historicize" Christian faith and praxis for Latin America, and the centrality of imagination in the Exercises, then we are warranted in asserting the complementarity of the theological argument, found in essays such as "Utopia and Propheticism in Latin America" (which, as I have argued, is about the healing of the social imagination), and the set of practices and vision of God and world (that is, the spirituality) opened up when one performs the Spiritual Exercises. This gives us a fuller portrait of Ellacuría, and helps us to see in a richer way the link between his practice as a theologian and his practice as administrator and public intellectual. The link is the transformed social imagination mediated by Ignatian spirituality.

The Spiritual Exercises *and "Orthopathy": Being Correctly Affected by Jesus*

I close this section on using the *Spiritual Exercises* to interpret Ellacuría and his theology with one final point, now one in which the *Spiritual Exercises* can help us understand the *life* of Ignacio Ellacuría. I do so with all due tentativeness, since henceforth we are talking not of texts but of a life, and of finding one's way to what Sobrino described as the "profoundest depths of a person ... that dimension of reality where a person finds himself or herself before a mystery, before God, and the faith that makes it possible to correspond to God. Or before an enigma, with questions that have no answer, or with the silence that can come with it."[180] Yet, it is important to attempt this, because otherwise our portrait of Ellacuría, including Ellacuría the philosopher and theologian, is incomplete. This is because, as Sobrino insists, it is not a text or even a spirituality, but the influence of a person, and preeminently the person of St. Oscar Romero, that opens up the profoundest understanding of Ellacuría's life and work.[181] Another Jesuit who knew Ellacuría well, Rodolfo Cardenal, makes a similar point, speaking of Ellacuría's ecclesiology:

> Ellacuría's ecclesiology is not a finished product, since it always developed in obedience to historical and ecclesial realities, namely, Vatican II, Medellín, Puebla, and his experiences of Monseñor

Romero, among others. His ecclesiology started from his experience of base communities, which he took to be a fundamental theological event and a new way of being church. Thus, Ellacuría does not begin with books as traditional theologies do but with a theology that springs from life itself.[182]

Given the breadth of his erudition and the resulting density of allusion to a multitude of books in his writings, this too might strike the reader as counterintuitive. Moreover, as true as it may be, such an observation seems to bring one to an interpretive barrier, insofar as that, unlike texts, this source is withdrawn into the personal and interpersonal dynamics of the author's dealings with friends, guides, and mentors. Yet the risk is worth taking for the sake of a richer understanding of the man, Ignacio Ellacuría, who produced the theology we study here, with its dialectical relationship to his lived understanding and interpretation of Ignatian spirituality. This understanding of the man, in turn, can suggest, with all care and tentativeness, some further conclusions about that synthesis.

I begin with further assistance from Sobrino, who himself has written extensively on spirituality and on the spirituality of Ignatius in particular.[183] His account is deeply influenced by Ellacuría's approach, but not identical in every detail. One of his most interesting comments on spirituality in relation to Christian faith and theology is found in the second volume of his mature Christology.[184] It comes in a section where he is considering the Christological titles. In addition to ones more traditionally treated—such as, Messiah, High Priest, Lord, Son of Man, Word of God—he considers one that is not so typically taken up: Jesus as *Eu-Aggelion*, "good news."[185] Christological titles intend to make Jesus intelligible and relevant to a given situation, and, Sobrino maintains, what our situation today most needs is the sense that it might be possible for there to be good news:

> We live in a world in which the news is not generally good, and in which goodness is not news. What is worse, while expectation of salvation—the coming of the kingdom of freedom, of the classless society, or whatever—was, in principle constitutive of modernity, now, postmodernity, neo-liberalism, and globalization are setting limits to, if not annulling expectation as such. The greatest hurdle facing evangelization is the lack of conviction that good news is possible.[186]

In such a situation, he goes on to argue, Jesus can and must be presented not only as Lord or Savior or Liberator, but as *Eu-Aggelion*, as good news. Such a presentation will highlight not just what he proclaimed and what he did, but also the *way* in which he did it: being honest to and with the real, being merciful and faithful, being joyful and ready to celebrate, attending to the smallest of needs while maintaining the greatest breadth of aspiration, combining tenderness and mercy with prophetic denunciation, confidence in God, and loneliness before God.[187] "Jesus is not only *good* at mediating the Kingdom, effective in his theory and practice, but a *good* mediator, welcoming, compassionate, trustworthy for the poor and afflicted, the recipients of the Kingdom."[188] If we do not understand that and how he is a good mediator, we will not fully understand what it was he mediated and not be able to "continue forward" (*proseguir*) the good news that he mediated.

This may sound trivial, obvious, or easy, but it is so far from being so for Sobrino that he adds a third characteristic of an authentic living out of Christian faith to the traditional pairing (and too often oppositional juxtaposing) of *orthodoxy* and *orthopraxis*: *orthopathy*. Examining the "good news" dimension of Jesus, Sobrino claims, "means that in our relationship to him we have to add what, for lack of a better word, we might call *orthopathy* to *orthodoxy* and *orthopraxis*. By *orthopathy* I mean the correct way of letting ourselves be affected by the reality of Christ."[189] This third element, according to Sobrino, cannot be reduced to the other two or replaced by them. This is because, ultimately,

> faith is not just an acceptance of an *interpretation*, nor is the act of faith in its deepest sense acceptance of a witness. When all is said and done it is the confrontation with and acceptance—in trust and in a willingness to make oneself available to it—of a historical reality that leads beyond itself, and that then can certainly be interpreted transcendentally and be an object of faith. The good news of Jesus in the New Testament is not only a belief—that the pasch brings salvation—but also an experience of a reality—that Jesus' mercy, honesty, loyalty and fidelity are good things for the human race.[190]

Appropriating this into theology is no easy thing, and, indeed, it involves "the most basic way of relating Christology [and with it, thus, theology] and spirituality."[191]

Let us follow this clue to shed further light on Ellacuría's spirituality and theology. In elaborating what he means by *orthopathy*, Sobrino considers Leonardo Boff, Karl Rahner, and Ellacuría. On Ellacuría, he quotes a recollection of a student in Ellacuría's classroom:

> In a theology lecture Fr. Ellacuría was analyzing Jesus' life, and suddenly reasoning departed and his heart took over. And he said: "The fact is that Jesus had the justice to go to the depths and at the same time he had the eyes and the bowels of mercy to understand human beings." Ellacu was silent for a while and then finished by saying of Jesus: "He was a great man."[192]

Reason did not, perhaps, so much depart as show its foundation in a deep and prior intuition, a spiritual one, and one essential for understanding what reason can and should produce. Let us apply our hypothesis on the mutual intercalation of Ellacuría's lived experience and interpretation of Ignatian spirituality, on the one hand, and his philosophical and theological production, on the other, in order to move a little bit further in understanding this deepest dimension of his life and work.

First, what Sobrino names "orthopathy," "the correct way of letting ourselves be affected by the reality of Christ," is the aim of the Spiritual Exercises as a whole and of the Second Week in particular. Sobrino agrees with Ellacuría that the key to understanding the *Spiritual Exercises* lies in its focus on "the historical Jesus" in the Second Week.[193] And the grace one asks for in the Second Week is "an intimate knowledge of our Lord, who has become human for me, that I may love him more and follow him more closely."[194] This is how the first moment of human sentient intelligence, which we discussed earlier ("realizing the weight of reality"), is manifest when engaging the historical reality of Jesus, and his humanity in particular, in which, Ellacuría asserts elsewhere, the entire mystery of the presence of God's transcendence and holiness in history is contained.[195] Insofar as this first moment is not present without the other two—the ethical and praxical—then "the correct way of letting ourselves be affected by the reality of Christ" cannot but unfold in "shouldering the weight of reality" as Jesus did, which means adopting his standard for making decisions, and, finally "taking charge of reality" as he did, which is to be placed with him by the Father as a disciple, even to the cross. Thus, for Ellacuría, as for Sobrino,

Ignatian spirituality details one way in which spirituality and theology (and Christian praxis) can interrelate: spirituality provides the starting point for allowing orthopathy to unfold into orthodoxy and orthopraxis.[196]

It is also true that, his earlier criticisms and opposition notwithstanding, Ellacuría felt himself compelled to let himself be deeply affected by Romero, as Sobrino states in his essay.[197] Ellacuría expressed this "being affected" in the most profound terms, perhaps speaking autobiographically: "There are many who are ready to follow his path, knowing that Monseñor Romero, in the last three years of his life, was an exemplary follower of Jesus of Nazareth."[198] And, most dramatically, "with Monseñor Romero God passed through El Salvador."[199]

On the one hand, keeping in view his interpretation of the Exercises, heavily inflected by his philosophy and theology, these statements come as no surprise. In his lectures on the Exercises six years earlier he had already argued that "a human presence and an historical action is always necessary to make God present"; and "it is in the historical following of the historical life of Jesus that the genuine Christian contemplation in action is going to be present."[200] Romero, the exemplary disciple, was thus, on Ellacuría's reading, the exemplary contemplative in action, which meant that Romero made God radically present both to Salvadoran reality and, we might venture to say, to Ellacuría himself, and was himself intimately united with God. Furthermore, if we turn to the exercise that is the locus for understanding contemplation in action, The Contemplation to Attain Love, we can understand Sobrino's claim that "ultimately, in my opinion, Ellacuría 'was carried' in his own faith by the faith of Monseñor Romero. By this I want to express the dimension of 'gift' and of 'grace' that became present in his life, and the way that it became present in him."[201] At risk of infringing on the mystery at the depths of this Basque Jesuit's relationship to God, I would venture a further elaboration of Sobrino's remarks by saying that in the lived Contemplation to Attain Love of God that describes Ellacuría's final years, the "exchange of gifts" that Ignatius defines as love (*SpEx* 231) manifested itself for him as an exchange in which the gift and grace that Romero was for him elicited the gift of his own life, given slowly in exhausting himself and his bodily energies in labor for peace and justice in El Salvador, and finally in the face of an assassin's M-16.

Yet it goes without saying that not all were affected by Romero in this way: not many of the wealthy elites in El Salvador, not most of the other Salvadoran bishops, the papal nuncio, and not many members of the Roman Curia. I would suggest that the option by which Ellacuría allowed himself to be affected by Romero in this way was an act of *discernment*. Sobrino argues that "without any kind of excessive piety at all (which he was not given to anyway), but rather with existential and intellectual conviction, he discerned in Monseñor Romero 'the true signs of the presence of God or of God's plans.' Monseñor Romero was a theologal sign of the times."[202] As we saw in the previous section, the imaginative work of discernment requires the transformation and healing of imagination that comes with engaging and embracing "the historical Jesus." Yet, if we follow Sobrino's line of argument, this means allowing oneself correctly to be affected by Christ: it requires orthopathy. In this discernment, which allowed and even required Ellacuría to say, "With Monseñor Romero God passed through El Salvador," Ellacuría was affirming, by a "personal adherence," a "historicization" of Jesus in a new time and situation, which deepens by historicizing in turn the "being affected by Christ" that is the purpose of the contemplations of the Second Week.[203]

This is one way of construing, with the help of the *Exercises* and Ellacuría's interpretation of them, what it might mean to say that, as Sobrino and Cardenal insist, it is just as important (perhaps more so) to attend to the *people* who had an influence on Ellacuría as it is to consider the many texts that he read and analyzed (even the text of the *Spiritual Exercises*). Monseñor Romero was a theological source for Ellacuría, not first or even primarily because of Romero's philosophical or theological insights (though they should not be disregarded), but because through his discerning attraction and commitment to Romero, Ellacuría was able to be affected correctly by Jesus, which is the furthest thing possible from a pious claim.[204] The same might be said of Pedro Arrupe and others too. Ultimately, it was the discerning commitment to the people, the poor in particular, of El Salvador that drove Ellacuría's work, for the same reason: in and through them he was affected by and attracted to Jesus.

It is this being affected deeply by Jesus, understood in the way that he understood it in his interpretation of the *Spiritual Exercises*, and the Second Week above all, that opened Ellacuría to the "more" that is possible in history, available to a healed and reinvigorated social imagination. It informed his rigorous analysis of the historical reality in which he lived, and the imagination with which he confronted it as a scholar, administrator, and public intellectual. In this way, echoing the points Rahner made in his essay on the motto *Ad majorem Dei gloriam*, Ellacuría made careful discernments and then decisive commitments: neither foolproof nor apodictic, always tentative, but never tentatively implemented, aiming at a more in history that comes into view when, as Sobrino concludes, using Ellacuría's own words, "these new human beings [of a new human being, a new heaven, and a new earth] keep on proclaiming firmly and steadfastly, although always in the darkness, an ever greater future, because beyond all the futures that follow one upon the other, they catch sight of the God who saves, the God who liberates."[205] In this he became good news in his own right, for a world that desperately needs it.

A Mysticism and Theology of the Historical Event

In a beautiful passage, Marie-Dominique Chenu, one of the great figures of *ressourcement* theology, described the importance of spirituality for theology:

> The fact is that in the final analysis theological systems are simply the expressions of a spirituality. It is this that gives them their interest and their grandeur.... One does not get to the heart of a system via the logical coherence of its structure or the plausibility of its conclusions. One gets to that heart by grasping it in its origins via that fundamental intuition that serves to guide a spiritual life and provides the intellectual regimen proper to that life.[206]

This is true of Ignacio Ellacuría. I have argued in this chapter that one of the goals of his philosophy and theology was to communicate a powerful "fundamental intuition" from the *Spiritual Exercises*, an intuition that was tested in the fires of violent persecution, and laboriously articulated and elaborated in long hours of scholarly research and writing. Within the *Spiritual Exercises*, I located this intuition more precisely in Ellacuría's commentary on the Second Week and the way it opens up an avenue to a properly historicized encounter with Jesus. I argued that Ellacuría offers a fundamental, novel, and compelling interpretation of the

Exercises using the philosophical and theological system he constructed over the course of a thirty-year academic career. Moreover, if we take seriously the connection between Ignatian spirituality and Ellacuría's thought, we are able to surface and elaborate three elements that are not often or correctly understood: that and how the encounter with the Jesus witnessed by scripture is essential not only to the Spiritual Exercises but also for theology; the power of Ignatian spirituality, and an academic theology that follows its lead, to heal a diseased social imagination; and the importance of interpersonal encounter, articulated in an "orthopathic circle," if I can put it that way, between "allowing oneself to be correctly affected by the humanity of Jesus" and allowing oneself to be affected by those persons and peoples today in whom the God of Jesus continues to "pass through" one's historical reality, wherever that is.

If we inquire more closely into the "fundamental intuition that serves to guide a spiritual life and provides the intellectual regimen proper to that life," the foregoing discussion leads to the conclusion that it corresponds to the strand in Ignatian spirituality, identified in chapter 3 with the help of Ewert Cousins's notion of a mysticism of the historical event as "a distinct form of mystical consciousness whereby one attempts to enter into a significant historical event of the past in order to tap its spiritual energies."[207] Cousins had suggested that Rahner might serve as the "Bonaventure" to Ignatius, integrating the latter's spirituality into the broader tradition of Christian spirituality and theology, as Bonaventure had for Francis.[208] Yet, we saw that Rahner's approach, though not completely ignoring "the historical Jesus," drew more on Neoplatonic strands. If we are looking for a theologian who integrated Ignatian spirituality, construed in terms of *this* decisive and novel mystical tradition, into theology, and attempted to make it available to the church, Ellacuría is a better candidate.

The contrast between Rahner and Ellacuría on discernment can make this point. In chapter 4, I argued (following Endean, Rubbelke, and others) that for Rahner the "touchstone" for discernment was the experience of consolation without prior cause. Granting whatever difficulties and ruptures (some of them inevitable when any rational conceptuality attempts to capture a core mystical experience) in the way Rahner theorized it, this experience is laid out in terms of indifference (with its earlier cognates in the mystical tradition of *Gelassenheit* and *Abgeschiedenheit*). Indifference, both as a fundamental structure of human being in the world and when accepted and embraced (in and by the power of the Holy Spirit), is disclosive of an immediate presence of God to the individual person, in all his or her particularity, as the core dynamism of the graced soul. By "comparing" this experience with one's affective-spiritual responses to the different options among which one is discerning, the one discerning gradually comes to identify one of them as more congruent to, or perhaps transparent to, this fundamental experience. This explanatory structure finds, as we saw, its theological and mystical genealogy in figures in the broad and complex Neoplatonic mystical stream: in the High and late Middle Ages, Ruusbroec, Tauler, Eckhart, and above all Bonaventure.

For Ellacuría, however, the touchstone experience for discernment is that of allowing oneself to be correctly affected by the humanity of Jesus, as this is facilitated by the contemplations on the life of Jesus in the Second Week, in particular, and urged on us as a decisive choice to be made by the Meditation on the Two Standards. It is what Sobrino named "orthopathy." The example of Ellacuría's appropriation of the process of discernment—in his philosophy, his theology, and his life—helps us understand the importance of placing the practice of discernment within the practices of contemplating the life of Jesus in the Second Week.

The latter practices bring about a healing and an attunement of one's imagination that then makes it possible for one to be correctly affected by the historical reality in which one is striving to make real one's following of Jesus, that is, to discern correctly. This discernment, reinforces that orthopathic relationship to Jesus in his humanity, which then refines one's capacity to correct errors in discernment more quickly. In both ways of thinking about discernment, one is able to give an account of how, over time, one can grow in wisdom and facility in discernment. This is the process that Ignatius captures beautifully with a metaphor toward the end of the Rules for Discernment: "In souls that are progressing to greater perfection, the action of the good angel is delicate, gentle and delightful. It may be compared to a drop of water penetrating a sponge. The action of the evil spirit upon such souls is violent, noisy and disturbing. It may be compared to a drop of water falling upon a stone" (*SpEx* 335).

Ellacuría's interpretation prescinds as much as possible from the Neoplatonism of which Rahner's is still redolent, and not surprisingly given the suspicions that Ellacuría learned from Zubiri about the dangers of this approach. Ellacuría's interpretation relies much more on the mystical tradition enacted by Francis of Assisi in his life and deeds, in which it is the mystical power inherent to the historical event, in its historicity (that is, to use Ellacuría's language, as historical reality), that empowers the mystical journey. This is an empowerment that arises from and remains within history, even though it discloses and, in however fragmentary and limited a way, actualizes ("historicizes") a graced "more" to history that corresponds to the "more" of the ever-greater God.

In this way too, Ellacuría moved much further in the direction of making Ignatian spirituality an instrument for corporate discernment, a way for the Church to historicize itself, particularly on the local level. Rahner had hinted at the need for this toward the end of his life. He also had suggested that one might be able to recapitulate the kind of argument that he had laid out in essays such as "The Logic of Concrete Existential Insight in Ignatius of Loyola" to this purpose, but had not realized that work himself, perhaps because it would have required too great a modification of the foundations of his own way of "theologizing" the Spiritual Exercises. Ellacuría attempted to do this in practice at the 1969 retreat of the Central American Vice Province, and articulated a philosophy and theology over the subsequent two decades that made some sense of how the Exercises can be turned to this task, so that his final essay, "Utopia and Propheticism from Latin America," which, I have argued, is about the healing of a diseased Christian social imagination, serves as a powerful complement and culmination of the work laid out in his lectures on the *Spiritual Exercises* a quarter century earlier.

In sum, what Ellacuría learned in the school of the *Spiritual Exercises* was the mysticism of the historical event. He used various tools, primarily taken from Zubiri, but also from Rahner, from Marx, from the poetry of Ángel Martínez, and from encountering the faith of Romero, to give conceptual expression to that mystical stance, but, in the process he "Ignatianized" those resources. He was, furthermore, in full agreement with the Franciscan/Bonaventuran insight that "there is no other path but through the burning love of the Crucified,"[209] with the important qualification that the place to encounter the crucified is in his crucified body in history: "the crucified people." He took up diverse philosophical and theological tools to offer this intuition to the Latin American Church as a real possibility. As a Jesuit, a university teacher and administrator, and a political actor on the troubled stage of Central America, he strove to deploy a healed social imagination and make it a transformative actuality—to "historicize" it, as he would say for his historical reality. This is the way that Ignatian spirituality served as a source and integrating center, not just for Ellacuría's theology, but for his entire life and work, and it is also the way in which he made a unique contribution to putting Ignatian spirituality, with its methodology for opening oneself to the grace of orthopathy, at the service of contemporary Christian theology (orthodoxy) and action (orthopraxis).

CHAPTER SIX

Pope Francis

Theology as an Instrument of Consolation

THEOLOGY, LEADERSHIP, IGNATIUS

On March 13, 2013, Jorge Mario Bergoglio, SJ, then the cardinal archbishop of Buenos Aires, was elected pope, succeeding the recently resigned Benedict XVI. When the tally of votes was completed, Giovanni Battista Re, the assistant cardinal dean, approached Bergoglio and asked him *"Acceptasne electionem de te canonice factam in Summum Pontificem?"* (Do you accept your canonical election as Supreme Pontiff?). Rather than the traditional (and simple) word of consent (*Accepto*), Bergoglio chose a longer response that signaled both the principal themes of his papacy and his roots in Ignatian spirituality: "I am a sinner, but I trust in the infinite mercy and patience of our Lord Jesus Christ, and I accept in a spirit of penance."[1] This formula echoes the opening line of the first substantive decree by the 32nd General Congregation of the Society of Jesus, which met from December 2, 1974, to March 7, 1975, and which Bergoglio attended as the provincial of the Jesuits of Argentina: "What is it to be a Jesuit? It is to know that one is a sinner, yet called to be a companion of Jesus as Ignatius was: Ignatius, who begged the Blessed Virgin to 'place him with her Son,' and who then saw the Father himself ask Jesus, carrying his Cross, to take this pilgrim into his company."[2]

The dual insight that one is a sinner and called to be a companion of Jesus is, to be sure, not exclusive to Ignatian spirituality. When he was named an auxiliary bishop of Buenos Aires twenty-one years earlier, Bergoglio embraced this truth in choosing his episcopal motto, using not Ignatius, but a line from a medieval theologian: *miserando atque eligendo* (by having mercy and by choosing him). As the pope himself explained in an interview, "The motto is taken from the *Homilies* of Bede the Venerable, who writes in his comments on the Gospel story of the calling of Matthew: 'Jesus saw a publican, and since he looked at him with feelings of love and chose him, he said to him, "Follow me."'" The pope then adds, "I think the Latin gerund *miserando* is impossible to translate in both Italian and Spanish. I like to translate it with another gerund that does not exist: *misericordiando* (mercy-ing)."[3]

Social, cultural, and political engagement on behalf of the poor, to which the Jesuits committed themselves in 1975, was also on the newly elected pope's mind.[4] A few days after the election, he gave his reasons for choosing the name "Francis":

> During the election, I was seated next to the Archbishop Emeritus of São Paolo and Prefect Emeritus of the Congregation for the Clergy, Cardinal Claudio Hummes: a good friend, a good friend! When things were looking dangerous, he encouraged me. And when the votes reached two thirds, there was the usual applause, because the Pope had been elected. And he gave me a hug and a kiss, and said: "Don't forget the poor!" And those words came to me: the poor, the poor. Then, right away, thinking of the poor, I thought of Francis of Assisi. Then I thought of all the wars, as the votes were still being counted, until the end. Francis is also the man of peace. That is how the name came into my heart: Francis of Assisi. For me, he is the man of poverty, the man of peace, the man who loves and protects creation; these days we do not have a very good relationship with creation, do we?[5]

The argument of this chapter is that as much as these and other features of Pope Francis's spirituality are the common patrimony of all Christians, and can be found in diverse schools of Christian spirituality, the ways that this pope has drawn on them as a leader in the Church are deeply shaped by his Jesuit formation and his embrace of Ignatian spirituality. Rendered in an Ignatian key, a list of these features would include his emphasis on the transformation that comes from encountering Jesus Christ, making one a "missionary disciple"; the acute awareness of one's sinfulness and limitations elicited by such an encounter, overmatched by the experience of mercy and of being sent that are integral to it; an unwavering commitment to the Church, including (but not solely) in its institutional dimension, in combination with a restless "going forth to the peripheries," frequently beyond the borders that some, at least, would draw for the Church; the restlessness that comes from taking the measure ever anew of whether one has succeeded in being a follower of Christ, taking this measure from the vantage point of a deeply consoling and also unsettling presence to the "ever greater God." These central lattices for his spirituality cannot be unified conceptually and then mechanically applied; they require, but also call forth and sustain, a crucial spiritual practice and disposition that the pope himself named as the most important element of Ignatian spirituality for him in his practice of ecclesial leadership: discernment.[6]

This is all well and good for a consideration of Ignatian spirituality and leadership, but Pope Francis might seem an odd man out when it comes to the topic of this book, which is Ignatian spirituality and contemporary theology. Unlike Rahner and Ellacuría, Pope Francis never completed a doctoral degree in either philosophy or theology. He was, to be sure, the rector of a major theological institute in Buenos Aires, the Colegio Máximo, but he never filled a teaching and research post fulltime, and few of his writings have been cast in the genre of academic theology. When he addresses or talks about theologians, he tends to use the second- or third-person plural, and not the first person.

Yet the pope has things to say about the current state of Catholic theology, and has said them both before and after his election in 2013. Part of the argument of this chapter is that, like other figures in the twentieth century and into the twenty-first, Pope Francis is concerned about the divorce that has come about between theology as a conceptual-argumentative praxis, focused on texts and other historical artifacts in the Christian tradition, and theology as an engagement with the pastoral and the local-contextual. The latter's object is the ways that people, as individuals and communities, struggle to be followers of Christ, "missionary disciples," in ever-shifting and challenging situations. This way of thinking about theology, which Francis often names "the pastoral dimension" (*lo pastoral*), overlaps in significant ways with what I have named "spirituality" in this book. And thus it is valid to say that an important issue for Francis is how to bridge the gap between academic theology and spirituality, even though he uses different terminology. If our other two authors sought to bridge this gap from the side of academic theology, Bergoglio has addressed it more from the other side of the divide. But in all three cases, it is Ignatian spirituality that provides materials to construct the bridge.

As I did with Rahner and Ellacuría, therefore, I will argue that Bergoglio has a unique and compelling interpretation of Ignatian spirituality that has been enriched by his intellectual formation, but also by his experiential-praxical formation as a religious superior and bishop. His writings and his practice shed light on the *Spiritual Exercises*. On the other hand, the *Spiritual Exercises* can be used as an interpretive tool in its own right to understand more deeply some of Pope Francis's theological positions. To be precise, I will argue that, in taking a point of view disclosed by this central text of Ignatian spirituality, Pope Francis has consistently pressed for academic theology (and, the practices and institutions that concretize the work of Christian education more broadly) to be an instrument of consolation in today's world, which it does by inviting those it serves into an experience of mercy. Moreover, in his practice as a religious leader he has incarnated a form of leadership and communal decision-making that draws on the Ignatian concept of discernment. Yet discernment, as I have already emphasized, cannot be considered or put into play without considering the other features that Ignatius interweaves with it over the course of the *Spiritual Exercises*: having an experience of mercy that opens oneself to a call to discipleship; encountering Christ in the concrete, which specifies and further energizes that call; and being faithful to that call, so specified, in order to seek and find consolation, for oneself and (with the same grace) for others, a consolation that, as the Third and Fourth Weeks make clear, is always cruciform-risen.

I begin with an overview of Pope Francis's life and intellectual formation in order to make the case (which perhaps hardly needs making) that Ignatian spirituality is an important, perhaps the most important, element in his development as a theologian, and a key to interpreting his thought and practice. Then I turn to his interpretation of Ignatian spirituality, focusing on a retreat that he give to the bishops of Spain, "in the manner of Ignatius of Loyola," in 2006, but also drawing on earlier retreats that he gave, and on lectures from his time as religious superior in the Society of Jesus and as pope.[7] Finally, I turn to one example of a theological issue in which using the *Spiritual Exercises* as a hermeneutical lens can shed significant light on his position: the relationship between mercy and justice in Christian faith.

Life of Pope Francis: The Pilgrim

It might seem paradoxical to give the name "pilgrim" to a man who, before being elected pope, had spent almost his entire life in Argentina, except for short stints in Chile, Spain, and Germany. And of those seventy-seven years, the majority were spent in Buenos Aires. Yet there is a restlessness about the first pope from the Global South, a restlessness he identifies with his favorite early Jesuit, second only to Ignatius himself: Pierre Favre. Moreover, in his own way, the pope has traversed diverse cultures as a pilgrim: from the traditional Italian-Argentinian Catholic milieu of his youth, to the religiously diverse, often chaotic, but also vibrant milieu of one of the world's great megacities, to the complex congeries of cultures that constitutes a pluralistic, global Church. He exemplifies the description that Nadal penned four hundred years before the young Jorge Mario Bergoglio entered the Society of Jesus: "The world is our house." Integral to the mindset of this pilgrim is the conviction that this diversity of cultures cannot be synthesized or grasped exclusively "from above" or from the "intellectual laboratory."[8] Real understanding requires that each culture be traversed and explored; the people nourished by it encountered, accompanied, and engaged in a dialogue that is based in empathy and appreciation, and desires to grow in them. Encounter, accompaniment, dialogue, appreciation: none of these terms, so pervasive in Pope Francis's writings and speeches, is the exclusive property of Ignatian spirituality, but it is nonetheless the case that he learned them and lived his way into them through learning Ignatian spirituality. He was formed by this spirituality and soon felt a desire to pass on its riches to others, which he endeavored to do first as a novice master and religious superior in the Society of Jesus, and then, in a different way, as a bishop, and finally as pope. Even more than for the other two Jesuits studied in this book, the most important "text" that Pope Francis has studied is the one made up of his life as a pilgrim. For this reason, a sketch of his pilgrimage through "the world our house" is vital. However brief it must be, this biographical sketch can also disclose the different modalities and the depth of his engagement with Ignatian spirituality.[9]

Jorge Mario Bergoglio was born in a suburb of Buenos Aires on December 17, 1936. His grandparents had emigrated from Italy about fifteen years earlier. Relatively prosperous at first, they, like many, were impoverished by the Great Depression and were forced to work hard to make ends meet. The first of five children, from an early age the young Jorge Mario was often sent to his grandmother for the day, and she had a profound influence on him. His insistence on the importance of the family (understood multigenerationally) has its experiential roots in these years. He was vigorous and well-liked, loved soccer and Samba, and the companionship of others. When he was seventeen, on the Feast of St. Matthew, he had a powerful experience in a confessional of a call to the priesthood.[10] Three years later he entered the diocesan seminary, which was run by the Society of Jesus, and within the year sought entrance into the Society itself. In March 1958 (after a serious illness that nearly took his life), he entered the novitiate.[11] After novitiate, he spent a year in Chile, where he had his first sustained exposure to radical poverty.[12] He then returned and took up residence in what is perhaps the most important Jesuit community and institution in Argentina: the Colegio Máximo.[13]

Continuing his Jesuit formation, Bergoglio studied both philosophy and theology at the Máximo, with the customary interlude of apostolic service, which he spent teaching literature in a Jesuit School in Santa Fé and another in Buenos Aires. He was ordained on December 13, 1969, and spent his final year of formation in Spain. By this time he had already been marked for leadership in the Argentinian province. He was named novice master in 1971, and then, remarkably, made provincial in 1973, at the age of thirty-six.

Looking ahead to his tenure as auxiliary bishop and then archbishop of Buenos Aires, and finally bishop of Rome, it is worth noting that Francis is the first pope not to have been integrally involved in Vatican II, either as a bishop (John XXIII, Paul VI, John Paul I, and John Paul II), or as a theological consultant (Benedict XVI). The young Jesuit watched the events of the Council unfold, albeit with great interest, from 7,000 miles away, while finishing his philosophy studies and then teaching in Santa Fé. He belonged to the first generation charged solely with interpreting and implementing the vision of the Council, rather than articulating it. Neither was he present at the CELAM meetings in Medellín and Puebla, even though, as we shall see, he was certainly just as caught up in the tumultuous and painful process of implementing the preferential option for the poor as Ellacuría was in El Salvador.

Unlike Ellacuría and the other young Jesuits who were initiated into Ignatian spirituality in the newly refounded novitiate in Santa Tecla, the future pope's early training followed more closely the ascetic and quasi-monastic model that was common in the Society of Jesus in those years. An important deviation from this pattern came when he was in philosophy training at the Colegio Máximo (1961–63), because of the influence of a remarkable Jesuit, Miguel Ángel Fiorito, who was the young Jesuit's spiritual director. Fiorito was deeply involved in the recovery of Ignatian spirituality in its original documents and practices, and is remembered in particular as a master of the interpretation and practice of Ignatius's Rules for Discernment of Spirits. Fiorito also brought back the practice of individually directed (rather than communal and preached) retreats using the *Spiritual Exercises*.[14] Bergoglio was part of a group of young Jesuits who formed around Fiorito and helped him start a journal of spirituality, in which Bergoglio himself published several essays.[15] During this period, Bergoglio was also exposed to Gaston Fessard's theological interpretation of the *Spiritual Exercises*. Fessard (1897–1978) wrote a commentary on the *Spiritual Exercises* that framed it in terms of a set of polarities and dialectics, for example, between shame and hope.[16] Bearing these polarities in mind, Fessard presented the *Spiritual Exercises* as a dialectics that cannot be systematized in a purely conceptual way, but only negotiated through the process of discernment actualized in a concrete commitment to a particular course of action. Fessard's approach became a cornerstone of Pope Francis's interpretation of the *Spiritual Exercises*.

Bergoglio had often expressed an aspiration to be involved in the formation of young Jesuits, an aspiration fulfilled when he was named novice master in 1971, but he was probably not prepared for being named provincial two years later. In a manner parallel to events unfolding in Central America, the Jesuits of Argentina had become deeply divided over how to implement Medellín and the mandate given by the Jesuit provincials in 1968. Tensions had risen to the point where Pedro Arrupe, the superior general, decided to find a new provincial, even though the current one, Ricardo O'Farrell, had only served four of the usual six years. But who? The older generation of Jesuits had been decimated by departures from the Society, so there was no figure among the more seasoned Jesuits who could unite the Province. As a result, the young Jesuit, just barely finishing his formation, was selected.

Reflecting with the benefit of forty years of hindsight, Pope Francis is brutally honest about those years:

> My style of government as a Jesuit at the beginning had many faults. That was a difficult time for the Society: an entire generation of Jesuits had disappeared. Because of this I found myself provincial when I was still very young. I was only 36 years old. That was crazy. I had to deal with difficult situations, and I made my decisions abruptly and by myself. Yes, but I must add one thing: when I entrust something to someone, I totally trust that person. He or she must make a really big mistake before I rebuke that person. But despite this, eventually people get tired of authoritarianism.... My authoritarian and quick manner of making decisions led me to have serious problems and to be accused of being ultraconservative. I lived a time of great interior crisis when I was in Cordova. To be sure, I have never been like Blessed Imelda [a goody-goody], but I have never been a right-winger.[17]

The difficulty of guiding a province divided over how to respond to Vatican II and to Medellín was made even worse by the onset of the so-called Dirty War in Argentina. This was the latest chapter in a complex history of Argentinian politics and society, which had revolved for almost thirty years around the figure of Juan Perón (1895–1974). Perón had first come to power when young Jorge was ten, with a rule that would last for nine years. Rising through the ranks of the military, Perón had spent time in Italy in the late thirties, where he studied the governments of Mussolini and Franco, and returned to Argentina convinced that the country could be governed by forging an alliance of labor unions, the military, and the Church. He advocated accelerated industrialization and nationalization of key industries, policies that favored the labor unions and gained the loyalty of workers, all presided over by the coercive power of the military and the moral and spiritual authority of the Church. Perón positioned himself to begin with as a champion of the "Catholic nation," and insisted that his government was structured according to Catholic Social Teachings, especially Pius XI's *Quadragesimo anno* (1931). For these reasons Perón's government was seen by many devout Catholics (including bishops and priests) as a welcome exception to many regimes in Latin America, which, with their liberal-secular viewpoint, were becoming increasingly hostile to the Catholic Church. Relations soured in the 1950s, however, culminating in a series of tense confrontations between Perón and the Argentinian Church in 1954 and 1955, the year in which a military coup ousted him.[18]

Held together largely by the force of Perón's personality and his political skills, Peronism fragmented into rightist and leftist factions. They began fighting one another after Perón was deposed by the military in 1955. For the next two decades politics in Argentina was dominated by the ways different parties and the military positioned themselves with regard to Perónism. In the process, "Perónism" came to mean not so much a political movement as a culture or a tradition. In its right-wing incarnation, this tradition envisioned an integralist union of Church and state built around the principles of Catholic Social Teachings and respect for the popular religious values of the people, while the left wing took Peronism's alliance with the working class in a Marxist direction and spurned alliance with the Church. This particular combination of politics, militarism, and religion was a volatile mixture, and it shaped the development of the young Bergoglio's views on politics and their relationship to Catholic faith. He was fascinated with politics, and though he dallied with communist literature, he soon settled back into the loyal right-wing Peronism that characterized his family—as it did many loyal Catholics who were put off by the vitriolic anti-Catholic rhetoric of the left-wing "Montoneros."[19] This preference would show itself when he became provincial, a preference that was quite evident (and provocative) to those Catholics and Jesuits who were troubled by the more radical and violent wing of this form of Peronism, or cast their lots with movements on the left wing of Peronism.

Perón briefly returned to power in 1973, but by that time the movement he had spawned had splintered beyond repair, with extremists on both sides forming death squads that rampaged through the neighborhoods of Buenos Aires. When a military junta overthrew the government, there was general relief on all sides. This lasted until the disappearances started. In the next seven years of the "Dirty War" (1976–83), somewhere between 10,000 and 30,000 Argentinians were arrested, tortured, and "disappeared," often dropped from planes into the estuary of the La Plata

River or into the Atlantic Ocean. The full story of the Church's role in the violence is yet to be told (and many Argentinians have hoped that Pope Francis will make documentation in the Vatican accessible for that purpose), but the general outlines are clear. Jeffrey Klaiber summarizes:

> During this period the official church denounced flagrant violations of human rights, but in general it did not take clear and decisive steps to back up those denunciations, as the church in Chile and Brazil did. And this in spite of the fact that many of the victims of this state terror were committed Christians, among them one or two bishops and several priests and religious women. What saves the image of the Argentinian church is the courageous effort on the part of a minority within the official church—some bishops and priests—and a great number of laypersons beyond the circle of the official church.[20]

Bergoglio followed the strategy of keeping a public silence, while making private objections to leaders of the military junta.[21] He also courageously sheltered those on governmental death lists and helped them flee the country, and worked doggedly for the release of some already imprisoned, often at great personal risk.[22] Assessing what Bergoglio did or did not do (which is all too easy from the distance of time, and the safety of relative peace and prosperity) is complicated by the entanglement of his actions during the Dirty War with his responses to the divisions within the province. As provincial he moved to reverse a number of the innovations that O'Farrell had put in place following what O'Farrell had judged that Medellín required. Bergoglio returned the houses of formation to more traditional patterns, instituting fixed schedules, requiring young Jesuits to wear clerical garb, and integrating manual labor into formation.[23] He also insisted on direct contact with the poor, of which the central component was gaining an appreciation for their popular religiosity. Pastoral work, in the narrowest sense of the term, dominated their work among the poor, a focus that was in marked contrast with new emphases on the promotion of justice integral to documents issued by the Latin American bishops at Medellín and the statement of the Latin American provincials in 1968. Bergoglio's decision also contrasted with the trend in other Latin American Jesuit provinces, including Central America. Bergoglio was suspicious of liberation theology and had its books removed from the shelves of the Colegio Máximo. He also took modern and postmodern philosophers such as Sartre, Heidegger, and Foucault off the syllabi in philosophy courses. He wanted his charges' intellectual formation to focus instead on more traditional philosophical approaches, and also on Argentinian literature and culture.

Bergoglio also had serious reservations about the work of the Center for Investigation and Social Action (CISA), one of a number of such institutes founded by the Jesuits around the world (and not unlike the Human Rights Institute—the IDHUCA—at the Jesuit University in San Salvador, founded by Ignacio Ellacuría and Segundo Montes in 1985). Bergoglio cut CISA's budget and staffing, and encouraged his successor as provincial to do the same.[24] Bergoglio's conflict with the staff at CISA put him out of step with other Latin American provinces, so much so that Pedro Arrupe sent one of his assistants, Michael Campbell-Johnston, to Buenos Aires in 1977 to discuss the matter and urge Bergoglio to change his policy. Bergoglio was unrepentant. He insisted that the situation in Argentina was different from Chile or El Salvador. It was also clear, however, that, regional differences aside, he disagreed on more fundamental grounds with the ways that other Jesuit provinces in Latin America were implementing Medellín and the decrees of the 32nd General Congregation. These grounds became clear in his conflicts with the sociologists and political scientists working at the CISA. He saw them as detached, armchair theorists, who wrote much about the poor, but never actually spent time with the poor.[25] They saw him as a throwback to an earlier era, in which the Church offered the consolations of religion and some palliative aid to the poor, while ignoring the deep, systemic causes of their poverty. This approach, in their minds, only continued the Peronist alliance of Church, state, and military, which, they were convinced, was at the root of the growing inequity and mounting violence in Argentinian society.[26]

Perhaps no case has continued to raise as many questions as the kidnaping and torture of two priests, Orlando Yorio and Franz Jalics. Three years before Bergoglio had become provincial, O'Farrell had given them, along with two other Jesuits, permission to set up a community in one of Buenos Aires's poor slums. They did their university lecturing and writing during the week (both had been Bergoglio's teachers at the Máximo), and on weekends worked in the slums where they lived. This apostolate included working with leftist-leaning groups, going well beyond the types of pastoral work that Bergoglio favored when he became provincial.

Bergoglio began closing communities such as theirs when he became provincial, but Yorio and Jalics balked. A protracted confrontation ensued, a difficult, tense process in which the two Jesuits appealed to Rome. Bergoglio's motives are difficult to sort out with clarity. On the one hand, he disapproved of the way they were carrying out their insertion among the poor; on the other, he felt that their work would draw the attention of the increasingly violent groups that were dominating the streets of Buenos Aires, endangering them and other Jesuits. He also thought it better, in the context of the Dirty War, to consolidate the province's Jesuits into fewer communities.

Whatever his motivations, the two priests felt their work was important and was being sacrificed on the altar of Bergoglio's retrograde theology and archaic understanding of the Jesuit mission. This was happening precisely at a time (the years of the 32nd General Congregation) when the Society of Jesus was opting more forcefully for the direct promotion of justice, and this is what Jalics and Yorio insisted they were about.[27] For Bergoglio, however, it finally came down to the authority of the provincial and the virtue (and vow) of obedience. The two Jesuits were given an ultimatum to leave the community or face dismissal from the Society. This difficult process was transpiring against the backdrop of the military coup of 1976 and the beginning of the "disappearances" that would take tens of thousands of Argentinian lives. The exact details of what happened next were disputed. Yorio and Jalics believed that Bergoglio had tipped off the military that they were being dismissed from the Jesuits. They also believed that their provincial had sabotaged their attempt to find refuge by becoming diocesan priests, thus exposing them to abduction and torture by the military, which presumed that the two had been cut free of any ecclesial protection.

Bergoglio has denied this accusation, and, to be sure, after the two were taken by the military he worked tirelessly behind the scenes for their release. It took five months, but they were released (but the degree to which Bergoglio's own intervention was the decisive factor is not clear). Bergoglio then helped them leave the country. Yorio went to his grave convinced that his provincial had betrayed him. Almost twenty-five years after the events, there was a meeting in Germany between Jalics and Bergoglio as archbishop of Buenos Aires, in which they celebrated Mass together and, as Jalics reported, "were reconciled" with one another. From that time forward, Jalics asserted that he no longer believed that Bergoglio had abandoned them to the military. Yet questions remain (and were raised both at the time of the 2005 conclave and when he was elected pope in 2013).[28] On balance, however, a fair judgment would sustain Bergoglio's innocence, at least when it comes to crimes of commission, in this and other cases. Yet it is hard not to think of cases like this when one reads in the interview with Spadaro: "My authoritarian and quick manner of making decisions led me to have serious problems."[29]

What comes into focus in reading the different accounts of these years is a portrait of a relatively young Jesuit thrust into leadership at a time in which there was something like a perfect storm of controversy among the Jesuits over the course that the renewal and commitment to social justice should take, combined with the mounting violence of the years leading up to and during the Dirty War. Bergoglio proved himself to be an extremely hard-working and decisive leader, with a powerful, charismatic personality. And the province did survive and even grew during his years. Yet, as he himself admitted later, his style was often authoritarian and he often showed little ability (or desire) to understand the views of those who disagreed with him. This took a toll.

After thirteen years of leadership, first as provincial and then as rector of the Colegio Máximo, his influence on many of the province's Jesuits had become so profound that it continued even after he stepped down as rector of the Máximo in 1986. At that point a new Jesuit superior general, Peter-Hans Kolvenbach, was becoming increasingly concerned over the polarization of Argentinian Jesuits into *bergoglianos* and *anti-bergoglianos*. He was also receptive to the complaints voiced by new leadership in the Province, which was trying to change some of the policies and commitments formed under Bergoglio. Perhaps to relieve some of the tensions caused by his presence, Bergoglio was sent in 1986 to the Jesuit theological school in Frankfurt. There he studied the work of Romano Guardini with a view to producing a dissertation and taking a doctorate. Yet, lonely and despondent, he returned after only six months, and once again began to exercise the influence in the Province that came from his long tenure in leadership, and that many in Argentina and in Rome found so problematic.

In 1990, drastic action was taken. Bergoglio was sent into a kind of internal exile in Córdoba, four hundred miles away from Buenos Aires. All contact with his former students was forbidden, and he was given no formal apostolic ministry besides finishing his dissertation and hearing confessions in the beautiful colonial-era Jesuit church there. In his interview with Spadaro, he called this a "time of great interior crisis."[30]

Those who lived with him or visited him during those years agree that he was deeply despondent, avoiding contact even with sympathetic members of the community. Some have suggested that Bergoglio went through something like a "dark night" during this period, but he himself has disavowed this label. Yet, it clearly was a crisis, and it changed him. He called it a time of "real purification" that gave him "greater tolerance, understanding, the ability to forgive, and a fresh empathy for the powerless. And patience, a lot of patience."[31] More than a decade later, when he was archbishop of Buenos Aires, he gave advice to a politician who had been defeated in an election and was struggling to deal with his exile from political office: "Live your exile," he advised. "I lived mine. And afterwards you will be back. And when you come back you will be more merciful, kinder, and will want to serve your people better."[32]

Bergoglio did, indeed, "come back" into a leadership role, but not among the Jesuits. He was picked by the archbishop of Buenos Aires, Antonio Quarracino, to be an auxiliary bishop in that megacity. Quarracino had been impressed by his personal austerity and holiness, and by retreats that Bergoglio had given to the priests of the archdiocese. At a high point of hostility toward liberation theology in the Vatican, Bergoglio also had impeccable credentials on that score from his years as provincial and rector.[33] He was ordained bishop in July 1992. Within a year, Quarracino had named Bergoglio vicar for the archdiocese, and in 1997 he persuaded John Paul II to appoint him coadjutor, which meant that he would succeed Quarracino. This he did, in 1998, upon the latter's death.

There were certainly continuities, but something had changed in Bergoglio's style of leadership. He still insisted on getting to know the people to whom one ministered. The shepherd must "smell like the sheep," as he would later remark as pope. But whereas he had used a car and chauffeur while provincial, as a bishop he drove himself, or even rode the subways to the various parishes that made up his archdiocese. Moreover, he became far more collaborative. He continued to insist on direct contact with the poor, bringing them the message of the gospel, and receiving it from them in turn, and, when needed, bringing them direct charitable aid. Yet, he also began now to see more clearly the need for the kind of economic and political analysis and critique that had been the hallmark of liberation theology (and of the Jesuits at the Center for Investigation and Social Action in Buenos Aires, with whom he had butted heads).

After the devastating crash of the Argentinian economy in 2001–2, Bergoglio began speaking of an economy that kills; he also used his power and position as archbishop to bring together Argentinian leaders to broker a solution to the country's pressing problems. He was also visible and unequivocal in his public criticism of the government, particularly on the rampant corruption that afflicted the political and civil spheres of Argentinian society.[34] As a Jesuit and former student, Rafael Velasco, who went on to become president of the Jesuit University in Córdoba, said, "Bergoglio was so very conservative that I was rather shocked years later when he started talking about the poor. It wasn't something which seemed at the top of his agenda at the time, but clearly became so as a bishop. Something changed."[35]

Bergoglio's skills in consulting others and in building consensus, rather than leading "in an authoritarian manner," also became evident in his work with ecclesial bodies, such as the World Synod of Bishops in 2001, and, above all, at the Fifth General Meeting of Latin American Bishops at Aparecida in 2007. Thus, even though the media was taken by surprise when Bergoglio was elected pope in 2013, in retrospect it is no surprise that by then the cardinals who gathered in Rome to choose Benedict XVI's successor had come increasingly to see him as a bridge-builder, someone who knew how to listen and who respected the unique challenges and resources in the different regions of a diverse, global Church. During the speeches at the General Congregations that preceded the actual voting, Bergoglio gave an address that presaged the approach that he would take in governing the Church as pope. It is worth quoting at length:

> The only purpose of the Church is to go out to tell the world the good news about Jesus Christ. It needs to "surge forth to the peripheries," not just geographically but to "the existential peripheries" where people grapple with "sin, pain, injustice, ignorance, indifference to religion and misery." Instead, the Church has gotten too wrapped up in itself. It is too navel-gazing. It has become "self-referential" which has made it sick. It is suffering a "kind of theological narcissism".... The Church is supposed to be "the *mysterium lunae*"—the mystery of the moon that has no light but simply reflects the light of the sun, and the mystery of the church is that it reflects the light of Christ. The Church must not fool itself that it has a light of its own; if it does that it gives in to the "spiritual worldliness" which

is what Henri de Lubac in *The Splendor of the Church* called "the worst evil that can befall the Church." That is what happens with a self-referential Church that believes it has its own light. Put simply, there are two images of Church: a Church that evangelizes and comes out of herself or a worldly Church, a Church living within herself, of herself, for herself. The next Pope should be someone who helps the Church surge forth to the peripheries, like a sweet and comforting mother who offers the joy of Jesus to the world, bringing "changes and reforms" for the salvation of souls.[36]

At the conclusion of this speech, Cardinal Christoph Schönborn, who had been a student of Josef Ratzinger's and general editor of the *Catechism of the Catholic Church*, leaned over to his neighbor and said, "That's what we need." Jorge Mario Bergoglio was on the way to becoming Pope Francis.[37]

Examining his work in detail as pope in the light of this vision is beyond the scope of this chapter. Moreover, to make it clear once again, I have no interest in claiming that this sort of vision could *only* be offered on the basis of Ignatian spirituality. My claim, rather, is that there is ample evidence that Bergoglio came to his unique vision on this basis, and that the specific textures of Ignatian spirituality provided the detailed contours of that vision. This can be given some initial plausibility by referring to an address he gave to the Jesuits gathered to elect a new superior general in 2016. He opened his address by recalling exhortations by Paul VI, John Paul II, and Benedict XVI for the Society to be faithful to its mission, "in full fidelity to your original charism."[38] In describing this mission and charism, the pope asserted that it is

> to walk together—free and obedient—moving *toward the margins of society* where no one else reaches, "under the gaze of Jesus and looking to the horizon which is the ever greater glory of God, who ceaselessly surprises us." As Saint Ignatius reminds us, a Jesuit is called "to think and to live in any part of the world where there is a greater need of service to God and assistance for souls" The fact is that "the Society must feel at home anyplace in the world," as Nadal used to say.[39]

These references first to the "ec-centric" impulse of evangelization and second to the priority of salvation of souls (which, in Jesuit idiom, is often rendered "assistance for souls" or "helping souls") are both central pillars of Ignatian spirituality, as are the importance of the gaze of Christ and the horizon of the ever-greater God. Moreover, as Bergoglio's speech before his election as pope shows, they became central to his vision for the Church. The embrace of the impulse "to help souls" can be seen in his conviction that "what the church needs most today is the ability to heal wounds and to warm the hearts of the faithful.... I see the church as a field hospital after battle."[40] These insights were first embraced by Bergoglio in his living out of Ignatian spirituality, but that embrace has clearly evolved over the course of his life's pilgrimage. This spirituality made up (to quote Chenu again) the "fundamental intuition that serves to guide a spiritual life" for Pope Francis, and hence has provided the "intellectual regimen" proper to his ecclesial praxis. We turn now to the different elements of this intellectual regimen.

Pope Francis's Intellectual Itinerary

As I have suggested, the primary text that shaped and continues to shape Pope Francis's thinking is the reality in which he has lived and exercised his vocation as Jesuit priest, superior, and bishop (including, ultimately, bishop of Rome). Pope Francis is one who, in Ignacio Ellacuría's words, has learned how to become aware of the weight of reality, take charge of the weight of reality, and shoulder the weight of reality. The priority of reality over disengaged theory is reflected in his own oft-stated maxim: "realities are greater than ideas."[41] By this he does not mean that ideas are unimportant, but that their relevance only proves itself when they are able to be put "at the service of communication, understanding and praxis."[42] Stated negatively, respecting the priority of reality over ideas means "rejecting the various means of masking reality: angelic forms of purity, dictatorships of relativism, empty rhetoric, objectives more ideal than real, brands of ahistorical fundamentalism, ethical systems bereft of kindness, intellectual discourse bereft of wisdom."[43]

For all of this emphasis on the priority of reality over ideas, Pope Francis's pilgrim itinerary has indisputably been guided in part by his reading and interpretation of a number of intellectuals—philosophers, theologians, social critics—of both European and Latin American provenance. A full-fledged intellectual biography is beyond the scope of this chapter.⁴⁴ However, a few indications of sources for Pope Francis's ideas provide a way of seeing how he has developed his own way of being honest to reality, and they also show how it is Ignatian spirituality, and its understanding of discernment in particular, that has configured the way the pope employs ideas "at the service of communication, understanding and praxis."

Massimo Borghesi provides a starting point for this overview in the following terms:

> *Bergoglio's entire system of thought is one of reconciliation*—not an irenic, optimistic, naively progressivistic thinking, but rather a dramatic thinking, marked by a tension, that, having matured during the course of his Ignatian studies in the 1960's, finds its first formulation in the 1970's, in the tragic context of an Argentina divided between a right-wing military and left-wing revolutionaries. It is a contrast that marks both the church and the Society of Jesus. From here grows his idea of a "polar," "antinomian" dialectic that constitutes the golden thread of Bergoglio's thought, his original, conceptual core.⁴⁵

Jorge Mario Bergoglio is a voracious reader, and a full account of how he developed his own intellectual synthesis would have to include his readings in history (for instance, on the Jesuit Reductions in Paraguay and Brazil), literature, and poetry.⁴⁶ Significant philosophical and theological contributions to this "polar, antinomian dialectic" came from his reading of Gaston Fessard, Alberto Methol Ferré, Amelia Podetti, Yves Congar, Henri de Lubac, Romano Guardini, and Luigi Giussani. He was also deeply influenced by, and indeed can be said to have contributed in his own way to, the "theology of the people," a distinctly Argentinian variant of the theology of liberation, pioneered by figures such as Lucio Gera, Rafael Tello, and represented today by (among others) Juan Carlos Scannone and Enrique Bianchi.⁴⁷ The intellectual development that emerges from this itinerary is not so much that of the gradual construction of an intellectual system as it is the discovery, ongoing refinement, and careful arrangement of a constellation of ideas that creates a shifting field of ideational attractions and repulsions.

It is within the intellective sensorium created by this constellation of ideas that Pope Francis has come to perceive and evaluate situations and challenges, and discern the proper response. The term "discern" is not used incidentally, insofar as it indicates the link to Ignatian spirituality. Pope Francis himself identifies discernment as the core contribution that Ignatian spirituality has made to his papacy, and it is a term that shows up often in his writings and addresses.[48] It also figures prominently in the first contributions to his constellation of ideas and arguments, as he began to put it together in the early 1960s. I now give some notes on what different intellectual figures contributed to this constellation of Bergoglio's.

Gaston Fessard: The Spiritual Exercises *as a Pedagogy for Engaging Historical Reality*

Bergoglio was mentored in his philosophical studies and beyond by Miguel Ángel Fiorito. Under his guidance, the young Jesuit began reading interpretations of the *Spiritual Exercises*, and of mysticism in general, which deeply shaped not only his spiritual but his intellectual development. He became aware of many of these writings from reading the recently founded French Jesuit journal *Christus*.[49] Among authors whom he encountered in this way is Michel de Certeau, whose translation of the *Memoriale* of Pierre Favre, along with the long introduction that Certeau wrote for it, became a lasting favorite of Bergoglio's.[50] But it was, above all, Gaston Fessard's *La Dialectique des "Exercises spirituels" de Saint Ignace de Loyola* that first provided Bergoglio with a model for a dialectical way of thinking, which he continued to refine over the next thirty years. It also set the pattern of working out his way of thinking in close conversation with the *Spiritual Exercises*. Some further consideration of Fessard's work is necessary for understanding how the intellectual and spiritual foundations were laid for Bergoglio's thought.

Fessard first composed his path-breaking interpretation of the *Spiritual Exercises* in the 1930s, at the same time that he was pursuing a close reading of Hegel's *Phenomenology of Spirit*. He decided to publish the book (expanded to two volumes) for the occasion of the 400th anniversary of the death of Ignatius in 1956. Like his contemporary Bernard Lonergan and later Ignacio Ellacuría, Fessard took as a principal concern constructing a philosophy and theology that took the foundational reality of history and human historicity more seriously than the regnant neoscholasticism was able to do. It is no accident, then, that although he often grappled with Hegel, appropriating and transforming Hegelian concepts, themes, and arguments, Maurice Blondel's *L'Action* (1893) provided the most important initial impetus and guide for Fessard's work on Ignatius. Starting with the primacy of human action as the crucible within which human freedom becomes real, Fessard gave an account of human freedom as not only thoroughly embedded within the structures and movements of history, but also at least relatively free with respect to them. Fessard took the actualization of freedom—both tied to and also relatively free with respect to history—to be the most effective locus from which to understand the way in which human beings respond to the unique vocation given to them by God. As Michael Schneider writes: "Fessard's chief concern, however, lay in the question of *the meaning of history*. This question stands at the center of his thought. He himself characterizes his efforts concerning 'the historical' as the 'central problem' of his own quest and research: how can human freedom actualize itself in history and be accountable to God?"[51]

In Fessard's philosophy and theology of history, history has a natural dimension (known, roughly speaking, through the natural sciences) and a dimension that arises from human historical action (or historical reality). The latter dimension of history is determined by past historical action (and by the structures of nature's history). Yet, in the moment of praxis and action, that past history is reshaped and redirected in novel ways. These ways are not fully determined by history's natural dimension, nor can they be predicted in advance solely on the basis of past human history. As a consequence, the dimension of human history cannot be known without reduction and distortion by the methods of the natural sciences alone. It can only fully be known interpretively and hermeneutically.

There is, however, a further and crucial dimension to history. Both of these forms or dimensions of history (the natural and the human-historical) are undergirded and given their ultimate context in supernatural history, which is constituted by the Christ event, by virtue of which all of history is oriented toward Christ, and ultimately taken up into Christ. History (both natural and human-historical) thus only receives its final unity and meaning from supernatural history. This foundational meaning, however, is not accessible in itself to human investigation, as are, in different ways, natural history and human history. It only becomes available to our understanding in the discrete moments of actualization of human freedom. A particular human choice, to the extent that it is authentically free, is a sort of window through which the meaning of supernatural history shines and illuminates historical reality as a whole, in however partial and perspectival a way.[52] Schneider summarizes:

> With the concept of *"historical reality"* Fessard intends to articulate both dimensions of human historicity: history as a totality of meaning as well as history as something that is always in play in the concrete here-and-now of the moment. The person recognizes in the historical actualization of his life that his life is oriented towards a totality. But he only grasps that totality little by little. In the present moment he must actualize his life ever anew and make a free decision, in order to bring the whole of the reality of his life into view.[53]

In other words, in each authentically free human act, the overarching meaning of history (which, recall, is Christocentric for Fessard) can be made available to human history, both to and for the individual, and also to and for her broader social context, insofar as the individual is able to discover and enact that meaning as it presents itself to her in the fixed parameters of the past, the exigencies of the present, and the possibilities of the future.

This description also does justice, in Fessard's view, to the dialectical union of divine and human freedom. Actualizing this union in an ineluctably individual way, but also in the presence of human finitude, failure, and sinfulness, constitutes the unique vocation to which each human being is called. This vocation provides the ultimate telos and fulfillment of human freedom and the leaven, as it were, for the process by which all of history is brought back to God in Christ. In this way, Fessard's is also a view of history that understands it to be a process of interaction of dialectical oppositions (as with Hegel and Marx), but it resists the tendency to find (or search for) an *intra*-mundane synthesis (or *"Aufhebung,"* to use the Hegelian term of art) of these dialectics, a synthesis closed to transcendence (closed, that is, to "supernatural history," using Fessard's terminology). Fessard argues that the attempt to construe the meaning of history in the latter, Hegelian or Marxist sense, as closed to "supernatural history," ultimately devolves into ideologies that fund different types of totalitarianism.[54]

Discernment of spirits then, for Fessard, is precisely the process in which this discovery and enactment of history's meaning takes place, immersed in the world's history, but in openness to supernatural history.

According to his interpretation, the *Spiritual Exercises* presents discernment by contextualizing it within an extended methodology (or a divine pedagogy, as Fessard names it) whereby a person can become more practiced in this art. He interprets the four weeks of the *Exercises* as a sort of roadmap (which succeeds not when one understands it analytically, but when one travels the route it lays out) for this process. The *Exercises* describes a dialectical process, in which each week includes and flows into the others, and in which the "end point" of a completed election (a realized discernment of spirits), fully actualized in the offering of love in the Contemplation to Attain Love, only sets the stage anew for taking up the implicit question posed in the Principle and Foundation, unleashing the process again.

We have Pope Francis's own testimony that Fessard was of fundamental significance for his thought: "The 'Hegelian' writer—but he is not Hegelian, though it may seem like he is—who had a big influence on me was Gaston Fessard. I've read *La Dialectique des "Exercises spirituels" de Saint Ignace de Loyola*, and other things by him, several times. That work gave me so many elements that later became mixed in [to my thinking]."[55] It is difficult to move with certainty into further specifics as to what precisely these elements are and at what points they shaped Bergoglio's intellectual system. The pope does not often explicitly cite the French Jesuit beyond adverting to his importance in these general terms.[56] Yet I suggest three points, at least, that we can identify with some confidence.

First, and perhaps most straightforwardly, there is the insight that the *Spiritual Exercises* and Ignatian spirituality as a whole can disclose a theology that responds to the challenges posed by modernity. Fessard was one of the first (along with Erich Pryzwara) to pursue this as a thesis and to produce a systematic commentary on the *Exercises* that attempts to disclose this theology in detail. From the very beginning of his intellectual development, Bergoglio thus was fascinated by the same thesis that gave inspiration to the work of Rahner and Ellacuría. Even when, later, he drank from other intellectual and literary wells, he often tested the reliability of what he was learning from this reading by applying it to new interpretations and applications of Ignatian spirituality. Fessard's work initiated this habit of the future pope's thinking, and the fundamental insights he took from Fessard remained among the most important structuring principles of his thought.

Second, Fessard mediated to the young Bergoglio Blondel's insight about the nature of doctrine and its relationship to lived Christian faith and praxis. That is, first of all, the most comprehensive context for the meaning of human life and history (individually and socially) is Christ-centered and Christ-formed, and it is given in revelation. It is thus, to be sure, subject to delineation and elaboration in doctrine and theological systems. Next, however, this meaning is not available in these doctrines and theological system as such. Indeed, it is neither available nor effective in *any* intellectual synthesis. Rather, it is most authentically and efficaciously available in the moment of choice, the moment of action, in which—perspectivally and with limits, but most fully and completely nonetheless—this meaning of the whole opens itself to the person acting (or persons); it is *given* to her, but only insofar as she opts for it. Finally this opening of oneself and opting is the core element of Ignatian spirituality, expressed in condensed form in the process of discernment.[57] This totality of meaning (supernatural history, as Fessard named it) is not available any other way. To depend exclusively on intellectual systems of ideas, however orthodox or exalted their theological provenance, is to short-circuit the process by which this meaning *is* available. This insight of Fessard's expresses the deeper theological-spiritual context for understanding Bergoglio's claim that (historical) reality is more important than ideas, and lies behind his resolute refusal to give in to his critics and enact his papacy only as a defense, or as a further definition and elaboration, of a system of ideas (dogma) abstracted from the concrete realities of human action and the discernment such action requires. It also gives us an understanding of what Bergoglio has in mind in warning of the dangers of "ideology." In addition, it also provides the background for his insistence that the doctrinal element of Christian faith and its pastoral element should not be set against one another; neither should the pastoral element be seen merely as the application of the doctrinal. The relationship between the two is far more intimate. We will consider this later.

Third, Fessard gave the young Jesuit an initial intellectual framing of the insight that conflicts and tensions within history cannot be resolved simply by overcoming in thinking the dialectical elements at play, whether that be by suppressing one or the other of them, by creating a synthesis that allegedly sublates their differences, or by forging a sort of "live and let live" or "least common denominator" compromise between them that ignores their capacity for further creative and generative interaction. Such attempts tacitly assume, on Fessard's reading, that these tensions can and ought to be solved by some synthesis that operates within the context of human history on its own resources—nature without grace, as it were. In fact, as Fessard insisted, their resolution is only available in terms of a dimension of history (supernatural history, or what others such as Rahner or Ellacuría call salvation history) that is absolutely real and present to human history, but is only available by the discernment that finds a realization of its meaning in the moment and substance of a choice, of an election. Yet this resolution of the dialectical polarities is always partial, always tentative, always opening up to an invitation, indeed an exigency to continued discernment. The resolution of dialectical tensions that make up human history will always happen by means of a process that we do not fully control, in which we must give ourselves over to the graced possibilities of temporality and historical process, rather than attempting to control the risks and openness of historical reality by freezing its elements in a rigidly controlled "space" defined by some abstract set of formulas.[58] Here, then, in Fessard's interpretation of the *Spiritual Exercises*, we find the roots of two other "mottos" for Pope Francis's framing of Christian action: "unity prevails over conflict" and "time is greater than space."[59]

The Theology of the People

In 1966, just after the close of Vatican II, the Argentinian Bishops Conference formed a pastoral commission, COEPAL (la Comisión Episcopal de Pastoral), with the task of interpreting the results of the council for the Argentinian reality. For the next seven years its members, led in particular by Lucio Gera, formulated the beginnings of a position that came to be known as the theology of the people, which was further worked out (sometimes in meetings at the Colegio Máximo) in the subsequent decades.[60] A variant of or close neighbor to liberation theology, it puts the emphasis on "the people" and sets its cultural response to and articulation of the gospel message as the starting point for theology and ecclesial praxis. "The people" was understood "as the entire people as a nation ... starting from the plural unity of a common culture, rooted in a common history, and projected forward toward a shared common good."⁶¹ Less interested in economic structures that created and reinforced inequity and distorted patterns of communication than other forms of liberation theology, the theology of the people focused instead on political domination, particularly as expressed through the ideological marginalization or suppression of the autochthonous culture of a people. Insofar as the theology of the people argued that this autochthonous culture is paradigmatically found among the poor, it shares the emphasis on the preferential option for the poor, but it is suspicious of ways of formulating it that draw on Marxist or revisionary Marxist theories.⁶²

Using the lens of a particular reading of *Lumen gentium* on the People of God, and of *Gaudium et spes* on culture, this approach provides a term that is frequently used by Pope Francis: the faithful people of God.⁶³ The future pope began using this term in the 1970s. In a speech to the opening of a meeting of Argentina's Jesuits, held in 1974 (not long after he began his term as provincial), Bergoglio gave a characteristic articulation of the term's importance and meaning for him:

> I would like, speaking personally, to express what this reality of the *faithful people* [*pueblo fiel*] means for me. By the *faithful people* I am simply talking about people who are believers, the people with whom our priestly mission and our religious witness lead us into particular contact. Of course, "the people" now has different meanings among us, deriving from ideological assumptions operative whenever people talk about or engage with the reality to which the term refers. But now I am talking, quite simply, about the *faithful people*. When I was studying theology ... I was very struck by one formulation in the Christian tradition: the *faithful people* is infallible *in credendo*—in its act of believing. From this I have derived a formula that may not be very precise, but which has been very helpful to me: when you want to know *what* Mother Church believes, go to the magisterium—because it is charged with teaching it infallibly. But when you want to know *how* the Church believes, go to the *faithful people*. The magisterium will teach you who Mary is, but our *faithful people* will teach you how to love Mary.⁶⁴

The theology of the people reinforced and theorized Bergoglio's conviction that the popular religiosity of the faithful people (whereby they instantiate *how* to love Mary) is a genuine *locus theologicus* and not a reality to be managed by theological experts from the outside. Indeed, Pope Francis will come to speak of a popular mysticism, the expression of the soul of a people.[65] His insistence that "the shepherds should smell like the sheep," then, is not just a sort of ecclesial variant of *noblesse oblige*, but has for him the force of an epistemological principle. The only way bishops and other leaders in the Church can participate in the privileged wisdom (flowing from this popular mysticism) found in the faithful people is to participate in their lives. Even though (as his addresses and writings after 2000 show) the pope has not been averse to pointing out the economic and political structures that divide, that privilege certain groups while turning others into "disposable persons," his starting point is still the unity found in the faithful people of God, understood primarily as a cultural phenomenon. The faithful people of God for him are united by a common history and a popular spirituality with which they express their faith through the symbol-system provided by that culture. These insights were decisive for the contributions that Bergoglio as cardinal archbishop of Buenos Aires made as principal editor of the concluding documents of CELAM V at Aparecida in 2007.[66]

Thinkers such as Amelia Podetti and Alberto Methol Ferré are also decisive for Bergoglio's vision, evident at Aparecida.[67] According to Austin Ivereigh, Podetti (along with Methol Ferré) was one of the most prominent philosophers of a group of thinkers who saw "the Church as key to the emergence of a new Latin American continental consciousness, *la patria grande*, which would take its place in the modern world and become an important influence on it. This was Bergoglio's intellectual family—a Catholic nationalism that looked to the *pueblo*, rather than to the state, and beyond Argentina to Latin America, and which saw Medellín as the beginning to the continent becoming a beacon for the Church and for the world."[68]

Trained in France, with expertise in German idealism, Podetti had critiqued Hegel's "universal history" as in fact still a European history. She argued for the importance of rediscovering Latin America in order to move beyond the European project, which from Descartes on had increasingly lost the authentically universalistic perspective opened up by the discovery of the Americas. What has come to be taken as peripheral (Latin America) is on her reading, in fact, central to the forward movement of history. Bergoglio himself states that he first began thinking in terms of a dialectic between center and peripheries because of Podetti's revisionary Hegelianism.[69] He was particularly interested in this theme for thinking about the inculturation of Christian faith in the culture and peoples of Argentina, an interest that links to his interest in Gera and the theology of the people.

Thinking about inculturation also drew him to the thought of Methol Ferré, whom he first met toward the end of his term as provincial. Methol Ferré argued, and Bergoglio agreed, that after centuries of being a "reflection church," which only imaged or reacted to what was happening in its "source" in the European Church, the Latin American Church was on the verge of becoming a "source church" in its own right, which had its own unique mission and its own contribution to make to the universal church.[70] This idea crystallized the energy and the vision that Bergoglio brought to bear in his work with the Aparecida documents. This notion also forms his understanding of the relationship of Rome to other regional churches around the globe. In understanding the relationship between universal and particular, he will refuse absolutely to prioritize any center, in terms of which peripheries would have to take their bearings. The image on which he draws to make this point is not that of a sphere or circle, because with this image all the points are still identified by their equidistance from some center. Rather, he uses the image of a polyhedron, with sides placed at different angles to one another, making up a whole in which the richness of the whole is diversely made available from the distinct perspectives offered from the different sides (or peripheries) along the perimeter.[71]

Romano Guardini and Diagnosing Modernity

When he was sent to Frankfurt in 1986 to study for a doctorate, Bergoglio focused on the German philosopher-theologian Romano Guardini, whom we have already encountered in our analysis of Rahner's understanding of modernity and the challenges it poses to Christianity. In a conversation with Antonio Spadaro, Bergoglio expressed his debt to Guardini in these terms:

> Speaking generally, I have to say that I love oppositions. Romano Guardini helped me with his book, *Der Gegensatz*, which was important to me. He spoke of a polar opposition in which the two opposites are not annulled. One pole does not destroy the other. There is no contradiction and no identity. For him, opposition is

resolved on a higher level. In such a solution, however, the polar tension remains.... Oppositions are helpful. Human life is structured in oppositional form. And we see this happening now in the church as well.[72]

Contradiction requires a decision (good over evil). Opposition, on the other hand, is "the lifeblood of concrete-living; it brings life and dynamism to its unity."[73] In the social context of the Church, applying the conceptuality of opposition (rather than contradiction) allows, indeed requires, seeing the Church as a complex, symphonic reality of positions-in-tension that are not to be ironed out or resolved in a monolithic synthesis, imposed from above. Rather, the oppositions are to be patiently brought into relationship with one another in a slow, dialogical process that will always have local nuances and differences, and, by the nature of the case, will not be without disagreement and conflict. It is not difficult at all to see this social ontology and epistemology reflected in Pope Francis's ecclesiology and in his pastoral practice and managerial style as bishop of Rome, particularly in his insistence that not every problem can or should be solved by a ruling from Rome, or in the way he has conducted himself at (and, as pope, organized) conferences and synods of bishops.

Guardini's thought provided Bergoglio with a further theoretical counterpart to the dialectical approach to Ignatian spirituality that he took from Fessard. It also seems very likely that the study of Guardini helped Bergoglio during his "time of interior crisis" in Córdoba from 1990 to 1992, when he was reflecting back on his period of leadership of the Jesuits of Argentina. It helped him to articulate a different style of leadership, one which he adopted when he became a bishop. A brief overview of Guardini's thought and Bergoglio's original appropriation of it can show its importance for this new style of leadership.

In *Der Gegensatz (The Opposition)*, Guardini constructs a set of eight oppositions that are fundamental to reality as a "living-concrete" unity. In the interest of rendering a social ontology, Bergoglio consolidates these down to three: fullness versus limit, idea versus reality, and globalization versus localization.[74] The opposition of fullness versus limit consolidates two of Guardini's oppositions: fullness and form, and act and structure.[75] Bergoglio used it to conceptualize one of the principles laid out in *Evangelii Gaudium* for making "progress in building a people in peace, justice, and fraternity": time is greater than space.[76] The most enigmatic of the four principles, the pope's explanation in *Evangelii Gaudium* helps understand what he means by it: "'Time' has to do with fullness as an expression of the horizon which constantly opens before us, while each individual moment has to do with limitation as an expression of enclosure."[77] The pope seems to mean something like this: any particular moment has constraints and challenges that ineluctably delimit our actions, but also, it is worth emphasizing, make action possible. On the other hand, for every action there is also a broader horizon, often presented to us as a utopian vision of a possible future, or, on Christian terms, as a call from an ever-greater God.[78] This horizon always calls us beyond the present moment. This opposition is present in every human action, individually and socially, and cannot be overcome or ignored. In the face of this opposition, one temptation is to embrace only the moment, scaling back one's actions and focusing on controlling the variables (and persons) that make it up. As he writes:

> One of the faults which we occasionally observe in sociopolitical activity is that spaces are preferred to time and processes. Giving priority to space means madly attempting to keep everything together in the present, trying to possess all the spaces of power and of self-assertion; it is to crystallize processes and presume to hold them back. Giving priority to time means being concerned about *initiating processes rather than possessing spaces*. Time governs spaces, illumines them and makes them links in a constantly expanding change with no possibility of return. What we need, then, is to give priority to actions which generate new processes in society and engage other persons and groups who can develop them to the point where they bear fruit in significant historical events. Without anxiety, but with clear convictions and tenacity.[79]

He does not make it explicit here, but the other temptation is to ignore "the moment," or "space," losing oneself in a dreamy (but ultimately unrealistic) gaze at the possibilities of a utopian future. The point of this principle, as with the others, is to establish a certain *priority* in negotiating the creative tensions that arise from the different oppositions, not simply to annul one or the other pole, or to establish a knee-jerk automatic choice of one over the other.

This becomes clear if we consider that to avoid the realities and limitations that are embedded in the exigencies of the moment (and metaphorically expressed as "space" in this principle) would be to ignore another of the pope's principles, to which we turn momentarily: realities are more important than ideas.[80] Giving priority to the fullness of graced human possibility, represented by "time" in this principle, is to allow oneself to be drawn forward into an unknown future by the ever-greater horizon of God's love without ignoring the hard work of considering the crucial, albeit limited, steps of the given moment by which we journey in that direction. This principle gives expression to the telos, the locus of the common good, that unites us, without ignoring or eliding the differences that give rise to conflict in the present moment (unavoidable given our situatedness within that moment, which will ineluctably render our visions of it both limited and potentially in conflict). Hence, as Borghesi notes, a second of Pope Francis's principles, "unity prevails over conflict," is also rooted in this creative-tensive opposition of fullness and limit.[81]

The third opposition, idea versus realities, is not present per se on Guardini's own list. As before, Francis's point in stipulating it is not that we should *ignore* ideas, but that we should prioritize reality and the ways that ideas are rooted in realities, and prove their value by how they enable us to engage those realities creatively, an insistence with which Ellacuría agrees in his own insistence on the priority of historical reality. This principle, Francis writes, "has to do with the incarnation of the word."[82] This calls to mind the centrality for the work of discernment of encountering the concrete, historical reality of Jesus Christ. Embedding the work of discernment in this encounter is the goal of the Second, Third, and Fourth Weeks of the Spiritual Exercises. It also reminds us of the pope's insistence at the beginning of *Evangelii Gaudium* on the necessity of an authentic encounter with Christ for Christian life and action (3).

The fourth opposition that Bergoglio formulated in his creative reading of Guardini is the opposition between globalization and localization, and it finds expression in *Evangelii Gaudium* in his principle that "the whole is greater than the part."[83] Borghesi argues that this corresponds to the opposition of individuality to totality in Guardini's system. Its particular formulation in *Evangelii Gaudium* manifests with great clarity the pope's engagement with the phenomenon of globalization, with which he had grappled earlier as archbishop of Buenos Aires and as a leader of the Latin American Church as a whole. He also uses it in his ecclesiology to talk about the relationship between the universal Church and local, particular churches. We saw how he uses the image of a polyhedron to capture this relationship. The differences between local churches from one another are irreducible and productive; moreover, they should not be understood in terms of their differences from a "center" (in Rome, or anywhere else, for that matter). As with the other oppositions, the tensions that result from this one cannot be resolved by a purely conceptual synthesis that does away with them. Rather, they need to be continually renegotiated in ever-new and creative resolutions, based on careful listening and dialogue, on attention to the other three oppositions, and on the spiritual practice of discernment.

In addition to his ontology and epistemology of oppositions, Guardini gave Pope Francis a phenomenology of the modern age. As was the case with Rahner, Guardini's *End of the Modern World* exercised a decisive influence on Pope Francis, in combination with Methol Ferré's critique of modernity.[84] Guardini's diagnosis of late modernity's predicament is clearly on display in *Laudato si'*. In that text, the mid-twentieth-century German theologian is the most frequently quoted contemporary theologian. Guardini had echoed a number of twentieth-century critics of modernity in asserting that the scientific and technological power gained during the Enlightenment have become ends in themselves, no longer subject to meaningful human oversight. This hypostatization of human powers that were originally intended to put an end to human subjection to natural forces has doubled back on humanity, instrumentalizing human beings and communities in such a way that these powers no longer truly serve human flourishing. Drawing on Guardini, the future pope's conclusion is that, on the intellectual plane, the solution is a more adequate anthropology.[85] On the practical-pastoral plane what is needed is a solidarity (which mediates the polarity of individual-community) that connects us with each other person, and each other living being, as a "thou," in the context of a transcendent dimension in which we relate to "the 'Thou' of God."[86] This sentence provides a good example of how multiple layers of the palimpsest that is Pope Francis's intellectual genealogy can be discerned in his current exercise of his teaching office.

Later Influences

In the two decades following his appointment as auxiliary bishop of Buenos Aires, Bergoglio refined the framework he learned from Guardini (building on his earlier reading) as he applied it to the difficult political and ecclesial situations facing him as a leader of the Church in Latin America. He drew on a number of other authors in the process, including Henri de Lubac, from whom he took the notion of "spiritual worldliness." From Hans Urs von Balthasar's theological analysis of Irenaeus, Bergoglio took an understanding of Gnosticism as Christianity's perennial opponent and most serious internal temptation. He often pairs it with Pelagianism.[87] For example, in his apostolic exhortation on the call to holiness *Gaudete et exsultate*, these two heresies are given to "represent an anthropocentric immanentism disguised as Catholic truth. Let us take a look at these two forms of doctrinal or disciplinary security that give rise 'to a narcissistic and authoritarian elitism, whereby instead of evangelizing, one analyzes and classifies others, and instead of opening the door to grace, one exhausts his or her energies in inspecting and verifying. In neither case is one really concerned about Jesus Christ or others.'"[88]

The pope reported to Borghesi that he was also instructed by Luigi Giussani on his understanding and diagnostic use of these two heresies:

> For me in the incarnation is found the weakness and concreteness of the Catholic faith. Pelagianism and Gnosticism are resolved in the incarnation. These heresies deny either the weakness of God or the power of God. Reading Giussani on this has helped me substantially. In the drafting of Aparecida these things appear. . . . Certainly I always liked to go to the incarnation to see the power of God against the Pelagian "power," and the weakness of God against the Gnostic "power." In the incarnation is found the right relationship. If we read, for example, the Beatitudes or Matthew 25, which is the protocol by which we will be judged, we find this: In the weakness of the incarnation human problems and heresies are resolved.[89]

Giussani was the founder of the Catholic religious movement Communion and Liberation. From Giussani's book *The Attractiveness of Jesus*, Pope Francis drew a number of themes that have become prominent in his writings and speeches in the twenty-first century: first, an understanding of nostalgia, of being called home, which echoes Augustine's well-known evocation of "the restless heart"; second, the indispensable place of encounter in human life, and of the encounter with Christ most of all; and the centrality of mercy.[90] To be sure, these themes were not completely new. What Giussani provided was a particularly compelling and clear articulation and interrelation of themes that were already important to

Bergoglio. For example, the centrality of mercy is already evident in the episcopal motto he chose in 1992: *miserando atque eligendo*. And one can find other sources for the insistence on encounter: Pope Benedict's 2005 encyclical, *Deus caritas est*, for example. In his work as final editor of the concluding documents of Aparecida, Bergoglio as cardinal of Buenos Aires quoted from Benedict's encyclical, and quoted the same line once again in *Evangelii Gaudium*: "Being a Christian is not the result of an ethical choice or a lofty ideal, but the encounter with an event, a person, which gives life a new horizon and a decisive direction."[91]

In this, as with other themes, it is difficult to draw clear and univocal lines of influence from one or another of the intellectual sources that I have just surveyed. Pope Francis's intellectual sources are many, and his use of their themes often has the character of a palimpsest, in which several sources can be discerned in a final result that is original to Francis himself. Moreover, he writes and speaks not to forge a philosophical or theological system of his own, but to express ideals, propose strategies, and exhort or encourage others in his work as an ecclesial leader, be it of the Jesuits in the 1970s and 80s, or as a bishop and then pope in the subsequent decades. He wants to move people to action. This, he tells us, is why he always includes a section on spirituality in his magisterial documents: "More than in ideas or concepts as such, I am interested in how [an ecological] spirituality can motivate us to a more passionate concern for the protection of our world. A commitment this lofty cannot be sustained by doctrine alone, without a spirituality capable of inspiring us, without an 'interior impulse which encourages, motivates, nourishes and gives meaning to our individual and communal activity.'"[92]

To use the Aristotelian categories, Francis is not so much interested in dialectic, the science of rigorous definition and proof, as he is in rhetoric, the art of effective persuasion. This makes him a true son of Ignatius, who, along with his first companions, prioritized a knowledge that touched both mind and heart over one that gave one intellectual mastery. Even when engaged in dialectic per se, as he was in his study of Guardini, his mind always moved to the latter pole of rhetoric. And the framework for attracting, inspiring, persuading, exhorting, and encouraging was ultimately, for him, provided by Ignatian spirituality, which also always provided the touchstone against which he tested the value of the abstract concepts and philosophical worldviews that he learned from such diverse sources.

Ignatian Spirituality: The Touchstone for Pope Francis's Intellectual Probings

As an example of this relationship between the development of Pope Francis's intellectual framework for understanding his world and his embrace of Ignatian spirituality, and as a transition into his appropriation and interpretation of that spirituality itself, let us consider an essay he wrote in 1988 on Decree 4 of the 32nd General Congregation ("Our Mission Today: The Service of Faith and the Promotion of Justice"), entitled "The Service of Faith and the Promotion of Justice."[93] Bergoglio had significant reservations about this decree and rarely referenced it in subsequent years as provincial and rector.[94] Twelve years after the decree was written (by which time he had stepped down from provincial leadership roles), Bergoglio argued that the document had been constitutively open to distorted interpretations. He judged that "these deviations in understanding and application of Decree 4 came, generally speaking, from a 'reduction' to a system of thought that was rather contradictory and exclusive, terminating in itself, the result of which, from the logical point of view, always entailed a disjunction, and, when it came to the analysis of reality, entailed slavery to an ideology."[95] The presence of Fessard (the ineluctable tendency for a contradictory constellation to reduce, when closed in on itself, without appeal to transcendence, to an ideology) is clear. Guardini's thought is also evident.

Guardini's phenomenology underwrites Bergoglio's further plotting of the problems that arose surrounding the decree. He laid out a series of tensions that have to be kept in mind in an authentic reading of the decree (the implicit critique being that the decree lends itself to being read exclusively from one or another of the poles in the tension, leading to distortion of the Ignatian charism it is meant to present). For example, Bergoglio argued that we need to keep in mind the opposition between universality and particularity when it comes to thinking about mission, or the opposition between conceptualization and reality (including the very real inspiration of the Holy Spirit that directs our engagement with reality) when it comes to thinking about doctrine.[96] Citing Guardini explicitly, he contended that these sorts of tension, which ultimately find their proper response in the logic of the Incarnation, are only resolved in a "concrete universal" or the "living concrete." The appeal to Guardini is elaborated in a footnote:

We are not talking about a concrete universal as a negation of the negation, which runs the danger of reducing the singular to a mere moment. Guardini approaches the problem of knowing the living concrete through the knowledge of a subject who is also living. Knowledge happens in the dialogal environment of encounter, and has a polar structure. The living concrete can be attained only if concept and intuition are applied simultaneously. A concept on its own would resolve the concrete into something abstract. Intuition alone would end up diluting it into something elusive. The two need to be united, but not externally, nor synthetically, but in the way that an opposite is united with the other opposite: in the tension of a concrete act. *What Guardini is talking about here is what happens in an Ignatian election.* Is this vision possible? The vision (*Anschauung*) of the concrete universal does not happen as a synthesis of opposites, but rather as a living, cognitive act that brings itself about in the maximal tension between two vital poles. And when it is an election confirmed by the good spirit and by the church it takes on the power of something that is truly universal and concrete.[97]

This extended reflection shows not only how much Guardini had helped Pope Francis to think in terms of creatively polarized oppositions, but also how important Ignatian spirituality continued to be for him in this thinking. The resolution of the poles does not come about in an intellectual synthesis, but in the concrete, living act of making an option, a commitment, or, as Ignatius would say, an election. The value and power of this concrete, living act comes to the extent that it is confirmed by "the good spirit" and by the Church. Ignatian spirituality provided the pedagogy (as the young Bergoglio had learned from Fessard over two decades earlier) for opening oneself to and seeking this kind of confirmation. Any intellectual system, or system of doctrines and theological truths, however orthodox they be, that is not opened up, interpreted, and applied in the light of this kind of pedagogy will inevitably collapse into sterile contradictions and polarizations, and fall victim to one or another ideology.

In sum, it has become clear in this review of Jorge Mario Bergoglio's intellectual pilgrimage how much he had learned from the intellectual, literary, and artistic wells from which he drank over the course of sixty years. What has also become clear is that the lodestone, the North Pole that oriented his application of what he learned was always Ignatian spirituality seen (as Fessard had argued) as a pedagogy for discernment. I now turn to a more explicit consideration of Pope Francis's interpretation of Ignatian spirituality, and the *Spiritual Exercises* in particular.

Pope Francis Interprets Ignatian Spirituality

> I feel a Jesuit in my spirituality; in the spirituality of the Exercises, the spirituality deep in my heart. I feel this so deeply that in three days I will go to celebrate with the Jesuits the feast of Saint Ignatius: I will say the morning Mass. I have not changed my spirituality, no. Francis, Franciscan, no. I feel a Jesuit and I think as a Jesuit. I don't mean that hypocritically, but I think as a Jesuit.[98]

In a number of decisive ways, the foregoing review of Bergoglio's pilgrimage has already demonstrated the thesis that Ignatian spirituality is inextricably woven into his theology. A brief review of two of the points made so far. First, under the influence of Fiorito, he became fascinated early on with Ignatius's theory and practice of discernment of spirits. This interest was complemented by his reading of Fessard's work, which taught him to understand discernment not only as a "spiritual" practice for making decisions about one's own vocation, but as a framework within which *any* actualization of graced human freedom should be understood and carried out, and thus as a privileged intersection point of profane history and salvation history. Second, it is discernment, understood as an anthropological-epistemological structure, that provided the exigency and the framework for Francis to embrace (as Borghesi names it) the "'polar,' 'antinomian' dialectic that constitutes the golden thread of Bergoglio's thought, his original, conceptual core."[99] In different ways, his reading of Podetti, Methol Ferré, and, above all, Guardini was guided by this exigency. Now we turn in a more focused way to the pope's interpretation of the *Exercises*.

Reading the different presentations (in interviews, articles, and retreat conferences) from which Pope Francis's interpretation of the *Exercises* can be derived, I believe that five points in particular stand out. First, the *Exercises* help us make important decisions in the ambiguous and often confusing situations in which we find ourselves today. Second, it gives a way of thinking that integrates the need for a community to have a center or focus of unity and the requirement that it be outward-directed in service. Third, it provides a way of making commitments that keeps an ever-greater horizon of possibilities in play while also paying attention to the fine details of carrying out the commitment one has made. Fourth, it provides a way of finding God's presence in our globalized world with the fragmentation and intermixing of cultures that characterizes it. Fifth, it provides a methodology for opening oneself to the transformative experience of God's mercy. The first four points are related in many ways, and can be connected to the value of Ignatian discernment in our complex, modern world; the fifth emerged later in the history of Pope Francis's interpretation of the *Exercises*, but has become as central to it as the focus on discernment, which was there from the beginning. As I elaborate each of these five points, I will also pay attention to the diversity of genres (such as interviews, lectures, sermons) in which Pope Francis's interpretation of the *Exercises* is found, and also to the development of his thinking on the *Exercises*.

First, the *Spiritual Exercises* is a pedagogy for making decisions within inherently ambiguous conditions, and it does so by making salvation history effectively present at a particular point in our history. The pope insists that the ethical, political, and spiritual dilemmas that confront us as individuals and corporately (be it as a Church or as a society) cannot be solved by the simple application of a conceptual framework that is purported to overcome or synthesize the oppositions involved, since such a framework inevitably fails adequately to recognize and value the oppositions involved. Neither is it adequate to adopt a least common denominator, "live and let live" compromise between them. Yet, such dilemmas can, and should, be resolved in a way that is neither irrational nor arbitrary. This is what discernment allows. It is not difficult, then, to understand why, upon being asked by Antonio Spadaro what element of Ignatian spirituality was most important to him in his exercise of the papacy, he named discernment: "My choices, including those related to the day-to-day aspects of life, like the use of a modest car, are related to a spiritual discernment that responds to a need that arises from looking at things, at people, and from reading the signs of the times. Discernment in the Lord guides me in my way of governing."[100] "The wisdom of discernment," he concludes, "redeems the necessary ambiguity of life and helps us find the most appropriate means, which do not always coincide with what looks great and strong."[101]

Second, the *Spiritual Exercises* is a pedagogy for holding the unity of a community ("center") in creative tension with the exigency that it be dispersed in service ("periphery"). Francis's frequent exhortation that the health of the Church depends on its willingness to go to the peripheries finds conceptual roots, as Borghesi notes, in the young Jesuit's reading of Podetti during the 1970s. This insistence on going to the peripheries could not but have been reinforced by the commitment of the Latin American Church to the option for the poor, so decisively stated at Medellín, at Puebla, and, with Bergoglio's own influence, at Aparecida. Here too, however, we can find an Ignatian connection. In an essay published in 1990 on the union of hearts (an important theme in Ignatius's articulation of Jesuit spirituality in the *Constitutions*), Bergoglio described Ignatius's "genius" in terms of a spirituality that unites the dialectical poles of dispersal and unity:

> Apostolic dispersal (born of mission and sustained by prayer and zeal for souls) will give consistency to belonging to the body [of the Society] and this belonging to the body—in turn—will make apostolic dispersal possible. In other words, in Saint Ignatius's mind, the Society is not preserved or increased either by Jesuits seeking "their perfection," individually or as a group, or by having many apostolic works. Rather, this happens because they are instruments constituted by the Society's two ends [perfection of one's own soul and the salvation and aid of the souls of one's neighbors].[102]

Bergoglio thus interprets Ignatius's spirituality as enacting the successful negotiation of the opposition of diversity versus unity, an interpretation that drew on his appropriation of Guardini's thought. Yet it is an enactment that is configured in specifically Ignatian terms as oriented around mission, around "helping souls." This gives one of the reasons why Pierre Favre is for Pope Francis the exemplary Jesuit. He is always on the move, driven by a "holy and beautiful restlessness," as Francis put it in a homily he gave on the occasion of the titular feast of the Society of Jesus, just a few weeks after he had canonized Favre.[103] The roots in Ignatian spirituality of the pope's understanding of the relationship between center and periphery are clear:

> The heart of Christ is the heart of a God who, out of love, "emptied" himself. Each one of us as Jesuits, who follow Jesus should be ready

to empty himself. We are called to this humility: to be "emptied" beings. To be men who are not centred in themselves because the centre of the Society is Christ and his Church. And God is the *Deus semper maior*, the God who always surprises us. . . . Because of this, to be a Jesuit is to be a person of incomplete thought, of open thought: because he thinks always looking at the horizon which is the ever greater glory of God, who ceaselessly surprises us. And this is the restlessness of our inner abyss. This holy and beautiful restlessness.[104]

"It was this restlessness," the pope continued, "that Peter Faber had, a man of great aspirations, another Daniel. . . . Faber experiences the desire 'to allow Christ to occupy the centre of his heart' (*Memoriale*, 63). It is only possible to go to the limits of the world if we are centred in God! And Faber travelled without pause to the geographic frontiers."[105] With Bergoglio as chief redactor of the Aparecida documents, this balancing of center and peripheries found expression in the theme of becoming and remaining "missionary disciples." As pope, it is amply evident in his focus on the exigency to "go to the margins" with the joy of the gospel as the antidote to a Church chronically closed in on itself.

Third, the *Spiritual Exercises* constructs a stance in which one can both envision ever-greater and more ambitious plans for the future, with the ever-greater God in view, and attend thoughtfully and lovingly to the concrete details of the situation in which one is called to enact them and take the next step, however modest. It is the way one appropriates the maxim "time is greater than space" without falling into an acedia that simply severs the connection between these by ignoring the exigencies of "space."

Pope Francis has only rarely written technical analyses of particular Ignatian texts. He often interprets Ignatius from particular phrases (we have already encountered the ever-greater God), some of which do not even derive immediately from the Basque saint himself. An example of this is a Latin phrase composed by an unknown Flemish Jesuit a century after Ignatius's death: *Non coerceri maximo, contineri tamen a minimo, divinum est* ("to suffer no restriction from anything, however great, and yet to be contained in the tiniest of things, that is divine").[106] As Peter Schineller writes, this maxim captures the spirituality of an Ignatius who "quietly worked in his room in Rome, writing and refining the myriad of details in the Constitutions, and at the same time sent Xavier around the globe to the Indies. Ignatius worked with kings and princes, popes and bishops, but at the same time ministered to the least, the women on the streets of Rome."[107]

In a retreat that Bergoglio gave to the Jesuits of Argentina in the late 1970s he referred to this maxim in a talk devoted to the Call of the King.[108] In a typically Bergoglian approach to expounding the *Exercises*, he keys on a phrase (which many might overlook) in the offering that concludes the exercise: "I wish and desire, and it is my deliberate decision" (*SpEx* 98). He explains: "'I wish' is in opposition to velleity; 'I desire' opposes acedia; 'it is my deliberate decision' opposes inconstancy."[109] He expands on each of these for several pages, explaining of acedia that "what is typical to all forms of acedia is something like a utopia, not taking account of the 'times, places and persons' that make up our pastoral activity."[110] He continues to explain that sometimes this problem manifests itself in a paralysis that is unable to accept the rhythms of everyday life. In a similar vein, it is found in the person who loses herself or himself in grand plans without paying attention to the concrete details in terms of which alone they could be executed. Conversely, it can show itself in a paralysis that comes from getting needlessly wrapped up in the minute details of every moment, without seeing the plan of God that both transcends them but also gives them their context and meaning. The importance of the seventeenth-century motto for interpreting Ignatius's sixteenth-century text comes at the conclusion of his reflections on acedia: "How true it is that we need to recover that epitaph of Ignatius's: 'Non coerceri a maximo, contineri a minimo, divinum est.'"[111]

Fourth, the *Spiritual Exercises* is a pedagogy for finding God's presence under conditions of globalization, with the fragmentation and intermixing of cultures that it entails.

Rahner did not use the motto *non coerceri a maximo, contineri a minimo, divinum est* to work it out, but he came to a very similar conclusion in reflecting on the Ignatian motto of *Ad maiorem Dei gloriam*.[112] Moreover, what Francis calls for in his interpretation of the motto is not unlike the "nameless virtue" that Rahner called for in an essay of this name.[113] Both were aware of the way that Ignatian spirituality could offer a response to what (following Anthony Giddens and Hartmut Rosa) I have called the disembedding of social processes and institutions from local time and geographical vicinity.[114] Nowhere is this disembedding more palpable than in the modern megacity. In this regard, Pope Francis's evocation of Ignatius in a 2011 talk titled "God Lives in the City" is particularly telling.[115] He reflects on the challenge of finding God's presence in a modern megacity such as Buenos Aires, and the need to develop a pastoral strategy for nurturing a more potent sense of that presence among its citizens. Francis described a certain perspective, a kind of theological imagination, essential to accomplishing this task. He concludes his discussion with a short commentary on the Contemplation of the Incarnation in the Second Week of the *Spiritual Exercises*: "The Contemplation of the Incarnation, which Saint Ignatius presents in his Spiritual Exercises, is a good example of the perspective we are proposing—a perspective that does not get bogged down in the dualism that constantly comes and goes as a result of the various diagnoses for planning, but that is dramatically involved in the reality of the city and is committed alongside it in a plan of action."[116]

With a further commentary reminiscent of Fessard's interpretation of the *Spiritual Exercises*, Francis cautions that the Contemplation on the Incarnation does not intend an ascent "from time into eternity in quest of the definitive beatific vision from which we will 'deduce' the ideal temporal order."[117] Rather, Bergoglio focuses on the rhythm of the contemplation, moving from the viewpoint (compassionate and efficaciously salvific) of the persons of the Trinity to the concreteness of the "'the house and rooms of Our Lady in the city of Nazareth, in the province of Galilee.'"[118] Entering into this rhythm nurtures a perspective that will "allow the Lord 'to become incarnate once again' in the world as it is."[119] This happens not by opening access to a comprehensive plan outside of history, but by positioning one for a discernment in which at this moment, in this concrete situation, one's decision can allow Christ to become incarnate again.[120] The *Exercises* makes this possible and enables one to avoid being paralyzed by the complexity of the modern world; even more, it enable one to find God's presence precisely in this modern world.

Fifth, the *Spiritual Exercises* provide a structure that opens us to the transformative encounter with God's mercy, which is the foundation for a productive life of loving service. This insight has come to be at the heart of the pope's interpretation of the *Exercises*, but he only arrived at it in the 1990s and 2000s (after his time in Córdoba).

The types of commentaries and applications of Ignatian spirituality that we have been considering so far in this section are typical of the way that Pope Francis's interpretation of the *Spiritual Exercises* manifests itself. He does not give it in a systematic treatise (such as Rahner's essay on the logic of concrete, individual knowledge, or even the earlier essay on "Ignatian Mysticism of Joy in the World"). Nor do we have a set of lecture notes (such as Ellacuría's notes from his course on the *Spiritual Exercises*). His references are occasional and concrete, but as they accumulate over the course of his career they make it clear that the *Exercises* offered him crucial resources to present to the Church on how to discern the most authentic way forward in the challenges posed to it in the post- or still-modern world.

We do have, however, some more extensive treatments in a different genre. Namely, there are texts of preached retreats he gave based on the *Spiritual Exercises*, which give us a few further clues for how he interprets Ignatian spirituality, and can highlight continuities and changes in his interpretation. Two sets of retreat conferences are from the late 1970s, one of them given to the Jesuits of the Argentinian province as a whole and a second given to superiors of communities.[121] A later set of retreat conferences comes from a retreat that Bergoglio gave to the bishops of Spain in January 2006.[122] There is a good deal of continuity between these presentations of the Exercises, separated as they are by three decades. Sometimes whole sections are repeated verbatim. There are significant differences, however. Most generally, the earlier retreat presentations evince a tendency to highlight more the "ascetic" dimension of Ignatian spirituality, whereas the later writings turn more toward the mystical side. Philip Endean has noted this about Bergoglio's earlier writings on Ignatius.[123] Subsequent to Pope Francis's insistence (in the 2013 interview with Spadaro) that he has in fact always embraced the "mystical" side of Ignatius, "over against 'an interpretation of the Spiritual Exercises that emphasizes asceticism, silence and penance,'" Endean modulated without fully retracting his earlier claim: "As far as the language of spiritual theology goes, I must of course stand corrected. But my conjecture, though articulated in terms of the ascetical and the mystical, arose less from Bergoglio's reading of Ignatian sources than from my sense of how a superior was dealing too harshly with his subjects, in particular with less robust personalities, and with people who thought differently from himself. There is, surely, a marked difference in leadership tone between Pope Francis's interview and Father Bergoglio's exhortations. The *maniera brusca* has modulated into a patient, vulnerable docility."[124]

Space precludes a full comparison of the "early Bergoglio" on Ignatius and the "later Bergoglio," and in what I have presented here on Pope Francis's interpretation of Ignatius I have drawn primarily on the later writings. Yet, on a first reading of texts from these different periods, the shift signaled by Endean's remarks is evident. Just one comparison will suffice to limn the difference and also to surface a highly significant theme in Pope Francis's mature (if I may put it that way) interpretation of the *Spiritual Exercises*: the theme of mercy. To this end, we consider and compare briefly Bergoglio's interpretations (separated by thirty years) of the themes of sin and conversion as they are given in the First Week of the *Exercises*.[125]

In the earlier retreat talks, Bergoglio uses the First Letter of John, and the tenor is severe. He writes of sin: "Everyone who commits a sin also commits iniquity. This is a word that has an eschatological meaning and designates the fundamental iniquity, the iniquity of the last days when the evil of the world under the dominion of the devil is manifested. More than a weakness of sin, it entails the fundamental rejection of the light.... What is essential to sin, which is iniquity, is the radical rejection of a liberty called forth by love."[126] Sin opposes God's plan, which founds us and integrates us into the Church. Sin creates, contrarily, "a foundation that disintegrates our belonging to the Lord and to our holy mother, the hierarchical Church."[127] The result is one or another species of despair, which Bergoglio also connects with an impatience that makes us unable to embrace the rhythms of everyday life, or drives us to seek magic solutions.

It is a stark presentation, and there is no doubt that there is much to the First Week to warrant such an interpretation. What is missing, however, and what is superabundantly present in the treatment of the same material thirty years later, is the insistence on God's mercy. A fuller discussion of the later Bergoglio's treatment will follow below, but the difference in tenor is evident from the outset of Cardinal Bergoglio's presentation of the First Week material to the bishops of Spain in 2006: "As we read the Gospels, a paradoxical pattern emerges: the Lord is more inclined to warn, correct, and reprimand those who are closest to him—his disciples and Peter in particular—than those who are distant.... In the context of the Lord's gratuitous choice and his absolute fidelity, to be reprimanded by him means that one is receiving a sign of God's immense mercy."[128] "From the hand of the Lord who corrects us comes his abundant mercy."[129] This marks the principal difference between the two iterations of Bergoglio's presentation of the First Week of the Exercises. Mercy is not mentioned once in the earlier retreat conferences on the First Week and on sin. Moreover, rather than focusing on a need to admit one's failures, even one's iniquity, and embrace conversion, the later Bergoglio emphasizes that one must first center on the gift of one's vocation and the closeness to Christ that it represents. An admission of failure will only succeed in the context of the prior recognition of the grace of one's call and a recognition that one's continuation in that call, one's sin notwithstanding, is a preeminent instance of God's faithful, merciful love. This is, perhaps, presumed in the earlier presentation, but in the later ones Francis makes it the organizing principle.

Matters of context surely explain some of the differences. The Jesuit leader in the 1970s was faced by a province that he feared was disintegrating into polarized factions, and in which there were currents (associated in his mind with liberation theology and the Movement of Third World Priests) that were harshly critical of the hierarchical Church. Yet the Spanish Church of the first decade of this century was not unfamiliar with divisions. And hopelessness, a major concern of the provincial in the 1970s, is still Bergoglio's gravest diagnosis of the danger at hand in the first decade of this millennium. Yet the patina of hopelessness in 2006 was not painted by divisions in the Society of Jesus or Church as a whole over how to respond to the Dirty War, but the accelerating secularization of Spanish society and the seeming helplessness of the hierarchical Church to stem this tide. In Spain he did not diagnose the problem by connecting hopelessness directly with iniquity and sin, but by situating it in a far more nuanced way. He used Mary's Magnificat, and recommended the choice of poverty, acceptance of humiliations, and embrace of humility as a way for the bishops to live into their vocations and exercise their office. This is, of course, the strategy recommended by Christ to his servants and friends in Ignatius's meditation on the Two Standards (*SpEx* 146). Bergoglio's use of this exercise evidences another difference of the pope's later presentation of the *Spiritual Exercises*: his willingness to intercalate elements from one week of the Exercises in materials proper to another (here: a reflection from the Second Week in material on sin in the First Week).

In sum, the most significant difference between the early and the late retreat conferences is the centrality of mercy, the hope and joy that it opens up (that is to say, consolation), and the apostolic efficacy that it uniquely unleashes. For the "later" Francis, the *Spiritual Exercises* opens one to the transformative experience of God's mercy, which, if embraced and enacted, brings consolation to oneself, and consequently to those whom one serves: hope, in the face of hopelessness; faith, in the face of paralyzing doubts pressed upon us by our secular age; an active, combative love that sends us "to the margins," and, as an ambient to all of this, deep joy.[130]

I will continue to elaborate this final and crucial feature of Pope Francis's interpretation of the *Spiritual Exercises*, with a further analysis of his interpretation of the First Week, but before doing so, a few more words about the general features of the 2006 retreat conferences are in order. Francis's presentation of the *Spiritual Exercises* to the Spanish bishops follows Ignatius's advice that the exercises be accommodated to the needs and capacities of the one making them (*SpEx* 18). He spends the greatest part of his time on the exercises of the Second Week.[131] With the materials of that week he spends little time with the contemplations on episodes from Jesus's life, devoting most of his attention to the week's less scripturally grounded exercises: the Call of the King, the Meditation on the Two Standards, the Meditation on Three Classes of Person, and the reflection on Three Ways of Being Humble. In his talks, Francis evinces a clear awareness of the challenges, perils, and pitfalls that face a bishop (unsurprisingly, since he had been facing them himself for more than fifteen years by the time he wrote his talks). He also shows an awareness of the dispiriting prospect that a rapidly secularizing Spanish society and culture presented its hierarchy. Many themes for which the future pope would come to be known and which we have encountered earlier in this chapter show up here: the dangers of corruption, clericalism, and spiritual worldliness; the need to pray for and cultivate a combative hope in the face of challenges facing the Church; and the importance of discernment. And, of course, mercy appears frequently and prominently.[132]

That Francis associates the First Week with the experience of mercy is clear from the very outset of the retreat. He chooses to frame the entire retreat with a reference to the Magnificat, "his mercy is from age to age": "As with Mary [he tells the bishops] our acts of thanksgiving, adoration and praise found our memory in the mercy of God that sustains us. With hope that is firmly rooted in him, we are thus prepared to fight the good fight of the faith and of love, on behalf of all those entrusted to our care."[133] The itinerary of the *Spiritual Exercises*, as the pope interprets and presents it here, is a remembering of God's mercy (First Week) giving rise to a hope that will enable the bishops to make the difficult pastoral discernments required of them to fulfill their calling and vocation (Second Week), strengthened by an awareness that, embracing the cross, we will understand that what seems weak and foolish is, in fact, the wisdom of God (Third Week), which finally makes it possible for us to open ourselves to the consolation of the risen Lord (Fourth Week), giving us a peace that "is the foundation and wellspring of apostolic courage (*parrhesia*) and apostolic patience (*hypomone*)."[134] The activist character of his approach is indicated by the kind of hope that he has in mind, which he marks as the outcome of the retreat: "the grace of a combative hope."[135] The influence of Fessard's articulation of the dialectic of mercy, shame, and hope is still abundantly in evidence.

One of the most interesting features of Francis's interpretation of the *Spiritual Exercises* is the way that he very tightly connects the First Week of the Exercises with the Second. That is, instead of seeing the First Week as a stage through which we pass and then leave behind in order to go on to the Second, he presents them as dialectically interrelated.

With this introductory overview of the shape and some of the features of the retreat conferences completed, I return to the passage discussed earlier, which is found in a chapter of *In Him Alone Is Our Hope* titled "The Lord Who Reprimands and Pardons Us." This chapter follows immediately on a chapter titled "The Lord Who Founds Us," which, as the verb indicates, presents Francis's elaboration of the theology of the Principle and Foundation. Thus, we are now encountering his interpretation of the keys to understanding (and experiencing!) the First Week. I quote here, once again, the opening passage, which shows the centrality of mercy in his presentation: "As we read the Gospels, a paradoxical pattern emerges: the Lord is more inclined to warn, correct, and reprimand those who are closest to him—his disciples and Peter in particular—than those who are distant. The Lord acts in this way to make it clear that ministry is a pure grace.... In this context of the Lord's gratuitous choice and his absolute fidelity, to be reprimanded by him means that one is receiving a sign of God's immense mercy."[136]

To illustrate this paradox, he uses what he calls "the first confession of Simon Peter" in the story of the miraculous catch of fish (Luke 5:1–11). The context, the pope notes, is evangelization—the Lord teaching the crowds from Peter's boat. The story is well known. Having completed his teaching, Jesus has the disciples put out into deep water and, their night of fruitless toil notwithstanding, has them throw their nets over one more time, only to have their nets filled to the bursting point. Francis's commentary on what follows is worth quoting in full:

> At the sight of this prodigy, Simon Peter confesses himself a sinner. And in this very act, the Lord converts him into a Fisher of men. Conversion and mission are thus intimately united in the heart of

> Simon Peter. The Lord accepts his *"Depart from me, Lord, for I am a sinful man"* (Lk 5:8), but he reorients it with his *"Do not be afraid, from now on you will be catching men"* (Lk 5:10). . . . From that moment on, Simon Peter never separates these two dimensions of his life: he will always confess that he is a sinful man and a fisher of men. His sins will not prevent him from accomplishing the mission he has received (and he will never become an isolated sinner enclosed within his own sinfulness). His mission will not allow him to hide his sin, concealed behind a pharisaical mask.[137]

This is for Francis the fruit of a genuine, graced experience of the First Week: "The Lord is the ever greater One: when he calls us to conversion, far from diminishing us, he is giving us stature in his Kingdom. From the hand of the Lord who corrects us also comes his abundant mercy."[138] This is, I suggest, Francis's way of taking into account the "colloquy before the cross" of the First Week, in which, fresh from the experience of God's faithful love and mercy even in the face of one's sin, one places oneself before the cross and asks vocation-oriented questions: "What have I done for Christ?" "What am I doing for Christ?" "What will I do for Christ?" The experience of mercy is not just the experience of being pardoned, but the experience of being "given stature in the Kingdom of God," being given the dignity of being not just the *object* of God's saving mercy and love, but its *subject*, making it a reality for oneself and for others. Thus, for the pope, an experience of mercy without an experience of being given a mission is incomplete.

On this reading of the *Spiritual Exercises*, the movement to the Second Week—with the so-called Call of the King, in which one imagines oneself along the model of a generous knight called into battle by a just king, and the "Two Standards" in which one contemplates the "logic" of Christ in contrast to the "logic" of Satan, the enemy of our human nature—is not a movement into something totally new, but simply an elaboration of a dynamic already unleashed in and by the First Week meditations on sin, mercy, and the call to conversion. They are bridges that allow that dynamic to flow into the precise articulation of *how* I will respond to God's mercy, which is the subject for discernment and choice during the Second Week.

There are other ways in which Francis's presentation of the *Spiritual Exercises* keep the First and Second Weeks tightly connected, connecting the experience of conversion in the First Week, with the commitment to a particular mission (the election) that is the subject of the discernment that happens in the Second Week. For example, chapter 4 ("The Spirit of the World or the 'Anti-Kingdom'") looks ahead to the Meditation on the Two Standards in the Second Week yet the chapter also keeps the focus on sin, and turns to the Colloquy before the Cross of the First Week.[139] When he begins his discussion of the meditation on the Call of the King, proper to the Second Week, he keeps the focus (rightly enough) on the way this meditation "frames the contemplations on the life of Jesus within the context of a great vocation," which refers back to his presentation of "the first call of Peter" in the reflections he drew from the First Week.[140]

Bearing in mind this linking of First and Second Weeks, of mercy and mission, can shed new light on the response that Pope Francis gave in accepting his election as pope, with which I began this chapter: "I am a sinner, but I trust in the infinite mercy and patience of our Lord Jesus Christ, and I accept in a spirit of penance." Recognizing that one is a sinner, and also recognizing that one is embraced by and called forth by God's mercy, enables one to accept one's vocation and live it joyfully. This response surely exemplifies Francis's avowal during the first year of his papacy: "I feel a Jesuit and I think as a Jesuit."[141]

The *Spiritual Exercises* Interprets Pope Francis

I have argued that over the course of his life, Pope Francis has developed a novel and compelling interpretation of Ignatian spirituality, one that has been crucial to his response to the particular situation of late modernity with which he has grappled in Argentina over the course of four decades as a leader of the Jesuits and then of the local Church, and which he is now drawing on as pope. First, Ignatian spirituality provides a way of making decisions within inherently ambiguous situations. Second, it provides a pedagogy for holding in creative balance the need for a community to be focused on itself ("center") but also be ready to go outside of itself in response to the mission that God gives it ("periphery"). Third, Ignatian spirituality encourages and opens one to a stance in which one can both envision a different future, drawn forward by the presence of the ever-greater God, and attend thoughtfully and lovingly to the concrete details and the particular persons that I deal with on a daily basis.

Fourth, it has provided for him a way of responding to the fragmentation and disintegrative pluralism that globalization has brought with it. These points highlight in different ways the centrality of Ignatian discernment in the pope's interpretation of Ignatius. Fifth and finally, in a more recent development of his interpretation of Ignatius, he finds in it a particularly effective means of opening oneself to God's steadfast love and mercy, which always brings with it the life- and joy-giving call to mission, which is the source of hope, joy, and faith (in other words, to consolation). It enables one, in other words, to be a contemplative in action.

Further verification of my thesis on the centrality of Ignatian spirituality to the pope's teachings and practice could be given by careful readings of his magisterial documents: *Evangelii Gaudium* and *Gaudete et exsultate*, in particular. Here, however, I attempt to show the productivity of the thesis by showing that certain puzzles about his doctrinal teachings can be illuminated by using the framework of the *Spiritual Exercises* to interpret them. I choose the issue of the relationship of mercy to justice.[142] This is a theme with a long and complex career in the history of theology.[143] I draw on *The Name of God Is Mercy*, a book that includes the bull *Misericordiae vultus*, which proclaimed the year of mercy, and also includes an interview with the pope on his thoughts and hopes about the jubilee year. My argument will be that his specific statements on the relationship between mercy and justice are underdetermined and ambiguous. A more satisfying understanding of what he has in mind can be obtained by reading those statements in the light of the close interweaving of the First and Second Weeks in his interpretation of the *Spiritual Exercises*.

When we take up the relationship between mercy and justice, we come quickly to the heart of the mystery of God's grace and confront perennial questions that arise when one plumbs that mystery: the relationship between God's mercy and God's justice, between God's merciful action and the response of human free will, and, looking at the latter, the relationship between the response of faith and the response of works, particularly works of justice. In *Misericordiae vultus*, Francis is spare in his comments on the relationship between justice and mercy. He starts by saying that they are "two dimensions of a single reality that unfolds progressively until it culminates in love."[144] He then distinguishes between justice as a principle in civil society and justice as the principle governing "that which is rightly due to each individual." Reading the Hebrew Bible with the latter definition in mind, he argues that there justice is understood as "full observance of the Law and the behavior of every good Israelite in conformity with God's commandments."[145] Yet, lest this become a legalistic rigorism (and not just when it comes to a caricatured Old Testament Judaism but, the pope is quite clear, for contemporary Catholicism), Francis adds that "we need to recall that in Sacred Scripture, justice is conceived essentially as the faithful abandonment of oneself to God's will."[146] I will return to this point insofar as it highlights an important bridge between the pope's thinking and the *Spiritual Exercises*. Looking at the New Testament in particular, Francis argues that "faced with a vision of justice as the mere observance of the law that judges people simply by dividing them into two groups—the just and sinners— Jesus is bent on revealing the great gift of mercy that searches out sinners and offers them pardon and salvation."[147] The "rule of life" for Jesus's disciples "must place mercy at the centre."[148] The pope frequently uses this kind of language: mercy is not only the defining feature of an action or a disposition to act, but an orienting center or a "rule of life." It is a key to the "logic" of God's gratuitous and overabundant love.

Mercy is thus "not opposed to justice, but represents God's way of reaching out to the sinner, offering him a new chance to look at himself, convert and believe."[149] It does not devalue justice or render it superfluous. "On the contrary: anyone who makes a mistake must pay the price. However, this is just the beginning of conversion, not its end, because one begins to feel the tenderness and mercy of God."[150] Mercy is also a marker of God's transcendence: "If God limited himself to only justice, he would cease to be God, and would instead be like human beings who ask merely that the law be respected."[151] God is not like human beings, because God acts with mercy, yet, this mercy does not deny justice. In and through mercy "God envelops [justice] and surpasses it, with an even greater event in which we experience love as the foundation of true justice."[152] "When there is mercy, justice is more just, and it fulfils its true essence."[153]

This cryptic set of statements is difficult to systematize, but the biblical background against which it is drawn, both from the Old Testament and the New, is clear. What does it mean for justice to be enveloped and surpassed? How precisely is justice "more just" where there is mercy? If justice and mercy are two parts of a single, unfolding reality, what are the stages of that unfolding, and how are the two parts related as this single reality unfolds? Two hints in *The Name of God Is Mercy* provide warrant to turn to the *Spiritual Exercises* for an interpretive framework in which to place and understand these statements. First, in the interview section of the book, when asked about the meaning and place of mercy in his own personal history, Francis makes reference to Fessard's work on the *Spiritual Exercises*, which is foundational for his understanding of the *Exercises* and set decisive and enduring parameters for his intellectual (including theological) development.[154] The pope tells his interviewer of the importance of Fessard's account of the dialectic interplay of shame, mercy, and hope, which (on Fessard's and Francis's reading) Ignatius expects to come into play when one stands before the cross of Christ. This associates the experience of mercy with the First Week and the Colloquy before the Cross (*SpEx* 53).

The second clue is Francis's claim "that in Sacred Scripture, justice is conceived essentially as the *faithful abandonment of oneself to God's will*."[155] This statement expresses the second of two purposes that Ignatius names for the *Spiritual Exercises*: "seeking and finding God's will in the ordering of our life for the salvation of our soul" (*SpEx* 1). As the Exercises unfold, this "seeking and following" takes shape as an exuberant liberality that seeks to place everything one has at God's service. This suggests that for Francis the full achievement of "justice" includes but goes beyond conformity to a particular codification of God's will to include "faithful abandonment" to that will. But what is faithful abandonment and how is it achieved? It is the fruit and goal of the spiritual life as a whole, and the *Spiritual Exercises* proposes a set of practices to move progressively closer to it. What is more, to the extent that the grace of experiencing mercy is central to the First Week of the Exercises, and to the extent that Ignatius insisted that if one did not find and embrace that grace she or he should not continue on, then we might say that *without* the experience of mercy, action for justice (which would be discerned in the Second Week election) will not fully succeed because one will not have been able fully to abandon oneself faithfully to God's will. Thus, in a negative voice, we have a rendering of Francis's claim: "Where there is mercy, justice is more just and fulfills its essence."[156]

What became clear from considering the 2006 retreat that he gave to the bishops of Spain is that on Francis's reading, the First and Second Weeks of the *Spiritual Exercises* are not most adequately understood as two stages through which one proceeds linearly, as it were, but represent a dialectical unity in which the experience of mercy unleashes a graced participation in God's saving work, which does not simply leave the experience of sin and frailty behind, but takes it up, albeit enframed in the experience of mercy. Let us take this close interrelating of First and Second Weeks, and the mutually implicatory experiences of mercy and of mission, to gloss and thus to interpret Francis's statements about mercy and justice.

First, justice and mercy "are two dimensions of a single reality that unfolds progressively until it culminates in love."[157] The *Spiritual Exercises* maps such an unfolding process, which begins with the transformative experience of mercy in the First Week, passes through the conforming of oneself with the will of God in the discernment and choice of life in the Second Week, continuing to be confirmed in the Third and Fourth Weeks, and culminates in love, expressed in the Contemplation to Attain Love at the end of the *Exercises*, an active love of the "contemplative in action."

Satisfying the demands of justice is the ever-renewed work of conforming one's life to God's will for oneself and for the world. Such work certainly requires attention to specific norms: "The Church remembers the mercies of God and therefore tries to be faithful to the Law. The Ten Commandments are the juridical aspect that provides a human framework for God's mercy."[158] But a graced response, as Ignatius envisions it in the *Spiritual Exercises*, and which Francis takes up in his retreat talks, also requires a discernment that is not only about applying those norms in and to the particularities of one's own situation, but of revising and extending them in response to an "ever-greater God." As we saw from Francis's interpretation of the Contemplation on the Incarnation, the fullest response is one in which we "allow the Lord 'to become incarnate once again' (*Spiritual Exercises*, 109), in the world as it is."[159] This is the fullness of justice, which requires the experience of mercy. The "ever-greater God's" call to act justly is heard more clearly and more radically (Second Week) the deeper our experience plumbs the depths of God's mercy as we come to terms more radically with the power of sin in the world and in our own lives (First Week). The process is not one driven by guilt or by demonizing oneself or others, but by the logic of gratitude and hope (as the Contemplation to Attain Love makes clear).[160] It is also a commitment to justice that never gives up on others, because it comes from the experience of mercy in which I realize that God has not given up on me. In short, as laid out by the dynamism of the Spiritual Exercises, "When there is mercy, justice is more just, and it fulfils its true essence."[161]

Finally, if we use this map for thinking about mercy and justice, we avoid the problem that mercy becomes a patronizing act of condescension on the part of someone in power toward the weak and powerless, which often ends up simply confirming the powerless in that state: mercy as a kind of divine *noblesse oblige*. The action of mercy, as Francis describes it by tying the First and Second Week closely together, is not just the forgiveness of a debt that the debtor cannot otherwise repay, but also, and indissolubly, an invitation to participate in God's own agency in the world.[162] Mercy's pardon is found precisely in a call to agency that confers a unique dignity on the one pardoned by calling him or her to join in the process of bringing others into this unfolding process. This is, I suggest, Pope Francis's way of doing justice to the quintessentially Catholic way of understanding grace: grace *heals* (including pardons) by *elevating*. This elevating, however, is not a removal from the world, but an elevation by plunging one into the world as a follower of Christ. Interpreted in this light, we can understand better the words with which Pope Francis begins his bull of indiction: "Jesus Christ is the face of the Father's mercy. These words might well sum up the mystery of the Christian faith."[163]

Theology at the Service of the Church as an Instrument of Consolation

In September 2015, Pope Francis recorded a message for a meeting of the International Congress of Theology, held in Buenos Aires on the occasion of the 100th anniversary of the founding of the theology faculty at the Catholic University of Argentina. In the course of this address he asserted the need for "reflection, discernment, taking the Church tradition very seriously and taking reality very seriously, putting the two in dialogue with one another." He continued, "In this context, I think that the study of theology is of the greatest importance. It is an irreplaceable service to the life of the Church."[164] Yet he has a very particular understanding of how to configure theology, which he begins describing by laying out a danger in the contemporary practice of this discipline:

> Not infrequently an opposition is generated between theology and pastoral thinking and action [*lo pastoral*], as if they were two opposing, separated realities that didn't have anything to do with one another. Not infrequently we identify the doctrinal mindset with being

conservative and retrograde; and, conversely, we think about the pastoral mindset from the perspective of adaptation, reduction, accommo-dation. As if they had nothing to do with one another. What gets generated in this way is a false opposition between the so-called "pastorally minded" and the "academics," between those on the side of the people and those on the side of doctrine. What gets generated is a false opposition between theology and thinking pastorally, between believing reflection and believing life. And then life has no room for reflection and reflection finds no room in life. The great fathers of the church, Irenaeus, Augustine, Basil, Ambrose, just to name a few, were great theologians because they were great pastors.[165]

The pope goes on to state that one of the main contributions of Vatican II was to overcome this opposition. Because of this, a theology that wants to serve the Church must take up "the arduous work of distinguishing the message of Life from its forms of transmission, from its cultural elements that have a time encoded within." He continues that "avoiding this exercise in discernment leads in one way or another to a betrayal of the content of the message. It causes the Good News to cease being new and, above all, to cease being good; it becomes sterile emptied of all its creative strength, its healing and resurrecting strength." He concludes, "This meeting of doctrine and the pastoral mindset is not optional, it is constitutive of a theology that aims to be ecclesial."[166]

This understanding of theology can be taken as a brief for the centrality of pastoral or practical theology to the work of academic theology, but I suggest that the twofold naming of discernment in his remarks also marks this as an appeal to the importance of spirituality. Discernment, whether defined precisely as Ignatius did it, or in conversation with another spiritual tradition, is in each case, a spiritual practice and not solely an academic enterprise; in discernment the spiritual and the academic are integrated.[167] This chapter has argued that discernment, as contextualized within a diverse set of other practices, along with those insights into the world that flow from and make sense of those practices (that is, a spirituality), is at the core of Francis's work as a leader in the Church and the theology he has developed to guide him. For him, as I have argued, it is Ignatian spirituality that provides the structure and pedagogy for uniting the doctrinal and the pastoral in Christian life and thought. To be clear, once again, this is not to discount the capacity of other spiritualities to do this work. The pope's drive to understand, embrace, and hand on Ignatian spirituality came from his diagnosis early on of a modernity fractured into contending oppositions that made any creative social action impossible and paralyzed the Church's ability to make of the good news something creative, life-giving, healing, and even resurrecting. He took up a diverse set of concepts and themes from different intellectual currents in Argentina and Europe in order to craft his own interpretation of Ignatian spirituality that was up to this task. Conversely, the thoughtful and "heartful" understanding of Ignatian spirituality that he crafted over the years has guided the careful thinking he has brought to his work of leading the Church—his pastoral theology, if you will (which, as he insisted in the address to the theologians gathered in Buenos Aires, is not opposed to academic theology).

The stakes for him are the same as they were for Ignatius: to open people to the grace of consolation that God desires to give them. He made this clear in his address to the Jesuits gathered at their 36th General Congregation:

> We can always improve in praying persistently for consolation. The Apostolic Exhortations *Evangelii Gaudium* and *Amoris Laetitia*, along with the Encyclical *Laudato Si'*, were meant to highlight the importance of joy. In the *Exercises*, Ignatius asks his companions to contemplate "the task of consolation" as something specific to the Resurrected Christ (*Spiritual Exercises*, 224). It is the specific task of the Society to console the Christian faithful and to help them in their discernment so that the enemy of human nature does not distract us from joy: the joy of evangelizing, the joy of the family, the joy of the Church, the joy of creation. . . . Let us never be robbed of that joy, neither through discouragement when faced with the great measure of evil in the world and misunderstandings among those who intend to do good, nor let it be replaced with vain joys that are easily bought and sold in any shop.[168]

He makes here the connection between consolation and joy. Joy is, after mercy, and, perhaps, hope, one of the most frequently used words in Francis's lexicon. Francis would agree with the words that John O'Malley used to describe the importance of consolation for the first Jesuits: "'Consolation,' if this occurred in the person unto whom Jesuits ministered, was the surest sign that all was well. Nadal, Polanco, and others had learned from the *Exercises* what this meant and how central it was. They had, in fact, learned it so well that I am tempted to dub their ministry a 'ministry of consolation,' and their spirituality a 'spirituality of consolation.'"[169]

The Church, for Francis, is called to be an instrument of consolation, *ad intra*, for its own members, but also *ad extra*, to all those "on the peripheries" to whom Francis has called the Church to go out and to minister.[170] To be sure, the pope understands the Church cannot be turned into a religious order (Jesuit or otherwise), but the fundamental dynamic of mercy-discipleship-consolation that Pope Francis came to articulate as the core spiritual intuition of Ignatian spirituality is one into which he has sought to bring the Church in his exercise of the papacy (in proclaiming the Year of Mercy in 2015–16, for instance, which could be interpreted as inviting the whole Church into the experience of the First Week). And the importance of discernment, a practice that has been a focus of his interest in Ignatius from his earliest years as a Jesuit, is clear from the way he makes decisions for himself and the ways that he has tried to facilitate decision-making in Church synods. In sum, I am tempted myself, following O'Malley, to name Francis's papacy a "papacy of consolation" and his grasp and application of Ignatian spirituality "a spirituality of consolation."

Pope Francis's interpretation of Ignatian spirituality and his incorporation of it into his theology has not been some kind of silver bullet that has magically solved all problems. There have been significant challenges for his papacy: the clergy sex abuse crisis and the corruption it has disclosed in the highest levels of the hierarchy prominent among them. His opponents misconstrue his interrelating of "the doctrinal" and "the pastoral" in Church teachings and theology to be a dismissal (or even transgression) of orthodoxy. I believe that in all of these, one can best understand how he is attempting to navigate this challenge by framing his decisions in the light of Ignatian spirituality. His original and creative appropriation of Ignatian spirituality for the sake of a theology that wishes to be of service to a Church that can and must understand itself as an instrument of consolation in a post- or still-modern world eminently merits him a place alongside Rahner, Ellacuría, and other Ignatian theologians. A theology that attends to his insights can discern in its own way how to become an instrument of consolation in turn, in service of the Church.

CHAPTER SEVEN

Ignatius and the Theologians

KARL RAHNER, IGNACIO ELLACURÍA, POPE FRANCIS:
IGNATIAN THEOLOGIANS

This book has sought to make a few steps toward a more fruitful relationship between two products of modernity: academic (or "scientific") theology and spirituality. Theology without a living relationship to spirituality risks devolving into a technical jargon reserved for experts, bereft of a capacity to propose or support an "art of living" (Hadot) that can attract and sustain contemporary men and women. Spirituality without a critical-constructive relationship to theology risks becoming a privatized bricolage of practices, which may construct an individualized haven in a heartless world, but in the end cannot unite men and women to imagine a different world, much less act effectively to instantiate it, in however fragmentary and yet hopeful a way. Without a more vital relationship between theology and spirituality, theologians may continue to interpret their texts, engage the findings of other academic disciplines, and construct their arguments for as long as increasingly secularized academic institutions will tolerate them. Spirituality may well continue to thrive as another category of popular commodity in the market, that increasingly preeminent force in our globalized world, defining the possibilities among which we choose to quiet our restless hearts, both individually and corporately, and which we consume in order to come to terms with the world we have constructed.

The conviction that has driven the argument of this book, however, is that such a state of affairs will eventually cripple both theology and spirituality. Without addressing this situation creatively both are rendered less able to serve the Church, the People of God, as it strives to announce the good news to the world and to act as a leaven in the world to imagine and enact, however fragmentarily, how that good news might take flesh. The church, as Hügel reminded us, needs both theologies that serve the intellectual element of faith and spiritualities that serve the mystical-volitional element. But it needs these in communication with one another.

The contribution of this book can only be a beginning, a few initial steps, because of the depth and complexity of the conditions of modernity that have produced the split I described in chapter 1. Indeed, part of the origin and growth of this split is the construction of the categories of theology and spirituality as we now have come to use them. Writing another book will not resolve the problem from the side of academic theology, any more than another workshop, webinar, or podcast will do it from the side of spirituality. The split is embodied in institutions, patterns of interaction, and a social imaginary that cannot be overcome from within. In the past, responding to such a situation was often done by new spiritualities, which engendered religious movements, some of which were endorsed by the institutional Church to become new religious orders. They proposed a new way of structuring the *vita evangelica*, and a new, creative, and at times also interruptive and disturbing social imaginary. Benedictines, Franciscans, Carmelites, Dominicans, and Jesuits, and many more have, as Johann Baptist Metz wrote, been those who have gone where the threat to the Church's life and mission is most dire, the stakes highest, the need for innovation greatest: "As I see it, Christianity is not some sort of postmodern sideshow, but rather the most perilous production of world history, since God Godself is involved in it. It is religious orders that step in whenever and wherever it turns particularly dangerous. *Historia docet.* What of the present? What does it mean when the Jesuit Jon Sobrino, who only by chance escaped the massacre of the Jesuits in El Salvador, immediately afterward came to Europe and just as matter-of-factly returned to an imperiled life with new community members."[1]

We are not without new religious movements and orders today, and in the Catholic Church, Vatican II articulated a broader mandate for the laity to heed the universal call to holiness, a call reiterated by Pope Francis, first as general editor of the documents of Aparecida and again as pope in his apostolic exhortation *Gaudete et exsultate*. My own modest contribution to such a reimagining and reconfiguring of Christian life has been to consider three men who were both invested in a particular spirituality and engaged in the work of theology. With them as examples, I have attempted to argue that it is possible to forge a more living circulation between the two, and that the result is deeply productive, not just for spirituality and theology, but, more importantly, also for the Church and its environing society. Moreover, all three were involved with what Hügel named the historical-institutional element of religion. Rahner was concerned to rethink seminary education, and, even more, was a pivotal figure in Vatican II's labor to rethink the Church in the modern world. Ellacuría was not only a university philosopher and theologian but was also at the center of the Central American Jesuits' labor to restructure their institutions. He spent ten years as rector of one of the most important of them: the UCA. Pope Francis was a leader of the Argentinian province of Jesuits and then bishop, cardinal, and pope.

Each of them became aware of the challenges for living a Christian life presented by this "age that does not know how to name itself" (David Tracy) in and from a particular place. Each man's place was constituted not only by geographical locale, but by social and institutional context, and by the way each one's engagement with Ignatian spirituality brought him to imagine his place and to discern what is required of him, in the manner of the Colloquy before the Cross of the First Week.[2] Each drew on scripture and the Christian tradition, and found and deployed an array of intellectual tools to deepen his imaginative construal of his place, and what needed to be done in it. These tools, given shape as a theology, also made that construal an offer to the broader publics of society, church, and academy.[3] As such, each one's theology can and should be evaluated in terms of the standards and canons of these publics, but it has been my argument that such an evaluation may well fall short of measuring the theology's full depth and contribution. A deeper understanding comes from asking how each theologian's engagement with Ignatian spirituality, in all its complexities, brought him to shape his theology in the particular way that he did, and how that shaping framed in turn a way that Ignatius's legacy can continue to be "a new gift by God's Spirit of the ancient Christianity to a new age."[4]

Of our three theologians, Rahner responded most focally and clearly to the challenge posed by secularism, more precisely, by what Taylor has described as "secularity 3": "a move from a society where belief in God is unchallenged and, indeed, unproblematic, to one in which it is understood to be one option among others, and frequently not the easiest to embrace."[5] It is unsurprising that Rahner would attend to this reality; many, many other European theologians and philosophers have done the same. Rahner grew up in a small, very Catholic town, and ended his career in a large European city, traversing geographically the epochal shift that Taylor has detailed.[6] He noted the difference between his own generation of seminarians and the generation coming to Innsbruck in the 1950s, for whom belief in God could no longer be unproblematic and always already intrinsically meaningful. Toward the end of his life he began to speak of the possibility that there would cease to be Christians in such a milieu at all, unless . . . unless they become mystics, unless they become practiced in adverting to a particular kind of experience, or modality of experience, that would enable them to break out, at least momentarily, of the disengaged stance, the buffered self, and hence the disenchanted world, which Taylor lists as principal components of the immanent frame that gives secularity 3 its power and its taken-for-grantedness.

Rahner's awareness of this problem was certainly sharpened by his encounter with Heidegger's diagnosis of modernity, Guardini's, and that of many others. I have argued that it was also given shape by his engagement with Ignatian spirituality. Even when he was not writing explicitly about Ignatius and his spirituality, Rahner's academic production was an attempt to make the kind of experience of oneself and the world that Ignatius had and formulated into the *Spiritual Exercises* available to modern Christians. This required a retrieval of the mystical aspect of Ignatius, in which Rahner collaborated with his brother, Hugo (albeit, not without errors, as Philip Endean has noted). It also required revising theology so that it had the conceptual tools to render with less distortion, and less flattening out of its astonishing and, for moderns, interruptive character, the Ignatian experience of being in a world that is grounded in a God who is both utterly beyond that world and found with utter intimacy in engaging that world. Prominent theological topoi for Rahner's revision of theology included the theology of grace, as an always tacit experience, never capable of complete isolation and instrumentalization, but vital and transformative nonetheless. Rahner also took up the theology of God, as Holy Mystery, the always greater "beyond-all-grasp" mystery of our being, which corresponds to our life itinerary of living ever-more fully "for the greater glory of God."

Ellacuría also found in the *Spiritual Exercises* a way toward an encounter with God and God's will, but it was not framed by the need to excavate a root experience of God still available in the disenchanted world of secularity 3. For Ellacuría it was the need to act in history, to heal a social imagination that had become entranced and systemically distorted by an inhuman set of values, which, as it becomes actualized in history ("historicized") traps the great majority of humankind in structures of death-dealing poverty and systemic violence. Martin Maier has perceptively noted that Ellacuría was deeply impressed by Rahner's theology insofar as it gestured toward an opening outward to transcendence within an individual's itinerary in a secularized world, but Ellacuría himself mined the *Spiritual Exercises* for such an opening outward that happened on the level of history as a whole, which human beings are charged to take up and move forward.[7] Such an emphasis is not unsurprising given Ellacuría's own place: living and working in one of the more violent corners of the world, during one of its more violent periods, in which the death-dealing consequences of structuring society according to the standard of the enemy of our human nature were horrifically evident. He was thoroughly versed from his studies and then collaboration with Xavier Zubiri in the phenomenological critique of modernity, but it is no surprise that he identified also with the diagnosis of modernity given by the Frankfurt School and other forms of critical theory: modernity's capacity to generate victims, precisely on the altars of Enlightenment values that it claimed to have constructed and implemented.

Ellacuría interpreted Ignatius's masterwork to propose a set of exercises that would open one to an encounter with a God who can only be encountered in history, indeed in historical action. He focused on the framing function of the Meditation on the Two Standards to move forward from this initial positing of the need for being a contemplative in action to an emphasis on how Ignatian spirituality presses one to be "a contemplative in the action of justice."[8] His focus on the Second Week and its exercises that aim for a "progressive historicization" of who Jesus was and is also indicates the centrality for him of what Jon Sobrino later named "orthopathy." Orthopathy means being correctly affected by the historical reality of Jesus, which links up with being correctly affected by our historical reality now, and by those persons in whom God passes through it (by Romero, for Ellacuría and for many other Salvadorans). Orthopathy lies at the root of the healing of the Christian social imagination and of discerning in which historical action we will, actually, encounter God. Orthopathy is also at the center of the Second Week and of the Exercises as a whole.

A spirituality configured in this way makes it possible, on Ellacuría's view, still to experience the fullness of faith, an experience of a world and a humanity transparent to the presence of a loving God, and to do this even, and precisely, in a crucified world that can (and should) be experienced as anything but this.[9] Ellacuría reconfigured philosophy and theology to make this set of exercises, or, perhaps better, the experience and historical action that is their *telos*, more easily subject to reflection, available to other Christians, and to implementation in a social and not just an individual context—as seen in his proposals to implement them in the corporate body of the Society of Jesus and in the institution of the modern university. To be sure, concepts and topics such as religation, the theologal, historicization, and the threefold task of human sentient intelligence when engaging the weight of historical reality have a rich intellectual background that deserves careful attention. Yet they take on an additional depth when we see them as the fruit of an extended effort on Ellacuría's part to make the spirit of the Exercises a living force in Central America and the world, to make the good news present in a world where, as Sobrino trenchantly put it, the news is not generally good and goodness is not news.[10]

If Rahner and Ellacuría attempted to bridge the divide between spirituality and theology from the side of theology, Pope Francis has done so from the side of the spiritual and the pastoral (*lo pastoral*, as he calls it). This too, should not surprise, since for most of his active life he has been a pastor. His writings on Ignatius were even more occasional in nature than those of the two other Jesuits in this book, but it is clear that Francis came increasingly to understand Ignatius's legacy to the Society of Jesus and to the Church as a set of exercises that opens one to living the Christian life that is threatened by the fragmentations and divisions that modernity has brought with it. In a time that oscillates between a "globalization of indifference," on the one hand, which rejects or trivializes the utopic visions of past centuries, and, on the other, an elevation of these visions to the status of ideologies that fund violent totalitarianisms, Francis turns frequently to Gaston Fessard's interpretation of the

Exercises. This interpretation, for Francis, lays out a pedagogy of discernment in which a transcendent, unifying meaning becomes present to one, animating her action, but always only episodically. This transcendent meaning only becomes real in the moment of committing oneself to its performance, humbly, in actions great or small.[11] Such meaning can never be grasped and instrumentalized, but only becomes available after the moment of commitment by renavigating the Exercises' graced pedagogy, with all that this entails for Ignatius. Throughout his career, Francis has been most open to and influenced by intellectual resources (such as those of Guardini) that explore this call (and capacitation) to decide in the midst of irreducible polarities, which ought to be (but too often are not) in creative tension with one another. He adopted these intellectual resources by testing them against his fundamental intuition about and experience of the *Spiritual Exercises*, and, if satisfied, used them as a part of a growing set of analytical tools for analyzing an expanding array of problems that he confronted as religious superior, bishop, and pope — from the disorienting reality of the modern megacity to global environmental crisis. As with Rahner and Ellacuría, the coherence of these tools and the cogency of the arguments constructed with them can and should be evaluated in their own terms; however, such an evaluation is deepened by appreciating how they flow out of a fundamental stance, a spirituality, defined by Ignatian spirituality.

As with Rahner, and Ellacuría too, in his own way, Pope Francis turned toward Ignatius the mystic rather than the ascetic. He was attuned to the need to deploy the resources of Ignatian spirituality to meet the needs of communal identity and discernment. In his essay on union of hearts, "Y Conforme a esta Esperanza: Algunas reflexiones acerca de la unión de los animos," he insisted that Ignatius taught us that the *ad intra* cohesion and identity of a community of disciples is not threatened by its dispersal in mission to others. This is another polarity that has been turned unhelpfully into a contradiction in modernity. This insight, nourished by Ignatian spirituality, has found expression in his papacy as an insistence that the Church loses its identity unless it "goes to the peripheries," the peripheries of suffering, of whatever kind, in order to bring consolation, an insistence that is behind what many critics interpret (incorrectly) and condemn as his diffidence toward, or even transgression of, the Church's dogmatic parameters. His is, as I have suggested, a papal ministry of consolation, which draws on Ignatian spirituality as a spirituality of consolation. In this he has come to see in the Exercises a spiritual itinerary that stretches from the transformative experience of mercy and being given a mission, in the First and Second Weeks, through to the deep experience of consolation in the Third and Fourth Weeks. If his engagement with Ignatian spirituality is not found so much in a theological system (as it is in Rahner and Ellacuría), it can certainly be discerned in the practical theology that orients his exercise of leadership in the Church.

Each Jesuit's work shows an awareness that Ignatian spirituality is a complex weave of different elements, which must be taken as a whole. Yet each also draws selectively from that weave, focusing on one particular part of the whole in order to offer that whole to the context within which he does theology. Rahner focused in particular on the Ignatian spiritual virtues of indifference and finding God in all things. Privileged exercises were the Principle and Foundation and the directives and rules for making an election—both the ways (or "times") in which an election can be made and the rules for discernment of spirits particular to the second way of making an election. The latter provided Rahner with an experiential field, that of consolation without prior cause, as a sort of laboratory to use to construct and test a theological anthropology, which, in turn, allowed the identification of a touchstone experience for what it is like to experience God in a world counted by many as irredeemably disenchanted. Though not wholly absent, less important in Rahner's intersecting of spirituality and theology are the contemplations on the life and ministry of Jesus in the Second Week.

As Ellacuría labored to make Ignatian spirituality fruitful for theology, and vice versa, he gravitated toward precisely these exercises of the Second Week, which he identified as the core of the *Spiritual Exercises*, and the locus of Ignatius's genius. As he interpreted it, the Meditation on the Two Standards enabled one to grasp the theologal dimension of historical processes and struggles, and the encounter with "the Jesus of history" in the other exercises of the Second Week made it possible for one to follow that Jesus by continuing his presence in and to history while attending to this theologal dimension. This making God present to history was at the same time making oneself present to God—it was a "mystical" encounter with God of profound depth and power. He does not ignore or excise them from his interpretation of the Exercises, but exercises of greater importance for Rahner (the Principle and Foundation, for instance) are of secondary importance for him.

Rahner and Ellacuría surface theologically in this way two major strands that Ignatius brought together in his Exercises. Rahner unfolded Ignatius's proposal for being a contemplative in action by developing the potentialities in the Neoplatonic tradition, which he had traced in his essays on the spiritual senses and spiritual touch in Bonaventure, and by deploying a notion of indifference with powerful resonances to Eckhartian mysticism. Ellacuría, on the other hand, drew on the current that Ewert Cousins has identified as the "mysticism of the historical event." Pope Francis, for his part, highlights another dimension of Ignatian spirituality: its incorporation of Renaissance humanism and the latter's emphasis on persuasion and attraction, rather than argument and debate (much less, coercion). His forefronting of the humanist stress on persuasion and attraction is evident in the pope's advocacy of Pierre Favre as a role model, with his capacity for "dialogue with all, even the most remote and even with his opponents."[12] It is also evident in Francis's emphasis on the need to encounter Christ, not just in one's head but in one's heart, as it orients his approach to the Second and Third Week contemplations of the life of Jesus and Ignatius's insistence that "what fills and satisfies the soul consists, not in knowing much, but in our understanding the realities profoundly and in savoring them interiorly" (*SpEx* 2). In the past two decades, Francis has also come to emphasize the experience of mercy, the grace of the First Week of the Exercises, unfolding into the grace of the Second Week to know (which means to be attracted by) and imitate Jesus more closely. I am tempted to say that in his guidance of the Catholic Church, the pope is heeding Ignatius's rule that one who has not been given the grace of the First Week should not go on to the rest of the Exercises and the election. *Mutatis mutandis*, the pope realizes that if the Church is to make an "election" on how to carry forward its ministry of consolation, of bringing the joy of the gospel to the world, it too must open itself as fully as possible to the grace of the First Week: the realized experience of mercy.

Finally, I have suggested that Ignatius had a finely developed sensorium for the novelty of modernity's conditions, and in his Exercises wove them into a tentative synthesis that makes it possible not only to appropriate them into Christian life, in their positive achievement, but to address their destructive underside. This provided a resource for the three Ignatian theologians treated here. Rahner was well aware of the challenges presented by what he named the "existentiality" of the modern age and the dizzying sense of provisionality to which it exposed modern persons.[13]

This awareness brought him to identify in Ignatian indifference a distinctively modern spiritual disposition (as opposed to being simply an age-old patrimony of the Christian spiritual tradition) that both mirrored and addressed this dilemma. The self that has made itself indifferent is far from the disengaged, buffered self that Taylor describes as a hallmark of modernity, disincarnate and taking up the "view from nowhere." The indifferent self is, on Rahner's view, by that very stance, also the self that is open to ("porous to," to use Taylor's language) the presence of God in particular elements of the world and its embodied existence in that world, an incalculable presence, utterly resistant to instrumentalization by any technique of self-surveillance or self-management.

Ellacuría's philosophy and theology resisted any appeal to a transcendence or source of fullness that is found outside history, but his is not a collapse into Taylor's immanent frame. The Ignatian articulation of the "mysticism of the historical event" provided him a realized (or "historicized") instance precisely of a transcendence that is embraced fully within history and historical action. Pope Francis is well aware of Ignatius's insight (articulated by Nadal) that "the world is our house" and of Ignatius's crafting of a spirituality that thrived in the midst of modernity's disembedding of social processes for circadian time and local space. Favre exemplifies for Francis the "holy and beautiful restlessness" into which this spirituality initiates its practitioner:

> We are called to this humility: to be "emptied" beings. To be men who are not centred on themselves because the centre of the Society [of Jesus] is Christ and his Church. And God is the *Deus semper maior*, the God who always surprises us. And if the God of surprises is not at the centre, the Society becomes disorientated. Because of this, to be a Jesuit means to be a person of incomplete thought, of open thought: because he thinks always looking to the horizon which is the ever greater glory of God, who ceaselessly surprises us. And this is the restlessness of our inner abyss. This holy and beautiful restlessness![14]

Yet, far from fragmenting the person's individual itinerary through life, and frustrating one's need for rootedness in time and space, and far from undermining communal decision and commitment, this restlessness and homelessness does finally have a place and a telos that can orient one and form community of action: it is the ever-greater glory of God, an "ever-greater" that, as Ignatius's Contemplation on the Nativity insists, expresses itself in effective mercy and redemptive action, ineluctably local, but with a global scene in view.[15]

In sum, each of the men we have considered crafted an original synthesis of theology and Ignatian spirituality, sensitive to context, and thus aware of Ignatius's dictum that the Spiritual Exercises always needs to be accommodated to the needs of the one to whom they are being given (*SpEx* 18). Each deployed a different subset of exercises, or a different strand of the cultures and spiritualities that Ignatius wove into his masterwork five centuries ago. Each found a way of expressing theologically the resources that Ignatius had discovered not only for living and thriving at the end of the modern age, but also for imagining, and enacting, however partially, a way of life that would contribute creatively to that age's transformation. Each deserves careful attention as a theologian, and that attention is enriched by attending to them as theologians fully in the Ignatian tradition: as Ignatian theologians.

An Ignatian Theology?

I have named Rahner, Ellacuría, and Bergoglio as Ignatian theologians. Is it possible to generalize on the basis of these three studies to propose, and perhaps delineate to some extent, the existence of an "Ignatian theology?" There are reasons to proceed with caution in this direction. First, it would be precipitous to generalize too robustly based on only three case studies, even if the figures they study have the depth and sophistication of the three Jesuits considered in the earlier chapters. There are, after all, many other figures who could have been chosen and should be chosen in making a broader claim about what it might mean to talk about an Ignatian theology. The three Jesuits treated here were chosen with a view to diversity: a Central European, a Central American (born in Europe), and a South American. Their training and intellectual context brought them into contact with a broad (albeit not exhaustive) cross section of twentieth-century philosophies and theologies. Their institutional context within the Church also varied. Moreover, the face of modernity that confronted them was different in each case. Gustavo Gutiérrez has identified three major challenges facing Christian faith and theology today: the modern mentality (secularization); the broad and systematic creation of "non-persons," people who don't count, who are disposable or surplus populations (injustice); and a deep and permanent religious pluralism. Rahner clearly focused on the first, Ellacuría was concerned with the second, and Francis represents something of a hybrid engagement with both (and a growing awareness of the third, particularly after becoming pope).

Thus I believe that this group of three theologians does give us important suggestions of what the lineaments of an Ignatian theology might be, if we were to propose it *ex hypothesi*. Yet there are others whose voices would need to be added. An incomplete list would include Bernard Lonergan, John Courtney Murray, Pierre Teilhard de Chardin, Henri de Lubac, Hans Urs von Balthasar, and William Lynch, and other figures who appeared in this study: Erich Pryzwara and Gaston Fessard. Other Jesuit theologians have confronted "the irruption of the poor," such as Jon Sobrino, Juan Luis Segundo, and Juan Carlos Scannone. If we posit the existence of an Ignatian theology, then it would have to be said that its work of engaging religious pluralism (which could perhaps be extended to include radical secularism) has only just begun, and I have not touched on what that work might mean. A start, but only a start, might come from considering Anthony DeMello, Jacques Dupuis, Aloysius Pieris, Michael Amaladoss, Roger Haight, and Agbonkhianmeghe Orobator. Finally, restricting inclusion among "Ignatian theologians" to members of the Society of Jesus is arbitrary, however convenient, at least as a starting point, as in this book. From the beginning, the first Jesuits sought collaborators in their works, men and women who have embraced in their own way the spirituality of Ignatius and the first companions. To be sure, this way necessarily differs because Ignatian spirituality is not mediated for these lay collaborators by incorporation and formation into that particular corporate embodiment of Ignatian spirituality defined by the Formula of the Institute and the *Constitutions*: the Society of Jesus. But it is arguably no less "Ignatian" for that fact. In an age in which academic theology — especially in Europe and North America, but elsewhere too — is becoming a work of the laity, the category of "Ignatian theologians" needs to be expanded to include those lay theologians who find inspiration in the gift of a new spirituality that Ignatius gave to the Church in the sixteenth century, and expanded to include members of other religious orders, particularly orders of religious women that early on embraced major elements of Ignatius's spirituality.

Thus, even if we were to gather together all the Jesuits who are doing theology that would not give us a precise sample from which to do the work of definition. Not only would it exclude lay Ignatian theologians and those of other religious orders, but it would presume that all Jesuits are in fact "Ignatian" in the way they do theology, a presumption that needs to be tested on a case-by-case basis, even if this testing should be done with a hermeneutic of generosity. My procedure in the three test cases presented here was to pick Jesuits not just because they were Jesuits who engaged in theology, but because there was good evidence that they knew and had striven to appropriate Ignatian spirituality, and that this appropriation rose to the level of systematic reflection and interpretation. Yet one can embrace a spirituality and still do theology without drawing on that embrace. And, it also seems possible that a theologian (Jesuit or otherwise) could in fact have appropriated Ignatian spirituality and come to a tacit or even focal awareness of its resources deep enough to inflect the way that she or he does theology, even if that awareness never expressed itself in written form in writings on the *Exercises* itself. Thus, the "test" of explicit writings on Ignatian spirituality might well fail to adequately identify the broadest field of Ignatian theologians.

This diversity should remind us of a diversity already accounted for in the initial definitions given for both spirituality and theology. I defined spirituality to be a constellation of practices, associated with an image- and narrative-laden portrayal of the world, our place in it, and our relationship to God that makes sense of—and is made sense of by—these practices. There are many ways in which the practices can be adopted in a given context, and the images, narratives, and ideas that make up the worldview may shift as a result. The latter themselves are inevitably taken selectively, with a corresponding spin on the whole. The spirituality may also shift because of the way one explores them with theology, in the work proper to it. Given the internal complexity of the elements brought together in Ignatian spirituality and the diverse ways it has been and can be appropriated in different contexts, and given the diversity of theologies, or even other spiritualities that can be intercalated with a chosen range of elements of Ignatian spirituality, and then brought to expression theologically, we should expect a great diversity of "Ignatian theologies."[16]

For all of these reasons, it seems most prudent to speak of Ignatian theology as a broad category, a diversity of theologies exhibiting a strong set of family resemblances. These family resemblances result from the ways the theologies draw on core features of Ignatian spirituality. What these features are can only be tentatively sketched at this point, but I would argue that the following seven would continue to surface even upon investigation of a broader group of Ignatian theologians.

1. An Ignatian theology would be "accommodated" to its particular context (*SpEx* 18). Each of our three theologians focused on a particular strand within Ignatian spirituality, and a certain subset of exercises, without absolutely excising or denying the others. Positively, this principle allows, or even encourages, a diversity of theological approaches. Negatively, if a particular theological approach makes it impossible to accommodate or at least be open to one or another central strand, then it would be excluded. Rahner thought that this was the case with some of the neo-scholastic theologies that he learned because they rejected the possibility of an experience of grace, which rules out the Ignatian understanding of discernment. Theologies that are unremittingly hostile to modernity and the possibilities of a framing of Christian faith under the conditions of modernity would, I argue, merit exclusion also, because they would make it impossible to express the "rhetorical turn" with its openness to culture and the theological-pastoral priority of attraction and persuasion rather than condemnation, so evident in Pope Francis's appropriation of Ignatian spirituality (even though, to be sure, Francis knows how to be critical of modernity).

2. An Ignatian theology will center on the challenge of "making an election" under the conditions of modernity and will work to deploy resources from the Ignatian understanding of discernment. This was the case in all three of the Jesuits we studied. Ellacuría, and less explicitly Pope Francis, explored how to make these resources available for a communal discernment, and Rahner was aware of the need to do this toward the end of his career. I am tempted to say that this element of Ignatian spirituality will be present in any Ignatian theology (and not just tacitly assumed) because "election" and "discernment" are absolutely central to the *Spiritual Exercises*, with its goal of "seeking and finding God's will in the ordering of our life for the salvation of our soul" (*SpEx* 1). In addition, the problem of coming to a good decision on issues touching on my sense of identity, my most intimate relationships with others, and my stance toward pressing ethical and political options has become extraordinarily complex and difficult under the conditions of modernity. All three of our Jesuit theologians were deeply aware of this, and it is hard for me to imagine an adequate Ignatian theology today that would not be.

I list a number of additional features because they emerged from the case studies above, but also because they point to a particularly Ignatian spin on a central element of Christian faith and theology.[17]

3. A sense for God as "ever-greater," which, as Rahner pointed out in his essay on the Ignatian motto of acting for the greater glory of God, has become present in modernity in a particularly acute way.[18]

4. Something like the dialectic between mercy and mission, which Pope Francis has articulated clearly in the past two decades, and which indicates a particularly Ignatian spin on the dialectic of sin and grace (and grace and works), opened up by the exercises of the First and Second Weeks.

5. An insistence on the irreplaceable work of encountering Christ (Pope Francis), and allowing oneself to be affected by that encounter (what Sobrino named "orthopathy"). This encounter will happen in a thickly imagined, historical mode, as presented in the exercises of the Second Week, and which Cousins articulated under the name of "mysticism of the historical event."[19] Ellacuría's was the most consistent and sophisticated theology to elaborate this Ignatian keynote, and even if Rahner's theology developed the encounter with Christ differently (more in line with the Neoplatonic tradition), he was aware of its importance nonetheless, and even made some gestures toward it later in his theological career. Such an inspiration should be detectable in any Ignatian theology that develops itself as a Christology.[20]

6. An awareness of the paschal mystery, of cross and resurrection, in which the way that "divinity veils itself" in the mystery of sin and death (Third Week) is juxtaposed with divinity being present "as consoler" (Fourth Week). This mystery makes itself present in one for whom the love of God and God's grace (consolation) are enough (*SpEx* 234). And it makes itself present in an action in history in which one finds a profound union with "the ever greater God" by making that consolation possible for others.

7. A theology of community, or an ecclesiology, which incorporates the profound "ex-centricity" evident in Nadal's phrase "the world is our house," ably explained by Pope Francis in his early essay on the authentically Ignatian understanding of the union of minds and hearts in the Society of Jesus, and later in his insistence that the Church only preserves its identity and flourishes when it "surges to the peripheries."[21]

These strike me as features or spins on central Christian doctrines (theology of God, theology of grace, Christology, soteriology, ecclesiology) to which any Ignatian theology would at least be open, and among which it would select one or a few on which to focus its attempts to meet the needs of its local context. It seems overly restrictive to expect that each would be equally present, but I would argue that the first two should be present, and not present only peripherally. But none should be rendered completely invisible or implausible by the framework of an Ignatian theology. The ways that they could be worked out are as diverse as the intellectual tools available to the theologian and the diversity of contexts within which she or he attempts to elaborate them.

I might add two further features that are more in the way of theological dispositions, and perhaps are not so much dispositions of an Ignatian theologian, but dispositions of any theologian for whom Ignatian spirituality provides a specific pedagogy and rationale (even if not the only one). First, the emphasis on rhetoric, on the insistence that the goal of theology is not so much to prove apodictically as it is to attract and persuade. Second, a "beautiful and holy restlessness" (to use Pope Francis's description of Pierre Favre), which keeps a theologian on the move, aware both of the mystery of God, beyond all grasp (Rahner), and, more proximately for an Ignatian theologian, aware of the many depths of the spirituality of Ignatius, which have given her access to that mystery and which she has left still untouched. This makes of "Ignatian theology," finally, an open-ended category, for which the few gestures to provide parameters above can provide only an initial and, I hope, relatively adequate identification, and which will no doubt always be expanded by surprising new entries. This is both a final reason for caution in making a final identification and reason to believe that this form of bringing together spirituality and theology has a fecund future ahead of it.

The Poverty of Theology Revisited: Spirituality and Academic Theology

I began this book by asserting the precariousness of theology. This precariousness is not resolved by an interrelation with spirituality, however creative. If anything, the theologies of our three Ignatian theologians became more precarious as they integrated with theology a spirituality that made of them persons "of incomplete thought, of open thought: because [they are] always looking to the horizon which is the ever greater glory of God, who ceaselessly surprises us."[22] What this integration *did* do, I have argued, was to make them aware of the hopes, anxieties, joys, fears, and needs of the Christians for whom they did the work of theology. For that, I think, the vantage point offered by Ignatius's spirituality was indispensable. It gave them a sensorium to what should, indeed, *must* matter to them as theologians, and how to bring that to mind and keep it in mind in whatever vocation they were given: philosopher, theologian, university administrator, bishop.

I must, however, remind the reader again that I have not been asserting that only Ignatian spirituality can do this work. That would be an untenable, indeed ridiculous claim. Other great spiritual traditions can do and have done this kind of work. Ignatius's has a particular aptness because, as I have contended, being forged on the threshold of modernity, it grappled with many of the paradoxes and painful challenges of modernity (and its achievements, it should not be forgotten) that vex contemporary theologians (and, of course, not just them). But spiritualities are malleable, and like any tradition of any depth and robustness, they can be reconfigured to engage a context or an age different from the one in which they were originally born. This is demonstrably true, I am convinced, of other great spiritual traditions in the Church's history, even though I have not had time or space to demonstrate this here. Moreover, other spiritualities may be more appropriate to certain dimensions of the challenges we face today. Carmelite spirituality, represented in the work of the great mystics of the sixteenth-century Teresa of Avila and John of the Cross, may well prove superior when it comes to charting the inner trajectories of the spiritual life, when properly retrieved today, precisely in the face of the very "modern" shape of the traumas that the soul faces in our violent age.[23] Consider, for example, the work of Constance Fitzgerald, OCD, in drawing on the conceptuality of the Dark Night to illuminate the different impasses of modernity and to enable us to grapple with them more creatively.[24] Franciscan and Benedictine spirituality have resources not found in Ignatius for confronting our (modern, northern Atlantic) tone-deafness when it comes to the cry of the Earth and crafting a way of life and theology appropriate to healing our breach with nature.[25] The Church needs all of these spiritualities, and needs them in concert with the theologies that plumb their resources, as did the Ignatian theologians treated earlier.

One need not be herself or himself a practitioner of Ignatian spirituality, or even deeply conversant with it, in order to appreciate the "Ignatian theologies" presented here. As I insisted early on, the elements of these theologies are not the property of any spiritual tradition; they are the patrimony of all Christians. They can be appreciated as such. My argument has been that one's appreciation of these theologies will be deepened, nonetheless, by uncovering the background constellation of practices and the social imaginary that both gives rise to them and makes sense of them. Turning from the interpretation of a theology to the production of a theology, it seems to me that at least a strongly suggestive case has been made that these theologians are worth imitating. This could, but need not, mean that one would find in one of the classics in the Church's array of spiritual traditions (Ignatian or otherwise) a similar animation of one's theological work.

Yet, I have not intended to imply that only "chemically pure" traditions (if such exist), of Benedictine, Franciscan, Carmelite, Ignatian provenance, among others, can do this work.[26] Spiritualities invite hybridity—indeed, I portrayed Ignatius's own contribution as a hybrid of a number of powerful spiritual currents in late medieval and Renaissance Europe. The ongoing vitality of a spiritual tradition is not threatened but reinforced by continued hybridization.[27] Hybridizations can, to be sure, disintegrate into cacophonous bricolage, but they can also be creative responses, inspired by God's spirit, to meet the needs of a new age. One service that theology can provide a spirituality is to propose critical questions and a framework for discerning the difference between creative hybridization and cacophony, which is not to force a spirituality to have the kind of logical-argumentative coherence appropriate for academic theology, but a kind appropriate for proposing an art of living, a mystagogy into a life of Christian discipleship under ever-shifting conditions.

Even someone who does not find herself or himself immediately identifying with one of these spiritual traditions (even in their hybrid forms) would, I suggest, do well to ask of his or her theology what it would look like to understand it as connected not just with theological debate and conversation over the sources and conversation partners for academic theology, but with an art of living, a way of being a Christian in troubled times. What would constitute a set of practices and an imaginative construal of ourselves, our world, and of how God's love encompasses both, the presence of suffering and sin notwithstanding, that could connect the theology with a way of life? I do not claim to have demonstrated that a theology must be an "Ignatian theology" (or a "Franciscan theology," or what have you) to take on the work of integrating spirituality and theology. I would contend that if one cannot carry out such an imaginative exercise, and could not pose in the process some questions that would drive the further development of her or his theology in order to make it more possible to do this, or to give a more adequate account of the exercises and the social imagination of what it might mean to be a Christian, then one's theology does fall on the "theological" side of the divide between theology and spirituality that I have endeavored to problematize in this book and for which I have attempted to argue a more creative alternative.

This creative alternative is nonetheless, to repeat my opening concession, only a small step toward a more comprehensive healing of divides that have opened up in our modern world, the split between theology and spirituality being one of them. These are enervating splits that have become internal to the Christian churches that are trying to proclaim the gospel. The further work requires the recrafting of the institutions and communal structures of the churches within which theologians cannot but only do their best to make their proposals. What this recrafting might look like is certainly beyond the scope of this book, and beyond the scope of what a theologian can do or perhaps even fully imagine. The most that a theologian can do, it seems to me, is to present, as clearly and foundationally as possible, as the heart of his or her theological work, the "fundamental intuition that serves to guide a spiritual life and provides the intellectual regimen proper to that life" (Chenu). He or she can only present this intuition, a spirituality, as in the final analysis, the graced presence of the Spirit of God in our world, which offers us a regimen for much, much more.

Notes

INTRODUCTION

1. For Gerson's complaints about the university, see Gerson, *Jean Gerson: Early Works*, 161–75. See also Maguire, *Jean Gerson and the Last Medieval Reformation*.

2. Thomas à Kempis, *The Imitation of Christ* 3.43 (149–50). To be sure, it is not learning itself that is the problem, but Kempis clearly believes that as it was institutionally structured in his time academic theology leads almost inevitably to distraction, strife, and pride (cf. 3.41).

3. Metz, *A Passion for God*, 184n7.

4. Hadot, *Philosophy as a Way of Life*, 272.

5. Hügel, *The Mystical Element of Religion*, 1:53.

6. The disastrous consequences of trying to defend these without such reference has been ably documented by Buckley, *At the Origins of Modern Atheism*.

7. At first glance, Pope Francis seems the odd man out on this list, insofar as he did not complete a doctorate in theology and never had a permanent teaching/research position in a university. Nonetheless, as I argue in chapter 6, he was very interested in the reformulation of theology and worked to bridge the gulf that is the subject of this book from the side of spirituality rather than from academic theology.

8. See McGinn, "The Letter and the Spirit," 1.

9. All quotations from the *Spiritual Exercises* will be taken from *The Spiritual Exercises of Saint Ignatius of Loyola*, trans. with commentary by George Ganss, SJ, using the now standard enumeration of sections: for example, *Spiritual Exercises*, 23 (abbreviated as *SpEx* 23). Where possible these references will be given within the text to cut down on notes. Furthermore, I follow the convention of using italics (*Spiritual Exercises*, or simply *Exercises*) to denote the text, and roman letters (the Exercises) to refer to all or some subset of the exercises contained therein, as given to someone for prayer.

10. Rahner, it is true, was familiar with a broader spectrum of writings of the founder of the Jesuits, in part because of the work of his brother, Hugo. Ellacuría, as a director of the training ("formation") of young Jesuits, and later as a delegate to the Jesuits' 33rd General Congregation, would also have had broader familiarity with Ignatius's opus. This would be even more true of Jorge Mario Bergoglio, who was novice master and then provincial for the Jesuits of Argentina. These qualifications will be treated as we come to the individual figures. Nonetheless, if we want to arrive at the heart of Ignatian spirituality as each of these men encountered it from novitiate on, it is appropriate to limit ourselves to the *Exercises*. This is in part because of the nature of Jesuit formation at the time these men entered the Society. Modern Jesuit training has not only benefited from the fruits of almost a century of historical scholarship, and the resultant availability of primary texts in translation, but has also been reconfigured in order to fulfill the mandate of Vatican II that religious orders root themselves anew in the charisms of their founders. This has meant a much greater attention to the full range of Ignatius's writings than was the case when the Jesuits treated here were trained. Even as important a document as the *Constitutions*, which Jesuits are required to study during the final period of their formation ("Tertianship"), was until recently treated in rather cursory fashion.

11. As we shall see, though, Ellacuría, however strong his critique of North Atlantic theology might be, maintained a respectful disposition toward Rahner's theology. Rahner, for his part, expressed his support of Gutiérrez's form of liberation theology, at least (see Rahner, "Letter to Cardinal Juan Landázuri Ricketts"). The complexity of the relationship—both the attractions and the aversions—between transcendental theology and political or liberation theology shows up far more strongly in the work of Rahner's student Johann Baptist Metz. I have examined this difference, also against the background of Ignatian spirituality, in Ashley, *Interruptions: Mysticism, Politics and Theology in the Work of Johann Baptist Metz*, chap. 6. Pope Francis's initial reserve and subsequent greater relative openness toward liberation theology will be detailed in chapter 6.

12. For one overview of those complex issues, see the articles in "Theology and Globalization," special issue, *Theological Studies* 69, no. 2 (2008).

13. See McGinn, "The Letter and the Spirit," 6–7; Principe, "Broadening the Focus," 1, 3–5; Philip Sheldrake, *Spirituality and History*.

CHAPTER ONE

1. The statistics for *The New Catholic Encyclopedia* are given in Alexander, "What Do Recent Writers Mean by Spirituality?," 247.

2. Downey, *New Dictionary of Christian Spirituality*.

3. This historical survey is based on Principe, "Toward Defining Spirituality"; Alexander, "What Do Recent Writers Mean by Spirituality?"; McGinn, "The Letter and the Spirit"; and Sheldrake, *Spirituality & History*, 34–56.

4. Jean Leclercq, "'Spiritualitas,'" *Studia medievali*, 3rd ser., 2 (1961): 293–94, cited in McGinn, "The Letter and the Spirit," 27.

5. On this convulsive event, which had a powerful effect not only on the history of spirituality but on the history of mysticism, see McGinn, *Crisis of Mysticism*.
6. On North American usage, see Alexander, "What Do Recent Writers Mean by Spirituality?," 248–49. On Scaramelli, see McGinn, "The Letter and the Spirit," 15.
7. Schmidt, *Restless Souls*, 20.
8. Ibid., 24.
9. Ibid., 29.
10. Wuthnow, *After Heaven*. Schmidt's salutary warning, then, is not to see "spirituality" as a sui generis phenomenon of the 1950s.
11. See McGinn's summary of this history as part of his review of methodological approaches to the study of mysticism, in McGinn, *Foundations of Mysticism*, 265–343.
12. For the latter, see Étienne Gilson, *Théologie et histoire de la spiritualité* (Paris: Vrin, 1943), cited in McGinn, "The Letter and the Spirit," 14.
13. For an overview of the process that focuses on Ignatian spirituality in Europe and then North America, see O'Malley and O'Brien, *Twentieth-Century Construction of Ignatian Spirituality*.
14. See, for example, Crossroad-Herder's series World Spirituality: An Encyclopedic History of the Religious Quest, which includes three volumes on Christian spirituality, volumes on Hindu spirituality, Confucian spirituality, South and Mesoamerican Native spirituality, and even a volume on "spirituality and the secular quest."
15. Tickle, *Re-discovering the Sacred*, 17–18. Her separate listing of spirituality and religion bears further discussion.
16. Jackson and Delehanty, *Sacred Hoops*.
17. A blurb from an issue of *People Magazine* on the back cover.
18. Hendricks and Ludeman, *Corporate Mystic*, xvii.
19. O'Murchu, *Quantum Theology*; Matt, *God and the Big Bang*.
20. Hendricks and Ludeman, *Corporate Mystic*, 9.
21. O'Murchu, *Quantum Theology*, 12n3.
22. Ibid., 13.
23. Wuthnow, *After Heaven*, 2.
24. There is evidence that the themes and language of spirituality have great appeal to scientists. See Ecklund and Long, "Scientists and Spirituality." For some critical comments on this literature, see Ashley, "A Post-Einsteinian Settlement," and the literature cited there.
25. Bellah et al., *Habits of the Heart*, 221.
26. McGuire, "Mapping Contemporary American Spirituality," 1, 3–8.
27. Ibid., 4.
28. See Wuthnow, *Sharing the Journey*, inter alia, 16–21, 31–40.
29. Mercadante, *Belief without Borders*.
30. She uses the categories of dissenters, casuals, explorers, seekers, and immigrants (Mercadante, *Belief without Borders*, 51–67). She also helpfully identifies generational differences between the greatest generation and GenX.

31. These are objections that were staple fare of Enlightenment critiques of religion in the seventeenth and eighteenth centuries.

32. Mercadante, *Belief without Borders*, 163, 167–68. On Schmidt, see earlier in this section. For Taylor's warnings on oversimplifying this phenomenon, see Taylor, *A Secular Age*, 516–35.

33. The story is different for investigations that use "spirituality" as a transcendental term applying across traditions and cultures. See, for example, Van Ness, *Spirituality and the Secular Quest*. In his introduction to this volume, Van Ness tells us that "being religious is not a necessary condition for being spiritual" (1). Of course, if it were, the volume would be incoherent. Van Ness contends, furthermore, that this presupposition follows from the definition of spirituality that governs the series as a whole. Ewert Cousins, the series editor, gives this definition in the general introduction to the series by defining its focus as "that inner dimension of the person called by certain traditions 'the spirit.' This spiritual core is the deepest center of the person" (Cousins, "Series Introduction," in *Spirituality and the Secular Quest*, xii). I shall touch on some of the difficulties in these sorts of "transcendental" definitions later in this section, but on the whole my focus will be on tradition-bound definitions.

34. McGinn, "The Letter and the Spirit," 16–19.

35. Principe, "Toward Defining Spirituality," 135 (original emphasis). He goes on to identify two other levels of spirituality: the elaboration of the first level into a doctrine or school by those who have and adhere to the first level experience, and the historical study of those doctrinal elaborations by those who, in principle, do not necessarily share that experience.

36. McGinn lists Sandra Schneiders as a principal example of this approach. She later proposed the name "hermeneutical approach" over "anthropological approach" as better capturing her position, but McGinn's description still largely applies. See Schneiders, "A Hermeneutical Approach to the Study of Christian Spirituality." Crossroad-Herder's series World Spirituality follows this approach.

37. Haight, *Spiritual and Religious*, 2–3 (emphasis original); cf. Haight, *Spirituality Seeking Theology*, 4.

38. McGinn, "The Letter and the Spirit," 18. This is the approach taken by McGinn's own seven-volume survey of Christian mysticism: *The Presence of God: A History of Western Christian Mysticism*, 7 vols. (New York: Crossroad, 1992–2021). It can also be seen in many of Paulist Press's 100-plus volume series Classics of Western Spirituality.

39. This problem shows up in popular literature on spirituality, as noted.

40. McGinn, "The Letter and the Spirit," 19.

41. Consider, for instance, the definition given by Walter Principe earlier in the section, or this definition, dense with terms from Christian theology, given by Richard McBrien: "*Spirituality* has to do with our experiencing of God and with the transformation of our consciousness and our lives as outcomes of that experience. Since God is available in principle to everyone, spirituality is not exclusively Christian. *Christian* spirituality is life in the Holy Spirit who incorporates the Christian into the Body of Jesus Christ, through whom the Christian

has access to God the Creator in a life of faith, hope, love, and service" (McBrien, *Catholicism*, 1058; emphasis original).

42. McGinn, introduction to McGinn, Meyendorff, and Leclercq, eds., *Christian Spirituality*, xvi.

43. This is, of course, a difficult distinction to render precisely, since sociologists, psychologists, including evolutionary psychologists, and anthropologists labor to understand phenomena of this sort immanently, without "immediate" reference to God.

44. A fascinating selection of definitions of spirituality can be found in Cunningham and Egan, *Christian Spirituality*, 22–28.

45. And, to reiterate, this does not mean that *we* can dismiss the term, or try simply to replace it with one of its older cognates, such as piety, devotion, or holiness. Linguistic ambiguity reflects deeper cultural ambiguity, and the latter cannot be resolved by ignoring or defining away the former.

46. For a helpful overview, see McGinn, "Introduction: Apostolic Renewal and the New Mysticism," in *The Flowering of Mysticism*, 1–30.

47. On the "discovery" of the individual in the Middle Ages, see Caroline Walker Bynum's critical overview of the literature: "Did the Twelfth Century Discover the Individual," in Bynum, *Jesus as Mother*, 82–109. On the growing interest in itineraries and methods of prayer, see Sheldrake, *Spirituality & History*, 40–44.

48. On monastic theology, see Leclercq, *The Love of Learning and the Desire for God*. On vernacular theology, see McGinn, "Meister Eckhart and the Beguines in the Context of Vernacular Theology," in McGinn, *Meister Eckhart and the Beguine Mystics*, 1–14, and McGinn, "Introduction: Apostolic Renewal and the New Mysticism."

49. McGinn, "Meister Eckhart and the Beguines," 9–10.

50. The concept of secularization has had a stormy career in the history of sociology as a whole, and the sociology of religion in particular. For a brief overview, and the concept of secularization I draw on here, see Casanova, *Public Religions in the Modern World*, 11–39. For a discussion oriented more by philosophy than sociology, see Taylor, *A Secular Age*.

51. For the understanding of modernity given here I draw on Anthony Giddens, *Consequences of Modernity*, and the sprawling analytical narrative in Taylor, *A Secular Age*. This story is also more provocatively told in the mode of intellectual history in Milbank, *Theology and Social Theory*.

52. Certeau, *The Mystic Fable*, 2. Compare with Newman's lament from *A Grammar of Assent*: "What strikes the mind so forcibly and so painfully, is His absence (if I may so speak) from His own world. It is a silence that speaks. It is as if others had got possession of His work"; cited in Louis Dupré, introduction to Dupré and Saliers, eds., *Christian Spirituality*, xviii.

53. See Dupré, introduction to Dupré and Saliers, eds., *Christian Spirituality*, xv. See also Dupré, *Passage to Modernity*, 221–23.

54. On Cusanus, see Bond, introduction to Nicholas of Cusa, *Selected Spiritual Writings*, 3–84. On the presence of mystical themes in Heidegger, see Caputo, *The Mystical Element in Heidegger's Thought*, and Prevot, *Thinking Prayer*, 37–69.

55. Taylor, *A Secular Age*, 594.
56. Moore, *The Soul's Religion*, xvi. Moore contrasts religion and spirituality, but he resists making that contrast absolute or turning it into an opposition.
57. Collins, introduction to *Best Spiritual Writings 2011*, xix (emphasis original).
58. Ibid., xx.
59. Sacks, *Gratitude*, 44.
60. On this phenomenon among the nones, see Drescher, *Choosing Our Religion*, 47–52. Drescher suggests that some of the nones who take this stance do so because they do not want to be associated with the negative portraits given of the "spiritual but not religious" in the scholarly and popular literature that began to study them in the 1980s and 90s.
61. The account of modernity sketched out here relies primarily on Dupré, *Passage to Modernity*; Giddens, *Modernity and Self-Identity*; Giddens, *The Consequences of Modernity*; Taylor, *Sources of the Self*, and Taylor, *A Secular Age*; Toulmin, *Cosmopolis*; and Bellah et al., *Habits of the Heart*.
62. This is the gist of Lynn White Jr.'s seminal critique of Christianity as the source of our ecological ills, in White, "The Historical Roots of Our Ecologic Crisis."
63. See, for example, Metz, *A Passion for God*, 132, 133.
64. Giddens, *Modernity and Self-Identity*, 75.
65. See Berger, Berger, and Kellner, *The Homeless Mind*. See also Robert Wuthnow's description of this phenomenon, using Michel Foucault's notion of "the dispersed self," in Wuthnow, *After Heaven*, 142–56.
66. Giddens, *Modernity and Self-Identity*, 83.
67. Dupré, *Passage to Modernity*, 119.
68. This idiomatic connotation of place is particularly telling given the fact that the temporal and spatial dislocations endemic to modernity make it impossible to define where one "is at" in terms of geographical locale or historical tradition.
69. Hendricks and Ludeman, *Corporate Mystic*, 12.
70. The overt instrumentalization of finding one's "true self" in this account distinguishes it from a similar conceptuality in Thomas Merton's writing. In the latter, the "true self" is constituted by a rootedness in God that always precedes, envelops, and not infrequently interrupts our projects of self-constitution and thus evade any instrumentalization for that purpose.
71. Taylor, *Sources of the Self*, 211–302.
72. Ibid., 213.
73. In *A Secular Age*, Taylor moves this shift at least incipiently back into the Middle Ages by identifying mendicant spiritualities as precursors in their intent to bring the *vita apostolica* out of the monasteries and into the worlds of the laity (93–95). He also places the affirmation of everyday life, and its insistence on the possibility of the highest forms of mystical assent for those outside the cloister, within the context of the broader desire for "reform," which, he argues, stems from "a profound dissatisfaction with the hierarchical equilibrium between lay life and renunciative vocations" (61).
74. See McGinn, *The Flowering of Mysticism*, 12–14.

75. More seriously, perhaps, he was unable to escape being associated with the transgression of patriarchal gender boundaries by medieval Beguines, who, in cases such as that of Margaret Porete, paid a much higher price for calling the prevailing hierarchical structures into question.

76. Baumer, "Stop Picking on Shoppers," 13–14.

77. Rosa, *Social Acceleration*, xxxviii.

78. Ibid. For a more popular and optimistic account of this world, see Friedman, *Thank You for Being Late*.

79. See Lasch, *Haven in a Heartless World*.

80. Slavin, "How Algorithms Shape Our World."

81. Ibid.

82. Wuthnow, *God and Mammon in America*, 5–6 (emphasis original).

83. Another response is represented by the spiritual literature that "reenchants" the world by populating it with angels or spirits that can, with the proper spiritual techniques, be contacted and called upon ("channeled"). On this, see Wuthnow, *After Heaven*, 115–41. For a contemporary example, see Crockford, *Ripples of the Universe*.

84. Jackson, *Sacred Hoops*, 12.

85. Steven James, dir., *Hoop Dreams* (Fine Line Features, 1994), DVD.

86. Hadot, *Philosophy as a Way of Life*, 83.

87. Ibid., 60.

88. Ibid., 64.

89. Ibid., 107–8.

90. See Gutiérrez, introduction to *On Job*. He writes there that "we must first establish ourselves on the terrain of spirituality and of practice; only subsequently is it possible to formulate discourse on God in an authentic and respectful way. Theology done without the mediation of contemplation and practice does not meet the requirements of the God of the Bible. The mystery of God comes to life in contemplation and in the practice of God's plan for human history; only in a second phase can this life inspire appropriate reasoning and relevant speech" (xiv).

91. The image is Origen's, from his homilies on Genesis (Homily X). See Origen, *Homilies on Exodus and Genesis*, 163. I am grateful to John C. Cavadini for giving me this reference.

92. Sandra Schneiders has raised this issue with regard to scripture in Schneiders, *The Revelatory Text*, in which she offers a sustained argument that and how "faith" ought to make a difference even (especially) for the "academic" interpretation of scripture. It is, in my view, no coincidence that she is also at the forefront of the scholarly movement for the recovery of spirituality in academic study.

93. For a brief explanation of the concept, see Jay, *Adorno*, 14–16.

94. See David Tracy's discussion of the classic and the religious classic, in Tracy, *The Analogical Imagination*, 99–130, 167–78.

95. To be sure, attaining further precision on how this telos presents itself in a given historical context, and defining more closely how a given set of spiritual practices can subserve that telos, is a theological task, which, on the view being propounded here, will entail a certain spirituality. The circularity thus defined can, but need not, be vicious.

96. So, for example, however you evaluate it, the practice of radical evangelical poverty by Francis of Assisi and his followers can be seen as a response to the changing situation of medieval Europe and to the incipiently developing market economy, in particular. See Little, *Religious Poverty and the Profit Economy in Medieval Europe*, or, with a more negative evaluation, Wolf, *The Poverty of Riches*. New spiritualities are often suspect, however, to the extent that, in foregrounding a certain set of practices, they are interpreted to be rejecting or denigrating others. Thus, the so-called heresy of the free spirit in the late Middle Ages was often taken to constitute a rejection of the medieval Church's sacramental structure. Whether it was or not is a question to be left to the historians; all that I argue in this way of defining spirituality is that it need not be.

97. Meister Eckhart's spirituality, for example, is expressed in rhetorically powerful vernacular sermons and intricate Latin scholastic treatises.

98. Gutiérrez, *A Theology of Liberation*, 4–5.

99. See Tracy, *The Analogical Imagination*, 3–31.

100. See Le Goff, *Time, Work and Culture in the Middle Ages*; Chenu, *Nature, Man, and Society in the Twelfth Century*.

CHAPTER TWO

1. Ignatius of Loyola, *A Pilgrim's Testament: The Memoirs of Ignatius of Loyola*, no. 50.

2. Ibid., no. 2.

3. Ibid., no. 30.

4. Gerhartz, "Von Jerusalem nach Rom," 98, translation mine.

5. O'Malley, *The First Jesuits*, 241, 242.

6. There are many commentaries and studies of Ignatius's master work. For a reliable beginning, one should consult the introduction and notes to Ganss, trans., *The Spiritual Exercises of Saint Ignatius*. Guibert, *The Jesuits: Their Spiritual Doctrine and Practice*, though dated, is still important and valuable. See also Coathalem, *Ignatian Insights*, and Ivens, *Understanding the Spiritual Exercises*. For a perceptive analysis of the Exercises that gives greater weight to what it is like actually to do them, see Fleming, *Like the Lighting*. Although it is written more in the style of retreat presentations, Martini, *Letting God Free Us*, has some valuable insights. The same is true of DeMello, *Seek God Everywhere*. For an interpretation based in liberation theology, see Brackley, *The Call to Discernment in Troubled Times*, and for essays that apply the interpretive lens of feminist theology, see Dyckman, Garvin, and Liebert, *Spiritual Exercises Reclaimed*. For a review of the sources of the *Spiritual Exercises* in Ignatius's life and context, see Plazaola, ed., *Las fuentes de los ejercicios espirituales de San Ignacio*, and Melloni, *The Exercises of St Ignatius Loyola in the Western Tradition*.

7. Cited in de Dalmases, *Ignatius of Loyola, Founder of the Jesuits*, 65. On the origins of particular parts of the *Exercises*, see Guibert, *The Jesuits*, 110–22; see also the introduction in Iparraguire and Dalmases, eds., *Obras Completas de San Ignacio de Loyola*, 187–92.

8. See McGinn, *Mysticism in the Golden Age of Spain*, 71.

9. O'Malley, *First Jesuits*, 37.

10. It should be noted that Ignatius himself did not often use the terms "director" or "retreat" but preferred circumlocutions such as "the one giving the Exercises." I use the former terms for the sake of economy of prose. Once again, the numbers in parentheses refer to the standardized numbering of Ignatius's texts, and not to page numbers.

11. Some of these prayerful reflections on the life of Jesus or on other events in the history of salvation (such as the first sin of the angels) are named "contemplations" and others "meditations." For the difference between the two, see the notes in Ganss, trans., *Spiritual Exercises*, 154n31, and 161–62n61.

12. Not even the "third time for an election" (described later in this section), in which one is to engage in a more rational-reflective tallying of the pros and cons of a decision, is done without the aid of the Holy Spirit.

13. Fairly early on, in order to press the case for the orthodoxy of the *Exercises*, the Jesuits connected the structure of weeks with the hallowed patterning of the three paths or ways of the spiritual life: the Purgative Way (First Week), the Illuminative Way (Second and Third Weeks), and the Unitive Way (Fourth Week). The only reference to this in Ignatius's own text is in the Introductory Explanations (*SpEx* 10), probably added near the end of the *Exercises*'s history of composition. See Ganss, trans. and ed., *Spiritual Exercises*, 144n8. Jerónimo Nadal stated in 1554 that "the method and order of the Exercises is purgation, illumination, and union" (see Palmer, trans. and ed., *On Giving the Spiritual Exercises*, 36). The identification is argued at length in chapter 39 of the "Official Directory of 1599," which was issued under the authority of the fourth superior general of the Society, Claudio Acquaviva (Palmer, ed., *On Giving the Spiritual Exercises*, 346–48).

14. *SpEx* 23. This is from the Principle and Foundation, a more philosophical and ahistorical reflection on the context of human choosing, which sets the stage for entering into meditations on the history of salvation. The exact status of this reflection within the structure of the *Exercises* is a matter of some debate. Its more philosophical language suggests composition during Ignatius's student years in Paris. What is more, in an early manuscript of the *Exercises*, dating from 1536 or 1537, it is found among the "Introductory Explanations," between an admonition that the retreatant enter the *Exercises* with "great spirit and generosity" (the fifth introductory explanation in the final version (*SpEx* 5) and that the giver and maker of the Exercises understand that "every good Christian ought to be more eager to put a good interpretation on a neighbor's statement than to condemn it" (*SpEx* 22). In a directory for giving the Exercises, dictated by Ignatius to Juan Alonso de Vitoria, Ignatius advised that it be given to the retreatant after Introductory Explanations 1 (the purpose of the Exercises), 5 (mentioned just above), 4, and 20 (on the length and nature of the "Weeks" of the Exercises). See Palmer, trans. and ed., *On Giving the Spiritual Exercises*, 21. It is only later that Ignatius, evidently becoming convinced of its greater importance, moved the Principle and Foundation to the beginning of the First Week. This has led to considerable debate over its importance to the *Spiritual Exercises* as a whole. For a summary of the

documentary history, see Guibert, *The Jesuits*, 119–21. For an argument that the Principle and Foundations is not only homologous with the rest of the Exercises, but central to them, see notes in Ganss, trans., *Spiritual Exercises*, 148n17; 208–14.

15. The significance of the General Confession of Devotion, which is out of proportion to its incidence in the text itself, provides an example of the importance of interpreting the *Spiritual Exercises* not simply as a written text but also as a set of practices whose full meaning emerges only as one engages in them.

16. On the first Jesuits' advocacy and practice of this exercise, and its roots in late medieval piety, see O'Malley, *First Jesuits*, 137–39. O'Malley points out that for them the primary goal of this form of confession was to dispose the penitent for a growth into consolation, a pivotal term in Ignatian spirituality.

17. See, for example, the directory dictated to Vitoria, where Ignatius insists that those who are "less well disposed" to a life of confession and Communion should be given additional exercises in order to bring them to realize the gravity of sin and to feel sorrow of their own sins. Furthermore, those who remain "obstinate" through the First Week should not, as a rule, continue, but should be gently dismissed (Palmer, trans. and ed., *On Giving the Spiritual Exercise*, 20).

18. O'Malley, *First Jesuits*, 40.

19. If for no other reason, this was true more or less by default, given that the young religious order did not have approved and legally binding constitutions for two and a half decades. Indeed, it had no constitutions of any form for its first decade, until Jerónimo Nadal began traveling around Europe in 1552, explaining the text that Ignatius produced (with the substantive help of Juan Polanco). Besides the highly condensed and laconic "Formula of the Institute," and copies of Ignatius's "autobiography," that Nadal carried with him on his peregrinations, the *Spiritual Exercises* was *the* book for the early Society.

20. Palmer, trans. and ed., *On Giving the Spiritual Exercises*, 24.

21. Ibid., 24–25.

22. Ibid., 9–10; cf. *SpEx* 189.

23. This issue touches on the broader issue of the objective of the *Exercises* as a whole. For a survey of the various positions developed, and a more fully articulated argument in support of the position I take here, see Cusson, *Biblical Theology and the Spiritual Exercises*, 81–93.

24. *SpEx* 93. The allusion to the Iberian *reconquista* and to the Crusades is unmistakable.

25. This is a good example of one of the dynamisms that David Fleming observes in the Exercises: from objective-observer stance to subjective-involved stance. The first meditation on sin takes up sin in history and the world around me; not until the second meditation does one take up one's own sin. Here the exercitant observes someone else making an offer; in later meditations (such as the Two Standards), he or she does it him- or herself. See Fleming, *Like the Lightning*, 26–27.

26. See Brackley, *The Call to Discernment in Troubled Times*, 61. This is an important point because it puts some distance between the military imagery used here and the type of response to which Ignatius is trying to lead the exercitant.

27. Thus, the Call of the King stands in the same preparatory, dispositive role with respect to the Second Week that the Principle and Foundation plays

for the Exercises as a whole. It is not itself a part of the Second Week. The first day of the Second Week starts with the Contemplation on the Incarnation.

28. *SpEx* 146. Thus, radical imitation, which was hinted at in the call of the eternal king and offered explicitly in the following offering, recurs now as the salvation strategy urged by Christ on his "servants and friends."

29. *SpEx* 166. Compare with the Principle and Foundation: "It is necessary to make our selves indifferent to all created things. . . . Consequently, on our own part we ought not to seek health rather than sickness, wealth rather than poverty, honor rather than dishonor, a long life rather than a short one, and so on in all other matters" (*SpEx* 23).

30. *SpEx* 167. To be sure, the "all other things being equal" is crucial. *If* it is for the greater praise and glory of God—which for Ignatius means that God be revealed in history as "good news," leading men and women to embrace God and God's salvific plan—one would, in fact, accept some material possessions or a position of prominence. On this issue, see Brian E. Daley, SJ, "'To Be More Like Christ': The Background and Implications of 'Three Kinds of Humility,'" *Studies in the Spirituality of Jesuits*, 27, no. 1 (1995): esp. 29–30. It should also be noted that this option for actual poverty over wealth is also present in the meditation on the three classes of person, not in the presentation of the three classes itself, but in the colloquy to be made. This colloquy is identical with that of the Contemplation on the Two Standards, in which the implicit tendency is to renounce wealth. It may be, however, that here the purpose of the colloquy is to overcome an inclination *not* to give up the wealth (typical of the second class of person) by acting against it (a classic case of the Ignatian method of *agere contra*). That is, it is a specific tactic for attaining the indifference of the third class of person or of the second way of being humble.

31. Again, this does not mean that one is operating by "nature alone." The fact that one finds oneself indifferent and at peace (both of which are graces), and that one offers it to God in the end, is sufficient indication that this approach is done under the guidance of the Holy Spirit.

32. This is evidently one of the purposes Ignatius envisioned for that consideration. By observing how a person reacts to this consideration, the director could judge whether he or she had achieved the requisite indifference for making a good election; see the *Autograph Directory*, no. 17, in Palmer, trans. and ed., *On Giving the Spiritual Exercises*, 9.

33. *SpEx* 313–51, see the discussion in "Discernment" in the next section.

34. Thus, it should be noted that discernment of spirits, which is proper to the second time of making an election, is not the same as discerning God's will, which can happen in any of the three times, with their differing methods of considering evidence, or even with a combination of them. And in the course of it one asks that the Holy Spirit enlighten one's intellectual musings.

35. H. Rahner, "Notes on the Spiritual Exercises," 301; Coathelem, *Ignatian Insights*, 193–94.

36. DeMello, *Seek God Everywhere*, 138–46.

37. Brackley, *The Call to Discernment in Troubled Times*, 86–91.

38. It is true, as José Carlos Coupeau points out, that the meaning of "consolation" when it is related to the verb, "to console," is not completely identical

with its usage as a noun, even though the two are related. See Coupeau, "Consolar (Ministerio de)," 428–35, esp. 429. See the discussion of "consolation" in the next section, "Discernment."

39. H. Rahner, *Ignatius the Theologian*, 3.

40. *SpEx* 95; cf. 96 and 97, which also speak of the *"trabajo."*

41. *SpEx* 108. The Spanish verb is *obrar*, which means "to do," "to bring about," or, when used as a transitive verb, "to work," as in "to work a miracle."

42. *SpEx* 116 (translation slightly emended).

43. This sense follows from making the other two comprehensive "offerings" in the *Exercises*: at the end of the Call of the King, which introduces the offer to imitate Jesus in bearing all injuries, humiliations, and actual poverty (*SpEx* 98), and the offer, expressed as a request, to serve under the standard of Christ, in actual poverty and in "bearing reproaches and injuries, that through them I may imitate him more" (*SpEx* 147).

44. Ignatius thus offers a unique contribution to the ongoing debate in Christian spirituality over the relationship between contemplation and action. For a survey of that debate up to the fourteenth century, see Dietmar Mieth, *Die Einheit von Vita activa und Vita contemplativa in den deutschen Predigten und Traktaten Meister Eckharts und bei Johannes Tauler* (Regensburg: Pustet, 1969). For a survey of the exegetical tradition concerning Martha and Mary, the key scriptural locus for carrying on this debate, see Giles Constable, "The Interpretation of Martha and Mary," in *Three Studies in Medieval Religious and Social Thought* (Cambridge: Cambridge University Press, 1995), 1–142.

45. The phrase is more properly attributed to Jerome Nadal. Speaking of Ignatius, Nadal said that he could "see and contemplate in all things, actions, and conversations the presence of God and the love of spiritual things, to remain a contemplative even in the midst of actions (*simul in actione contemplativus*)"; quoted in Guibert, *The Jesuits*, 45.

46. See Jacques Guillet, Gustave Bardy, et al., *Discernment of Spirits*, trans. Sr. Innocentia Richards (Collegeville, MN: Liturgical Press, 1970). This gives the article on the same subject from the *Dictionnaire de spiritualité*.

47. Schreiner, *Are You Alone Wise?*, 270. As Schreiner demonstrates, although Ignatius's contribution is most well known, articulations of different rules or principles for discernment showed up all across the variegated religious landscape of Ignatius's times, be it from Ignatius, Martin Luther, or Thomas Müntzer. See Schreiner, "Unmasking the Spirit of Light," 261–321.

48. Buckley, "Structure of the Rules for Discernment," 219–37, esp. 220–23. See also Schreiner, *Are You Alone Wise?*, 270–85. For a full commentary on the rules for discernment, see Toner, *A Commentary on Saint Ignatius's Rules for the Discernment of Spirits*. Also helpful is DeMello, *Seek God Everywhere*, 84–137, and Brackley, *The Call to Discernment in Troubled Times*, 126–73. Finally, Brian McDermott, SJ, has argued for a more delimited interpretation of consolation as "spiritual consolation," in McDermott, "Spiritual Consolation and its Role in the Second Time of Election."

49. Buckley, "Structure of the Rules for Discernment," 223.

50. *SpEx* 315. An obstacle of this sort came to Ignatius while at Manresa, when "a forceful thought came to trouble him by pointing out the hardships

of his life, like a voice within his soul, 'How will you be able to endure this life for the seventy years you have to live?'" See Ignatius of Loyola, *A Pilgrim's Testament*, no. 20.

51. The anthropological implications and phenomenological features of such an "experience," in which God alone is active, without any other mediation external or internal to the self, are by no means easy to tease out, and there is endless interpretive and theological debate over what Ignatius meant by it, as we shall see in the discussion of Karl Rahner (chapter 4). For an initial orientation on the debate, see notes in Ganss, trans., *Spiritual Exercises*, 194–95n154.

52. On this temporal dimension, see Buckley, "Structure of the Rules for Discernment," 228–29.

53. In a letter to Francis Borgia, he includes tears over others' sins (Ganss, ed., *Ignatius of Loyola: Spiritual Exercises and Selected Works*, 348).

54. Corella, "Consolación" (all translations are my own).

55. Ibid., 413.

56. Ibid., 415.

57. Ibid., 417.

58. Ibid.

59. Ibid., 418.

60. The resonances with the Principle and Foundation are evident in the mention of "the things on the face of the earth" and "his [Christ's] praise and service." The language of the third categorization of consolation also seems redolent of the Contemplation to Attain Love.

61. Ibid., 416.

62. McDermott, "Spiritual Consolation." He aligns himself with Jules Toner's position in Toner, *A Commentary on Saint Ignatius' Rules for the Discernment of Spirits*, and Toner, *Discerning God's Will*. In the process he gives helpful summaries of Toner's arguments.

63. McDermott, "Spiritual Consolation," 15, 26. And, of course, it can be authentic or false and deceptive, the substance of the rules (of the second week in particular) providing guidelines to tell the difference.

64. Buckley adduces the unpleasant experience of the sting of conscience mentioned in the first rule (*SpEx* 314) as a kind of consolation, while the joyous experience of a person going from one sin to another is not; see Buckley, "The Structure of the Rules for Discernment," 225–26.

65. McDermott, "Spiritual Consolation," 27.

66. Ibid., 26.

67. See, for example, O'Malley, "Some Distinctive Characteristics of Jesuit Spirituality in the Sixteenth Century," 7–8; Mateo, "Imitación de Cristo," in García de Castro, ed., *Diccionario de Espiritualidad Ignaciana*, 1:994–1001, esp. 998–1001.

68. McDermott, "Spiritual Consolation," 21, 26.

69. It also is difficult to see how tears over others' sins (which Ignatius recommended to Borgia) can be interpreted as sweet and peaceful. Perhaps an example. When Oscar Romero experienced grief and even tears over the suffering of the poor of El Salvador, and the hardness of heart of the wealthy and the army, this was a grief that, as heart-wrenching as it was, strengthened his resolve to be a

voice for the voiceless. I would argue that Ignatius would consider this a form of spiritual consolation.

70. McDermott, "Spiritual Consolation," 25. He cites Toner, *A Commentary on Saint Ignatius' Rules for Discernment of Spirit*, 103–7, and Ivens, *Understanding the Spiritual Exercises*, 216.

71. See Coupeau, "Consolar (Ministerio de)." Here, the range of ways in which the God of mercy has consoled God's people and the self-diffusive way that this consolation spreads through the ministries of consolation shape the Ignatian understanding of consolation (429–30).

72. Cited in O'Malley, "Some Distinctive Characteristics of Jesuit Spirituality in the Sixteenth Century," 18. Cf. O'Malley, *The First Jesuits*, 19–20, 41–43, 82–84.

73. Thus, I still find myself persuaded by Buckley's position, for reasons I've given.

74. In what follows, when I use "spiritual consolation" or "consolation," unless otherwise noted, I intend *authentic* consolation, or consolation that arises under the influence of the good spirit.

75. Ignatius gives a traditional list of reasons why one might fall into desolation. We may do so because of our tepidity or laziness, but it may also be a way that God tests us, and a source of genuine self-knowledge and humility (that consolation comes from God and is not in our power). The latter two could be present in someone who, on the whole, still embraces, and is still embraced by, God's loving presence (*SpEx* 322).

76. This is clear from the "additional directives" given for each of the weeks and from the frequent places where Ignatius instructs the retreatant to labor to feel the particular emotion that corresponds to the consolation appropriate to the given week. For example, in the second additional directive for the First Week, Ignatius instructs the retreatant "to strive to feel shame" for his or her sins by use of imaginative examples, such as that of a knight who has failed or offended his king (*SpEx* 74). In the sixth additional directive, the retreatant is warned against thinking about "pleasant or joyful things, such as heavenly glory or Resurrection, for if we desire to experience pain, sorrow, and tears for our sins, any thought of happiness or joy will be an impediment" (78). In the Fourth Week, on the other hand, one is "to endeavor to feel joyful and happy," and is to call to mind precisely those things that were proscribed during the First Week. One is even to attend to one's environment, making use of "the refreshing coolness in summer or the sun or heat in winter" in order to mold one's affect (78). This makes it evident that in this context we can and should distinguish spiritual consolation from consolation that arises out of our natural experience of the world, as McDermott notes (see McDermott, "Spiritual Consolation," 12), but the character of the boundary between the two (that is, whether there is overlap, and whether the boundary is permeable or impermeable) depends on one's theology of grace.

77. It should be noted that the first time of election, in which God directly moves the intellect and will in such a way that the person cannot doubt the conclusion, need not be an affective movement, so that one could envision it happening by means of a "consolation without prior cause," but not necessarily so.

78. This is a controversial point. Rahner, as we shall see, takes the position I lay

out here, but Jules Toner takes the position that a decision made in the "third time," by the use of one's reason alone (but not unaided by grace), is fully self-sufficient and need not be confirmed by appeal to movements of consolation and desolation. See Toner, *A Commentary on Saint Ignatius's Rules for the Discernment of Spirits*, 291–313. Much depends on whether and how one factors in the temporal-historical feature of discernment that Buckley highlights. The indubitability of a decision made on the basis of a "consolation without prior cause" immediately opens into a "penumbral moment," in which the enemy, according to Ignatius, can twist and distort the decision, thus requiring continual vigilance in "tracking" one's affective movements. In a similar way, I would argue, a decision made in "the third time" can require further discernment and confirmation. It could indeed be true that the decision made in the third time is sufficiently confirmed in itself, but the temporal threshold between that decision and its ongoing implementation, when it becomes susceptible to diversion and distortion (just as is the case for a decision made under the influence of a consolation without prior cause), is razor thin and asymptotically close to the decision itself. Ignatius thus proposes that one act preemptively and proactively to present one's decision to the master and giver of consolation, on the premise that the enemy will try immediately to stir up counter-movements in the soul.

79. It is worth noting that it is a cognate form of the verb *sentir*, which occurs often in the *Exercises*: for example, in the title of the section on "discernment of spirits" (*SpEx* 313).

80. Dulles, "The Ignatian 'Sentire cum Ecclesia' Today," 20.

81. John O'Malley notes that the rules are "among the few indications that the religious situation in Paris made an impression on Ignatius" (O'Malley, *First Jesuits*, 49).

82. *SpEx* 353. On his use of these titles, see Dulles, "The Ignatian 'Sentire cum Ecclesia' Today," 27–28.

83. *SpEx* 362. It may be good, Ignatius adds, to bring the problems to the attention of "persons who can bring about a remedy" (362).

84. See O'Malley, *First Jesuits*, 243–53, 264–66.

85. Ibid., 50.

86. Both may be found in Ganss, ed., *Ignatius of Loyola: Spiritual Exercises and Selected Works*. There are significant interpretive issues with authorship of the "autobiography." These problems do not lessen its importance as a document in early Jesuit spirituality, but they do make it less reliable as a source for Ignatius's own spirituality. See O'Malley, *First Jesuits*, 8–9.

87. *Constitutions of the Society of Jesus*, trans. with intro. and notes George Ganss, SJ (St. Louis: Institute of Jesuit Sources, 1970). Here too there are problems of authorship. Ignatius is undoubtedly responsible for the final text, but the effect of Polanco's collaboration should not be underestimated.

88. And some might wonder whether I am anachronistically imposing a tacit distinction by using the term "Ignatian spirituality" at all—that is, contrasting it with "Jesuit spirituality," for which it would certainly be necessary to consult the *Constitutions* at length, and much of Ignatius's later correspondence. It would also require detailed attention to others: Jerónimo Nadal, Juan Polanco, Pierre

Favre, and so on. It is certainly true that Ignatius's first followers would not have recognized a distinction between "Ignatian spirituality" and "Jesuit spirituality." Indeed, they would not have called "our way of proceeding" a spirituality at all, for reasons we detailed in chapter 1. The distinction makes eminent sense today, when there are perhaps more "non-Jesuits" appropriating Ignatius's heritage than members of the Society of Jesus, for whom the *Constitutions*, say, is certainly suggestive, but not determinative the way the *Spiritual Exercises* is. Yet this does not mean that applying the term to Ignatius's time is arbitrary or purely an exercise in anachronism. He composed the *Spiritual Exercises* as a layman, and even as he and his first companions refined it for the purpose of their new "Society of Jesus," they thought it relevant for those who were not members of their company.

89. Still worth consulting in this regard is Guibert, *The Jesuits*. More recently, one can look to Lonsdale, *Eyes to See, Ears to Hear*. Also helpful is Burke and Burke-Sullivan, eds., *The Ignatian Tradition*.

90. Even in Tertianship, according to John O'Malley, the coverage of the *Constitutions* and other foundational documents would have been extremely cursory at best during the times when these men underwent this final stage of their formation (interview with the author, Boston, November 1997).

91. Two brief anecdotes may serve to illustrate this. When the Jesuits of the United States engaged in sustained reflection in the early 1970s concerning the methods and goals of Jesuit education, there was an almost complete lack of reference to the *Constitutions*. Since part IV deals at length with Ignatius's own understanding of the apostolate of education in the Society, this lack is remarkable and also telling (see Buckley, *The Catholic University as Promise and Project*, 56–57). Similarly, when the Central American Jesuits gathered in 1969 to decide how to implement in their own works the challenges laid down by the Latin American bishops at Medellín, Ignacio Ellacuría and Miguel Elizondo, both extremely learned Jesuits, used the *Spiritual Exercises* to focus the reflections, with virtually no reference to the *Constitutions* at all (see chapter 5, section titled "Introduction: Making Theology Latin American and Ignatian").

92. See the discussion in Arrupe, *The Trinitarian Inspiration of the Ignatian Charism*, 6–12.

93. O'Malley, *First Jesuits*, 372.

94. This policy was made mandatory at the Sixth General Congregation in 1606 (see O'Malley, *First Jesuits*, 360).

95. See Guibert, *The Jesuits*, 45, 206. We shall see that this is the case for Pope Francis's appropriation of Ignatian spirituality, keying on an "Ignatian" motto penned a century after the saint's death: *Non coerceri maximo, contineri tamen a minimo, divinum est* ("to suffer no restriction from anything, however great, and yet to be contained in the tiniest of things — that is divine"). See chapter 6, section titled "Pope Francis Interprets Ignatian Spirituality."

96. Schineller, "The Pilgrim Journey of Ignatius" (henceforth, "Pilgrim Journey"). He appeals to a similar argument in Marjorie O'Rourke Boyle's analysis of Ignatius's autobiography in Boyle, *Loyola's Acts*.

97. Schineller, "Pilgrim Journey," 3–4.

98. Segundo, "Ignatius Loyola: Trial or Project?," 167. Segundo's views are elaborated at greater length in his *The Christ of the Ignatian Exercises*. In this

fourth volume of Segundo's five-volume Christology, the broader theological agenda behind Segundo's interpretation of Ignatius becomes clear.

99. The following could also be taken as an argument for the legitimacy of the term "Ignatian spirituality" itself, since it seems more appropriate to name the spirituality that results when one includes the *Constitutions* and Ignatius's correspondence as general, as "Jesuit spirituality." Arguing the cogency and self-sufficiency of the *Spiritual Exercises* as a source for identifying a particular spirituality is important for giving content to the term "Ignatian spirituality," as opposed to "Jesuit spirituality" (which has its own legitimacy).

100. Segundo, "Ignatius of Loyola, Trial or Project?, 175.

101. Ibid., 153.

102. Ibid., 174.

103. Ibid., 165. Segundo calls this "a very serious distortion of what the Gospels (principally the synoptics) present as the Christian memory of Jesus' public life."

104. Ibid., 167. He asserts that this is in disregard of the Pauline doctrine stated in Romans 8 that the created world is incomplete and in bondage.

105. Segundo does note the recommendation (damning, in his view) to read the *Imitation of Christ*, but passes over in silence the far more pervasive *requirement* that one read and meditate on the scriptures.

106. Even for those who do not go past the First Week and the General Confession of Devotion, Ignatius directed that they be given instruction in prayer, and he presumed that they were engaged in the sacramental life of the Church. Thus, even for them the christic function of the earlier materials would be fulfilled. It must never be forgotten that Ignatius did not intend the Exercises for just anyone, but only for those who were at least at the beginnings of the journey toward Christian perfection and capable of following it through rather than "stalling" at one stage. Ignatius made Pierre Favre, one of his most promising first companions, wait for several months before making the Exercises, precisely because Ignatius judged he was not ready to perform the exercises even of the First Week, without too great a risk of getting stuck there (because of his affliction with scruples).

107. So that the "Second Week" is, in fact, generally the longest of the four measured in terms of days.

108. Schineller's approach is more nuanced, but its reliance on Segundo's interpretation (for example, Schineller "Pilgrim Journey," 2–3, 15, 23) makes the novelty of his approach less persuasive.

109. Schineller, "Pilgrim Journey," 13–14.

110. This is not just a hypothetical question, as we shall see when we discuss Ignacio Ellacuría in chapter 5. It was precisely this kind of situation that the Jesuits in Central America, including Ellacuría, and later Dean Brackley, confronted from the 1960s through the 1990s, and beyond. Brackley's commentary on the *Spiritual Exercises, Discernment in Troubled Times*, starts from this perspective. On the other hand, the new situation faced in Latin America or Africa may require a shift in metaphor in the direction that Schineller prefers. My contention here is that it is not the particular root-metaphors that indicate a more or less mature Ignatian spirituality, but the ways they are taken up and implemented based on the spirituality mapped out by the *Spiritual Exercises*.

111. For a representation of just such a set of spiritualities, some within the Society of Jesus and others expanding beyond its boundaries, see Burke and Burke-Sullivan, eds., *The Ignatian Tradition*.

CHAPTER THREE

1. Ignatius wrote to Paschale Broët and Alfonso Salmerón, appointed as papal legates to Ireland: "So we with a good purpose can praise or agree with another concerning some particular good thing, dissembling whatever else may be wrong. After thus gaining his confidence, we shall have better success. In this sense we go in with him his way but come out our own" (*Letters of St. Ignatius of Loyola*, 51). This is a mirror image of the strategy that Ignatius attributes to the evil angel in the *Spiritual Exercises*: "It is characteristic of the evil angel . . . to enter by going along with the devout soul in order to come out by his own way with success for himself" (*SpEx* 332).
2. See Eisenstadt, ed., *Multiple Modernities*.
3. In his analysis of Ignatian spirituality and modernity, Cristopher van Ginhoven Rey emphasizes the axis of nature and grace—more precisely, of human agency and the divine grace—that empowers it. See Van Ginhoven Rey, "The Jesuit Instrument: On Saint Ignatius of Loyola's Modernity," in Maryks, ed., *A Companion to Ignatius of Loyola*, 198–215. In the same volume, Moshe Sluhovsky focuses on the turn to the subject: Sluhovsky, "Loyola's *Spiritual Exercises* and the Modern Self," in ibid., 216–47. These are both apt candidates, even though they are expansive and internally complex enough to require further articulation and discrete treatments of their elements.
4. See, for example, Ignatius of Loyola, *A Pilgrim's Testament*, nos. 15, 39, 49, 52, 96, 98, and 99.
5. Dulles, "Saint Ignatius and the Jesuit Theological Tradition," 16. See also Dulles, "The Ignatian Charism and Contemporary Theology," in *Avery Dulles: Essential Writings from America Magazine*, 151–66.
6. Hans Blumenberg, for example, argues that modernity arose after and because the medieval synthesis collapsed under its own weight; see Blumenberg, *The Legitimacy of the Modern Age*. On his reading, late medieval nominalism is the first key player in this drama, a view shared by Gillespie, *Theological Origins of Modernity*. Dupré, *Passage to Modernity*, argues that nominalism provided a key deconstructive step, adding as a complement the positive move made by Renaissance humanists. Toulmin, *Cosmopolis*, sees in the sixteenth-century humanists a first flowering of modernity, with a more open, tolerant, and self-consciously context-bound understanding of reason. This first shoot withered in the flames of religious war in the seventeenth century. The modernity associated with Descartes, Leibniz, and Newton grew up in the seared cultural and intellectual landscape that these wars left behind.
7. This follows Dupré's framing of the issue in Dupré, *Passage to Modernity*. For his own brief but evocative portrayal of Ignatius's spirituality as a provisional synthesis, see 224–27. See also the sketch of Ignatius's sources in Molloni, *Exercises of St Ignatius Loyola in the Western Tradition*.

8. The Oñaz-Loyola family was one of the chief clans (*parientes mayores*) in Guipuzcoa, associated with the *oñacitos*, and locked in struggle with the *gamboínos* for control of the region. Even in this backwater region, however, the transition to modernity was on the horizon, as the *parientes mayores* struggled to contain the burgeoning power of the new towns with their rising middle-class populations. See Dalmases, *Ignatius of Loyola*, 15–24.

9. Ignatius of Loyola, *A Pilgrim's Testament*, no. 1.

10. See Juan Manuel Cacho Bleuca, "Del gentilhombre mundano al caballero 'a lo divino': Los ideales caballerescos de Ignacio de Loyola," in Plazaola, ed., *Ignacio de Loyola y su Tiempo*, 129–59.

11. On the latter, see Wolter, "Elements of Crusade Spirituality in St. Ignatius," in Wulf, *Ignatius of Loyola*, 97–134.

12. *SpEx* 97.

13. The *Castillano*, Juan Luis Segundo, SJ, captured this in his reflections on Contemplation of the Kingdom of Jesus Christ. See Segundo, "Ignatius Loyola: Trial or Project," 160–61.

14. Cited in Cusson, *Biblical Theology and the Spiritual Exercises*, 20.

15. Later in life, in Rome, Ignatius confided that one of the saints who particularly caught his imagination was one St. Honofrio, who lived for seventy years in the desert, "with his hair flowing down to the ground and naked except for a girdle of foliage" (Caraman, *Ignatius of Loyola*, 28).

16. For a brief discussion of this book and its influence on Ignatius, see Shore, "The *Vita Christi* of Ludolph of Saxony and Its Influence on the *Spiritual Exercises* of Ignatius of Loyola." See also, Cusson, *Biblical Theology and the Spiritual Exercises*, 10–19.

17. See Cousins, "Francis of Assisi: Christian Mysticism at the Crossroads"; also, Cousins, "The Humanity and the Passion of Christ," 375–91. For the relationship of this mysticism to Ignatius, see Cousins, "The Franciscan Roots of Ignatian Meditation."

18. See Cousins, "Franciscan Roots of Ignatian Meditation," 55–59.

19. Ibid., 60. Cousins cites his essay, "Francis of Assisi: Christian Mysticism and the Crossroads."

20. See Cousins, "Humanity and Passion of Christ," 376–80.

21. See Cousins, "Francis of Assisi," 175–88.

22. Cousins, "Franciscan Roots of Ignatian Meditation," 63. He suggests that Bonaventure might do this work still for Ignatius, or a modern-day theologian, influenced by Bonaventure: Karl Rahner.

23. In contemplating the Nativity, for instance, I am encouraged "to make myself a poor, little, and unworthy slave, contemplating them [the Holy Family], and serving them in their needs, just as if I were there" (*SpEx* 114). Ignatius learned this method of making oneself an actor in the scene from Ludolph of Saxony.

24. Cited in Cusson, *Biblical Theology and the Spiritual Exercises*, 12–13. Compare this with the grace asked for in the Second Week of the *Spiritual Exercises*, in which the contemplation of the life of Christ figures so prominently: "an interior knowledge of our Lord, who became human for me, that I may love him more intensely and follow him more closely" (*SpEx* 104).

25. In the latter, Ignatius suggests that one "imagine Christ our Lord eating

in company with his apostles, and to observe how he eats, how he drinks, how he looks about, and how he converses, and then to try to imitate him" (*SpEx* 214).

26. See Chenu, "Theology and the New Awareness of History," in *Nature, Man, and Society in the Twelfth Century*, 162–201.

27. Gillespie, *The Theological Origins of Modernity*, 2. Peter Harrison has also argued that the Protestant rejection of symbolic and allegorical readings of scripture expands into a similar rejection of such a way of reading "the book of nature," which makes possible the rise of modern science. See Harrison, *The Bible, Protestantism, and the Rise of Natural Science*.

28. See Taylor, *A Secular Age*, 54–61.

29. As Otto Gründler points out, "the institutions and literature of the *devotio moderna* represent a revival of traditional monastic spirituality rather than a radical innovation" (see Gründler, "*Devotio Moderna*," in Raitt, ed., *Christian Spirituality: High Middle Ages and Reformation*, 179).

30. John O'Malley identifies the following points of convergence between Ignatius's spirituality and the Modern Devotion, as the latter is exemplified in the *Imitation of Christ*: recommendation of frequent Communion and confession, examination of conscience, a focus on interiority, and an insistence on personal appropriation of religious truth in holiness of life. See O'Malley, *First Jesuits*, 264–66.

31. See Josef Sudbrack, "'Gott in allen Dingen finden': Eine Ignatianische Maxime und ihr metahistorischer Hintergrund," in Plazaola, ed., *Ignacio de Loyola y su Tiempo*, 343–44.

32. See Ozment, *Mysticism and Dissent*.

33. *SpEx* 357.

34. *SpEx* 14, 15.

35. A "hypergood" serves as an ordering source or locus for leading a truly worthy or excellent human life. It does so by organizing the various goods that we perceive and seek in the various diverse spheres of human life. The affirmation of everyday life has as its necessary corollary the dethroning of those hypergoods (knightly valor or solitary contemplation, for example) that define a life that transcends, and is to some extent in tension with, the everyday work of reproducing and sustaining life. See Taylor, *Sources of the Self*, 63–73, 211–18.

36. Thus in the matters for election that Ignatius proposed for persons already committed to a certain state of life. See chapter 2, section titled "The Structure and Dynamism of the *Spiritual Exercises*."

37. Cousins, "Francis of Assisi," 165.

38. Ibid., 175–88.

39. See Evennett, *The Spirit of the Counter-Reformation*, 60–63.

40. However, whether it reflects Aquinas or Ockham (as Van Ginhoven Rey argues it does; see "The Jesuit Instrument," 205) is probably undecidable from the text itself. "Scholasticism" at Paris was a variegated phenomenon, which reflected the state of the school, with a strong current of eclectic nominalism dominant in Paris.

41. O'Malley, "Some Distinctive Characteristics of Jesuit Spirituality in the Sixteenth Century," 9. Cf. O'Malley, *The First Jesuits*, 244–53.

42. Here the preference is for the scholasticism of the high Middle Ages. Ockham and other late medieval nominalists are not to be found on Ignatius's list.

43. *SpEx* 2. The Spanish verbs are *sentir* and *gustar*.

44. See O'Malley, "Renaissance Humanism and the First Jesuits," in Plazaola, ed., *Ignacio de Loyola y su Tiempo*, 381–403; O'Malley, *The First Jesuits*, 253–72.

45. Rules 2 through 9 of the Rules for Thinking with the Church appear to draw from the acts of the Council of Sens (1528), which were directed in large measure against Erasmus (see Dulles, "The Ignatian 'Sentire cum Ecclesia' Today," 22). For a description of the University of Paris while Ignatius was there, see James K. Farge, "The University of Paris in the Time of Ignatius Loyola," in Plazaola, ed., *Ignacio de Loyola y su Tiempo*, 221–44.

46. For an extended analysis of this "turn" using Ignatius's *Autobiography*, see Boyle, *Loyola's Acts*.

47. See, for example, *SpEx* 4, 17, 18. The same principle of accommodation is pervasive to the *Constitutions*.

48. *SpEx* 145, 146 (emphasis added). This contrasts with the strategy that the enemy gives to the demons he sends out into the world: "to lay snares for men and bind them with chains" (142).

49. O'Malley makes this point in O'Malley, "Some Distinctive Characteristics," 13.

50. For a discussion of the history of Jesuit historiography, including both the ways the Jesuits portrayed themselves and how they were portrayed by others, see O'Malley, "The Historiography of the Society of Jesus."

51. This was a potent strategy to counter the ongoing attacks on the Jesuits from within the Catholic Church, by figures such as the Dominican Melchior Cano.

52. O'Malley, "Historiography of the Society of Jesus," 25.

53. On this issue, see O'Malley, *First Jesuits*, 272–87.

54. See O'Malley, "Historiography of the Society of Jesus," 18–24.

55. No one expressed this more eloquently in his own life and work than Pierre Favre, who wrote to Lainez that in dealing with "the heretics" (as he did, indeed, name the Protestant Reformers), "We need to win their goodwill, so that they will love us and accord us a good place in their hearts. This can be done by speaking familiarly with them about matters we both share in common and avoiding any debate in which one side tries to put down the other. We must establish communion in what unites us before doing so in what might evince differences of opinion.... A man who can speak with them on how to live well... will do them more good than another who is filled with theological authorities for confounding them" (quoted in Burke and Burke-Sullivan, eds., *The Ignatian Tradition*, 40).

56. See Sluhovsky, "Loyola's *Spiritual Exercises* and the Modern Self," 227–30, and the literature cited there.

57. *SpEx* 14, 15.

58. See O'Malley, "Early Jesuit Spirituality," 20.

59. Ibid., 8.

60. "The history of Loyola's *Spiritual Exercises* is thus a history of both the emergence of a new sense of modern individual subjecthood and of the anxiety this novelty brought with it" (Sluhovsky, "Loyola's *Spiritual Exercises*," 228). See also Schreiner, *Are You Alone Wise?* Taylor captures this tensive relationship between the affirmation of the possibility of perfection in the everyday and the move toward ever-more thorough techniques of surveillance in his discussion of the three different levels of "reform" that accompanied the dissolution of a hierarchically ordered categorization of states of perfection. See Taylor, *A Secular Age*, 90–145.

61. Cited in O'Malley, "Some Distinctive Characteristics of Jesuit Spirituality in the Sixteenth Century," 15.

62. This is not to imply that other classic spiritual schools, such as the Carmelite, Benedictine, or Dominican spiritualities, are not modern, or better, that they have not become so in their own distinctive ways.

63. Taylor, *A Secular Age*, 38.

64. As I argued in discussing the Contemplation to Attain Love, particularly its third point (*SpEx* 236). See chapter 2, section titled "The Structure and Dynamism of the *Spiritual Exercises*."

65. Caraman, *Ignatius of Loyola*, 186. Typically enough, however, after fifteen minutes in prayer Ignatius emerged from the chapel calm and collected, having found the presence of God even in this development.

66. See my discussion of the Contemplation on the Incarnation in chapter 2.

67. *Constitutions*, no. 671 (see Ganss, ed., *Ignatius of Loyola*, 310). The echo of the fourth point of the Contemplation to Attain Love (*SpEx* 237) is unmistakable.

68. See chapter 2, section titled "The Structure and Dynamism of the Spiritual Exercises," toward the end.

69. Cited in O'Malley, *First Jesuits*, 243.

70. Chapter 1, section titled "Spirituality and the Wells of Vision."

71. Both of these (contrition and sorrow, and grateful love) can be the occasion for the "gift of tears," so important to Ignatius, and are involved in the spiritual disposition of *acatamiento* ("affectionate awe"), so central to his spirituality. *Acatamiento* captures both the deep sense of intimacy and familiarity with God that was characteristic of Ignatius and his sense of God's awe-ful transcendence and holiness. Joan Nuth points out *acatamiento's* similarity to Julian of Norwich's insistence that God's love is both "courtly" and "homely," and also its resonances with Rudolf Otto's articulation of the experience of the Holy as *fascinans et tremendum*; see Nuth, "*Acatamiento*: Living in an Attitude of Affectionate Awe." Bernard McGinn points to its genealogy in the mystical disposition of compunction, which has a twofold appearance as the compunction of fear (for Ignatius, *acatamiento temero*, from the First Week) and compunction of love (for Ignatius, *acatamiento amoroso*, of the Second through Fourth Weeks, but above all in the Contemplation to Attain Love); see McGinn, *Mysticism in the Golden Age of Spain*, 98. See also Rogelio García Mateo, "Acatamiento-Reverencia," in García de Castro, ed., *Diccionario de espiritualidad ignaciana*, 1:77–79.

72. See Tanner, *Theories of Culture*, 3–60.

73. See John W. Padberg, SJ, "Predicting the Past, Looking Back for the

Future," in O'Malley, Padberg, and O'Keefe, *Jesuit Spirituality*, 21–44.

74. See Toulmin, *Cosmopolis*, 30–38. It was also at this time that the Jesuits had charge of one of their most famous pupils, René Descartes.

75. For the history of this recovery of the sources that led to a new configuration of Ignatius's legacy, see O'Malley and O'Brien, *The Twentieth-Century Construction of Ignatian Spirituality*.

CHAPTER FOUR

1. Rahner, *Karl Rahner in Dialogue*, 191. This particular interview took place in March 1979.

2. Many authors have argued for the importance of Ignatian spirituality to Rahner's theology. Among the most important are the following: Fischer, *Der Mensch als Geheimnis*; Egan, "Karl Rahner: Theologian of the 'Spiritual Exercises'"; Zahlauer, *Karl Rahner und sein "produktives Vorbild" Ignatius von Loyola*; Endean, *Karl Rahner and Ignatian Spirituality*; Batlogg, *Die Mysterien des Lebens Jesu bei Karl Rahner*; and Fritz, *Freedom Made Manifest*, esp. chap. 3 (128–79). My debts to these authors, and to Endean's magisterial study in particular, will be noted in what follows. An important contribution on Rahner's mystical theology, which treats not only the influence of Ignatius but also of other important mystics, is found in Rubbelke, "A Constant Closeness to *This* God." I have learned much from this dissertation.

3. For example, we have a list of readings that Rahner read over and above the required texts while in his theology studies in Valkenburg, from 1929 to 1933. Among the names that appear on that list are Jan van Ruusbroec, Heinrich Suso (a disciple of Meister Eckhart), John of the Cross, Francis de Sales, Blaise Pascal, John Henry Newman, and W. Sierps, *Ignatianische Wegweisung* (Freiburg: Herder, 1929). See Neufeld, *Die Brüder Rahner*, 99.

4. These began as an essay in a *Festschrift* written by Karl and his brother Hugo for their father on the occasion of his sixtieth birthday (1928). The textual history is quite complex; see Zahlauer, *Karl Rahner*, 97–100. With some modifications, this material was eventually published in *Theological Investigations* 16:81–134. Henceforth, the twenty-three volumes of *Theological Investigations* will be abbreviated as *TI*, followed by the volume number. The German series, *Schriften zur Theologie*, of which its volumes are a translation, will be abbreviated *SzT*, with the volume number (1–16).

5. Rahner, *Faith in a Wintry Season*, 19. His first published work dealt with prayer: "Warum uns das Beten nottut" ("Why We Need to Pray"); see Zahlauer, *Karl Rahner*, 86–96.

6. See Neufeld, *Die Brüder Rahner*, 61.

7. Rahner, "Lebenslauf," 32; cited in Zahlauer, *Karl Rahner*, 89n16.

8. Quoted in Endean, *Karl Rahner and Ignatian Spirituality*, 2. Nothing ultimately came of the project; see ibid., 1–3.

9. Przywara, *Deus Semper Maior*. For an overview of the relationship between his reading of Ignatian spirituality and his theology, see O'Meara, *Erich Przywara, S.J.*, 150–57, and the literature cited there. See also Lagger,

Dienst: Kenosis in Schöpfung und Kreuz bei Erich Przywara SJ. For a very helpful article-length treatment, see Dunkle, "Service in the *Analogia Entis* and Spiritual Works of Erich Pryzwara."

10. For a complete listing of Rahner's writings on Ignatian spirituality, consult the bibliography in Endean, *Karl Rahner*, 268–74. The notes giving the historical context and textual issues for each contribution are particularly valuable.

11. With some minor changes it was published as Rahner, "Ignatian Mysticism."

12. Rahner, "The Logic of Concrete Individual Knowledge in Ignatius of Loyola." This essay was first written for Wulf, *Ignatius von Loyola*, 343–405. This was a book of essays composed on the occasion of the 400th anniversary of Ignatius's death. Rahner then published it in *Das Dynamische in der Kirche*, 74–148. Henceforth cited as "Logic."

13. These were group retreats in which the retreat director gave what amounted to lectures on the different meditations, contemplations, and reflections of the *Spiritual Exercises*, which the retreatant was then to mull over during his or her free time. As a result of the 31st and 32nd General Congregations of the Society of Jesus (1964–65 and 1975–76, respectively), the original Ignatian intention that retreats be individually directed was reemphasized as the norm. Up until that time such individually directed retreats were much less common.

14. Rahner, *Spiritual Exercises*. There are a number of difficulties with the text; see Endean, *Karl Rahner*, 270. Primary among these is that, as Rahner himself notes, he did not exert much control over the transcription of the original retreat lectures or on their subsequent editing into a book; see Rahner, *Spiritual Exercises*, 7. Thus, a prudent use of the text will consider general themes that appear in the text as authentically Rahner's own but will put rather less weight on specific wordings or nuances of smaller portions of the texts.

15. Rahner, *Meditations on Priestly Life*. Rahner himself prepared this text for publication. For further details on both texts, see the comments by Batlogg, Herzgsell, and Kiechle, eds., in Rahner, *Sämtliche Werke XIII*, xx–xxvii. Both *Betrachtungen zum ignatianischen Exerzitienbuch* and *Einübung priesterlicher Existenz* may be found in this volume of Rahner's collected works.

16. Rahner, "Rede des Ignatius von Loyola an einen Jesuiten von Heute." This essay was subsequently published under the same title in *Schriften zur Theologie*, but was not translated and included in the corresponding volumes of *Theological Investigations*. There is an English translation (in *Ignatius of Loyola*, ed. Paul Imhof, trans. Rosaleen Ockenden), but I will provide my own translations using the German original in *Schriften zur Theologie*, citing it as "Rede des Ignatius."

17. Rahner, *Faith in a Wintry Season*, 104.

18. Dych, "Theology in a New Key," 2.

19. For overviews, besides O'Donovan, *A World of Grace*, see Marmion and Hines, eds., *A Cambridge Companion to Karl Rahner*, and O'Meara, *God in the World*.

20. This story is told in McCool, *Nineteenth-Century Scholasticism*. The subsequent history and internally driven fragmentation of this position is described in the successor volume: McCool, *From Unity to Pluralism*. For an abbreviated version of parts of this story and a sketch of Rahner's place in it,

see McCool, "Karl Rahner and the Christian Philosophy of St. Thomas Aquinas."

21. *Aeterni Patris* required that Thomism (which meant the neoscholastics' interpretation of his thought) be taught in all seminaries. This did not extend to nonseminary theological training, but the Society of Jesus embraced this requirement for all its educational initiatives.

22. See Neufeld, *Die Brüder Rahner*, 65–85, 94–103.

23. Indeed, Rahner sometimes called Maréchal "my own 'Father of the Church.'" See Coreth, "Philosophische Grundlagen der Theologie Karl Rahners," 528.

24. Rahner, *Hearer of the Word*.

25. For example, he wrote essays that came out of the dialogue with scientists, and subsequently revisionary Marxists, in which he engaged as a participant in meetings sponsored by the "Paulusgesellschaft."

26. Rahner, *Foundations of Christian Faith*, 9. Cf. Rahner, "The Current Relationship between Philosophy and Theology," in *TI* 13:61–79.

27. For a description of this traditional theological method from the neoscholastic manualist approach, see Schüssler Fiorenza, "Systematic Theology: Task and Methods," 20–26.

28. Rahner, *Foundations of Christian Faith*, 9–10.

29. Besides the already cited introduction to *Foundations of Christian Faith*, see Rahner, "Reflections on the Contemporary Intellectual Formation of Future Priests," in *TI* 10:113–38, especially, 123–28.

30. This is a version of the story that Taylor, *A Secular Age*, tells in his analysis of "secularity 3," in a story that charts "a move from a society where belief in God is unchallenged and indeed, unproblematic, to one in which it is understood to be one option among others, and frequently not the easiest to embrace" (3).

31. See, for example, Rahner, "Possible Courses for the Theology of the Future," *TI* 13:32–60, esp. 40–42, and Rahner, "Notwendigkeit einer neuen Mystagogie."

32. The converse is also true, as I will argue in greater detail in the rest of the chapter.

33. Rahner, "The Ignatian Mysticism of Joy in the World," in *Theological Investigations*, 3, *The Theology of the Spiritual Life*, trans. Karl-H.[einz] and Boniface Kruger (New York: Crossroad, 1982), 277–93. The version published in *Schriften zur Theologie* 3 in 1956 (and translated for *TI* 3) differs slightly from the original, with the addition of updated footnotes and the substantive revision and expansion of one of its paragraphs. The original was published in 1937: Rahner, "Die ignatianische Mystik der Weltfreudigkeit."

34. Rahner wrote it as a thesis on Aquinas, but Honecker ultimately rejected it for being unduly influenced by modern philosophical currents. It would be published anyway two years later: Karl Rahner, *Geist in Welt* (Innsbruck: Verlag Felizian Rauch, 1939). In an interesting illustration of another way in which Rahner's systematic and spiritual theologies were interdependent, *Geist in Welt* was published with a subvention using funds garnered from the publication of Rahner's book, *Worte ins Schweigen*; translated into English as *Encounters with Silence*, trans. James Demske (Westminster, MD: Christian Classics, 1984).

35. Translated into English as Rahner, *Hearer of the Word*.

36. Rahner, "Ignatian Mysticism," 290. To be precise, Rahner uses "ignati-

anische Frömmigkeit" (Ignatian piety). "*Spiritualität*" does not become widely used in German for some decades (as is the case in English), and Rahner never used it with great frequency or enthusiasm. I treat "piety" here as synonymous with "spirituality."

37. Ibid.

38. It is possible that Rahner may have gotten the idea of setting forth Ignatian spirituality in terms of a polarity from Erich Pryzwara, since this is perhaps *the* principal methodological strategy of Rahner's elder compatriot and fellow Jesuit.

39. This is one of the few places where Rahner cites from the *Constitutions*. The passage in question is paragraph 101 of the "General Examen" of the *Constitutions*. See Ganss, ed., *Ignatius of Loyola: Spiritual Exercises and Selected Works*, 286.

40. Rahner, "Ignatian Mysticism," 283 (translation slightly emended).

41. One cannot but think here of Heidegger's definition of the authentic mode of human being as "anticipatory resoluteness," which is brought to the fore by confronting authentically the disclosure of our radical contingency as beings always oriented toward the nonbeing of death, an "authentic Being towards the possibility which we have characterized as Dasein's utter impossibility" (see Heidegger, *Being and Time*, 378). It is relevant in this regard that Rahner gave a lecture on existential philosophy in Vienna on the same visit in which he gave this lecture on Ignatian spirituality.

42. Rahner, "Ignatian Mysticism," 286.

43. Ibid., 287. This claim recurs frequently and insistently, even up to the last essay we treat, "St Ignatius of Loyola Speaks to a Jesuit Today" (1977), in which Rahner has Ignatius say, "I will simply say this: I have experienced God, the nameless and unfathomable, holding silent, and yet near, in the three-foldness of God's self-bestowal to me" (Rahner, "Rede des Ignatius," 374).

44. Rahner, "Ignatian Mysticism," 287.

45. He has in mind here the opening contemplation of the First Week: *SpEx* 50–51.

46. Rahner, "Ignatian Mysticism," 287–88. Emphasis has been added to highlight the fact that Rahner had already come to the conviction that the heart of the *Spiritual Exercises*, and thus of Ignatian spirituality, lies in the rules for discernment of spirits. His allusion to the inadequacy of "general moral principles" for this work also presages his argument about discernment in the 1950s.

47. Among other things this would be far too Pelagian a rendering: as if we could "force" God to grant us salvation by our own strenuous rejection of the world.

48. Rahner, "Ignatian Mysticism," 289 (emphasis original).

49. Ibid., 291 (emphasis original). The different stances that Ignatius and Francis took toward the gift of tears is a favorite case that Rahner cites often, even down to his last writings.

50. Ibid., 291–92. It is worth noting that Rahner is aware that this motto (*in actione contemplativus*) does not come from Ignatius himself. Rahner has more than a novice's familiarity with the sources of Ignatian spirituality.

51. This gives the text a hybrid character: on the one hand it is philosophical, as a kind of Kantian transcendental analysis, but on the other hand it is not, since its starting point is not some universal human activity, such as knowing or willing,

but the historically conditioned act of appropriating revelation (mediated through scripture and tradition).

52. Rahner, "Ignatian Mysticism," 283, 285.

53. Ibid., 287.

54. Here a dual focus appears that Rahner never resolves, perhaps because it cannot be. As he has Ignatius put it in "Rede des Ignatius," there is a kind of "external irrigation system" created and maintained by the Church to water the heart and maintain faith, and this includes the preaching and mystagogical deepening of the awareness of the Christ event in the hearts of believers. Yet, "besides religious indoctrination, above and beyond the doctrines about God and God's commandments, to which belong also the Church, the words of Scripture, the sacraments, and so on, there is, as it were, a deep well in these fields [of the heart] themselves, so that out of such a font, bored in this way, within the fields themselves, the water of the living Spirit bubbles up into eternal life (which is really what we already find in John)" ("Rede des Ignatius," 379). Both sources have evidentiary power, as it were, for the Christian life of faith; their relationship is not entirely clear and has been the source of no little argument among interpreters of Rahner.

55. At the time when Rahner delivered this lecture (early in the year 1937), Hitler had just formally renounced the Treaty of Versailles. The Spanish Civil War, which Hitler and Mussolini were using as a proving ground for their militaries, had reached its full savagery. Indeed, the attack on Guernica, made famous by Picasso's painting, was just a few months away.

56. Rahner, "Ignatian Mysticism," 279. Rahner says that the title of the talk was given to him in advance (277n), which suggests that, had he had the liberty to do so, he would have titled it differently.

57. Ibid., 280.

58. Rahner, "Die ignatianische Mystik," 122 (translation mine).

59. Rahner, "Ignatian Mysticism," 279.

60. Michael Rubbelke has shown that Rahner's reluctance and manifest scruples when defining the sense in which Ignatius was a mystic derives from Rahner's complex and not yet fully resolved (to his satisfaction) negotiation of a number of ongoing debates about the nature and status of mysticism in the late nineteenth and early twentieth centuries. See Rubbelke, "A Constant Closeness to *This* God," chaps. 1 and 2.

61. It is of course possible that he was already aware of this at the time he wrote the earlier essay, but did not want to include technical theological questions in a lecture given to nonspecialists.

62. See the clear and helpful discussion in Endean, *Karl Rahner*, 32–67.

63. Karl Lehmann claims that this task of working out the possibility and actuality of the experience of grace is the heart of Rahner's system as a whole; see Lehmann, "Karl Rahner: A Portrait," esp. 27–30.

64. From Rahner, *De gratia Christi*, quoted in Endean, *Karl Rahner and Ignatian Spirituality*, 39.

65. Endean, *Karl Rahner*, 22–31, 42–43; Zahlauer, *Karl Rahner und sein "produktives Vorbild,"* 97–157.

66. This analogy comes from Wiseman, "I Have Experienced God," 28; quoted in Endean, *Karl Rahner*, 32.

67. Guardini, *The End of the Modern World*. The German title is *Das Ende der Neuzeit*. English translators render "Neuzeit" variously as "the modern world," "the new age," and "modernity." When I speak in what follows of "modernity," this should be borne in mind.

68. Ibid., 69.

69. See, for instance, Guardini, *Letters from Lake Como*, which date from 1927. For an overview of the development of Guardini's stance toward modernity, including a summary of these letters, see Krieg, *Romano Guardini*, 161–82.

70. The text is cited in several places, including Rahner, "Ignatian Spirituality and Devotion to the Heart of Jesus"; Rahner, "Being Open to God as Ever Greater: On the Significance of the Aphorism 'Ad majorem Dei gloriam,'" in *TI* 6:25–46; and Rahner, "Modern Piety and the Experience of Retreats," *TI* 16:135–55.

71. Rahner, "Ignatian Spirituality and Devotion to the Heart of Jesus," 180–81.

72. Ibid., 181.

73. Ibid., 185.

74. Guardini, *End of the Modern World*, 56–57.

75. He cites Goethe and quotes from his poetry at several key points, not only as exemplary of the "modern" experience of subjectivity, but also of nature; see Guardini, *End of the Modern World*, 54–55, 58, 60, 69–70, 75. Frederick Wilhelmsen, the volume's editor, helpfully points out that the Goethe bicentennial had just been celebrated, which may explain in part Guardini's focus on him.

76. Bellah et al., *Habits of the Heart*, 33–35.

77. Taylor, *Sources of the Self*, 368–81.

78. Guardini, *End of the Modern World*, 75–92. One cannot but be reminded of roughly contemporaneous works in American sociology: Riesman, *The Lonely Crowd*; Whyte, *The Organization Man*; and Wilson, *The Man in the Gray Flannel Suit*.

79. Guardini, *End of the Modern World*, 79. Guardini suggests that those individualists who bemoan the passing of "the Individual" suffer from a hidden elitism, since that ideal was only really realizable for a few "Great Men," while the majority of the human race was tacitly abandoned to a purported mediocrity (82). He believes, moreover, that "mass man" has virtues proper to it: the comradery and community that arise from the collective effort to subdue nature in the service of the common good of humanity as a whole (83–84).

80. Ibid., 80.

81. Rahner, "Ignatian Spirituality and Devotion to the Heart of Jesus," 184. This may also constitute a tacit parry of Jacques Maritain's critique of Ignatius and Ignatian spirituality in Maritain, *Integral Humanism*, where he associates it with the Promethean humanism that, on his view, arose with the Renaissance. On Maritain's critique (and a rebuttal), see Buckley, *Catholic University*, 76–79. John O'Malley has asserted a much stronger connection between Ignatian spirituality and Renaissance humanism in O'Malley, *The First Jesuits*.

82. Rahner, "Ignatian Spirituality and Devotion to the Heart of Jesus," 184 (emphasis added).

83. Ibid., 185–86.
84. Rahner, *Spirit in the World*, xlix.
85. Ibid., li.
86. Rahner, "Being Open to God as Ever Greater," in *TI* 7:25–46; cf. the German in *StZ* 7:32–53. This was originally an address given to a Jesuit meeting at Rottmanshöhe during Easter Week 1959.
87. Ibid., 32–33.
88. Ibid., 27–28.
89. Ibid., 28.
90. As we shall see in chapter 5, Ignacio Ellacuría names this historical process "possibilitization": in which a phenomenon which is always a latent possibility in history only becomes truly possible because of certain historical realities. See below the subsection "Philosophical Underpinnings," in the section "Ellacuría's Intellectual Project: A Philosophy and Theology of Historical Reality."
91. Rahner finds it significant that the *Suscipe* begins with the offer of "all my liberty," before offering the traditional triad of memory, understanding, and will (*SpEx* 234).
92. Ibid., 36. For the German, see *SzT* 7:43.
93. Ibid., 37.
94. That Rahner was thoroughly familiar with this terminology can be seen in his article on "existential philosophy," which he equated with Heidegger's philosophy; see Rahner, "The Concept of Existential Philosophy in Heidegger," esp. 132–33. The article dates from 1940, but it goes back to a lecture that Rahner gave in Vienna in 1937, at the same time he lectured on Ignatian spirituality.
95. Heidegger, *Being and Time*, 174.
96. Ibid., 185.
97. Rahner, "Being Open to God as Ever Greater," 38–39 (translation slightly emended).
98. Ibid., 40.
99. Ibid., 41.
100. See Rahner, "Ignatian Spirituality and Devotion to the Heart of Jesus," 189–90, Rahner, "Being Open to God as Ever Greater," 43–45.
101. One detects echoes here of Dostoyevsky's Grand Inquisitor.
102. Rahner, "The Concept of Existential Philosophy in Heidegger," 137.
103. For bibliographical information on this essay, see note 12, above. Henceforth cited as "Logic," or, for the German original, "Logik."
104. For Endean's review of these criticisms and his own articulation of them, see Endean, *Karl Rahner*, 131–34, 157–82. Jules Toner's strong critique is found in Toner, *Commentary on Saint Ignatius' Rules for Discernment of Spirits*, 291–313.
105. Rahner, "The Concept of Existential Philosophy," 135.
106. This is a more literal rendering of the German title: "Die Logik der existentiellen Erkenntnis bei Ignatius von Loyola." The translator renders "existentiell" as "concrete particular."
107. Rahner, "On the Question of a Formal Existential Ethics," in *TI* 2:217–34. A word on terminology: "existential" in the title of this essay refers to a general approach to philosophical and theological anthropology. When Rahner uses

"existentiell" in the essay on Ignatian discernment, he intends the distinction between "existential" and "existentiell," as terms of art *within* "existential philosophy." Broadly speaking, an "existential" refers to a structure that is always actualized wherever there is Dasein (such as "thrownness" or "fallenness"), whereas "existentiell" refers to the specific way it is actualized and "felt" in a given person when she enacts her existence, always in a way unique to her situation. Thus "existentielle Erkenntnis" (which the translator renders as "concrete individual knowledge") refers to a specific insight into my human existence as I attempt to enact it in a particular situation or challenge. It is very much an individual affair, but it is still characterized by certain basic structures ("existentials") that can be disclosed by the appropriate phenomenological analysis. It is an important distinction, but I will not attempt to transfer it into English. The context will be sufficient to indicate which meaning is intended by "existential."

108. Rahner, "On the Question of a Formal Existential Ethics," 219. He cites the condemnation of this approach in *Humani generis*. For further discussion of the controversy surrounding situation ethics and Rahner's place in it, see Endean, *Karl Rahner*, 103–11.

109. These decisions would not have the gravity they do if human beings as individuals, in their concrete particularity, were not destined for intimate union with God. In a world not determined by such a destining of human beings by God (that is, a world not already suffused by grace), these decisions would be important but not have ethical-spiritual weight. However, as with "pure nature," this kind of world only exists by an act of logical abstraction that follows the premise of the absolute gratuitousness of grace. In fact, it *is* God's will that I, as an individual, in my concrete embodiment, as this is shaped by all my decisions, be united with God. This will of God adds a further moral and spiritual dimension to decisions that otherwise would lack it. This argument is not unlike his argument on how the lack of original justice in humans after the fall can be experienced as something that "ought not to be," even though original justice is not a perfection owed to human beings by their nature (that is, the relative "dis-integration" entailed by concupiscence does not in itself make human nature defective or evil). The answer lies in the graced ordination of human beings toward union with God, which elicits and ought to elicit a fuller, integrated response of the person. In this light, human beings experience this way of existing as something alien and unnatural. See Rahner, "The Theological Concept of Concupiscencia," in *TI* 1:347–82, esp. 376–79.

110. Rahner, "On the Question of a Formal Existential Ethics," 227. Cf. Rahner, "Logic," 89–90.

111. Rahner, "On the Question of a Formal Existential Ethics," 229.

112. Ibid.

113. Ibid., 231 (translation slightly emended).

114. Rahner, "Logic," 110.

115. Ibid., 85.

116. See chapter 2, section titled "The Structure and Dynamism of the *Spiritual Exercises*."

117. Rahner, "Logic," 104.

118. Ibid., 105.

119. See Endean, *Karl Rahner*, 176–78.

120. Rahner, "Logic," 89, 169.

121. Ibid., 116–17.

122. The "first time" of making an election might have this character, but Rahner argues that Ignatius understood it to be relatively rare. Normally one discerns only in the aftermath of this kind of direct divine communication, in its penumbra, as it were, using the more complex, tentative procedures of the second time.

123. In Thomistic epistemology, the "formal object" of a cognitive power is the modality of being under which a particular entity (the "material object") is present to that power. For example, color is a formal object of human vision, as opposed to that of some other animals: objects are present to our vision as having this or that color. I see this flower (a material object) as colored (formal object). By nature, human knowing has being as its formal object; elevated by grace, human knowing has nothing less than God Godself as its formal object, so that our experience of the created world now is modulated by the virtue of faith, and ultimately we are capable of the beatific vision.

124. That is, though this elevation of our consciousness is a pervasive element of the way we are aware (*Bewußtheit*), this is different from its being susceptible to reflective identification and analysis (*Reflektbarkeit*). See Rahner, "Logic," 126. In Bernard Lonergan's words, it is not something we can identify by "taking a good look."

125. Ibid., 130.

126. Ibid., 131 (translation slightly emended; see Rahner, "Logik," 115) — a typically Rahnerian understatement, given the diverse interpretations that had been offered for this form of consolation, even at the time he wrote this essay.

127. Rahner worries that adverting to some sudden, apparently interruptive recollection, mood, or insight as coming from God precisely on the basis of its suddenness is fatally vulnerable to a counterexplanation of its origins from depth psychologies (ibid., 141–42). Later he connects this with a concern that Ignatius's spirituality not fall victim to a demythologization that would look askance at the mention of "good and evil spirits," and so on (see ibid., 164).

128. Ibid., 133 (translation slightly emended). Rahner also cites textual evidence in his support and a series of commentators who take this position (ibid., 133n28).

129. This suspicion is unfortunately abetted by the fact that the translator here often chooses to render "*ungegenständlich*" quite unhelpfully as "non-conceptual," rather than as, say, "unrelated to an object," which would be a more literal rendering.

130. Endean, *Karl Rahner and Ignatian Spirituality*, 138, 158.

131. Ibid., 133n28 — a footnote that goes on for more than 500 words!

132. Ibid. (translation emended); see Rahner, "Logik," 117n.

133. Endean, *Karl Rahner and Ignatian Spirituality*, 144. Here I render *Offenheit* as "openness" rather than "receptivity." At this point we have moved to matters treated decades earlier in Rahner, *Hearer of the Word*.

134. In other words, to paraphrase the Principle and Foundation, it is the graced capacity to see all things in the world as "created for human beings, to help

them in working toward the end for which they are created" (*SpEx* 23), with the proviso that this end is participation in the Trinitarian life of God.

135. This whole discussion leads us into the topic of Rahner's aesthetics, which has been woefully underappreciated and underdeployed in understanding his work. For an important exception, see Fritz, *Karl Rahner's Theological Aesthetics*.

136. Rahner, "Logic," 149.

137. Ibid., 151. He does not detail what these might be. If we keep in mind the framework of this essay—that we are dealing with an *existentiel* dimension and not *existential* matters—then it seems plausible to suggest that the "higher" instances are not higher in the sense of manifesting a more fundamental phenomenon in the relationship between God and the human (what could be higher than the coming into awareness of our union with God?), but are "higher" in the sense that they evince a higher level of integration of this kind of consolation with the specific constitution of a particular individual and her journey into God. But, by the nature of the case, one cannot generalize on what such an individual, "existentielle" form would be. I am indebted to Michael Rubbelke for this suggestion.

138. Ibid., 155–56.

139. Ibid., 158.

140. In this sense, God's word of address to me in prayer is my whole created being and the environing world within which I have been "thrown." See Rahner, "Dialogue with God?," in *TI*, 18:122–31. Dialogue with God is not some kind of inner dialogue in my head, however spiritually elevated, but rather the "dialogue" between my being in the world, on the one hand, as the word God addresses to me as a gift within which God offers Godself, and, on the other hand, my own response by the life I embrace in response. Not unsurprisingly, in his final articulation of what an unmythological understanding of dialogue with God might mean, the *Spiritual Exercises* of Ignatius provides an exemplary source and actualization of the answer (see ibid., 130–31).

141. That is, for example, Rahner's use of the three times for making an election is overly forced. All three bear the marks of the weighing of graced, affective movements most (but not *exclusively*) characteristic of the second. I am, however, more sympathetic to Rahner's language about what cannot be put into language than Endean appears to be in arguing that "Rahner's 'first principle' must be understood in less extravagant terms than his rhetoric may suggest, as a regulative truth applicable to all experience, and Christologically specified" (Endean, *Karl Rahner and Ignatian Spirituality*, 225). Rahner claims that there is an experience in which "the absence of object in question is utter receptivity to God, the inexpressible experience, apart from any object, of the love of God who is raised transcendentally above all that is individual, all that can be mentioned, of God as God"; Rahner, "Logic," 135 (slightly emended); cf. Rahner, "Logik," 117–18. It is true that this type of experience threatens to rupture the epistemological and anthropological framework of Rahner's theology, but this is the risk one must take if one is going to attempt to capture what finally cannot be captured in a theology. Rahner opted, I contend, to leave it be, unruly and dangerous as it is, rather than to domesticate it so as to preserve the theological framework that is supposed to be

at its service (a domestication of which he accused previous generations of Jesuit theologians, as we will see).

142. A major exception is his transcription and reworking of retreat notes that he gave to ordination candidates in 1961, which appeared (in English translation), in 1973. See Rahner, *Meditations on Priestly Life*.

143. The first such claim to appear in print was from Karl Fischer; see Fischer, *Der Mensch als Geheimnis*. As Endean notes, this work, which began as a doctoral thesis, took up the claim made in a 1970 essay by Karl Lehmann that the guiding thread of Rahner's theology is the attempt to understand the reality and consequences of the experience of grace. As we have already seen, however, Rahner always associated questions concerning the "experienceability of grace" with the questions of the nature and experience of "Ignatian mysticism."

144. Rahner, "Rede des Ignatius," 373–74. All translations are my own. Some variant of this claim is repeated on almost every page, but see, in particular, 377, 380, 382, 394.

145. Ibid., 377.

146. Rahner, "Weihnacht im Licht der Exerzitien," in *SzT* 12:330. This is my translation; cf. Rahner, "Christmas in the Light of the Ignatian Exercises," in *TI* 16:4. The theme of "homelessness" is a common one in these late texts on Ignatius.

147. Rahner, "On the Hiddenness of God," in *TI* 16:227–43, and Rahner, "An Investigation on the Incomprehensibility of God in St. Thomas Aquinas," in *TI* 16:244–54. These essays date from 1974.

148. See Gaspar Martinez, *Confronting the Mystery of God: Political, Liberation, and Public Theologies* (New York: Continuum, 2001), 1–20.

149. See Rahner, "The Doctrine of the 'Spiritual Senses' in the Middle Ages," in *TI* 16:104–34; 117–27 deal with "ecstasy." The material in this section was first published in 1934, and it goes back almost a decade earlier; see Endean, *Karl Rahner*, 24–29.

150. Rahner, "The Doctrine of the 'Spiritual Senses' in the Middle Ages," 118–20.

151. Ibid., 123.

152. Ibid., 128–31.

153. Cf., for instance, Rahner, "Rede des Ignatius," 381: "Without God we would wander around anxiously and eternally uncertain within the realm of our freedom and our decisions, since anything we might choose is after all finally something finite and can always be superseded by something else, and thus remains equivalent. Yet my experience was that in the sphere of my own freedom and its possibilities the infinitely free God embraced this before that one among them with God's special love, allowed it to be transparent to Godself, in distinction from the others, in such a way that it did not disguise God but rather allowed it to be loved in God and God in it and in this way was shown to be the 'will of God.'"

154. Rahner, "Unmittelbare Gotteserfahrung in den Exerzitien," 27 (my translation); cf. *Karl Rahner in Dialogue*, 176.

155. Rahner, "Unmittelbare Gotteserfahrung in den Exerzitien," 28.

156. See Rahner, "Rede des Ignatius," 379. Using the metaphor of drawing water from a well goes back, of course, to John's Gospel (John 4), as Rahner

himself says. It can also be found in Origen, Bernard of Clairvaux, Bonaventure, and Teresa of Avila, among many others. He may have taken the image of the two sources of water from Teresa of Avila's *Interior Castle* in her description of the fourth dwelling places. See Teresa of Avila, *The Interior Castle*, 74.

157. Ibid. Recall that in this essay Rahner is having Ignatius address Jesuits; thus, "your theologians" refers to Jesuit theology.

158. Ibid., 380.

159. Rahner, "A New Task for Fundamental Theology," in *TI* 16:156–66.

160. Ibid., 165. In an interesting note, Rahner suggests that Pierre Rousselot, one of the "fathers" of transcendental Thomism, investigated the possibility, "almost unconsciously," of translating Ignatius's rules for election and discernment into a method for fundamental theology (ibid., 163n8).

161. Ibid., 166 (translation emended).

162. Rahner, "Moderne Frömmigkeit und Exerzitienerfahrung," in *SzT* 12:176. In some cases, I will offer my own translations of this work, giving the relevant page in the English translation: Rahner, "Modern Piety and the Experience of Retreats," in *TI* 16:138. This was originally a talk given to retreat directors in Vienna in 1974.

163. "Moderne Frömmigkeit und Exerzitienerfahrung," 181, my translation (English translation, 142).

164. "Moderne Frömmigkeit und Exerzitienerfahrung," 186, my translation (English translation, 146).

165. Rahner, "Unmittelbare Gotteserfahrung," 29. Rahner freely admits that when he himself presented the Spiritual Exercises in the 1950s, he did not really present them authentically as a structured occasion for the individual to encounter God in solitude (ibid.); cf. Rahner, *Spiritual Exercises*, 8–9.

166. Rahner, "Modern Piety and the Exercise of Retreats," 146. This is for Rahner essential if the human race is to successfully manage the global crises that threaten its very survival.

167. Ibid., 146.

168. Ibid., 145–46.

169. Ibid., 152–53.

170. See Rahner, "Rede des Ignatius," 378–80.

171. Rahner, "Ignatius of Loyola."

172. Rahner, "Rede des Ignatius," 387–88.

173. Rahner, "Ignatius of Loyola," 336, 338.

174. Ibid., 336; cf. Rahner, "Rede des Ignatius," 388–90.

175. See Metz, *Followers of Christ*. Rahner has Ignatius cite Metz by name and refer to this text (Rahner, "Rede des Ignatius," 391).

176. See *Documents of the 31st and 32nd General Congregations of the Society of Jesus* (St. Louis: Institute of Jesuit Sources, 1977).

177. We will visit this controversy in greater detail when we deal with Pope Francis in chapter 6.

178. Rahner, "Rede des Ignatius," 391–92.

179. Rahner, *Karl Rahner in Dialogue*, 188.

180. On this, see Rubbelke, "A Constant Closeness to *This* God."

181. Metz, *A Passion for God*, 32.

182. Rahner, "Ignatian Mysticism," 287. This passage is identical in the original 1937 lecture-text.

183. See the discussion in the section titled "Early Engagement with Ignatian Spirituality: 'Ignatian Mysticism of Joy in the World.'" The tentativeness of Rahner's introduction of the term is perhaps indicated by his placing it in scare quotes.

184. Rahner, *Spiritual Exercises*, 130–31.

185. Ibid., 129 (my translation); cf. Rahner, *Betrachtungen zum ignatianischen Exerzitienbuch*, 132.

186. Rahner, *Spiritual Exercises*, 119. Rahner cites the controversies over the imitation of Jesus's poverty among the first generations of followers of Francis of Assisi.

187. Ibid., 120–23. Rahner's portrait of the "historical Jesus" here sounds very much like Harnack's in his well-known 1900 lectures on "the essence of Christianity." Jesus's life is "scandalous" in its utter everydayness. Jesus is not concerned with politics or science. He lives an unremarkable life on those standards. He was not like ascetics who live life out of *ressentiment*. He is, rather, the indifferent man par excellence.

188. For a fuller account of this Christological approach, see Endean, *Karl Rahner and Ignatian Spirituality*, 116–23, at the conclusion of which he puzzles over "why, in other contexts, Rahner remains almost silent on Christ's role in Ignatian discernment" (ibid., 123). Rahner does return briefly to the "thickly" historical character of Jesus in his last major essay on Ignatius: see Rahner, "Rede des Ignatius," 384–86.

189. On Heidegger in this regard, see Caputo, *The Mystical Element in Heidegger's Thought*.

190. Zahlauer, *Karl Rahner und sein "produktivisches Vorbild."*

191. Rahner, *Karl Rahner in Dialogue*, 191.

192. See Rahner, "Rede de Ignatius," 405–7.

193. If Rahner is "optimistic" about the prospects of Christianity in the modern world, and of the modern world itself, it is a cruciform optimism, as Rahner makes clear in the retreat talk he gave on the prayer exercise of Ignatius's that is, on the surface, most supremely optimistic about God's presence in the world: the Contemplation to Attain Love: "Truly to find God in the hard, cruel, divided, and threatening world, despite and even because the world's oppressive contradictions to search out a reconciliation in love—a person can only do that if he does not shun the cross of the Savior, and if he believes in God's love, even though he himself must hang on a cross in this world. Finding God in all things and experiencing the transparency of things toward God is accomplished only by the person who meets this God at the point where He descended into utter darkness and abandonment: on the cross of Jesus Christ!" (Rahner, *Spiritual Exercises*, 271–72).

CHAPTER FIVE

An earlier version of portions of this chapter appeared in Ashley, "Ignacio Ellacuría and the *Spiritual Exercises* of Ignatius Loyola." I am grateful for the permission of the editors of *Theological Studies* to reuse some of that material. I am also very grateful to Michael E. Lee, Kevin Burke, SJ, and Robert Lassalle-Klein for extensive comments on an earlier draft of this chapter.

1. The following account of the "province retreat" is taken from Lassalle-Klein, *Blood and Ink*, 32–52, and Beirne, *Jesuit Education and Social Change in El Salvador*, 84–87.

2. "El tercer mundo como lugar óptimo de la vivencia de los *Ejercicios*" (*ET* 4:222). Ellacuría's theological works, some of them otherwise unpublished, have been gathered in four volumes of *Escritos teológicos* as a part of his collected works. I will generally cite from these volumes, abbreviating as *ET* and the volume number. In some cases, I will also cite from other sources that might be more generally available (such as the *Revista Latinoamericana de Teología*). All translations from the Spanish are my own unless otherwise noted.

3. Ellacuría even suggests that were Ignatius to rewrite the meditation on the Kingdom today, he would use the example not of a feudal king proposing to his vassals the conquest of his enemies, but of coming to the service of the Third World (ibid.).

4. Ibid., 228–33.

5. Ellacuría, "El problema del traslado del espíritu de los *Ejercicios* a la Viceprovincia," *ET* 4:202–3.

6. For an overview of this transformation, see Gutiérrez, "The Meaning and Scope of Medellín," in *The Density of the Present: Selected Writings*, 59–101.

7. Latin American Provincials of the Society of Jesus, "The Jesuits in Latin America," 78.

8. The so-called *Deliberatio primorum Patrum*. See Toner, "The Deliberation That Started the Jesuits."

9. Lassalle-Klein, *Blood and Ink*, 49.

10. Ibid., 50.

11. The resistance became so vociferous that at one point the superior general of the Jesuits, Pedro Arrupe, intervened. See Beirne, *Jesuit Education*, 85–86. Arrupe supported the change in direction, but was concerned that it not be carried through a way that deepened divisions among the Central American Jesuits.

12. Lassalle-Klein, *Blood and Ink*, 48.

13. His changes provoked such a reaction that Arrupe felt compelled to order Ellacuría removed from that position less than four years later. Ellacuría turned his energies to the Central American University instead. See Whitfield, *Paying the Price*, 58–59.

14. See Cardenal, *Historia de una esperanza*, 103–8.

15. There had been discussions for some years of the Jesuits turning over control to the dioceses, but the discomfort engendered by Jesuits such as Grande and the new rector, Amando López, accelerated the process. Romero was named to be the new rector, but most of the administrative work was done by Freddy Delgado. The bishops executed a clean sweep not only of faculty but of students, with most of the theology and philosophy students being either sent elsewhere or dismissed. The seminary did not thrive under the new regime; indeed, it closed within a year. Romero later apologized to López for his role in the affair. López himself had been a compromise candidate when the Salvadoran bishops balked at

the Jesuits' nomination of Rutilio Grande as new rector. It was a very dispiriting experience for Grande, whose next assignment was as pastor in the church in Aguilares. See Brockman, *Romero: A Life*, 51–52.

16. Romero was once again at the center. The Jesuit provincial at the time, Miguel Estrada, had an angry confrontation with Romero, demanding to know why Romero had acted this way when Estrada and the staff of the *Externado* had kept Archbishop Chávez y González, Romero's ecclesial superior, fully informed of the changes that had been made. Romero was unmoved. Indeed, he was not pleased when Chávez y González instructed him to print the commission's report exonerating the high school in the diocesan paper. Romero gave only nominal obedience, while still attacking the Jesuits at the *Externado*. See Brockman, *Romero*, 48–49; Whitfield, *Paying the Price*, 53–55.

17. See Beirne, *Jesuit Education*, 126–27.

18. Whitfield, *Paying the Price*, 243, 251–53. For another account of Ellacuría's vision and activity as university president, and an interpretation of how it could be applied today, see Quinn, "Is a Different Kind of Jesuit University Possible Today"?

19. The editorial was titled "A sus órdenes, mi capital," which loosely translates as "Aye, aye, my capital!" See Whitfield, *Paying the Price*, 66–70; Beirne, *Jesuit Education*, 129–135.

20. In June 1977, for instance, a right-wing death squad called the "White Warriors Union" issued a blanket proclamation threatening death to any Jesuit who did not leave the country within thirty days. See Whitfield, *Paying the Price*, 109–10.

21. For a brief introduction to Rutilio Grande, including the transformative effect of his martyrdom on Romero, see Brackley, "Rutilio and Romero: Martyrs for Our Time." For a biography, see Cardenal, *Historia de una esperanza*. On Grande's broader influence on the Salvadoran Church, see Kelly, *The Gospel Grows Feet*.

22. The story of the Romero's remarkable conversion that came at the beginning of his three years as archbishop of San Salvador, albeit prepared by his years as bishop of the diocese of Santiago de Maria, has been told elsewhere; see Lee, *Revolutionary Saint*. On Maura Clark, Dorothy Kazel, Ita Ford, and Jean Donovan, see Noone, *The Same Fate as the Poor*; Carrigan, *Salvador Witness*; Glavac, *In the Fullness of Life*; Ford, *Here I Am, Lord*; Markey, *A Radical Faith*.

23. See Ellacuría, "Is a Different Kind of University Possible?"

24. The best accounts of Ellacuría's career set against the backdrop of his Central American political context and his institutional setting as Rector of the Jesuits' university in Salvador may be found in Whitfield, *Paying the Price*, and Lassalle-Klein, *Blood and Ink*. For an introduction to his theology, with extensive notes and bibliography, see Burke, *The Ground beneath the Cross*. A recent collection on various dimensions of Ellacuría's thought may be found in Burke and Lassalle-Klein, eds., *Love That Produces Hope*. Among the more helpful introductions in Spanish are Sobrino and Alvarado, eds., *Ignacio Ellacuría*; Samour, *Voluntad de liberación*; Sols Lucia, *La teología histórica de Ignacio Ellacuría*. See also the essays collected in Ashley, Burke, and Cardenal, eds., *A Grammar of Justice*.

25. This is the principal claim Ellacuría makes in an essay he wrote for students beginning the study of philosophy, "What Is the Point of Philosophy?"

26. For biographical information on Ellacuría, see Burke, *Ground beneath the Cross*, 15–42. See also Whitfield, *Paying the Price*, 15–70, and Sols Lucia, *La teología histórica*, 21–47.

27. Elizondo was at various times novice master, spiritual director, provincial, and tertian director (tertianship is the final one-year period of Jesuit training). Among other things, he also directed Romero in the full thirty-day retreat in the mid-1950s.

28. Sols Lucia, *La teología histórica*, 21.

29. Interview with Cesar Jeréz, in Whitfield, *Paying the Price*, 21.

30. Ibid., 24. The novice to which Whitfield refers and whom she quotes is Cesar Jeréz, who was provincial during the late 1970s, when Romero was archbishop and Grande was murdered.

31. Sols Lucia points out that another formative figure in Ellacuría's training was Ángel Martínez Baigorri, a Jesuit poet, who inspired in him an abiding love of poetry. See Sols Lucia, *La teología histórica*, 23. On Martínez's importance, see Prevot, *Thinking Prayer*, 258–61.

32. Maier, "Karl Rahner: The Teacher of Ignacio Ellacuría."

33. "Historia de la salvación," in *ET* 1:604. The last sentence is quoted by Maier, "Karl Rahner," 138.

34. Ellacuría, *Conversión de la Iglesia al Reino de Dios*, 266; cited in Maier, "Karl Rahner," 136. This is the core insight that finds expression in the important concept of "historicization," to which we will turn in due course.

35. Ellacuría, "Pedro Arrupe, renovador de la vida religiosa," esp. 6–9.

36. Ibid., 12.

37. Ibid. (emphasis original). For further discussion of Arrupe's influence on Ellacuría, see Burke, *Ground beneath the Cross*, 25–26.

38. Sobrino, "Ignacio Ellacuría: El hombre y el cristiano," 86.

39. Burke, *Ground beneath the Cross*, 24.

40. Cited in ibid.; see Sobrino, "Ignacio Ellacuría," 86.

41. Sobrino, "Ignacio Ellacuría," 85.

42. Rahner, "Logic of Concrete Individual Knowledge," 86.

43. I rely here on Samour, "Filosofía y libertad," in Sobrino and Alvarado, eds., *Ignacio Ellacuría*, 103–49; Samour, *Voluntad de liberación*. See also Burke, *Ground beneath the Cross*, 43–99; Lee, *Bearing the Weight of Salvation*; Lassalle-Klein, *Blood and Ink*, 201–27; and Prevot, *Thinking Prayer*, 248–79. On Zubiri as a fundamental theologian, see Shah, "Disciplining Theology."

44. Ellacuría, "La superación del reduccionismo idealista," 409.

45. See Samour, *Voluntad de liberación*, 45–46 (translations of Samour are mine).

46. In this sense, Zubiri's open materialist realism is not unlike the position outlined by Rahner, "Christology within an Evolutionary View of the World," in which he argues that the human "soul," as the marker of transcendence (whose ultimate term is God Godself), is not an "addition" to the human body but, precisely as spirit, is an actualization of a potency immanent to matter. In this sense, Rahner suggests, one can affirm that the human being as a whole is a result of evolution (and not just the physical form, as Pius XII had maintained in 1950 in *Humani generis*, 36).

47. Zubiri and Ellacuría distinguish between the verbs *inteligir*, *conocer*, and

entender. The first is cognate with the English noun "intelligence." The latter two can be translated "to know" and "to understand." I shall follow Kevin Burke in translating the first term as "apprehend intelligently."

48. Samour, *Voluntad de liberación*, 49.
49. Ellacuría, "Laying the Foundations of Latin American Theological Method."
50. Ibid., 79.
51. Ibid., 80 (emphasis original). The idioms in the original text that operate with cognates of the Spanish *cargo* and *cargar* are virtually untranslatable into English. Other translations have been proposed, some of which flow more naturally in English. The advantage of the one proposed here (first crafted by Kevin Burke) is that it carries over the tight connection between the three "moments" of the engagement of reality, which Ellacuría expressed by using the closely related terms, *cargar, cargo*, and *encargarse*.
52. Ibid.
53. Ellacuría, "Laying the Foundations," 82.
54. According to Héctor Samour and Antonio González, this shift of emphasis from reality to *historical* reality represents the key point at which Ellacuría went beyond his teacher, Xavier Zubiri; see Samour, "Filosofía y libertad," 108–9; González, "Assessing the Philosophical Achievement of Ignacio Ellacuría," in Burke and Lassalle-Klein, eds., *Love That Produces Hope*, 80.
55. These have tended to be the privileged vantage points in modernity, leading to recurring conflicts between materialism, with its focus on material reality, and idealism, with its focus on individual subjectivity.
56. Samour, "Filosofía y libertad," 104. These appropriations then make new possibilities available for a subsequent appropriation: a process Ellacuría names "possibilitization."
57. Ellacuría, *Filosfía de la realidad histórica*, 169. I am grateful to Robert Lassalle-Klein for bringing this dimension of historicization to my attention and for the citation from *Filosfía de la realidad histórica*.
58. It is usually clear which sense of historicization Ellacuría has in mind when he uses the term. The fact that there is some ambiguity or overlap in usages, however, indicates that Ellacuría (following Zubiri) will not make a clean distinction between human life (at which historicization in the first sense given above is at work) and thought (in which this sense comes to the fore). This is not the place to carry on a detailed comparison of Rahner and Ellacuría, but I am tempted to propose that the place that "existentiality" played in the later (from the 1950s forward) description that Rahner gave of the human condition is taken in Ellacuría by the notion of historicization.
59. One thinks here of the classic discussion of the relationship of ideology to utopia in Karl Mannheim's book by that name. For a discussion of this historical line of thought, see Ricoeur, *Lectures on Ideology and Utopia*.
60. Ellacuría, "The Historicization of the Concept of Property," 109 (emphasis original).
61. For Ellacuría's critical contextualization (historicization) of human rights, see Ellacuría, "Historicización de los derechos humanos."
62. I make this distinction as a heuristic device. Ellacuría was firmly opposed

to any rigid dichotomy between nature and history, but his solution was not so much to "naturalize" history (as, say, sociobiologists tend to do), but to "historicize" nature.

63. Sobrino frequently expresses this insight theologically in these terms: "There is also, finally, *human hubris*—the tendency to manipulate the truth and suppress it for our own advantage. According to Paul's dialectic in Romans 1:18ff., the original act of oppressing the truth results in the darkening of the heart. Then the original lie leads to the institutionalized lie" (Sobrino, *Principle of Mercy*, 35).

64. Ellacuría, "What Is the Point of Philosophy?," 18 (emphasis original).

65. On Zubiri's complicated relationship to theology, see Shah, "Disciplining Theology," 86–95. As Shah notes, Ellacuría named his teacher a "theologal philosopher" (100).

66. Ellacuría, "The Historicity of Christian Salvation," henceforth, "Historicity." This essay is translated by Margaret Wilde. When I offer my own translations, I will use the Spanish version in *ET* 1:535–96. The essay appeared originally in the very first issue of the theological journal that Ellacuría founded in 1984 as rector of the UCA, *La Revista Latinoamericana de Teología*. Ellacuría produced this essay in an ecclesial atmosphere tense with expectation of the imminent publication of a document from the Congregation for the Doctrine of the Faith (CDF) in Rome that would be highly critical of liberation theology. Thus, he wrote it with extreme care in order to parry critiques already mounted, and others that he knew would be forthcoming. For these reasons, this essay can well serve as a precis of his understanding of liberation theology.

67. Ellacuría, "Historicity," 138.

68. International Theological Commission, "Declaration on Human Development and Christian Salvation."

69. Thus, even though Ellacuría conceded, indeed insisted, that the theology of liberation was a theology from and for the Latin American continent, its fundamental structures were of more universal scope for any theology that wanted to take history seriously. For a sustained argument for this thesis, see Sols Lucia, *La teología historica de Ignacio Ellacuría*.

70. Ellacuría, "Historicity," 146 (my translation); see *ET* 1:571.

71. Ibid., 142

72. Ibid., 142, 150. Here one can already discern a strong "elective affinity" between Ignatian spirituality and Ellacuría's historical soteriology. Ignatius makes the same point when it comes to God's action in the soul. The "intervention" of the good Spirit, that is to say, the way that God "deals immediately" with the human soul, is fundamentally different when the context is predominantly one of sin, as opposed to one of grace. This is why the rules for discernment are different for the First Week, when a person is trying to free herself or himself from a context dominated by sin, in contrast to the rules for the Second Week, when she or he is growing more fully into a life oriented by the love of God and neighbor.

73. Ibid., 150–53. The precise nature of this presence will become clearer when we consider Ellacuría's interpretation of the Fourth Week of the *Spiritual Exercises* and its Contemplation to Attain Love.

74. Ibid., 151. The difficulties of speaking about creation, along with the solution worked out by Aquinas, are helpfully discussed in Burrell, *Freedom and Creation in Three Traditions*.

75. Ibid. (my translation, see *ET* 1:578). I use "giving-itself-shape" to render *plasmación*. This is a very difficult noun to translate. As Michael Lee notes, it is the nominal form of the verb *plasmar*, which has a variety of meanings, including "giving form to something" and "giving expression to" or "reflecting or representing an idea or feeling in a physical form." See Lee, *Bearing the Weight of Salvation*, 57; 183n97.

76. Ellacuría, "Historicity, 151 (my translation) (*ET* 1:578).

77. Ibid., 152 (my translation) (*ET* 1:578–79).

78. Ibid. (my translation) (*ET* 1:579).

79. Zubiri coined the word "*religación*" to express this "being-tied-back-to" that is constitutive of human being as *personal* being. It is a neologism consciously chosen for its connection with *religión*. Religion, on this view, is itself the *plasmación*, the expression or giving shape *ad extra* of the Trinitarian life into this most intimate human reality. For a more detailed analysis of this, and of the discursive strategies whereby Zubiri and Ellacuría seek to avoid having this scheme collapse into pantheism or a gnostic emanationist scheme, see Lee, "Liberation Theology's Transcendent Moment." For an analysis of Zubiri's use of *religación*, in particular, against a backdrop of a fundamental theology that sheds light on Ellacuría's project, see Shah, "Disciplining Theology," 118–48.

80. Ellacuría, "Historicity," 153. Of course, this frustration is only penultimate. The presence of the Trinitarian life cannot ultimately be excised or paralyzed; rather, that presence takes the form of prophetic denunciation, hopeful annunciation, and the bearing of sin that has the paschal mystery as its paradigmatic instance. In his own life, Ellacuría found this in Romero. Hence his observation: "With Oscar Romero God passed through El Salvador" can be parsed in this way. God continued to be present in the Salvadoran reality, marked as it was by sin: especially the root-sin of idolatry (of national security, of wealth, of armed force) that Romero so frequently uncovered and denounced in Salvadoran society.

81. Ibid., 154. Elsewhere he calls theology "the ideological moment of Christian ecclesial praxis," using ideology in its nonpejorative sense as the necessary conceptual and ideational self-reflection by human beings on their action that must accompany any genuinely human praxis. See Ellacuría, "Theology as the Ideological Moment of Christian Ecclesial Praxis," in *Ignacio Ellacuría*, 255–73.

82. Ellacuría, "Historicity," 154.

83. See the essays collected in three large volumes: *Veinte años de historia en El Salvador*.

84. See, above all, Ellacuría, "The Crucified People." The prior discussions of what Ellacuría means by "history" and "historical" can serve to alert one as to the complexity of an *historical* soteriology.

85. Ellacuría, "Historicity," 158.

86. See his concluding presentation at the retreat of Central American Jesuits in Ellacuría, "El tercer mundo como lugar óptimo de la vivencia cristiana de los *Ejercicios*," esp. 227–28. Also, as early as 1969, Ellacuría manifested a preference for the Suffering Servant Songs in Second Isaiah as a way of articulating this scheme (ibid., 219).

87. Ellacuría, "Historicity," 160.

88. Ibid., 163–64.

89. It should be emphasized again that God is always present, even in contexts of sin, but the mode of that presence (the form that God's grace may take) will differ—that presence is configured according to the scheme of cross-resurrection.

90. See, Ellacuría, "The Church of the Poor," and Ellacuría, "The Crucified People."

91. The more primordial human labor of historicization, which is a "making of history from nature and with nature" (Ellacuría, *Filosfía de la realidad histórica*, 169) is the praxis of the church as the people of God as a whole, in which theology contributes in the way specific to it through "historicizing" concepts and practices in order to enable the church as a whole to "historicize" by turning history more in the direction of the Kingdom of God.

92. However much there are structural similarities between Ellacuría's articulation of what ideology critique is about and Marx's, or ideology critique as worked out in the different variants of post-Marxian critical theory, it should be emphasized here that Ellacuría's theory of ideology critique rests firmly on Zubiri's philosophy, as he (Ellacuría) extended it into a philosophy of historical reality. This is not to claim immunity from critique, but simply to assert that a critique of Ellacuría's approach based on affinities to Marxism will be wide of the mark unless it takes into account the underlying *Zubirian* structure, particularly with its "thickly" Trinitarian theism.

93. Ellacuría, "A Latin American Reading of the *Spiritual Exercises* of Saint Ignatius." Henceforth "Latin American Reading."

94. Ibid., 206. Both senses of historicization given above are in play here.

95. Ibid., 208.

96. Ibid.

97. Ibid., 206.

98. Ibid., 207.

99. Ibid., 239n5, where he footnotes Rahner, "The Logic of Concrete Individual Knowledge in Ignatius Loyola."

100. See Ellacuría, "Tesis Sobre Posibilidad, Necesidad y Sentido de una Teología Latinoamericana."

101. Ellacuría, "Latin American Reading," 205–6.

102. Ibid., 207–8.

103. Ibid., 208.

104. Ibid.

105. Ibid. This appeal to the historical Jesus requires careful interpretation to avoid confusing it with appeals to "the historical Jesus" in any of the "quests for the historical Jesus." See the next section.

106. Ibid., 211.

107. Ibid., 212.

108. This reproduces in his interpretation of the *Spiritual Exercises* the claim he made in "Historicity of Christian Salvation," that the most appropriate framework for understanding transcendence in history is not constructed by the dyad of nature/supernature, but the dyad of sin/grace.

109. This is for Ellacuría the significance of Ignatius's inclusion of the sin of the angels (Ellacuría, "Latin American Reading," 214). Some contextual light can be shed by noting that Ellacuría is intervening here in a debate in Latin America

concerning "development" (these lectures were composed and given not long after the conclusion of the "decade of development"). He here registers his deep and oft-stated disagreement with "theologies of development" and their counterparts in political theory and economic policy. Such theories either asserted or assumed that Latin America was simply "underdeveloped" and had to "catch up" with the more developed first world. The theological interpretive rule that Ellacuría claims to derive here from Ignatius is that historical process is never only the development of a good always already there, but, as infected by sin, the reversal of an evil. History, just as much as the individual, always stands in need of conversion.

110. "A Meditation Using the Three Powers of the Soul about the First, Second, and Third Sins" (*SpEx* 45–54).

111. Thus: "The cross of Jesus is the world's act of negating God and it is God's act of negating the world; in both cases it is a matter of an historical negation, even though it has a significance that exceeds history" (Ellacuría, "Latin American Reading," 216).

112. Ibid., 217, 218.

113. Ibid., 218.

114. Ibid.,

115. Ibid., 217.

116. Or perhaps it might be more precise to say that the praxis of Christian discipleship (rather than theological conceptualization and argument alone) best reflects the complex, threefold phenomenon of human sentient intelligence, discussed earlier as it engages the historical reality of God's action in history, decisively and unsurpassably mediated by Jesus.

117. Ibid.

118. Ibid., 221.

119. Here Ellacuría plays on the Spanish words for "follow" (*seguir*) and "continue" (*proseguir*).

120. See Ellacuría's opening remarks in these lectures on "the Christian necessity of rendering theology and pastoral practice Latin American" (Ellacuría, "Latin American Reading," 204). In these remarks one can detect Ellacuría's running dispute with those who accused him of reducing Christian theological analysis and action to Marxist analysis and revolutionary praxis. He also objects, however, to those who see this work as "something that has to develop here and now in complete dependence on social-economic and cultural reality," because they "do not take the proper character of Christian salvation seriously enough" (ibid.).

121. Ellacuría, "Latin American Reading," 221.

122. After his comment at the end of the fourth lecture, concerning the need for an historical discernment of spirits, he concludes by asserting that "the orienting principles of this discernment are already there" (ibid.). This provides the segue into the Meditation on the Two Standards as the place where these criteria are "already there."

123. Ibid., 223. Later he will speak of a culture with values that either promote or render unexceptionable the existence of vast majorities that confront death-dealing poverty, as a "possessed culture" (225).

124. Ibid., 222.

125. Ibid., 223.

126. Ibid., 221.

127. Ibid., 223.

128. See Matthew 4:1–11; Luke 4:1–13. Just a year earlier he had published a book in which he focused on those temptations: see Ellacuría, *Freedom Made Flesh*, 56–60.

129. See Ellacuría, "Las bienaventuranzas, carta fundamental de la Iglesia de los pobres," in *Conversión de la Iglesia al Reino de Dios*, 129–51.

130. Ellacuría, "Latin American Reading," 222.

131. This was a point that Ellacuría had pressed with great vigor in his talks before and during the 1969 province retreat.

132. Ellacuría, "Latin American Reading," 224.

133. Ibid., 225.

134. Ibid., 226–30.

135. Ibid., 227.

136. Ibid., 229.

137. Ibid., 231.

138. Ibid., 232.

139. Ibid., 234. In both cases, the preposition "for" translates *por*, which can also be translated "because of" or "due to." Keeping this plurality of possible meanings in mind we should not automatically read the second affirmation ("Jesus died 'for' our sins") in terms of an atonement soteriology (which is what the English "died for our sins" almost always leads to). On the whole Ellacuría is suspicious of this kind of soteriology, even though he does not reject it tout court.

140. Ibid.

141. Ellacuría, "Latin American Reading," 235–39. Sobrino gives a fuller elaboration on this theme, under the rubric of "living like already resurrected ones" in Sobrino, *Christ the Liberator*, 74–78.

142. Ellacuría, "Latin American Reading," 235.

143. Ibid.

144. As we have seen, the most graphic and horrifying instantiation of this is named as such by Ellacuría in his essay on the global, scandalous presence of the poor as "the crucified people."

145. Ellacuría, "Latin American Reading," 236; cf. *SpEx* 231, 232.

146. Ellacuría, "Latin American Reading," 236. The still ongoing confrontation with policies focusing on the "development" of the Third World is evident in this quote. The clear implication is that this development is not manifesting or resulting in a "communication" of nature's gifts with all the people of Latin America.

147. Ibid., 237.

148. This is itself, of course, part of a long Christian tradition of interrelating the *vita contemplativa* and the *vita activa*. For an analysis of Ellacuría's place in that tradition, see Ashley, "Contemplation in the Action of Justice."

149. Ibid., 238.

150. "Dios se hace presente al hombre haciendo y el hombre hace presente a Dios y se hace presente a Dios haciendo" (Ellacuría, "Lectura latinoamericana," in *ET* 4:146). Perhaps the following, more awkward English translation is appropriate, not only for the way it captures the interrelations, but also for the way it

emphasizes that "acting" for Ellacuría is always a historical action that "makes," that gives rise to a concrete result, that historicizes: "God makes Godself present to the person making and the person makes God present and makes him- or herself present to the God making."

151. Ibid., 239.

152. Ignacio Ellacuría, *Fe y Justicia*, 210 (my translation).

153. Ellacuría, "Latin American Reading," 234.

154. Meier, "Bible as a Source for Theology," 7. For a summary overview of critiques of liberation theology's use of the Bible, see McGovern, *Liberation Theology and Its Critics*, 62–82. Sobrino's own response to these sorts of critique may be found in Sobrino, *Jesus the Liberator*, 36–63.

155. Ellacuría, "The Church of the Poor," 228. Note again Ellacuría's play on the Spanish words *seguir* (follow) and *proseguir* (continue).

156. Ibid. (translation slightly emended). For the Spanish original, see Ellacuría, "La Iglesia de los Pobres," 127.

157. Ellacuría, *Freedom Made Flesh*, 26 (emphasis added and translation emended); cf. *Teología Política*, 13.

158. Ignatius followed the established medieval tradition of referring to them by this name (see, for example, *SpEx* 261).

159. Ascetical theology was contrasted with mystical theology, which concerned extraordinary divine gifts of mystical rapture and the like (the unitive way). See Sheldrake, *Spirituality and History*, 44–47. The terminology of spiritual, ascetical, and mystical theology dominated Roman Catholic seminaries during the time when Ellacuría studied theology.

160. Ellacuría, "Latin American Reading," 217.

161. See Blondel, "History and Dogma." Ellacuría left behind an unfinished manuscript on Blondel, composed in the early 1960s, that shows his early concern with this issue: "Introducción al problema del milagro en Blondel."

162. For a recent text by a scripture scholar that intends to do precisely this, see Neyrey, *Imagining Jesus in His Own Culture*.

163. For a different but complementary argument for this claim, see Tracy, *The Analogical Imagination*, 238–39. To respond in a rather polemical way to Meier's own polemical remarks, not only would it prove impossible for any theologian to draw on the Bible exclusively by means of historical Jesus research, but *any* realized knowledge of Jesus would have to move beyond the "the historical Jesus." In a more constructive vein, it seems clear that the problem here lies in what is meant by "historical Jesus." Neither Ellacuría nor Sobrino uses it with the reconstructions created by modern scripture scholars in mind. The deep metaphysical resonances of the adjective "historical" in Ellacuría's work make it clear that "the historical Jesus" cannot be for him a construction governed by the rather thin positivism that characterizes the historical Jesus project. Sobrino says as much in his later Christology (see Sobrino, *Jesus the Liberator*, 60–63). For a careful discussion of the problematic terminology surrounding "the historical Jesus," and a counterproposal, see Schneiders, "Preface to the Second Edition," in *Revelatory Text*, xvii–xl. I would propose that what she names the "proclaimed Jesus" would correspond in Ellacuría's system to "the historicized Jesus."

164. Haight, *Dynamics of Theology*, 207–8.
165. Sobrino, *Principle of Mercy*, 3.
166. Haight, *Dynamics*, 208.
167. Jennings, *Christian Imagination*, 4.
168. Ibid., 5.
169. Ibid., 6–7. And he adds (as a student, professor, and academic dean) that "one crucial site where I have watched the display of this interrupted social imagination is in the theological academy" (7).
170. And tied closely to this is a healing of memory, given the close linkage of memory and imagination. Both memory and imagination are inherently creative. Memory reconfigures and reorchestrates the past for the sake of the imagination's work of projecting a different, more creative future.
171. Ellacuría, "Utopia and Propheticism from Latin America," 11. This was Ellacuría's last theological writing, written in 1989, the year of his death, after more than twenty years of labor for a society more worthy of and welcoming to human beings.
172. Ibid., 33–55.
173. Ibid., 13.
174. Ibid.
175. See Ellacuría, "Is a Different Kind of University Possible?"
176. Lassalle-Klein shows the deep paradigm shift—a shift of imagination—regarding the function and *telos* of the UCA that arose out of the fundamental reimagining of 1969: a shift from "developmentalism" to an option for the poor that operated out of a paradigm of liberation. See Lassalle-Klein, *Blood and Ink*, 53–101.
177. On this reading, it does indeed seem more appropriate, as Toner and Endean suggest, to understand all three "times" for making an election as complementary and, indeed, as approaches that interpenetrate one another. The third time, in particular, makes use of the imagination, but is not without affective elements, and a full application of discernment in the second time would require some considerations of the "objects" (which would be the imaginative renderings of the different futures) that are arousing either consolation or desolation. This certainly seemed to be the case in Ignatius's own discernment on his sickbed in Loyola between a future as a knight in the courts of Spain or as a "knight" in the divine court. Moreover, the kinds of precisions about "spiritual consolation" that Toner and McDermott advocate also find a powerful context of application, even if I would continue to suggest that the kind of mourning and lamentation that belong to the prophetic healing of imagination should be included under the category of "spiritual consolation."
178. "The Contemplation to Attain Love shows—from the perspective of faith—the real possibility of finding God in creation and the possibility of recovering creation as the presence of God" (Ellacuría, "Latin American Reading," 236).
179. He could and did, however, deploy powerful images: most famously, his imagining of the poor as "the crucified people" (see Ellacuría, "The Crucified People: An Essay in Historical Soteriology"). And we need to keep in mind the importance of the poetic imagination for Ellacuría, which was awakened by his studies with Aurelia Espinoza Pólit in Quito, and was further nourished by the

poet Ángel Martínez. On the latter, see Prevot, *Thinking Prayer*, 259–61.

180. Sobrino, "Monseñor Romero's Impact on Ignacio Ellacuría," 57.

181. In a panel discussion with Sobrino and others, in which I presented on Ellacuría's interpretation of the *Spiritual Exercises*, Sobrino agreed with what I said, but then added, "You know, really what was much more important for him than the encounter with a text, even the text of the *Exercises*, was the encounter with *people*, and particularly with Romero."

182. Cardenal, "The Church of the Crucified People," 147.

183. See Sobrino, *Spirituality of Liberation*, and Sobrino, "Spirituality and the Following of Jesus." On Ignatian spirituality in particular, see Sobrino, "The Christ of the Ignatian Exercises."

184. See Sobrino, *Christ the Liberator*.

185. Ibid., 209–18.

186. Ibid., 215 (translation slightly emended); cf. Sobrino, *La fe en Jesucristo*, 309.

187. Sobrino, *Christ the Liberator*, 215–16. "Being honest to and with the real" corresponds closely to the first "moment" of sentient intelligence in Ellacuría's account: "realizing the weight of reality."

188. Ibid., 216 (emphasis original).

189. Ibid., 210.

190. Ibid., 212 (translation emended; emphasis original). See Sobrino, *La Fe en Jesucristo*, 305.

191. Sobrino, *Christ the Liberator*, 213.

192. Ibid., 214.

193. Sobrino, "Christ of the Ignatian Exercises," 401, 404.

194. *SpEx* 104.

195. See Ellacuría, "Historicity of Christian Salvation," 158–59.

196. Orthopathy clearly involves the aesthetic dimension of Christian faith, and could well provide the most fruitful point from which to develop an Ellacurian aesthetics that could be put into conversation with his erstwhile theological opponent, Hans Urs von Balthasar.

197. Sobrino, "Monseñor Romero's Impact on Ignacio Ellacuría," 57–76.

198. Ellacuría, "Monseñor Romero: One Sent by God to Save His People," 292.

199. This is from a homily that Ellacuría preached not long after Romero's death. See Sobrino, "Monseñor Romero's Impact on Ignacio Ellacuría," 66.

200. Ellacuría, "Latin American Reading," 219, 240.

201. Sobrino, "Monseñor Romero's Impact," 58.

202. Ibid., 60. Sobrino is citing here *Gaudium et spes*, 11.

203. See Ellacuría, "Latin American Reading," 219–20.

204. Looking ahead to Pope Francis, "being affected correctly by Jesus" is the principal topic of his apostolic exhortation *The Joy of the Gospel*, in which he begins by inviting "all Christians everywhere, at this very moment, to a renewed personal encounter with Jesus Christ, or at least an openness to letting him encounter them; I ask all of you to do this unfailingly each day. . . . May nothing inspire more than his life, which impels us onwards" (3).

205. Sobrino, "Monseñor Romero's Impact," 76, quoting the final words of

Ellacuría, "Utopia and Propheticism from Latin America," 55.

206. Chenu, *Une Ecole de Théologie*, 75; cited (translated into English) in Gutiérrez, *We Drink from Our Own Wells*, 147n2.

207. Cousins, "Franciscan Roots of Ignatian Spirituality," 52.

208. Ibid., 63.

209. Bonaventure, *Itinerarium mentis in Deum* 7.2. See Cousins, ed., *Bonaventure*, 112.

CHAPTER SIX

1. Vallely, *Pope Francis*, 155. See also Pope Francis, *A Big Heart Open to God*, 9.

2. General Congregation 32, Decree 2, 1–2. See Padberg, ed., *Jesuit Life & Mission Today*, 291.

3. Pope Francis, *A Big Heart Open to God*, 8.

4. Immediately after the passage quoted above, the decree goes on to specify being a companion of Jesus: "And what is it to be a companion of Jesus today? It is to engage, under the standard of the Cross, in the crucial struggle of our time: the struggle for faith and that struggle for justice which it includes" (Decree 2, §2). Padberg, ed., *Jesuit Life & Mission Today*, 291.

5. Francis, "Address to Representatives of the Communications Media," Vatican City, March 16, 2013, http://w2.vatican.va/content/francesco/en/speeches/2013/march/documents/papa-francesco_20130316_rappresentanti-media.html.

6. Pope Francis, *A Big Heart Open to God*, xx.

7. For the 2006 retreat, see Pope Francis, *In Him Alone Is Our Hope*. The early lectures and retreat conferences may be found in Papa Francisco, *Meditaciones para religiosos*.

8. See, for example, his reflections in "God Lives in the City," in Pope Francis, *Only Love Can Save Us*, 33–48.

9. There are a number of biographies of Pope Francis. I follow here primarily Ivereigh, *The Great Reformer*, and Vallely, *Pope Francis*. Also useful are Rubin and Ambrogetti, *Pope Francis: Conversations with Jorge*; and Piqué, *Pope Francis: Life and Revolution*. For an intellectual biography, see Borghesi, *The Mind of Pope Francis*.

10. See Ivereigh, *The Great Reformer*, 35–36, and Rubin and Ambrogetti, *Pope Francis*, 34. The way he describes it gives warrant to consider it under the category of the "first time" of making an election described in the *Spiritual Exercises* (175). The experience remained powerfully in his memory, such that when he chose an episcopal motto thirty-nine years later, he chose a line from a commentary of the Venerable Bede precisely on the call of Matthew: *miserando atque eligendo*.

11. He describes this illness as a crisis that "changed the way I saw life." See Pope Francis, *Let Us Dream*, 39.

12. Ivereigh, *The Great Reformer*, 69–71.

13. It is often called simply "the Máximo"; Ivereigh describes this massive community and its apostolates in these terms: "Set in a 120-acre estate, it had rooms for 180 Jesuits, a cavernous church, and endless little chapels for the priests to say their daily Mass on their own. For there was a large community of priests

and brothers there, in addition to the students.... Its main purpose, however, was study. The Máximo was one of the most important Catholic centers of teaching and research in South America: researchers and doctoral students came to use its immense world-class library and archive. Next door was the Jesuit-run National Observatory, and three buildings were dedicated to scientific research. There was an active printing press, which ran off the highly respected theology journal *Stromata*" (Ivereigh, *The Great Reformer*, 72).

14. On Fiorito's influence on the young Jesuit, see Ivereigh, *The Great Reformer*, 92–93, and Borghesi, *The Mind of Pope Francis*, 2–3, 9–12.

15. The journal is the *Boletín de Espiritualidad*. For a list of his publications in it, see Pope Francis, "Writings on Jesuit Spirituality I," 12. A number of these essays were translated in this issue of *Studies in the Spirituality of Jesuits* and in the following one: "Writings on Jesuit Spirituality II." Philip Endean's commentaries are particularly helpful in "Writings on Jesuit Spirituality I," 1–12, and in "Writings on Jesuit Spirituality II," 39–43.

16. Fessard, *La Dialectique des "Exercices spirituels" de saint Ignace de Loyola*. An extended summary and analysis of Fessard's interpretation is available in Pousset, *Life in Faith and Freedom*. See also Borghesi, *Mind of Pope Francis*, 6–12.

17. Pope Francis, *A Big Heart Open to God*, 23. Elsewhere he judges that he "did a few good things, but I could be very harsh" (Pope Francis, *Let Us Dream*, 41).

18. On Perón, see Vallely, *Pope Francis*, 31–33; Ivereigh, *The Great Reformer*, 18–30; and Klaiber, *The Church, Dictatorships, and Democracy in Latin America*, 70–75.

19. In his follow-up to *The Great Reformer*, Ivereigh suggests that many elements of Pope Francis's political strategies, whether it be with recalcitrant curial cardinals or with the media, were learned by observing Perón's political maneuverings in Argentina; see Ivereigh, *Wounded Shepherd*, 34–39.

20. Klaiber, *The Church, Dictatorships, and Democracy in Latin America*, 66. For a far more critical appraisal (including of the provincial, Bergoglio), see Fermin Mignone, *Witness to the Truth*.

21. In this, his was not unlike the stance and practice taken up by Oscar Romero as bishop of Santiago de Maria, a stance that changed dramatically when Romero was named archbishop of San Salvador and confronted the judicial murder of Rutilio Grande. On this change, see Lee, *Revolutionary Saint*, 57–60.

22. See Scavo, *Bergoglio's List*. See also Vallely, *Pope Francis*, 57–84; Ivereigh, *The Great Reformer*, 129–64.

23. Vallely, *Pope Francis*, 39.

24. According to Vallely, Bergoglio even tried to close the Institute at one point, but was overruled from Rome; see Vallely, *Pope Francis*, 49–50.

25. In a retreat that he preached to the Jesuits of Argentina, in language that could hardly be mistaken when it came to whom he had in mind, he said that "the worst thing that can happen to a human being is to let himself be swept away by the 'lights' of reason. He will end up being an ignorant intellectual or detached 'expert.' The mission for our minds, rather, is to discover the seeds of the Word in the midst of humanity, the *lógoi spermatikoí*"; see Papa Francisco, *Meditaciones para religiosos*, 134 (translation mine).

26. Their suspicions, which were shared by other Argentinian Jesuits, had

already been aroused when Bergoglio turned over one of the Jesuits' universities (the Universidad del Salvador) to a center-right Peronist group, the Iron Guard, in 1974. This was a decision for which, as one of Bergoglio's aides observed, "many Jesuits have never forgiven him." And matters were made worse when the university subsequently gave an honorary doctorate to Admiral Emilio Massera, one of the three members of the military junta that orchestrated the dirty wars. See Vallely, *Pope Francis*, 44–45. Ivereigh gives a more positive reading of this episode in Ivereigh, *The Great Reformer*, 104–6, 116–17, 148–49. As with so many episodes during this period, both accounts are plausible, and both have support from witnesses in Argentina at the time. Whatever his motivations, however, decisions like these polarized the province, and his "authoritarian" way of making them (his own word) alienated many.

27. The 32nd General Congregation met from December 1974 to March 1975, with Bergoglio present as provincial. Bergoglio's attitude toward its decrees, particularly Decree 4, "Our Mission Today: The Service of Faith and the Promotion of Justice," was complex. However, it is not unfair to generalize by saying that he was suspicious of Decree 4 in particular, and did not prioritize its implementation. See Valley, *Pope Francis*, 45–48; Ivereigh, *The Great Reformer*, 119–23. Bergoglio was not alone among Jesuits in worrying about seemingly putting the promotion of faith and of justice on the same level. He far preferred Paul VI's 1975 apostolic exhortation *Evangelii nuntiandi*, but he interpreted it by so focusing on the pope's insistence that evangelization has at its center the proclamation of Jesus Christ and the liberation from sin that he overlooked the equally strong insistence that evangelization "would not be complete if it did not take account of the unceasing interplay of the Gospel and of man's concrete life, both personal and social. That is why evangelization involves an explicit message, adapted to the different situations constantly being realized ... about international life, peace, justice and development–a message especially energetic today about liberation" (*Evangelii nuntiandi*, 29). I discuss Bergoglio's concerns about Decree 4 in the section below titled "Ignatian Spirituality: The Touchstone for Pope Francis's Intellectual Probings."

28. See Ivereigh, *The Great Reformer*, 151–64; Vallely, *Pope Francis*, 57–80. For the pope's own account of these events, see Ambrogetti and Rubin, *Pope Francis*, 203–8.

29. Pope Francis, *A Big Heart Open to God*, 23.

30. Ibid.

31. Pope Francis, *Let Us Dream*, 42.

32. Vallely, *Pope Francis*, 125. The mention of mercy is significant. From this point on this term, and what it represents, became more and more important for him.

33. The instructions on liberation theology from the Congregation for the Doctrine of the Faith were issued in the 1980s, but the campaign from Rome to rein in what were seen as excesses of liberation theology came to a head in the 1990s with Rome's assertion of control over the fourth meeting of Latin American bishops in Santo Domingo in 1992. See Ivereigh, *The Great Reformer*, 235–36. Ivereigh interprets this as an instance of Roman resistance to the collegiality represented by such regional meetings of bishops, but it is amply evident that the preferential

option for the poor, as articulated at Medellín and Puebla, was equally in the crosshairs, if not more so.

34. See Bergoglio, "Corruption and Sin," in *The Way of Humility*, 7–56. This essay was originally penned in 1991, while in Córdoba, reflecting on a particularly egregious instance of judicial corruption. He also comments on the difference between sin and corruption in Pope Francis, *The Name of God Is Mercy*, 81–88. He describes corruption in the latter as "not an act, but a condition, a personal and social state in which we become accustomed to living" (83). In some ways the category of corruption has become the way that the concepts of "structures of sin" and "social sin," which were seldom present in his earlier work, entered into his theological lexicon.

35. Quoted in Vallely, *Pope Francis*, 128. A debate over whether Bergoglio experienced "a conversion" while at Córdoba seems pointless; however, framing it in the terms that Lee suggests with respect to Romero's "conversion" is illuminating; see Lee, *Revolutionary Saint*, 44–85.

36. Quoted in Vallely, *Pope Francis*, 151–52.

37. Ibid.

38. See "Address of His Holiness Pope Francis to the 36th General Congregation of the Society of Jesus."

39. Ibid. (emphasis added). He is quoting here first from a homily he gave on January 3, 2014, the Feast of the Most Holy Name of Jesus, which is the titular feast of the Society of Jesus, and, second, from the *Constitutions*, §304. The quote from Nadal is in the same speech in which Nadal insisted that "the world is our house" (see O'Malley, "Some Distinctive Characteristics of Jesuit Spirituality in the Sixteenth Century," 15).

40. Pope Francis, *A Big Heart Open to God*, 30.

41. See *Evangelii Gaudium*, 231–33.

42. Ibid., 232.

43. Ibid., 231.

44. For this, see Borghesi, *The Mind of Pope Francis*. For more focused studies on particular regions of Pope Francis's thought, see Rourke, *The Roots of Pope Francis's Social and Political Thought*, and Luciani, *Pope Francis and the Theology of the People*.

45. Borghesi, *The Mind of Pope Francis*, xxiv, emphasis original. "Antinomian" does not, in this context, mean "opposed to law." Rather it means that the pope's thinking works in terms of antinomies.

46. A favorite text of his is the monumental nineteenth-century epic poem *El Gaucho Martín Fierro* by José Hernández. During his years as a teacher of Spanish literature, he was able to bring the poet Jorge Luis Borges (future winner of the prestigious Miguel de Cervantes prize) to his classroom in August 1965. See Ivereigh, *The Great Reformer*, 80–82.

47. See Luciani, *Pope Francis and the Theology of the People*. For a brief overview, see Scannone, "Pope Francis and the Theology of the People."

48. See, for example, Pope Francis, *Let Us Dream*, which can be read as a book-length commentary on how he understands discernment.

49. Borghesi, *The Mind of Pope Francis*, 4. On the importance of *Christus* in

the recovery of Ignatian spirituality in its original documents, see O'Malley and O'Brien, "Twentieth-Century Reconstruction of Ignatian Spirituality," 21.

50. Borghesi, *The Mind of Pope Francis*, 5–6, 236–43.

51. Schneider, *"Unterscheidung der Geister,"* 135 (translation mine; emphasis original). The following summary is based on Schneider's presentation of Fessard's theology of the *Spiritual Exercises*. All translations are mine.

52. Fessard would often speak of *"l'actualité historique,"* which I translate here as "historical reality." When the term is used by Pope Francis, its source and meaning is in Fessard, a different stream of thought than the one that led Ellacuría to use a similar term, even though the two trajectories often end up making very similar claims about human action, the meaning of history, and the importance of discernment.

53. Schneider, *"Unterscheidung der Geister,"* 138 (emphasis original).

54. For Fessard, writing in the 1930s and 40s, these were the uncreative and closed totalities represented by secular liberalism, communism, and National Socialism. Indeed, with regard to the last, Fessard spoke of his research as the search for a mode of "spiritual resistance" to Nazism. This assertion of Fessard's shows the thoroughly social and political dimension of his work, a dimension that could not have been lost on his young Argentinian reader in the charged political atmosphere of the early 1960s, and amidst the enduring danger in Argentina of collapsing into totalitarian ideologies, whether it be that of the far right or the extreme left iterations of Peronism.

55. From an audio recording sent to Borghesi, quoted in Borghesi, *The Mind of Pope Francis*, 36.

56. For one brief instance in which he does, see Pope Francis, *The Name of God Is Mercy*, 10.

57. Speaking of Fessard, Schneider writes, "The person cannot constitute and ground the meaning of his life on his own. Rather, he must let it be given to him, in order subsequently to be able to realize it. Every discernment of spirits has, accordingly, a passive *and* an active element. On the one hand, a person is given the meaning of her life in the encounter with Christ; on the other hand, she must grasp this meaning and realize it in the existential engagement with her life" (Schneider, *"Unterscheidung der Geister,"* 144).

58. This view of discernment is clearly evident in the pope's understanding of authentic synodality, as he makes clear in his own descriptions of the synods over which he has presided; see Pope Francis, *Let Us Dream*, 81–94.

59. He most fully defined these guidelines conceptually as he appropriated Guardini's philosophy, but they go back to his initial reading of Fessard in the 1960s.

60. Here I follow Luciani, *Pope Francis and the Theology of the People*, and Scannone, "Pope Francis and the Theology of the People." See also the discussion in Borghesi, *The Mind of Pope Francis*, 44–55. Borghesi's method of defining the theology of the people by contrasting it with the work of Gustavo Gutiérrez is seriously flawed.

61. Scannone, "Pope Francis and the Theology of the People," 121.

62. Defining the relationship between liberation theology and the theology of the people is a complex task. Gera was an important theological voice both at

Medellín and at Puebla, as were (other) liberation theologians, such as Gustavo Gutiérrez. As Scannone notes, it is an oversimplification to characterize the relationship between the theology of the people and liberation theology as the contrast between a cultural paradigm and a socioeconomic one. Referring to a meeting held in 1996 in Schönstatt, Germany, on the future of theology in Latin America, Scannone recalls that he "asked Gutiérrez for his opinion [on whether there had been a paradigm shift in liberation theology from a socioeconomic paradigm to a cultural one], and he told me that the issue of culture had been present from the beginning, and that there had not been a change in paradigm, but only in emphasis. That was the response of the majority of the meeting's participants" (see Scannone, "Pope Francis and the Theology of the People," 125).

63. See Luciani, *Pope Francis and the Theology of the People*, 1–6; Scannone, "Pope Francis and the Theology of the People," 121–22. Sometimes the pope will say or write "holy, faithful people of God."

64. Jorge Mario Bergoglio, "Una institución que vive su carisma," in *Meditaciones para religiosos*, 46–47 (my translation; emphasis original). This essay is translated by Philip Endean, SJ, in "Writings on Jesuit Spirituality I," 16–17. I have drawn on this English translation, with some modifications. Endean notes that the formula on which Bergoglio draws is from *Lumen gentium*, 12. For another description of what he means by "the people," see *Let Us Dream*, 97–107.

65. Luciani, *Pope Francis and the Theology of the People*, 22–24; Scannone, "Pope Francis and the Theology of the People,"123.

66. See Luciani, *Pope Francis and the Theology of the People*, 85–89. They are also the structuring insights of his most recent apostolic exhortation, *Querida Amazonia*: chapter 2, "A Cultural Dream" (28–40), and chapter 4, "An Ecclesial Dream" (61–110).

67. On Podetti, see Borghesi, *Mind of Pope Francis*, 28–36; on Methol Ferré, see Borghesi, *The Mind of Pope Francis*, 85–99: Ivereigh, *The Great Reformer*, 233–37.

68. Ivereigh, *The Great Reformer*, 106; quoted in Borghesi, *The Mind of Pope Francis*, 29.

69. Borghesi, *The Mind of Pope Francis*, 33.

70. Ibid., 292. The distinction between being a "source church" and being a "reflection church" comes originally from a Brazilian Jesuit, Henrique de Lima Vaz. See ibid., 156.

71. It is worth noting too that Pope Francis does not reference a *regular* polyhedron, in which the sides are still symmetrically arranged with respect to some center.

72. Quoted in Borghesi, *The Mind of Pope Francis*, 105. See also the pope's references to Guardini in Pope Francis, *Let Us Dream*, 55–57, 79. His references make it very clear that Guardini provides the philosophical backdrop to the strategy and tactics that the pope is using to promote synodality in the Church.

73. Borghesi, *The Mind of Pope Francis*, 106. My discussion of Guardini relies on Borghesi's presentation in ibid., 101–41.

74. This appropriation of Guardini is found in Pope Francis, "Toward a Bicentennial of Justice and Solidarity: We as Citizens, We as a People," in *In Your Eyes I See My Words*, 1:116–35. The other clearest indication of Bergoglio's

reading of Guardini is a lecture delivered at the Universidad del Salvador in 1989, which, according to Ivereigh, "was the skeleton of what would have been, had he written it, his doctoral thesis" (Ivereigh, *The Great Reformer*, 202). This text is titled "Necesidad de una Antropología política: Un problema pastoral" (The Necessity of a Political Anthropology: A Pastoral Problem). See Pope Francis, *Reflexiones en Esperanza*, 257–88. It is worth noting of this latter essay that, typical for Bergoglio, a theoretical issue is approached as "a pastoral problem."

75. Borghesi, *The Mind of Pope Francis*, 113.

76. *Evangelii Gaudium*, 221–25. This principle, and the other three, go back even to the 1960s, and are found in many of Bergoglio's addresses and writings from the 1970s forward.

77. Ibid., 222.

78. There are unmistakable echoes here of Fessard's presentation of the dialectic of human freedom, in which "the moment" represents the tangential contact point of the conjoint reality of natural and human history, on the one hand, with the constraints it brings with it, and supernatural history, on the other, which shapes the other two dimensions of history, but only by means of human choice, and does so authentically to the extent that this choice is the result of a process of discernment like the one structured by Ignatius's *Spiritual Exercises*.

79. *Evangelii Gaudium*, 223 (emphasis original).

80. Which is not to say that the fullness of the future is not a part of reality, but that it loses its reality when we articulate it in terms of ideas that ignore the limitations of the moment.

81. Borghesi, *The Mind of Pope Francis*, 115.

82. *Evangelii Gaudium*, 231.

83. Ibid., 234–37.

84. Whereas Rahner appropriated Guardini's warnings about the disintegration of the Renaissance ideal of personality, this side of Guardini's diagnosis of the challenge that modernity poses to Christian faith is less evident in Rahner.

85. As Borghesi points out, the pope resists both a Promethean anthropocentrism and a biocentrism characteristic of so-called Deep Ecology (see Borghesi, *Mind of Pope Francis*, 140).

86. Pope Francis, *Laudato si'*, 119.

87. See, for example, Pope Francis, "Two Subtle Enemies of Holiness," chap. 2 of *Gaudete et exsultate*, 35–62.

88. Ibid., 35. The pope quotes from *Evangelii Gaudium*, 94. Anthropocentric immanentism recalls Fessard's warnings about attempts to understand and enact the meaning of human history that are closed to supernatural history. This provides another way in which different elements of Pope Francis's intellectual thought are multiply determined by the many different sources on which he draws.

89. From an audio recording of the pope's; quoted in Borghesi, *Mind of Pope Francis*, 284–85 (translation slightly emended). For the Italian original, see Borghesi, *Jorge Mario Bergoglio*, 277. In the same recording, the pope indicates the influence of his reading of the Italian Catholic monthly *30 Giorni*, which was published between 1981 and 2012, and, starting in 2002, published several interviews with and articles by Cardinal Bergoglio. See Borghesi, *The Mind of Pope Francis*, 284n73.

90. Luigi Giussani, *L'Attrattiva Gesù* (Milan: Editoriale Rizzoli, 1999). See

Borghesi, *The Mind of Pope Francis*, 276–80, 284–86.

91. Pope Benedict, *Deus caritas est*, 217; quoted in *Evangelii Gaudium*, 7.

92. *Laudato si'*, 216. He quotes from *Evangelii Gaudium*, 261, introducing a chapter on "spirit-filled evangelizers."

93. Jorge Mario Bergoglio, "Servicio de la Fe y Promoción de la Justicia," *Stromata* 44, no. 1/2 (1988): 7–22. All translations are my own.

94. See Ivereigh, *The Great Reformer*, 131; Vallely, *Pope Francis*, 47–48.

95. Bergoglio, "Servicio de la Fe y Promoción de la Justicia," 13.

96. Ibid., 14–16.

97. Ibid., 19n22, emphasis added.

98. From a press conference with Pope Francis, July 28, 2013, http://www.vatican.va/content/francesco/en/speeches/2013/july/documents/papa-francesco_20130728_gmg-conferenza-stampa.html.

99. Borghesi, *The Mind of Pope Francis*, xxiv.

100. Pope Francis, *A Big Heart Open to God*, 14.

101. Ibid.

102. Pope Francis, "Y Conforme a esta Esperanza: Algunas reflexiones acerca de la unión de los animos," in *Reflexiones en Esperanza*, 205 (translation mine). See also the texts in the *Constitutions* on this theme in Ignatius of Loyola, *Constitutions of the Society of Jesus*, 285–93.

103. See Pope Francis, "Homily for the Mass of the Liturgical Memorial of the Most Holy Name of Jesus," January 3, 2014, http://www.vatican.va/content/francesco/en/homilies/2014/documents/papa-francesco_20140103_omelia-santissimo-nome-gesu.html.

104. Ibid. This passage, which is focused on the centrality of a God who ceaselessly surprises us, bears comparison to Ellacuría's description of Pedro Arrupe, given above (see chapter 5, section titled "The Formation of a Contemplative in Action for Justice").

105. Ibid.

106. For a brief commentary, see Hugo Rahner, *Ignatius the Theologian*, 23–25. It could well be that Pope Francis first encountered this maxim through his reading of Fessard, who commented at length on it in Fessard, *La Dialectique des "Exercices spirituels,"* 167–77.

107. See Schineller, "Pope Francis—Deeply Ignatian and Deeply Jesuit."

108. Pope Francis, "El Reino de Cristo," in *Meditaciones para Religiosos*, 152–57 (all translations mine). He repeats this meditation almost verbatim in the retreat given to the bishops of Spain in 2006: *In Him Alone Is Our Hope*, 51–60.

109. Pope Francis, "El Reino de Cristo," 154.

110. Ibid., 156.

111. Ibid.

112. See the discussion in chapter 4, section titled "The 1950s: Ignatius as a Prophet of the End of the Modern World" (first of the two subsections of this section).

113. Rahner, "Plea for a Nameless Virtue," in *TI* 23:33–37. The nameless virtue provides an alternative between skeptical relativism and ideological fanaticism.

114. See chapter 1, section titled "Early Modernity and the Origins of Spirituality."

115. Pope Francis, "God Lives in the City," in *Only Love Can Save Us*, 33–48.

He takes the title from a section of the Concluding Documents of Aparecida titled "Urban Ministry" (sections 509–19).

116. Ibid., 47.

117. Ibid. (translation slightly emended). See Jorge Mario Bergoglio, "Dios vive en la ciudad," http://es.catholic.net/op/articulos/43353/dios-vive-en-la-ciudad.html#modal.

118. Ibid., quoting *SpEx* 103.

119. Ibid.

120. Discernment is mentioned explicitly a page earlier: Pope Francis, *Only Love Can Save Us*, 45.

121. See Pope Francis, *Meditaciones para religiosos*, 119–211, for the first set of retreat conferences, and 215–57, for the retreat conferences for religious superiors.

122. Pope Francis, *In Him Alone Is Our Hope*.

123. Endean writes, "For most of Jesuit history, authority figures have been 'ascetics,' the approach which our author [the young Bergoglio] intelligently exemplifies" (see Endean, "Translator's Introduction," in *Writings on Jesuit Spirituality I*, 8).

124. Endean, "Translator's Afterword," in *Writings on Jesuit Spirituality II*, 40 (citing Pope Francis, *A Big Heart Open to God*, 18). The attempt to make a distinction between the young Bergoglio's interpretation of Ignatian spirituality and his application of that spirituality in his style of governance is fair enough as far as it goes. However, it goes against the grain of Francis's insistence that "the doctrinal" (here, interpretation) and "the pastoral" (governance) cannot be separated in any straightforward way.

125. The relevant passages from the retreat conferences from the late 1970s are found in Pope Francis, *Meditaciones para religiosos*, 139–46. In the 2006 retreat, see Pope Francis, *In Him Alone Is Our Hope*, 29–42.

126. Pope Francis, *Meditaciones para religiosos*, 139–40. All translations are mine.

127. Ibid., 142. In both sets of retreat conferences, early and late, the pope plays with different usages of "foundation" and "found," drawing out what he takes to be implicit connotations of the "Principle and Foundation" (*SpEx* 23), and linking it with subsequent weeks of the *Exercises*.

128. Pope Francis, *In Him Alone Is Our Hope*, 29.

129. Ibid.

130. I suggested in the overview of influences in Francis's intellectual itinerary (see "Later Influences") that Giussani's, *L'Attrattiva Gesù* is one source of the later Francis's focus on mercy, but also that his shift to focus on the importance of mercy can be discerned in his choice of episcopal motto in 1992, *miserando atque eligendo*.

131. After a brief introduction, a chapter is devoted to the Principle and Foundation (14 pages), two chapters to the First Week (20 pages), and six chapters to the Second Week (56 pages). One chapter treats death and resurrection—that is, Third and Fourth Weeks—together (12 pages), with a final chapter given to the Contemplation to Attain Love, which concludes the Fourth Week and folds in material on the Rules for Thinking with the Church (16 pages). So, a little more

than 40 percent is devoted to the Second Week.

132. It figures prominently in the openings lines of his talks: Pope Francis, *In Him Alone Is Our Hope*, 9; and also 29, 33, 88, 116 (quoting Jas. 3:17), 122, 124.

133. Ibid., 9. He also chooses this because of a document that the Spanish bishops themselves had penned. The quote from Luke 1:50 is in a passage from a document approved by the Spanish Bishops Conference in November 1999: *La fidelidad de Dios dura siempre. Mirada de fe al siglo XX*.

134. Pope Francis, *In Him Alone Is Our Hope*, 115.

135. Ibid., 10.

136. Ibid., 29.

137. Ibid., 30.

138. Ibid., 29.

139. Ibid., 48–49.

140. Ibid., 51.

141. Press conference with Pope Francis, July 28, 2013, http://www.vatican.va/content/francesco/en/speeches/2013/july/documents/papa-francesco_20130728_gmg-conferenza-stampa.html.

142. An earlier version of this argument appeared in Ashley, "Pope Francis as Interpreter of Ignatius's Spiritual Exercises." I am grateful to the editors of *Spiritus* for permission to use sections of that article in the current presentation of the argument.

143. For a review of this complex history, see Kasper, *Mercy*, 52–55, 75–129.

144. Pope Francis, *Misericordiae vultus*, §20. I will cite from the text of the bull printed as an appendix to *The Name of God Is Mercy*, 138.

145. Ibid.

146. Ibid.

147. Ibid., §20, p. 140.

148. Ibid.

149. Ibid., §21, p. 141.

150. Ibid., §21, p. 142–43.

151. Ibid., §21, p. 142.

152. Ibid., §21, p. 143.

153. Pope Francis, *The Name of God Is Mercy*, 80.

154. Ibid., 10.

155. Pope Francis, *Misericordiae vultus*, §20, p. 138 (emphasis added).

156. Pope Francis, *The Name of God Is Mercy*, 80.

157. Pope Francis, *Misericordiae vultus*, §20, p. 138.

158. Pope Francis, *In Him Alone Is Our Hope*, 124.

159. From Pope Francis, "God Lives in the City," in *Only Love Can Save Us*, 47.

160. Francis begins his reflection on this famous Contemplation thus: "When Saint Ignatius asks us to renew our memory of 'the blessings of creation and redemption, and the special favors I have received' (*Sp. Ex.*, 234) he wants us to go much further than merely giving thanks for all that we have received. He wants to teach us to have *more love*" (Pope Francis, *In Him Alone We Hope*, 119; emphasis original).

161. Ibid., p. 80.

162. Although Francis does not himself draw attention to this, what is remarkable in the story of Peter's "first call" is that Jesus does not deny Peter's confession of sinfulness in Luke 5:8, but neither does he respond with explicit words of forgiveness; the act of forgiving is implicit to the call to follow him.

163. Pope Francis, *Misericordiae vultus*, §1, p. 105.

164. See "Video Message of His Holiness Pope Francis to Participants in an International Theological Congress Held at the Pontifical Catholic University of Argentina." I have modified the translation slightly based on the Spanish original. The pope (when he was still cardinal archbishop of Buenos Aires) made a very similar point in an address to the Pontifical Commission for Latin America in February 2009: Pope Francis, "The Importance of Academic Formation," in *Only Love Can Save Us*, 139–49, esp. 143–45.

165. Pope Francis, "Video Message."

166. Ibid.

167. It is worth pointing out also that "believing life" (*vida creyente*) echoes many of the definitions of spirituality we discussed in chapter 1.

168. "Address of His Holiness Pope Francis to the 36th General Congregation of the Society of Jesus."

169. O'Malley, "Some Distinctive Characteristics," 19.

170. And this *ad intra* and *ad extra* do not make up a zero-sum game, but a creative opposition (in Guardini's sense) for which Ignatian spirituality gives the key for unlocking, as I argued above, using Bergoglio's 1990 address, "Y Conforme a esta Esperanza: Algunas reflexiones acerca de la union de los animos."

CHAPTER 7

1. Metz, "A Passion for God: Religious Orders Today," in *A Passion for God*, 153. Among the Jesuits massacred, mentioned by Metz, was Ignacio Ellacuría.

2. In my use of the notion of "place" I draw on Jon Sobrino's reflections on "Theology and Its Place," in Sobrino, *The Principle of Mercy*, 31–35.

3. See Tracy, *Analogical Imagination*, 30–31.

4. Rahner, "The Logic of Concrete Individual Knowledge in Ignatius of Loyola," 86.

5. Taylor, *Secular Age*, 3.

6. Speaking of his own similar experience, Rahner's student Johann Baptist Metz has written, "One comes from far away when one comes from there. It is as if one were born not fifty years ago, but somewhere along the receding edges of the Middle Ages" (Metz, "Productive Noncontemporaneity," 171).

7. See Meier, "Karl Rahner: The Teacher of Ignacio Ellacuría," 128–43, and the discussion in chapter 5 herein.

8. See his discussion "Contemplation in the Action of Justice," in Ellacuría, *Fé y Justicia*, 207–16.

9. The experience of fullness found in the Fourth Week and its Contemplation to Attain Love never, ever leave the experiences of the prior weeks behind, including the experience of the crucified Christ in First and Third Weeks, in which "divinity

is veiled," as Ignatius puts it, and sin seems to have triumphed: "In order for it [the experience of fullness proper to the Fourth Week] to be authentic, all the things are necessary that Saint Ignatius places in his Spiritual Exercises, before proposing the 'Contemplation to Attain Love.' There is no Christian contemplation without the first three Weeks, without abandoning sin, the world, one's own passions and interests, and so on" (Ellacuría, *Fé y Justicia*, 215; translation mine).

10. Sobrino, *Christ the Liberator*, 215.

11. Hence the pope's favorite Ignatian motto: *Non coerceri maximo, contineri tamen a minimo, divinum est* ("to suffer no restriction from anything however great, and yet to be contained in the tiniest of things, that is divine").

12. Pope Francis, *A Big Heart Open to All*, 22.

13. See the discussion of Rahner's talks on the devotion to the Sacred Heart and on the motto, *Ad maiorem Dei gloriam* in chapter 4, section titled "The 1950s: Ignatius as a Prophet for the End of the Modern World."

14. See his homily for a Mass celebrating Favre's canonization: "Holy Mass for the Liturgical Memorial of the Most Holy Name of Jesus: Homily of Pope Francis," January 3, 2014, http://w2.vatican.va/content/francesco/en/homilies/2014/documents/papa-francesco_20140103_omelia-santissimo-nome-gesu.html.

15. See the discussion of this Contemplation in chapter 3, section titled "Ignatian Spirituality and the Conditions of Modernity." Pope Francis appeals precisely to the Contemplation to Attain Love in proposing how the Church can act and thrive in the bewildering complexity of the modern megacity. See Pope Francis, "God Lives in the City," 33–48, esp. 46–47, and the discussion of this essay in chapter 6, section titled "Pope Francis Interprets Ignatian Spirituality."

16. Anthony DeMello's interpretation of the *Spiritual Exercises*, for instance, is recognizably Ignatian, even though it combines Ignatian spirituality with elements of Buddhism and Hinduism. See DeMello, *Seek God Everywhere*.

17. By "spin" I refer to the particular way that doctrines common to the Christian tradition as a whole are given in a particular and particularly strong way by the exercises carefully knit together in the *Spiritual Exercises*. The same doctrines are certainly present in other spiritualities (Benedictine and Franciscan spirituality, for example), but not in the same way.

18. See Rahner, "Being Open to God as Ever Greater," in *TI* 7:25–46, and the discussion in chapter 3 herein. This God is a Trinitarian God, as both Rahner and Ellacuría made clear. See also Arrupe, "Trinitarian Inspiration."

19. In this sense, this feature could be considered one held in common between Ignatian and Franciscan spirituality.

20. Sobrino's Christology is a fine example of this.

21. A further understanding of this feature in its origins would indeed require a closer examination of the *Constitutions* and Ignatius's voluminous correspondence, materials that I bracketed in this study, for reasons indicated in the Introduction.

22. Pope Francis, "Holy Mass for the Liturgical Memorial of the Most Holy Name of Jesus."

23. I learned in a particularly powerful way that John of the Cross's mystical itinerary is fully relevant to thinking about (and enacting) the healing of the wounds of violence and trauma so endemic today from Heather M. DuBois, "To Be More

Fully Alive: John of the Cross and Judith Butler on Transformation of the Self."

24. See the essays collected in Cassidy and Copeland, eds., *Desire, Darkness and Hope*, which demonstrate the power of this tradition for grappling with phenomena as diverse as racism, climate change, and pandemic.

25. This is probably why Francis of Assisi is the central figure for Pope Francis's writing on our ecological crisis: *Laudato si'*.

26. I also trust its goes without saying that although my own location as a Roman Catholic theologian has brought me to frame this initial inquiry thinking of spiritualities located primarily in that church, this is in no way to deny that there are potent instances of theology-animating spiritual traditions in other churches.

27. Think of the creativity of Bede Griffith's (Swami Dayananda's) creative hybridization of Benedictine and Hindu spiritualities, found also, for Ignatian spirituality, in Anthony DeMello's work.

Bibliography

Alexander, Jon. "What Do Recent Writers Mean by Spirituality." *Spirituality Today* 32 (1980): 247–56.
Arrupe, Pedro, SJ. "The Trinitarian Inspiration of the Ignatian Charism." *Studies in the Spirituality of Jesuits* 33, no. 3 (2001).
Ashley, J. Matthew. "Contemplation in the Action of Justice: Ignacio Ellacuría and Ignatian Spirituality." In Burke and Lassalle-Klein, eds., *The Love That Produces Hope*, 144–65.
———. "Ignacio Ellacuría and the *Spiritual Exercises* of Ignatius Loyola." *Theological Studies* 61, no. 1 (2000): 16–39.
———. *Interruptions: Mysticism, Politics and Theology in the Work of Johann Baptist Metz.* Notre Dame, IN: University of Notre Dame Press, 1998.
———. "Pope Francis as Interpreter of Ignatius's Spiritual Exercises." *Spiritus: A Journal of Christian Spirituality* 17, no. 2 (2017): 165–79.
———. "'A Post-Einsteinian Settlement?' On Spirituality as a Possible Border Crossing between Religion and the New Science." In *Theology: Expanding the Borders*, Vol. 43 of *The Annual Publication of the College Theology Society*, edited by Roberto Goizueta and Maria Pilár Aquino, 80–108. Mystic, CT: Twenty-Third Publications, 1998.
Ashley, J. Matthew, Kevin F. Burke, SJ, and Rodolfo Cardenal, SJ, eds. *A Grammar of Justice: The Legacy of Ignacio Ellacuría.* Maryknoll, NY: Orbis, 2014.
Battlog, Andreas. *Die Mysterien des Lebens Jesu bei Karl Rahner: Zugang zum Christusglauben.* Innsbruck: Tyrolia, 2001.
Baumer, Patricia Hughes. "Stop Picking on Shoppers." *U.S. Catholic* 59, no. 1 (1994): 13–17.
Beirne, Charles. *Jesuit Education and Social Change in El Salvador.* New York: Garland, 1996.
Bellah, Robert, Richard Madsen, William Sullivan, Ann Swidler, and Steven Tipton. *Habits of the Heart: Individualism and Commitment in American Life.* Updated edition with a new introduction. Berkeley: University of California Press, 1996.

Berger, Peter, Brigitte Berger, and Hansfried Kellner. *The Homeless Mind: Modernization and Consciousness*. New York: Vintage Books, 1974.
Blondel, Maurice. "History and Dogma." In *The Letter on Apologetics and History and Dogma*, translated and edited by Alexander Dru, 219–90. Grand Rapids, MI: Eerdmans, 1994.
Blumenberg, Hans. *The Legitimacy of the Modern Age*. Translated by Robert Wallace. Cambridge, MA: MIT Press, 1983.
Borghesi, Massimo, *The Mind of Pope Francis: Jorge Mario Bergoglio's Intellectual Journey*. Translated by Barry Hudock with a foreword by Guzmán Carriquiry Lecour. Collegeville, MN: Liturgical Press Academic, 2018. Originally published as *Jorge Mario Bergoglio: Una biografia intelletuale* (Milan: Editorale Jaca, 2017).
Boyle, Marjorie O'Rourke. *Loyola's Acts: The Rhetoric of the Self*. Berkeley: University of California Press, 1997.
Brackley, Dean, SJ. *The Call to Discernment in Troubled Times: New Perspectives on the Transformative Wisdom of Ignatius of Loyola*. New York: Crossroad, 2004.
———. "Rutilio and Romero: Martyrs for Our Time." In *Monsignor Romero: A Bishop for the Third Millennium*, edited by Robert S. Pelton, CSC, 79–100. Notre Dame, IN: University of Notre Dame Press, 2004.
Brockman, James. *Romero: A Life*. Maryknoll, NY: Orbis, 1989.
Buckley, Michael, SJ. *At the Origins of Modern Atheism*. New Haven, CT: Yale University Press, 1987.
———. *The Catholic University as Promise and Project: Reflections in a Jesuit Idiom*. Washington, DC: Georgetown University Press, 1998.
———. "The Structure of the Rules for Discernment." In Sheldrake, ed., *The Way of Ignatius of Loyola*, 219–37.
Burke, Kevin F., SJ. *The Ground beneath the Cross: The Theology of Ignacio Ellacuría*. Washington, DC: Georgetown University Press, 2000.
Burke, Kevin F., SJ, and Robert Lassalle-Klein, eds. *Love That Produces Hope: The Thought of Ignacio Ellacuría*. Collegeville, MN: Michael Glazer, 2006.
Burke, Kevin F., SJ, and Eileen Burke-Sullivan, eds. *The Ignatian Tradition: Spirituality in History*. Collegeville, MN: Liturgical Press, 2009.
Burrell, David, CSC. *Freedom and Creation in Three Traditions*. Notre Dame, IN: University of Notre Dame Press, 1993.
Bynum, Carolyn Walker, *Jesus as Mother: Studies in the Spirituality of the High Middle Ages*. Berkeley: University of California Press, 1982.
Caputo, John. *The Mystical Element in Heidegger's Thought*. New York: Fordham University Press, 1978.
Caraman, Philip, SJ. *Ignatius of Loyola: A Biography of the Founder of the Jesuits*. San Francisco: Harper & Row, 1990.
Cardenal, Rodolfo, SJ. "The Church of the Crucified People: The Eschatology of Ignacio Ellacuría." In Ashley, Burke, and Cardenal, eds., *The Grammar of Justice*, 147–60.
———. *Historia de una esperanza: Vida de Rutilio Grande*. San Salvador: UCA Editores, 1985.

Carrigan, Ana. *Salvador Witness: The Life and Calling of Jean Donovan.* New York: Simon and Schuster, 1984.
Casanova, Juan. *Public Religions in the Modern World.* Chicago: University of Chicago Press, 1994.
Cassidy, Laurie, and M. Shawn Copeland, eds. *Desire, Darkness, and Hope: Theology in a Time of Impasse, Engaging the Thought of Constance Fitzgerald, OCD.* Collegeville, MN: Liturgical Press, 2021.
Certeau, Michel de. *The Mystic Fable: The Sixteenth and Seventeenth Centuries.* Translated by Michael B. Smith. Chicago: University of Chicago Press, 1992.
Chenu, Marie-Dominique, OP. *Nature, Man and Society in the Twelfth Century: Essays on New Theological Perspectives in the Latin West.* Edited and translated by Jerome Taylor and Lester Little. Chicago: University of Chicago Press, 1968.
Coathalem, Hervé, SJ. *Ignatian Insights: A Guide to the Complete Spiritual Exercises.* Translated by Charles McCarthy, SJ. Taichung, Taiwan: Kuangchi Press, 1971.
Collins, Billy. Introduction to *Best Spiritual Writings 2011.* Edited by Philip Zaleski. New York: Penguin, 2010.
Congregation for the Doctrine of the Faith. "Instruction on Certain Aspects of the 'Theology of Liberation.'" In Hennelly, ed., *Liberation Theology,* 393–414.
Corella, Jesús, SJ. "Consolación." In García de Castro, ed., *Diccionario de Espiritualidad Ignaciana,* 413–25.
Coreth, Emerich, SJ. "Philosophische Grundlagen der Theologie Karl Rahners." *Stimmen der Zeit* 212 (1994): 525–36.
Coupeau, José Carlos. "Consolar (Ministerio de)." In García de Castro, ed., *Diccionario de espiritualidad ignaciana,* 1:428–35.
Cousins, Ewert. "Francis of Assisi: Christian Mysticism at the Crossroads." In *Mysticism and Religious Traditions,* edited by Steven Katz, 163–91. New York: Oxford University Press, 1983.
———. "The Franciscan Roots of Ignatian Meditation." In *Ignatian Spirituality in a Secular Age,* edited by George Schner, SJ, 51–64. Waterloo, ON: Wilfrid Laurier University Press, 1984.
———. "The Humanity and the Passion of Christ." In *Christian Spirituality: High Middle Ages and Reformation,* edited by Jill Raitt, 375–91.
Crockford, Susannah. *Ripples in the Universe: Spirituality in Sedona, Arizona.* Chicago: University of Chicago Press, 2021.
Cunningham, Lawrence S., and Keith J. Egan. *Christian Spirituality: Themes from the Tradition.* New York: Paulist Press, 1996.
Cusson, Giles, SJ. *Biblical Theology and the Spiritual Exercises: A Method toward a Personal Experience of God as Accomplishing within Us His Plan of Salvation.* Translated by Mary Angela Roduit and George E. Ganss, SJ. St. Louis: Institute of Jesuit Sources, 1988.
Dalmases, Candido de, SJ. *Ignatius of Loyola: Founder of the Jesuits.* Translated by Jerome Aixalá. St. Louis: Institute of Jesuit Sources, 1985.

DeMello, Anthony, SJ. *Seek God Everywhere: Reflections on the Spiritual Exercises of St. Ignatius*. Edited by Gerald O'Collins, SJ, Daniel Kendall, SJ, and Jeffrey La Belle, SJ. New York: Image/Doubleday, 2010.
Downey, Michael, ed. *The New Dictionary of Catholic Spirituality*. Collegeville, MN: Liturgical Press, 1993.
Drescher, Elizabeth. *Choosing Our Religion: The Spiritual Lives of America's Nones*. New York: Oxford University Press, 2016.
DuBois, Heather. "To Be More Fully Alive: John of the Cross and Judith Butler on Transformation of the Self." PhD diss., University of Notre Dame, 2018.
Dulles, Avery, SJ. *Avery Dulles: Essential Writings from "America" Magazine*. Edited by James T. Keane. Notre Dame, IN: Christian Classics, 2019.
———. "The Ignatian 'Sentire cum Ecclesia' Today." *Review of Ignatian Spirituality* 25, no. 2 (1994): 19–35.
———. "Saint Ignatius and the Jesuit Theological Tradition." *Studies in the Spirituality of Jesuits* 14, no. 2 (1982).
Dunkle, Brian, SJ. "Service in the *Analogia Entis* and Spiritual Works of Erich Pryzwara." *Theological Studies* 73, no. 2 (2012): 339–62.
Dupré, Louis. *Passage to Modernity: An Essay in the Hermeneutics of Nature and Culture*. New Haven, CT: Yale University Press, 1993.
Dupré, Louis, and Don E. Saliers, eds. *Christian Spirituality: Post-Reformation and Modern*. World Spirituality: An Encyclopedic History of the Religious Quest 18. New York: Crossroad, 1991.
Dych, William, "Theology in a New Key." In O'Donovan, ed., *A World of Grace*, 1–16.
Dyckman, Katherine, SNJM, Mary Garvin, SNJM, and Elizabeth Liebert, SNJM. *Spiritual Exercises Reclaimed: Uncovering Liberating Possibilities for Women*. Mahwah, NJ: Paulist Press, 2001.
Ecklund, Elaine Howard, and Elizabeth Long. "Scientists and Spirituality." *Sociology of Religion* 72, no. 3 (2013), 253–74.
Egan, Harvey, SJ. "Karl Rahner: Theologian of the 'Spiritual Exercises.'" *Thought* 67, no. 266 (1992): 257–70.
Eisenstadt, S. N., ed. *Multiple Modernities*. New Brunswick, NJ: Transaction, 2002.
Ellacuría, Ignacio, SJ. "The Church of the Poor, Historical Sacrament of Liberation." In Ellacuría, *Ignacio Ellacuría*, 227–53.
———. *Conversión de la Iglesia al Reino de Dios para anunciarlo y realizarlo en la historia*. San Salvador: UCA Editores, 1985.
———. "The Crucified People: An Essay in Historical Soteriology." In Ellacuría, *Ignacio Ellacuría*, 195–24.
———. "El problema del traslado del espíritu de los *Ejercicios* a la Viceprovincia." In *Escritos teológicos*, 4:197–213.
———. "El tercer mundo como lugar óptimo de la vivencia de los *Ejercicios*." In *Escritos teológicos*, 4:215–34.
———. *Escritos teológicos*. 4 vols. San Salvador: UCA Editores, 2002–2004.
———. *Fe y Justicia*. Con estudio introductorio por Jon Sobrino. Bilbao: Descleé de Brouwer, 1999.

———. *Filosfía de la realidad histórica*. Edited by Antonio González. Madrid: Trotta, 1990.

———. *Freedom Made Flesh: The Mission of Christ and the Church*. Translated by John Drury. Maryknoll, NY: Orbis, 1976. Originally published as *Teología política*. San Salvador: Ediciones del Secretariado Social Interdiocesano, 1973.

———. "The Historicity of Christian Salvation." Translated by Margaret Wilde. In Ignacio Ellacuría, *Ignacio Ellacuría: Essays on History, Liberation and Theology*, ed. Michael E. Lee, 137–68. Originally published as "La Historicidad de la Salvación Christiana." *Revista Latinoamericana de Teología* 1 (1984): 5–45.

———. "Historicización de los derechos humanos desde los pueblos oprimidos y las mayorías populares." *Estudios Centroamericanos* 45 (1990): 589–96.

———. "The Historicization of the Concept of Property" (translated by Phillip Berryman). In Hassett and Lacey, eds., *Towards a Society That Serves Its People*, 105–37.

———. *Ignacio Ellacuría: Essays on History, Liberation, and Salvation*. Edited with an introduction by Michael E. Lee, with commentary by Kevin F. Burke, SJ. Maryknoll, NY: Orbis, 2013.

———. "Introducción al problema del milagro en Blondel." In *Escritos filosóficos*, 1:545–48. San Salvador: UCA, 1996.

———. "Is a Different Kind of University Possible?" In Hassett and Lacey, eds., *Towards a Society That Serves Its People*, 177–207.

———. "La Iglesia de los Pobres, Sacramento histórico de Liberación." In *Mysterium Liberationis: Conceptos fundamentales de la teología de la liberación*, edited by Ignacio Ellacuría and Jon Sobrino, 2:127–54. San Salvador: UCA Editores, 1991.

———. "La superación del reduccionismo idealista." In *Escritos Filosóficos*, 3:403–30. San Salvador: UCA Editores, 2001.

———. "A Latin American Reading of the *Spiritual Exercises* of Saint Ignatius." Translated by J. Matthew Ashley. *Spiritus: A Journal of Christian Spirituality* 10, no. 2 (2010): 204–41. Originally published as "Lectura Latinoamericana de los *Ejercicios Espirituales* de san Ignacio." *Revista Latinoamericana de Teología* 8 (1991): 111–47.

———. "Laying the Foundations of Latin American Theological Method." Translated by J. Matthew Ashley and Kevin F. Burke. In Ellacuría, *Ignacio Ellacuría: Essays on History, Liberation, and Salvation*, 63–91.

———. "Pedro Arrupe, renovador de la vida religiosa." *Revista Latinoamericana de Teología* 8, no. 22 (1991): 5–23.

———. "Tesis Sobre Posibilidad, Necesidad y Sentido de una Teología Latinoamericana." In *Teología y Mundo Contemporáneo: Homenaje a Karl Rahner*, edited by Antonio Vargas-Machuca, 325–50. Madrid: Ediciones Cristiandad, 1975.

———. "Utopia and Propheticism from Latin America." Translated by J. Matthew Ashley and Kevin F. Burke, SJ. In Ashley, Burke, and Cardenal, eds., *A Grammar of Justice*, 7–55.

---. *Veinte años de historia en El Salvador (1969–1989): Escritos políticos*. 3 vols. San Salvador: UCA Editores, 1991.
---. "What Is the Point of Philosophy?" Translated by Michael McNulty, SJ. *Philosophy & Theology* 10, no. 1 (1997): 1–18.
Endean, Philip, SJ. *Karl Rahner and Ignatian Spirituality*. New York: Oxford University Press, 2001.
Evennett, H. Outram. *The Spirit of the Counter-Reformation*. Notre Dame, IN: University of Notre Dame Press, 1968.
Fermin Mignone, Emilio. *Witness to the Truth: The Complicity of Church and Dictatorship in Argentina, 1976–1983*. Maryknoll, NY: Orbis, 1988.
Fessard, Gaston, SJ. *La Dialectique des "Exercices spirituels" de saint Ignace de Loyola*. Paris: Aubier, 1956.
Fischer, Klaus. *Der Mensch als Geheimnis: Die Anthropologie Karl Rahners. Mit einem Brief von Karl Rahner*. Freiburg: Herder, 1974.
Fleming, David L., SJ. *Like the Lighting: The Dynamics of the Ignatian Exercises*. St Louis: Institute of Jesuit Sources, 2004.
Ford, Ita. *Here I Am, Lord: The Letters and Writings of Ita Ford*. Edited by Jeanne Evans. Maryknoll, NY: Orbis, 2005.
Francis, Pope (Jorge Mario Bergoglio, SJ). "Address of His Holiness Pope Francis to the 36th General Congregation of the Society of Jesus." http://www.vatican.va/content/francesco/en/speeches/2016/october/documents/papa-francesco_20161024_visita-compagnia-gesu.html.
---. *A Big Heart Open to God: A Conversation with Pope Francis*. Interview by Antonio Spadaro, SJ. New York: HarperCollins, 2013.
---. *Evangelii Gaudium* (2013). https://www.vatican.va/content/francesco/en/apost_exhortations/documents/papa-francesco_esortazione-ap_20131124_evangelii-gaudium.html.
---. *Gaudete et exsultate* (2018). https://www.vatican.va/content/francesco/en/apost_exhortations/documents/papa-francesco_esortazione-ap_20180319_gaudete-et-exsultate.html.
---. *In Him Alone is Our Hope: Spiritual Exercises Given to His Brother Bishops in the Manner of Saint Ignatius of Loyola*. New York: Magnificat, 2013.
---. *In Your Eyes I See My Words: Homilies and Speeches from Buenos Aires*. 3 vols. Edited by Antonio Spadaro, SJ. New York: Fordham University Press, 1999–2021.
---. Laudato si' (2015). https://www.vatican.va/content/francesco/en/encyclicals/documents/papa-francesco_20150524_enciclica-laudato-si.html.
---. *Let Us Dream: The Path to a Better Future*. In conversation with Austin Ivereigh. New York: Simon and Schuster, 2020.
---. *Meditaciones para religiosos*. Bilbao: Ediciones Mensajero, 2014.
---. *Misericordiae vultus* (2015). https://www.vatican.va/content/francesco/en/apost_letters/documents/papa-francesco_bolla_20150411_misericordiae-vultus.html.
---. *The Name of God Is Mercy: A Conversation with Andrea Tornielli*. New York: Random House, 2016.
---. *Only Love Can Save Us: Letters, Homilies, and Talks of Cardinal Jorge Bergoglio*. Translated by Gerard Seromik. Huntington, IN: Our Sunday Visitor, 2013.

———. *Querida Amazonia* (2020). https://www.vatican.va/content/francesco/en/apost_exhortations/documents/papa-francesco_esortazione-ap_20200202_querida-amazonia.html.

———. *Reflexiones en Esperanza*. Vatican City: Libreria Editrice Vaticana, 2013.

———. "Servicio de la Fe y Promoción de la Justicia." *Stromata* 44, 1, no. 2 (1988): 7–22.

———. "Video Message of His Holiness Pope Francis to Participants in an International Theological Congress Held at the Pontifical Catholic University of Argentina." https://www.vatican.va/content/francesco/en/messages/pont-messages/2015/documents/papa-francesco_20150903_videomessaggio-teologia-buenos-aires.html. Spanish original: http://w2.vatican.va/content/francesco/es/messages/pont-messages/2015/documents/papa-francesco_20150903_videomessaggio-teologia-buenos-aires.html.

———. *The Way of Humility*. Translated by Helena Scott. San Francisco: Ignatius, 2014.

———. "Writings on Jesuit Spirituality I," by Jorge Mario Bergoglio. Translated and edited by Philip Endean, SJ. *Studies in the Spirituality of Jesuits* 45, no. 3 (2013).

———. "Writings on Jesuit Spirituality I," by Jorge Mario Bergoglio. Translated and edited by Philip Endean, SJ. *Studies in the Spirituality of Jesuits* 45, no. 4 (2013).

———. "Y Conforme a esta Esperanza: Algunas reflexiones acerca de la unión de los animos." In Pope Francis, *Reflexiones en Esperanza*, 199–237.

Friedman, Thomas. *Thank You for Being Late: An Optimist's Guide to Thriving in the Age of Accelerations*. New York: Palgrave Macmillan, 2016.

Fritz, Peter. *Freedom Made Manifest: Rahner's Fundamental Option and Theological Aesthetics*. Washington, DC: Catholic University of America Press, 2019.

———. *Karl Rahner's Theological Aesthetics*. Washington, DC: Catholic University of America Press, 2014.

Ganss, George, SJ, ed. *Ignatius of Loyola: Spiritual Exercises and Selected Works*. Translated by George Ganss, SJ, and Martin Palmer, SJ. Mahwah, NJ: Paulist Press, 1991.

García de Castro, José Carlos, ed. *Diccionario de espiritualidad ignaciana*. 2 Vols. 2nd ed. Bilbao: Ediciones Mensajero, 2007.

Gerhartz, Johannes G., SJ. "Von Jerusalem nach Rom: Der Weg des Ignatius zu seiner Kirchlichkeit." In *Ignatius von Loyola und die Gesellschaft Jesu: 1491–1556*, edited by Andreas Falkner and Paul Imhof, 93–104. Würzburg: Echter, 1990.

Gerson, Jean. *Jean Gerson: Early Works*. Translated with an introduction by Brian Patrick McGuire. New York: Paulist Press, 1998.

Giddens, Anthony. *Consequences of Modernity*. Stanford, CA: Stanford University Press, 1990.

———. *Modernity and Self-Identity: Self and Society in the Late Modern Age*. Cambridge: Cambridge University Press, 1991.

Gillespie, Michael. *The Theological Origins of Modernity*. Chicago: University of Chicago Press, 2008.

Glavac, Cynthia. *In the Fullness of Life: A Biography of Dorothy Kazel, O.S.U.* Meadville, PA: Dimension Books, 1996.

Guardini, Romano. *Der Gegensatz: Versuche zu einer Philosophie des Lebendig-Konkreten.* 4th ed. Stuttgart: Matthias Grünewald, 1998.
———. *The End of the Modern World: A Search for Orientation.* Translated by Joseph Theman and Herbert Burke. Edited with an introduction by Frederick D. Wilhelmsen. New York: Sheed & Ward, 1956.
———. *Letters from Lake Como.* Translated by Geoffrey W. Bromiley. Grand Rapids, MI: Eerdmans, 1994.
Guibert, Joseph de, SJ. *The Jesuits, Their Spiritual Doctrine and Practice: A Historical Study.* Edited by George E. Ganss, SJ, and translated by William Young, SJ. St. Louis: Institute of Jesuit Sources, 1994.
Guillet, Jacques, Gustave Bardy, et al. *Discernment of Spirits.* Translated by Sr. Innocentia Richards. Collegeville, MN: Liturgical Press, 1970.
Gutiérrez, Gustavo, OP. *The Density of the Present: Selected Writings.* Maryknoll, NY: Orbis, 1999.
———. *On Job: God-talk and the Suffering of the Innocent.* Translated by Matthew J. O'Connell. Maryknoll, NY: Orbis, 1987.
———. *A Theology of Liberation: History, Politics, and Salvation.* 2nd rev. ed. Translated and edited by Sister Caridad Inda and John Eagleson. Maryknoll, NY: Orbis, 1988.
Hadot, Pierre. *Philosophy as a Way of Life: Spiritual Exercises from Socrates to Foucault.* Edited with an introduction by Arnold I. Davidson. Translated by Michael Chase. Oxford: Basil Blackwell, 1995.
Haight, Roger, SJ. *Dynamics of Theology.* Mahwah, NJ: Paulist Press, 1990.
———. *Spiritual and Religious: Explorations for Seekers.* Maryknoll, NY: Orbis, 2016.
———. *Spirituality Seeking Theology.* Maryknoll, NY: Orbis, 2014.
Harrison, Peter. *The Bible, Protestantism, and the Rise of Natural Science.* Cambridge: Cambridge University Press, 1998.
Hassett, John, and Hugh Lacey, eds. *Towards a Society That Serves Its People: The Intellectual Contribution of El Salvador's Murdered Jesuits.* Washington, DC: Georgetown University Press, 1991.
Heidegger, Martin. *Being and Time.* Translated by John Macquarrie and Edward Robinson. San Francisco: Harper & Row, 1966.
Hendricks, Gay, and Kate Ludeman. *The Corporate Mystic: A Guidebook for Visionaries with Their Feet on the Ground.* New York: Bantam Books, 1996.
Hennelly, Alfred T., SJ, ed. *Liberation Theology: A Documentary History.* Maryknoll, NY: Orbis, 1990.
Hügel, Friedrich von. *The Mystical Element of Religion as Studied in Saint Catherine of Genoa and Her Friends.* 2 vols. New York: E. P. Dutton, 1909.
Ignatius of Loyola. *Constitutions of the Society of Jesus.* Translated with introduction and notes by George Ganss, SJ. St. Louis, MO: Institute of Jesuit Sources, 1970.
———. *Ignatius of Loyola: Spiritual Exercises and Selected Works.* Edited by George Ganss, SJ. Mahwah, NJ: Paulist Press, 1991.
———. *Letters of Ignatius of Loyola.* Selected and translated by William J. Young, SJ. Chicago: Loyola University Press, 1959.

———. *Obras completas de San Ignacio de Loyola*. 4th ed. Translated and edited by Ignacio Iparraguire, SJ, and Cándido de Dalmases, SJ. Biblioteca de autores cristianos. Madrid: Editorial Cátolica, 1982.

———. *A Pilgrim's Testament: The Memoirs of Ignatius of Loyola*. Translated by Parmananda Divarkar. St. Louis: Institute of Jesuit Sources, 1995.

———. *The Spiritual Exercises of Ignatius of Loyola: A Translation and Commentary*. Translated with an introduction and commentary by George Ganss, SJ. Series I: Jesuit Primary Sources in English Translations 9. St. Louis: Institute of Jesuit Sources, 1992.

International Theological Commission. "Declaration on Human Development and Christian Salvation." In Hennelly, ed., *Liberation Theology*, 205–19.

Ivens, Michael, SJ. *Understanding the Spiritual Exercises*. Leominster, UK: Gracewing, 1998.

Ivereigh, Austin. *The Great Reformer: Francis and the Making of a Radical Pope*. New York: Henry Holt & Company, 2014.

———. *Wounded Shepherd: Pope Francis and His Struggle to Convert the Catholic Church*. New York: Henry Holt & Company, 2019.

Jackson, Phil, and Hugh Delehanty. *Sacred Hoops: Spiritual Lessons of a Hardwood Warrior*. New York: Hyperion, 1995.

James, Steven, dir. *Hoop Dreams*. New York: Criterion Collections, 2005. DVD.

Jay, Martin. *Adorno*. Cambridge, MA: Harvard University Press, 1984.

Jennings, Willie James. *The Christian Imagination: Theology and the Origins of Race*. New Haven, CT: Yale University Press, 2010.

Kasper, Walter. *Mercy: The Essence of the Gospel and the Key to Christian Life*. Translated by William Madges. New York: Paulist Press, 2014.

Kelly, Thomas. *The Gospel Grows Feet: Rutilio Grande, SJ, and the Church of El Salvador: An Ecclesiology in Context*. Maryknoll, NY: Orbis, 2013.

Kelly, William, ed. *Theology and Discovery: Essays in Honor of Karl Rahner, S.J.* Milwaukee: Marquette University Press, 1980.

Kempis, Thomas à. *The Imitation of Christ*. Translated with an introduction by Leo Sherley-Price. New York: Penguin, 1952.

Klaiber, Jeffrey, SJ. *The Church, Dictatorships, and Democracy in Latin America*. Maryknoll, NY: Orbis, 1998.

Krieg, Robert. *Romano Guardini: A Precursor of Vatican II*. Notre Dame, IN: University of Notre Dame Press, 1997.

Lagger, Christian. *Dienst: Kenosis in Schöpfung und Kreuz bei Erich Przywara SJ*. Innsbruck: Tyrolia, 2007.

Lasch, Christopher. *Haven in A Heartless World: The Family Besieged*. Rev. ed. New York: W. W. Norton, 1995.

Lassalle-Klein, Robert. *Blood and Ink: Ignacio Ellacuría, Jon Sobrino, and the Jesuit Martyrs of the University of Central America*. Maryknoll, NY: Orbis, 2014.

Latin American Provincials of the Society of Jesus. "The Jesuits in Latin America." In Hennelly, ed., *Liberation Theology*, 77–83.

Leclercq, Jean. *The Love of Learning and the Desire for God: A Study of Monastic Culture*. 2nd rev. ed. Translated by Catherine Misrahi. New York: Fordham University Press, 1974.

Lee, Michael E. *Bearing the Weight of Salvation: The Soteriology of Ignacio Ellacuría.* New York: Crossroad, 2009.
———. "Liberation Theology's Transcendent Moment: The Work of Xavier Zubiri & Ignacio Ellacuría as Non-Contrastive Discourse." *Journal of Religion* 83, no. 2 (2003): 226–43.
———. *Revolutionary Saint: The Theological Legacy of Oscar Romero.* Maryknoll, NY: Orbis, 2018.
Le Goff, Jacques. *Time, Work and Culture in the Middle Ages.* Chicago: University of Chicago Press, 1980.
Lehman, Karl. "Karl Rahner: A Portrait." In *The Content of Faith: The Best of Karl Rahner's Theological Writings*, edited by Karl Lehmann, 1–42. New York: Crossroad, 1993.
Little, Lester. *Religious Poverty and the Profit Economy in Medieval Europe.* Ithaca, NY: Cornell University Press, 1978.
Lonsdale, David. *Eyes to See, Ears to Hear: An Introduction to Ignatian Spirituality.* Chicago: Loyola University Press, 1990.
Luciani, Rafael. *Pope Francis and the Theology of the People.* Maryknoll, NY: Orbis, 2017.
Maguire, Brian Patrick. *Jean Gerson and the Last Medieval Reformation.* University Park: Pennsylvania State University Press, 2005.
Maier, Martin, SJ. "Karl Rahner: The Teacher of Ignacio Ellacuría." In Burke and Lassalle-Klein, eds., *Love That Produces Hope*, 128–43.
Markey, Eileen. *A Radical Faith: The Assassination of Sister Maura.* New York: Nation Books, 2016.
Marmion, Declan, and Mary E. Hines, eds. *A Cambridge Companion to Karl Rahner.* New York: Cambridge University Press, 2005.
Martini, Carlo-Maria, SJ. *Letting God Free Us: Meditations on the Ignatian Exercises.* Translated by Richard Arnandez, with a foreword by George A. Maloney, SJ. New Rochelle, NY: New City Press, 1993.
Maryks, Robert Aleksander, ed. *A Companion to Ignatius of Loyola: Life, Writings, Spirituality.* Brill's Companions to the Christian Tradition 52. Boston: Brill, 2014.
Matt, Daniel. *God and the Big Bang: Discovering the Harmony between Science and Spirituality.* Woodstock, VT: Jewish Lights, 1996/2016.
McBrien, Richard P., *Catholicism.* Rev. ed. San Francisco: HarperSanFranciso, 1994.
McCool, Gerald, SJ. *From Unity to Pluralism: The Internal Evolution of Thomism.* New York: Fordham University Press, 1992.
———. "Karl Rahner and the Christian Philosophy of St. Thomas Aquinas." In Kelly, ed., *Theology and Discovery*, 63–93.
———. *Nineteenth-Century Scholasticism: The Search for a Unitary Method.* New York: Fordham University Press, 1989.
McDermott, Brian, SJ. "Spiritual Consolation and Its Role in the Second Time of Election." *Studies in the Spirituality of Jesuits* 50, no. 4 (2018).
McGinn, Bernard. *The Crisis of Mysticism: Quietism in Seventeenth-Century Spain, Italy, and France.* Vol. 7 of *The Presence of God: A History of Western Christian Mysticism.* New York: Crossroad-Herder, 2021.

———. *The Flowering of Mysticism*. Vol. 3 of *The Presence of God: A History of Western Christian Mysticism*. New York: Crossroad-Herder, 1998.

———. *The Foundations of Mysticism*. Vol. 1 of *The Presence of God: A History of Western Christian Mysticism*. New York: Crossroad, 1991.

———. "The Letter and the Spirit: Spirituality as an Academic Discipline," *Christian Spirituality Bulletin* 1, no. 2 (1993): 13–22.

———, ed. *Meister Eckhart and the Beguine Mystics*. New York: Continuum, 1994.

———. *Mysticism in the Golden Age of Spain, 1500–1650*. Vol. 6 of *The Presence of God: A History of Western Christian Mysticism*. New York: Crossroad-Herder, 2017.

McGinn, Bernard, John Meyendorff, and Jean Leclercq, eds. *Christian Spirituality: Origins to the Twelfth Century*. New York: Crossroad, 1985.

McGovern, Arthur. *Liberation Theology and Its Critics: Toward an Assessment*. Maryknoll, NY: Orbis, 1989.

McGuire, Meredith. "Mapping Contemporary American Spirituality: A Sociological Perspective." *Christian Spirituality Bulletin* 5, no. 1 (1997): 1, 3–8.

Meier, John. "The Bible as a Source for Theology." *Catholic Theological Society of America Proceedings* 43 (1988).

Mercadante, Linda. *Belief without Borders: Inside the Minds of the Spiritual but Not Religious*. New York: Oxford University Press, 2014.

Metz, Johann Baptist. *Followers of Christ*. Translated by Thomas Linton. Mahwah, NJ: Paulist Press, 1978.

———. *A Passion for God: The Mystical-Political Dimension of Christianity*. Edited and translated with an introduction by J. Matthew Ashley. New York: Paulist Press, 1997.

———. "Productive Noncontemporaneity." In *Observations on "The Spiritual Situation of the Age,"* edited by Jürgen Habermas; translated with an introduction by Andrew Buchwalter, 169–77. Cambridge, MA: MIT Press, 1984.

Milbank, John. *Theology and Social Theory: Beyond Secular Reason*. New York: Blackwell, 2006.

Moore, Thomas. *The Soul's Religion: Cultivating a Profoundly Spiritual Way of Life*. San Francisco: HarperCollins, 2002.

Neufeld, Karl. *Die Brüder Rahner: Eine Biographie*. Freiburg: Herder, 1994.

Neyrey, Jerome, SJ. *Imagining Jesus in His Own Culture: Creating Scenarios of the Gospel for Contemplative Prayer*. Eugene, OR: Cascade Books, 2018.

Nicholas of Cusa. *Selected Spiritual Writings*. Translated and edited with an introduction by H. Lawrence Bond. Classics of Western Spirituality. New York: Paulist Press, 1997.

Noone, Judith. *The Same Fate as the Poor*. Maryknoll, NY: Orbis, 1995.

Nuth, Joan. "*Acatamiento*: Living in an Attitude of Affectionate Awe—An Ignatian Reflection on the Unitive Way." *Spiritus: A Journal of Christian Spirituality* 10, no. 2 (2010): 173–91.

O'Donovan, Leo, SJ, ed. *A World of Grace: An Introduction to the Themes and Foundations of Karl Rahner's Theology*. Washington, DC: Georgetown University Press, 1995.

O'Malley, John, SJ. "Early Jesuit Spirituality: Spain and Italy." In Dupré and Saliers, eds., *Christian Spirituality*, 3–27.
———. *The First Jesuits*. Cambridge: Cambridge University Press, 1993.
———. "The Historiography of the Jesuits: Where Does It Stand Today?" In O'Malley et al., eds., *The Jesuits*, 3–37.
———. "Some Distinctive Characteristics of Jesuit Spirituality in the Sixteenth Century." In O'Malley, Padberg, and O'Keefe, eds., *Jesuit Spirituality*, 1–20.
O'Malley, John, Gauvin Bailey, Steven Harris, and T. Frank Kennedy, eds. *The Jesuits: Cultures, Sciences, and the Arts, 1540–1773*. Toronto: University of Toronto Press, 1999.
O'Malley, John, SJ, and Timothy W. O'Brien, SJ. "The Twentieth-Century Construction of Ignatian Spirituality: A Sketch." With an Introduction by José C. Coupeau, SJ. *Studies in the Spirituality of Jesuits* 52, no. 3 (2020).
O'Malley, John, John Padberg, and Vincent O'Keefe, eds. *Jesuit Spirituality: A Now and Future Resource*. Chicago: Loyola University Press, 1990.
O'Meara, Thomas. *Erich Przywara, S.J.: His Theology and His World*. Notre Dame, IN: University of Notre Dame Press, 2002.
———. *God in the World: A Guide to Karl Rahner's Theology*. Collegeville, MN: Michael Glazier Books, 2015.
O'Murchu, Diarmuid. *Quantum Theology: Spiritual Implications of the New Physics*. New York: Crossroad, 1997/2004.
Origen. *Homilies on Exodus and Genesis*. Translated by Robert E. Heine. The Fathers of the Church 76. Washington, DC: Catholic University of America Press, 1982.
Ozment, Steven. *Mysticism and Dissent: Religious Ideology and Social Dissent in the Sixteenth Century*. New Haven, CT: Yale University Press, 1973.
Padberg, John, SJ, ed. *Jesuit Life & Mission Today: The Decrees of the 31st–35th General Congregations of the Society of Jesus*. St. Louis: Institute of Jesuit Sources, 2009.
Palmer, Martin, SJ, ed. and trans. *On Giving the Spiritual Exercises: The Early Jesuit Manuscript Directories and the Official Directory of 1599*. St. Louis: Institute of Jesuit Sources, 1996.
Paul VI. *Evangelii nuntiandi* (1975). https://www.vatican.va/content/paul-vi/en/apost_exhortations/documents/hf_p-vi_exh_19751208_evangelii-nuntiandi.html.
Piqué, Elisabetta. *Pope Francis, Life and Revolution: A Biography of Jorge Bergoglio*. Chicago: Loyola University Press, 2014.
Plazaola, Juan, ed. *Las fuentes de los ejercicios espirituales de San Ignacio. Actas del Simposio Internaciona*. Bilbao: Mensajero, 1998.
Pousset, Édouard. *Life in Faith and Freedom: An Essay Presenting Gaston Fessard's Analysis of the Dialectic of the Spiritual Exercises of St. Ignatius*. Translated by Eugene Donahue. St. Louis: Institute of Jesuit Sources, 1980.
Prevot, Andrew. *Thinking Prayer: Theology and Spirituality Amid the Crises of Modernity*. Notre Dame, IN: University of Notre Dame Press, 2015.
Principe, Walter. "Broadening the Focus: Context as Corrective Lens in Reading Historical Works in Spirituality." *Christian Spirituality Bulletin* 2, no. 1 (1994): 1, 3–8.

———. "Toward Defining Spirituality." *Sciences religieuses* 12, no. 2 (1983): 127–41.

Pryzwara, Erich, SJ. *Deus Semper Maior. Theologie der Exerzitien*. 3 vols. Freiburg: Herder, 1938.

Quinn, Kevin P., SJ. "Is a Different Kind of Jesuit University Possible Today? The Legacy of Ignacio Ellacuría, SJ," with an introduction by Robert Lassalle-Klein. *Studies in the Spirituality of Jesuits*, 53, no. 1 (2021).

Rahner, Hugo, SJ. *Ignatius the Theologian*. Translated by Michael Barry. San Francisco: Ignatius Press, 1991.

———. "Notes on the Spiritual Exercises." Translated by Louis Mouteer, SJ. Woodstock Letters 5. Washington, DC: Woodstock College Press, 1956.

Rahner, Karl, SJ. "Christology within an Evolutionary View of the World." In *TI* 5:157–92.

———. "The Concept of Existential Philosophy in Heidegger." *Philosophy Today* 13 (Summer 1969): 126–37.

———. "Die ignatianische Mystik der Weltfreudigkeit." *Zeitschrift für Aszese und Mystik* 12 (1937): 121–37.

———. *Faith in a Wintry Season: Conversations and Interviews with Karl Rahner in the Last Years of His Life*. Edited by Paul Imhof and Hubert Biallowons; English translation edited by Harvey D. Egan. New York: Crossroad, 1990.

———. *Foundations of Christian Faith: An Introduction to the Idea of Christian Faith*. Translated by William Dych. New York: Crossroad, 1982.

———. *Hearer of the Word: Laying the Foundation for a Philosophy of Religion*. Translated by Joseph Donceel. New York: Continuum, 1994. Originally published as *Hörer des Wortes: Zur Grundlegung einer Religionsphilosophie*. Munich: Verlag Kösel-Pustet, 1941.

———. "The Ignatian Mysticism of Joy in the World." In *TI* 3:277–93.

———. "Ignatian Spirituality and Devotion to the Heart of Jesus." In *Mission and Grace*, translated by Cicely Hastings, 3:176–210. London: Sheed and Ward, 1966.

———. "Ignatius of Loyola." In Karl Rahner, SJ, *The Great Church Year: The Best of Karl Rahner's Homilies, Sermons, and Meditations*, translated by Frederick G. Lawrence, 329–40. New York: Crossroad, 1994.

———. *Karl Rahner in Dialogue: Conversations and Interviews, 1965–1982*. Edited by Paul Imhof and Hubert Biallowons; English translation edited by Harvey D. Egan. New York: Crossroad, 1986.

———. *Karl Rahner: Spiritual Writings*. Edited and translated by Philip Endean, SJ. Modern Spiritual Masters. Maryknoll, NY: Orbis, 2004.

———. "Lebenslauf." *Entschluß* 31, no. 10 (1977): 32.

———. "Letter to Cardinal Juan Landázuri Ricketts of Lima, Peru." In Hennelly, ed., *Liberation Theology*, 351–52.

———. "The Logic of Concrete Individual Knowledge in Ignatius of Loyola." In *The Dynamic Element of the Church*, translated by W. H. O'Hara, 84–168. New York: Herder, 1964. Originally published as *Das Dynamische in der Kirche*. Edited by Karl Rahner and Heinrich Schlier. Questiones Disputatae 5. Freiburg: Herder, 1958.

———. *Meditations on Priestly Life*. New York: Sheed and Ward, 1973.

———. "Notwendigkeit einer neuen Mystagogie." In *Handbuch der Pastoraltheologie*, Vol. II, Part 1, edited by Franz Xavier Arnold, Karl Rahner, Viktor Schurr, and Leonhard M. Weber, 269–71. Freiburg: Herder, 1966.

———. "Rede des Ignatius von Loyola an einen Jesuiten von Heute." In *Ignatius von Loyola*, edited by Paul Imhof, 9–38. Freiburg: Herder, 1978. Also published in *Schriften zur Theologie XV: Wissenschaft und christlicher Glaube*, 373–408. Zürich: Benziger, 1983. Translated by Rosaleen Ockenden as "Ignatius of Loyola Speaks to a Modern Jesuit." In *Ignatius of Loyola*, edited by Paul Imhoff. London: Collins, 1979.

———. *Sämtliche Werke XIII: Ignatianischer Geist. Schriften zu den Exerzitien und zur Spiritualität des Ordensgründers*. Edited by Andreas R. Batlogg, Johannes Herzgsell, and Stefan Kiechle. Freiburg: Herder, 2006.

———. *Schriften zur Theologie*. 16 vols. Einsiedeln: Benziger, 1962–1984.

———. *Spirit in the World*. Translated by William Dych. New York: Continuum, 1994.

———. *Spiritual Exercises*. Translated by Kenneth Baker. New York: Herder, 1965. Originally published as *Betrachtungen zum ignatianischen Exerzitienbuch*. Munich: Kösel-Verlag, 1965.

———. *Theological Investigations [TI]*. 23 vols. New York: Crossroad, 1974–1992.

———. "Unmittelbare Gotteserfahrung in den Exerzitien." In *Horizonte der Religiosität*, edited by Georg Sporschill, 25–35. Vienna: Herold, 1984.

Raitt, Jill, ed. *Christian Spirituality: High Middle Ages and Reformation*. World Spirituality 17. New York: Crossroad, 1989.

Ricoeur, Paul. *Lectures on Ideology and Utopia*. Edited by George Taylor. New York: Columbia University Press, 1986.

Rosa, Hartmut. *Social Acceleration: A New Theory of Modernity*. Translated by Jonathan Trejo-Mathys. New York: Columbia University Press, 2013.

Rourke, Thomas R. *The Roots of Pope Francis's Social and Political Thought: From Argentina to the Vatican*. New York: Rowman & Littlefield, 2016.

Rubbelke, Michael. "'A Constant Closeness to *This* God': Karl Rahner's Experience of God and Contemporary Mystical Theology." PhD diss., University of Notre Dame, 2018.

Rubin, Serio, and Francesca Ambrogetti. *Pope Francis: Conversations with Jorge Bergoglio*. New York: Penguin/New American Library, 2014.

Sacks, Oliver. *Gratitude*. New York: Alfred A. Knopf, 2015.

Samour, Héctor. *Voluntad de liberación: El pensamiento filosófico de Ignacio Ellacuría*. San Salvador: UCA Editores, 2002.

Scannone, Juan Carlos, SJ. "Pope Francis and the Theology of the People." *Theological Studies* 77, no. 1 (2016): 118–35.

Scavo, Nello. *Bergoglio's List: How a Young Francis Defied a Dictatorship and Saved Dozens of Lives*. Translated by Bret Thoman. Charlotte, NC: Saint Benedict Press, 2014.

Schineller, Peter, SJ. "The Pilgrim Journey of Ignatius: From Soldier to Laborer in the Lord's Vineyard and its Implications for Apostolic Lay Spirituality." *Studies in the Spirituality of Jesuits* 31, no. 4 (1999).

———. "Pope Francis—Deeply Ignatian and Deeply Jesuit." Salt and Light Media. https://slmedia.org/blog/pope-francis-deeply-ignatian-and-deeply-jesuit.

Schmidt, Leigh Eric. *Restless Souls: The Making of American Spirituality*. 2nd ed. with a new preface. Berkeley: University of California Press, 2012.

Schneider, Michael. *"Unterscheidung der Geister": Die ignatianischen Exerzitien in der Deutung von E. Przywara, K. Rahner und G. Fessard*. Innsbruck: Tyrolia Verlag, 1983.

Schneiders, Sandra. "A Hermeneutical Approach to the Study of Christian Spirituality." *Christian Spirituality Bulletin* 2, no. 1 (1994): 9–14.

———. *The Revelatory Text: Interpreting the New Testament as Sacred Scripture*. 2nd ed. with a new preface. San Francisco: HarperSanFrancisco, 1991.

Schreiner, Susan. *Are You Alone Wise? The Search for Certainty in the Early Modern Era*. Oxford: Oxford University Press, 2010.

Schüssler Fiorenza, Francis. "Systematic Theology: Task and Methods." In *Systematic Theology: Roman Catholic Perspectives*, edited by Francis Schüssler Fiorenza and John Galvin, 2nd ed., 1–75. Minneapolis: Fortress, 2011.

Segundo, Juan Luis, SJ. *The Christ of the Ignatian Exercises*. Edited and translated by John Drury. Jesus of Nazareth Yesterday and Today, 4. Maryknoll, NY: Orbis, 1987.

———. "Ignatius of Loyola: Trial or Project?" In *Signs of the Times: Theological Reflections*, edited by Alfred Hennelly, SJ, 149–75. Maryknoll, NY: Orbis, 1993.

Shah, Vinod Bruno, OP. "Disciplining Theology: Critically Retrieving Xavier Zubiri's Fundamental Theology of Experience." PhD diss., University of Notre Dame, 2019.

Sheldrake, Philip, ed. *Spirituality and History: Questions of Interpretation and Method*. New York: Crossroad, 1992.

———. *The Way of Ignatius of Loyola: Contemporary Approaches to the Spiritual Exercises*. St. Louis: Institute of Jesuit Sources, 1991.

Shore, Paul. "The *Vita Christi* of Ludolph of Saxony and its Influence on the *Spiritual Exercises* of Ignatius of Loyola." *Studies in the Spirituality of Jesuits* 30, no. 1 (1998).

Slavin, Kevin. "How Algorithms Shape Our World." TedGlobal 2011. https://www.ted.com/talks/kevin_slavin_how_algorithms_shape_our_world/transcript.

Sluhovsky, Moshe. "Loyola's *Spiritual Exercises* and the Modern Self." In Maryks, ed., *A Companion to Ignatius of Loyola*, 216–47.

Sobrino, Jon, SJ. "The Christ of the Ignatian Exercises." In *Christology at the Crossroads: A Latin American Approach*, 396–424. Maryknoll, NY: Orbis, 1978.

———. *Christ the Liberator: A View from the Victims*. Translated by Paul Burns. Maryknoll, NY: Orbis, 2001. Originally published as *La Fe en Jesucristo: Ensayo desde las víctimas*. Madrid: Trotta, 1999.

———. "Ignacio Ellacuría: El hombre y el cristiano." In Ellacuría, *Fe y Justicia*, 11–109.

———. *Jesus the Liberator: A Historical-Theological Reading of Jesus of Nazareth*. Translated by Paul Burns and Francis McDonagh. Maryknoll, NY: Orbis, 1993.

———. "Monseñor Romero's Impact on Ignacio Ellacuría." Translated by J. Matthew Ashley. In Ashley, Burke and Cardenal, eds., *The Grammar of Justice*, 57–85.

———. *The Principle of Mercy: Taking the Crucified People from the Cross*. Maryknoll, NY: Orbis, 1994.
———. "Spirituality and the Following of Jesus." In *Mysterium Liberationis: Fundamental Concepts of Liberation Theology*, edited by Ignacio Ellacuría and Jon Sobrino, 677–701. Maryknoll, NY: Orbis, 1993.
———. *Spirituality of Liberation: Toward Political Holiness*. Translated by Robert Barr. Maryknoll, NY, Orbis, 1988.
Sobrino, Jon, SJ, and Rolando Alvarado, eds. *Ignacio Ellacuría: Aquella libertad esclarecida*. San Salvador: UCA Editores, 1999.
Sols Lucia, José. *La teología histórica de Ignacio Ellacuría*. Madrid: Editorial Trotta, 1999.
Tanner, Katheryn. *Theories of Culture: A New Agenda for Theology*. Minneapolis, MN: Augsburg Fortress, 1997.
Taylor, Charles. *A Secular Age*. Cambridge, MA: Belknap, 2007.
———. *Sources of the Self: The Making of Modern Identity*. Cambridge, MA: Harvard University Press, 1989.
Tickle, Phyllis. *Re-discovering the Sacred: Spirituality in America*. New York: Crossroad, 1995.
Toner, Jules, SJ. *A Commentary of Saint Ignatius's Rules for the Discernment of Spirits: A Guide to the Principles and Practice*. St Louis: Institute of Jesuit Sources, 1982.
———. "The Deliberation That Started the Jesuits: A Commentary on the *Deliberatio primorum Patrum*." *Studies in the Spirituality of Jesuits* 6, no. 4 (1974).
———. *Discerning God's Will: Ignatius of Loyola's Teaching on Christian Decision Making*. St. Louis: Institute of Jesuit Sources, 1991.
Toulmin, Stephen. *Cosmopolis: The Hidden Agenda of Modernity*. New York: Free Press, 1990.
Tracy, David. *The Analogical Imagination: Christian Theology and the Culture of Pluralism*. New York: Crossroad, 1981.
Underhill, Evelyn. *Mysticism: A Study in the Nature and Development of Man's Spiritual Consciousness*. New York: E. P. Dutton, 1911.
Vallely, Paul. *Pope Francis: The Struggle for the Soul of Catholicism*. New York: Bloomsbury, 2015.
Van Ness, Peter H., ed. *Spirituality and the Secular Quest*. World Spirituality 22. New York: Crossroad, 1996.
White, Lynn, Jr. "The Historical Roots of Our Ecological Crisis." *Science* 155, no. 3767 (1967): 1203–7.
Whitfield, Teresa. *Paying the Price: Ignacio Ellacuría and the Murdered Jesuits of El Salvador*. Philadelphia: Temple University Press, 1995.
Wiseman, James, OSB. "'I Have Experienced God': Religious Experience in the Theology of Karl Rahner." *American Benedictine Review* 44, no. 1 (1993): 22–57.
Wolf, Kenneth Baxter. *The Poverty of Riches: St. Francis of Assisi Reconsidered*. Oxford: Oxford University Press, 2003.
Wulf, Friedrich, SJ, ed. *Ignatius of Loyola: His Personality and Spiritual Heritage*,

1556–1956. St. Louis: Institute of Jesuit Sources, 1977. Originally published as *Ignatius von Loyola: Seine geistige Gestalt und sein Vermächtnis*. Würzburg: Echter, 1956.

Wuthnow, Robert. *After Heaven: Spirituality in America since the 1950s*. Berkeley: University of California Press, 1998.

———. *God and Mammon in America*. New York: Free Press, 1994.

———. *Sharing the Journey*. New York: Free Press, 1994.

Zahlauer, Arno. *Karl Rahner und sein "produktives Vorbild" Ignatius von Loyola*. Innsbruck: Tyrolia, 1996.

Index

acatamiento (affectionate awe), 330n.71
acedia, 271, 272
Achaerandio, Luis, 176
Acquaviva, Claudio, 317n.13
Adorno, Theodor, on constellations, 31–32
Alcott, Amos Bronson, 4
Alexander, Jon, on spirituality, 3
Alumbrados, 68
Amaladoss, Michael, 300
Ambrose, St., 286
American Transcendentalists, 3–4
Aparecida Conference (CELAM V), 247–48, 258, 259, 264, 265, 270, 271, 291
apophaticism, 155–56, 169
Aquinas, Thomas, 13, 70, 328n.40
 on knowledge, 187
 on nature and grace, 90
 Rahner on, 133–34, 141, 145, 148, 153, 161, 166, 333n.21
Argentina
 Catholic Church in, 240–41, 242, 256
 Colegio Máximo, 238, 356n.13
 Dirty War in, 240, 241–42
 economic conditions, 247
 Peronism in, 240–41, 243, 360n.54
 theology of the people in, 250, 256–59, 360n.60, 361n.62
Arrupe, Pedro, 239, 243, 344n.11, 363n.104
 relationship with Ellacuría, 183–84, 227
asceticism, 239, 343n.187, 364n.123
 ascetical theology, 215, 353n.159
 of Ignatius, 35–36, 74, 96–97, 108, 111, 113, 206, 274, 295
atheism, 17, 18, 159, 195
Augustine, St., 13, 29, 264, 286
Azcue, Segundo, 175

Basil, St., 286
beatific vision, 125, 126, 127, 339n.123
Bede the Venerable, *Homilies*, 234, 356n.10
Beguines, 14, 88, 315n.75
Bellah, Robert, 8–9, 131
Benedictine spirituality, 305, 306, 330n.62, 367n.17, 368n.27

387

Benedict XVI, 233, 238, 248
  Deus caritas est, 265
Berger, Peter, on pluralization of life-worlds, 21
Bernard of Clairvaux, 13, 86, 341n.156
Bianchi, Enrique, 250
Blondel, Maurice, 216, 255, 353n.161
  L'Action, 252
Blumenberg, Hans, 326n.6
Boff, Leonardo, 225
Bonaventure, St., 70, 132, 341n.156
  Cousins on, 85, 89, 229, 327n.22
  and Rahner, 127, 148, 156–57, 161, 166, 169, 230, 297, 327n.22
  on spiritual touch, 127, 148, 156–57, 167
  Tree of Life, 84, 85
Borges, Jorge Luis, 359n.46
Borghesi, Massimo, 250, 262, 264, 268, 270, 360n.60, 362n.85
Brackley, Dean, on *Spiritual Exercises*, 53, 325n.110
Buckley, Michael, 321n.64, 322n.73, 322n.77
  on consolation and desolation, 62, 63
  on times for election, 59
Buddhist spirituality, 367n.16
Burke, Kevin, 184

Campbell-Johnston, Michael, 243
Cano, Melchior, 329n.51
Cardenal, Rodolfo, 222–23, 227
Carmelite spirituality, 305, 306, 330n.62
Catholic Encyclopedia, 2
Catholicism
  and academic theology, ix–x, xiv
  Congregation for the Doctrine of the Faith (CDF), 348n.66, 358n.33
  Counter-Reformation, 92–94
  the Eucharist, 33, 46, 163, 164
  and faith, 30
  mysticism in, 4–5
  preferential option for the poor, 175, 177, 239, 257, 270, 358n.33
  sex abuse crisis, 288
  Social Teachings, 240–41
  vocation in, 24
  See also Vatican II
Center for Investigation and Social Action (CISA), 243, 246, 357n.24
Certeau, Michel de, 251
  on mysticism, 16
Chávez y González, Luis, 176, 345n.16
Chemnitz, Martin, 92
Chenu, Marie-Dominique, xiv, 5, 228, 249, 307
Christus, 251, 360n.49
Clement of Alexandria, 125
Coathelem, Hervé, on *Spiritual Exercises*, 52
COEPAL (la Comisión Episcopal de Pastoral), 256
Coleridge, Samuel, 131
Collins, Billy, on spirituality, 18, 24
Communion and Liberation, 264
Congar, Yves, xiv, 5, 250
consolation
  Buckley on, 62, 63
  Corella on, 61–62, 63, 65, 66
  Coupeau on, 319n.38
  Ellacuría on, 66
  God's role in, 60, 61–62, 65, 68, 146–47, 149, 150, 303, 322n.75
  in *Imitation of Christ*, 63–64, 65
  Jesus as consoler, 55
  McDermott on, 62–65, 66, 320n.48, 321n.62, 63, 322n.76, 354n.177

Pope Francis on, 66, 236, 281, 287–88, 295–96, 297
Rahner on, 66, 146–53, 164, 167, 168, 229, 296, 321n.51, 339n.126, 340n.137
in *Spiritual Exercises*, 51–52, 55, 59, 60–66, 67, 68, 101, 107, 146–53, 164, 167, 168, 229, 236, 296, 303, 318n.16, 319n.38, 320n.48, 321nn.51, 60, 62, 63, 69, 322nn.71, 74–77, 339n.126, 354n.177
as without prior cause, 66, 146–53, 164, 167, 168, 229, 296, 321n.51, 322n.77, 339n.126, 340n.137
Corella, Jesus, on Ignatian consolation, 61–62, 63, 65, 66
Corporate Mystic, The, 7–8, 22
Council of Sens, 329n.45
Council of Trent, 92
Counter-Reformation, 92–94
Coupeau, José Carlos, on consolation, 319n.38
Cousins, Ewert
on Bonaventure, 85, 89, 229, 327n.22
on mysticism of the historical event, 84–85, 89, 229, 297, 298, 303
on spirituality, 312n.33
culture
popular culture and spirituality, 7–10, 13, 27, 32, 289
relationship to theology, ix, xi, xiii–xiv, xviii, 302
Renaissance humanism, 91, 94, 102, 103, 119, 297
and Society of Jesus, 41–42, 80, 91, 92, 106, 107, 119, 180–81, 237
See also modernity

Daniélou, Jean, 5
Deep Ecology, 362n.85

Delgado, Freddy, 344n.15
de Lubac, Henri de, 5, 248, 250, 264, 300
DeMello, Anthony, 300, 367n.16, 368n.27
on *Spiritual Exercises* and unselfing the self, 53, 54
Descartes, René, 82, 95, 326n.6
Cartesian *cogito*, 21
Diccionario de espiritualidad ignaciana, 61
Dictionnaire de spiritualité, 5
Dionysius the Areopagite, 85
discernment
Ellacuría on, 200, 205–8, 221, 227, 228, 229, 230–31
Fessard on, 252–53, 360n.57
Pope Francis on, 235, 236, 250–51, 255, 262, 263, 267, 268, 269, 280, 281, 286, 287, 288, 295, 302, 359n.48, 360nn.52, 58
Rahner on, 112, 122, 124, 133, 144, 146–48, 150–51, 157, 160, 163, 164, 165, 169, 170, 175, 182, 200, 229–30, 256, 302, 334n.46, 343n.188
Schneider on, 360n.57
Schreiner on, 320n.47
Spiritual Exercises' Rules for the Discernment of Spirits, 52, 58–70, 95, 98, 99, 112, 122, 124, 133, 144, 146–48, 150–51, 157, 160, 163, 164, 165, 169, 200, 205, 221, 230–31, 239, 268, 269, 279–80, 296, 302, 319n.34, 320n.47, 323n.79, 326n.1, 334n.46, 342nn.160, 188, 348n.72, 354n.177, 362n.78
discipleship
Ellacuría on, 199, 202, 203, 204–5, 212, 235, 351n.116

discipleship *(cont.)*
  in *Spiritual Exercises*, 76, 86, 94–95, 105–6, 123, 202, 236, 306
Dominican spirituality, 330n.62
Drescher, Elizabeth, 27, 314n.60
Dulles, Avery, 69
  on Ignatian spirituality, 82
Dupré, Louis
  on the modern self, 21
  on nominalism, 326n.6
  Passage to Modernity, 326n.7
  on spirituality, 16–17
Dupuis, Jacques, 300
Dych, William, 113, 114, 117

Eckhart, Meister, 15–16, 23, 157, 230, 297, 315n.75, 316n.97, 331n.3
  vs. Ignatius, 87–88, 89
Elizondo, Miguel, 174, 218, 324n.91
  relationship with Ellacuría, 175, 180, 346n.27
Ellacuría, Ignacio
  on agrarian reform, 177
  assassination of, 178, 366n.1
  on consolation, 66
  on contemplation in action, 196–97, 199
  on development of Third World, 350n.109, 352n.146
  on discernment, 200, 205–8, 221, 227, 228, 229, 230–31
  on discipleship, 199, 202, 203, 204–5, 212, 235, 351n.116
  ecclesiology of, 222–23
  on encountering Jesus, 213, 214, 216, 221, 228, 229, 231, 235, 296, 350n.105
  and *Estudios Centroamericanos (ECA)*, 176, 196
  Filosfía de la realidad histórica, 189
  on God as Trinity, 193–95
  "The Historicity of Christian Salvation," 192–97, 207, 348n.66
  on history and historicization, 182–83, 184, 189–91, 192–201, 203, 205, 206–7, 210–12, 214–17, 220, 222, 225, 227, 228, 231–32, 251, 262, 293, 294, 296, 298–99, 337n.90, 346n.34, 347nn.54, 56, 58, 62, 348nn.66, 69, 72, 349n.84, 350nn.91, 105, 351nn.116, 122, 352n.150, 353n.163, 360n.52
  on ideology, 198–99, 349n.81, 350n.92
  and Ignatian spirituality, xiv–xv, xvi, xvii–xviii, xix, 35, 108, 173–74, 178–79, 183, 193–94, 196–97, 199–229, 231, 254, 291, 293, 296, 298, 299, 302, 303, 304–5, 310n.10, 324n.91, 325n.110, 348n.72
  on imagination, 217–22, 227, 227–28, 231–32, 354nn.169, 170
  on intelligence, 186–87, 188–90, 196, 200, 216, 225, 294, 355n.187
  on Latin American Church, 183, 200, 203, 204–5, 208, 214, 215, 221, 231
  and liberation theology, xviii, 192–93, 213–14
  and modernity, xiv–xv, xix, 178–79, 206, 293, 299–300, 302
  on philosophy, 191–92
  vs. Pope Francis, 235, 236, 237, 239, 262, 274, 288, 291, 294, 295, 296, 299, 302, 303, 310n.10, 360n.52, 363n.104
  on possibilitization, 337n.90, 347n.56
  on poverty, 195–96, 198, 207, 208, 351n.123, 352n.144, 354n.179
  on private property, 191
  on propheticism and utopia, 220, 222

vs. Rahner, 178–79, 193, 195, 200, 217, 228, 229, 230, 231, 291, 293, 296–97, 299, 302, 303, 310n.11, 347n.58
on reading the signs of the times, 182, 183, 184, 197
on reality, 186–87, 188–89, 196, 197–98, 200, 203–4, 211, 216, 225, 227–28, 231, 232, 249, 262, 294, 347n.51, 355n.187, 360n.52
relationship with Arrupe, 183–84, 227
relationship with Elizondo, 175, 180, 346n.27
relationship with Espinoza, 181
relationship with Martínez Baigorri, 346n.31
relationship with Montes, 243
relationship with Rahner, 182–83
relationship with Romero, 183, 184–85, 222–23, 226–27, 231, 349n.80, 355n.181
relationship with Zubiri, 181, 185–86, 230–31, 293, 347nn.54, 58, 348n.65, 349n.79, 350n.92
at retreat of Central American Vice Province (1969), 173, 180, 183, 196, 201, 220, 231
and *Revista Latinoamericana de Teología*, 176–77
on salvation, 192–97, 198, 202, 207, 216, 256, 348n.66, 349n.84, 351n.120, 352n.139
on sin, 173, 193, 195–96, 202–3, 206, 209–10, 220, 349n.80, 350nn.108, 109, 351n.111, 352n.139
on *Spiritual Exercises*, 173–74, 199–212, 213, 214, 215, 217, 220–21, 222, 225, 226, 227, 228–29, 231, 274, 296, 344n.3, 348n.73, 350nn.108, 109, 355n.181

Spiritual Exercises and life of, 222–28
on theologal dimension, 192, 194, 203–4, 206–7, 209, 212, 294
theology of, 192–99, 202, 203, 207–8, 212–22, 223, 225–26, 228–32, 291, 296, 298–99, 310n.11, 349n.79, 350n.91, 351n.120
at UCA, 176, 177–78, 291, 348n.66
on union with God, 211
"Utopia and Propheticism in Latin America," 222, 231, 354n.171
El Salvador
Jesuits in, 175–78, 180–81, 183–84, 239, 290, 344n.15, 345n.20
murders in, 177
ruling elites in, 175, 176, 177, 226, 321n.69
Emerson, Ralph Waldo, 4, 131
Endean, Philip, 354n.177, 361n.64
on Pope Francis, 274, 364n.123
on Rahner, 126, 127, 148, 154, 164, 166, 229, 292, 340n.141, 341n.143
Enlightenment, x, xii, 131, 190, 263, 293, 312n.31
Erasmus, Desiderius, 90, 91, 329n.45
Espinoza Pólit, Aurelio, 181, 354n.179
Estrada, Miguel, 345n.16
Estudios Centroamericanos (ECA), 176, 177
Eucharist, 33, 46, 163, 164
Evennett, Outram, 90

faith, 30–31, 33, 125, 315n.92, 335n.54, 354n.178
Falla, Ricardo, 174, 175
Fathers of the Church, 70, 87, 132, 161
Favre, Pierre, 323n.88, 329n.55
Memoriale, 251
and Pope Francis, 237, 270, 271, 297, 298, 304

Favre, Pierre *(cont.)*
   relationship with Ignatius, xv, 325n.106
Fessard, Gaston
   La Dialectique des "Exercises spirituels" de Saint Ignace de Loyola, 251, 254, 363n.106
   on discernment of spirits, 252–53, 360n.57
   on history, 251–54, 255–56, 360n.52, 362n.78
   on human freedom, 252–53, 268, 362n.78
   on Nazism, 360n.54
   and Pope Francis, 239, 250, 251–56, 260, 266, 267, 268, 273, 278, 283, 294–95, 360nn.52, 54, 59, 78, 362n.88, 363n.106
   on *Spiritual Exercises*, 239, 251–56, 267, 268, 283, 294–95
Fiorito, Miguel Ángel, 239, 251, 268
Fischer, Karl, 341n.143
Fitzgerald, Constance, 305
Fleming, David, 318n.25
Foucault, Michel, 243
Franciscans, 39, 89, 305, 306, 367nn.17, 19
Francis of Assisi, St., 84–85, 86, 89, 229, 231, 316n.96
   on gift of tears, 123, 130, 334n.49
   Pope Francis on, 234, 368n.25
   Rahner on, 123, 130, 334n.49, 343n.186
Francis, Pope
   Amoris Laetitia, 287
   and Aparecida Conference (CELAM V), 247–48, 258, 259, 264, 265, 270, 271, 291
   as archbishop of Buenos Aires, 233, 234, 244, 246, 247, 258, 262, 263–64, 265, 356n.10, 364n.130
   on being a Jesuit, 233, 268, 280
   on center and periphery, 259, 262–63, 270–71, 280, 295, 303, 361n.71
   on Christian communities, 295, 298, 302
   on the Church, 247–49, 257–58, 260, 262–63, 275, 277, 285–88, 290–91, 295, 297, 303
   at Colegio Máximo, 235, 238, 239, 243, 245, 246
   on consolation, 66, 236, 281, 287–88, 295–96, 297
   on conversion, 275, 278–79
   in Córdoba, 245–46, 260
   on corruption, 247, 359n.34
   and Decree 4 of 32nd General Congregation, 266, 358n.27
   during Dirty War, 242, 244–45
   on discernment, 235, 236, 250–51, 255, 262, 263, 267, 268, 269, 280, 281, 286, 287, 288, 295, 302, 359n.48, 360nn.52, 58
   election as pope, 233, 247–49, 280
   vs. Ellacuría, 235, 236, 237, 239, 262, 274, 288, 291, 294, 295, 296, 299, 302, 303, 310n.10, 360n.52, 363n.104
   on encountering Jesus, 235, 262, 297, 303, 355n.204
   Endean on, 274, 364n.123
   episcopal motto *miserando atque eligendo*, 234, 356n.10, 364n.130
   Evangelii Gaudium, 260–61, 262, 265, 281, 287, 362nn.76, 78, 88
   on faithful people of God, 257–58, 361nn.63, 64, 66
   and Favre, 237, 270, 271, 297, 298, 304
   and Fessard, 239, 250, 251–56, 260, 266, 267, 268, 273, 278, 283,

294–95, 360nn.52, 54, 59, 78, 362n.88, 363n.106
Gaudete et exsultate, 264, 281, 291
and Giussani, 264–65, 364n.130
on globalization and localization, 262–63, 281
on Gnosticism and Pelagianism, 264
on God as surprising, 270–71, 363n.104
on God's mercy, 273, 275–76, 277–79, 280, 281, 364n.130
and Guardini, 259–64, 265, 266–67, 268, 270, 295, 360n.59, 361nn.72, 74, 362n.84, 366n.170
on ideology, 255, 266, 267
and Ignatian spirituality, xiv–xv, xvi, xvii–xviii, xix, 108, 233–36, 237–38, 239, 248–49, 250–51, 254–55, 260, 262, 263, 266–81, 282–88, 291, 294–96, 297, 298, 299, 302, 303, 304–5, 310n.10, 324n.95, 364n.124, 365n.160
In Him Alone Is Our Hope, 278, 365n.160
intellectual influences on, 249–68
on joy, 287
The Joy of the Gospel, 355n.204
on justice, 237, 281–85
Laudato si', 263, 287, 368n.25
leadership style, 240, 245, 246, 260, 265, 274, 296, 357nn.17, 19, 358nn.26, 27, 364n.124
Let Us Dream, 359n.48
and liberation theology, xviii, 242, 246, 276, 310n.11
and mercy, 234, 237, 265, 273, 275–76, 277–79, 280, 281–85, 288, 296, 297, 303, 358n.32, 364n.130
Misericordiae vultus, 281–82, 285
and modernity, xiv–xv, xvii–xviii, xix, 263, 273–74, 287, 294, 298, 299, 302, 367n.15

and motto *Non coerceri maximo, contineri tamen a minimo, divinum est*, 271, 272, 324n.95, 367n.11
The Name of God is Mercy, 281, 282–83
on oppositions, 260–63, 266–67, 270, 285–87
on the pastoral dimension, 235–36, 255, 285–86, 288, 294, 361n.74
as pilgrim, 237–49
and Podetti, 250, 258–59, 268, 270
and politics, 241, 247
on the poor, 234, 242, 243, 244, 246, 247
as provincial, 240–44, 246, 257, 259, 276, 357n.25, 358n.26
Querida Amazonia, 361n.66
vs. Rahner, 235, 236, 237, 254, 263, 272, 273, 288, 291, 294, 295, 296, 299, 302, 303, 310n.10, 362n.84, 363n.113
as reader, 250
on reality and ideas, 249, 255, 262, 362n.80
on reason, 357n.25
relationship with Fiorito, 239, 251, 268
relationship with Yorio and Jalics, 243–45
retreat given in 2006, 236–37, 274, 275–76, 277, 283–85
on salvation, 248–49
"The Service of Faith and the Promotion of Justice," 266–68
on sin, 233–34, 275–76, 278–79, 280, 303, 359n.34
on *Spiritual Exercises*, 268–80, 281, 282–85, 287, 294–96, 364nn.127, 131, 365n.160, 367n.15
on spirituality, 265
on St. Francis of Assisi, 234, 368n.25

Francis, Pope *(cont.)*
  theology of, 235–36, 250, 283, 285–88, 291, 296, 299, 309n.7
  on time and space, 256, 260–62, 298
  on unity and conflict, 256, 262
  "Y Conforme a esta Esperanza," 295
Frankfurt School, 293
Frentz, Emmerich Raitz von, 112

Galileo Galilei, 82
Gandhi, Mohandas, 4
Gera, Lucio, 250, 256, 259, 361n.62
Gerhartz, Johannes, 40–41
German idealism, 17, 117
German Romanticism, 131
Gerson, Jean, ix
Giddens, Anthony, 20, 100, 272
Gillespie, Michael, on modernity, 86, 326n.6
Gilson, Étienne, 5
Giussani, Luigi, 250
  The Attractiveness of Jesus, 264–65, 364n.130
  and Pope Francis, 264–65, 364n.130
Gnosticism, 264
God
  as Creator, 46, 61, 120, 121, 125, 127, 142, 152, 168, 193–94, 202, 210, 339n.134
  goodness of, 101
  grace of, 52, 53–54, 55, 105, 114, 115, 121, 122–23, 126–27, 146, 149, 151, 153, 156, 158–59, 160, 161, 163, 167, 168, 169, 170, 182, 193, 195, 197, 230, 285, 287, 292, 302, 303, 322n.76, 326n.3, 335n.63, 338n.109, 339n.123, 341n.143, 348n.72, 350nn.89, 108
  immediate experience of, 146, 155–57, 158, 161, 163, 167, 168, 230, 296, 302, 339nn.122, 124, 127, 340n.141, 341n.156
  incomprehensibility of, 156
  justice of, 281–85
  as loving, 58, 281, 282, 294, 303, 341n.153, 343n.193
  mercy of, 233, 235, 236, 269, 273, 275–76, 277–79, 280, 281–85, 296, 322n.71, 364n.130
  as mystery, 183, 185, 292–93, 304
  presence and goodness of, 56, 57
  relationship to history, 192–96, 197–98, 293, 351n.116
  response to sin, 45, 46, 48–49, 53, 54, 105, 121–22, 204
  revelation in world, 120–21, 122–24, 127, 144, 145, 168, 170, 182–83, 196, 334n.51
  role in consolation, 60, 61–62, 65, 68, 146–47, 149, 150, 303, 322n.75
  transcendence of, 120, 123, 127, 282, 330n.71
  as Trinity, 28, 48, 104, 192, 193–95, 197, 204, 273, 339n.134, 349nn.79, 80, 350n.92
  union with, 23, 58, 63, 88, 97, 100, 142, 152, 156, 163, 164, 211, 303, 320n.44, 338n.109, 340n.137
  will of, 96, 132, 145, 146, 149, 152, 200, 201, 212, 221, 282, 283, 284, 293, 302, 319n.34, 338n.109, 341n.153
Goethe, Johann Wolfgang von, 131, 336n.75
Gonçalves da Câmera, Luís, 81
González, Antonio, 347n.54
Grande, Rutilio, 176, 177, 344n.15, 357n.21
Griffith, Bede, 368n.27
Gründler, Otto, on Modern Devotion, 328n.29

Guardini, Romano
  The End of the Modern World, 128–29, 130–31, 132–33, 135, 140, 153, 159, 161, 163, 167, 263, 292, 336n.79, 362n.84
  Der Gegensatz (The Opposition), 259–63
  Letters from Lake Como, 336n.69
  on personality and personhood, 130–31, 132, 362n.84
  and Pope Francis, 245, 250, 259–64, 265, 266–67, 268, 270, 295, 360n.59, 361nn.72, 74, 362n.84, 366n.170
Gutiérrez, Gustavo
  and liberation theology, 310n.11, 360n.60, 361n.62
  on modernity and Christian faith, 299–300
  on poverty, 198
  on spirituality, 30, 315n.90
  on theology, 34–35, 315n.90

Hadot, Pierre
  on classical philosophy, 28–29, 31
  Philosophy as a Way of Life, xi
  on spiritual exercises as transformation, 80
  on spirituality and theology, 289
Haight, Roger, 300
  on imagination and theology, 217–18
  on spirituality, 11
Harnack, Adolf von, 343n.187
Harrison, Peter, 328n.27
Hegel, G. W. F., 102, 186, 254
  on *Aufhebung*, 123, 253
  on history, 253, 258
  Phenomenology of Spirit, 251–52
Heidegger, Martin, 17, 186, 243
  on anxiety, 141, 152, 168
  on authenticity, 334n.41
  Being and Time, 124, 137–38, 337n.94
  on *Dasein*, 124, 137, 141, 150, 334n.41, 337n.107
  and Rahner, 118, 124, 137–38, 140, 141, 150, 159, 167, 168, 170, 292, 337nn.94, 107
heresy of the free spirit, 23–24, 316n.96
Hernández, José, *El Gaucho Martin Fierro*, 359n.46
Hindu spirituality, 367n.16, 368n.27
Holy Spirit, 45, 58, 100, 160, 214, 220, 221, 230, 266, 312n.41
  gifts of, xvi, 28, 63
  role in election/choice, 317n.12, 319n.31
Honecker, Martin, 118, 333n.34
Honofrio, St., 327n.15
Hoop Dreams, 27
Hügel, Friedrich von
  The Mystical Element of Religion as Studied in Saint Catherine of Genoa and her Friends, 5
  on spirituality and theology, 290
  on three elements of living religion, xii–xiii, 5, 291
human freedom, 281, 341n.153
  Fessard on, 252–53, 268, 362n.78
  Zubiri, 187–88
Hummes, Claudio Cardinal, 234
Husserl, Edmund, 186
  on transcendental ego, 22

Ibisate, Francisco, 176
ideology, 222, 253, 294, 347n.59
  Ellacuría on, 198–99, 349n.81, 350n.92
  Pope Francis on, 255, 266, 267
Idoate, Florentino, 174
Ignatius of Loyola
  asceticism of, 35–36, 74, 96–97, 108, 111, 113, 206, 274, 295

Ignatius of Loyola *(cont.)*
  autobiography, xv, 71, 323n.86
  and Christian Neoplatonism, 56, 85, 87, 89, 169, 297, 303
  conversion in 1521, 40, 43, 68
  correspondence, xv, 71, 73, 74, 90, 323n.88, 325n.99, 326n.1
  early life, 83, 327n.8
  on gift of tears, 123, 130, 330n.71, 334n.49
  in Holy Land, 39–41, 69, 81
  on St. Honofrio, 327n.15
  on love as exchange of gifts, 226
  at Manresa, 40, 41, 43, 52, 71, 72, 73, 84, 320n.50
  and modernity, 81–95, 108, 161, 272, 299
  mysticism of, 35–36, 84–85, 87–88, 89, 108, 111–12, 113, 118–28, 155–57, 159, 162, 167, 168, 171, 229–30, 251, 274, 292, 295, 335n.60, 341n.143
  in Paris, 40, 43, 44, 69–70, 90, 91, 92–93, 104, 317n.14, 323n.81
  as pilgrim, 81–82, 233
  on positive theology and scholasticism, 70, 90–91
  relationship with Favre, xv, 325n.106
  relationship with Laínez, xv, 43
  relationship with Nadal, xv, 72, 104
  relationship with Paul IV, 100, 330n.65
  relationship with Polanco, 47, 71, 72, 90, 104, 323n.87
  and scholasticism, 70, 90–91, 94, 328n.40, 329n.42
  Spiritual Diary, xv, 52, 71, 153
  as superior general, 40, 41–42, 71, 72, 73–74, 97–98
  as theologian, 104–8
  See also Spiritual Exercises

Imitation of Christ, The
  Book on Interior Consolation, 63
  vs. *Spiritual Exercises*, 44, 63–64, 65, 70, 87, 95, 325n.105
  on theology, ix, 70, 309n.2
indifference
  vs. apathy, 45
  vs. mystical *Gelassenheit*, 87, 229, 297
  Rahner on, 119, 123, 127, 129–30, 132, 139, 156, 165, 166, 168, 170, 229–30, 296, 297, 298
  relationship to finding God in all things, 87–88, 119, 123, 127–28, 164, 166, 168, 171, 296
  in *Spiritual Exercises*, 45, 50–51, 87, 99, 119–20, 123, 127–28, 129–30, 132–33, 139, 156, 164, 165, 166, 168, 170, 171, 229–30, 296, 297, 319nn.29–32
Institute of Public Opinion (IUDOP), 177
Irenaeus, 264, 286
Ivens, Michael, 64
Ivereigh, Austin, 258, 356n.13, 357n.19, 358nn.26, 33, 361n.74

Jackson, Phil, *Sacred Hoops*, 7, 27
Jacobus de Voragine, *Golden Legend/ Flos sanctorum*, 40, 41, 84
Jalics, Franz, 243–45
Jansenists, x
Jennings, Willie
  The Christian Imagination, 219–20
  on social imagination, 219–20, 221
Jesus Christ
  Beatitudes, 206
  as consoler, 55
  Ellacuría on discipleship, 202, 203, 204–5, 212, 235, 351n.116
  Ellacuría on encountering Jesus, 213, 214, 216, 221, 228, 229, 231, 235, 296, 350n.105

and God's mercy, 282, 285
God's self-communication in, 124–25
as good news, 223–24, 294
"the historical Jesus," 52, 70–71, 86, 89, 106, 177, 201, 207–8, 210, 211–12, 213–17, 225, 227, 229, 343n.187, 350n.105, 353n.163
imitation of, 35, 40, 48, 49, 51, 52–53, 54, 56, 58, 73, 84, 86, 87, 89–90, 98, 100, 155, 165, 170, 201, 204–5, 207–8, 211–12, 214, 297, 319nn.28, 30, 320n.43, 327nn.24, 24, 343n.186
Incarnation, 48, 53, 57, 85, 120, 125, 265, 266, 284
orthopathy regarding, 224–26, 227, 229, 230, 232, 293–94
passion and death, 46, 47, 52, 54, 64, 196, 203, 204, 208, 303, 343n.193, 351n.111
Pope Francis on encountering Jesus, 235, 262, 297, 303, 355n.204
poverty of, 51, 320n.43, 343n.186
Resurrection, 46, 52, 55, 62, 196, 204, 208–10, 287, 303
and Simon Peter, 278–79, 366n.162
temptation in the desert, 206, 352n.128
See also discipleship
1 John 4:10–12, 55, 58
John of Choux, *Meditationes vitae Christi*, 84
John of the Cross, 101, 125, 305, 331n.3, 367n.23
John Paul I, 238
John Paul II, 238, 246, 248
John XXIII, 238
Julian of Norwich, 330n.71
on soteriology, 28
Julius III, 93

Exposcit debitum, 66

Kant, Immanuel, 117, 119, 127, 142–43, 148, 186, 334n.51
Kierkegaard, Søren, on the self, 21
King, Martin Luther, Jr., 4
Klaiber, Jeffrey, 242
Kleutgen, Joseph, x, 114
Kolvenbach, Peter-Hans, 245

Lainez, Diego, xv
Lassalle-Klein, Robert, 354n.176
lay confraternities, 14, 96
Leclercq, Jean, xiv
The Love of Learning and the Desire for God, 15
Lee, Michael, on *plasmación*, 349n.75
Lehmann, Karl, 335n.63, 341n.143
Leibniz, Gottfried Wilhelm, 326n.6
Leo XIII, x, 114
Aeterni Patris, 115, 333n.21
liberation theology, 34, 218, 348nn.66, 69, 358n.33
and Ellacuría, xviii, 192–93, 213–14
and Gutiérrez, 310n.11, 360n.60, 361n.62
and Pope Francis, xviii, 242, 246, 276, 310n.11
and Rahner, xviii, 310n.11
vs. theology of the people, 256–57, 361n.62
Libertore, Matteo, x, 114
Lima, Henrique de, on source church vs. reflection church, 361n.70
Llasera, Javier, 175
Lombard, Peter, 70
Lonergan, Bernard, 75, 251, 300, 339n.124
López, Amando, 178, 344n.15
López Vallecillo, Italo, 176
López y López, Joaquín, 178
Lucifer, 49–50

Ludolph of Saxony, *Life of Christ*, 84, 86, 87, 327n.23
Luke
　5:1–11, 278–79, 366n.162
　10:41–42, 157
Luther, Martin, 88, 92, 320n.47

Maier, Martin, on Ellacuría and Rahner, 182–83, 293
Mannheim, Karl, 347n.59
Maréchal, Joseph, 167, 170, 333n.23
　Le point de départ de la métaphysique, 115
Maritain, Jacques
　on Ignatian spirituality, 336n.81
　Integral Humanism, 336n.81
Martín Baró, Ignacio, 176, 177, 178
Martínez, Ángel, 231, 354n.179
Martínez Baigorri, Ángel, 346n.31
Marx, Karl, 102, 231, 253
Marxism, 154, 176, 205, 241, 257, 350n.92, 351n.120
Matt, Daniel, *God and the Big Bang*, 7
Mayorga, Ramón, 176
McBrien, Richard, on spirituality, 312n.41
McDermott, Brian, on Ignatian consolation, 62–65, 66, 320n.48, 321n.62, 63, 322n.76, 354n.177
McGinn, Bernard
　on mysticism, 23, 330n.71
　on spirituality, xv, 10–12, 36, 312nn.36, 38
　on vernacular theology, 15
McGuire, Meredith B., 9
Medellín conference, implementation by Society of Jesus, 174, 177, 183, 200, 223, 239, 242, 243, 258, 270, 324n.91, 358n.33, 361n.62
meditation, 4, 21
Meier, John, 213, 353n.163

Mercadante, Linda, on spirituality, 9–10, 26, 311n.30
mercy
　of God, 233, 235, 236, 269, 273, 275–76, 277–79, 280, 281–85, 296, 322n.71, 364n.130
　and Pope Francis, 234, 237, 265, 273, 275–76, 277–79, 280, 281–85, 288, 296, 297, 303, 358n.32, 364n.130
　relationship to justice, 237, 281–85
Merton, Thomas, 314n.70
Methol Ferré, Alberto, 250, 258, 259, 263, 268
Metz, Johann Baptist, 20, 75, 164, 290, 366n.1
　on identity, 20
　relationship with Rahner, 165, 310n.11, 366n.6
　on theology, x, 167
Modern Devotion, 91, 94, 328nn.29, 30
　and *The Imitation of Christ*, ix, 63, 70, 87, 328n.30
modernity
　affirmation of everyday life in, 19, 23–24, 88–89, 95, 96–97, 100, 157, 168, 314n.73, 328n.35
　beginning of, 82, 326n.6
　and Ellacuría, xiv–xv, xix, 178–79, 206, 293, 299–300, 302
　historical consciousness in, 86–87, 179
　identity of self in, 20–23, 24, 25–26, 95, 168, 314nn.68, 70
　and Ignatius, 81–95, 108, 161, 272, 299
　individualism in, 19–22, 95–97, 98–99, 131, 162–63, 336n.79
　labor in, 101–3
　materialism in, 347n.55
　methodological canons in, 20

and Pope Francis, xiv–xv, xvii–xviii, xix, 263, 273–74, 287, 294, 298, 299, 302, 367n.15
and Rahner, xiv–xv, xix, 110, 113–18, 128–54, 155, 156, 159–65, 166, 167, 171, 172, 259, 263, 291–92, 297–98, 299–300, 302, 303, 343n.193, 362n.84
relationship to spirituality, xiii, xiv–xvi, xvii–xviii, xix–xx, 1–13, 41–43, 78, 79–83, 86–87, 88–89, 91, 94–103, 106–8, 110, 157–65, 171, 178, 181, 216, 254, 280, 289, 290, 294, 305, 307, 326n.3
relationship to theology, x–xi, 113–18, 159–60, 166–72, 254, 289, 290, 307
religious liberalism in, 3–4, 6
secularization in, 16, 17, 114, 117, 118, 158, 159, 166–72, 277, 291–92, 300, 313n.50, 333n.30
and Society of Jesus, 80, 106, 326n.3
subjectivity in, 130–32, 131–32, 135–38, 140–42, 143, 145, 161–63, 167, 168, 329n.60, 336n.75, 347n.55
transience and rootlessness in, 19, 24–26, 95, 97–98, 100–101
monastic spirituality, 15, 29, 87, 120, 125, 328n.29
Montes, Segundo, 176, 177, 178, 243
Moore, Thomas, 314n.56
Care of the Soul, 17–18
on transcendence, 17–18
Moreno, Juan Ramón, 175, 178
Movement of Third World Priests, 276
Müntzer, Thomas, 88, 320n.47
Murray, John Courtney, 300
mystagogy, 31, 32–33, 117, 306, 315n.95

mysticism, xii–xiii, 7, 23–24, 158, 292, 353n.159
definition, 125–26
Hügel on mystical-volitional element in religion, xii–xiii, 290
of Ignatius, 35–36, 84–85, 87–88, 89, 108, 111–12, 113, 118–28, 155–57, 159, 162, 167, 168, 171, 229–30, 251, 274, 292, 295, 335n.60, 341n.143
McGinn on, 23, 330n.71
mysticism of the historical event, 84–85, 89, 169–70, 229, 231, 297, 298
relationship to spirituality, 3, 4–5, 16
role of solitude in, 3, 4

Nadal, Jerónimo, 92, 98, 111, 287–88, 317n.13, 318n.19, 320n.45, 323n.88
on Formula of the Institute, 66
relationship with Ignatius, xv, 72, 104
on "the world is our house," 237, 248, 298, 303, 359n.39
nation-states, 16, 80
nature, 4, 10, 20, 85, 98, 328n.27
and grace, 90, 114, 115, 182, 256
and history, 190, 191, 193, 347n.62
Neoplatonism, Christian
and Ignatius, 56, 85, 87, 89, 169, 297, 303
and Rahner, 169, 170, 229, 230, 297, 303
neoscholasticism, 114, 116, 117, 145–46, 166, 215, 251, 333n.21
New Dictionary of Catholic Spirituality, 2
Newman, John Henry, 313n.52, 331n.3
Newton, Isaac, 326n.6

Nicholas of Cusa, 17
Nietzsche, Friedrich, on the modern soul, 21
nominalism, 16, 326n.6, 328n.40, 329n.42
nouvelle théologie, 128
Nuth, Joan, 330n.71

Ockham, William of, 328n.40, 329n.42
O'Farrell, Ricardo, 239, 242, 243
O'Malley, John
   on first Jesuits, 90, 287, 318n.16
   on Ignatius and asceticism, 96–97
   on Ignatius and Renaissance humanism, 336n.81
   on Modern Devotion, 328n.30
   on Society of Jesus, 41–42, 318n.16, 324n.90
   on *Spiritual Exercises*, 44, 47, 70, 323n.81
O'Murchu, Diarmuid, *Quantum Theology*, 7, 8
Origen, 127, 341n.156
Orobator, Agbonkhianmeghe, 300
orthopathy, 224–26, 227, 229, 230, 232, 293–94, 303, 355n.196
Otto, Rudolf, 330n.71

Parker, Theodore, 4
Pascal, Blaise, x, 331n.3
Paul, St.
   on created world, 325n.104
   on living according to the spirit, 2
Paulist Press, Classics of Western Spirituality, 5
Paul III, 44, 93
Paul IV, 100, 330n.65
Paul VI, 238, 248
   Evangelii nuntiandi, 358n.27
Pelagianism, 134, 264, 334n.47
Perón, Juan, 240–41, 357n.19

Philo of Alexandria, on Judaism as *patrios philosophia*, 29
philosophy
   Ellacuría on, 191–92
   Greek philosophy, 190
   Hadot on, xi, 28–29, 31
   relationship to spirituality, 28–30, 179
   relationship to theology, xi, 113, 114–15, 116, 117, 127–28, 133–34, 153, 170, 179, 192–99
Pieris, Aloysius, 300
Pius IX, x, 114
Pius XI, *Quadragesimo anno*, 240–41
Pius XII, *Humani generis*, 346n.46
plasmación, 195, 349nn.75, 79
Plotinus, 29
pluralism, xviii, 114, 116, 158, 159, 281, 300
Podetti, Amelia, 250, 258–59, 268, 270
Polanco, Juan, 287–88, 318n.19, 323n.88
   relationship with Ignatius, 47, 71, 72, 90, 104, 323n.87
Porete, Margaret, 15–16, 88, 315n.75
positive theology, 70, 87, 90
postmodernity, 141, 143, 163
poverty, 218–19, 227, 238, 316n.96, 319n.30
   Ellacuría on, 195–96, 198, 207, 208, 351n.123, 352n.144, 354n.179
   of Jesus, 51, 320n.43, 343n.186
   Pope Francis on, 234, 242, 243, 244, 246, 247
   preferential option for the poor, 175, 177, 239, 257, 270, 358n.33
preferential option for the poor, 175, 177, 239, 257, 270, 358n.33
Principe, Walter, on spirituality, 11, 312nn.35, 41
Protestantism, 92, 328n.27

and faith, 30
and spirituality, 3–4, 6
and university theology, ix–x
Pryzwara, Erich, 254, 334n.38, 112
Puebla conference, 223, 239, 270, 358n.33, 361n.62
Puente, Luis de la, *De la perfección del christiano en todos sus estados*, 96

Quarracino, Antonio, 246

Rahner, Hugo, 111, 115, 153, 167, 292, 310n.10, 331n.4
Rahner, Karl
  on Aquinas, 133–34, 141, 145, 148, 153, 161, 166, 333n.21
  and Bonaventure, 127, 148, 156–57, 161, 166, 169, 230, 297, 327n.22
  on Christian communities, 162–64, 169, 171, 231, 302
  and Christian Neoplatonism, 169, 170, 229, 230, 297, 303
  "Christmas in the Light of the Exercises," 156
  on consolation without prior cause, 66, 146–53, 164, 167, 168, 229, 296, 321n.51, 339n.126, 340n.137
  criticisms of, 144–45, 153–54
  "Dialogue with God?," 340n.140
  on discernment, 112, 122, 124, 133, 144, 146–48, 150–51, 157, 160, 163, 164, 165, 169, 170, 175, 182, 200, 229–30, 256, 302, 334n.46, 343n.188
  on election/choice, 144–45, 151–52, 153, 154
  vs. Ellacuría, 178–79, 193, 195, 200, 217, 228, 229, 230, 231, 291, 293, 296–97, 299, 302, 303, 310n.11, 347n.58
  Endean on, 126, 127, 148, 154, 164, 166, 229, 292, 340n.141, 341n.143
  on ethics, 142–44, 145–47, 157, 159, 182, 200, 337n.107, 338n.108
  on existentiality, 129, 130, 132, 347n.58
  on existentiel insight, 142, 143–44, 147, 337n.107, 340n.137
  on St. Francis of Assisi, 123, 130, 334n.49, 343n.186
  Geist in Welt, 333n.34
  on God as mystery, 183, 292–93, 304
  on God's grace, 121, 122–23, 126–27, 335n.63, 341n.143
  Habilitationsschrift, 112, 118–19
  Hearer of the Word, 115, 119, 124, 127, 195, 339n.133
  and Heidegger, 118, 124, 137–38, 140, 141, 150, 159, 167, 168, 170, 292, 337n.94, 337nn.94, 107
  and history, 128–29, 132, 133–35, 153–54, 160, 167, 169–70, 343nn.183, 187
  on human soul, 346n.46
  "The Ignatian Mysticism of Joy in the World," 112, 118–28, 129, 134, 136, 139, 149, 165, 167, 169, 273, 335nn.55, 56
  and Ignatian spirituality, xiv–xv, xvi, xvii–xviii, xix, 5, 88, 108, 109, 110–13, 117–28, 129–32, 134–65, 166–72, 231, 291, 292–93, 296–97, 298, 299, 302, 303, 304–5, 310n.10, 331n.2, 333n.36, 334nn.38, 41, 46, 49, 50, 335n.60
  on immediate experience of God, 146, 155–57, 158, 161, 163, 164, 167, 168, 229–30, 296, 302, 339nn.122, 124, 127, 340n.141, 341n.156

Rahner, Karl *(cont.)*
  on indifference, 119, 123, 127, 129–30, 132, 139, 156, 165, 166, 168, 170, 229–30, 296, 297, 298
  and liberation theology, xviii, 310n.11
  "The Logic of Concrete Individual Knowledge in Ignatius of Loyola," 140–54, 185, 200, 231, 332n.12, 337n.106
  on marginality, 164–65, 171
  and modernity, xiv–xv, xix, 110, 113–18, 128–54, 155, 156, 159–65, 166, 167, 171, 172, 259, 263, 291–92, 297–98, 299–300, 302, 303, 343n.193, 362n.84
  on motto *Ad maiorem Dei gloriam*, 118, 134–39, 152, 153, 272, 293, 303, 337n.91
  on nature and grace, 182
  vs. Pope Francis, 235, 236, 237, 254, 263, 272, 273, 288, 291, 294, 295, 296, 299, 302, 303, 310n.10, 362n.84, 363n.113
  relationship with Ellacuría, 182–83
  relationship with Metz, 165, 310n.11, 366n.6
  on Renaissance and Ignatius, 131–32
  on the sacraments, 158, 163, 164, 171
  "Saint Ignatius of Loyola Speaks to a Jesuit Today," 155–56, 165, 334n.43, 335n.54, 341n.153, 342n.157
  on salvation, 127, 256
  on Society of Jesus, 109, 154–55, 162, 164–65
  Spirit in the World, 127, 133–34, 145, 148, 149, 166
  on *Spiritual Exercises*, 52, 56–57, 110, 111, 112–13, 121–22, 125, 143, 144–45, 146–47, 157, 158, 160–62, 164, 169–70, 332n.14, 340n.141, 342n.165
  theology of, 109–19, 126–27, 143–44, 145–46, 153–55, 159–60, 166–67, 231, 291–92, 296, 299, 331n.2, 333nn.32, 34, 335n.61, 340n.141, 341n.143
  and timelessness, 125
  and Vatican II, 115–16, 333n.25
Ramos, Celina, 178
Ramos, Elba, 178
reason and revelation, 114, 115
Reformation, 23, 59, 81, 88, 92–94, 329n.55
Renaissance humanism, 91, 94, 102, 103, 119, 297, 326n.6, 336n.81
rhetoric, 91–92, 302, 304
Romero, Oscar, 176, 177, 294, 321n.69, 344n.15, 345n.16, 346n.27, 357n.21
  relationship with Ellacuría, 183, 184–85, 222–23, 226–27, 231, 349n.80, 355n.181
Rosa, Hartmut, 272
  on modern time structures, 24–25, 97
Rousellot, Pierre, 167, 170, 342n.160
Rubbelke, Michael, 229, 331n.2, 335n.60, 340n.137
Ruusbroec, John, 28, 230, 331n.3

Sacks, Oliver, *Gratitude*, 18
Sales, Francis de, 331n.3
salvation, 10, 32, 70, 93, 98, 334n.47
  Ellacuría on, 192–97, 198, 202, 207, 216, 256, 348n.66, 349n.84, 351n.120, 352n.139
  Pope Francis on, 248–49
  Rahner on, 127, 256

in *Spiritual Exercises*, 44, 45, 47, 50, 51, 52, 53, 55, 56, 57, 65, 71, 73, 76, 104, 283, 302, 317n.11, 319nn.28, 30
Samour, Héctor, 187, 347n.54
Sartre, Jean-Paul, 243
Scannone, Juan Carlos, 250, 300, 361n.62
Scaramelli, Giovanni Battista, 3
Schelling, Friedrich Wilhelm Joseph, 186
Schineller, Peter, on Ignatian spirituality, 72–73, 76–77, 271–72, 325nn.108, 110
Schmidt, Leigh Eric, 10, 26, 27
  on mysticism, 5
  on religious liberalism, 3, 4, 6, 311n.10
  Restless Souls, 3
Schneider, Michael, 252, 253
  on discernment, 360n.57
Schneiders, Sandra, 312n.36
  The Revelatory Text, 315n.92, 353n.163
scholasticism, 2, 14–15, 41
  and Ignatius, 70, 90–91, 94, 328n.40, 329n.42
  neoscholasticism, x, 113, 114, 116, 117, 145–46, 166, 215, 251, 333n.21
Schönborn, Christoph Cardinal, 248
Schreiner, Susan
  on discernment, 320n.47
  on spiritualism, 59
science, 12, 82, 116, 252, 328n.27
  relationship to spirituality, 7, 8, 311n.24
  scientific revolution, 132
  social sciences, 197
Segundo, Juan Luis, 300
  on Ignatian spirituality, 73–76, 201, 325nn.105, 108
  on *Spiritual Exercises*, 206, 324n.98, 325nn.103, 104
self-identity
  buffered self vs. porous self, 98–99, 105, 298
  in modernity, 20–23, 24, 25–26, 95, 168, 314nn.68, 70
self-surveillance, 20, 21, 22–23, 95–96, 97, 168, 298
Shah, Vinod Bruno, 348n.65
Sierps, W., 331n.3
Simons, Menno, 88
sin, 197, 321nn.53, 69, 350n.89
  Ellacuría on, 173, 193, 195–96, 202–3, 206, 209–10, 220, 349n.80, 350nn.108, 109, 351n.111, 352n.139
  God's response to, 45, 46, 48–49, 53, 54, 105, 121–22, 204
  Jesus and Simon Peter, 278–79, 366n.162
  Pope Francis on, 233–34, 275–76, 278–79, 280, 303, 359n.34
  in *Spiritual Exercises*, 45–47, 48–49, 53–54, 59–60, 61, 105, 121–22, 212, 221, 303, 318n.25, 322n.76, 348n.72
Slavin, Kevin, on computer algorithms, 25
Sluhovsky, Moshe, 329n.60
Sobrino, Jon, 176, 213, 218, 222, 290, 352n.141, 353n.163
  Christology of, 367n.20
  on Ellacuría, 184–85, 225, 226, 227, 228, 355n.181
  "The Historical Jesus," 177
  on human hubris, 348n.63
  on Jesus as good news, 223–24
  on orthopathy, 224–26, 227, 230, 293–94, 303

Society of Jesus, xxi, 17, 47–48, 66, 100–101, 221, 248, 356n.4
  in Argentina, 175, 239–40
  in Central America, 173–78, 175–78, 180–81, 183–84, 220, 239, 290, 325n.110, 344n.11, 344n.15, 345n.20
  Constitutions, xv, 71, 73, 74, 77, 78, 90, 100, 101, 120, 180, 270, 300, 310n.10, 323nn.87, 88, 324nn.90, 91, 329n.47, 334n.39, 359n.39
  and Counter-Reformation, 92–94
  and culture, 80, 91, 92, 106, 107, 119, 180–81, 237
  first Jesuits, 47, 61, 65–66, 70, 72, 78, 90, 91, 92, 107, 119, 163, 181, 201, 287–88, 300, 318n.16
  Formula of the Institute, 66, 93, 300, 318n.19
  General Congregation (31st), 332n.13
  General Congregation (32nd), 165, 233, 243, 244, 266, 332n.13, 358n.27
  Ignatius as superior general, 40, 41–42, 71, 72, 73–74, 97–98
  and Medellín conference, 174, 177, 183, 200, 223, 239, 242, 243, 258, 270, 324n.91, 358n.33, 361n.62
  and modernity, 80, 106, 326n.3
  motto *Ad maiorem Dei gloriam*, 118, 134–39, 152, 153, 272, 293, 303, 337n.91
  motto of contemplation in action, 58, 62, 72, 108, 123, 170, 196, 196–97, 199, 211, 212, 226, 281, 284, 293, 297, 320n.45, 334n.50
  Rahner on, 109, 154–55, 162, 164–65
  and retreats, 44, 96, 113, 162, 164, 175, 236–37, 239, 317n.10, 332n.13, 346n.27
  Tertianship, 72, 310n.10, 324n.90
  tradition of finding God in all things, 35, 72, 87–88, 89, 119–20, 123, 127–28, 136, 151, 163, 164, 166–72, 168, 171, 211, 212, 296, 343n.193
  vow of obedience to the pope, 94
Soderberg, Axel, 176
Sols Lucia, José, 346n.31
Spadaro, Antonio, 245, 259, 269, 274
Spain
  Civil War, 335n.55
  reconquista, 83, 84, 318n.25
Spiritual Exercises, xv, xvi, 42–43, 96, 98, 180, 236, 288, 325n.99, 353n.158, 367n.17
  Colloquy before the Cross, 280, 283, 291
  composition, 43–44, 69, 317nn.13, 14, 323n.88
  Contemplation of the Kingdom of Jesus Christ/Call of the King, 49, 52, 57, 70–71, 74, 83, 93, 100, 102, 170, 208, 272, 277, 279, 280, 318n.27, 319n.28, 344n.3, 367n.15
  Contemplation on the Incarnation, 57, 100, 102–3, 273, 284, 318n.27
  Contemplation on the Nativity, 298–99, 327n.23
  Contemplation to Attain Love, 35, 36, 55–58, 62, 72, 74, 75, 87, 102, 169, 199, 204, 209, 210, 211–12, 221, 226, 254, 284, 321n.60, 330nn.64, 67, 71, 343n.193, 348n.73, 354n.178, 364n.131, 365n.160, 366n.9
  desolation in, 51–52, 59, 60, 62, 63, 64, 66–67, 322nn.75, 77
  discipleship in, 76, 86, 94–95, 105–6, 123, 202, 236, 306
  election/choice in, 45, 48–49, 50, 51–52, 53, 54, 55, 56, 57, 59, 63, 67, 68, 75, 99, 104, 105, 144–46,

151–52, 153, 154, 201, 205, 230, 254, 256, 267, 279–80, 284, 296, 302, 317nn.11, 12, 319nn.31, 32, 34, 322nn.77, 78, 339n.122, 340n.141, 342n.160, 354n.177, 356n.10, 362n.78

First Week, 46–47, 48, 49, 52, 53–54, 55–56, 57, 58, 59–60, 61, 74, 75, 173, 201, 202, 212, 221, 275, 276, 277, 278, 279–80, 281, 283–85, 288, 291, 296, 297, 303, 317nn.13, 14, 318n.17, 322n.76, 325n.106, 330n.71, 334n.45, 348n.72, 364n.131, 366n.9

Fourth Week, 46, 52–53, 54–55, 58, 62, 208, 211, 212, 236, 262, 277–78, 284, 296, 303, 317n.13, 322n.76, 330n.71, 348n.73, 364n.131, 366n.9

General Confession of Devotion, 46, 55–56, 60, 318nn.15, 16, 325n.106

goals of, 44–45, 47, 50, 52, 53, 70, 91, 283, 302, 318n.23

grace of God in, 105

vs. *Imitation of Christ*, 44, 63–64, 65, 70, 87, 95, 325n.105

imitation of Jesus in, 48, 49, 51, 52–53, 54, 56, 58, 73, 86, 87, 89–90, 97, 100, 165, 170, 201, 204–5, 207–8, 211–12, 214, 297, 319nn.28, 30, 320n.43, 327nn.24, 25

Introductory Explanations, 83, 88, 90–91, 317nn.13, 14

labor in, 101–3

vs. Ludolph's *Life of Christ*, 84, 86, 87, 327n.23

Meditation on the Two Standards, 36, 49, 92, 93, 100, 174, 199, 205–6, 208, 230, 276, 277, 279, 280, 293, 296, 318n.25, 319n.30, 329n.48, 351n.122

Meditation on Three Classes of Person, 277

On the Three Classes of Persons, 50

as open-ended, 77–78

Presupposition, 94

Principle and Foundation, 36, 50, 51, 62, 73, 74, 75, 83, 90, 169, 170, 201–2, 203, 204, 210, 254, 278, 296, 317n.14, 318n.27, 319n.29, 321n.60, 339n.134, 364nn.127, 131

relationship to classical rhetoric, 91–92

role in Ignatian spirituality, 71–77

role of persuasion in, 91–92, 94

Rules for Eating, 86, 327n.25

Rules for the Discernment of Spirits, 52, 58–70, 95, 98, 99, 112, 122, 124, 133, 144, 146–48, 150–51, 157, 160, 163, 164, 165, 169, 200, 205, 221, 230–31, 239, 268, 269, 279–80, 296, 302, 319n.34, 320n.47, 323n.79, 326n.1, 334n.46, 342nn.160, 188, 348n.72, 354n.177, 362n.78

Rules for Thinking with the Church, 58, 69–71, 88, 90, 93–94, 99–100, 323n.83, 329n.45, 364n.131

salvation in, 44, 45, 47, 50, 51, 52, 53, 55, 56, 57, 65, 71, 73, 76, 104, 283, 302, 317n.11, 319nn.28, 30

Second Week, 46–47, 48–49, 53, 54, 56, 57, 58, 59, 60, 67, 75, 76, 83, 85, 86, 102, 165, 170, 173–74, 199, 201, 203, 204–5, 208, 211, 212, 214, 215, 216–17, 221, 225, 227, 228, 230, 262, 273, 276, 277, 278, 279–80, 281, 283–85, 293, 294, 296, 297, 303, 317n.13, 318n.27, 321n.63, 325n.107, 327n.24, 330n.71, 348n.72, 364n.131

Spiritual Exercises (cont.)
   sin in, 45–47, 48–49, 53–54, 59–60, 61, 105, 121–22, 212, 221, 303, 318n.25, 322n.76, 348n.72
   structure and dynamism, 44–58
   Third Week, 46–47, 52–55, 56, 57, 58, 64, 67, 86, 208–9, 211, 212, 236, 262, 277, 284, 296, 297, 303, 317n.13, 330n.71, 364n.131, 366n.9
   Three Ways of Being Humble, 50–51, 74, 100, 174, 207, 277
   See also consolation; discernment; Ignatius of Loyola; indifference

spirituality
   as constellation of practices, 31–33, 36–37, 105, 109, 301
   definition of, xv, 2–13, 31–37, 105–6, 109, 312nn.33, 35, 41, 313n.43, 316n.96, 366n.167
   as gift of Holy Spirit, xvi, 28
   and hybridization, 306
   as mystagogy, 31, 32–33, 105
   openness and multidimensionality of, xvi–xvii
   relationship to faith, 31, 33
   relationship to modernity, xiii, xiv–xvi, xvii–xviii, xix, 1–27, 41–43, 78, 79–83, 86–87, 88–89, 91, 94–103, 106–8, 110, 157–65, 171, 178, 181, 216, 254, 289, 290, 294, 305, 307, 326n.3
   relationship to mysticism, 3, 4–5, 16
   relationship to philosophy, 28–30, 179
   relationship to popular culture, 7–10, 13, 27, 32, 289
   relationship to religious orders, 290
   relationship to science, 7, 8, 311n.24
   relationship to scripture, xviii
   relationship to theology, ix–x, xiii–xvi, xix–xxi, 5, 14–16, 27–30, 34–35, 71, 73, 78, 81–82, 104–8, 109–11, 113, 117–18, 123–24, 125–27, 144, 145–47, 153–54, 157–60, 166–72, 214, 217, 221–22, 223, 224–26, 228–32, 235–36, 254, 280, 283, 285–88, 289–307, 315nn.90, 95, 331n.2, 333n.32
   sense of time and history in, 86–87
   as set of exercises, xix, 28–30, 31–34, 35–37, 75–76, 94–95, 104, 153–54, 283, 294, 318n.15
   the "spiritual but not religious," 6, 8, 9–10, 22, 314n.60
   as transformative, 1, 28, 30, 31, 34, 37, 43, 76, 78, 80, 221–22, 227, 231–32, 235, 273, 276, 284, 296, 312n.41
   and Vatican II, 5, 37, 108, 310n.10
Stewart, Potter, xv
Stoicism, 21, 28
Suscipe prayer, 337n.91
Suso, Heinrich, 88, 331n.3

Tauler, Johannes, 88, 230
Taylor, Charles
   on affirmation of everyday life, 23, 168, 314n.73
   on the buffered self, 98–99, 107, 298
   on higher time, 100
   on hypergoods, 89, 328n.35
   on the immanent frame, 17, 18, 19, 26, 75, 298
   on modernity, 86, 97, 98–99, 107, 298
   on secularization, 291–92, 333n.30
   Sources of the Self, 131
Teihard de Chardin, Pierre, 300
Tello, Rafael, 250
Teresa of Avila, 101, 125, 305, 341n.156
Theologia Germanica, 88
theological virtues, 63, 64, 66–67, 151
theology

definition of, xv, 34
of Ellacuría, 192–99, 202, 203, 207–8, 212–22, 223, 225–26, 228–32, 291, 296, 298–99, 310n.11, 349n.79, 350n.91, 351n.120
future of, x–xi, xii
Ignatius as theologian, 104–8
of Pope Francis, 235–36, 250, 283, 285–88, 291, 296, 299, 309n.7
of Rahner, 109–19, 126–27, 143–44, 145–46, 153–55, 159–60, 166–67, 231, 291–92, 296, 299, 331n.2, 333nn.32, 34, 335n.61, 340n.141, 341n.143
relationship to culture, ix, xi, xiii–xiv, xviii, 302
relationship to faith, 30–31
relationship to history, 128–29
relationship to imagination, 217–22
relationship to modernity, 113–18, 159–60, 166–72, 254, 289, 290, 307
relationship to philosophy, xi, 113, 114–15, 116, 117, 127–28, 133–34, 153, 170, 179, 192–99
relationship to spirituality, ix–x, xiii–xvi, xix–xxi, 5, 14–16, 27–30, 34–35, 71, 73, 78, 81–82, 104–8, 109–11, 113, 117–18, 123–24, 125–27, 144, 145–47, 153–54, 157–60, 166–72, 214, 217, 221–22, 223, 224–26, 228–32, 235–36, 283, 285–88, 289–307, 315nn.90, 95, 331n.2, 333n.32
See also liberation theology, vs. theology of the people; scholasticism
theology of the people, 250, 256–59, 361n.62
Thomas à Kempis. *See Imitation of Christ, The*

Thoreau, Henry David, 4
Tickle, Phyllis, 7
Tillich, Paul, on faith as ultimate concern, 11
Toner, Jules, 62, 64, 321n.62, 322n.77, 354n.177
Toulmin, Stephen
on modernity, 326n.6
on philosophy, 107–8
Tracy, David, 106, 291

UCA. *See* Universidad Centroamericana José Simeon Cañas
Underhill, Evelyn, *Mysticism*, 5
Ungo, Guillermo, 176
United States, spirituality in, 3–4, 5, 7–8, 10, 22, 27
Universidad Centroamericana José Simeon Cañas (UCA), 176–78, 291, 354n.176
Universidad de El Salvador, 176
University of Alcalá, 91, 104
Urs von Balthasar, Hans, xiv, 5, 264, 355n.196

Vagad, Guaberto, 84
Vallely, Paul, 357n.24
Van Ginhoven Rey, Cristopher, 326n.3, 328n.40
Van Ness, Peter H., 312n.33
Vatican I, 115
Vatican II, 129, 154, 182, 183, 223, 238–39, 240, 286, 290
Gaudium et spes, 257
Lumen gentium, 257, 361n.64
and Rahner, 115–16, 333n.25
relationship to spirituality, 5, 37, 108, 310n.10
Velasco, Rafael, 247
Velásquez de Cuéllar, Juan, 83
vernacular theology, 15–16, 19

Vitoria, Juan Alonso de, 317n.14, 318n.18

Weber, Max, on charism and institution, 12
Wesley, John, x
White, Lynn, Jr., 314n.62
Whitfield, Teresa, 180, 346n.30
Wuthnow, Robert
    God and Mammon, 26
    on spirituality, 4, 8, 9

Yorio, Orlando, 243–45

Zahlauer, Arno, 127, 166, 171
Zubiri, Xavier
    on entification of reality, 186
    on human freedom, 187–88
    on human intelligence as sentient intelligence, 186–88, 190, 200
    on logification of intelligence, 186
    on reality, 186–88, 346nn.46, 54
    relationship with Ellacuría, 181, 185–86, 230–31, 293, 347nn.54, 58, 348n.65, 349n.79, 350n.92
    on *religación*, 349n.79
    theology of, 192–93

J. MATTHEW ASHLEY is associate professor of systematic theology at the University of Notre Dame. He is the author and editor of a number of books, including Take Lord and Receive All My Memory: Toward an Anamnestic Mysticism.

www.ingramcontent.com/pod-product-compliance
Lightning Source LLC
Chambersburg PA
CBHW071435300426
44114CB00013B/1447